CONNECTING
CANADIANS

CONNECTING CANADIANS

Investigations in Community Informatics

Edited by | *Andrew Clement* | *Michael Gurstein*
Graham Longford | *Marita Moll* | *Leslie Regan Shade*

AU PRESS

Published by AU Press, Athabasca University
1200, 10011 – 109 Street, Edmonton, AB T5J 3S6

ISBN 978-1-926836-04-1 (print) 978-1-926836-05-8 (PDF) 978-1-926836-42-3 (epub)

Cover design by Michel Vrana.
Printed and bound in Canada by Marquis Book Printers.

Library and Archives Canada Cataloguing in Publication
Connecting Canadians : investigations in community informatics /
edited by Andrew Clement ... [et al.].

Issued also in electronic format.
ISBN 978-1-926836-04-1

1. Information technology — Social aspects — Canada.
2. Telecommunication — Social aspects — Canada.
3. Computer networks — Social aspects — Canada.
4. Community life — Technological innovations — Canada.
5. Social change — Canada.
I. Clement, Andrew Howard, 1947–

HN110.Z9I563 2012   303.48'330971   C2011-901001-1

We acknowledge the financial support of the Government of Canada through the Canada Book Fund (CBF) for our publishing activities.

 Canada Council   Conseil des Arts
for the Arts   du Canada

Assistance provided by the Government of Alberta, Alberta Multimedia Development Fund.
**Government
of Alberta** ■

CONTENTS

PART VII Public Policy

ILLUSTRATIONS

Tables

Figures

ACKNOWLEDGEMENTS

This book represents the culmination of many years of work conducted under the auspices of the Canadian Research Alliance for Community Innovation and Networking (CRACIN). Any major long-term research project inevitably accumulates a long list of debts of gratitude to those who have contributed to the endeavour, often in unseen ways. The fact that CRACIN is a research alliance means that the list is not only long but unusually broad in terms of the institutional affiliations of the many key players. We can't thank by name every individual to whom we're grateful, but let's begin.

As with most research projects, much of the hard work was put in by graduate students. In this case, we had the pleasure of working with many fine young scholars in the making, spread across five universities: Brandi Bell, Chris Bodnar, Elise Chien, Stéphane Couture, Diane Dechief, Adam Fiser, Mel Hogan, Nicholas Lecomte, Robert Luke, Susan MacDonald, Ryan Mac-Neil, Rachel Miles, Catherine Parrish, Katrina Peddle, Alison Powell, Oriane Regus, Paula Romanow, John Stevenson, Craig Stewart, Ken Werbin, Frank Winter, and Matt Wong. We are also grateful to our research collaborators, Marco Adria, Nadia Caidi, Arthur Cordell, and Serge Proulx, for leading subprojects and supervising several of these graduate students.

We were fortunate to have as our official advisors Mark Surman and Heather Hudson, who generously made time in their busy schedules to share their extensive experience. We also appreciated the feedback given by other community informatics experts along the way: Anne Bishop, Jack Carroll, Peter Day, Bruce Dienes, Bill Dutton, Maurita Holland, Bill McIver, Susan O'Donnell, Ken Pigg, Christian Sandvig, Richard Smith, Sharon Strover, and Wal Taylor.

A novel, and vital, aspect of this project was the key role that community networking initiatives and their leaders played. We had the privilege of collaborating with extraordinarily committed and talented community innovators across Canada, who opened doors and gave liberally of their time. From west to east they were: Steve Chan and Peter Royce (Vancouver Community Network); Lucy Pana (The Alberta Library); Brian Beaton and Brian Walmark (K-Net); Rick Egan, Maureen Fair, Susan Piggott, and Randall Terada (St. Christopher House); Damien Fox and Steve Wilton (Wireless Nomad); Sandra Huntley (Sm@rtSites Ottawa); Michael Lenczner (Île Sans Fil), Monique Chartrand and Ariane Pelletier (Communautique), Janet Larkman (Western Valley Development Agency); and Sheila Downer (SmartLabrador).

Complementing the academic and community legs of the research project was our long-term relationship with the federal government departments most actively involved in the Connecting Canadians agenda. What made this relationship work was the openness and dedication of public officials who belied the stereotype of the uncaring faceless bureaucrat: Prabir Neogi (Industry Canada); Maureen Doody and Natalie Frank (Canadian Heritage); Rob Mastin and Michael Williamson (Human Resources and Skills Development Canada); and Heather Clemenson (Agriculture Canada). Prabir, in particular, saw the CRACIN project through from beginning to end, offering sage counsel and keen insights at every step along the way.

Keeping the research records straight, juggling expenses, maintaining the project website, organizing events, and quietly seeing to a myriad of other details were a succession of conscientious graduate students who took their turn as CRACIN coordinator: Diane Dechief, Christie Hurrell, Stephanie Hall, Susan MacDonald, and Alison Powell. They were succeeded by two more graduate students who worked as editorial assistants: Nicole Desaulnier and Yannet Lathrop. The administrative staff in the (then) Faculty of Information Studies were also invaluable in managing this large and sprawling project. We are especially grateful to Kathy Shyjak, whose rare but much appreciated combination of patience, attention to detail, extensive knowledge of financial arcania, and savvy sense of the doable saved us from imminent death by accounting entanglement on more than one occasion.

This project was primarily funded by an Initiative for the New Economy grant from the Social Sciences and Humanities Research Council. Our principal contact at SSHRC, Gordana Krcevinac, was a pleasure to work with. Three federal government departments also contributed financially, mainly for workshops: Canadian Heritage, Human Resources and Skills Development Canada, and Industry Canada.

The final stage of the project was to produce the volume you are now reading. In this we were very fortunate to find the Athabasca University Press, with its open access policy and its highly professional, able, and personable staff. Walter Hildebrandt offered vital encouragement and guidance at key moments in the process. Pamela MacFarland Holway cheerfully went above and beyond in providing detailed editorial correction and advice. Three anonymous reviewers contributed bracing but invaluable comments and critiques.

CONNECTING CANADIANS

1 CONNECTING CANADIANS?
Community Informatics Perspectives on Community Networking Initiatives

Graham Longford, Andrew Clement, Michael Gurstein, Leslie Regan Shade

This volume of essays addresses the question of how citizens and communities in Canada are responding to the opportunities as well as the challenges presented by rapid technological change, particularly in the areas of information and communication technologies (ICTs). Since the 1990s, many commentators have extolled the virtues of the information or knowledge-based society that has emerged in recent decades and of the technological developments—microcomputing, data-processing, software, the Internet, and so on—underpinning it (Drucker 1994; Negroponte 1995; Tapscott 1997). Corporations, entrepreneurs, and governments have embraced these technologies in their pursuit of growth, innovation, efficiency, and global competitiveness, a process typified by the US retailer Wal-Mart's highly successful use of ICTs to rationalize and streamline its operations (Gurstein 2007; see also chapter 2 in this volume). In addition, citizens, consumers, and skilled workers have taken advantage of ICTs to enhance their own knowledge, skills, and communicative capacities, in the process developing new, more mobile, flexible, and collaborative patterns of work, consumption, learning, and communication (Jenkins 2006; Mitchell 2000; Tapscott 2008; Urry 2007).

The transition to the information age is, however, fraught with risk, for individuals, firms, communities, and entire regions of the globe. Globalization and rapid technological change pose enormous challenges, including wrenching economic restructuring and dislocation, growing imbalances of wealth and power, and the marginalization and exclusion of whole regions and populations that lack the infrastructure, resources, knowledge, and skills needed to participate and thrive in the information society. Manuel Castells, among others, calls attention to the threat of economic and social exclusion posed by the "digital divide," that is, the inability of certain regions, communities, and populations to connect to and insert themselves within the vital networks of investment, production, consumption, education, and governance that serve as the central nervous system of contemporary global society (Castells 1998, 1999).

While Castells's work focuses on the risks of marginalization and exclusion facing large parts of the developing world that find themselves on the wrong side of the digital divide—the so-called "black holes" of the network society (see Castells 1998, chap. 2)—similar risks exist within developed countries as well, differing only in degree. In Canada, for example, recent studies and reports have found that a significant number of citizens and communities remain without access to broadband Internet infrastructure or supports and services, this despite the fact that the country began the millennium as a global leader in broadband availability (National Broadband Task Force 2001; National Selection Committee 2004; Telecommunications Policy Review Panel 2006; Howard, Busch, and Sheets 2010). Rural and remote regions of Canada, as well as marginalized communities and populations (such as Aboriginal Canadians and the urban poor), are in danger of being excluded as new, technology-enhanced economic, social, and educational opportunities pass them by. Recognizing the potential economic and social benefits of universal connectivity, many developed countries have over the past decade implemented national Internet and, more recently, broadband access strategies, including Australia, New Zealand, Denmark, and South Korea, to name a few. Many countries, including Estonia and Finland, have also proclaimed broadband connectivity to be a basic human right.[1]

However, as this book demonstrates, many communities at risk of being excluded from the information society are far from passive spectators to socio-technical transformation and are unwilling to leave their fate either to market forces or to government largesse. *Connecting Canadians: Investigations in Community Informatics* focuses on the active role that citizens, civic organizations, and communities can play in overcoming digital divides and connecting to the network society on their own terms, in ways designed to promote local economic and social development, community learning and innovation, civic participation, and social cohesion. This book reflects on and documents some of the findings of the Canadian Research Alliance for Community Innovation and Networking (CRACIN), a research partnership funded by the Social Sciences and Humanities Research Council of Canada (SSHRC) from 2003 to 2007. (Details of this partnership are presented below.) As this book highlights, and notwithstanding the risks outlined above, increasingly well-organized and self-conscious grassroots technology movements, or community networks (CNs), have emerged over the past couple of decades in North and South America, Europe, and Asia to work on behalf of and with communities to mitigate some of the dangers of economic and social exclusion accompanying the emergence of the network society.

The essays in this volume document how specific civil society groups are engaged in diverse socio-technical projects designed to enable local communities to develop on their own terms within the broader context of global economic, social, and technological transformation (see Schuler and Day 2004). This is accomplished through various "community informatics," or community-based ICT initiatives,[2] ranging from neighbourhood technology centres and public Internet access sites to community web portals, e-learning applications, and community-owned broadband and wireless networks. In Northwestern Ontario, for example, the Aboriginal-owned and -controlled Kuh-ke-nah Network, or K-Net, operates a terrestrial and satellite broadband network that, among other things, supports distance learning and Telehealth applications, thus enabling the members of their participating remote communities to receive educational and health services online. Along with other goals, these services are designed to stanch ongoing outflows of youth, the elderly, and their families who, until recently, were compelled to travel great distances to receive such services, at a heavy cost to the social integrity of their local communities.

Community networks in Vancouver and Toronto, meanwhile, recruit volunteers from among skilled new immigrants to conduct computer and Internet training workshops and to develop community web portals populated with information relevant to other new migrants, including settlement, employment, health, and legal information, while at the same time allowing new migrants to gain necessary Canadian work experience. As well, in downtown Montréal, Île Sans Fil, an all-volunteer group of "hacktivists," students, and artists operates a network of some 150 Wi-Fi Internet "hotspots," providing free Internet access to more than 50,000 users.

Such initiatives are not conducted in a vacuum, as we shall see. Important ingredients to the success of community informatics initiatives include community support and engagement; fruitful partnerships with local non-profit and community organizations, the private, and public sectors; well-designed and adequately funded government programs; and a broader public policy environment that is supportive of the goals of universal access and community-based technology development.

This book will be of interest to multiple audiences. It will appeal to the academic community, in furthering empirical community informatics studies and in detailing Canadian public policy initiatives designed to ameliorate the digital divide. It will also be of interest to the practitioner community, especially in its documentation of successes in empowering community members through ICTs as well as its analysis of how communities fostered technological innovation while dealing with difficulties engendered by the politics of both community and federal funding strictures.

COMMUNITY INFORMATICS IN CANADIAN AND INTERNATIONAL PERSPECTIVE

Broadly speaking, as both a practice and an academic discipline, community informatics (CI) refers to the use of information and communication technologies to enable communities to reach their social, economic, cultural, and political goals (Gurstein 2007). Applications of CI include such activities and services as community Internet access provision, community information sharing, local online content development, online civic participation, online community service delivery, community economic development and e-commerce support, formal and informal learning networks, ICT training, and telework support.

Exemplifying the operational approach to CI is community networking, which historically has played a central role in the development of CI initiatives on the ground. Schuler (2000) defines community networks as enabling electronic environments that promote citizen participation in community affairs. Gurstein (2004, 231) describes a community network as "a locally-based, locally-driven communication and information system" designed to enable "community processes and [to achieve] community objectives."

Community networks began to emerge in the 1970s and 1980s, initially as experiments in the use of computers and other networked digital technologies to support local communities. These included both grassroots efforts, such as the Community Memory project (Kubicek and Wagner 2002) and the online community The Well (Rheingold 2000) in California, and large-scale government initiatives to develop public information systems, such as France's Minitel (Feenberg 1995) and Canada's Telidon projects (Clement 1981). CNs often take the form of community-based ICT-enabled organizations supporting universal access to the Internet and the use of ICT systems to promote local economic and social development, civic participation, social inclusion, and community learning.

Ranging from basic public computing and Internet access sites to full-service community technology centres and interactive web-based community information systems, CNs share in common the broad ideals of promoting economic and social participation by using ICTs to enhance the communication and informational resources available to people living in cities, towns, and specific neighbourhoods, as well as in rural and remote communities (Gurstein 2007; Keeble and Loader 2001b). Best practices in community networking treat community members as active designers of their network and as producers of local content, while at the same time striving, through training and other forms of support, to transform community members into skilled agents in the use of ICTs so that they can pursue individual and collective goals (Gurstein 2004; Pinkett 2003; Ramírez et. al. 2002).

Among the thousands of community networking projects initiated worldwide, some of the better known, most thoroughly documented, and successful examples include the Digital City Amsterdam (De Digitale Stad) (Lovink 2004), the Seattle Community Network (Silver 2004), Blacksburg Electronic Village, in Virginia (Kavanaugh and Patterson 2002), the Milan Community Network (Rete Civica di Milano) (De Cindio 2004), and the Public Electronic Network (PEN) of Santa Monica, California (Dutton and Guthrie 1991). A rich CI literature has begun to emerge, covering a broad range of issues and focusing on the benefits of these and other CNs in North America, Europe, Latin America, Africa, Asia, and Australia (Gurstein 2000; Keeble and Loader 2001a; Marshall, Taylor, and Yu 2004; McIver 2003; Schuler and Day 2004).

Alongside studies of CN practices, scholarship interrogating the implications of the Internet for community formation, identity, and social cohesion is voluminous. Indeed, the last decade of the twentieth century was rife with utopian and dystopian prognostications on the nature of virtual communities and debates over the problematic nature of the increasing incursion of commercial models onto public platforms (Shade 1998). Today, so-called Internet Community Studies is well entrenched in interdisciplinary scholarship, as is evident in the proclivity of researchers studying both the micro and macro dynamics wrought by the inherently collaborative nature of the Internet for individual empowerment and collective mobilization (Burnett, Consalvo, and Ess 2010; Wellman 2004). As Cavanagh (2009) also argues, Internet Community Studies has generated much methodological innovation, while lively debates on the politics of community within networks has opened up space for fresh interrogations of ongoing themes in community research, among other areas.

While the origins of CI in Canada can be traced back to a number of experiments in community networking in the early 1970s (Clement 1981), dramatic growth took place in the early 1990s as personal computers and modems became increasingly affordable. The early use of computer networking as a tool for social action and mobilization across constituent groups was recognized by women's groups (Balka 1992) and by the labour movement (Mazepa 1997). While the development of commercial residential networking and Internet service was slow to take off, early adopters and technology enthusiasts formed grassroots CNs to provide dial-up Internet access and local information services (Shade 1999). One of the first and, initially, most successful CNs in Canada was Ottawa's National Capital FreeNet (NCF), established in 1992 as a community-based, non-profit co-operative project by a group of enthusiastic volunteers, university professors, and private industry donors. In addition to providing free dial-up Internet access, NCF offered access to information posted by over 250 community organizations and government agencies and hosted listservs for dozens of specialized interest groups (Shade 1999; Weston 1997).

Modelled on this and other successful initiatives, dozens of other CNs were established in communities across Canada in the early 1990s. The first international conference on community networking was held at Ottawa's Carleton University in August 1993, bringing together a range of community activists, policy makers, and early "free-net" entrepreneurs to discuss the technical, social, and policy aspects of this nascent movement. This was followed by a second conference in August 1994 that established Telecommunities Canada, an umbrella group for all CNs in Canada.[3] Occurring during the early "information highway" policy debates that coalesced under the federal Information Highway Advisory Council (IHAC), the conference also brought together federal government policy makers, while generating a space for public interest activists to meet and organize.

The specific use of community-based ICTs as a basis for local and regional economic development was pioneered by a Natural Sciences and Engineering Research Council (NSERC) / SSHRC Research Chair in the Management of Technological Change at the University College of Cape Breton (UCCB), which in turn provided the support for the Centre for Community and Enterprise Networking at UCCB. The research and other outputs of the chair and the centre contributed significantly to an understanding of the link between community ICTs, community innovation, and local economic development, on regional, national, and global scales (Graham 2005; Gurstein 1999, 2002).

By the mid-1990s, thirty-five CNs were flourishing across the country, located in major cities as well as a number of regional centres and smaller communities and serving as many as a half million users (Shade 1999). Early CNs took a variety of organizational forms but typically comprised a few paid staff members, a voluntary board of directors, and a larger group of volunteers responsible for activities such as training, technical support, fundraising, and content development. In addition, early CNs in Canada were often affiliated with public institutions such as universities and public libraries (see chapter 17), as well as with non-profit community organizations such as social service agencies. Funding and other forms of material support have typically been provided through a pastiche of membership fees, government programs, cash and in-kind donations, volunteer labour, and equipment donations from corporate benefactors (Moll and Shade 2001; Rideout and Reddick 2005). Typical services offered by these networks included free or low-cost dial-up Internet access, email accounts, bulletin boards and listservs, access to public computer terminals, ICT training sessions, content development, and, eventually, web hosting and online training and discussion forums.

While novel in terms of the adoption and use of networked computing technologies for community development and engagement, the emergence of CNs in Canada can be considered within a broader tradition of using communication technologies for community development, including Canada's early leading role in the development of community-based media initiatives. While community media initiatives often are subsumed under the rubric of "alternative," "activist," or "independent" media (Skinner 2010), all with interrelated and sympathetic concerns for the use of non-corporate media for social change, one imperative of community media is their abiding concern with access to and participation in the means of communication for citizens (Rennie 2006). Beginning in the early 1940s, for example, adult educators, farmers' groups, and the Canadian Broadcasting Corporation (CBC) collaborated to create the Farm Radio Forum, a series of moderated, face-to-face discussion groups composed of rural Canadians who would meet to discuss important social and economic issues of the day, the proceedings of which were then broadcast across the country over the CBC radio network (Sim 1964). Perhaps the most widely known community media project, however, emanated from the National Film Board (NFB) of Canada's Challenge for Change / Société nouvelle program. The program was launched in 1967 by the federal government, with the explicit goal of using documentary film to address the issue of increasing poverty in Canadian communities. According to Waugh, Baker, and Winton (2010, 4), Challenge for Change brought together an unlikely partnership of "government bureaucrats, documentary filmmakers, community activists and 'ordinary' citizens." The objective was "to engender social change through media, and aspiring filmmakers of the New Left rose to the challenge. . . . Filmmakers working with citizens would take on many issues, from women's rights to housing to First Nations struggles to agriculture." The production and dissemination of 145 films and videos over fourteen years resulted from an evolving research process in which filmmakers went into the communities themselves to develop media in a form of participatory action research. Dubbed the "Fogo Island" process, this involved an iterative approach wherein a filmmaker worked with a community development officer to identify a low-income community, who in turn worked with community members in order to identify grassroots solutions to their local problems. During the production process, emphasis was given to involving community members in the final editing decisions. Another integral part of the process was the playback of the film to the community, with government participation, so as to encourage conversation and problem solving (Wiesner 2010).

Television is another communications technology that Canadians made pioneering use of in the field of community development, through the creation of community cable television stations during the 1970s. Community television in Canada was unique in that its inception and growth was mandated by a funding obligation imposed upon cable companies in 1975 as a condition of their licensing by the Canadian Radio-television and Telecommunications Commission (CRTC). As community television activist Kim Goldberg (1990) documented, however, despite the popularity and use of local community stations for community action and social change, government responses in the 1980s toward maintaining community television were tepid at best, influenced by the advent of nationwide cable companies. With enthusiasm for the use of traditional communications media and technology for social change waning in the 1980s, activists and community development practitioners began to turn to newer communication technologies to foster social change, including networked computers, thanks to their increasing affordability.

In the mid-1990s, community networking received a significant boost in support through the federal government's Connecting Canadians initiative, a suite of programs designed to make Canada a global leader in Internet connectivity. A steady stream of progressively more elaborate programs such as SchoolNet, the Community Access Program (CAP), and the Smart Communities pilot program had the broad objective of providing primarily technical Internet access from locations such as community centres, public libraries, and schools. Other federal programs made available either through or in conjunction with the Connecting Canadians agenda pursued related goals, such as rural broadband connectivity, online training and education, and the development of Canadian online content. (For a brief overview of the Connecting Canadians initiative, see Appendix C.) Altogether, more than $900 million has been spent through these programs in support of over 10,000 community-based ICT initiatives (see chapter 19).

A number of community networking organizations were significant recipients of funding under the Connecting Canadians initiative and became lynchpins in the development and success of many projects. CNS were natural partners for community organizations such as libraries and community centres seeking to establish public Internet access sites under the CAP program, and, today, community networks manage hundreds of such sites across the country. Community networks also played a leading role in a number of federally funded Smart Communities demonstration projects, such as the Western Valley Development Agency (Nova Scotia) and the aforementioned K-Net (Northwestern Ontario), which resulted in the deployment of broadband infrastructure and applications in a number of rural and remote communities throughout Canada. In addition, CNS have been highly active in providing computer training, technical support, and content development for many CAP sites, as well as at community centres, libraries, and schools, particularly in rural, remote, and Aboriginal communities across the country (Moll and Shade 2001).

Well-known Canadian examples of successful community networks include, among others, the National Capital FreeNet (Ottawa), the Vancouver Community Network, the Chebucto Community Network (Halifax), Communautique (Montréal), the Victoria FreeNet, and the Aboriginal-owned K-Net. Working in partnership with these and other community organizations, along with the private sector and other levels of government, the federal government's Connecting Canadians initiative succeeded in placing Canada as an early leader among those nations pursuing the goal of universal access to the Internet, the deployment of ubiquitous broadband connectivity for their citizens, and the design and development of citizen-oriented ICT-enabled services.

By the late 1990s, Canada was consistently among the top five countries in the world for Internet penetration, and the Connecting Canadians strategy was marketed as a template for bridging the digital divide in other countries, particularly in the developing world. During the early 2000s, meanwhile, a handful of researchers and practitioners endeavoured to document the achievements and benefits of and the challenges facing publicly supported CI initiatives in Canada. Work by Gurstein (1999, 2002, 2004), Moll and Shade (2001), Ramírez et al. (2002), and Rideout and Reddick (2005) highlights the many contributions of these initiatives to local civic participation, social inclusion, information sharing, community learning, local and regional economic development, and human and social capital development.

For all its success, however, the CI sector in Canada stands at a crossroads as of this writing. With household Internet access rates approaching 75 percent and commercial broadband availability covering over 90 percent of the country (Telecommunications Policy Review Panel 2006), the relevance and necessity of publicly funded, community-based technology initiatives have been called into question, jeopardizing the long-term sustainability and survival of CI organizations across the country. As several chapters (see, especially, chapters 3 and 21) as well as Appendix B in this book document, in 2004 the federal government announced major budget cuts and program closures affecting CI initiatives. This heralded a significant withdrawal of federal support for the sector over the next few years, despite a number of studies pointing to the continuing necessity of public funding for the sustainability of CI initiatives and the need for government support to ensure equitable access (and use) of the Internet by marginalized populations throughout Canada, particularly those in remote and rural regions, Aboriginal peoples, the elderly, and recent immigrants (Telecommunications Policy Review Panel 2004; Rideout and Reddick 2005).

Waning government interest in the sector has placed thousands of community-based ICT initiatives across Canada in jeopardy and threatens to undermine the significant progress recently made in closing the digital divide and enabling individuals and communities to access the benefits of new ICTs. This atmosphere of increasingly tenuous funding and public policy gave rise to the research presented in this volume.

CRACIN: THE CANADIAN RESEARCH ALLIANCE FOR COMMUNITY INNOVATION AND NETWORKING

The Canadian Research Alliance for Community Innovation and Networking (CRACIN) was established in 2003 as a research partnership between academics, practitioners, and public sector representatives, with the aim of investigating and documenting the status and achievements of CI initiatives in Canada. Based in the Faculty of Information Studies at the University of Toronto, CRACIN was funded through a four-year grant from the SSHRC under its Initiative on the New Economy (INE) Research Alliance program (File #538-2003-1012). Co-principal investigators for CRACIN included Andrew Clement (at the University of Toronto), Michael Gurstein (then at the New Jersey Institute of Technology, in Newark, and now at the Centre for Community Informatics Research, Development and Training, in Vancouver), Marita Moll (Telecommunities Canada), and Leslie Regan Shade (at Concordia University).

As a research alliance, CRACIN brought together CI researchers, practitioners, and government policy specialists from all across Canada, forming a network of expertise comprising some twenty academic researchers and graduate students, eleven community partner organizations, and representatives from three federal government departments.[4] Case study sites and community partners for CRACIN included the following (listed roughly west to east across Canada):

- Vancouver Community Network (Vancouver, British Columbia)
- The Alberta Library (Edmonton, Alberta)
- The Keewatin Career Development Corporation (KCDC) (La Ronge, Saskatchewan)
- K-Net Services (Sioux Lookout, Ontario)
- St. Christopher House (Toronto, Ontario)
- Wireless Nomad Inc. (Toronto, Ontario)
- Communautique (Montréal, Québec)
- Île Sans Fil (Montréal, Québec)
- SmartLabrador (Forteau, Newfoundland and Labrador)
- Western Valley Development Agency (Cornwallis, Nova Scotia)

Case study sites were chosen based on, among other factors, a desire to reflect the geographic and demographic diversity of the country. Selected sites represented a broad range of organizational characteristics (e.g., paid versus volunteer staff), users/clients (e.g., Aboriginal, rural, and urban), and core missions (e.g., rural adjustment and development, Aboriginal connectivity, social inclusion, and civic participation).

CRACIN also included policy and program specialists from three federal government departments with a history of involvement in CI initiatives: Industry Canada, Human Resources and Social Development Canada,[5] and Heritage Canada. Detailed community and government partner profiles are provided in Appendix A.

CRACIN researchers conducted three different kinds of research studies: (1) in-depth structured case studies of leading Canadian CI initiatives, (2) broad-based studies on themes or issues of relevance to CI generally, and (3) integrative studies addressing themes and issues that cut across two or more of the case study sites and provided a basis for undertaking systematic comparisons and drawing integrative conclusions. Overall, CRACIN was guided by the principles of participatory action research, and thus the researchers intended to co-design research questions, studies, and evaluation frameworks with community and government partners. In addition, the results were to be shared with and disseminated amongst CRACIN partners in order to maximize their potential benefits for both the CRACIN membership and the broader community of CI researchers and practitioners. Periodic CRACIN workshops over a three-year period served as venues for discussion and refinement of research studies and presentation of final results. Specifically, CRACIN case study research examined the role of CI initiatives in the following areas:

- Ameliorating Canada's multi-faceted "digital divide"
- Fostering local civic participation, social inclusion, and the creation of social capital
- Facilitating both formal and informal community learning
- Promoting rural economic adjustment and development
- Enhancing economic, social, and cultural participation by Canada's Aboriginal peoples
- Developing community-oriented informational resources and cultural content
- Encouraging local innovation in the development of ICT infrastructure, software, and applications tailored to meet local needs.

In addition, CRACIN researchers pursued broad-based and more integrative research on the following themes:

- The sustainability of community informatics initiatives
- Gender and youth perspectives on community networking
- Community networks and civic participation
- Community networking and the role of public libraries
- Community informatics theory
- Community networks as public goods
- ICT policy and policy making in Canada
- Community networking and immigrants.

Finally, the founders of CRACIN pursued a broader set of research objectives that were focused on establishing the nascent field of community informatics, building research capacity within community organizations, and informing and influencing government policy. CRACIN researchers actively engaged in the development of case studies, conceptual frameworks, theoretical approaches, and curriculum materials for use within the field, both in Canada and internationally. CRACIN also supported the launch, in September 2004, of the *Journal of Community Informatics* (under the editorship of Michael Gurstein) as a venue for the publication of peer-reviewed research in the field. Furthermore, as directed by the grant supporting the project, the training and employability of graduate student researchers was enhanced through diverse opportunities to build knowledge and expertise through hands-on field research and related experience.

CRACIN investigators also sought to foster networks and the sharing of information, resources, and expertise with partners beyond academia, including community practitioners and government policy and program specialists. One goal of this effort was to enhance the capacity of community-based organizations to conduct research on their own and to engage in self-assessment as a means to reinforce the decision-making and problem-solving capacities of local organizations and communities. A final objective of the CRACIN project was to evaluate the impact and effectiveness of government programs in support of CI initiatives, with a view to informing future policy and program developments both in Canada and abroad.

COMMUNITY INFORMATICS: CONCEPTUAL AND METHODOLOGICAL APPROACHES

The broad conceptual and methodological approach reflected in this volume is that of community informatics. As an emerging interdisciplinary research field, CI is concerned with the study of the enabling uses of information and communication technologies in communities—in short, how ICTs can help a community to achieve its social, economic, cultural, and political goals (Gurstein 2000). An emphasis on community is explicitly foregrounded: community informatics "combines an interest in the potentially transforming qualities of the new media with an analysis of the importance of community social relations for human interaction" (Keeble and Loader 2001b, 3). Although bridging the digital divide by assuring universal access to broadband networks is a central concern, CI encompasses a broader range of issues than mere technical connectedness to computer hardware and carriage facilities: CI explores how and under what conditions universal access to ICTs can be made as usable and useful as possible, particularly for the purposes of local economic and social development, social inclusion, civic participation, and political empowerment within marginalized populations and communities.

Two useful and complementary conceptual frameworks for understanding CI are Clement and Shade's "access rainbow" (Clement and Shade 2000) and Gurstein's concept of "effective use" (Gurstein 2004). Clement and Shade have argued that achieving mere technical connectedness to the Internet, as has been the goal of many government-sponsored connectivity programs and initiatives, is no guarantee that an individual or community will succeed in appropriating new ICTs in ways that promote their development, autonomy, or empowerment in a meaningful way. Achieving such empowerment calls for an approach that is attentive to a broader set of access issues affecting how ICTs can be effectively appropriated. Clement and Shade refer to this broader set of concerns as an access rainbow, which they envision as a multi-layered socio-technical model for universal access to ICTs. This access rainbow is modelled as seven layers, beginning with the underlying technical elements of connectedness and moving upward through layers that increasingly stress the requisite social infrastructure of access, such as training and public policy:

1. Carriage—the infrastructure for transporting the data
2. Devices—the computers and other devices used by individuals
3. Software tools—the browser, email program, and other software needed to use the Internet
4. Content/services—online databases and website repositories of information; email and e-commerce services
5. Service/access provision—local ISPs and community access points
6. Literacy / social facilitation—text and computer literacy; training and support services
7. Governance—public consultation on policy issues; social impact assessments.

Clement and Shade (2000) argue that their access rainbow model illustrates the multifaceted nature of the concept of access. Inspired by the layered models used for network protocols, the lower layers emphasize the conventional technical aspects. These have been complemented with additional upper layers emphasizing the more social dimensions. The main constitutive element is the service/content layer in the middle, since this is where the actual utility is most direct. However, all the other layers are necessary in order to accomplish proper content/service access.

As many of the case studies in this volume illustrate, mere technical connectedness to computer hardware and an Internet connection does not guarantee that users will become skilled users and/or active creators and producers of online information and services. Meaningful access to new ICTs calls for the development of a complementary social infrastructure of access to accompany the technical one. The community networks profiled in the following chapters, and others like them, lie at the heart of this social infrastructure.

Gurstein, meanwhile, defines *effective use* as "the capacity and opportunity to successfully integrate ICTs into the accomplishment of self or collaboratively identified goals" (Gurstein 2003). Gurstein's concept of effective use makes a similar point about the limitations of conceiving of the digital divide as a problem of mere technical connectedness (Gurstein 2003). A preoccupation with the digital divide as a problem of technical connectedness more often than not serves the commercial interests of Internet service providers (ISPs), without necessarily empowering or addressing the critical needs of those one is striving to connect. Achieving the latter demands that attention be paid to how connectivity is used to empower and enable marginalized and disenfranchised populations and communities, to support local economic development, social justice, and political empowerment, to improve access to education and health services, and to enable local control of the production and distribution of information and cultural material. It is, Gurstein writes more recently, "what is and can be done with the access that makes ICT meaningful" (Gurstein 2007, 13).[6]

Community informatics research and practice are also informed, either directly or indirectly, by a certain theoretical understanding of the development of technology that recognizes the social shaping of technology. Theories of the social shaping or social construction of technology, as exemplified in the works of theorists such as Bijker and Latour, reject technological determinism, which tends to treat technology as an autonomous force acting on society in a one-way relationship, in favour of the view that society and technology are mutually conditioning (Bijker and Law 1992; Latour 1996; MacKenzie and Wajcman 1999). Thus, technological systems and artifacts are shaped by broad social forces such as class, race, and gender relations, as well as by more discrete factors such as the culture of the scientific and engineering professions. Accordingly, CI research and practice treat ICTs not as something that happens to communities—that is, something to which communities are forced to adapt—but rather as tools and resources that have the potential to be socially appropriated or democratically shaped to meet the self-defined needs and goals of communities themselves. CI research, including the contributions in this collection, bears witness to the ways in which, at times against heavy odds, civil society organizations and communities are "shaping the network society" (Schuler and Day 2004).

From a methodological standpoint, CI research is marked by a close relationship with the practice of enabling communities through ICTs (Gurstein 2007). CI researchers endeavour to conduct research *with* as opposed to *on* community networks and users and to produce research results that are valued by practitioners and communities, not simply by other researchers. As a result, partnership and collaboration with communities are central principles of CI research. CRACIN researchers adopted an explicit commitment to participatory action research (PAR) methods, in which community partners were enlisted as active agents in identifying research questions and designing appropriate instruments and evaluation methods so that the research carried out would yield outcomes that were valued by communities as well as by the research community.[7] In a similar vein, they also enlisted the participation of government partners, with the goal of producing policy-relevant research findings. PAR provides a means to engage and integrate community participants and civil servants in the research process and is designed to ensure that recommendations arising from the research have both community and policy relevance. A PAR approach also helps to transfer knowledge and bridge the gaps between communities of practice, research institutions and academics, and government policy makers. The methods deployed by the researchers whose work is presented here was primarily qualitative in nature, relying on ethnographic approaches to participant observation, interviewing, group meetings, and document analysis.

Inevitably, the tripartite nature of CRACIN's structure and the associated research activities revealed tensions and fault lines among the partners, with their disparate priorities, resources, clients, expectations, and organizational mandates, accountabilities, and timeframes. Inequality of resources (such as paid staff, person hours, overhead, and expense budgets), as between non-profit community partners on the one hand and academic researchers and government partners on the other, became evident on occasions when requests for community partners to make interview subjects, data, or organizational reports, evaluations, or other documents available to researchers and/or government program administrators placed burdens on community networks' human resources. A collaborative approach to identifying research questions and the deployment of research students to conduct fieldwork, gather data, and conduct interviews helped in part both to alleviate this burden on community partners and also to ensure that they valued research outcomes.

Fruitful tension also emerged within the alliance around issues of evaluation and the identification of project "success" or "failure." The relationship between community partners and government funders is particularly complex and fraught in this regard, with researchers often caught in the middle. CRACIN provided an opportunity to observe interactions and to engage partners in discussions about the intricate dance between community organizations and their funders. For the past decade, community networking organizations in Canada have been heavily reliant on various government grants and other funding mechanisms in order to deliver their services and programs. At the same time, government funding agencies rely on community partners to deliver services and meet government policy objectives and are responsible for administering funding programs in a cost-effective manner. (For additional discussion, see chapter 19.)

There is little tolerance for project "failure" in such an environment, in which perceived project failures can jeopardize future funding for community partners and likewise have the potential to publicly embarrass government officials. Heightened sensitivity to the potential for scandal in the wake of recent high-profile cases of mismanagement in the Canadian public sector resulted in increased project reporting and evaluation burdens on funding recipients, burdens seldom offset by increased funding or administrative support.

Both parties often look to academic researchers as third-party observers who document and evaluate certain projects or programs. But academic evaluations can be a double-edged sword for community and government partners alike. Positive reports help to validate the community organization's activities (thus helping to secure continued or additional funding) as well as the administration and outcomes of government programs. Community and government partners are increasingly invested in the production of so-called success stories about the projects that have received funding. For community partners, success means not only positive outcomes in the community but also meeting the funders' requirements, thus enhancing the potential for new or continued funding for the organization and ongoing employment for staff and other community members. A successful project for government validates its public policies and offers proof of managerial competence on the part of program staff and government officials. In this context, academic and other third-party reports on project "failures" can do damage to community partner funding opportunities and to the future prospects of government funding programs and their associated administrative staff. CRACIN academic researchers were mindful of these issues and worked with care in order to "do no harm" to our partners, while trying at the same time to provide space for frank discussion of these sensitive topics, usually face to face and off the record.

CRACIN researchers set out explicitly to document the positive outcomes of community partners' activities as well as the implementation of government connectivity policies. However, project outcomes that fell short of expectations were probed as well, on the principle that there is as much to be learned from what does not work as from what does. In this respect, the CRACIN approach was to try to recast the discussion of project failure or success in terms of innovation and learning. Indeed, many of the community initiatives and activities studied involved a considerable degree of social as well as technological innovation and experimentation. K-Net, for example, is trying to develop a sustainable, community-owned satellite broadband network in Northern Ontario and to develop broadband applications in the areas of education and health care that are shaped by the needs of community members. The all-volunteer Île Sans Fil (ISF) has developed and is expanding a large network of Wi-Fi Internet access hotspots in downtown Montréal. St. Christopher House, in downtown Toronto, recruits and trains skilled new immigrants to develop and maintain its own open-source online community portal and content management system to support the organization's community outreach and social service programs. Given the experimental nature of these and other initiatives, it became clear to CRACIN researchers that evaluating outcomes solely on the basis of standard measures of success (cost/benefit analysis, number of network users trained, positive and measurable "impacts" on communities, and so on) risked obscuring some of the most important lessons to be learned from these activities.

INTEGRATIVE RESEARCH THEMES
AND CHAPTER OVERVIEWS

While CRACIN research was primarily conducted as individual in-depth case studies of particular community networking initiatives, thematic issues were also pursued that cut across the various sites, including community innovation, civic participation, participatory design, open source development and community wireless networking, rural and remote community broadband, libraries and community networking, and public policy. It is around these themes that much of the present collection is organized. The themes are situated within wider research contexts and informed by a variety of conceptual approaches.

Contexts

To set the stage for the community networking case studies to follow, this collection begins with an overview of three distinct areas relevant to research on recent CI initiatives in Canada. While they appear at the front of the collection, they were developed over the course of the research itself and thus represent summative views, rather than prior foundations.

In chapter 2, "Toward a Conceptual Framework for a Community Informatics," Michael Gurstein anchors CI in a larger socio-technical context and critique, suggesting that CI is in fact an emergent alternative paradigm to existing practices (the default position) as understood and articulated by a broad range of information society commentators and commentaries. In chapter 3, "Keeping in Touch: A Snapshot of Canadian Community Networks and Their Users," Marita Moll and Melissa Fritz report on the results of their survey of users of Canadian community networks, most of which were established under the federal program that has the widest community reach, the Community Access Program (CAP). In chapter 4, "Canadian and US Broadband Policies: A Comparative Analysis," Heather Hudson provides a comparative analytic overview of Canadian and American broadband policies and strategies that are striving, in particular, to meet the needs of rural and remote communities. She describes funding programs and policies in the two countries, the definitional tensions around what constitutes high-speed broadband, and the National Broadband Plan announced by the US government in March 2010.

Conceptual Approaches

This volume demonstrates not only the current emergent character of CI but also the diversity and the energy that it manifests. While CI research and researchers forge critical perspectives on the received wisdom and approaches to Internet and information society research, the clear emphasis in this work is neither on theory development nor on displays of methodological dexterity and rigour for their own sake. Rather, in both intention and result, these studies are concerned with engaging with, reflecting on, and ultimately informing the practice of using ICTs for enabling and in many cases empowering communities as the ultimate ICT users.

As well, the research undertaken within the CRACIN framework can be seen as a most useful and evidence-based contribution to ongoing policy discussions in areas of continuing national interest, including ICT and social equity (the digital divide), the gender gap in technology, and the appropriate directions for innovation policy in Canada, as well as rapidly emerging issues such as extending and maintaining a sustainable national presence in rural and remote regions of the country. In exploring the questions concerning community and technology posed by studies carried out in rural Nova Scotia, low-income Toronto, rural and remote Northern Ontario, urban Montréal and Vancouver, mid-Northern Saskatchewan, and coastal Labrador, CRACIN researchers have not only carried on the traditions and concerns of the early "frontier," "communications," and "staple economy" researchers in Canada—Dawson, Innis, McLuhan, Smythe, Watkins—but have also begun the process of extending this into the information age.

The tensions in Canada as an "information society" are now often tensions between those who have access to and are able to use new technologies to pursue their economic and social ends and those who do not, rather than between those able to immediately direct or influence the exploitation, distribution, production, and pricing of commodities, goods, and services and those who, separated by divisions of class and geography, are able only to respond to the outcome of these directions. It is the task of CI and the objective of the CRACIN project to identify, document, and, where possible, intervene into those information gaps in an effort at least to understand the processes that are at work, if not to correct them.

But, in this, CRACIN is only a first step. Serge Proulx, in chapter 5, "Information Technology as Political Catalyst," explores the manner in which technology, on the one hand, and social and political activism grounded in electronic communities, on the other, interact so as to mutually reinforce and provoke one another in heretofore unrealized directions, with potentially significant consequences that support broader social and political change. In chapter 6, "'The Researcher Is a Girl': Tales of Bringing Feminist Labour Perspectives into Community Informatics Practice and Evaluation," Katrina Peddle, Alison Powell, and Leslie Regan Shade draw on two case studies to begin a process of examining the role of gender as an intervening variable in the sometimes very tentative initial programs that use ICTs for local development—economic development in the one case, and software development, in the other. In both instances, they bring to the surface underlying assumptions about women and technology, as well as the tensions and difficulties generated by the inclusion of female perspectives. In chapter 7, "What Are Community Networks an Example Of?" Christian Sandvig provocatively poses the question of what overarching (and meta-CI) framework we might fit community networks and networking into, pointing out that, while at this stage there are many possibilities, none are as yet fully realized.

Community Innovation I: Participatory Design, Open Source Development, Civic Engagement

Innovation is one of the most frequently and persistently proclaimed ideals of the so-called information age and, more specifically, of the knowledge-based economy and society and the overarching social imaginary of the Canadian government's Connecting Canadians program. (On the vision of Canada as a knowledge-based economy and society, see chapter 16.) However, the dominant discourse generally treats innovation as occurring only in private enterprises that develop and sell new digitally enabled products and services. Largely absent from this discussion is the way that other actors, notably community-based organizations, also foster innovation. To redress this imbalance, the CRACIN project pursued community innovation, broadly construed, as one of its central themes, expanding use of the concept to include marginalized actors and social innovations tied more to new forms of practice than to new technologies per se.

As community-based organizations become more ambitious in their efforts to adopt and adapt ICTs to meet their various goals, they confront novel challenges. In chapter 8, "Systems Development in a Community-Based Organization," Susan MacDonald and Andrew Clement examine how St. Christopher House, a well-established community and social services agency in downtown Toronto, tackled the building of a content management system (CMS) to support a range of community learning and internal administration activities.

While the study at St. Christopher House focused mainly on the internal staff dynamics around the development and use of a new ICT capacity, this is an intermediate concern. It is rather the question of whether the capacities and relationships among the wider community are strengthened that is of primary importance and that provides the ultimate basis for assessing the implications of CNs. A number of CRACIN researchers and community practitioners were particularly interested in the role played by CI initiatives in fostering civic participation, the growth of social capital, and a sense of belonging within local communities. The recent decline in civic participation and social capital visible across Western liberal democracies has provoked concern among social commentators, policy makers, and community leaders. The role played by ICTs in either hastening or combatting this decline has been debated. Concerns have also been raised about the impact of the digital divide, which threatens to widen existing power and participation gaps between information haves and have-nots.

Surveys, documentary research, participatory observation and qualitative interviews with CN staff, volunteers, and users were conducted at three CRACIN case study sites: Vancouver Community Network, St. Christopher House (Toronto), and Île Sans Fil (Montréal). CRACIN research has yielded some intriguing insights, particularly with regard to the civic participation and community-building activities of new immigrants and youth, two groups that are typically less engaged and involved in their local communities than many other Canadians. In chapter 9, "Vancouver Community Network as a Site of Digital and Social Inclusion," Diane Dechief explores how both human and social capital are built within the Vancouver Community Network (VCN) and how participation in the network's CI initiatives has contributed to the social inclusion and integration of its new immigrant volunteers. Later, in chapter 11, "Wi-Fi Publics: Defining Community and Technology at Montréal's Île Sans Fil," Alison Powell describes the findings of a participatory, ethnographic research project on the members and users of Île Sans Fil, a grassroots, community wireless network (CWN) in downtown Montréal dedicated to providing free wireless Internet access in public places and to the use of wireless networks to engage citizens with their local communities. Powell's analysis of the achievements of CWNs in terms of civic participation provides a welcome tonic to some of the heady rhetoric of "community" and "digital inclusion" that has accompanied the emergence of CWNs as a self-conscious movement.

In summary, the essays by Dechief and Powell focus on the ways in which CI initiatives promote the civic participation and engagement of potentially marginalized groups: new immigrants and youth. By providing volunteer opportunities, job-related experience, and a sense of community for new immigrants, who are often technically skilled but under- or unemployed, VCN promotes their integration into the local community. Île Sans Fil, meanwhile, has succeeded in mobilizing technically skilled youth in Montréal around community Wi-Fi projects, encouraging civic participation within a demographic that is typically disengaged. Most noteworthy among the findings from this research, and one that is seldom explored or appreciated in existing research on community networking and civic participation, is the extent to which much of the civic participation and community building that CRACIN researchers observed was taking place in physical spaces dedicated to ICTs and their use, rather than through ICTs and the online communities to which they afford access. This suggests that the social affordances of community access sites as physical places, where community members encounter and engage with one another and develop social networks face to face, may be more consequential for developing social capital and fostering a sense of community among new immigrants and youth than merely providing access to ICT hardware and Internet connections (Dechief et al. 2008). Community informatics research on the social affordances of ICTs would do well to pay closer attention to this phenomenon, which has been obscured by recent fascination with the nature and impact of online community.

Community Innovation II: Community Wireless Networking

Notwithstanding the primacy of social engagement over technical connectedness, and not to divorce them into disjointed realms, the actual technologies of information and communication do matter greatly. In this respect, community-based ICT initiatives have a long history of innovation dating back to the 1970s (Clement 1981). In such cases as bulletin board systems and public access to the Internet and information services more generally, locally oriented, non-profit initiatives have preceded commercial offerings and have indeed paved the way for them by demonstrating their value to people. This has most recently been the case with community wireless networking. The development in the late 1980s and the 1990s of the IEEE (Institute of Electrical and Electronic Engineers) 802.11 standard and compliant equipment (better known as Wi-Fi, short for Wireless Fidelity) for intermediate range (10m to 100m) digital wireless communication over the 2.4 GHz unlicensed spectrum was aimed initially at creating local area networks (LANs) within households and enterprises. Community-oriented technology activists were among the first to exploit Wi-Fi's potential for sharing network access outside the walls of individual establishments and into the surrounding neighbourhoods. These kinds of technologically innovative initiatives were still very much alive when the CRACIN research began. CRACIN researchers studied the patterns of community and municipal Wi-Fi developments across Canada, as well as examining in-depth two urban community Wi-Fi projects that pursued quite different approaches.

In chapter 10, "Community and Municipal Wi-Fi Initiatives in Canada: Evolutions in Community Participation," Alison Powell and Leslie Regan Shade introduce community Wi-Fi projects as forms of community infrastructure, aiming to serve a variety of purposes. They begin by discussing various Wi-Fi networking models and the current state of Canadian spectrum policy. Their exploration of how Wi-Fi development and innovation is occurring within urban Canadian communities, in the context both of municipal government projects and of grassroots community technology initiatives, provides the basis for comparison with developments elsewhere, notably in the

United States. As mentioned earlier, Alison Powell adopted an ethnographic, participant-observer approach to studying one of Canada's most successful community wireless networking initiatives, Île Sans Fil (see chapter 11). Its development of the open-source WiFiDog "captive portal" software represented a critical ingredient in enabling the organization to convert existing business wireline Internet access points into free hotspots in over 150 locations across Montréal. (See http://dev.wifidog.org/wiki/Community.) In chapter 12, "Wireless Broadband from Individual Backhaul to Community Service," Matt Wong looks at a small Toronto based co-operative, Wireless Nomad, that took a very different approach to turning existing broadband backhaul into a form of community infrastructure by having individuals share their signals on a mutual-benefit basis. Without a financially sustainable subscriber base, and beset by a variety of technical setbacks, the co-op folded in March 2009. However, it did succeed in showing that there are technically viable alternatives for providing universal access to Internet service in dense urban areas at a price substantially below that of present commercial offerings.

Rural and Remote Community Broadband

One of the most enduring preoccupations of Canadian telecommunications policy is ensuring that high-quality communications services reach Canadians in rural and remote areas. This emphasis on equity has deep historical roots in Canada, perhaps dating back to concerns with communications along immensely long trade routes into the poorly known central region of the continent, and, perhaps unsurprisingly, equity continues to be a concern with contemporary high-speed Internet access. As noted above, the CRACIN project included several case studies across Canada that looked into the challenges of providing broadband services to communities where "market forces" would not, and what such services meant for members of those communities.

In chapter 13, "'We Were on the Outside Looking In,'" Brandi Bell, Philipp Budka, and Adam Fiser explore the development of MyKnet.org, a loosely structured system of personal home pages, blogs, and other web-based devices. Established as a major component of K-Net Services, Canada's most prominent rural/remote community network, MyKnet.org is youth based and built around the communities' need to maintain social ties across great distances and intractable wilderness. The remarkable rise of K-Net is the subject of chapter 14, "A Historical Account of the Kuh-ke-nah Network," by Adam Fiser and Andrew Clement. The chapter presents a history and institutional analysis of the broadband network, which currently comprises over one hundred points of presence (POPs) in Aboriginal communities and organizations across Ontario, Québec, and Manitoba. Of interest to proponents of community networking, the K-Net broadband deployment model institutes a decentralized ownership structure that accommodates a community-owned local loop, "last-mile" infrastructure within a co-operatively controlled gateway to wide area networking and broadband e-service delivery over terrestrial and satellite carriers. In chapter 15, "Atlantic Canadian Community Informatics," Katrina Peddle takes up two rural/remote community networking initiatives in Atlantic Canada, that, as with K-Net, received major funding from the federal Smart Communities program but were not as fortunate in their partnerships and did not survive as viable, sustainable networks. In chapter 16, "Reverse English," Frank Winter engages with another project that received major federal funding for rural/remote community networking, this time in Saskatchewan: the Keewatin Career Development Corporation (KCDC). Again the focus is on the complexities of multi-stakeholder relationships, but in this case Winter explores the way that the community networking organization resisted and reshaped the dominant federal discourse of the so-called knowledge-based economy and society.

Libraries and Community Networking

The relationship between community networking initiatives and public libraries is another of the integrative themes that CRACIN researchers pursued. While some clear distinctions can be drawn between community networks (CNs) and public libraries, an appreciation for the overlaps and interplay between these two organizational forms is important not only for understanding the emergence of CNs in recent decades but also for the future prospects of both CNs and public libraries.

In chapter 17, "Community Networks and Libraries," Nadia Caidi, Susan MacDonald and Elise Chien examine the larger issues at stake. Their guiding questions focus on how public libraries and CNs compare in terms of their ideals and practices, on whether there are identifiable dimensions along which to compare synergies and tensions, and on what the prospects are for various forms of collaboration between libraries and CNs. They draw upon their extensive involvement in the CRACIN project to review many of the individual case sites, looking for illustrations of how the CN initiatives did or did not interact with the libraries in their locales.

One example of an explicit joint library and community networking initiative is reported on by Marco Adria in chapter 18, "The Library Ideal and the Community Network." Echoing the recurring calls for using ICTs, and broadband networking in particular, to better connect rural and remote communities with each other (see also chapters 13, 14, and 16), Adria's research team partnered with the Alberta Library to experiment with video conferencing in public libraries in four rural communities participating in the province-wide Alberta SuperNet project.

Public Policy

The public policy and regulatory environment in which community informatics organizations operate is extremely important, as it creates policy and regulatory conditions that can both nurture and undermine their work. Policy research in areas such as telecommunications and community development shed light on the changing fortunes of the CI sector and help to identify policy and regulatory changes and administrative reforms to government programs that can create more fertile conditions for the growth of the sector. In keeping with its participatory and action-oriented approach, CRACIN sought to pursue policy research that was relevant to both community and government partners in terms of the policy environment in which CI organizations and projects in Canada were situated. Comparative and international perspectives were also explored. Common themes that emerged from the research included the precarious situation of community networks in the current policy environment of deregulation and increasing reliance on market forces to roll out advanced telecommunications services, the negative implications of cuts to major government connectivity programs (such as CAP), and the active, if not always effective, role that community networks and other public interest and civil society groups have played in trying to intervene in and influence the policy agenda.

In chapter 19, "Community Networking Experiences with Government Funding Programs," Susan MacDonald, Graham Longford, and Andrew Clement delve more deeply into the CI sector's experience in partnering with the federal government to deliver connectivity programs and services as part of the Connecting Canadians initiative (1997–2004). In chapter 20, "Communautique: Action and Advocacy for Universal Digital Access," Nicolas Lecomte and Serge Proulx explore the experiences of people involved with the Québec-based community networking organization Communautique as it emerged both as a key agent in the delivery of provincial government programs and as a vocal advocate on behalf of universal access and digital rights for all citizens and communities. In chapter 21, "There and Back to the Future Again," Graham Longford, Marita Moll, and Leslie Regan Shade provide an historical overview of a decade and a half of ICT policy making and reform in Canada, with a focus on the changing fortunes of the CI sector.

CONCLUSION

The CRACIN project was inaugurated at a critical juncture in the history and development of CN and CI in Canada. The past decade and a half has been marked by laudable government efforts to close the digital divide and explosive growth in community-based ICT initiatives as a result. Together, these have led to many benefits for communities across the country.

FIGURE 1.1 CRACIN case study site map

Ⓐ Vancouver Community Network
Ⓑ The Alberta Library
Ⓒ Keewatin Career Development Corporation
Ⓓ Kuh-ke-nah Network (K-Net)

Ⓔ St. Christopher House, Wireless Nomad
Ⓕ Communautique, Île Sans Fil
Ⓖ Western Valley Development Agency
Ⓗ Smart Labrador

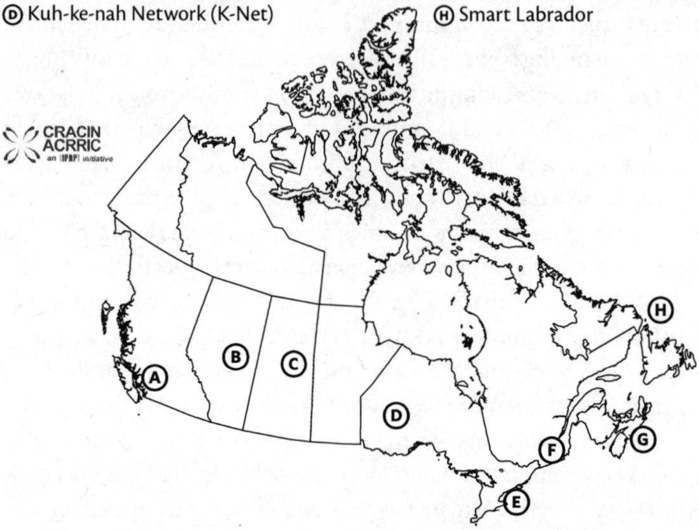

CRACIN
ACRRIC
an IPRP initiative

However, the realization of increasingly affordable and widespread technical access has provoked doubts about the continuing need for public access initiatives, and government ICT policies and programs seem increasingly shifting and uncertain. In addition, the sustainability of thousands of community-based ICT initiatives has been called into question. Thus, the need to systematically document and assess the accomplishments, unique contributions, and challenges of CNs in Canada has seldom been more compelling. With the narrowing (but not closing) of digital divides in Canada and elsewhere, a shift in focus from access in the technical sense to access in a richer, socio-technical sense, such as that developed in Clement and Shade's access rainbow model or Gurstein's concept of effective use, is called for on the part of CN researchers, policy makers, and practitioners alike. Mere access is not the end in itself for community networking; rather, it is the beginning of the pursuit of real ends, enabling the accomplishment of communally identified goals in economic, social, and cultural life. How are CNs using ICTs to meet the economic, learning, civic, and cultural needs of communities? What successes have been achieved, and what challenges do they face? What policy and program changes at the governmental level will best support the effective use of ICTs to build community in Canada? CRACIN began the work of generating both practical and theoretical responses to questions such as these and, by feeding into other research networks and bodies of CN and CI literature that are emerging internationally (for example, from CIRN, the Community Informatics Research Network), helped to share research and practical experiences with CN and CI academics as well as practitioners in other jurisdictions who face similar challenges.

The research reported here was conducted as the major federal government funding programs in Canada were winding down. However, the renewed attention in North America to issues of national broadband policy and the digital economy (see chapter 4), prompted by the election of President Obama and by the growing recognition that Canada and the United States are "falling behind" other advanced economies in terms of Internet performance and adoption, makes the CRACIN research approach and findings especially pertinent for current community practitioners and policy makers.

NOTES

1   See Oana Lungescu, "Tiny Estonia Leads Internet Revolution," BBC News, 7 April 2004, http://news.bbc.co.uk/2/hi/europe/3603943.stm; and Nick Higham, "Delivering Finland's Web 'Human Right,'" BBC News, 24 January 2010, http://news.bbc.co.uk/2/hi/8477572.stm.

2   For a definition and more detailed explanation of this emerging field of practice and research, see Gurstein 2007.

3   The conference agendas are available at http://www.ncf.ca/ip/freenet/conferences/com-net93/agenda.txt and at http://www.ncf.ca/ip/freenet/conferences/com-net94/agenda.

4   During the course of the project, as additional community groups saw the benefit in developing an affiliation, the number of community partners increased from the original group of seven to include Île Sans Fil, the Keewatin Career Development Corporation (KCDC), Wireless Nomad, and SmartLabrador. One original community partner, Sm@rtSites Ottawa, was dismantled just prior to the beginning of the project owing to the elimination of its funding.

5   This department is now called Human Resources and Skills Development Canada. It has been renamed several times over the years: see the Glossary.

6   This insistence on looking past "technical connectedness" to focus as well on the social dimensions of access may seem obvious, even banal, but it is remarkable how technological imaginaries and funding programs often concentrate almost exclusively on the technical aspects.

7   For a description and examples of PAR, see, for example: Peter Reason and Hilary Bradbury, eds., *Handbook of Action Research: Participative Inquiry and Practice* (Thousand Oaks, CA: Sage, 2000); and Yoland Wadsworth, "What Is Participatory Action Research?" Action Research International Paper no. 2 (1998), http://www.scu.edu.au/schools/gcm/ar/ari/p-ywadsworth98.html.

REFERENCES

Balka, Ellen. 1992. Womentalk goes on-line: The use of computer networks in the context of feminist social change. PhD diss., Simon Fraser University.

Bijker, Wiebe, and John Law, eds. 1992. *Shaping technology/building society: Studies in socio-technical change*. Cambridge, MA: MIT Press.

Burnett, Robert, Mia Consalvo, and Charles Ess, eds. 2010. *The handbook of Internet studies*. Malden, MA: Wiley-Blackwell.

Castells, Manuel. 1998. *End of millennium*. Vol. 3 of *The information age: Economy, society, and culture*. London: Blackwell.

——. 1999. The informational city is a dual city: Can it be reversed? In *High technology and low-income communities: Prospects for the positive use of advanced information technology*, ed. D. B. Schon, B. Sanyal, and W. Mitchell, 25–43. Cambridge, MA: MIT Press.

Cavanagh, Allison. 2009. From culture to connection: Internet community studies. *Sociology Compass* 3(1): 1–15.

Clement, Andrew. 1981. Community computing. *Journal of Community Communications* 4(1): 10–15.

Clement, Andrew, and Leslie Regan Shade. 2000. The access rainbow: Conceptualizing universal access to the information/communications infrastructure. In *Community informatics: Enabling communities with information and communications technologies*, ed. Michel Gurstein, 1–20. Hershey, PA: Idea Group Publishing.

Dechief, Diane, Graham Longford, Alison Powell, and Kenneth C. Werbin. 2008. Enabling communities in the networked city: ICTs and civic participation among immigrants and youth in urban Canada. In *Augmented urban spaces*, ed. Alessandro Aurigi and Fiorella de Cindio, 155–70. Farnham, UK: Ashgate.

De Cindio, Fiorella. 2004. The role of community networks in shaping the network society: Enabling people to develop their own projects. In *Shaping the network society: The new role of civil society in cyberspace*, ed. Doug Schuler and Peter Day, 199–225. Cambridge, MA: MIT Press.

Drucker, Peter. 1994. *Post-capitalist society*. New York: Harper-Collins.

Dutton, William, and Kendall Guthrie. 1991. Constructing an electronic city hall: Santa Monica's Public Electronic Network. In *ITCA Teleconferencing Yearbook 1991*, compiled by Charles W. Steinfield and Tricia S. Ehlers, 91–107. Washington D.C.: International Teleconferencing Association.

Feenberg, Andrew. 1995. *Alternative modernity: The technical turn in philosophy and social theory*. Berkeley: University of California Press.

Goldberg, Kim. 1990. *The barefoot channel: Community television as a tool for social change*. Vancouver: New Star Books.

Graham, Garth. 2005. Community Networking as Radical Practice. *Journal of Community Informatics* 1(3): 4–12.

Gurstein, Michael. 1999. Fiddlers on the wire: Music, electronic commerce and local economic development on a virtual Cape Breton Island. In *Doing business on the Internet: Opportunities and pitfalls*, ed. Celia T. Romm and Fay Sudweeks, 193–207. Berlin: Springer Verlag.

——, ed. 2000. *Community informatics: Enabling communities with information and communication technologies*. Hershey, PA: Idea Group Publishing.

Gurstein, Michael. 2002. A community innovation system: Research and development in a remote and rural community. In *Knowledge, clusters and regional innovation systems*, ed. D. Wolfe and A. Holbrook. Montreal and Kingston: McGill-Queen's University Press.

——. 2003. Effective Use: A community informatics strategy beyond the digital divide. *First Monday*, Special Issue no. 8 ("A Web site with a view—The Third World on First Monday"), http://firstmonday.org/htbin/cgiwrap/bin/ojs/index.php/fm/article/view Article/1798/1678.

——. 2004. Effective use and the community informatics sector: Some thoughts on Canada's approach to community technology/community access. In *Seeking convergence in policy and practice: Communications in the public interest*, vol. 2, ed. Marita Moll and Leslie Regan Shade, 223–43. Ottawa: Canadian Centre for Policy Alternatives.

——. 2007. *What is community informatics (and why does it matter)?* Milan: Polimetrica.

Howard, Philip N., Laura Busch, and Penelope Sheets. 2010. Comparing digital divides: Internet access and social inequality in Canada and the United States. *Canadian Journal of Communication* 35(1), http://www.cjc-online.ca/index.php/journal/article/view/2192.

Jenkins, Henry. 2006. *Fans, bloggers, and gamers: Media consumers in a digital age*. New York: New York University Press.

Kavanaugh, Andrea, and Scott Patterson. 2002. The impact of community networks on social capital and community involvement in Blacksburg. In *The Internet in everyday life*, ed. Barry Wellman and Caroline Haythornthwaite, 325–44. London: Blackwell Publishing.

Keeble, Leigh, and Brian D. Loader. 2001a. Community informatics: Themes and issues. In Keeble and Loader 2001b, 1–10.

——, eds. 2001b. *Community informatics: Shaping computer-mediated social relations*. New York: Routledge.

Kubicek, Herbert, and Rose M. Wagner. 2002 (September). Community networks in a generational perspective: The change of an electronic medium within three decades. *Information, Communication and Society* 5(3): 291–319.

Latour, Bruno. 1996. *Aramis, or the love of technology*. Cambridge, MA: Harvard University Press.

Lovink, Geert. 2004. Polder model in cyberspace: Amsterdam public digital culture. In *Shaping the network society: The new role of civil society in cyberspace*, ed. Doug Schuler and Peter Day, 111–35. Cambridge, MA: MIT Press.

MacKenzie, Donald, and Judy Wajcman, eds. 1999. *The social shaping of technology*. Buckingham, UK: Open University Press.

Marshall, Stewart, Wal Taylor, and Xinghuo Yu, eds. 2004. *Using community informatics to transform regions*. Hershey, PA: Idea Group Publishing.

Mazepa, Pat. 1997. The Solidarity Network in formation: A search for democratic alternative communication. MA thesis, Carleton University.

McIver, William, Jr. 2003. A community informatics for the information society. In *Communicating in the information society*, ed. Bruce Girard and Seán Ó Siochrú, 33–64. Geneva: United Nations Research Institute for Social Development.

Mitchell, William. 2000. *e-Topia*. Cambridge, MA: MIT Press.

Moll, Marita, and Leslie Regan Shade. 2001. Community networking in Canada: Do you believe in magic? In *E-commerce vs. e-commons*, vol. 1 of *Communications in the public interest*, ed. Marita Moll and Leslie Shade, 165–81. Ottawa: Canadian Centre for Policy Alternatives.

National Broadband Task Force. 2001. The new national dream: Networking the nation for broadband access. Ottawa: Industry Canada.

National Selection Committee, BRAND. 2004. Stronger communities for a stronger Canada: The promise of broadband. Report of the National Selection Committee, Broadband for Rural and Northern Development Pilot Program, 31 March 2004. Ottawa: Industry Canada.

Negroponte, Nicholas. 1995. *Being digital*. New York: Knopf.

Pinkett, Randal. 2003. Community technology and community building: Early results from the Creating Community Connections Project. *The Information Society* 19: 365–79.

Ramírez, Ricardo, Helen Aitkin, Galin Kora, and Don Richardson. 2002. Community engagement, performance measurement and sustainability: Experiences from Canadian community based networks. Paper presented by at the Global CN Community Informatics Mini-conference, Montréal, October.

Rennie, Ellie. 2006. *Community media: A global introduction.* Lanham, MD: Rowman and Littlefield.

Rideout, Vanda N., and Andrew J. Reddick. 2005. Sustaining community access to technology: Who should pay and why. *Journal of Community Informatics* 1(2): 45–62.

Rheingold, Howard. 2000. *The virtual community: Homesteading on the electronic frontier.* Rev. ed. Cambridge, MA: MIT Press.

Schuler, Douglas. 2000. New communities and new community networks. In *Community informatics: Enabling communities with information and communication technologies,* ed. Michael Gurstein. Hershey, PA: Idea Group Publishing.

Schuler, Douglas, and Peter Day, eds. 2004. *Shaping the network society: The new role of civil society in cyberspace.* Cambridge, MA: MIT Press.

Shade, Leslie Regan. 1998. www.nondigerati.com: who are you? Paper presented to the Canadian Cultural Research Network Colloquium, "Cultural Policies and Cultural Practices: Exploring the Links Between Culture and Social Change," Theme Two: "Virtual" Communities and Identities in an Information Society, 3 June 1998, University of Ottawa. http://ccm.uwaterloo.ca/ccrn/documents/colloq98_shade.html.

——. 1999. Roughing it in the electronic bush: Community networking in Canada. *Canadian Journal of Communication* 24(2), http://www.cjc-online.ca/index.php/journal/article/view/1095/10.

Silver, David. 2004. The soil of cyberspace: Historical archaeologies of the Blacksburg Electronic Village and the Seattle Community Network. In *Shaping the network society: The new role of civil society in cyberspace,* ed. Douglas Schuler and Peter Day, 301–24. Cambridge, MA: MIT Press.

Sim, R. Alex, ed. 1964. *Canada's Farm Radio Forum.* Paris: UNESCO.

Skinner, David. 2010. Minding the growing gaps: Alternative media in Canada. In *Mediascapes: New patterns in Canadian communication,* vol. 3, ed. Leslie Regan Shade, 221–36. Toronto: Nelson Education.

Tapscott, Don. 1997. *The digital economy: Promise and peril in the age of networked intelligence.* Toronto: McGraw-Hill Ryerson.

——. 2008. *Grown up digital: How the net generation is changing your world.* New York: McGraw-Hill.

Telecommunications Policy Review Panel. 2006. Telecommunications Policy Review Panel: Final Report 2006. Ottawa: Industry Canada.

Urry, John. 2007. *Mobilities.* Malden, MA: Polity Press.

Waugh, Tom, Michael Baker, and Ezra Winton, eds. 2010. *Challenge for change: Activist documentary and the National Film Board of Canada.* Montreal and Kingston: McGill-Queen's University Press.

Wellman, Barry. 2004. The three ages of Internet studies: Ten, five and zero years ago. *New Media and Society* 6(1): 123–29.

Weston, Jay. 1997. Old freedoms and new technologies: The evolution of community networking. *The Information Society* 13: 195–201.

Wiesner, Peter K. 2010. Media for the people: The Canadian experiments with film and video in community development. In *Challenge for change: Activist documentary and the National Film Board of Canada,* ed. Tom Waugh, Michael Baker, and Ezra Winton, 73–102. Montreal and Kingston: McGill-Queen's University Press.

PART I

Context

2 TOWARD A CONCEPTUAL FRAMEWORK FOR A COMMUNITY INFORMATICS

Michael Gurstein

Much of what is unique in Canadian social science can be traced to attempts to make sense of the country's history as a "staple economy," one reliant on natural resources spread across a vast territory on the periphery of empire.[1] Harold Innis (1950) and others wrestled with the larger questions of understanding the nature of commodity production and distribution in a vast hinterland, as well as the practical and localized (that is, physically contextualized) community responses to such an economy within a context of externally imposed and coordinated conditions of power and economic exploitation.

It should not be surprising that those who have systematically attempted to understand the social and economic interactions of Canadians have historically been preoccupied with communications and transportation—that is, with the management and deployment of distribution systems. The concern has been with supply and delivery networks over vast distances under frequently harsh physical and commercial conditions and with the technology that provided their underpinnings. Of equal significance on the human side of the equation have been questions concerning the development and maintenance of the communities that populated and were the provisioners of the commodity and other contents of these networks in the midst of often unforgiving climates, both physical and economic.

But we are no longer in the era of traditional staples that Innis describes. With the advent of computerization, particularly the Internet, we are now in an era of a new form of staple, information, which stands as the primary resource in an information society. And, equally, we are now concerned with understanding the manner in which information as a new form of productive resource is created, packaged, and distributed via the electronic trade routes of the Internet. As well, we ask questions concerning the implications of this new trade for those communities that are thus interconnected and the new (but perhaps old) structures of power and control that are manifest and played out in this new information-as-a-resource economy (Schiller 1988).

My intention here is to look forward rather than backward in order to discern the underlying structures and tensions in the dynamics of these relationships—relationships between centre and periphery and between those who control the technology-based means of information production and distribution and those who have privileged access to opportunities for the development and deployment of information and communications technologies (ICTs). In these dynamics, there are also those who must either find a place within the resulting structures and patterns of dominance and resistance or else create alternative structures more in keeping with their goals and requirements. This chapter provides a set of concepts to make explicit the dynamics that underlie what I consider to be the very "traditional" and very distinctively "Canadian" approach to the development, deployment, and use of ICTs for local benefit, which is the central concern of community informatics (CI).

As community informatics researchers, the members of the Canadian Research Alliance for Community Innovation and Networking (CRACIN) began their examination at the grassroots, looking to see how those at the economic and geographic peripheries are responding to the risks and opportunities presented by the new information economy. As documented in this volume, CRACIN researchers have undertaken studies in rural Nova Scotia, in low-income sections of downtown Toronto, among First Nations peoples in rural and remote areas of northern Ontario, in the small towns of rural Alberta, among low-income and recent immigrant residents of urban Montréal and Vancouver, among the Métis in mid-northern Saskatchewan, and in the tiny and very isolated communities of coastal Labrador. In this they have built on the recognition that in Canada, as an "information society," tensions are prominent between those who have access to and are able to use the new technologies to pursue their economic and social ends and those who do not have such access and ability. It is the task of community informatics and a primary objective of the CRACIN project to identify, document, and, where possible, to intervene in those information gaps, in order at least to understand those processes if not necessaily to correct them.

What follows is a framework for situating community informatics within this broader Canadian context. It should be seen as an attempt to develop a theoretical basis for a community informatics, while at the same time providing a very broad framework for understanding and situating the individual research papers that follow in this collection.

Community informatics is by no means unique to Canada; rather, it is an overall approach to the research and practice of the design, implementation, and operation of ICTs in a global variety of local and national contexts. However, it was in Canada that the Community Access Program (CAP) was developed (Gurstein 2003), and this achieved a particular resonance within the broad periphery of Canada's vast rural and remote areas and their populations and communities, including First Nations, as well as among the marginalized poor and some ethnic populations of Canada's cities. This in turn has stimulated some of the research and thinking that prompted the development of community informatics in Canada.

THE DIGITAL DIVIDE IN CANADA

As elsewhere, considerable attention has been addressed to the so-called digital divide in Canada. Statistics Canada has published a series of useful documents providing statistical insight into the division that exists between those who have access to the Internet (and other communications technologies) and those who do not. In these studies, issues of cost and location have been particularly identified as barriers to ICT access (Birdsall 2000; Middleton and Sorenson 2005; Sciadas 2002).

However, from a community informatics perspective, the issues surrounding the digital divide are only background to the larger question as to whether there is a systematic exclusion of certain economically, socially, or locationally identifiable groups who are, for whatever reason, unable to make "effective use" (Gurstein 2003) of information and communication infrastructures—that is, to go beyond simple access to ensure that the ICTs are useable, useful, and being used—in support of personal and community-based objectives. By shifting the ground from matters of access to matters of effective use, CI research adds a design, an education and training, and a social or organizational support component to discussions of ICTs in society, as well as providing the kind of background for policy and programmatic intervention that the more general digital divide studies are unable to do (Reddick, Boucher, and Groseilliers 2000).

The research undertaken by CRACIN has not specifically focused on the issues of access or the digital divide in Canada. Rather, it has for the most part addressed the central concern that many in Canada's physical peripheries and among the economically and socially marginalized have been addressing: how to manage and control the tools and opportunities presented by ICTs to realize meaningful benefits for those individuals and communities both distant geographically and culturally from the central, dominant drivers of the primary networks of which the information society in Canada is constituted.

In an information society, technology globalization (Leavitt 1993) acts not simply as a metaphor but as a defining condition of both the dominant structures of the emerging economy and their associated social structures (Giddens 1984). *Globalization* in this context refers to the creation of ICT-enabled, centrally coordinated networks of producers and consumers, of supply chains and distribution networks. The very rapid rise to national and increasingly global dominance of a select number of comprehensively electronically enabled corporations and organizations is perhaps the defining example of these processes (Ross 1998). In the retail sector, Wal-Mart is one of the most visible and successful of these corporations and serves as the poster child for this trend.

I argue in this chapter that CI provides the conceptual framing (or perhaps even "theory") to support the use of ICT as resistance, offering an alternative approach to understanding the current environment of ICT-driven and -enabled economic totalization and engulfment. As well, CI may form the basis of an alternative strategy for incorporating and using ICTs in modern society, where the exercise of mediated power and control might only be resisted (and possibly overcome) through the development of equally powerful, technology-mediated forces anchored in communities both physical and increasingly virtual.

In this context, Wal-Mart and similar organizations are less companies than they are electronic infrastructures for managing the flow of goods from producers in low-cost countries to consumers in higher-cost countries while extracting profit from the "arbitrage" between these two sides of the equation.[2] Thus, the defining characteristic of Wal-Mart is the efficiency, scope, and depth of its IT infrastructure, integrated with its material logistics and distribution infrastructure, and the continuous internal drive within its IT processes to enhance these efficiencies and the market power that results. By creating a relatively seamless supply chain internally and a low overhead relationship between producers and consumers, the company has mastered the central elements of a consumer economy (Kalakota and Robinson 2001).

Since, in important respects, community informatics is positioned as offering a critique of and alternative to the globalized ICT-based production and distribution model exemplified by Wal-Mart, and the closely related sociological phenomenon of "networked individualism," we examine these in turn before outlining the core concepts and principles of community informatics.

What is characteristic of Wal-Mart, and all of the organizations strategically linked into similar webs of electronic and business alliances of suppliers and subsuppliers, is the very high degree of centralization and centralized control that they exert even through their highly dispersed operations.[3] It is this control as exerted through the direct use of ICTs that is characteristic of the information age and of the role of ICT in the current globalizing world economy.

A notable characteristic of these organizations is that they are not only "globalized" enterprises but also "globalizing" and "totalizing" enterprises—actively proselytizing and reorganizing systems and businesses in support of these initiatives and approaches and totally incorporating economic and even social processes that are captured within their technology net(work). The very fact of this integration, coupled with the intensive centralization and overwhelming drive toward expansion, has meant that these organizations (and similar integrated structures in a variety of other industrial sectors, such as the automotive, electronic, and financial) have integrated their suppliers into their "value chains" (Kalakota and Robinson 2001). This also puts significant pressure on their suppliers to integrate *their* own suppliers into these ever-expanding information networks/value chains, similarly using common electronic platforms and integrated information systems. The overall effect of this is that a very significant and increasingly large component of the US economy, as well as substantial elements of the global economy, are becoming integrated into a single, ever-expanding, technologically driven and efficiency-seeking electronic infrastructure with attendant processes of highly aggressive cost-reduction and profit maximization, all cascading into these electronically enabled behemoths. As well, these technology drivers have their ideological, organizational, management, and human resource counterparts.

Contrary to earlier industrial production processes, however, the actual physical production of goods can now be highly dispersed and decentralized, with the centre maintaining simply a coordinating role, less through specific direction and more through the establishment of targets (production, cost, quality) and standards. Local or dispersed nodes—suppliers, producers, retail outlets—have considerable autonomy in how they achieve their results, as long as the results are achieved.

Equally, the employee relationships and work activities related to these goods production and distribution processes are not necessarily externally coordinated or framed in an aggregated fashion, as in a context such as an assembly line, where all employees are treated alike and are equally subject to external coordination. Rather, in this circumstance, the managerial practice and ideology is of "individuation"—of employee supervision and of the relationship of the employee to the employer more generally. Employees in value-chain enterprises are not called workers, or even employees; they are identified as "associates," which suggests independent contractors negotiating terms with the employer on a one-to-one basis.[4]

In this way, at least nominally, an illusion (and to some degree the reality) is presented of employee autonomy within a larger, centrally coordinated framework. In the modern iteration, of course, this coordination takes an increasingly technological form, as opposed to, for example, management coordination through direct oversight.[5] In the Wal-Mart-style formulation, each employee ("associate") has his or her separate contract, including output quotas, with the employer maintaining the right to monitor the employee's performance against these quotas (with technology giving the employer an increased opportunity for such monitoring). This individualized arrangement stands in contrast to the more traditional collective output requirements leading to collective labour agreements (Tsui and Wu 2005).

NETWORKED INDIVIDUALISM AND THE POLITICS OF THE CONSUMPTION OF INTANGIBLES

How then are we to understand the status and mode of "being in the world" of these associates? In the earlier classical formulations, notions of individualism and the creation of individualized identities and individualized methods of participating in the various activities and realities of daily and communal life were formulated by, among others, John Locke and David Hume (Macpherson 1962). In these earlier formulations, the origin of such individualism can be seen as deriving from the breakdown of feudal modes of production and social relationships and the rise of individualized, contract-based relationships through industrial production, as well as the end of legal and religious ties to the land and to central religious value systems.

We can perhaps see a direct parallel here with the evident rise of individualized relations between employer and employee as characterized by Wal-Mart's associates' status, but we can also see it in the formulation presented by sociologist Barry Wellman and his colleagues (Stalder 2010; Wellman et al. 2003) concerning the nature of the status of and relationships among individuals within electronic networks per Wellman's notion of "networked individualism."[6] The Wal-Mart employee is compelled to a form of individualism quite unknown in earlier management-employee relationships. The development of this new individualism has been made possible by the fact that, rather than managers and management organizations, it is the electronic infrastructure, the "network," that provides the basis for the coordination and organization of labour activities.[7]

Wellman's notion of networked individualism as the way in which identity manifests itself in the networked society is useful in that it highlights both the manner in which the network links into the individual in an unmediated fashion and the manner in which the individual both experiences and interacts with the dispersed and (from his/her perspective) centreless network directly, rather than through the mediation of social groupings or other social constructs. This is becoming increasingly prominent in the context of the widespread integration of social media tools such as Facebook and Twitter as central elements in inter-individual communication and social group mediation.

Networked individualism also gives a sense that the individual, in the context of an environment in which she is engaged in multiple electronically enabled networks such as Facebook or YouTube, is in turn a construct linking fragmented identities/individualisms that are structured, created, or responsive to and within networks, each of which is only partially, if at all, overlapping. Thus the creation of the self in this context may (and can be generally understood) as an act of individual will, which may take different forms for different individuals or even on different occasions (Wellman and Hampton 1999). Within this context individual action also takes place within and through the individual networks in which the self is able (or available) to act (or interact) with others but this action is simultaneously circumscribed by and within the very limited areas of linkage/interconnection that are available in individual networks. For example, an individual buying or selling on eBay performs their respective actions within the parameters defined by the interaction between the individuals as per their "profile" within eBay and within eBay's prescribed and technologically enforced rules of interaction, or policies.[8]

The notion of identity vis-à-vis individual action as a "networked individual" is thus peculiar because, while the individual may define their specific "identity" within the context of a specific network (the definition of the individual's "profile" within that network), the manner in which that identity may in turn execute or perform actions within that network is directly a function of the centrally determined and prescribed standards or regulations—or "code"—of that network (Lessig 1999). The individual may control their profile (that is, their identity), but they can do so only within rules over which they have no direct influence and which they can resist or ignore only at the risk of being de-networked. If they were to be "de-networked," they would be completely *erased* from participating in the network, which, in network terms, is tantamount to being obliterated—not simply killed or destroyed, in which cases traces may be allowed to remain within the network, but obliterated, that is, utterly removed, including all historical traces or fragments.[9]

In the case of Facebook, for example, the individual's relationship to the network is a result of the conditions that govern their participation in the network. Once the company has determined that those conditions are no longer being met, the participation by the individual in the network may be terminated, and the individual (or, in case of an employment contract with, say, Wal-Mart, the "associate") has no residual connection or involvement with the other party and no residual responsibility or contractual, paternalistic, or other linkages. This example is perhaps equally striking with respect to Wal-Mart, Facebook, and eBay, where, the individual having ceased to be a member of the network, the act of termination immediately triggers a series of electronically (and network-) enabled actions, particularly the changing of passwords. This has the immediate effect of denying individuals access to previously accessible information networks (including both physical and, increasingly, electronic networks, along with the information resources stored in such networks, including information created by the individual), as well as work premises, email accounts, data files, and so on. The effect, of course, is to forcibly and irrevocably expunge all of the related elements of identity (and selfhood) in a networked and electronic environment.[10]

Resistance and Building Alternatives

In this context, the individual is truly powerless to resist this more or less complete (network) obliteration, since the network itself is centrally controlled, and this capacity to block or delete or suspend is a centrally managed function or feature of such networks. Even prior to such a measure, the capacity to resist or to organize within the network is in itself a feature determined and circumscribed by the network's code. This code in turn determines in what manner individuals are allowed to individually interact and coordinate their behaviour outside of the centrally prescribed coordination as determined by the rules and standards of the networks.

It is only by stepping outside of these networks and drawing upon or creating a unique individualism or a non-networked identity that the type of inter-action through which non-(centrally) networked inter-individual interaction, and thus collaboration or non-network subordinated organizing can begin to take place. For individuals whose identities are largely structured in relation to these externally driven networks—those for whom employment, gaming, socializing, or purchasing networks are the sum of their individualism—little may be left as a residual base of identity on which to form such non-externally coordinated interrelationships (that is, non-externally dependent networks). Thus there is little or no basis from which can arise "resistance," or alternatives, to arbitrary, abusive, or exploitative actions from the centre or, more simply, to enhance employee opportunities for financial or social well-being.[11]

And yet we are seeing manifestations of coordinated resistance to these networks and their impacts on individuals as well as physical communities where their presence is most evident. Notably, the only effective resistance to the Wal-Mart juggernaut, including competitive resistance in the market place, has come initially from place-based communities and, in general, integrated, relatively small communities that have mounted active resistance to the location of a Wal-Mart store within their immediate environment. It is at these local, face-to-face community levels that the most successful resistance to these organizations as global intensively networked behemoths has been possible,[12] although it should be noted that this success has been extremely limited in scope and volume (Porter and Mirsky 2003). Furthermore, it is through the building of and involvement in communities that individuals are able to conceive of and tentatively create alternatives to the fragmentation that comes through a total involvement in the networked individualism that is characteristic of the information society (Castells 1994).

From Resistance to Theory

The electronically enabled, centrally controlled networks that underpin contemporary advanced economies and cultures are, at their very core, totalizing systems whose inner life is one of extreme and even cancerous and explosive growth. Through such growth, networks absorb and transform ever-wider circles of production and consumption into extensions of these ever-expanding network chains. It is thus not surprising that the resistance and alternatives to this totalization comes from opportunities and frameworks that enable the individual to overcome this fragmentation and to integrate their identity and, more importantly, find the means for entering into collaborative relationships with others. This process of reintegration is necessarily, theoretically, and practically the discovery or rediscovery of community and of organic and integrated inter-individual relationships, rather than purely contractual and electronically fragmented internetworked connections.[13] This, of course, has the effect of overcoming contractually structured and fragmented networked relations in favour of organic and network-enabled production and distribution. These relationships of networked community response can be seen not simply as reactions but as dialectically produced and structured responses to the invasive electronic networks engendered as part of the production and distribution process of electronically enabled enterprises.

Networked communities may take either of two forms. They may be virtual communities that exist only in and through the communications networks that enable them, or they may be physical communities that are enabled both internally and in their relationship with the outside world via ICTs.[14] The terms *virtual* and *electronic* point to these communities' origins in the act of networking and of interindividual communication as between peers. In many cases, these communities reflect a repurposing of top-down, centrally driven e-networks in which individuals as network end-users/participants begin to bypass the central authority and enter into direct peer-to-peer communication. This occurs even though centrally driven networks are almost universally structured so as to preclude the possibility of peer-to-peer connections, recognizing that this type of organizing would be of little advantage and could potentially present threats to the networks themselves.[15]

In the second case, physical communities are enabled in a variety of ways and for a variety of purposes through the use of ICTs. In these instances, the community, as a series of ongoing peer-to-peer connections, may exist over a long period of time. However, the application or introduction of ICTs to support these processes, and particularly to support the various outcome-oriented activities of such communities, may be relatively new (Gurstein 2000).

Furthermore, as the use of ICTs to support electronically enabled communities becomes commonplace, and as experience in enabling physical communities with ICTs is acquired, there is emerging a convergence or overlap between these. In these instances, electronically enabled communities begin to seek out ways of becoming linked more directly via physical interactions and physical processes. As well, ICT-enabled physical communities begin to enhance and extend their activities and reach by incorporating elements of virtual relationships as aspects of their ongoing physical and face-to-face relationships.

Thus the basis for a *community informatics* is not simply that communities along with groups and organizations come to use ICTs as tools for their development, but rather that communities have a different status or ontology from other entities, and as such, both enable and require a unique perspective and approach to ICT design and development, namely, a *community* informatics rather than a generic *informatics* as applied to communities. Networked communities thus can provide the basis for resistance or an alternative to the centrally controlled networks and a means through which individuals can develop their capacities for effective action in a networked society.

COMMUNITY AS ALTERNATIVE, RESISTANCE, AND ONTOLOGY

Ontology has to do with the nature of fundamental being (Strawson 1990) that is the base from which other phenomena derive or which provides the basis for the continued persistence of other phenomena or activities. In this context, the question is: What are the ontological foundations for an understanding of the current structure of action/reaction, extension (propagation), and resistance within the domain?

Within Wellman's and Castells's models of networked individualism, and Manuel Castells's model of the networked society, the primary ontological mover, whether independent agent or source of independent action/agency, is the network itself, as it is the network that underlies the construction of all other relations. The individual in Wellman's formulation is simply the sum of the fragments of an individual's participation in the various externally driven networks (of production, consumption, and even socialization) of which he or she is a member, or with which s/he has contractually or digitally mediated relations. In this world, the network is everything.

Beyond the world of social analysis, however, externally driven networked relationships are only one element of a complex interconnection of social forces. In addition to such networked relationships, there are self-initiated (or self-organized) and participatory networks that interlink individuals not on the basis of fragments of identity but on the basis of self-initiated and self-realized identities. These networks function as communities through which action may be undertaken, projects realized, and reality confronted and modified, and thus they provide an alternative and collaborative social construction in contrast to the individualism of conventional network-driven social relations.

These communities, both physical and electronically enabled, represent an additional and structurally oppositional ontology to the network ontology as described, for example, by Wellman et al., and as such, seem to flow, at least potentially, alongside and in partial opposition to a Facebook/YouTube set of socially networked interindividual relationships. These communities provide the basis for the construction of an alternative reality—a set of organizational, economic, and social structures operating independently of the centrally controlled networks (such as Wal-Mart) or the technologically facilitated fragmentation of "socially networked software" (such as Facebook).

The assertion here is that communities can and should be seen as primary and autonomous. That is, they do not depend on any other social formation and are thus capable of acting as the platform or conceptual agent on the basis of which one could (and should) undertake technical design vis-à-vis hardware and software. In this way, one can specifically develop information, communications, and networking systems that provide the means for communities being enabled and empowered to effect collaborative action in the world, and this is the conceptual foundation for a community informatics. This directly parallels and provides an alternative to the way in which ICTs are designed to enable and empower corporations and individuals, while also integrating as a design element the differences in the presuppositions of the different platforms (Gurstein and Horan 2005).

THE NATURE OF NETWORKED COMMUNITIES

Networked communities, as well as community networks, have a variety of essential or ideal typical characteristics that differentiate them from other networks, centrally determined networks, and networked individuals. In fact, several of the case studies provided in this volume provide useful illustrations.

Bottom-up

Networked communities are "bottom-up," which is to say they are derived and developed by the users or participants themselves rather than being centrally initiated or externally driven. What this means is that users or participants are actors in the networks and these networks in turn are community-based, developing through pre-existing or self-presented individualism rather than with the interindividual connections being externally defined and elicited. In this way, participation in a community is rather more rounded and integrated from the participant's perspective than the fragmented and largely contractual or rule-based relationships of the individualism-based networks, as defined by Wellman and others. This in turn gives the nature of the community participation a stronger and fuller grounding in the lived context. The communities and individuals within K-Net, for example (see chapters 13 and 14), are concerned with using ICTs as a basis for expressing and maintaining their local culture and language and for the economic survival of their communities. In these contexts, the use of the ICT platform is as a means for people to assert themselves and the elements of their communities in the context of overwhelming environments where these differences are not understood or easily assimilated from administrative and other perspectives.

Voluntary

Participation in networked communities is voluntary and self-initiated; that is, individuals choose to participate in these communities (in the case of physical communities it is often in the form of choosing not to *not participate*), and participation is based on individual decision and volition rather than through entering into contractual relationships. While there may be an exchange of value through a networked community, in the form of cash, goods, or services, in fact there is very often a considerable such exchange, but it is not the basis of the participation in the community, and the relationships are with the community as a whole rather than on a bilateral basis, where there may be an enforced or enforceable structured value exchange relationship. The role of the Vancouver Community Network (VCN) of providing an electronic platform and including volunteers to support broader community use of ICTs, as Diane Dechief demonstrates in chapter 9, is a useful example of this as is the small and medium sized communities described in Adria's discussion of applications of the Alberta SuperNet (see chapter 18).

Collaborative

In communities, goals and the methods for achieving them are the result of collaborative decision-making processes, recognizing of course, that even within communities there may be significant differences in power and position. These processes may differ significantly from context to context, but in each case there is an element of participation by those involved, and of responsiveness to the decisions made. In practice, such processes for the most part reflect some form of consensus position on the part of the participants, although the achievement of formal consensus may or may not occur, and in many communities there are a variety of more or less formalized structures for decision-making. Katrina Peddle's discussion of the Labrador community (see chapter 15) reflects this type of internal community decision-making and the role that the use of ICT can play in supporting it.

Autonomous

Community networks are autonomous and capable of independently initiating action. In this context, networked communities function at the "edge" of the larger networks in which they are participants. As with the Internet itself, intelligence, together with the related capacity for autonomous action and independent (that is, non-coerced) participation in the network, is found at the edges of the network. This stands in contrast to coercive, top-down, centrally coordinated networks, in which the centre alone is capable of autonomous action, while those at the periphery are capable of action only within a coordinated, centrally determined set of parameters, standards, and code. In chapter 16, Frank Winter examines the role that the KCDC takes upon itself as an independent actor amidst significant outside companies in the context of the Saskatchewan telecommunications ecology.

Emergent

Networked communities are emergent in that they often come into existence in response to some external condition or circumstance. That they are emergent does not mean that they do not or have not persisted over time, but rather that they may have lain nascent until called forward into formalized existence by social entrepreneurship, self-initiated problem solving, or similar external stimuli or internal processes. Similarly, networked communities evolve over time and move into and out of existence in formalized terms. That no formal external structures of a networked community can be externally identified does not mean that the networked community does not exist, but rather that it is still nascent and waiting to be called forth in structured form. Powell's description of the ongoing operation of Île Sans Fil is a good example of this although the Île Sans Fil community might not have the complexity or multiplicity of internal connections that characterize other more physically situated communities.

Emergent communities provide a means for understanding the sustainability paradox, and while the formal structures of communities may or may not be sustainable (Simpson 2005) over time, the community itself may be sustaining and spring to life, reemerging in the form of formalized structures at a future, unpredictable occasion. This suggests the obvious but frequently overlooked conclusion that communities are not defined simply by their structures, but rather are the connections that persist over time as between members of the community, with structures being simply formalizations of these connections. Connections between the members of Île Sans Fil give us some means for understanding such a community (see chapter 11).

THE DESIGN OF COMMUNITY INFORMATICS RESEARCH

The research and design issues and strategies for the application of information systems (IS) in a community context are somewhat more complex than for more traditional IS. The design of IS for communities requires that the assumptions and characteristics of themselves as communities must be made explicit and included as elements and assumptions within the context of the research (Gurstein and Horan 2005; Nnadi and Gurstein 2007). Thus, the research and design component requires an understanding and sensitivity toward the social elements of computing and communication in addition to the technical elements (Kling and Lamb 2002). There is also a need to break away from received research designs and assumptions, given that communities may be seen at some levels as being in a dialectical relationship with the dominant, intrusive, and engulfing forces of the centrally coordinated organizations and structures (Mann 1984).

The nature of the research driving much of this advance in information systems has of course been technical in nature. The basic managerial assumptions on which this technical research is founded, such as centralization of decision making, exclusionary access to information, operational efficiency, and extension in the span of control, are deeply embedded and taken as axiomatic and commonplace ("This is how organizations are and how they necessarily function"). There is suspicion and even incomprehension of any suggestion that these assumptions are anything other than necessary and non-problematic. Such an approach equally applies to the design and use of IS in not-for-profit enterprises.

The practice of community informatics (CI) research will thus have certain characteristics that are different from those in other areas of IT or applications research, but will instead take the form of participatory action research (PAR), which is discussed elsewhere in this collection and which provides the basic methodology for many of the case studies discussed.

Dialectical Approach

The concept of dialectical research (Mann 1984; Piven and Cloward 1979) is a relatively unconventional one in the context of current research activities, and likely even less familiar in the context of technical or informatics research. Nevertheless, it is crucial as an element in CI research. The challenge of CI research is not simply to enable or empower communities as persistent formalized structures. In fact, as we have already noted, communities in this context are neither permanent nor fully realized; rather, as already noted, they are emergent, particularly in the context of responding to the presentation of opportunities or threats from the larger environment. Notably, the centrally driven networks in the larger environment also operate with a continuous drive to encroach and engulf all areas of activity including whatever small areas of autonomous action communities might be able wrest from these pressures and encroachments. The struggles around these areas of enablement or empowerment are continuous and pervasive.

The role and objective of CI research thus is to document such areas of struggle, identify those areas of small victory (where autonomous community-enabling activities and objectives are realized), and, on the basis of this research, identify strategies that have achieved success and suggest means for replicating, reproducing, and extending them. The area of technology and enabling technology is crucial to such endeavours, of course, and, designing, developing, and implementing the technology as tools and supports for these types of developments is also highly significant. Additionally, the opportunity for appropriating, integrating, and repurposing existing technology as community supports, while equally facilitating the development of technologies that in their very design reflect the specific ontology of communities, presents significant challenges and opportunities for CI researchers (de Moor and De Cindio 2007).

A dialectical approach provides the larger framework and context into which each of the individual initiatives might be placed nationally, globally, and in terms of the broad development of community informatics initiatives overall. Thus, rather than seeing the success or outcome of individual initiatives as slight, particularly when looked at only in their specific local environments, outcomes of struggle with the truly massive forces of the centralized and encroaching technologies of enforced dependency (including of course, the technologies of e-Government and e-Service delivery) can be reinterpreted as being true successes. Furthermore, when seen in this latter perspective and through the application of research and analysis, the basis of this success can be understood and made available elsewhere for similar communities equally seeking to exert an autonomous role in the midst of pervasive monopolistic centralization and corporate domination. Thus, for example, the developments by K-Net of the range of their applications, particularly the development of a self-managed ICT platform, represent a significant victory not only for themselves but for First Nations people throughout Canada who are currently learning from and acting to implement similar initiatives, as well as inspiring Indigenous people outside of Canada as to what is possible when Indigenous communities act and are able to empower themselves through the use of ICTs (see chapter 14).

Iterative Process

The networked community is in its nature iterative, because it changes—grows, evolves, shrinks, disappears—in a recurrent and responsive fashion. The various instances of its substantiation (i.e., formalization) may also, and very often do, grow from and in response to one another. Given that electronically enabled, networked communities are based on technology platforms, it is not surprising that the communities that emerge and are enabled into existence by means of such platforms will evolve along with the technologies on which they are based. Thus networked communities and community networks change over time, and design and analytical processes applied to these must recognize and make provision for such iterations and evolutions.

What this means is that CI research is by its nature partial, temporal, and even context specific, providing insight and direction for future developments and activities but necessarily reflecting and representing reality as based on a recognition and interpretive understanding of the nature of the local social and technology context, and how this mediates any development or application. Thus, as findings and insights are realized, they may have value in guiding and informing future action as well as system design and implementation, which in turn will be the subject of further research, and so on. However, at no stage can it be taken as given that CI research has made a one-time discovery or identified results that are universally necessary rather than locally contingent.

This type of iterative research implies a specific relationship between the researcher and the researched, one of partnership and knowledge sharing, as well as humility in the manner in which research is presented and reported. Research and results are never final and definitive but always partial and exploratory. They are always the result of collective efforts including necessarily a partnership with the community with whom the research is being conducted, and whose understanding of the research question and the interpretation of its results are co-equal with that of the professional researcher. Finally, there is a necessary recognition that results will always be evolving and that ultimately their value will come from the insight they provide as a basis for future action by the community, rather than as a one-time development of universally applicable models or theories. The above of course parallels directly the PAR methodological approach (Baskerville 1999).

Holistic Orientation

Community informatics research is necessarily holistic, paying specific attention to and being explicit concerning the particularities of the social context. For CI, the goals of the application are also at least in part linked directly to the requirements of the networked community, through the complexity of responding to the emergent requirements of communities in their diversity and the specificity of their functioning as communities. CI goals are necessarily diffuse and of course, include various specific elements required to reflect and ensure the continuity of the community for which an application is being developed. Thus, research conducted in Cape Breton began as research on the use of ICTs in direct job creation and quickly evolved into how to use ICTs as a support for a primary local resource—in this instance, the local music industry (Gurstein 1999). Only by adapting the initial expectations and requirements was it possible to make the local CI intervention useful, both practically and from a research perspective. This holistic approach requires, therefore, an understanding and insight into the broader social, physical, and technological community environment into which the application is being introduced.

Practice-driven Research

The nature of the research conducted within the context of CI is driven primarily by practice, i.e., outcome, rather than by methods or theory. CI research is generally concerned with developing the means to achieve specific outcomes.

In the academic research context, these outcomes may be somewhat less immediately practical, yet they are structured to link to practical or usable outcomes even if only at a later stage.

In management information systems (MIS) research, outcomes are linked in relation to business or organizational applications or business practice, and the ultimate measure of success is the degree to which an application provides usable and useful results in this context. For CI, the practice of research is parallel but the measure is the degree of usefulness or usability by end-user communities. As above, given the emergent and impermanent nature of networked communities, there is a clear need for continuous and structured linkages, feedback, and "feed-forward" mechanisms between researchers and community users.

The notion of partnerships between community users and researchers is powerful but is one with which certain difficulties are associated, as Susan MacDonald and Andrew Clement discuss in chapter 8. Differences in short-term objectives and achievement criteria (e.g., users looking for applications, researchers requiring formalized institutional acknowledgements, language, cultural norms and practices, incommensurable schedules and timelines between users and researchers, and so on) make the relationship between researchers and practitioners a somewhat difficult but not impossible barrier to working partnerships.

Theory as Pragmatic Practice / Theory as Process

Theory in CI, as in other areas of applied research, has a primary role of informing and guiding practice, and giving guidance to research in relation to practice. Specifically, in CI research, theory is needed to provide insight into the particular areas where the community as a primary social structure presents design or application challenges that diverge from those underlying other areas of applied technology. That is, it is a question of how factors specific to communities as ontological entities can be included in the understanding or analysis of particular CI applications or activities. For example, how can one understand, conceptualize, and model dispersed and consensus-based decision making as a basis for collaborative action and as design criteria for technology systems to enable such processes?

In this context, the deeper and more formalized understanding of collective and non-hierarchical decision making and consensus building, and the effects of electronically mediated communication on these processes, all will inform the outcome, and thus can inform the research in relation to the outcome as practice. Since there are deep interplays between the specific nature (affordances) of individual technologies and the related interactive processes, these understandings (formulations or theories) are works in progress rather than universal insights. These understandings may also readily take the form of inductive constructs (models) or deductive propositions leading to formalized conclusions. The ultimate test of theory in this context is its usefulness and appropriateness of fit in relation to ongoing and evolving practice, and so theory itself has to be seen as an ongoing and evolving set of formulations, which respond to both changes in the technology environment and to the specific situations and contexts of its application.

COMMUNITY INFORMATICS RESEARCH: GUIDING PRINCIPLES

It is possible to identify a number of working principles or general guidelines that inform CI research practice:

Research Use Must Be Built into Research Design

CI research is not generally conducted simply for the sake of doing research. As with Participatory Action Research more generally, CI research is usually done in relation to a specific, practical outcome or action and this means the research use generally must be integral to the research design. Thus, questions such as the following are necessary background to the formulation of CI research strategies and programs:

- What are the anticipated findings, and how can these be made usable?
- Who are the research results designed to be used by, and how do we include them as co-developers/partners in the research?
- What research questions are of interest to the practitioners currently, are there questions they may not anticipate but that will be of value in the medium and longer term, and how can the research inform those questions?
- Is there a policy-related significance to the research, and what specific type of research-based information will be required to inform and influence policy?
- Who will be the carriers, or distributors, of this information, and in what form?
- Who will be the anticipated end users or targets of the information?

Knowledge Sharing and Collaborative Knowledge Building

A key element of CI research is the contribution that it makes to the larger CI research and practitioner community. Underlying elements of the research design must include the identification of a strategy for contributing to and participating in knowledge sharing and collaborative knowledge building with the community partners, among others. This suggests that CI research is generally done in conjunction with the broader knowledge community of CI researchers and practitioners, and that this community both contributes to and derives benefits from the ongoing practice of the research. As well, it implies that recognition of the necessary role of and relationship with the community partners should be built into the research at its outset.

Researcher as Part of a Network

The basic model of CI research (explicated by CRACIN) is that of the collaborative research network. This includes academic researchers, practitioners, and those involved in policy, all of whom contribute to the research in their own way and also derive specific benefits from the outcome of the research. The research model is thus not that of the solitary "hero" researcher, gathering knowledge and bringing it forth in authoritative pronouncements to a waiting and expectant universe. The collaborative research approach is difficult to maintain since so much of institutional practice, including the constraints of research funding and the reward system for research in the academic context, has typically been designed around the model of the heroic individual researcher. Nevertheless, in a collaborative CI model, these pressures should be resisted and the power differentials between partners openly identified.

Non-Researchers as Research Peers

Similarly, the recognition and acceptance of non-researchers as research peers, as equal partners in the design, conduct, and analysis of research, is a difficult and counter-normative position. Yet in the context of applied research, as with that of CI, such recognition and acceptance is necessary at all stages if the research is to successfully achieve its goals. Again, this can be seen in the CRACIN research model, in which the non-research community partners were in most instances acting as peer partners in the overall design and conduct of the research, rather than, as in most other research instances, being passive research "subjects."

Research as Process

So, CI research can be seen ideally as a process rather than as a product; that is, an ongoing and iterative engagement between the researcher and the practitioner/partner in the research. The research thus moves back and forth in an iterative fashion between problem definition, information collection, analysis, engagement at the level of practice, assessment, and feedback, and then back again to problem definition and so on. CRACIN would have benefitted from the opportunity of being able to operate in a more iterative manner; but in this it was constrained by the formal requirements of its research funding (focused primarily on support for graduate students), its limited research lifespan (four years' funding with little possibility of extension), its only partially effective relationship with its government policy partners, and so on. In the end, CRACIN was constrained to having a very strong research product focus, even when a more process-oriented structure might have been desirable, from the perspective of providing support to the community partners, and even in ensuring a more comprehensive and insightful research output.

Technology as an Instrument of Power

As discussed above, the basis of the dialectical nature of networked communities is their struggle for existence and autonomy within the broader context of encroachments and external engulfments, through the use of the technology as an instrumentality of power. In this sense, technology is not neutral. CI-oriented technology is technology that enables communities to achieve a degree of persistence and autonomy in the midst of attempts to eliminate these zones of independence and autonomous action. The use of the broadband infrastructure by K-Net in support of its locally based high school is one example of a CI approach to the use of ICTs to realize this type of autonomy as centralized educational administrations try to provide a unified educational experience for students, whether they live in isolated First Nations communities or in southern, predominantly white suburbs.

Thus, while individual items of technology may in themselves be neutral for use by either side of such struggles, the broad force of the technology and thus the manner in which it is specifically instantiated either supports or undermines networked communities. This means that for the researcher, there is considerable pressure to redesign technologies according to the community ontology, or to redesign or repurpose existing technologies in order to provide similar affordances, or to act as enablers in a similar fashion. Given that these are areas of continuing struggle between the forces of encroachment and autonomy, the researcher has the added obligation to be explicit and concrete in the formulation and presentation of their research design, methods, and results. This formulation is necessarily constructed within the contexts of the community's struggles for social and economic power and autonomy, as potentially enabled by the technology, and including the means to determine modes of operation, structures of decision making, enforced dependencies, and so on.

CRACIN AND THE CANADIAN ROOTS OF COMMUNITY INFORMATICS

Each chapter in this volume exemplifies various observations as made above. As a whole, the collection provides a strong indication of the deeper connections between a community informatics approach to linking ICTs with communities, the broad Canadian historical experience of critiquing advanced technologies, and, more importantly, to directly appropriating and assimilating these technologies in support of local community values and objectives. Adam Fiser and Andrew Clement (chapter 14) examine how a collaboration of isolated Aboriginal communities in the Canadian hinterland were able to achieve significant opportunities and local benefits from ICTs through the development of a strongly autonomous set of interests, in turn reflecting the retention (and creation) of strong community identities even in the midst of a wide range of powerful external influences. Peddle (chapter 15) presents a similar case in the context of a similarly "peripheral" Labrador, equally in a position to obtain inordinately significant benefits from ICTs, but only as a result of a clear articulation of a local and autonomous identity and set of local interests. Winter (chapter 16), who deals with another peripheral region, northern Saskatchewan, examines the process of managing institutional development and evolution in support of ICTs through a clear articulation of local goals and norms.

Each of these papers, and others in this volume, can be seen as falling clearly within a grand tradition of Canadian social science that has as its primary concern understanding the processes underlying the extraction, management, and distribution of resources in peripheral regions and for marginalized populations, although of course in the modern era the resource being examined is information and communications rather than furs or wheat.

CONCLUSION

Research is the very core of community informatics, and at the heart of CI research is a recognition of the dialectical role of networked communities within the contemporary environment. Once, communities were a necessary and taken-for-granted element of lived society, isolated within themselves, often with only precarious links to the outside world. In the modern world, it is the external environment that is pervasive, and communities exist precariously, struggling to occupy contested spaces within and between globally pervasive and invasive electronic networks.

The "Wal-Mart" and "Facebook" effects, as models of how the "new economy" and the new technology environment is being deployed, exemplify how little space exists for community, when communities only exist through an act of assertion, will, and ultimately struggle—and notably a struggle against almost overwhelming odds. That there is an ever-extending structure of such networks both parallel and interconnected through e-governments, e-commerce systems, and e-learning structures is a condition of our time and provides both framework and backdrop for the development of community informatics as a critical discipline, and for community informatics research as one of the tools in these overall efforts in responding to and resisting these encroachments.

1   This argument is usually made in the context of Canadian political economy, with its roots in Mackintosh, Innis, Shortt, and, more recently, Mel Watkins and others of the "staples" school (see Mel Watkins, "Staple Thesis," *The Canadian Encyclopedia*, http://www.thecanadianencyclopedia.com/index.cfm?PgNm=TCE&Params= A1ARTA0007659). The argument is less often made but is equally pertinent in providing roots to and a distinctive flavour for Canadian social science in general, as in the work of Carl Dawson, Marius Barbeau, and Harold Innis, in examining the relationship between the extractive economy and the development and evolution of the associated human settlements (Donald Whyte and Frank Vallee, "Sociology," *The Canadian Encyclopedia*, http://www.thecanadianencyclopedia.com/index.cfm?PgNm=TCE& Params=A1ARTA0007537#SEC828331, and "Canadian Sociological Perspectives—I," http://uregina.ca/~gingrich/250a403.htm).

2   The technical and management literature on Wal-Mart's supply chain is large and, of course, extremely laudatory. An interesting example is "You Gonna Be a Greeter?' (http://www.almc.army.mil/alog/issues/janfeb97/ms046.htm), which examines what the US Army can learn from Wal-Mart's logistics. The significance of these global supply chains, and specifically Wal-Mart, in the area of management information systems (MIS) cannot be over-emphasized. In fact, a colleague suggested (in conversation) that all MIS research today was in one form or another concerned with the management and deployment of the Wal-Mart infrastructure.

3   This control takes the form of either contracting or not contracting. That is, a company either conforms to the technical requirements and standards of Wal-Mart or else it doesn't do business with Wal-Mart. Given the massive significance of Wal-Mart as a purchaser, this means that conformity is not voluntary but is a compulsory aspect of staying in business.

4   See http://walmartstores.com/Diversity/309.aspx.

5   This coordination is done through continuous monitoring of employee behaviour and particularly through the monitoring of employee outputs against norms. See Kalikota and Robinson (2001) concerning this type of employee "management" as being the characteristic form for electronically enabled business.

6   Citing Wellman's "Changing Connectivity: A Future History of Y2.03K" (2000), Jan van Dijk presents a very useful explication of Wellman's theory of networked individualism, as follows:

> This means that the individual in one of its roles increasingly is the most important node in the network and not a particular place, group or organization. The social and cultural process of individualization is strongly supported by the rise of social and media networks. Using them the individual creates a very mobile lifestyle and a crisscross of geographically dispersed relations. Every mobile phone user knows that (s)he does not any longer reach a place, but a particular person in one of its roles. This practice may be very liberating and self-empowering, but there also is a less positive side to it. Less and less people have a view of us as a whole person: one only knows one or a few sides of our personality playing a particular role (Wellman 2000). Presently, the last refuge where one is supposed to know each other more completely, the family household, is dispersed also. In families husbands and wives, parents and children

are engaged with ever more different activities in other social and media networks. Effects to be observed might be an increase of loneliness, alienation, uncertainty and the feeling of not being understood by others. This might happen in spite of, or because of (?), the virtual explosion of means of communication available.

See Jan van Dijk, "Outline of a Multilevel Approach of the Network Society," Department of Communication, University of Twente, The Netherlands, http://www.gw.utwente.nl/vandijk/research/network_theory/network_theory_plaatje/a_theory_outline_outline_of_a.doc/.) Wellman's essay appeared in *Sociological Research Online* 4(4), http://www.socresonline.org.uk/4/4/wellman.html.

7   In this as in other areas, when we are discussing externally driven networks based on centralized decision making, we should include as direct parallels the processes of the transfer into electronic format of government services ("e-government") without the parallel development of enhanced means for enabling citizen participation and control at the community level of these services ("e-governance"). For an elaboration of this discussion, see Gurstein 2005.

8   See http://pages.ebay.com/help/policies/hub.html?ssPageName=home:f:f:US.

9   For example, a person suspended from eBay loses all membership privileges. A suspended individual is not permitted to participate on the eBay site using any existing account or to register new accounts with eBay. A suspension from eBay may be for a fixed length of time, indefinitely, or permanently. Suspensions remain in effect until removed by eBay. See also http://pages.ebay.com/help/policies/rfe-previously-suspended.html. Apparently, some quarter of a million individuals and businesses are currently deriving a majority of their livelihood from transactions on eBay. Thus, being suspended from eBay, without right of notice or appeal, is potentially an extremely significant sanction and gives those who enforce such rules enormous economic and social power.

10   It should be noted that while the individual is denied access to his or her self-created information, this information, at least in the case of Facebook, is extremely difficult to have removed.

11   I am grateful to my colleague Andrew Clement for pointing out the role of "alternatives" as parallel to "resistance" in the dialectic of communities and ICTs.

12   There are, of course, other areas in which Wal-Mart's actions and policies have been extensively criticized. The company has, for example, been taken to task for its policies concerning gender and race and for its approach to human rights, including the manner in which the company has dealt with documented abuse of their subcontractors in various countries. For an interesting depiction of one instance of resistance to Wal-Mart, see Sergeo Kirby's 2006 National Film Board of Canada film *WAL-TOWN*, at http://www.nfb.ca/film/wal_town/.

13   Cf. Wellman's references to contractual, or *Gemeinschaft*, relationships, as per Durkheim's notions of the defining characteristic of his networked individualism postulate (Hampton and Wellman 1999).

14   Of course, virtual, physical, and geo-local communities existed and made use of communications media such as the telephone, radio, print, and so on long before the development of digital media. What is discussed below and elsewhere in this chapter should be seen to include these forms of virtual and physical communities alongside those with a more specifically electronic platform and connections.

15 A number of companies in the dot-com period and immediately after created online forums in which customers were given the opportunity to present feedback to the company, with the intention of creating "communities" around the various products or brands, as promoted by Hagel and Armstrong in their influential book, *Net Gain: Expanding Business Through Virtual Community* (Boston, MA: Harvard Business School Press, 1997). Most such communities were quickly shut down when the customers began to interact with each other to form groups of customers, many of which were directly critical of particular company offerings. A number of such critical groups eventually reemerged in the "sucks.com" phenomenon (see, for example, http://www.mycarsucks.com/).

REFERENCES

Baskerville, Richard L. 1999. Investigating information systems with action research. *Communications of the AIS* 2(3), http://aisel.aisnet.org/cais/vol2/iss1/19.

Birdsall, William F. 2000. The digital divide in the liberal state: A Canadian perspective. *First Monday* 5(12), http://firstmonday.org/htbin/cgiwrap/bin/ojs/index.php/fm/article/viewArticle/820.

Castells, Manuel. 1994. European cities, the informational society and the global economy. *New Left Review* 204: 19–32.

de Moor, Aldo, and Fiorella De Cindio. 2007. Beyond users to communities: Designing systems as though communities matter. *Journal of Community Informatics* 3(1), http://www.ci-journal.net/index.php/ciej/article/view/434/312.

Giddens, Anthony. 1984. *The constitution of society: Outline of the theory of structuration.* Berkeley: University of California Press.

Gurstein, Michael. 1999. Fiddlers on the wire: Music, electronic commerce and local economic development on a virtual Cape Breton Island. In *Doing business on the Internet: Opportunities and pitfalls*, ed. Celia T. Romm and Fay Sudweeks, 193–207. Berlin: Springer Verlag.

———. 2003. Effective use: A community informatics strategy beyond the digital divide. *First Monday*, Special Issue no. 8 ("A Web site with a view—The Third World on First Monday"), http://firstmonday.org/htbin/cgiwrap/bin/ojs/index.php/fm/article/viewArticle/1798/1678.

———. 2005. From e-Government to e-Governance: An approach from effective use. Paper prepared for "Paving the Road to Tunis," Conference on Canadian Civil Society and the World Summit on the Information Society, Canadian Commission for UNESCO, Winnipeg.

———, ed. 2000. *Community informatics: Enabling communities with information and communications technologies.* Hershey, PA: Idea Group Publishing.

Gurstein, Michael, and Thomas Horan. 2005. Why community information systems are important to the future of Management Information Systems and the field of Information Science (IS). Paper presented to the Gordon Davis Series on the Future of Information Systems Academic Discipline: Opportunities and Directions.

Innis, Harold A. 1950. *Empire and communications.* Toronto: Ryerson.

Kalakota, Ravi, and Marcia Robinson. 2001. *E-Business 2.0: Roadmap for success.* Boston: Addison-Wesley Longman.

Kling, Rob, and Roberta Lamb. 2002. IT and organizational change in digital economies: A socio-technical approach. In *Understanding the digital economy: Data, tools and research*, ed. Erik Brynjolfsson and Brian Kahin, 295–324. Cambridge, MA: MIT Press.

Lessig, Lawrence. 1999. *Code and other laws of cyberspace.* http://www.code-is-law.org.

Levitt, Theodore. 1993. The globalization of markets. In *Readings in international business: A decision approach,* ed. Robert Z. Aliber and Reid W. Click, 249–66. Cambridge, MA: MIT Press.

Macpherson, Crawford B. 1962. *The political theory of possessive individualism: Hobbes to Locke.* London: Oxford University Press.

Mann, Michael. 1984. The autonomous power of the state: Its origins, mechanisms and results. *European Journal of Sociology* 25: 185–213.

Middleton, Catherine A., and Christine Sorensen. 2005. How connected are Canadians? Inequities in Canadian households' Internet access. *Canadian Journal of Communication* 30(4), http://www.cjc-online.ca/index.php/journal/article/viewArticle/1656/1794.

Nnadi, Nkechi, and Michael Gurstein. 2007. Towards supporting community information seeking and use. *Journal of Community Informatics,* Special Issue on Community Informatics and Systems Design, 3(1), http://www.ci-journal.net/index.php/ciej/article/view/325/304.

Piven, Frances Fox, and Richard A. Cloward. 1979. *Poor people's movements: Why they succeed, how they fail.* New York: Vintage Books.

Porter, David, and Chester L. Mirsky. 2003 *Megamall on the Hudson: Planning, Wal-Mart and grassroots resistance.* Victoria, BC: Trafford Publishing.

Reddick, Andrew, Christian Boucher, and Manon Groseilliers. 2000. *The dual digital divide: The information highway in Canada.* Ottawa: Public Interest Advocacy Centre.

Ross, D.F. 1998. *Competing through supply chain management: Creating market-winning strategies through supply chain partnerships.* Norwell, MA, and Dordrecht: Kluwer Academic Publishers.

Schiller, Dan. 1988. How to think about information. In *The political economy of information,* ed. Vincent Mosco and Janet Wasko, 27–43. Madison: University of Wisconsin Press.

Sciadas, George. 2002. *The digital divide in Canada.* Ottawa: Statistics Canada, http://www.statcan.gc.ca/pub/56f0009x/56f0009x2002001-eng.pdf.

Simpson, Lyn E. 2005. Community informatics and sustainability: Why social capital matters. *Journal of Community Informatics* 1(2): 102–19.

Stalder, Felix. 2010. Autonomy and control in the era of post-privacy. In *Beyond privacy: New notions of the private and public domains,* Open 19, http://www.skor.nl/artefact-4808-en.html.

Strawson, P.F. 1990 [1959]. *Individuals: An essay in descriptive metaphysics.* London: Routledge.

Tsui, Anne S., and Joshua B. Wu. 2005. The new employment relationship versus the mutual investment approach: Implications for human resource management. *Human Resource Management* 44(2): 115–21.

Wellman, Barry, and Keith Hampton. 1999. Living networked in a wired world. *Contemporary Sociology* 28(6): 648–54.

Wellman, Barry, Anabel Quan-Haase, Jeffrey Boase, Wenhong Chen, Keith Hampton, Isabel Isla de Diaz, and Kakuko Miyata. 2003. The social affordances of the Internet for networked individualism. *Journal of Computer Mediated Communication* 8(3), http://jcmc.indiana.edu/vol8/issue3/wellman.html.

3 **KEEPING IN TOUCH** A Snapshot of
Canadian Community Networks and Their Users — Report
on the CRACIN Survey of Community Network Users

Marita Moll, Melissa Fritz

How the Internet affects social capital is neither a trivial nor an obscure question.
— Wellman et al. (2001, 436)

The concept of social capital emphasizes the notion of "investments and assets that bring benefits that are not fully appropriated by the individuals making the investments" (Helliwell 2001, 6). Social capital is created through the actions of individuals, and yet it is not only, or even necessarily, the individual who stands to benefit as a result: the benefits accrue to the entire community. As sociologist Robert Putnam points out (1993, 170): "This means that social capital, unlike other forms of capital, must often be produced as a by-product of other social activities."[1] In other words, whereas financial capital is usually privately held, and individuals deliberately seek to create it, social capital is a public good.

In this chapter, we argue that community networks can be considered among the "investments and assets" to which Helliwell refers. Government investment in community networks, both nationally and internationally, indicate that they are considered a public good, a critical part of the infrastructure of communities in an information society. (For additional discussion, see Appendix B.)

THE CRACIN COMMUNITY NETWORK SURVEYS: RATIONALE AND METHODOLOGY

In 2003, the CRACIN group began to assess the development of community-oriented ICT capacity and services and to document the contribution of community networks to local learning, to the strengthening of relations in and between communities, and more generally to community-focused social and economic development (Clement et al. 2003, 1).

As part of the CRACIN research, a survey of administrators and users of community networks was designed to collect information that could inform other researchers and policy makers in areas of community technology and economic development, social development, and communications. The goal was to provide the kind of micro-level data that Jeff Frank (2003), then project director and lead for the Social Capital as a Public Policy Tool project, suggests is necessary to gauge the impact of public investment in community communications technologies.[2]

The CRACIN survey described in this chapter consisted of two parts. The user survey, on which we report here, collected information concerning various user characteristics: why and how users use the service and the social and community activities in which users engage. In addition, an administrator survey collected general information about community networking sites and the people who run them. It included questions related to the size and characteristics of the site or sites, questions about funding, questions about goals and objectives, as well as questions about community impact. Information collected from the site administrator survey is available on the CRACIN website (Moll and Fritz 2007).

The surveys were undertaken for a number of reasons:

- To broaden the generalizability of the CRACIN research findings
- To provide a more quantitative basis for policy recommendations
- Investigate possible "public good" outcomes
- To explore patterns of interaction emerging from the new "connected" community.

The preparation and implementation of the surveys included:

- Collecting information about related surveys
- Developing possible indicators of social capital in the context of community technology initiatives
- Validating the surveys through focus groups (organized by two CRACIN partners, Communautique, in Montréal, and St. Christopher House, in Toronto)
- Seeking ethics clearance through the University of Toronto Ethics Committee.

Potential survey candidates were located through various personal networks, which included CRACIN community partners, members of Telecommunities Canada, and personal and professional contacts.

It was our goal to find forty-two cooperating administrators to complete the English language administrator survey. Given that survey overload is a major problem for this sector because of a constant round of data gathering required to satisfy the government accountability process (see chapter 19 for further discussion), responses to the CRACIN request to complete yet another lengthy survey were not always enthusiastic. In the end, we were able to contact thirty-three administrators from whom we received sixteen completed administrator surveys. Of these, twelve agreed to approach a few users about completing the user survey. It would have been impossible for the authors to do the kind of travelling necessary to contact users individually, so the co-operation of administrators was essential, despite the issues surrounding the validity of gathering data in this way. For example, the data set comes from users who had the time and opportunity to complete the survey, and who may have felt a commitment to or dependence on the site and/or had a good relationship with the administrator.

In the end, we received eighty-five user surveys from twelve sites across Canada, seventy-nine of which are included in this analysis. As this represents only a tiny fraction of the actual CAP site users at any time, this survey makes no claim to represent the entire population of users. To provide a wider perspective, results from the much broader but less detailed Industry Canada survey (Ekos Research Associates 2004) have, where relevant, also been included in this analysis, as have certain results from a BC survey of rural CAP sites conducted by GPI Atlantic (Colman 2002a, 2002b). The CRACIN survey provides an up-close and personal perspective on the use made of these sites by those who responded, including users' direct comments, which often offer helpful clarification.

The survey responses were collected between January 2007 and February 2008 from five sites in Ontario, two in British Columbia, one in Nova Scotia, two in Prince Edward Island, one in Manitoba, and one in the Northwest Territories. Of the respondents, 60 percent were from rural/remote sites, and 40 percent were from urban/inner-city sites.

THE CRACIN USER SURVEY

The following are tales from two community networks.

> The only thing I'd like to share is that I'm grateful that I have access to these computers. When I wasn't working, I was bored and felt useless. But I would go to the Community House and look for a job. Then [a CAP worker] told me where to go [to find a job] and I did. I'm very happy that I got a job to help my family of 3 kids. I was a stay at home dad and now I can help support my family.

Also, I love to keep in touch with friends and family by emailing them. Please don't take away these computers. You should be giving us better ones. I mean could you give us newer ones? Also the printer does break down a lot. That is the only real problem. Thank you.

—A respondent in the 21-to-30 age group, living in Ontario

I can't live without my Community Learning Network. It provides a number of essential services beyond the Internet. It provides IP telephony, video conferencing, online learning platforms, web hosting, email, telemedicine, searching, etc., which I use every day. I feel that I am a part of the network planning process; it meets my needs because I have contributed to its design and I know that many other people can say that as well. The staff are incredible in ensuring the network is working smoothly and are always looking to the future for expansion, improving access and services. My Network is thriving because [it] is for everyone and anyone can contribute to it.

—An Aboriginal respondent, also in the 21-to-30 age group

Community networks are as different as the communities that host them— some are well endowed technologically, others are barely keeping pace. But these users offer us a taste of how their lives have been changed by their access to the community sites. It is obvious that they share a sense of ownership and a sense of belonging with respect to the site. These users are exhibiting some of the fundamental characteristics of social cohesion. Social cohesion can be defined as "a set of social processes that help instill in individuals the sense of belonging to the same community and the feeling that they are recognised as members of that community" (Jenson 1998, 4).

The CRACIN user survey collected a wide range of information on user characteristics, activities, and preferences. Particular emphasis was placed on determining common activities and on the role that staff and volunteers played in helping users engage in these activities. We were also interested in documenting community crossover activities, that is, how activities at the sites interacted with the broader community. One of the goals was to paint a picture of the value of these sites in the everyday lives of these users.

This survey is one of the few that collected results directly from users of community networking sites. Another is an online survey of 7,004 CAP site users conducted by Industry Canada's Information Highway Applications Branch (IHAB) in 2003, the results of which were incorporated into an evaluative study of the CAP program carried out by Ekos Research Associates (2004). We see a remarkable consistency between the results for similar questions, suggesting that, although relatively small in comparison, our survey reached a similar population of users.

Demographic Details

Age, gender, and education. Despite the difficulties inherent in finding people within a constantly changing user population who are willing to fill out a lengthy survey for no compensation, the responses we received do provide valuable information about the users who participated in the survey and their activities at the site:

- Female participation slightly exceeded male participation in community networking sites: 55.3% of our respondents were women (Ekos = 56.0%).
- 41.0% of the respondents to the CRACIN survey were under 30; 14.1% were under 20 (Ekos = 29% under 24).
- The largest group of users was the 21–30-year-old category.
- 62.4% of the respondents were under 40.
- 12.9% were over 50 (Ekos = 15% over 55).
- Of all the users aged 30 years or under, 34% were male and 66% were female.

Although the age and gender distributions in this survey are not an indication of who comes to the site but rather of who was willing to take the time to fill out the questionnaire, CRACIN survey responses present a demographic very similar to the much larger Industry Canada survey reported on by Ekos Research Associates.

Community network users were well educated, but there were interesting gender differences in education levels:

- 16% of users had high school education or less.
- 34% had some post-secondary education.
- 37.8% of male users and 18.2% of female users had completed a bachelor's degree.
- Female users were more likely to have incomplete post-secondary or university education.
- 14.9% females and 8.1% males were more likely to have incomplete bachelor's level education, a reverse of the trend for the post-secondary/university level.

In comparison, only 11 percent of the general Canadian population surveyed in the 2001 census reported that they had a bachelor's degree. However, of that 11 percent, more than half (6.8%) were under the age of 44 (Statistics Canada 2003). The relatively high level of education among our respondents could thus be due to the fact that 41 percent of CRACIN respondents were under the age of 30.

In addition, we know that, as a result of the screening process, immigrants to Canada tend to be relatively well educated, and the use of these sites by immigrants might also help to explain the high levels of education among respondents. Speaking about how volunteering at the Vancouver Community Network allows newcomers to Canada to improve language and technical skills, Diane Dechief notes in chapter 9: "Even though the volunteers are already skilled and knowledgeable, gaining some experience with these skills in Canada seems to enhance their human capital and to benefit their job-seeking processes. Volunteer contributions to the network—while resulting in enhanced technical skills and practice with English language skills—also build social capital." This serves as a good example of Coleman's theory that social capital is a by-product of other social activities (Coleman 1990, 317). Similarly, one respondent to the CRACIN survey noted that the site was "very good for newcomers and for the people in-between jobs."

- 28.2% of respondents indicated they were not born Canadian citizens.
- 30% of these indicated that they were recent immigrants (they had arrived in Canada on or after 1 January 2000).
- 83% of the immigrants responding to this survey were from urban sites; 17% were from rural sites.
- 41% of immigrants were male while 54% were female; this mirrors the gender breakdown in general respondents (55.3% female).
- Immigrants were, on the whole, a little older than the respondents overall. The largest group of immigrants was the 31–40-year-old category (29.2%), followed by the 41–50 group (25.0%). Only 20.8 percent were in the 21–30-year old category.
- Immigrants were also somewhat better educated: 33.3% had completed a bachelor's degree (survey overall = 24.7%).

Industry Canada did not collect information on immigrants in its user survey. The Ekos evaluative report does, however, note that 11 percent of administrators agreed with the statement that new immigrants used their site to "a large extent" (Ekos Research Associates 2004).

We know that community networking sites located in urban and inner-city areas play an important role in helping recent immigrants assimilate. As Diane Dechief concludes her study of immigrant volunteers at the Vancouver Community Network by commenting:

> The VCN, communities within the Lower Mainland, and the volunteers themselves all benefit as interactions at the VCN contribute to newcomers' settlement processes. These contributions include involving recent immigrants in a not-for-profit organization, supplying training for volunteer roles, offering a space in which to interact and share information with others, and providing a means to gain 'Canadian experience' including references for potential employers. . . . Collectively, these interactions create social capital and enhance social inclusion at a community level.

Aboriginals. 11 percent of respondents identified themselves as Aboriginal (First Nations, Métis, or Inuit) (Ekos = 7%).

Income. Income distribution analysis of the user population represented in both the CRACIN and Industry Canada surveys reveals remarkable similarities. Both surveys showed that 56 percent of users had an income of $29,000 or less. The CRACIN survey allowed for a more detailed breakdown of this group:

- A considerably higher percentage of women than men earned $29,000 or less (66% versus 49%).
- 53% of all respondents over the age of 40 had an annual household income of less than $20,000. It is worth noting that $20,000 is near or below (depending on region) the before-tax low-income cut-off established by Statistics Canada for 2005 (National Council on Welfare 2006).[3]
- Almost 26% of CRACIN respondents had an annual household income of less than $9,999 per year, well below the poverty line by any definition.
- More women than men were earning less than $9,999 per year (32% versus 23%).

As a point of comparison with the general population at the time, according to Statistics Canada, the median total income of couple families (a couple living together with children) in metropolitan areas was $67,600 in 2005.[4] The national median income for lone-parent families was $30,000 (Statistics Canada 2007). The Canadian Internet Use Survey showed that income is a factor in Internet use: "About 88% of adults with household incomes of $86,000 or more used the Internet last year, well above the proportion of 61% among adults living in households with incomes below $86,000" (Statistics Canada 2006).

These results show that community networks are serving a group that is, by and large, economically disadvantaged and that the women in this group tend to be even more disadvantaged than the men. Women struggling at the low end of the economic scale know that they need to acquire new information and communication skills in order to improve their situation and are seeking help in a community setting, as women often do, to overcome technological disadvantages. It makes the continuation of CAP sites and community networks a gender equity issue as well as an economic and social issue. (See chapters 6 and 10 for more on the gender dimensions of community networking.)

Governments have an obligation to remedy major disparities in access to communications technologies. This is recognized in the telecommunications sector through basic service obligations imposed on incumbent telecommunications carriers. Recognizing the need for remediation in the area of new and emerging technologies, the *Final Report* of the Telecommunications Policy Review Panel (TPRP) recommended a national ICT adoption strategy "focused on using ICTs to increase the productivity of the Canadian economy, the social well-being of Canadians and the inclusiveness of Canadian society" (2006, 7-20). It also noted that such an adoption strategy needed to be focused on the acquisition of new skills as well as on physical access to the tools (2006, 7-29). Perhaps some of these recommendations could become part of the basic service obligation currently under review by the Canadian Radio-television and Telecommunications Commission (CRTC) (2010). Such a policy shift would give a program such as CAP the long-term stability it needs to continue serving those who depend on these services.

General Activities

We asked respondents to tell us a little bit about their basic usage patterns at the site and their overall satisfaction with the site. The majority (80%) of respondents made use of the site at least a few times per week; 40 percent said they used the site every day. In addition, 65 percent of users indicated the site always met their computing needs in terms of availability and hours of service.

TABLE 3.1 Computer and internet activities: Frequency of use

Activity	Every day	At least once a week	At least once a week, as reported by Ekos Research Associates (2004)
Send and receive e-mail	49.4%	83.5%	78%
Surf the internet for fun or general interest	25.9%	70.5%	
Read news from Canadian sources	18.8%	57.6%	
Type letters using a word processing program	24.7%	57.6%	38% (word processing and Internet research)
Search for information about local events	23.5%	55.3%	
Read news from other countries	11.8%	48.2%	
Search for government information	15.3%	44.7%	46% (federal) 34% (other levels)
Engage in independent study	15.3%	37.6%	55% (personal development/interests)
Seek health-related information	8.2%	28.2%	34%
Play games	3.5%	28.2%	
Play music	4.7%	23.5	
Purchase or sell goods and/or services	2.4%	9.4%	13%

We were also looking for specific patterns of use related to twelve common computer activities. These activities are listed in table 3.1 and in figure 3.1. Not surprisingly, sending and receiving email was the most popular activity, closely followed by surfing the Web for no special reason other than enjoyment. But the respondents also used the community sites for a variety of other purposes.

FIGURE 3.1 Weekly use of community network sites by activity

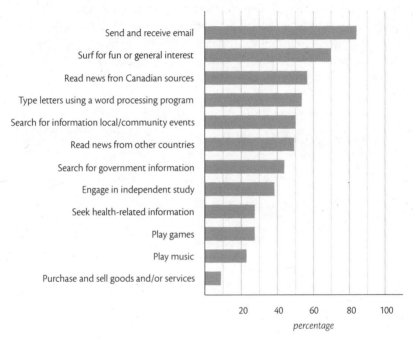

Typing letters. We were surprised to find typing letters using a word processing program so high on this list, with 24.7 percent indicating that this was a daily activity, and 57.6 percent engaging in this activity at least once per week. Users may be coming to the sites for this purpose because they need help using computers and printers. Although many users (61%) did have computers at home, they may not have had printers or word processing software, or what software they had may have lacked certain needed features (one user mentioned multi-lingual character sets). Responses to other questions indicate that job searching and, therefore, résumé building are important activities. The sites are also used by students, and, as one student noted, "schools expect a lot of projects to be typed and the CAP site lets me do that." Clearly, then, community sites are important for reasons beyond Internet searches and email.

Searching for information about local and community events. A little over half (55.3%) of the respondents said they had made use of the site to search for information on local events at least once a week, if not more frequently (see table 3.1). This is considerably higher than the 42 percent of respondents to the Canadian Internet Use Survey (which surveyed 30,000 Canadians), who said they had used the Internet to research community events at least once during that year (Statistics Canada 2006).

Are community network users more connected to their communities than the general public? Along with other evidence presented in this chapter, the relative frequency with which users of these sites sought information about community events (see figure 3.2) suggests that this may indeed be the case. Further analysis showed that rural users were just as likely to use the site to search for community events as were respondents from urban areas.

FIGURE 3.2 Frequency of searches for community information

How often do you use this CNS to search for information on local community events?

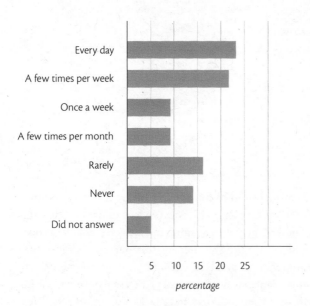

percentage

As we show further on, community networks, which offer access to the new technologies combined with the in-house support that enables effective use of those technologies, also function as social enablers. This effect was also reported by the Ekos Research study (2004, 4), which found that one of the benefits of the CAP network model was "the fuller integration of citizens into society and greater social cohesion."

Searching for government information. Government at all levels now relies heavily on websites for distributing information. A little time spent searching government websites will often turn up needed information in a fraction of the time it takes to contact someone by phone. Having made this commitment to the online delivery of information, government now has a responsibility to ensure that all citizens have access to the knowledge and tools needed to search for this information and to communicate with the government online.

Our results show that searching for government information is an important activity for these respondents:

- 44.7% used the site to search for government information at least once per week.
- 64.7% searched for government information at least a few times per month.
- Age distribution of those seeking government information seekers was quite even: 66% under 40 and 60% over 40 searched for government information at least a few times per month.

In comparison, 52 percent of respondents to the Canadian Internet Use Survey indicated that they had searched for government information during the year (Statistics Canada 2006). Ekos also reported a high percentage of users searching for such information.

Community networks are important distribution sites for government information. This is certainly one very good reason to offer these sites some core funding. As we learned from the administrator surveys and through talking to site administrators, funding instability is an enormous drawback that really hampers program delivery:

> The CAP funding... enables us to keep all five sites open and pays for much of the administrative work that keeps the partnerships running smoothly. Without it, we would have fewer services and staff would be working even longer hours with probably less pay. Our ability to manage all these services would be substantially reduced (Pam Gliatis, administrator of the Sea to Sky Public Access Network in Squamish, BC, quoted in Moll 2007, 12).

See chapter 19 for a thorough discussion of community networking experiences with government funding.

Seeking health-related information. Although relatively few respondents (8.2%) searched for health-related information on a daily basis, this was a fairly common activity among users.

- 83.5% of survey respondents had used the community networking site to search for health-related information at some time. In comparison, 58% of Canadians surveyed for the Canadian Internet Use Survey reported having used the Internet over the course of the previous year to search for medical or health-related information (Statistics Canada 2006).

- 28.2% of respondents to the CRACIN survey (Ekos = 34%) indicated they searched for health-related information once per week or more.

The growing use of the Internet as a resource for such information suggests that users want to have a better understanding of health-related issues, presumably so that they can have more input into (and hence control over) health-related decisions. This raises the question of what community network users do with this health-related information and how they evaluate the information they find on the Internet.

"The key finding from the individual/micro-level research is that there is a very clear and very robust relationship between individual income and individual health," says Shelley Phipps in her review of research literature on the impact of poverty on health (Phipps 2003, iii). Given that community networks users are often economically disadvantaged and possibly at greater risk for health problems, community networks could serve these users better if they were more fully integrated into the public health network. There is an excellent opportunity for partnerships between community networking sites and community health organizations, which could perhaps lead to workshops and information sessions on searching for and evaluating such information and applying it to personal situations.

The Importance of Community Networking Sites

I don't have the Internet at home so this resource has been very important to me (as well as a lot of my neighbourhood friends) because I am able to do the research I need for school.
—A survey respondent who was attending high school

Although this respondent did have access to the Internet through the public library and at school, as was the case for many other respondents, the CAP site was clearly a critical part of her educational support system. She indicated that she could only use the site several times a week for completing homework, as it was not open every day.

Respondents were asked to consider how important these sites were for various online information search needs. The results presented in table 3.2 indicate the percentage of respondents who said the sites were either important or very important for specific information needs, as compared with other sources of information.

Respondents are telling us quite clearly that new information and communication technologies have quickly assumed a very important place in their lives. In the next few years, we can only expect these numbers to go up as the Internet becomes increasingly integrated into the daily information stream. Any citizens who do not have effective access to such services will be at a serious disadvantage, an issue that needs to remain a priority at all levels of government.

TABLE 3.2 Relative importance of community network sites for information needs

Online activity	Ranked as important or very important
Communicating with people (versus by phone or post)	78.3%
Looking for employment information (versus via newspaper, TV, or radio)	72.3%
Helping find employment (versus through training, peer support, networking)	63.9%
Looking for local information (versus via newspaper, TV, or radio)	63.9%

Engaging in Individual Support and Personal Networking Activities

It has helped me keep in touch with family and friends, that I grew close to while living in the North . . . and with new friends that I have made throughout the past years. It is great to know that this is a quicker way to keep in touch, instead of waiting for the regular snail mail from the post office. . . .

I would like to share that having this technology that we have in place now, is GREAT. I have learned quite a bit the past few years, in the knowledge that I have gained in the work place where I pretty well learned, and am pleased with what I know now. . . .

Having access to video conference is GREAT, as I am thinking of using this technology to keep in touch with my immediate family, who doesn't live with me, but I still would like to keep in touch with them, just to see their faces, and of course, with my beautiful grandchildren.

—An Aboriginal respondent, in the 41-to-50 age group

We were interested in the extent to which users engaged in self-directed learning activities at the sites as well as the extent to which the sites facilitated interaction with other people, both online and off. We posed the question, "Did using the computers at this site help you to . . ." and then provided a list of activities that focused on individual growth and improvement activities as well as on personal networking activities that users might undertake at or through the site. The results appear in table 3.3 and figure 3.3.

TABLE 3.3 Role of staff and volunteers in effective use of community network resources

Did the staff/volunteers at this site help you to…	Yes	No	Not applicable
Improve your computer skills?	72.6%	11.9%	14.3%
Improve your Internet skills?	75.0%	8.3%	14.3%
Stay in contact with non-local friends and family?	47.6%	25.0%	20.2%
Stay in contact with local friends and family?	48.8%	22.6%	21.4%
Learn about community events?	71.4%	10.7%	14.3%
Find health-related information?	53.6%	16.7%	20.2%
Further your employment skills?	50.00%	13.1%	32.1%
Prepare a résumé or employment letter?	53.5%	15.5%	26.2%
Look for employment?	42.5%	11.9%	39.3%
Deal with personal challenges?	57.8%	16.9%	20.5%
Improve your basic literacy skills?	29.8%	27.4%	38.1%
Help you meet new people?	56.5%	12.9	23.5%
Connect with support groups?	38.1%	23.8%	32.1%

FIGURE 3.3 Use of community network sites to address specific personal needs and goals

Did using computers at this site help you …

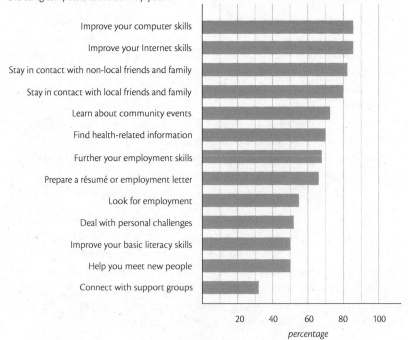

Finding health-related information. To no one's surprise, improving computer and Internet skills and email activities that allow users to stay in contact with friends and family locally and abroad are the primary activities at community sites. But "finding health-related information" still ranks fairly high in the positive responses to the activities on this list. As noted earlier, important synergies between community health programs and community networking sites seem to be emerging and should be explored.

Learning about community events. In their 1999 ethnographic study of "Netville," an early wired Toronto suburb, Hampton and Wellman (1999, 12) found that "the local network brought neighbours together to socialize, helped them arrange in-person gatherings. . . . The high rate of online activity led to increased local awareness." The CRACIN survey likewise found that respondents used community networking sites to connect with community events. Of all the respondents, 72.9 percent said computers at the site helped them learn more about events, groups, services, and issues in their local community (see figure 3.2), and 55.3% had previously indicated that they searched for local information at least once per week (see table 3.1).

Of the people who found the site useful for learning about community events, 63 percent were from rural sites, and 37 percent were from urban sites. This rural-urban split suggests that there was relatively little difference between rural and urban users with respect to using the sites to find local information. In fact, we had expected urbanites to make heavier use of community event listings if only to sort through the choices. However, in comparison to urban dwellers, who see posters and have easy access to local, on-street newspapers, rural users may have fewer readily available sources of information about community events. Online community event listings would thus appear to be an important source of this kind of information in rural areas. A report from a BC survey of rural CAP sites highlights the importance of these sites to everyday life in the areas they serve: "CAP sites also play an important role in strengthening rural communities, enhancing communication and reducing isolation, facilitating inclusion of youth, seniors, and disadvantaged groups, promoting equity, and providing opportunities for education, employment, and local learning" (Colman 2002b).

Facilitating personal networking. As the quotation that opens this chapter suggests, the effect of Internet communications on how individuals and communities function socially is an important field of study for Internet researchers. In their 1998 survey of 39,211 visitors to the National Geographic website, Wellman et al. (2001, 450) found that "Internet use supplements network capital by extending existing levels of face-to-face and telephone contact. . . . Most Internet contact is with people who live within an hour's drive."

The CRACIN user survey was particularly interested in how the sites facilitated personal networking and face-to-face interaction. In response to the question, "Do you find that using the computers or Internet at this community networking site helped you to stay in contact with family/friends in the local community/outside the local community?" over 80 percent of respondents indicated that they used the site for such purposes. Delving deeper into community connections, it appears that the sites were also instrumental in helping these users extend their local social networks. We asked whether the computers at the site had helped respondents meet new people: nearly half (49.4%) of the respondents said yes. Although the sites are used more for "maintaining" than for "extending" personal relationships, as suggested by Wellman et al. (2001), this result is still a good indication that community networking sites do serve as local meeting places. This was further supported by the findings in the administrator portion of the CRACIN survey. Providing a meeting place was the third most important goal of the sites surveyed, and one at which administrators felt they had been quite successful (Moll and Fritz 2007).

Events organized at the sites included the following:

- Computer classes and teas for seniors
- Graduations
- Semi-annual community gatherings
- Reading and literacy programs
- Local history and children's programs
- Bi-monthly presentations by participants that are open to the public
- Award sponsorship
- Fundraising events, such as a dance or a concession

The Ekos report included a telephone survey of 503 "site representatives" (volunteers, paid staff, administrators). According to these site reps, users of CAP sites experienced:

- Improved computer skills (95%)
- Improved Internet skills (95%)
- Better integration into the community (72%)
- Improved economic situation (53%)

Although less detailed, this information from a much larger group of CAP users strongly supports the often unrecognized social role such sites play in their communities.

The Role of Staff and Volunteers

In August 2008 the Northern News Service carried a report on Rankin Inlet's CAP program, established in 2005. Rankin's free computer sites were now facing a serious shortage of cash and a lack of adequate staffing. The report quoted Darlene Thompson, CAP administrator for Nunavut, who noted that "being under-funded is standard for pretty much every CAP site across the territory." The report continued:

> A few years back, six communities in Nunavut did get added funding through regional Inuit organizations and Human Resources Development Canada. That money allowed them to hire a site supervisor. . . .

> "It made a huge difference for those communities and those CAP sites," she [Thompson] said. "They were able to do a whole lot of programs that they couldn't otherwise have done."

> In Clyde River, for instance, the site supervisor helped establish a media centre and train local youth in computer editing. Now filmmakers and visiting researchers can hire "youth not just as load bearers, but as camera people and editors," she said. (Mackenzie 2008)

The importance of the effective use of new technologies—"the capacity and opportunity to successfully integrate ICTs into the accomplishment of self or collaboratively identified goals" (Gurstein 2003)—is well documented in community informatics literature and has been recognized by policy makers as a strategic element of success in a networked society. For example, in 2006, the final report of the Telecommunications Policy Review Panel (TPRP) acknowledged that the social infrastructures that enable the use of ICTs are at least as important as the technical infrastructure and that the community is the key provider of the social infrastructure:

> A new generation of ICT applications allows communities to adapt ICTs to their own situations, develop local content, and access and use content created by others. However, none of this will happen in the absence of e-literacy and technology skills at the community level. . . . The Canadian Research Alliance for Community Innovation and Networking noted in its submission to the Panel that community networks and other community-based organizations provide both technological and social infrastructures for ICT development and innovation. Through training programs, for example, they help ensure that all Canadians, particularly those most at risk of being left behind, have the necessary skills to participate in a networked economy. (Telecommunications Policy Review Panel 2006, 7-43)

In the CRACIN survey, users were asked to indicate whether staff and volunteers had helped them with the individual support and personal networking activities already listed in figure 3.3.

From the responses, it is clear that the staff and volunteers at the sites played an important role in enabling users to tap the available resources effectively. Staff and volunteers helped respondents improve their computer and Internet skills, which in turn would make them less dependent on assistance with basic computer activities such as email. Of the 86 percent who said using the computers at the site helped them with their Internet and computer skills, 75 percent and 72.6 percent, respectively, said that staff and volunteers were important in facilitating these activities (see table 3.3 and figure 3.4).

FIGURE 3.4 Assistance provided by community network staff and volunteers

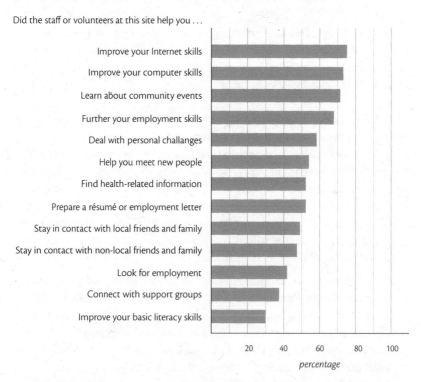

An unexpectedly high rate (over 50%) of positive responses regarding assistance of staff and volunteers was found for the categories "dealing with personal challenges" (57.8%) and "help you meet new people" (56.5%). This seems to indicate that the volunteers in community networking sites do much more than help people find their way around computers and onto the Internet. Write-in comments about the staff and volunteers confirmed this:

The staff as well as the volunteers of the community networking program have helped me in a way to be more confident, helped me tap into those inner computer skills that I thought I lost way back in school. They also helped me enjoy myself on the computers instead of making it feel like such a chore.

—A respondent, in the 21-to-30 age group, who was taking college courses though a CAP site in BC

As noted in a 2003 report on the social and economic impacts of CAP networks, one of the key benefits of the CAP model was "the fuller integration of citizens into society and greater social cohesion," as well as "community capacity building through the creation of a critical mass of knowledge over time on how to integrate ICT into community social and economic development programs/services" (SECOR Group, quoted in Ekos 2004, 4). The CRACIN survey provides further evidence for these impacts.

As CRACIN researcher Diane Dechief (2005, 14) observes in her study of volunteering at the Vancouver Community Network, volunteers, too, see a substantial payback: "It is important to note that social capital building and increased social inclusion take place in the physical environs of VCN, in a face to face manner. While all of the volunteers I spoke to have the digital skills required to keep in touch with friends and family in their home countries and to find online information about living in Canada, they are looking to connect with people *in-person*" (emphasis in the original).

Searching or Sharing

For those who reported that they were using the resources at the site to look for health-related information (see figure 3.3), further analysis showed that the information seeking, not information sharing, appeared to be the major activity in this area. The survey included a specific set of questions asking users whether they participated in discussion groups on politics, cultural issues, health issues, lifestyle issues, and economic issues. Only between 19 and 26 percent indicated that they did participate in such discussions (see figure 3.5). When asked if they posted to newsgroups, websites, and/or blogs in the areas mentioned, politics scored at the low end of the scale (4.7%), while, after "Other," cultural issues scored highest (21.2%) (see figure 3.6).

The results show that, for the most part, respondents rarely used the sites to formally post content in these areas. When they did participate in online discussions, it was mainly on health and lifestyle issues. Male and female participation in online discussion on these topics was almost equal, with men scoring slightly higher than women in cultural discussions (27% versus 21%, respectively), and women scoring slightly higher than men in health discussions (28% versus 24%).

FIGURE 3.5 Use of community network sites to participate in online discussions

Do you use this CNS to participate in discussions about . . .

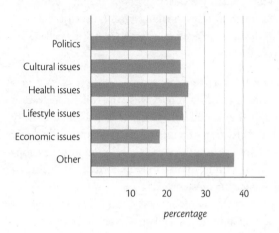

percentage

FIGURE 3.6 Use of community network sites to post information online

Do you use this CNS to post information to a listserv/blog/website about . . .

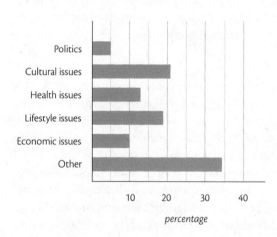

percentage

Community Networks and Skills Acquisition

We know from the administrator surveys that most responding sites had some programs targeted to the needs of the unemployed. As already noted (see figure 3.3), looking for employment, furthering employment skills, and writing résumés were common activities pursued by the respondents. In the words of one respondent:

I was able to determine the direction of my career by learning about what employment options are available to me and what appropriate aptitudes and skills I possess. . . . The staff and volunteers were very helpful and friendly. I am very proud to say that [this community network] has given me new insights and opened new opportunities for me.

—An immigrant from the West Indies, in the 41-to-50 age group

Respondents were asked whether they had "ever taken courses or classroom instruction provided by this community network." Responses showed that 40 percent of the respondents had taken at least one course at the site. Of these respondents, 35 percent had taken courses on how to use the Internet and computers, but only 25 percent had taken courses on how to look for employment. In addition, 31 percent had taken courses on computer software training. Other types of courses mentioned by respondents included reading, group literacy, accounting, website design, hardware troubleshooting, drafting software, digital camera use, and project management. Some indicated they would have liked to have access to courses on graphic production related to business cards and related activities.

A further analysis showed that 50 percent of users over 40 years of age with a household income of less than $20,000 had used the computers at the site to look for employment and further employment skills. However, only 19 percent of these users had taken a course on how to look for a job. Although we do not know whether users were taking such courses elsewhere, it seems reasonable to conclude that there could be a role for community networks in doing more follow through with programs that enable users to take advantage of new skills learned.

Civic Engagement

According to Internet researchers Quan-Haase and Wellman (2004, 113), civic engagement and social contact are two complementary uses of social capital. Social capital, as explained earlier, relates to collective benefits that accrue to the community as a whole. "Life is easier in a community blessed with a substantial stock of social capital," says social science researcher Robert Putnam. "In the first place, networks of civic engagement foster sturdy norms of generalized reciprocity and encourage the emergence of social trust" (Putnam 1995, 67).

Quan-Haase and Wellman (2004, 113) define civic engagement as "the degree to which people become involved in their community, both actively and passively, including such political and organizational activities as political rallies or book and sports clubs." In order to explore the extent to which community networks support strong communities, the CRACIN survey asked questions concerning two types of civic engagement: political engagement and community volunteer activities.

Political engagement. In this section, we asked about users' political activities, both on- and offline. We chose, as examples of such activities, voting in elections, attending public meetings or meetings of political parties, communicating with politicians, writing letters to local newspapers on political issues, engaging in discussions with friends and/or neighbours about political issues, and participating in political action by delivering flyers, donating money, attending demonstrations, or joining boycotts.

Results showed that over half (between 56% and 57%) of the respondents had voted in at least one of the most recent federal, provincial, and/or municipal elections. In comparison, 59 percent of eligible Canadians voted in the 2008 federal election, and 52.6 percent of eligible Ontarians voted in the October 2007 Ontario provincial election. However, for the most part, that remained the extent of their political involvement. Only 11 percent of respondents to this survey indicated they had worked for or attended meetings of a political party. Moreover, other than discussions or debates with friends and neighbours (in which 13.4% had engaged), virtually none of the respondents had participated in activities such as contacting local politicians, attending public meetings, writing letters to newspaper editors, or becoming involved in local political action or community groups.

In examining the importance of the community networking site to the respondents in helping them participate in political activities, most indicated the site was less important or not at all important compared to other resources. There was, however, some indication of indirect impacts. One respondent noted that community network staff had made an effort to notify users of upcoming elections by sending notices through email. Another said that the Internet made it possible to find out "what was going in the world."

In the Statistics Canada 2003 General Social Survey (GSS): Social Engagement, which canvassed 25,000 Canadians 15 years of age and older, respondents were asked whether they had participated in specific types of political activities during the year prior to the survey: "About 28% of Canadians reported that they had signed a petition, while 26% had searched for information on a political issue. About one-fifth had attended a public meeting. Similarly, about one-fifth had boycotted or chosen a product for ethical reasons. About 13% had expressed their views on an issue by contacting a newspaper or a politician, while 6% had participated in a march or demonstration" (Statistics Canada 2004). Of the respondents to the CRACIN survey, 11 percent had attended a public meeting. There was virtually no activity in the other categories. Although they represented only a small proportion of the respondents (14.1%), users less than 20 years of age were more likely to have engaged in political discussions, attended political meetings, or communicated with politicians.

The GSS survey also made a positive connection between level of education and household income and involvement in political activities. Although many respondents to the survey were well educated, the low income levels reported, combined with a high proportion of recent immigrants (who may not yet be Canadian citizens and therefore cannot vote), are one possible explanation for the low level of formal political activity reported by these users.

Volunteering. A very different view of civic engagement emerged in the responses to questions about volunteering activities among respondents and how, or whether, they found support for these activities through the sites. As we discovered, 71 percent of respondents had volunteered in some form or another in the previous twelve months, with their time commitments evenly distributed across the response categories (more than 15 hours, 5–15 hours, or 1–4 hours per month). In a snapshot of some of the types of volunteering activities undertaken, we see the following:

- 52% helped organize or supervise events for an organization
- 30% did administrative work for an organization
- 29% taught or coached in an organization
- 23% collected/delivered/served food and other goods
- 30% sat on a board or executive committee

When asked about the relative importance of the site to their volunteering activities, approximately 58 percent of the respondents indicated that email and Internet access at the site was as important as other resources, if not a very important resource. Approximately 59 percent of respondents indicated that the site's staff and volunteers were at least an equally important source of support compared to other sources, with many saying they were very important.

In comparison to the 71 percent of the CRACIN survey respondents who reported engaging in volunteer activities, the 2003 GSS found that 61 percent of Canadians belonged to at least one group or organization, such as sports or recreational groups (hockey leagues, health clubs, and so on); unions and professional associations; cultural, education or hobby groups (such as book clubs); religiously affiliated groups (such as church choirs); and school-, neighbourhood- or community-associated groups (Statistics Canada 2004).[5]

The GSS also made a positive connection between level of education and household income and involvement in local activities. Despite generally low incomes, the users of community networks we surveyed reported a high level of involvement in their local community. Given Quan-Haase and Wellman's definition of civic engagement (see above), these users were displaying a high level of such engagement and were substantially contributing to the circulation of social capital in their communities. It is an interesting result, one that would benefit from further study.

The GPI (Genuine Progress Index) Atlantic survey of rural CAP sites in British Columbia, which was designed to assess the value of the voluntary work generated by BC's rural CAP sites, indicated that CAP volunteers contributed an estimated 630,000 hours of voluntary time each year to BC's rural CAP sites (Colman 2002a, 3). "These volunteer hours are worth $9.5 million annually, and are the equivalent of 330 full-time jobs," according to the economic evaluation of the survey results (Colman 2002b, 2).

Assessing the economic value of CAP sites, Colman (2002a, 32) points out that this kind of community activity is often underestimated and undervalued:

> The strength of society's commitment to voluntary work is, for many social scientists, a touchstone of social health, stability, and harmony. A weak civil society, by contrast, is more subject to social unrest, alienation, and disintegration. It is associated with higher rates of crime, drug abuse, and other dysfunctional activities, which eventually produce high social and economic costs. From this perspective, wise investments in community and other voluntary associations can help strengthen the fabric of civil society, and produce long-term economic savings.

Community Networks Are People Networks

Respondents were asked whether they had a computer at home. If they indicated they did, we asked them to comment on why they chose to use the community networking site rather than their home computer. In reply, 61 percent (Ekos = 51%) of our respondents said they had a computer at home, mainly for personal use, rather than for work or education. Their reasons for using a community site are broadly summarized as follows:

- They had no Internet access or slower Internet access with their home computer.
- Their home computer wasn't always working.
- Using the community site allowed them to take advantage of the training and software course offerings.
- The staff at the site could assist them with online searches.
- They enjoyed their personal contact with the staff.
- A few indicated their computer at home was shared and they preferred the privacy of the community networking site.
- One respondent noted that the computer at home was not equipped to read Chinese characters, whereas the computers at the site could.

One respondent said that the community networking site provided "a professional place to look for a job without being interrupted or disturbed by family and friends." The privacy reason is, perhaps, a surprising one, given that these are public sites. However, this response is supported by interviews collected in a recent study on the complexity of online privacy (Viseu, Clement, and Aspinall 2004). Just as the public library offers many services beyond the lending of books, it appears that community networking sites serve many roles in the community beyond simple access to computers and Internet resources.

According to CRACIN researcher Ken Werbin (2006, 15), whereas CAP sites "were designed to provide people with ICT access and training," these sites "have in fact been operating in a completely different way than was intended." His research suggested that that "successful community-networking initiatives tended to actively encourage, support and maintain the 'third spaces' emerging around ICT in the community center" (2006, 15–16). Werbin found that "access to such valuable, physical, on-the-fly 'third spaces,' where site users have the chance to meet others and develop social networks, plays a far greater role in fostering a sense of community than mere technological access and training alone" (2006, 24). As one survey respondent put it: "The computer resources here have greatly improved my knowledge about the community and people around us. I've met new people and made some new friends."

CONCLUSION

The results of the CRACIN survey provide a closer look at who uses community networking sites and how they use them. In our survey, the largest demographic segment was female and under 40 years old, and the levels of income were very low. The sites were used for many different activities beyond email and web searching, and the staff and volunteers were a key element in the success of these sites. The level of political engagement among these users was generally low, but the level of community engagement, in the form of volunteering, was unusually high. Our results demonstrated that the resources available at the site were an enabling factor in this high rate of volunteerism and that community networking sites play a significant role in facilitating face-to-face local social interaction for these users. In other words, community networking sites are places where social capital is invested and accumulated and the process of developing a community of shared values is well established. Our research adds to the growing evidence that these sites are important hubs around which communities help their members find economic and social stability in the new information society.

Some of the most convincing evidence, however, comes to us from stories contributed by the sites themselves. One such story is from Sanikiluaq, the southernmost community in Nunavut, located near the southeastern corner of Hudson Bay. In this community of eight hundred people, 98 percent are Inuit.

The government is the main employer. Soapstone carving and other Inuit arts and crafts are local economic mainstays, but marketing them is a challenge:

> In this small isolated community, homes are more likely to have cable TV than telephones and, increasingly, more likely to have computers than cable TV or telephones. Located in the school and the daycare centre, the CAP site offers an interface by maintaining a local cable TV channel. In addition to local cultural and educational programming, it serves as a local shopping channel used to move needed items around inside a community where you can't just drive down to the local Canadian Tire to replace a snowmobile part. Locals bring their wares to the CAP site, have them photographed and put on PowerPoint slides which are then broadcast on the channel. In an unusual version of the "moccasin telegraph," Channel 3 also serves as a way for the school to contact parents who don't have a phone—a message is broadcast from the CAP site and, if the parents don't see it, a friend or neighbour most certainly will.
>
> Supported by grants from Canadian Heritage but using the CAP resources, students have made and sold videos of local knowledge about making the famous fish skin dolls which are unique to Sanikiluaq and about Inuit methods of starting fires with friction. The CAP site has also been instrumental in facilitating the marketing of the fish skin dolls and the unique local baskets to international customers, bringing much-needed revenue into the community.
>
> It is not just about buying and selling, but also about making outside training programs available locally. Through their school and the CAP site, local youth have been able to participate in an Internet-based competition aimed at Aboriginal students in Grades 10 to 13 across the country. The goal of the Business Development Bank of Canada's E-spirit Aboriginal Youth Business Plan Competition is to expose Aboriginal youth to the potential of entrepreneurship and the Internet. (Moll 2007, 13)

Supported by the Industry Canada and GPI surveys, the CRACIN user survey provides further evidence that these new actors on the community stage can and do play a role in the creation and exchange of social capital in their communities. As Tom Schuller, a professor of lifelong learning at the University of London's Birkbeck College, argues (2001, 20), it is important to look at social capital as a policy instrument because it provides a balance to other policy instruments that can be too narrow to deal with the complexities of modern life: "Technological innovation and human capital are both very powerful in their own terms, and essential features of prosperity, but they cannot be taken out of their contexts of social relationships. Social capital demands a wider focus. . . . It deals with the social infrastructure that enables other policies to be effective." When viewed from this perspective, community networking sites should be on the radar of governments at all levels, as part of the critical infrastructure needed to build strong communities in an information society.

ACKNOWLEDGEMENTS

We know that it was not easy for CAP site administrators to find users willing to respond to a very detailed survey. We thank those administrators for taking time out of an already overloaded work schedule to assist in this study.

NOTES

1 Putnam cites James Coleman (1990, 317), who argues: "Social capital is an important resource for individuals and can greatly affect their ability to act and their perceived quality of life. They have the capability of bringing such capital into being. Yet because many of the benefits of actions that bring social capital into being are experienced by persons other than the person so acting, it is not to that person's interest to bring it into being. The result is that most forms of social capital are created or destroyed as a by-product of other social activities."

2 The Policy Research Initiative (PRI) was created in 1996 as a government-wide exercise intended to identify key medium-term pressure points for the government's policy agenda and to foster collaboration across departments. The social capital stream released its report on this issue in 2005. More information is available at http://www. policyresearch.gc.ca/page.asp?pagenm=rp_sc2.

3 A low-income household is one that spends a disproportionate amount of its income on the necessities of life, such as food, shelter, and clothing (National Council of Welfare 2006). "Fact Sheet: Definitions of the Most Common Poverty Lines Used in Canada, June 2003," http://www.ncwcnbes.net/documents/researchpublications/ OtherFactSheets/PovertyLines/2003DefinitionsPovertyLinesENG.htm.

4 The median income is the middle value in the range of family incomes. In other words, half of all families had an income greater than $67,600, and half had less.

5 For more information on volunteering activities in Canada, see Statistics Canada 2004, "Survey on Giving, Volunteering and Participating," http://www.givingandvolunteering. ca/pdf/CSGVP_Highlights_2004_en.pdf. See also the statistics based on this survey presented by Human Resources and Skills Development Canada, "Indicators of Well-being in Canada," http://www4.hrsdc.gc.ca/indicator.jsp?lang=en&indicatorid=74.

REFERENCES

Canadian Radio-television and Telecommunications Commission. 2010. Proceeding to review access to basic telecommunications services and other matters. Telecom notice of consultation CRTC 2010-43. http://www.crtc.gc.ca/eng/archive/2010/2010-43.htm.

Clement, Andrew, Michael Gurstein, Marita Moll, and Leslie Shade. 2003. Canadian Research Alliance for Community Innovation and Networking (CRACIN). A proposal submitted to the Initiative on the New Economy (INE) Research Alliances program of the Social Sciences and Humanities Research Council (SSHRC). July 2003.http:// archive.iprp.ischool.utoronto.ca/cracin/Final_proposal.pdf.

Coleman, James S. 1990. *Foundations of social theory.* Cambridge, MA: Harvard University Press.

Coleman, Ronald. 2002a. Impact of CAP sites on volunteerism. GPI Atlantic. January. http:// www.gpiatlantic.org/pdf/misc/bc-cap.pdf.

——. 2002b. Economic value of CAP sites as investments in social capital: An analysis based on GPI Atlantic's survey of British Columbia's rural CAP sites and the report "Impact of CAP sites on volunteerism" (January 2002). GPI Atlantic. March. http://www.gpiatlantic.

org/pdf/misc/econvalue-cap.pdf (full report; an abstract is available at http://www.
gpiatlantic.org/publications/abstracts/econvalue-cap-ab.htm).

Dechief, Diane. 2005. Recent immigrants as an "alternative civic core": How VCN provides
Internet services and Canadian experiences. CRACIN Working Paper no. 8. October.
Toronto: Canadian Research Alliance for Community Innovation and Networking.
http://archive.iprp.ischool.utoronto.ca/cracin/publications/pdfs/WorkingPapers/
CRACIN%20Working%20Paper%20No%208.pdf.

Ekos Research Associates. 2004. Evaluation Study of the Community Access Program (CAP).
Industry Canada, Audit and Evaluation Branch, 16 January. http://archive.iprp.ischool.
utoronto.ca/cracin/policy/policy/polmap-ic1.pdf.

Frank, Jeff. 2003. "Counting connections that count: Measurement challenges and data
gaps." Horizons 6(3): 70–72. http://www.horizons.gc.ca/doclib/HOR_v6n3_200311_e.
pdf.

Gurstein, Michael. 2003. Effective use: A community informatics strategy beyond the digital
divide. First Monday 8(12) (1 December). http://firstmonday.org/htbin/cgiwrap/bin/ojs/
index.php/fm/article/view/1107/1027.

Hampton, Keith N., and Barry Wellman. 1999. Netville online and offline: Observing and
surveying a wired suburb. American Behavioral Scientist 43(3) (November): 475–92.

Helliwell, John. 2001. Social capital. Isuma: Canadian Journal of Policy Research 2(1) (Spring):
6–7.

Jenson, Jane. 1998. Mapping social cohesion: The state of Canadian research. CPRN Study
No. F/03. http://www.cprn.org/documents/15723_en.pdf.

Mackenzie, Karen. 2008. Computer site hurting for cash. Northern News Services, 20 August. http://www.nnsl.com/frames/newspapers/2008-08/aug20_08cs.html.

Moll, Marita. 2007. The good news about CAP. Making Waves 18(2) (Summer): 10–13. http://
www.tc.ca/GoodNewsaboutCAP.pdf.

Moll, Marita, and Melissa Fritz. 2007. Community networks and Canadian public policy:
Preliminary report on the CRACIN survey of community networks. Draft. 4 September.
http://archive.iprp.ischool.utoronto.ca/cracin/Moll_Fritz_Info-incan.pdf.

National Council of Welfare. 2006. Poverty Profile, 2002–2003. Statistics Canada's before-
tax low income cut-offs (1992-base) for 2005.

Phipps, Shelley. 2003. The impact of poverty on health: A scan of research literature. Canadian Institute for Health Information. June. http://secure.cihi.ca/cihiweb/products/
CPHIImpactonPoverty_e.pdf.

Putnam, Robert D. 1993. Making democracy work: Civic traditions in modern Italy. Princeton,
NJ: Princeton University Press.

——. 1995. Bowling alone: America's declining social capital; An interview with Robert
Putnam. Journal of Democracy 6(1) (January): 65–78. http://xroads.virginia.edu/~
HYPER/DETOC/assoc/bowling.html.

Quan-Haase, Anabel, and Barry Wellman. 2004. How does the Internet affect social capital? In Social Capital and Information Technology, ed. Marleen Huysman and Volker
Wolf, 113–31. Cambridge, MA: MIT Press.

Schuller, Tom. 2001. The complementary role of human and social capital. Isuma: Canadian
Journal of Policy Research 2(1) (Spring): 18–24.

Statistics Canada. 2003. 2001 Census. Detailed Highest Level of Schooling (20), Age Groups
(13B) and Sex (3) for Population 15 Years and Over, for Canada, Provinces, Territories,
Census Metropolitan Areas and Census Agglomerations, 2001 Census—20% Sample
Data. Catalogue no. 97F0017XCB2001001. Release date 11 March 2003.

——. 2004. General social survey: Social engagement. *The Daily*, 6 July. http://www.statcan.gc.ca/daily-quotidien/040706/dq040706b-eng.htm.

——. 2006. Canadian Internet use survey. *The Daily*, 15 August. http://www.statcan.gc.ca/daily-quotidien/060815/dq060815b-eng.htm.

——. 2007. Family Income. *The Daily*, 29 May. http://www.statcan.gc.ca/daily-quotidien/070529/dq070529e-eng.htm.

Telecommunications Policy Review Panel. 2006. *Final Report*. Ottawa: Industry Canada.

Viseu, A., A. Clement, and J. Aspinall. 2004. Situating privacy online. *Information, Communication and Society* 7(1) (March): 92–114.

Wellman, Barry, Anabel Quan-Haase, James Witte, and Keith Hampton. 2001. Does the Internet increase, decrease or supplement social capital? Social networks, participation and community commitment. *American Behavioral Scientist* 45(3) (November): 436–55.

Werbin, Kenneth C. 2006. Where is the "community" in "community-networking initiatives"? Stories from the "third-spaces" of Connecting Canadians. CRACIN Working Paper no. 11. Toronto: Canadian Research Alliance for Community Innovation and Networking. http://archive.iprp.ischool.utoronto.ca/cracin/publications/pdfs/Working Papers/CRACIN%20Working%20Paper%20No%2011.pdf.

4 CANADIAN AND US BROADBAND POLICIES A Comparative Analysis

Heather E. Hudson

Broadband is becoming increasingly important for rural economic activities and for the delivery of education, health care, and other social services. Industry Canada (2009) notes: "Broadband Internet access is viewed as essential infrastructure for participating in today's economy, as it enables citizens, businesses and institutions to access information, services and opportunities that could otherwise be out of reach." On a nationwide basis, Canada currently ranks tenth among Organisation for Economic Co-operation and Development (OECD) nations in broadband access, and the United States ranks fifteenth. At the same time, both Canada and the United States have major gaps in broadband availability in rural areas.

Both countries have long recognized the importance of communications for social and economic development. The Canadian Department of Communications' *Instant World* report in 1970 heralded a new era of interconnected citizens and instantaneous access to information long before the Internet came into being. Both countries invested in experimental communications satellites, and supported projects to explore their potential for telemedicine, distance education, and cultural exchanges. Commercial satellites were then launched to provide national television distribution and voice and video services for remote areas, primarily in the North. In the 1990s, the United States proposed a National Information Infrastructure (NII) initiative to connect

Americans to the Internet. Canada proposed a national information highway that would link Canadians and provide access to new information services. Currently, Industry Canada is proposing a new initiative on the so-called digital economy that would focus on applications and impacts of information and communication technologies (ICTs), including broadband (Industry Canada 2009b).

Both countries recognized internal digital divides that left rural and remote communities and low-income households cut off from these new opportunities, and both have adopted policy and funding strategies to attempt to bridge these gaps. Canadian federal initiatives have brought broadband to remote Indigenous communities across the Arctic and to remote regions of some Canadian provinces. The United States has provided subsidies for broadband access to communities through schools and libraries, and grants and loans to rural carriers to upgrade their networks for Internet services. However, access can be expensive and quality of service inadequate in these remote areas. Also, there are still rural areas, typically with low population density, that do not have broadband access or where broadband is only available via individual satellite installations. For example, the Canadian Radio-television and Telecommunications Commission's (CRTC) 2009 *Communications Monitoring Report* states that some 6 percent of Canadian households currently lack broadband (1.5 Mbps) access. In rural areas, that figure is closer to 22 percent (Canadian Radio-television and Telecommunications Commission 2009).

BROADBAND: A MOVING TARGET

Industry Canada (2009a) has defined broadband as a speed of at least 1.5 Mbps (presumably downstream). It further defines unserved Canadians as "those without Internet access or with dial-up service only" and underserved Canadians as "those who may be able to access the Internet using a connection with a speed less than 1.5 Mbps." It notes that "at 1.5 Mbps, a customer can make a voice call over the Internet, download an audio CD in seven minutes and experience video-quality streaming / video conferencing. It is also possible to use multiple applications at the same time, enabling consumers to make a voice-over-Internet telephone call while downloading a document" (Industry Canada 2009c).

The United States has adopted a higher speed target of actual download speed of 4 Mbps for universal broadband in its National Broadband Plan, although the plan also calls for a much higher target: 100 million households with 100 Mbps by 2020 (Federal Communications Commission 2010a). Other countries have chosen targets from 0.5 Mbps to 2 Mbps (see table 4.1).

TABLE 4.1 Universal broadband speed goals for selected countries

	Download speed	Target date
United States	4 Mbps	2020
United Kingdom	2 Mbps	2012
Australia	2 Mbps	2018
Canada	1.5 Mbps	2010?
South Korea	1 Mbps	2008
Finland	1 Mbps	2009
Ireland	1 Mbps	2010
Germany	1 Mbps	2010
Australia	0.5 Mbps	2010
Denmark	0.5 Mbps	2010
France	0.5 Mbps	2010

SOURCE: Federal Communications Commission 2010a, 135.

MORE BANDWIDTH BUT LIMITED COMPETITION

Each country typically has very little broadband competition, with a duopoly of DSL and cable in most urban areas, and only one provider in rural areas that have broadband service. Both countries rely primarily on facilities-based competition, with little use of unbundling. In Canada, according to CRTC data, incumbent cable companies receive 48 percent of Internet access revenues, and incumbent telecom companies receive 40 percent. The top five Canadian ISPs (most owned by the incumbent carriers) captured 76 percent of Internet access revenues in 2008 (Canadian Radio-television and Telecommunications Commission 2009).

Fixed wireless was considered a promising means to increase competition, but most community wireless networks have not been sustainable (Hudson 2009a). New high-speed mobile networks may offer a competitive option, but are not likely to reach isolated residents. The CRTC estimates that 91 percent of Canadians are covered by mobile broadband (Canadian Radio-television and Telecommunications Commission 2009). Canada's major mobile carriers claim that mobile broadband will be available to 90 percent of their current mobile coverage areas (CRTC, pers. comm. 2009). However, mobile broadband pricing is considerably higher than fixed service, and quality of service is variable.

Satellite service is another option, particularly for remote areas. The United States and Canada have national satellite coverage that can provide two-way broadband, although the signal delay using geostationary satellites (located 36,000 km above the equator) is noticeable, and prices tend to be higher than for terrestrial services. Both countries use satellites to reach remote communities, and satellite services using small terminals (VSATS) are available for otherwise unserved households, businesses, and organizations. Ubiquitous broadband could be made available today throughout North America by providing a sub-sidy for satellite access, if needed, but neither country has adopted this approach.

Satellite proponents argue that the next generation of satellites will have much greater capacity at only slightly higher costs so that the costs (and ostensibly price to end users) of satellite bandwidth should be significantly cheaper (Barrett Xplore, pers. comm. November 2009). Yet rural and remote providers are increasingly opting for terrestrial facilities to replace satellite service. Alaskan consortia have won two stimulus grants to install terrestrial wireless middle mile and last mile networks to provide broadband connectivity to more than sixty villages, and a consortium including KNet (see chapter 14 in this volume), Bell Aliant, and public sector entities requested federal stimulus funding to install optical fibre to link remote communities in Northwestern Ontario.

RURAL INFRASTRUCTURE INVESTMENTS

The Canadian federal government sponsored several innovative initiatives to extend broadband to rural and remote areas in the 1990s, such as BRAND (Broadband Access for Rural and Northern Development Pilot Program). However, no new funding has been provided to continue or replace BRAND. The government has subsidized satellite service for northern communities through its Northern Satellite Initiative, which continues through 2011 (Industry Canada 2004). Satellite broadband is also available throughout much of rural Canada, but at prices significantly higher than comparable service (on the same Anik satellite) in the United States.

Strategies to achieve universal broadband in Canada have focused on capital subsidies, with the apparent assumption that availability is all that is required to achieve access. The CRTC took steps to fund rural broadband when it required incumbent local exchange carriers (ILECs) to use established deferral accounts after the introduction of price cap regulation in 2002. Up to CAD $650 million from the accounts was to be used to support initiatives to expand broadband services to rural and remote communities and improve accessibility of telecommunications services for persons with disabilities (Canadian Radio-television and Telecommunications Commission 2008).

Two US federal agencies provide funding for rural telecommunications infrastructure. The Rural Utilities Service (RUS), in the Department of Agriculture, provides low-interest loans and some grants to rural communications carriers to extend and upgrade their networks. The National Telecommunications and Information Administration (NTIA), in the Department of Commerce, has administered several grant programs that included support for rural broadcasting and communications.

In 2009, both countries announced broadband infrastructure grants as part of national economic stimulus initiatives. The US American Recovery and Reinvestment Act (ARRA), signed in February 2009, appropriated USD $7.2 billion "to begin the process of significantly expanding the reach and quality of broadband services." NTIA received USD $4.7 billion to address the following goals:

- Provide access in unserved areas and improved access in underserved areas
- Provide broadband education, awareness, training, access, equipment, and support
- Improve access and use by public safety agencies
- Stimulate broadband demand, economic growth, and job creation.

Grants were to be awarded for infrastructure, public computer centres, projects to foster sustainable broadband adoption, and for broadband data collection and mapping. The RUS received USD $2.5 billion specifically for *rural* infrastructure projects. Other stimulus initiatives include funding for electronic health record systems, ICTs in education, "smart grids" to manage distribution and utilization of energy, and communication systems for public safety and security (American Recovery and Reinvestment Act of 2009).

In September 2009, Industry Canada announced "Connecting Rural Canadians," a CAD $225 million stimulus program to extend "essential infrastructure" in remote and rural areas. Projects required a 50 percent match in funds, except for programs serving First Nations, and a five-year sustainability plan (Industry Canada 2009a). Industry Canada has adopted 1.5 Mbps as a baseline definition for broadband service availability and has developed a map of broadband availability.

STATE AND PROVINCIAL INITIATIVES

Meanwhile, faced with frustrated residents, businesses, and social service providers who were without broadband access, many American states decided to tackle the problem of getting broadband to all their residents. Several have authorized task forces to examine the status of broadband recommendations and to recommend policies to accelerate deployment. Among the strategies adopted or being proposed are various types of grants, deregulatory bargains, tax credits, and public-private partnerships. Several states have also made efforts to address barriers to adoption among lower-income, elderly, and minority populations through various programs and grants for training, outreach, and content development (Hudson 2008).

Like US states, many Canadian provinces have recognized the importance of broadband to their economic development and are providing various forms of support to extend broadband access, particularly in rural areas. For example, Ontario has an e-government initiative known as Digital Ontario that includes support for community projects. Ontario and the federal government provided CAD $170 million to extend broadband throughout counties in eastern Ontario (Eastern Ontario Warden's Caucus 2009). The British Columbia government has provided subsidies to Telus to extend rural broadband infrastructure through its Network BC initiatives. Alberta's SuperNet is a public-private partnership with carriers and industry that has built a broadband backbone throughout the province. Nova Scotia, New Brunswick, and Prince Edward Island have created incentives for investment from regional carriers, while government-owned SaskTel is extending broadband facilities throughout rural Saskatchewan.

AFFORDABILITY

Access requires both availability and affordability. A Canadian consumer representative noted that not everyone could afford to pay for the Internet: "There is a difference between service existing and service being available to all" (quoted in Ditchburn 2010). As noted below, affordability remains an issue even where broadband is available to individual households, especially if service is delivered by satellite or mobile wireless.

In both countries, broadband via satellite and wireless is substantially more expensive than that offered by DSL and cable providers, although US prices are generally substantially cheaper. Satellite broadband for individual households is an option in rural and remote areas where neither terrestrial DSL/cable nor line-of-site wireless is available. However, the price of satellite equipment and service can be prohibitively expensive for some households. For example, the price of basic satellite broadband (download *up to* 512 Kbps) using XPlornet is CAD $50 per month, plus initial charges for equipment ranging from CAD $99 with a three-year contract to CAD $399 with no contract, plus installation charges, a CAD $99 set-up fee, and CAD $75 annual universal service fee.[1] Thus a person who did not want a three-year contract would have to pay CAD $500 for equipment and initial fees, plus an installation charge, plus more than CAD $50 per month for service at best one-third the speed designated as broadband by Industry Canada.

The CRTC estimates that 91 percent of Canadians are covered by mobile broadband (Canadian Radio-television and Telecommunications Commission

2009). Canada's major mobile carriers claim that mobile broadband will be available to 90 percent of their current mobile coverage areas (CRTC, pers. comm. November 2009). However, at present, mobile broadband pricing is considerably higher than fixed service, and the quality of service is variable. For example, Telus Mobility currently charges CAD $65 per month for maximum data usage of 5 GB, plus 5 cents for each additional MB with no specified speed, while for DSL with speeds of 1.5 to 6 Mbps, Telus charges CAD $37 per month for 60 GB usage plus CAD $2 per additional GB.[2]

SUSTAINABILITY

In addition to having sufficient capital investment and offering affordable rates, broadband services must operate sustainably. In Canada, although there have been intermittent federal projects to contribute to the costs of connectivity, to date there has been no long-term strategy for the sustainability of rural/remote Internet and broadband connectivity. Examples of operating support include federally subsidized satellite service for northern communities through the Northern Satellite Initiative, which continues through 2011, but no follow-on support has been announced (Industry Canada 2004). Another federal initiative, the Community Access Program (CAP) has facilitated free community Internet access at more than three thousand locations across Canada since 1994. The federal government announced severe cuts to the CAD $14-million-a-year program that would halt funding for 93 percent of the CAP sites in March 2010, although it subsequently rescinded the cuts, stating that funding would come from other sources (apparently, Connecting Rural Canadians).

In discussing the decision to continue CAP support in the near term, Tony Clement, the minister for Industry Canada, noted: "We don't want to get anybody left in the lurch by having the funding cut this year, while the broadband strategy to households is still rolling out" (quoted in Ditchburn 2010). He added that funding for libraries and community centres would be decreased when more Canadians have the opportunity to pay for high-speed Internet at home. Yet such services may not only be unaffordable for some residents but unsustainable for providers in some high-cost or low-revenue areas.

UNIVERSAL SERVICE SUPPORT

The means of financing expansion of services to high-cost and/or low-income regions traditionally was cross subsidies, generally internal cross-subsidies from high margin services. Typically, a regulator would designate regions to be served or quality of service (QOS) targets to be met as a condition of granting or renewing a license and would authorize tariffs designed to generate revenue from services such as international calls or domestic long distance that could be then directed to subsidizing expansion of or rates for services in other areas. With the introduction of competition, subsidies had to become explicit so that providers could not transfer revenues from still-monopolized services to competitive offerings in order to drive out competitors. Funds for such subsidies could come from government budgets, but to avoid relying on governments, mechanisms were set up to channel some revenue from all the carriers (or all in a certain category) into a fund for redistribution as subsidies to address universal service or access.

US universal service programs were originally designed to subsidize voice telephony access for low-income residents and to extend reasonably priced telephone services to rural and other underserved areas. The Telecommunications Act of 1996 expanded the definition of universal service to include schools, libraries, and rural health care facilities, and access to "advanced services" (Telecommunications Act of 1996). The goal was to provide opportunities for students and community residents to take advantage of these advanced services, even if they were not yet available in their homes, to help bridge what came to be called the digital divide. Funds come from telecommunications carriers, which are required to contribute a set portion of their revenues to the universal service funds (USF) (Hudson 2009b). Other USF support is provided for carriers in high-cost regions and for low-income residents. These programs are likely to be modified in the implementation of the 2010 National Broadband Plan (see below).

In the United States, the E-Rate (short for "education rate") created by the Telecommunications Act of 1996 provides discounts on a wide variety of telecommunications, Internet access and internal connections for schools and libraries. The applicable discount rate is based on a school's economic need and whether it is located in an urban or rural area. Up to USD $2.25 billion worth of discounts can be made available each year. Approved costs are billed directly to the Universal Service Administrative Company (USAC), up to the limit of the subsidy. Schools and libraries are responsible for the remainder, and must demonstrate that they can cover their portion of the costs (Hudson 2009b).

Approved schools and libraries post their requirements online, where they are open for competitive bids. If no competitors respond during the designated time period, the school or library may contract with the local incumbent operator. The result in many small communities has been that the school has become an anchor tenant for Internet access. In Alaska, which has many remote villages similar to Indigenous communities in the Canadian North, the E-Rate subsidy had brought Internet access to most village schools. One of the competitive providers concluded that the school subsidy was critical to its business case to bring broadband to the villages (primarily by satellite), and subsequently installed broadband wireless to cover the villages, with price for individual access not to exceed the price in Anchorage, the largest city (Hudson 2006).

Connectivity for rural health services is also supported from universal service funds in the United States. In Alaska, the AFHCAN Telehealth System relies on this subsidy to connect more than 250 sites, including links between more than 150 village clinics and regional hospitals (Hudson 2006). Up to USD $2.25 billion per year is available for schools and libraries. A further USD $400 million is available for rural health care but has been significantly underutilized. In 2007, the Federal Communications Commission (FCC) announced a one-time allocation of more than USD $417 million for construction of statewide or regional broadband telehealth networks (Hudson 2009b). Other USF support is provided for carriers in high-cost regions and for low-income residents. These programs are currently under review.

Although Industry Canada has underwritten some connectivity costs for rural and remote areas for limited periods, there is no Canadian equivalent of the US E-Rate program, which is in effect a mandated sustainability subsidy targeting service for schools and libraries.

NATIONAL BROADBAND POLICIES

As required in the US stimulus legislation, the FCC announced a National Broadband Plan in March 2010 (Federal Communications Commission 2010a). Its proposals include creation of a Connect America Fund and reform of current universal service policies to provide incentives to extend broadband services. The plan's goals included:

- At least 100 million US homes should have affordable access to actual download speeds of at least 100 megabits per second and actual upload speeds of at least 50 megabits per second.
- Every American should have affordable access to robust broadband service and the means and skills to subscribe if they so choose.
- Every community should have affordable access to at least 1 Gbps broadband service to anchor institutions such as schools, hospitals, and government buildings.

The plan also provides a detailed analysis of the steps the FCC has determined will be required to achieve these goals under four major headings:

- Establishing competition policies, including pricing, privacy, and transparency
- Ensuring efficient allocation and use of government-owned and government-influenced assets, such as spectrum and rights-of-way
- Creating incentives for universal availability and adoption of broadband
- Updating policies, setting standards, and aligning incentives to maximize use for national priorities, in fields such as health, education, and public safety

Of these, the most relevant goals and targets for comparison with Canadian broadband policy concern broadband access, including changes to universal service definitions and support mechanisms.

The National Broadband Plan states that the FCC's long-term goal should be "to replace all the legacy High-Cost programs with a new program that preserves the connectivity that Americans have today and advances universal broadband in the 21st century" (Federal Communications Commission 2010a, 145). Following the publication of the Broadband Plan, the FCC accordingly announced a 2010 Broadband Action Agenda with steps identified to achieve the four key goals. The steps designed to achieve universal access to broadband include:

- Carry out a "once-in-a-generation transformation of the Universal Service Fund over the next ten years to support broadband service . . . by converting existing subsidy mechanisms over time from 'POTS' (plain old telephone service) to broadband, without increasing the size of the fund over the current baseline projection."
- Upgrade the E-Rate program (which subsidizes Internet connectivity for schools and libraries: see above) to benefit students and others across the country by making broadband more accessible (possibly by providing support for additional means of community access through schools or other local institutions).
- Reform and upgrade current rural health connectivity subsidies "to connect more public health facilities to high-speed Internet facilities and to foster telemedicine applications and services."
- Create a Health Care Infrastructure Fund to support the deployment of dedicated health care networks to underserved areas.
- Create a "Connect America Fund to extend broadband service to unserved areas of the nation and to ensure affordable broadband service in high-cost areas." The goal is provision of affordable broadband with at least 4 Mbps of actual download speed.
- Create a Mobility Fund to upgrade wireless coverage throughout the country to 3G or better. (Federal Communications Commission 2010b)

The National Broadband Plan concludes that private investment alone is unlikely to extend broadband in some areas of the country with low population density (Federal Communications Commission 2010a). The FCC began the universal service reform process through a Notice of Inquiry and Notice of Proposed Rulemaking on these universal service proposals in April 2010 (Federal Communications Commission 2010c).

In contrast, Canada lacks an explicit broadband policy. Industry Canada is proposing a new initiative on the digital economy that would focus on applications and impacts of ICTs, including broadband. Although considered a regulator rather than policy maker, the Canadian Radio-Television and Tele-communications Commission also plays a role in policy. As noted above, the CRTC has designated deferral account funds of up to CAD $650 million for rural broadband upgrades and in February 2010 announced its intention to review its definition of basic service, last updated in 1998 (Canadian Radio-Television and Telecommunications Commission 2010).

BEYOND INFRASTRUCTURE

Although there are still gaps in availability of broadband in both Canada and the United States, the next steps in closing the digital divide and deriving socio-economic value from infrastructure investments are to increase adoption and to develop and implement applications that address social and economic needs for information, e-services, access to markets, consultation with specialists, and so on. National data in the United States shows lower levels of broadband adoption among lower-income, rural, and some minority populations. Among non-adopters, lack of relevance is cited as main reason for not having broad-band at home (Federal Communications Commission 2009). In both countries, research is needed to increase our understanding of the reasons for non-adoption, to develop strategies to encourage adoption, and to identify or develop relevant applications for users with limited ICT or English-language skills.

The United States and Canada are investing significant public funds in extending and upgrading broadband infrastructure and in providing regulatory incentives for carriers to extend broadband facilities. These initiatives should be evaluated to assess impacts the increased access has had on availability and effectiveness of health services, education and training, government programs and services, new or increased economic activities, and so on.

The next step in research should be to examine national level impacts, or barriers to impact. There are some macro-economic studies (see, for example, Waverman and Dasgupta 2009), but little field research exists that examines how broadband and related access to ICTs and applications can improve productivity, contribute to new economic activity, and help to grow and diversify regional and national economies. In both countries, we will need such research to foster a digital economy.

NOTES

1 Prices posted at www.xplornet.ca in April 2010. Italics added. In the United States, prices for satellite equipment from WildBlue that accesses the same Anik satellite are considerably lower and more flexible (no installation fee and an option to lease the equipment). See www.wildblue.com.
2 See www.telusmobility.com and www.telus.com. Prices quoted are for unbundled services in British Columbia in April 2010.

REFERENCES

American Recovery and Reinvestment Act of 2009. Public Law 111-5, 111th Cong., 1st sess. (17 February 2009). http://www.recovery.gov/Pages/home.aspx.

Canadian Radio-television and Telecommunications Commission. 2008. Decision CRTC 2008-1. http://www.crtc.gc.ca/eng/archive/2008/dt2008-1.htm.

——. 2009. Communications monitoring report 2009. http://www.crtc.gc.ca/eng/publications/reports/policymonitoring/2009/cmr.htm.

——. 2010. Notice of consultation and hearing: Proceeding to review access to basic telecommunications services and other matters. 28 January. www.crtc.gc.ca/eng/archive/2010/2010-43.htm.

Ditchburn, Jennifer. 2010. Industry Minister announces reprieve for library Internet access program. *Globe and Mail*, 17 March, www.theglobeandmail.com/news/politics/industry-minister-announces-reprieve-for-library-internet-access-program/article1503146/.

Eastern Ontario Warden's Caucus. 2009. Advancing Eastern Ontario's digital possibilities. www.eodigitalpossibilities.org/index.html.

Federal Communications Commission. 2009. Presentation at September commission meeting, 29 September. http://reboot.fcc.gov/open-meetings/2009/september.

——. 2010a. *Connecting America: The National Broadband Plan.* March. Washington, DC. http://www.broadband.gov/download-plan/.

——. 2010b. National Broadband Plan: Connecting America. Broadband action agenda. http://www.broadband.gov/plan/broadband-action-agenda.html.

——. 2010c. Notice of inquiry and proposed rulemaking: In the matter of Connect America Fund, a national broadband plan for our future, high-cost universal service support. 21 April. http://www.nasuca.org/archive/BB Cost Model Comments 7-12-10.pdf.

Hudson, Heather E. 2006. *From rural village to global village.* New York: Routledge.

——. 2008. Broadband: The state imperative. Paper presented at the Telecommunications Policy Research Conference, Washington, DC, 27–28 September.

——. 2009a. Municipal wireless broadband: Lessons from San Francisco and Silicon Valley. *Telematics and Informatics* 27(1): 1–9.

——. 2009b. The future of the E-Rate: U.S. Universal Service Fund support for public access and social services. In *And communications for all: An agenda for a new administration,* ed. Amit Schejter, 239–62. Lanham, MD: Lexington Books.

Industry Canada. 2004. Government of Canada announces broadband access via satellite for 52 remote communities. http://www.ic.gc.ca/eic/site/ic1.nsf/eng/02381.html.

——. 2009a. Broadband Canada: Connecting Rural Canadians. www.ic.gc.ca/eic/site/719.nsf/eng/home.

——. 2009b. Canada's digital economy: Moving forward. Background paper. 22 June. www.ic.gc.ca/eic/site/ecic-ceac.nsf/vwapj/background_paper.pdf.

——. 2009c. Backgrounder: Broadband Canada: Connecting Rural Canadians—Call for Applications. 1 September. http://www.ic.gc.ca/eic/site/ic1.nsf/eng/04943.html.

Telecommunications Act of 1996. Public Law 104-104, 104th Cong., 2nd sess. (8 February 1996). http://www.fcc.gov/telecom.html.

Waverman, Leonard, and Kalyan Dasgupta. 2009. Connectivity Scorecard 2009. http://www.connectivityscorecard.org/images/uploads/media/TheConnectivityReport2009.pdf.

PART II

Conceptual Frameworks

5 INFORMATION TECHNOLOGY AS POLITICAL CATALYST From Technological Innovation to the Promotion of Social Change

Serge Proulx

User-centred innovation research by scholars such as Eric von Hippel (us) and Christophe Aguiton and Dominique Cardon (France) has demonstrated how, by freely sharing ideas and artifacts, innovative users develop dense communications links to bind themselves within larger communities of innovators. Research in that tradition has thus far been concerned chiefly with technological innovation. In examining the mechanics of innovative processes within the social field, in this chapter, we turn to how user innovations in the technological sphere have transitioned to innovations that resonate in the sociocultural sphere. In a research project undertaken at LabcMO in Montréal from 2005 to 2007, we observed and described the activities of two groups of users innovating within the technological sphere. The first group operates in the free software domain; the second group's activities involve urban wireless networking. Paired with their joint technological innovation, however, members of these groups—"techno-activists"—have developing joint ideological platforms oriented toward social change.

That ideological platform is built around specific activities, values, and beliefs; involvement with international networks and exchanges, rather than solely with a local community of user-innovators; a heterarchical structure of work organization, not an exclusively hierarchical one; an ambivalent economic relationship with existing capitalistic structures; and a set of social representations of the technological world used as a foundation upon which to construct a politically progressive platform—one driven by political and economic contradictions. These activists position their technological practices as an opportunity to renew social forms of organization, collaboration, and communication. In criticizing the prescriptive and normative composition of technical devices marketed by large-scale software and telecommunication providers, they foreground deliberation as an essential innovation mechanism within the community of users. The sociological questions we address involve the extent to which these new forms of organizing collaboration are permeable with respect to other groups and communities with which these techno-activists interact. In what ways can techno-activist practices influence other groups already engaged in social and political action? Do such practices play a significant role in transforming the public sphere more generally?

THE PROCESS OF APPROPRIATING A TECHNOLOGY AS A THEORETICAL MODEL FOR COMMUNITY INFORMATICS

If community informatics is designed to provide means and clues about how information and communication technologies (ICTs) can empower ordinary people in relation to the achievement of their own goals (Gurstein 2007; see also chapter 2 in this volume), the concept of appropriating a technology appears to be useful to the understanding of that kind of social process. The concept of appropriating a technology also fits well with what Max Weber (1949, 90) has termed an ideal type, one that is "formed by the one-sided accentuation of one or more points of view and by the synthesis of a great many diffuse, discrete, more or less present and occasionally absent concrete individual phenomena, which are arranged according to those one-sidedly emphasized viewpoints into a unified analytical construct." To establish that a genuine appropriation of technology is taking place, one prerequisite—access to the technical device—and the following five conditions must be satisfied:

1. Technical and cognitive mastery of the artifact
2. Meaningful integration of the device's use into the user's everyday practices
3. Innovation: using the device introduces new creative avenues into the individual's social practices, rather than merely participating in them
4. Community mediation: learning processes and support are shared within a mobilized collective or community of practice with which the user identifies
5. Political representation: social appropriation presupposes that user collectives are adequately represented, a matter that regards both public policy and innovation markets.

Regarding the second condition, it is here that I introduce the distinction between mere use of a technical device, on the one hand, and a user's enrolment of it in social practice, on the other. Using word processing software as a technical device, for instance, is distinct from the user practice of writing, in which that software participates.

Satisfying all of these conditions signifies successful appropriation. Yet unless the prerequisite requirement, access to the technical device, is fulfilled, appropriation will be impossible. Cognizance of this prerequisite alongside the conditions allows us to distinguish appropriation from mere access, a distinction that comparative national statistics on technology penetration often confuse. Access to a device does not necessarily imply mastering its use.

THE CONTEXT FOR TECHNO-ACTIVIST SOCIAL INNOVATION

The Emergence of Informational-Cognitive Capitalism

Social experiments in "informational co-operation," whose analysis is central to our research, echo the position that some groups of social actors have taken in the ongoing transformation of highly digitized societies. Analysts describe certain emergent forms of the mode of production in contemporary societies as belonging to a new "informational capitalism" (Aigrain 2005), by which they mean that our current societies tend to yield a particular type of industry—those industries that capitalize on the ownership of the code, such as the software, pharmaceutical, or media industries (see Ghosh 2005; Lessig 1999; Weber 2004). Activists engaged in co-operative projects in the information and communication fields question the legitimacy of this new dominance (Blondeau and Latrive 2000; Moody 2001). As opposed to a proprietary definition of information, these actors maintain that information is a public good. It is this commitment to values such as gift economies, accessibility, open exchange, and communication—all first linked to information by software pioneers—that anchors the commitment of so-called code activists or techno-activists (Proulx, Couture, and Rueff 2008). Some analysts use the term *cognitive capitalism*, coined by Yann Moulier-Boutang (2008), to describe that present transformation of our contemporary economic structures.

Our research aims to situate the innovative practices of these techno-activists within the broader context of emergent social protest movements that denounce the code-owning industries in the context of informational capitalism (Castells 2002; Granjon 2001). We seek to identify the extent to which code activists are part of a process of civic negotiation of our societies' digitization (Boltanski and Chiapello 1999). Some contemporary thinkers have located a novel perspective on democratization in civic forms of technological appropriation (Feenberg 2004; Loader 1998). Our study is an opportunity to grasp the values put into play by these processes of innovation, from their initiation, negotiation, and coagulation to their wider public deployment.

Innovation by Use

Most of the time, technological objects issued from ICTs are perceived by users as "black boxes," which is to say that ordinary users pay scant attention to the objects' inner workings. Code activists, in contrast, act as a sort of technical handyman; they do not hesitate to look inside codes or devices to take an active role in how informational objects work, particularly through computer programming and the design and dissemination of new technological devices. Technologies' network organization favours co-operation between users and designers, facilitating not only acts of appropriation, diversion, and tinkering (Certeau 1980; Perriault 1989; Proulx 2005) but also those of co-construction (Neff and Stark 2003; Oudshoorn and Pinch 2003), rising even to the level of tangible technological innovations linked tightly to innovative usage. Set in motion from below, these innovations break with prescribed uses, emerging to respond to users' ad hoc needs. Considered decisive by creative process analysts, these innovations are known as "ascendant" because they proceed upward and onward from the exploration of users seeking to improve what they can do with already-existing technologies (Cardon 2005; Von Hippel 2001, 2005). Born of the ordinary practices of resourceful users, these innovations diffuse through networks of user exchange.

Technical Innovation and Social Change

Analysts of innovation posit a complex linkage between it and social change. In-depth analysis of socio-technical controversies (Callon 1981) has demonstrated both the non-linear, socially constructed character of innovation, and some of the mechanisms by which the ideological and political challenges these innovative processes mobilize are staged in public (Latour 2001). Usage studies (Proulx 2005) have, for their part, demonstrated the non-linear manner in which technological objects are distributed (Rogers 1995), underlining users' ability to divert (Certeau 1980), to reinterpret (Bijker and Law 1992), and to socially appropriate (Proulx 1994, 2002) the technology. New principles for collective action emerge from these hybridizations of social and technical spaces. Only those uses of technology that lead to tangible change in social practice can be characterized, according to Tuomi (2002), as innovation.

A RESEARCH PROJECT: TECHNO-ACTIVIST PRACTICE AS A SOURCE OF INNOVATION

Main Objectives of the Project

Anchored in a participative approach associating our team directly with the groups connected to this research, our project sought to provide detailed description and analysis of groups of persons within Canada experimenting with what we call informational co-operation. The research focuses on the practices and values of so-called code activists creating non-proprietary devices that, as alternatives to the code industries, produce social innovation. The project's main theme is to evaluate the transferability of the values associated with these practices of technical innovation into other spheres of activity (Brand 2005; Himanen 2001; Lessig 2004). To what extent can these technologically innovative practices provoke socially innovative practices in the political sphere of citizen and democratic action?

Our analysis centres on two groups located in Montréal. They operate at the intersection of the Québec community movements and free software movement. Their activities are highly technological but, at the same time, are oriented toward social change. Members of the two groups agreed to join our team as part of a participative approach that involved them as full participants in the research process:

Île Sans Fil (ISF) is a Montréal-based volunteer organization, founded in 2003 by three university students, which now forms a municipal network of over a hundred Internet access points provided free of charge in public spaces such as bars, restaurants, and cafés. ISF is a non-profit organization whose goals are to promote free public access to Wi-Fi-based Internet, to create and maintain a network of Wi-Fi access points in public locations, and to use Wi-Fi as a tool to promote art and cultural content and social applications. Thirty active volunteers contribute to hardware and software development, install equipment in public places, and manage marketing, communications, and public relations. In the past two years, the working model of ISF has been lauded, and its hotspot management software has been held up as an innovation worthy of reproduction (Powell 2006). The group considers wireless technology to be a means of creating social networks. In 2007 and 2008, ISF focused its efforts on two infrastructure projects. The first of these is the deployment of hotspots in public spaces, such as parks and cafés. The second is the creation of open access, roof-to-roof high-speed Internet infrastructure. The group was awarded the Montréal Social Innovation prize in 2005 and currently has close to 10,000 users. (See also chapters 10 and 11 in this volume.)

Koumbit is a Montréal-based volunteer organization founded in 2002 whose mission is to promote the appropriation of free and open software by social groups in Québec, in Canada, and abroad. This group works on the development of a collective software platform and provides support for users of free and open software (see Goldenberg 2006). The name "Koumbit" is a derivation of the Haitian Creole word konbit, which can be translated as an association of people working toward the realization of a common goal. On their website, the group describes its founding principles as follows:

Collectively managed. We believe in a greater autonomy for people and collectives. We believe that it is essential for groups and individuals to manage by themselves their direction, life, and authority.

Educational space. We believe that our organization must not be a simple service company but must also integrate continuing education of workers and members to new technologies, along the principles of participative organization like ParEcon and other horizontal organizational techniques.

Transparency. We believe that organizations should be transparent toward their members but also toward society at large. No organization evolves in a void and all our actions have consequences. Therefore, it is essential that the public can follow on the actions and decisions of the different organizations that make up society. We believe that the flow of information coming out of organizations must not be blocked, but be broadcasted so that citizens can take enlightened decisions on the issues that affect them.

Copyleft (free software). We believe in developing free and open source software. Free software is a matter of freedom (as in speech): everyone should be free to use software for any socially useful purposes. Software is not a tangible material object, like a chair, sandwich, or oil, so it can be copied and changed easily. Those possibilities render software useful as such; we believe that software users must be able to appropriate those possibilities.

Self-sufficiency. We believe that our organization must be self-sufficient and not depend exclusively on one big customer or state to finance itself. We are always looking for ways to diversify our sources of income and believe in partnership to develop durable and functional links with other organizations. Similarly, we offer technological solutions that empower people with their own tools within their organizations.

Solidarity. We believe that our organization must support citizen initiative and those left behind in our society. We also believe that people in an organization must build it in support and respect of each other, their integrity, and dignity. We also believe that some sacrifices must be made so that the organization doesn't harm mankind and nature as a whole. "Above all, do no harm."

Equity and equality. We believe that everyone must have the same chances not only at the start of but also during the race. We are trying to eliminate inequities between individuals, and compensate for iniquities that are impossible to eliminate.

Participatory economics. We believe in balanced job complexes, variable modes of decision, participation of workers in the definition of their workplace, and participation of parties affected by the services of the organization in its orientation. In short, we are strongly inspired by the Participatory Economics model elucidated by Michael Albert.

Some studies on governance and cooperation models in activist groups exist (Aguiton and Cardon 2006; Auray 2005; Conein and Delsalle 2005; Granjon 2001). The study of informational co-operatives, however, must take into account how these localized practices are articulated with the militant ambitions expressed in international networks of activists and global social forums. Since the local groups are simultaneously bound to international networks, we sought to analyze their local activities in light of broader debates concerning the so-called information society that have unfolded in the global arena (Fontan 1998). Our ethnographic descriptions, produced in collaboration with the actors in a participatory approach, have the following four objectives:

1. To explain the context in which these groups situate their activities and describe how they seek to innovate socially and technologically
2. To analyze how the groups define the modalities of democratization through informational co-operation, and the transferability of their innovations into other spheres of activity
3. To identify the controversies that emerge in thus-constituted local public spaces and their interaction with the broader questions that inform contemporary debate
4. To trace the prospects for generalizing these practices and innovations to contribute to the common good.

Methodology: Participative Ethnography

Using a participative approach (Barnsley and Elis 1992; Dallaire 2002), our ethnographic descriptions were compiled by two observers. Each observer first clearly identified herself to the group as an observer and a university student. After some time, and on a voluntary basis, each observer became a full member of the organization. This obviously gives rise to several questions about the relationship between the observer and the observed. We are aware that the knowledge we generate about each group teaches the group about itself and thus stimulates self-analysis within groups regarding clarification of their missions and organizational models. Our observations brought key points to the fore about group identity, sources of controversy, and mission. Each observer simultaneously played both the role of a conveyor of information between the research team and the observed group and of an actor who prompted the group to engage in self-reflection and self-analysis.

This participative ethnography tends toward a progressive appropriation by the observed group of the research goal's (re)definition in line with the group's specific interests. We reject the dominant sociological position that requires that researchers adopt a "suspended" position in order to study the group under observation. The precautionary principle characteristic of our approach lies in seeking not to impose the researcher's vocabulary on actors in the field. We contemplate a reciprocal enrichment of worldviews and a reciprocal contribution to knowledge between the research team and the observed group. The purpose of our methodological approach is to understand the meaning that the actors themselves ascribe to their identity, project, and activities in order to support a reflexive approach within each of the target groups. This approach thus presupposes an epistemological (re)articulation between the production of scientific knowledge and its potential use by users in the field. How can our results be incorporated back into the activities and reflexivity of the target group? How can socio-political commitment be articulated in conjunction with scientific rigour?

Toward a Politicization of Technology

Code activists offer users the possibility of approaching technological culture in a different way. They suggest a new way to represent technology. They reconceptualize technology not simply as a set of tools to be used to further a project of personal or social emancipation but rather as a culture or set of devices and apparatuses that are not neutral tools but are, on the contrary, value laden and organized into technical configurations that encode power relations, promoting one type of activity to the detriment of other possible types. Technological devices are not neutral. The innovation process operated by these activists is part of a transformation of the relationship between users and the technological world (Bencheikh 1986; Jouët 1987). Yet once technology is conceived of as a culture (Simondon 1958), representing the technological world as this type of transformation becomes profoundly political and is therefore disposed to provoke significant change within the broader register of social values (Lessig 2001).

Can these new representations of technological culture help carve out new spaces of citizenship inside the public sphere (Feenberg 2004)? Informational co-operation projects import a taste for change into a technological world whose reigning incumbents, who value the large, proprietary code industries that police its borders, would prefer that we accept passively. More radically, Cardon and Granjon (2003) note that a politicized segment of the techno-activist population presents itself as a militant counter-culture in which collective software production, technical process, and anti-institutional digital insurrection coalesce. Code activists in this sense produce new spaces for collective action and, through their actions, put forward a model for extended participation in which developers and users can participate jointly in the collective production of public technological and informational goods. We hypothesize that this construction of new public space around technologies could lead to citizen empowerment. As our earlier research regarding the free culture controversies revealed, activist practice in the technological sphere is a source of social innovation, particularly from the standpoint of collaborative practices established in how work is organized (Proulx and Couture 2006).

Innovations in Informational Cooperation

In experimenting with new forms of collaboration around the organization of their production work, code militants act politically. Analysis of these collective practices suggests that such models of action and involvement are neither unified nor stabilized. As in some scientific communities, multiple controversies over how technology uses are articulated into work organization appear to stimulate group activity among code activists. For some of them, the opening up of technological apparatuses is a technological victory; for others it is a measure of democracy. As the search for consensus within activist groups reveals, informational co-operation's pragmatic objectives invite a novel deliberative process around themes such as the decentralization of technological action, procedural governance, and collective management of training (Proulx, Couture, and Rueff 2008; Proulx, Rueff, and Lecomte 2007).

CONCLUSION: WHAT SORT OF DIGITAL WORLD ARE WE CONSTRUCTING?

Grassroots digital technology movements have a role to play in the construction of a bottom-up alternative to the top-down dominant view expressed through the promotion of a so-called global information society. Homilies repeated for the past thirty years on the apparently inevitable rise of an information society have made this rhetoric commonplace, entrenching the quasi-certainty of this inevitably in the popular imagination. A similar message has issued forth from national governments, international organizations, and the large electronic entertainment, software, and telecommunications industries. Critics have demonstrated that this rhetoric is bound to a pervasive groupthink-style approach steeped in neo-liberalism and appeals to globalization (Mattelart 2003; Proulx 2007). Such representation of a global information society has become the dominant *top-down* model for describing the future of Western societies.

The activities of the techno-activists described here contribute to a *bottom-up* model that anticipates the rise of a network of shared knowledge groups (Ambrosi, Pimienta, and Peugeot 2005). This alternative representation of the future information society contrasts with the unitary vision for an information society conceived in the boardrooms and cube farms of global multinationals. The bottom-up alternative was in evidence in Tunis in December 2005, during the last World Summit on the Information Society (WSIS); it is a vision that expresses the position adopted by "organized civil society" as part of what economist Eli Noam has called a third wave of Internet leaders (Noam 2005), more politicized than those of the first wave, who emerged from the military, university, and hacker milieu, or those of the second, who were wedded to the Internet's encasement by market logics. The alternative vision of an information society associated with "shared knowledge collectives" is rooted in the social practices of community-based exchange and knowledge sharing; these emerge from groups, collectives, and small societies asserting their cultural diversity against a standard of cosmopolitanism (Beck 2006).

ACKNOWLEDGEMENT
I am grateful to Bram Abramson, who translated the text from the original French.

REFERENCES

Aguiton, Christophe, and Dominique Cardon. 2006. L'équipement technologique des débats altermondialistes. In *Communautés virtuelles: Penser et agir en réseau*, ed. Serge Proulx, Louise Poissant, and Michel Sénécal, 335–49. Québec: Presses de l'Université Laval.

Aigrain, P. Philippe. 2005. *Cause commune: L'information entre bien commun et propriété*. Paris: Fayard.

Ambrosi, Alain, Daniel Pimienta, and Valérie Peugeot. 2005. Vers des sociétés de savoirs partagés. In *Enjeux de mots: Regards multiculturels sur les sociétés de l'information*, ed. Alain Ambrosi and Valérie Peugeot, 23–33. Caen: C&F Éditions.

Auray, Nicolas. 2005. Le sens du juste dans un noyau d'experts: Debian et le puritanisme civique. In *Internet, une utopie limitée: Nouvelles régulations, nouvelles solidarités*, ed. Serge Proulx, Françoise Massit-Folléa, and Bernard Conein, 71–94. Québec: Presses de l'Université Laval.

Barnsley, Jan, and Diana Eliss. 1992. *La recherche en vue de stratégies de changement: Guide de recherche-action pour les groupes communautaires*. Vancouver: Women's Research Center.

Beck, Ulrike. 2006. *Qu'est-ce que le cosmopolitisme?* Paris: Aubier.

Bencheikh, Touhami. 1986. Construit social et innovation technologique. *Sociologie du travail* 28(1): 41–57.

Bijker, Wiebe, and John Law, eds. 1992. *Shaping technology/building society: Studies in socio-technical change*. Cambridge, MA: MIT Press.

Blondeau, Olivier and Florent Latrive, eds. 2000. *Libres enfants du savoir numérique*. Paris: L'Éclat.

Boltanski, Luc, and Eve Chiapello. 1999. *Le nouvel esprit du capitalisme*. Paris: Gallimard.

Brand, Ralf. 2005. The citizen-innovator. *The Public Sector Innovation Journal* 10(1): 1–11.

Callon, Michel. 1981. Pour une sociologie des controverses technologiques. *Fundamenta Scientiae* 12(4): 381–99.

Cardon, Dominique. 2005. L'innovation par l'usage. *Vécam*, http://vecam.org/article588.html.

Cardon, Dominique, and Fabien Granjon. 2003. Les mobilisations informationnelles dans le mouvement altermondialiste. Colloque international: Les mobilisations altermondial-istes, Paris. http://www.afsp.msh-paris.fr/activite/sei/collsei231003.html.

Castells, Manuel. 2002. *La galaxie Internet*. Paris: Fayard.

Certeau, Michel de. 1980. *L'invention du quotidien*, vol. 1, *Arts de faire*. Paris: UGE, collection 10/18.

Conein, Bernard, and Sebastien Delsalle. 2005. Le logiciel libre comme communauté de connaissance: Normes épistémiques et normes sociales. In *Internet, une utopie limitée: Nouvelles régulations, nouvelles solidarités*, ed. Serge Proulx, Françoise Massit-Folléa, and Bernard Conein, 39–69. Québec: Presses de l'Université Laval.

Dallaire, Marlène. 2002. Cadre de collaboration en approches participatives en recherché. Recension d'écrits, Chaire Approches communautaires et inégalité de santé, FCRSS/IRSC. Montréal: Université de Montréal.

Feenberg, Andrew. 2004. *(Re)Penser la technique: Vers une technologie démocratique*. Paris: La Découverte.

Fontan, Jean-Marc. 1998. Innovation sociale et société civile québécoise. *Possibles* 22(3–4): 116–35.

Ghosh, Rishab Aiyer, ed. 2005. *Code: Collaborative ownership and the digital economy*. Cambridge, MA: MIT Press.

Goldenberg, Anne. 2006. *Les pratiques collaboratives de Koumbit*. Final report. Montréal: LabCMO, UQAM, 24 July.

Granjon, Fabien. 2001. *L'Internet militant: Mouvement social et usages des réseaux téléma-tiques*. Rennes: Apogée.

Gurstein, Michael. 2007. *What is community informatics (and why does it matter)?* Milan: Polimetrica.

Himanen, Pekka. 2001. *L'éthique hacker et l'esprit de l'ère de l'information*. Paris: Exils.

Jouët, Josiane. 1987. Le vécu de la technique: La télématique et la micro-informatique à domicile. *Réseaux* 25: 119–41.

Latour, Bruno. 2001. *L'espoir de Pandore: Pour une version réaliste de l'activité scientifique*. Paris: La Découverte.

Lessig, Lawrence. 1999. *Code and other laws of cyberspace*. New York: Basic Books.

———. 2001. *The future of ideas: The fate of the commons in a connected world*. New York: Random House.

——. 2004. *Free culture: The nature and future of creativity.* New York: Penguin.

Loader, Brian. 1998. *Cyberspace divide: Equality, agency and policy in the information society.* London: Routledge.

Mattelart, Armand. 2003. *Histoire de la société de l'information,* 2nd ed. Paris: La Découverte.

Moody, Glyn. 2001. *Rebel code: Inside linux and the open source revolution.* New York: Perseus Publishing.

Moulier-Boutang, Yann. 2008. *Le capitalisme cognitive: La nouvelle grande transformation.* Paris: Éditions Amsterdam.

Neff, Gina, and David Stark. 2003. Permanently beta: Responsive organization in the Internet era. In *Society on line: The Internet in control,* ed. Philip Howard and Steve Jones, 173–88. Thousand Oaks, CA: Sage.

Noam, Eli. 2005. The Internet's third wave. *Financial Times* (New York), 28 November.

Oudshoorn, Nelly, and Trevor Pinch, eds. 2003. *How users matter: The co-construction of users and technologies.* Cambridge, MA: MIT Press.

Perriault, Jacques. 1989. *Logique de l'usage.* Paris: Flammarion.

Powell, Alison. 2006. *Île Sans Fil as a digital formation.* Final report, *Pratiques collaboratives.* Montréal: LabCMO, UQAM, 20 July.

Proulx, Serge. 1994. Les différentes problématiques de l'usage et de l'usager. In *Médias et nouvelles technologies: Pour une sociopolitique des usages,* ed. André Vitalis, 149–59. Rennes: Apogée.

——. 2002. Trajectoires d'usages des technologies de communication: Les formes d'appropriation d'une culture numérique comme enjeu d'une société du savoir. *Annales des télécommunications* 57 (3–4): 180–89.

——. 2005. Penser les usages des TIC aujourd'hui: Enjeux, modèles, tendances. In *Enjeux et usages des TIC: Aspects sociaux et culturels,* vol. 1, ed. Lise Vieira and Nathalie Pinède, 7–20. Bordeaux: Presses universitaires de Bordeaux.

——. 2007. Interroger la métaphore d'une société de l'information: Horizon et limites d'une utopie. *Communication and Langages* 152(2): 107–24.

Proulx, Serge, and Stéphane Couture. 2006. Pratiques de coopération et éthique du partage à l'intersection de deux mondes sociaux. In *Intelligence collective: Rencontres 2006,* ed. J.M. Penalva, 137–52. Paris: Les Presses de l'École des Mines de Paris.

Proulx, Serge, Stéphane Couture, and Julien Rueff. eds. 2008. *L'action communautaire québécoise à l'ère du numérique.* Québec: Presses de l'Université du Québec.

Proulx, Serge, Julien Rueff, and Nicolas Lecomte. 2007. La redéfinition du tiers secteur québécois à l'aune du militantisme technique. *Hermès* 47: 107–14.

Rogers, Everett. 1995. *Diffusion of innovations,* 4th ed. New York: Free Press.

Simondon, Georges. 1958. *Du mode d'existence des objets techniques.* Paris: Aubier.

Tuomi, Ilkka. 2002. *Networks of innovation: Change and meaning in the age of Internet.* Oxford: Oxford University Press.

Von Hippel, Eric. 2001. Innovation by user communities: Learning from open source software. *Sloan Management Review* 42(4): 82.

——. 2005. *Democratizing innovation.* Cambridge, MA: MIT Press.

Weber, Max. 1949. *The methodology of the social sciences.* New York: Free Press.

Weber, Steven. 2004. *The success of open source.* Cambridge, MA: Harvard University Press.

6 "THE RESEARCHER IS A GIRL"
Tales of Bringing Feminist Labour Perspectives into Community Informatics Practice and Evaluation

Katrina Peddle, Alison Powell, Leslie Regan Shade

Community informatics (CI) analyzes the enabling uses of ICTs to achieve community social, economic, cultural, or political goals. By bringing together various stakeholders—community activists and groups, policy makers, users/citizens, artists, and academics—it implicitly foregrounds its emphasis on community. CI "combines an interest in the potentially transforming qualities of the new media with an analysis of the importance of community social relations for human interaction" (Keeble and Loader 2001, 3). It is "concerned with the development, deployment and management of information systems designed with and by communities to solve their own problems"(McIver 2003, 33), and via incorporation of "the user and his [*sic*] community into the system design process introduces 'stakeholders' into an extended approach to ICT design, development, and implementation" (Gurstein 2000, 6). CI applications include community Internet access, delivery of community information, online civic participation, community economic development, and development of learning networks (see O'Neil 2002, as well as chapter 2 in this volume).

In this chapter we argue that the field of CI would be strengthened by further acknowledging feminist contributions in science and technology studies (STS) (see Wajcman 2007 and 2010 for a panoramic overview of the scholarship to date) and by welcoming new feminist interventions in practice and evaluation. In her examination of the intersection of feminist-oriented STS with digital technologies, Suchman (2008, 153) provides evidence of energetic engagement, ranging "from questions regarding received assumptions to dialogic interventions and more directly experimental alternatives," that have both practical and political "implications for how we conceptualize and configure practices of information technology design and use and the relations between them." Given STS's critical interdisciplinarity, as well as feminist scholarship's attention to the nuances of power and the dissenting discourses at work in the domain of science and technology, STS is well positioned to align with CI.

Eubanks throws out a challenge to STS scholars: "If we take seriously science and technology studies' claims that science and technologies are socially shaped, then we must also explore the converse: how our social problems are technologically shaped, mediated, and produced, and how we can redirect our technological politics and practices to increase social justice" (Eubanks 2007a, 136). In assessing the use of participatory action research (PAR) to develop a popular technology training program for women living in transitional circumstances in upper state New York, Eubanks argues that the "distributive paradigm" is at the foreground of much CI work. She contends that this paradigm limits the dispersal of ICT resources because it cannot adequately account for the various socio-technical access dynamics and that its "commodity focus precludes understanding ICT as a 'technology of citizenship'" (Eubanks 2007b). In her own interventions, she discovered how the way in which "digital divide interventions have been framed acts to obscure the kinds of day-to-day interactions low-income women have with technology; and how the powerful symbolism equating computers with technological and social progress contradicts these women's experiences, resulting in a critical ambivalence towards technology" (Eubanks 2007b).

COMMUNITY INFORMATICS: FEMINIST PERSPECTIVES

CI perspectives that integrate gender highlight capacity building in relation to women's empowerment, strengthening learning communities for sustainability, instituting social literacy, access, training, and content efforts, and the importance of design in user-technology relations. Salient CI literature that is explicitly feminist in orientation includes Webb and Jones's analysis (2004) of Women Connect, a London CN that uses diverse communication tools to strengthen the skills and development of women within their local communities. They stress the value of capacity building in evaluation and, especially, in interrogating whether women have influenced policies that affect their lives. Also drawing from Women Connect, Page and Scott (2001) argue that CI needs to mainstream feminist approaches in order to make CNS sustainable and to recognize that learning communities should be conceptualized and strengthened as dialogic and playful spaces where learners can inform themselves about new ideas and events and engage critically and creatively with their differences, while constructing new models of learning. As they observe: "Such communities work with the realities of gendered power relations, aiming to challenge and to change them. To achieve this, quality facilitation is needed, encompassing both political and relational skills. These skills are often the province of women, and are traditionally undervalued in organizations" (550).

Bishop et al. (2001) in their Afya participatory action research project, which aimed to help African American women increase their access to community health information and services, stress the importance of bridging the technological and the social aspects of the digital divide:

> As members of diverse communities, we all must look to change in our social literacy, access, training, and content efforts. In terms of social literacy, we must learn how to read each other, how to grant respect and validity to diverse funds of knowledge and social capital. We need to be socially accessible, opening ourselves to new relationships. Social training must occur as stakeholders throughout a community model and practice a shared vision of social justice.

Likewise, in her review of women's contributions to Ireland's flagship information society initiative, the community-based Ennis Information Age Town project (1997–2002), McQuillan identified an "archetypal triad"—technicians, tacticians, and tattlers—to describe the multiple roles women assumed in engagement and agency in ICT, bridging both the technical and the social. As McQuillan noted, these women were variously "'technicians,' contributing knowledge, expertise and skills; 'tacticians,' functioning as mediators and influencers of policy and practice; and 'tattlers,' increasing understanding, visibility, and presence" (McQuillan 2008, 3). Digital inclusion, participation, and contributions to community ICT projects were thus strengthened by women acting multifariously and interchangeably as agents, innovators, and mediators.

To understand barriers to use of technologies by specific users, Oudshoorn, Rommes, and Stienstra (2004) advocate a semiotic approach to user-technology relations. Grounding their case study in an analysis of Amsterdam's Digital Staad (DDS), they identify gaps between the rhetoric and the practice of design for democratic purposes. For instance, did the placement of computers in public spaces increase access for all? In fact, DDS terminals were eventually removed from some public spaces because of concerns about their increased use by "tramps," thus detracting from DDS's image as an innovative and culturally hip system. The authors also argue that even when users are not involved in the design stages of technological artifacts, envisioning how designers imagine and configure their users is a useful strategy. Focusing on the gender identities of the designers and users can shed understanding on how products constrain specific users, particularly women.

In evaluating ICT projects that seek inclusive participation of citizens, and particularly the strengthening of women's involvement, Lennie (2005a, 18) highlights the need for rigorous analyses that examine the gendered power-knowledge dynamics of community-based projects that "can reveal both the empowering and disempowering impacts and effects of new technologies on women's lives and experiences." It is in this spirit of her call for "an eclectic feminist framework" that we examine the many particularities of labour involved in community ICT projects both by women working within the organizations themselves and by those researching the communities as academic participants.

THE WESTERN VALLEY DEVELOPMENT AGENCY

As Peddle details in chapter 15, the Western Valley Development Agency (WVDA) was considered an international innovator. As a core-funded, community-based organization, it was active in community development, particularly with ICTs. In 2005 it closed because of lack of municipal support. Because the WVDA was a regional development agency administered under the Regional Development Authority Act (RDA Act), municipalities contributed one-third of the organization's core funding, which was essential for obtaining matching provincial and federal monies for its operating budget. Core funding was supplemented by project funding from programs with a CI focus. Project funding exceeded core funding by a factor of ten to one—especially with the Smart Community project, one of ten national multimillion dollar demonstration projects designed to make communities "smart" in their use of ICTs. Here we outline how the invisibility of feminized community development work relates to the closure of the WVDA and discuss perceptions of who can engage in business development. The decision to close WVDA must not be reduced to essentializing notions of gender difference. Rather, it is important here to reflect on the role of gendered forms of work.[1]

The WVDA had a sustained commitment to capacity building, while municipal stakeholders felt that business development investment yielded better regional results. Two salient issues are (1) capacity building work is feminized and therefore invisible and (2) the lack of municipal support is not only indicative of the invisibility of WVDA's capacity building activities but also underscores a lack of confidence in the organization's ability to work on business development.

Situating and Critiquing Capacity Building

Capacity building is the "increase in community groups' abilities to define, assess, analyse and act on health (or any other) concerns of importance to their members" (Labonte and Laverack, quoted in Gibbon, Labonte, and Laverack 2002, 485). Cook and Smith (2004) consider capacity building an essential element of CI. While acknowledged and supported at the theoretical level, in practice capacity building often involves caring work that is typically undervalued. While demands are placed on CI organizations to provide quantitative results of their work, these are problematic in the broader context of CI initiatives, in which outputs are often social in nature and thus hard to measure.

Lennie (2005b) underlines the importance of participative frameworks in community development and of iterative engagement that allows for meaningful contributions by community members, arguing for the importance of the process rather than simply of an end goal (such as job creation). It can be argued that the WVDA was a participatory organization, engaging in a participatory evaluation process in which decisions regarding the organization's direction were informed by interviews with 150 stakeholders. Collective visioning is closely aligned with capacity building, a leadership style considered by municipal representatives to lack focus (interview with municipal councillor, 2005).

Given conflicts over what is recognized as legitimate community development activities, capacity building needs to be situated within a broader understanding of empowerment of community members, predicated on valuing participation. Key influences in the empowerment paradigm include emancipatory pedagogy, feminist pedagogy, and participatory action research, with a focus on the community versus the individual level.

Capacity building has been criticized for being difficult to define, operationalize, and measure (Gibbon, Labonte, and Laverack 2002) and thus exemplary of the invisible nature of community development work. Invisible work refers to "work that remains unseen and unrecognized," including "work done by invisible people, routine work, and informal work processes" (Nardi and Engeström 1999). In view of this, one can understand capacity building as a form of feminized labour typically undervalued and often unseen (Stall and Stoeckler 1998).

The feminization of capacity building is a phenomenon that has yet to be illuminated in CI literature. The literature on caring work has long critiqued the dominant societal perception that caring is an essentially "feminine" characteristic. It is rather via gender socialization that women learn to care in both paid and unpaid labour (Baines, Neysmith, and Evans 1991). Caring work is typically undervalued and invisible, and we argue here that much of the capacity building work done by both women and men at the WVDA falls into this category. Critically assessing the theoretical basis of capacity building furthers reflection on the role of invisible labour in CI organizations.

Community Informatics at the WVDA

Created at a time of high unemployment and change in Nova Scotia's Western Valley, the WVDA made a dedicated effort to build community resources and secure projects for the region. The WVDA focused on building individual capacity through youth intern and computer training programs and on building business capacity through its e-business program. However, a concern with confidentiality (for example, in meetings with individuals seeking to start businesses) limited the organization's capacity to measure outputs quantitatively. This focus on process as a vehicle for community development was a source of conflict between WVDA staff and certain municipal partners, who expressed frustration with "too much capacity building" and urged the WVDA to instead focus on local business expansion. While attracting new businesses into the region was a WVDA priority, municipal representatives stressed that WVDA should perform its mandate with accountability for how and with whom its time was spent. This reflects a move away from a process-oriented approach to a managerial focus on products. Indeed, a collaborative team approach, predicated on a positive attitude, group accountability, and inclusion, was key to work at the WVDA—an approach that differs from traditional top-down leadership models.

The WVDA significantly contributed to the local region through partnerships to support community learning, notably for an online library catalogue that significantly increased the number of people accessing the collection. One community resource person, a librarian, recounted her work as a member of a WVDA Smart Community advisory group:

> It was quite a diverse group, but it was great. You learned a lot—well I did—from the other members. It was really good. In that advisory role strictly, they [the WVDA] sort of wanted a community-based governance. Well, it was not governance, because it was not governed by us, but they just wanted input from the community in general to make sure they were going in the way the community would have wanted, rather than just the organization taking it on. . . . They didn't have to strike an advisory committee; they just felt that they wanted to have that capacity, which was good, especially in the first couple of years of that project while things were taking shape.

Although the WVDA valued capacity building, it also was active in larger-scale business negotiations. Following several years of lobbying the incumbent telco (telecommunications company) to extend broadband service to the region,[2] the WVDA, in partnership with the municipalities and a large post-secondary institution, succeeded in negotiating with two small telcos to create a community-owned broadband fibre network. In the same year that the network was secured, the municipalities began to voice serious concerns about the organization's approach to community economic development. One municipal councillor explained his concerns with capacity building with this example:

> [Those at the WVDA] have done a very commendable job, and they should be commended for it. But . . . when I was younger there wasn't much money around . . . and a lot of people, you would see them build a basement and then move into it, and they would live in the basement for one, two, three years, while they were collecting money to build the house on the basement. . . . I had an uncle who built a basement, and he lived in the basement so long without building a house on it that the walls of the basement actually started to crumble because it didn't have the structure to hold it together. And that's where I feel our area is at that point now. I feel as far as the foundation for a business environment, the WVDA has built an excellent one, and they're to be commended for the job they've done. But now is that time that we have to stop working on a basement or stop living in our basement and start building the businesses that use the structure. The development agency has been focused on capacity building.

The perspective he articulates asserts that capacity building would actually hinder the community and ignores the large infrastructure project that the WVDA had championed. It also dismisses the organization's ability to work with businesses. With a more specific focus on explicitly business-related activities, there was less room for broad-based CI initiatives that were a substantial part of the WVDA's mandate.

Feminized Labour and Invisible Work in Community Informatics

It initially seems that an ideological clash over what counts as legitimate development activities was at the heart of WVDA's closure. Page and Scott (2001) argue that a shared vision of social justice is critical to CI, and in this instance such a common vision was palpably absent.

The refocusing of priorities at the WVDA belies a deeper conflict around what type of work is valued. It is clear that the work of business attraction, retention, and expansion were the priorities of the municipalities, with the assumption that this would further social development in the area. Municipal partners did not see the WVDA as an organization that could adequately focus on building businesses, despite its many successes in regional development and its notable accomplishments in establishing community-owned broadband infrastructure. This demonstrates a lack of municipal faith in the organization's leadership and also points to assumptions about who can perform this type of work.

Women played important leadership roles at the WVDA. Given the white, masculinized fields of engineering and computer science (Cockburn 1999), the contributions of women leaders to CI trouble traditional gender roles around work (Meiners and Fuller 2004). Analysis of gender roles in community development is scarce, reflecting a conceptual marginalization of the role of gender in this process generally (Leavitt 2003).

Feminist approaches to community development emphasize collaboration, a perspective that was in conflict with the desire for "hard outputs" (for example, a quantitative record of how many businesses were started in the area as a direct result of working with the WVDA) articulated by certain municipal partners. Another challenge to measuring outputs was the collaborative and facilitative nature of the WVDA's work. However, it is difficult to dismiss the conflict between the organization and its municipal funders as a simple lack of interest in business-related activities, given the WVDA's success in negotiating large telecommunication partnerships. Rather, the conflict is more indicative of assumptions about who is capable of engaging in business than it is of a lack of business orientation at the WVDA.

The municipalities attempted to rationalize community development by bringing it under more direct municipal control. This move away from capacity building activities requested by municipal funders devalues the relational aspects of community development work and parallels the ways in which caring work has been unseen in other arenas of paid labour, including nursing and teaching (Graham 1983). One WVDA staff member elaborated on the challenges of doing work that is neither visible nor easily quantified, but still relates to business development:

> I have other things that I have been involved in that I think are very strategically important for the organization, like the broadband. We need somebody to keep pushing that. I mean, what is really important now is that we get users, that we have demonstration projects, and it is kind of like, we thought we could build it and people would start coming to it, but . . . the applications aren't there yet, and the timing is just not quite right yet, so you have to keep demonstrating how people can use it, to engage people, and that is just like, that is not an easy task, you know, lot of behind the scenes things that people don't see but people are working on it all the time.

Given the frustration of municipal representatives at the alleged lack of "tangible" outputs from WVDA, it is apparent that this invisibility of everyday development activities was a factor in their concerns. This lack of recognition is surprising, given the WVDA's aggressive marketing of the Western Valley and promotion of its activities, which won it national and international recognition.

It is clear that, at the WVDA, participation and the work that facilitates it was an important priority that did not fit into tightly monitored and rationalized visions of community development. The WVDA's struggle with doing "too much capacity building" in community development highlights how feminized forms of labour are largely invisible and ignored in the CI context.

GENDER, DIFFERENCE, AND PARTIAL PERSPECTIVES IN COMMUNITY TECHNOLOGY DEVELOPMENT

As compared to funded projects within established community organizations such as the WVDA, grassroots community technology projects present different contexts for the gendering of work—and the gendering of technology development. As a rule, few non-specialists have a chance to participate in the design of ICTs. A look at the gendered nature of a non-commercial ICT production environment adds an explicit focus on cultural power to a feminist political economy of communications. Through reflexive participant observation as a research method and a focus on the gendered aspects of ICT production in a non-hierarchical, non-commercial setting, the analysis becomes more subtle, as the expected conceptual link between masculinity, power, knowledge, and technology is broken. Community informatics research shifts the perspective on technology production away from an exclusive focus on materialism and consumption. Projects such as Île Sans Fil (ISF), in which technology production occurs outside of commercial settings and open-source software is produced by voluntary contributions, appear to provide examples of more democratic, community-oriented technology production. Yet as the participatory, "embedded" research with ISF indicates, even such an environment requires a negotiation of situated, partial knowledge in order to fully break down the association between masculinity and technological mastery.

Here we reflect on participatory research conducted with the community wireless networking group ISF. ISF is a group of volunteers centred in downtown Montréal who create and maintain a network of a hundred Internet access points, managed by a piece of open-source software they created. (For further discussion, see chapters 10 and 11.) The software presents a unique portal, or opening web page, at each of the access points, on which news and images pertinent to the location appear. ISF's founders wanted to connect public Internet use to location-based services and the delivery of local media content. To achieve their goal, they partnered with business owners to offer free Wi-Fi to clients and developed the functionalities of their software to distribute "ultra-local" news and emerging local art on the portal pages. The software also managed overall use of the network. The entire project was run on volunteer labour. Volunteers were for the most part young, male, self-identified "hackers" or "geeks"—people who liked, understood, and engaged with tech- nology, and identified this engagement as a key part of their identity.

Geeks and hackers are key actors in some community technology pro- jects, where the official hierarchies of expertise characteristic of large research and development organizations are absent. While women have long worked in industrial technical design as researchers (Suchman 1987), the woman researcher in community ICT development, who is engaged primarily in re- flecting on the practices taking place, is both a token and simultaneously "one of the boys"—both inside and outside the inner circle. This position within the group mirrors the theoretical and philosophical position that Haraway (1991) describes as "partial perspective"—the ability and necessity to see non- objectively. As she sees it, partial perspective breaks down the hegemonic, masculine myth of the objective observer and situates the viewer as always in the process of becoming and always in the process of creating the loca- tion of her vision, which does not presume its necessary objectivity. It seems possible that the negotiated role of embedded researcher might help such a partial perspective to develop—although, when partial perspectives are not integrated into the development culture, the work of the embedded research becomes less visible. The following sections describe, from such a perspec- tive, the social and technical negotiations that constitute community-based, grassroots ICT design and development.[3]

Many community wireless networks such as ISF have members who are actively engaged in research and reflection, and a disproportionate number of these are women. The presence of an embedded researcher in fact played an important role in creating legitimacy for ISF. Academic affiliation helped the group when it applied for funding or submitted conference proposals. Yet for many of the group's members, research activities were not considered as real contributions to their central projects—building their network and developing their software. Research, like other "non-technical" activities associated with technical development, is often gendered as female. Still, by constructing the research position as explicitly embedded in the group, the CRACIN project attempted to promote a perspective wherein different perspectives might be brought to bear on technology development.

Boys and Toys: Gendered Technocultures

Many social and cultural practices mark ISF's culture as predominantly mas- culine. Members meet in a bar to drink beer and talk about technology. They use jargon and technical language to communicate and often spend their time together gazing at their computer screens. They like to make things work well, or at least better, and are fascinated with new technological developments. Knowing about technology and being able to use it to change things makes them feel strong. As Cockburn (1983), Wacjman (2004), and Faulkner (2001) point out, gender identity and technology are mutually constituted. As Faulkner comments: "The fact that popular images of both science and technology are strongly associated with the masculine side of [gender] dualisms must be one of the reasons why, in a deeply gender divided world, most girls and women don't consider a career in engineering" (11). A mastery of technology is associated with a certain type of masculinity, with control and detachment.

However, at ISF, technology is also fun—a leisure activity that members pursue in their spare time. The group nourishes a certain kind of masculinity that valourizes its members. This is positive for male members of ISF, but it poses questions about whether such a community technology project provides the same benefits to female members who do not conceive of their engagement with technology in the same manner. The joy that many male members draw from working with technology may exclude women who do not express their engagement with technology in the same way. Mellström (1995) writes that "engineering practice tends to reproduce patterns of homosociality." Women are not exactly part of the club —even if they are invited in with good intentions.

"The Researcher Is a Girl": Women in Community ICT

No member of ISF would claim that the group excluded women, and to say so would be untrue. About 10 percent of the volunteers are women, and many of them made significant contributions to ISF's projects by raising grant money, curating art projects, proposing usability studies of the portal page, coordinating media relationships, and creating marketing packages. Yet no female members of ISF were programmers or software developers. Considering that these activities carried a high social value, it was difficult to explain or quantify the contribution of women volunteer's activities to the advancement of ISF's projects. For the most part, they were opaque to the rest of the volunteers, who were not able to reconcile their utility or functionality as compared to the utility of producing code or other technical developments. In part, the prioritization of technical work is linked into the ability to gain status and financing through the development and promotion of the group's software, which grew into a separate revenue-generating project. Yet this prioritization of "difficult" technical work is also linked into the gendered culture of ISF. When faced with a question about the small number of women in the group, one ISF member responded, "Well, the researcher is a girl." Indeed, within the group, certain actions related to the production of technology, such as programming, are already gendered as male, while others, such as design, marketing, or social research, are gendered as female. For example, a female member created a new user interface for the portal page that she hoped could replace a previous interface. Despite her presentation of it at several meetings, she was perpetually ignored or even dismissed. No one responded to the messages she posted on the mailing list. Her interface design work, which combines analysis of human behaviour with software programming, transcended the categories of "masculine" software development and "feminine" research and design work. Since it was impossible to get a clear definition of how to position her boundary-crossing work, other members may have just ignored it until they could better define it. She finally completed the new interface design in partnership with another member—a male web designer.

The modes of relation between ISF were also gendered, with direct and assertive communication styles prioritized—in the "talk louder and faster" mode of relationship that has been observed in engineering schools (see Hacker 1990). Male members of ISF indicated that they would have liked to promote the inclusion of a more diverse group of people, but many of them, trained in engineering schools and private single-sex institutions and accustomed to mediating their relationships through technology, just simply "didn't know how to talk to girls." The relationship to gender is conceived of as a problem of "how to get more girls to be geeks," with a presumption that "girls" in ISF would behave, conceive of, and communicate in the same manner as the "boys" who currently make up most of its members. This perspective is typical of what Faulkner (2001) calls the "women in technology" movement, which essentializes gender, assigning masculine qualities to technology and posing as its central problem the lack of women in science and technology, as opposed to interrogating the culture of gender in science and technology.

It is clear that women within ISF have made contributions to the group's organization and to the design and structure of its software products. However, as Suchman and Jordan (1989) point out, these contributions are not always valued, since women's perspectives on technological development are not recognized as "actual work." Suchman (2005) calls for an inclusion of feminist frameworks in technology to provide a wider interpretation of work roles that take into account the situatedness of work tasks: "Feminist research displaces traditional preoccupations with abstracted and decontexualized forms of knowledge in favour of particular, specifically situated practices of knowing in action. . . . It directs attention always to the labours (particularly those previously ignored) that are an essential and ongoing aspect of sociotechnical assemblages" (6).

Masculine Technocultures Versus Sexism: Where Is the Line?
The development of a gendered design environment produced moments in which masculine culture edged toward sexism. At one point, a member of ISF distributed a message on the listserv implying that the women members

might be willing to perform sexual favours to promote ISF. It was a joke, of course, but the women members (affectionately called "les filles sans fil" or "wireless girls") were not amused. Responses ranged from quiet shock to a questioning of one's involvement in ISF. The member who originally posted the message apologized in due course, and several "filles sans fil" continued to work with ISF, but the email underlined the difficulty of working for progressive gender politics at ISF.

In all-male spheres, sexual humour is often tolerated and even considered to be the norm; the author of the email likely assumed that everyone was part of the "ISF gang." But the difference introduced by integrating women into an environment marked as masculine made this assumption difficult to support. In short, the "wireless girls" were not men, and our troubled response to the email reiterated that our presence required a different kind of social code than the "natural" sexual humour of an all-male social group. The tension that this difference produced and the sense that ISF remained, despite apologies and attempts at inclusion, a masculine space reveal the deeply complex cultural engagements between gender and technology. The environment created at ISF, with its apparent horizontality and simultaneous negotiation between heterarchy and hierarchy, created a social environment that made it more difficult for female members to negotiate our "extraordinary juxtapositions of positive and negative feelings about technologies" (Faulkner 2001).

By focusing on the essential difference between masculine geeks and "wireless girls" rather than on the way that each member's partial perspective contributed to the development of ISF's technical and social projects, ISF failed to capitalize on the potentially radical ability of a community organization to reshape technical development.

CONCLUSION

In this chapter we argue that gender is an important element of CI research, one that is currently under-theorized in the CI literature. What types of labour are acknowledged and considered legitimate (and thus visible) must be further investigated. CI is a field predicated on participation, and questions regarding who participates and in what ways they participate must inform the growing literature.

Certainly, women involved in community technology projects, especially if they are not technicians or technical "experts," are not necessarily approaching their involvement from the same perspective as their male colleagues. Assuming that it is possible for women to seamlessly become "one of the boys" undermines their potential contributions to the cultures of community technology projects. Creating a dynamic, innovative, social organization that works on developing technology appropriate for its environment is as important as its technical development. This requires discussion and engagement within a set of multiple perspectives. Community technology projects, which often already exist outside of the business structures that require return on investment or strict hierarchical structure, might provide the potential to capitalize on these multiple perspectives.

CI organizations also must be accountable to the bodies that fund them, and thus they face pressures to conform to a business orientation. Powell's research with ISF indicates that the gendered nature of technology work creates cultural structures that can more easily reinscribe difference than open multiple perspectives. This finding is closely tied to the invisibility of capacity building work noted in the case of the WVDA. Indeed, the two cases highlighted in this chapter demonstrate a devaluing of feminized labour in both a funded and non-funded CI organization. It is therefore essential for CI researchers to examine the exclusions inherent in the invisibility of the everyday (Balka 2002) when conceptualizing participation in CI initiatives and organizations.

NOTES

1   Research for WVDA was conducted over a one-month intensive field study in 2005. Observations emerged from semi-structured interviews and insights garnered from lunch conversations, municipal council meetings, board meetings, and other community interactions. A grounded theory approach was employed where research themes were based on the data (Strauss and Corbin 1998). In addition to interviews with WVDA staff and municipal councillors, snowballing methods were used to find interview participants from the broader community.

2   Broadband access is often a prerequisite for many businesses to locate in an area and was cited by one local businessperson as dramatically enhancing her ability to interface with larger markets such as Halifax, the provincial capital.

3   Inspired by the PAR tradition, a two-year research project was oriented toward providing feedback to advance social goals and organizational change. Research included observation and participation in meetings, monitoring of the group's email mailing list, and supervision of an undergraduate intern, as well as participation in conference presentations.

REFERENCES

Baines, Carol, Sheila Neysmith, and Patricia Evans, eds. 1991. *Women's caring: Feminist perspectives on social welfare.* Toronto: McClelland and Stewart.

Balka, Ellen. 2002. The invisibility of the everyday: New technology and women's work. In *Sex and money: Feminism and political economy in the media,* ed. Eileen Meehan and Ellen Riordan, 60–74. Minneapolis: University of Minnesota Press.

Bishop, Ann Peterson, Imani Bazzell, Bharat Mehra, and Cynthia Smith. April 2001. Afya: Social and digital technologies that reach across the digital divide. *First Monday* 6(4), http://firstmonday.org/issues/issue6_4/bishop/index.html.

Cockburn, Cynthia. 1983. *Brothers: Male dominance and technological change.* London: Macmillan.

———. 1999. Caught in the wheels: The high cost of being a female cog in the male machinery of engineering. In *The social shaping of technology*, 2nd ed., ed. Donald MacKenzie and Judy Wajcman, 12–33. Philadelphia: Open University Press.

Cook, John, and Matt Smith. 2004. Beyond formal learning: Informal community eLearning. *Computers and Education* 43(1–2): 35–47.

Eubanks, Virginia E. 2007a. Popular technology: Exploring inequality in the information economy. *Science and Public Policy* 34(2) (March): 127–38.

———. 2007b. Trapped in the digital divide: The distributive paradigm in community informatics. *Journal of Community Informatics* 3(2), http://ci-journal.net/index.php/ciej/article/view/293.

Faulkner, Wendy. 2001. The technology question in feminism: A view from feminist technology studies. *Women's Studies International Forum* 24(1) (January–February): 79–95.

Gibbon, Marion, Ronald Labonte, and Glenn Laverack. 2002. Evaluating community capacity. *Health and Social Care in the Community* 10(6): 485–91.

Graham, Hilary. 1983. Caring: A labour of love. In *A labour of love: Women, work and caring*, ed. Janet Finch and Dulcie Groves, 13–30. London: Routledge and Paul Kegan.

Gurstein, Michael. 2000. Community informatics: Enabling community uses of information and communications technology. In *Community informatics: Enabling communities with information and communication technologies*, ed. Michael Gurstein, 1–32. Hershey, PA: Idea Group Publishing.

Hacker, Sally. 1990. *Doing it the hard way: Investigations of gender and technology.* London: Unwin Hyman.

Haraway, Donna. 1991. Situated knowledges: The science question in feminism and the privilege of partial perspective. In *Simians, cyborgs and women: The reinvention of nature*, Donna Haraway, 183–201. New York: Routledge.

Keeble, Leigh, and Brian Loader. 2001. Community informatics: Themes and issues. In *Community informatics: Shaping computer-mediated social relations*, ed. Leigh Keeble and Brian Loader, 1–10. New York: Routledge.

Leavitt, Jacqueline. 2003. Where's the gender in community development? *Signs: Journal of Women in Culture and Society* 29: 207–31.

Lennie, June. 2005a. An eclectic feminist framework for critically evaluating women and communication technology projects. In *Topical issues in communication and media research*, ed. Kwamena Kwansah-Aidoo, 117–42. Hauppauge, NY: Nova Science Publishers.

———. 2005b. An evaluation capacity-building process for sustainable community IT initiatives: Empowering and disempowering impacts, evaluation. *The International Journal of Theory, Research and Practice* 11(4): 390–414.

McIver, William, Jr. 2003. A community informatics for the information society. In *Communicating in the information society*, ed. Bruce Girard and Seán Ó Siochrú, 33–64. Geneva: United Nations Research Institute for Social Development.

McQuillan, Helen. 2008. Refracting gender and ICT theories through community lenses: Women as innovators and change agents. In *2008 IEEE international symposium on technology and society*, 1–9. Proceedings of ISTAS 2008, Fredericton, New Brunswick, 26–28 June. Institute of Electrical and Electronics Engineers.

Meiners, Erica, and Laurie Fuller. 2004. Empowering women? Engaging a technology grant for social change. *Journal of International Women's Studies* 5(4): 1–19.

Mellström, Ulf. 1995. *Engineering lives: Technology, time and space in a male-centred world.* Linköping: Linköping Studies in Arts and Science, no. 128.

Nardi, Bonnie A., and Yrjö Engeström. 1999. A web on the wind: The structure of invisible work. *Computer Supported Cooperative Work* 8(1–2): 1–8.

O'Neil, Dara. 2002. Assessing community informatics: A review of methodological approaches for evaluating community networks and community technology centers. *Internet Research: Electronic Networking, Applications and Policy* 12(1): 76–102.

Ottoson, Judith M., and Lawrence W. Green. 2005. Community outreach: From measuring the difference to making a difference with health information. *Journal of the Medical Library Association* 93(4): s49–s56.

Oudshoorn, Nelly, Els Rommes, and Marcelle Stienstra. 2004. Configuring the user as everybody: Gender and design cultures in information and communication technologies. *Science, Technology, and Human Values* 29(1): 30–63.

Page, Margaret, and Anne Scott. 2001. Change agency and women's learning: New practices in community informatics. *Information, Communication and Society* 4(4): 528–59.

Scott, Katherine. 2003. *Funding matters: The impact of Canada's new funding regime on nonprofit and voluntary organizations.* Ottawa: Canadian Council on Social Development.

Stall, Susan, and Randy Stoeckler. 1998. Community organizing or organizing community? Gender and the crafts of empowerment. *Gender and Society* 12(6): 729–56.

Strauss, Anselm, and Juliet Corbin. 1998. *Basics of qualitative research: Grounded theory, procedures, and techniques,* 2nd ed. Thousand Oaks, CA: Sage.

Suchman, Lucy. 1987. *Plans and situated actions: The problem of human-computer communication.* Cambridge: Cambridge University Press.

——. 2005. Agencies in technology design: Feminist reconfigurations. http://www.lancs. ac.uk/fass/sociology/papers/suchman-agenciestechnodesign.pdf.

——. 2008. Feminist STS and the sciences of the artificial. In *The handbook of science and technology studies,* 3rd ed., ed. Edward J. Hackett, Olga Amsterdamska, Michael Lynch, and Judy Wacjman, 139–63. Cambridge, MA: MIT Press.

Suchman, Lucy, and Brigitte Jordan. 1989. Computerization and women's knowledge. In *Women, Work, and Computerization,* ed. M. Tijdens, I. Jennings, I. Wagner, and M. Weggelaar, 153–60. Amsterdam: North Holland.

Wajcman, Judy. 2004. *Technofeminism.* Cambridge, MA: Polity Press.

——. 2007. From women and technology to gendered technoscience. *Information, Communication and Society* 10(3) (June): 287–98.

——. 2010. Feminist theories of technology. *Cambridge Journal of Economics* 34: 143–52.

Webb, Susan, and Kate Jones. 2004. Women Connect: Lessons from practice. *Journal of Community Informatics* 1(1): 89–117.

7 WHAT ARE COMMUNITY NETWORKS AN EXAMPLE OF? A Response

Christian Sandvig

In a recent research project studying community wireless organizers in the UK, I ran across a case that changed my thinking about community networking generally. I was talking to a local organizer who (with a group of confederates) had spent two years of painstaking effort lobbying regional development authorities and local councils to make them aware of the economic and community benefits that would come from an investment in wireless networking. His two years of meetings, emails, and letters had just paid off, but my interlocutor was deeply unhappy. The tide had turned, some elected officials fell into line, the bureaucracy was convinced, and a regional development authority announced that it was going to pay BT to build a wireless system (that is, British Telecom, the incumbent telecommunications operator).

His battle was won and lost on that day. The epiphany for me was that the community organizers wanted the network but they would never be happy with a network operated or built by BT. While one might say that he had just won a long fight—he had convinced the government to make the investments that he wanted—he felt that he had lost, and lost totally.

Most consumers love to hate the incumbent, and some of the organizers objected to BT in ways that were not based on reason—not that they were *ir*rational, but that they unreflectively objected to any relationship with the dominant commercial carrier because of their feelings about large companies. He would continue to object to BT, it became clear, even if he got to write the government's contract, and to specify exactly what BT was required to do. Even if the community organized itself and, through representative government, used public funds to build exactly the network that the people desired, in this view if the network was built by BT then the community had failed.

Many of the reasons that community activists mistrust BT are entirely sensible and well founded. But the larger point is that my own case study of these groups was hopelessly incomplete without consideration of this relationship with BT. The group's resistance to the status quo defined everything that they did, even when they didn't mention it. This chance to revisit my own change of perspective, as a researcher, is my response to the excellent research presented in this volume by CRACIN.

Choosing the context within which to contextualize CRACIN case studies is a difficult problem, but it is essential that we address it. The larger context helps to develop practical and policy suggestions, ensures that this writing will be useful to the next generation of researchers, and suggests ways to think about what the future might hold. For an academic researcher it might seem that the use of grounded theory, an exploratory perspective, or a pilot study avoids the hard problem of asking (or answering) larger questions, but in fact these tactics just delay the problem. (Grounded theory, for example, demands that new theory be the result of the research process—a tall order!)

More controversially, I think it is very difficult to usefully contextualize community networks in relation to each other. While comparison across similar projects might be practically useful, all of these cases still beg for some larger idea to sit inside. One way of considering this problem is to ask the question, "What are community networks an example of?" (Or even, "What is Wi-Fi an example of?" "What is the Internet an example of?" and so on). For community networks, there are many useful answers. Let me briefly introduce four.

THE NETWORK AS AN EXAMPLE OF REVOLUTIONARY INFRASTRUCTURE CREATION

It may be that community Wi-Fi projects (or any projects that are an architecturally distinct form of community Internet) aspire to replace other systems of communication. Sawhney (1992, 1993, 1999) developed a theoretical model to explain the process by which infrastructures replace each other over time. For instance, railroads were originally seen as a "last-mile" solution for the canal network, and canal owners invested in the railroad technology that would ultimately usurp them because they could not foresee a long-distance railroad as a realistic technological possibility or as a threat. Similarly, telephones were the "last-mile" technology for the telegraph system, and roads were a "last-mile" technology for the railroads.

To take Wi-Fi as an example, we currently can't see Wi-Fi as a long-distance technology, but it may be that research into long links and new protocol developments will cause Wi-Fi to follow the same pattern. For example, amateur experimentation includes Wi-Fi range contests at the annual DEFCON hacker conference, while WiMax is a more recent protocol that aims in part to increase the range of Wi-Fi. It isn't impossible to think that these small cases of wireless community networks may be the beginning of large networks that will usurp and replace today's infrastructure. Sawhney, the author of the model, has in fact made this connection between local wireless projects and revolutionary infrastructure development himself (Sawhney 2003).

THE NETWORK AS AN EXAMPLE OF
USER AUTONOMY AND PROTEST

In this second view, these networks are the result of specific features or services being unavailable to a given population. The network itself is a kind of user protest: The dissatisfied users probably do not want to operate their own telecommunications networks, but they see no other way to obtain any service at all—or access to specific features. Elsewhere (Sandvig 2004), I have previously developed the comparison between community wireless projects and the telephone co-operatives in Claude Fischer's (1994) work on the development of the telephone in rural America and Canada (Sandvig 2006).

In history, community co-operatives have introduced a stunning array of important infrastructures, particularly in remote areas. While we think of infrastructure as inherently a project of big government or big business, the evidence suggests that big, elaborate systems often start small (Hughes 1983). The first roads, telephones, and Internet services in many areas were introduced by community co-operatives, typically (according to Fischer) because these people were forced to act on their own if they wanted any service at all. Currently, many community networks pride themselves on offering services where no other options are available, or services that are unavailable from incumbent carriers, such as symmetric broadband Internet service, service that can be legally resold, or Internet access without port blocking. In this instance the Wi-Fi co-op is heir to the early Internet service providers with the same motives.

THE NETWORK AS AN EXAMPLE
OF PROFESSIONALIZATION

There was a time when "electrician" was not a recognizable job title, and electrical tinkerers were not popularly differentiated from electrical magicians who put on powerful shows with lights and electrical fire (Marvin 1988). Partly as a response, a community of electrical "hobbyists" organized themselves in a quest for respect, better job opportunities, and class mobility. This motive, over a long period, transformed some electrical "charlatans" and tinkerers into professional "electrical engineers" with certification examinations, unions, professional associations (such as the IEEE), and high pay.

Although electrical history may seem far removed from the present moment, a variety of forms of "amateur" association related to technology have been found to comprise this drive for professionalization and upward class mobility. The same process can be seen in recent years, including the travails of those with the now-defunct job title "webmaster" or "web designer" (Kotamraju 1999, 2002, 2003). From this perspective, community networks could be an attempt to professionalize and create respect and certification for a set of popularly devalued skills such as "community capacity builder" (see chapter 6 in this volume) or "wireless network designer" (see chapter 12, Wong's example of Wireless NOMAD). Another example could be the drive to legitimate community informatics itself in the curriculum of library and information schools.

To again take the case of Wi-Fi, founders of wireless community networks may have a big stake in the institutionalization of titles such as "wireless network engineer," a job that (at least in reference to computing) did not exist until very recently. There is evidence that despite their revolutionary or countercultural ideological commitments, at least some participants in community networks leverage their experiences into well-paid, mainstream information technology (IT) jobs (Sandvig 2005, 16–17).

THE NETWORK AS A LEARNING COMMUNITY

The instrumental value of tinkering with technology has been developed in some detail in the economics literature on learning communities (see Greenstein 2004, especially chapter 3). Specifically, economists have found that technological systems spawn user groups that "learn by doing" (Rosenberg 1982, especially chapter 6). Related work in economics has focused on the way that these communities return innovations as inputs into the process of product development (von Hippel 1988, 2005). While this is a similar perspective to that of professionalization (discussed above), the research on professionalization focuses on the individual's motivation for status and class mobility, while within the learning community perspective from economics, in contrast, the benefit is systemic (to the technology or to the user's organization). For instance, learning communities create new user-driven (to use von Hippel's phrase) innovations of the technology, but these may not be commodified by the users themselves. Instead, entrepreneurs or dominant firms in the area might "harvest" innovations by closely examining the learning communities among their own users for new product or service ideas. The user-innovators may get nothing at all beyond the pleasure of tinkering and the utility of the individual product that they built or modified. In communication history, this perspective could be readily applied to the invention of the mass audience for radio broadcasting—a practice pioneered by amateur groups that was then commodified by large corporations and transformed into commercial broadcasting as we know it today (Douglas 1989).

THE ALTERNATIVE: CONTEXT OF NO CONTEXT

Although for this chapter we promised four perspectives, a fifth deserves mention: the context of "no context."[1] Many projects compare community networks to nothing (the isolated case study) or to each other via recent, similar examples. These researchers might answer that their particular community network is an example of a community network (Schuler 1994, 1996; for a review, see O'Neil 2002). This is not as useful as it at first appears. Rather than an analytic move, it is instead a circular appeal to the way that these networks define themselves. And if community networking is to be taken seriously as a perspective for analytic comparison, this demands serious assessment and consideration of the successes and failures of earlier waves of community networking projects.[2] Such rigorous evaluation has typically not happened.

There are other more practical problems with this approach. To again take wireless community networks as an example, if one wanted to argue that community wireless networks are examples of community networks or the community networking movement, why don't community networks and community wireless networks like each other very much? Why didn't the wired form adapt into the wireless form? Are wireless community networks a more recent example of the Freenet movement? Public access centres? Independent media centres? Universal service policy?

The most important point to be made here is that whatever you choose as an answer, the question, *What are community networks an example of?* has important implications. Although some answers are complementary and could be simultaneously true, other answers logically preclude each other. Either a new infrastructure is revolutionary, or it is not.[3] For some answers to be right, some have to be wrong, though it may not be possible to know enough at this stage to determine which ones.

Let me again stress that there are many more useful answers to the questions of context. The contexts I have chosen are idiosyncratic and arise from my own reading. I notice now that they are also all crudely functionalist. I am not listing them here in order to endorse these specific answers to the question of context, but to raise the point that some choice needs to be made by Wi-Fi researchers. Here, I have tried to suggest a few examples that seem readily applicable, and also to choose theoretical frameworks that offer some overlap but also some tension so as to highlight the necessity to choose one over another.

Choosing an answer to this essay's title should lead a researcher to ask different questions when conducting research, and to interpret the data that has already been collected in a different way. For instance, if Sawhney's revolution between competing systems is in the offing, researchers should focus on the development of long links and the complementarities of these systems with other systems. If Rosenberg or Greenstein are to be believed, researchers should look for technological features of these networks that grant users benefits the more familiar they get with them ("learning by doing"). That is, what specific skills are Île San Fil members building as they try to connect with each other? (See chapter 10 in this volume.) If Marvin is instead a guide, the status of the professions involved should be examined, and special attention should be paid to trans-group associations and the methods by which members delimit insiders and outsiders.

To return to the anecdote that introduced this comment, without addressing the larger context it may be impossible to make sense of these data, or a researcher may miss data that are essential to understanding a case. For instance, Fischer contextualized early telephone co-ops as resistance to the telephone companies of the day, and this led him to go beyond co-ops in his data collection. He unearthed memoranda in telephone company archives that explained why telephone companies did not serve the rural areas where co-ops began, providing a much more compelling explanation for the co-ops.[4] A key explanation for the existence of the co-ops wasn't located in the co-ops themselves, and could not be obtained without looking outside them.

Many ways of answering the question of context suggest that it might *not* be particularly useful to ask the people of community networking what they think they are doing. If we kept, for instance, von Hippel's model of user-driven innovation in mind, it would be entirely plausible that user-innovators would not see themselves in this role, or would even deny it. That is, user-innovators may work for their own benefit, and not be able to see the external value of their own invention. While they might delight in tinkering, they may not be the ones who are able to eventually capitalize on their innovation. In a learning community as described by Rosenberg (1982), the main benefit returned to a community network would be an increase in the group member's own skills, and any references they made to addressing the digital divide or other external goals would be simply beside the point (see chapter 10).

The answer to the question of context also has critical public policy consequences and implications for practitioners. If particular networks are examples of user autonomy and protest (after Fischer [1994]), we would expect the networks to go away as soon as the missing service or feature is made available by other carriers. The network's role in the development of the overall system would have been accomplished—perhaps by embarrassing a larger operation into offering a new feature or extending its service to a remote area—but the network that prompted the change would not need to survive, or to keep doing the same thing. Several of the perspectives outlined above suggest that these networks will not scale, that they are instead useful as influential examples or prototypes that are soon to be reconstituted within some larger sort of agglomeration. For a practitioner, creating publicity for one novel and influential example could be a far better use of resources than attempting to scale a service that is overly similar to offerings already provided by others.

In the policy context, if we see these networks as sources of innovation (von Hippel's term again) rather than service delivery, then most government programs funding these community networks are designed in the wrong way. That is, to spur innovation we should encourage diversity among sites, not homogeneity or "best practices." For innovation theory, giving grant money to unusually organized (or disorganized) groups that fall outside what is normal for a government program would be an asset, not a drawback. Forcing the groups to modify their organization to become more like everyone else could in fact eliminate their chance of producing a useful innovation.

NOTES

1 Apologies to George W. S. Trow for borrowing his excellent title.
2 This insight is Michael Gurstein's.
3 Although the work of both Fischer and Sawhney could be used to explain Wi-Fi as an example of infrastructure development, in Sawhney's model the power relationships among complementary infrastructures undergo a reversal or revolution, while in Fischer's framework complementary infrastructures only have the power to slow each other's growth. Fischer relates the telephone to the automobile in this way.
4 Fischer makes a convincing case that rampant anti-rural sentiment led telephone companies to refuse service to rural areas. See Sandvig (2006).

REFERENCES

Clement, Andrew, Michael Gurstein, Graham Longford, Robert Luke, Marita Moll, Leslie Regan Shade, and Diane Dechief. 2004. The Canadian Research Alliance for Community Innovation and Networking (CRACIN): A research partnership and agenda for community networking in Canada. *Journal of Community Informatics* 1(1): 7–20, http://www.ci-journal.net/index.php/ciej/article/view/207/163.

Douglas, Susan J. 1989. *Inventing American broadcasting, 1899–1922*. Baltimore: Johns Hopkins University Press.

Fischer, Claude S. 1994. *America calling: A social history of the telephone to 1940*. Berkeley: University of California Press.

Greenstein, Shane. 2004. *Diamonds are forever, computers are not: Economic and strategic management in computing markets*. London: Imperial College Press.

Hughes, Thomas P. 1983. *Networks of power: Electrification in Western society, 1880–1930*. Baltimore: Johns Hopkins University Press.

Kotamraju, Nalini P. 1999. The birth of web site design skills: Making the present history. *American Behavioral Scientist* 43(3): 464–74.

——. 2002. Keeping up: Web design skill and the reinvented worker. *Information, Communication and Society* 5(1): 1–26.

——. 2003. Art versus code: The gendered evolution of web design skills. In *Society online: The Internet in context*, ed. Philip E. N. Howard and Steve Jones, 189–200. Thousand Oaks, CA: Sage.

Marvin, Carolyn. 1988. *When old technologies were new: Thinking about electric communication in the late nineteenth century*. New York: Oxford University Press.

O'Neil, Dara. 2002. Assessing community informatics: A review of methodological approaches for evaluating community networks and community technology centers. *Internet Research* 12(1): 76–102.

Rosenberg, Nathan. 1982. *Inside the black box: Technology and economics*. Cambridge: Cambridge University Press.

Sandvig, Christian. 2004. An initial assessment of cooperative action in Wi-Fi networking. *Telecommunications Policy* 28(7/8): 579–602.

——. 2005. The return of the broadcast war. Paper presented at the 33rd Annual Telecommunications Policy Research Conference on Communication, Information, and Internet Policy, Arlington, Virginia, USA, 23 September. http://web.si.umich.edu/tprc/papers/2005/479/Broadcast_War.pdf.

——. 2006. Disorderly infrastructure and the role of government. *Government Information Quarterly* 23(3–4): 503–6.

Sawhney, Harmeet. 1992. Public telephone network: Stages in infrastructure development. *Telecommunications Policy* 16(7): 538–52.

——. 1993. Circumventing the center: The realities of creating a telecommunications infrastructure in the USA. *Telecommunications Policy* 17(7): 504–16.

——. 1999. Patterns of infrastructure development in the U.S. and Canada. In *Progress in Communication Science*, vol. 15, *Advances in Telecommunications*, ed. H. Sawhney and G. Barnett, 71–91. Stamford, CT: Ablex.

——. 2003. Wi-Fi networks and the rerun of the cycle. *Info: The Journal of Policy, Regulation, and Strategy for Telecommunications* 5(6): 25–33.

Schuler, Douglas. 1994. Community networks: Building a new participatory medium. *Communications of the ACM* 37(1): 39–51.

——. 1996. *New community networks: Wired for change*. New York: Addison-Wesley.

von Hippel, Eric. 1988. *The sources of innovation*. Oxford: Oxford University Press.

——. 2005. *Democratizing innovation*. Cambridge, MA: MIT Press.

PART III

Community Innovation I: Participation and Inclusion

8 SYSTEMS DEVELOPMENT IN A COMMUNITY-BASED ORGANIZATION
Lessons from the St. Christopher House Community Learning Network

Susan MacDonald, Andrew Clement

Since the 1990s, organizations in the non-profit sector have increasingly adopted information and communication technologies (ICTs) to support a growing range of organizational activities. Generally this has involved installing and configuring standardized hardware and software packages for common administrative and communicative tasks. Still relatively rare, however, are community-based organizations (CBOs) that undertake major software development projects for strategic purposes, aimed at significantly transforming their operations and the ways they relate to their constituencies. This chapter reports on a case study of one such organization, St. Christopher House (St. Chris), which embarked on an ambitious ICT development project that promised fundamental capacity and service improvement. St. Chris is an urban community and social services agency in Toronto that, in 2002, received $300,000 in funding from the federal government to design and implement a content management system, or a Community Learning Network (CLN), to support organizational processes and the learning needs of the community they serve. Here, we consider the particular ways that a non-profit organization with a history of nearly a century of community service is learning with and about information and communication technologies.

How are non-profit organizations adopting and adapting ICT to build their own community networks?

St. Chris is a not-for-profit agency of the United Way that has served the southwest quadrant of downtown Toronto through a rich network of connections since 1912. It is widely recognized as a "pioneer organization of Canadian social services and community development . . . and has influenced community work across the country through innovative program development" (Shillington 2001). St. Chris offers a range of services and resources to disadvantaged community members of all ages, including computer and Internet access; counselling, employment, and skills training; nutrition, language, and literacy courses; and legal, recreation, and supportive housing services. The organization delivers over thirty direct service programs and community development projects. In 2001, before the project began, St. Chris was serving an average of over 10,000 community residents each year (Terada 2001). By 2009, it was serving 16,000 annually. Over 800 volunteers, many of whom work in the field, extend the reach of St. Chris further into the community to facilitate program delivery. Complementing its service work, St. Chris is also active in social policy advocacy.

In 1999, St. Chris formally engaged with ICTs when it received funding from Industry Canada to establish Community Access Program (CAP) sites,[1] which provide public access to the Internet as well as hardware, software, and computer training. The addition of the CAP site, known as Bang the Drum, to St. Chris's ICT infrastructure expanded their capacity for learning with *and* about ICTs. The objectives of Bang the Drum were:

- to raise the level of digital literacy and improve basic computer skills of community members,
- to promote life-long learning by breaking down barriers posed by differential access to knowledge by providing free online interactive learning tutorials, and
- to ensure all people become empowered, active digital citizens of the Internet regardless of age, race, ethnicity, class, or ability (Terada 2001, section 2.3).

By 2007, St. Chris had seven Bang the Drum locations providing community access to over seventy computer terminals with high-speed Internet service.

Building on their successes with providing Internet access and in an effort to enhance the long-term financial sustainability of the CAP sites, St. Chris applied to the federal Office of Learning Technologies' (OLT) Community Learning Networks Initiative in 2001. This program, launched in 1998 by Human Resources Development Canada (HRDC), was designed to support pilot projects that made use of existing network technologies. St. Chris was not unique in pairing these funding programs; almost half (44%) of the approximately one hundred projects funded by the Community Learning Networks

Initiative were directly linked to existing CAP sites (Human Resources and Skills Development Canada 2002).[2] Two other CRACIN community partners that similarly combined CAP and CLN funded projects case study were Vancouver Community Network and K-Net (see chapters 13 and 14 in this volume).

WHAT IS A COMMUNITY LEARNING NETWORK?

Community Learning Networks are, in official terms, "locally controlled structures that support community development and aspire to enhance the lives of their members through lifelong learning" (Government of Canada 2003, 29). A background paper prepared for an OLT policy discussion on the future of the Community Learning Network Initiative in relation to Canada's National Strategy on Innovation in 2003 noted that CLNs come in many forms and are as varied as there are definitions of *community*: "While many players are engaged in the overall governance, one organization usually acts as champion for the overall effort and the diverse learning activities upon which the community decides to embark" (Government of Canada 2003, 30). In this case, St. Chris was clearly the champion of their CLN initiative, developed largely to meet organizational needs.

St. Chris envisioned its CLN as both a process and a product. In the first instance, it was an experiment in open source software engineering, pursued with participatory design elements involving key stakeholders (community members, staff, volunteers, funders, software developers, and academic researchers). In the second, it was a content management system (CMS), a website and database that supports the creation, publication, and archiving of online content, which would offer new ways of learning for and with their constituents. Like many other organizations, corporate and not-for-profit alike, in the early 2000s St. Chris had difficulty maintaining its website, characteristically having "out of date material, poor control over design and navigation, a lack of authority control, and the constriction of the Webmaster bottleneck" (Browning and Lowndes 2001, 1). And too, like many organizations, St. Chris sought a solution in a CMS. In this regard, St. Chris's broad objectives were twofold:

- Create an interactive CLN in which each program area could develop a distinct Internet presence encouraging community feedback and participation through the use of interactive tools, for which staff and volunteers are trained to administer and publish content, and program participants and community members gain computer skills and learn about the resources on the Internet.
- Build the capacity of St. Chris to use the Internet by establishing a "co-ordinated community-based training methodology" (Terada 2001, section 2.7).

To realize these two objectives, St. Chris senior management focused on the learning needs of staff who needed to be comfortable using ICTs before they could teach and support community members' use of the CLN. Consequently, development focused intensively on working with and addressing the needs of St. Chris staff. In a later phase of the project, St. Chris expected to enable community members, especially those who are socially marginal, to use the CLN to find information and to communicate with one another. Organizations taking on these kinds of projects sometimes choose a group amenable to the role they could play in the overall long-term development of a project. For example, an initiative to develop the information design of a community network's website focused on "innovators and early adopters" who served as "catalysts for the design" and "provided a means by which to gather community oriented feedback" (Vaughan and Schwartz 1999, 590).

In this chapter we seek to better understand the challenges facing non-profit sector organizations when adopting new technologies. Simpson (2005), in citing Dabinett (2000), reports that ICT initiatives in community settings typically confront: a variety of challenges, including tension between commercial and community aspects of networks, poor communications, unrealistic expectations, conflicting agendas, shortage of capital, and inadequate strategic and operational management. ICT initiatives in CBOs are also often characterized by an underlying desire to reflect organizational values of learning and participation. This raises a couple of questions: What are the particular challenges that CBOs, such as St. Chris, face in the development and use of custom-designed information systems? What can other CBOs learn from St. Chris's CLN venture when undertaking organization-wide ICT initiatives that reflect the values of learning and participation? In this chapter, we proceed by drawing on the literatures of organizational learning, and management and community informatics, followed by a brief discussion of our research method. Based on our interviews with St. Chris staff, we highlight several recurring issues focused primarily on current use. We close with some suggested lessons to be drawn.

ICT ADOPTION IN COMMUNITY SETTINGS: PARTICIPATION AND LEARNING

While there is a desire for organizational innovation and transformation in many ICT initiatives, in corporate settings the failure rate for such initiatives is estimated to be as high as 75 percent (Davenport 1993, cited in Boonstra and Vink 1996). Some suggest that a balance is needed "between a top-down formulation of goals and coordination of the change process and bottom-up self-designing activities in which organizational members manage the change process themselves" (Boonstra and Vink 1996, 374). Change processes can be further complicated when competing or conflicting organizational values coexist (Iivari and Huisman 2007). For example, participatory practices in development stages of ICT initiatives may conflict with an organization's need to assert hierarchical controls in implementation. Similarly, CBOs must strike a balance between expert and participatory processes in development and implementation, particularly since ICT initiatives in community settings are often as much an expression of organizational values as they are about technology (Venkatesh and Chango 2007). Consequently, success in community settings in particular is very much tied to an organization's ability to realize its values in new organizational practices and structures.

Elmholdt (2003) suggests that different *types* of organizational learning must also be balanced. This is especially true when social networking-based sharing systems that rely on participation are combined with an acquisitional approach to "capture" knowledge. When organizations take on new practices that conflict with existing norms a "double loop" of learning is needed to reconcile the differences. Organizational learning is understood to take place "when members respond to changes in the environment by detecting errors and correcting errors through modifying strategies, assumptions, or norms" (Choo 1998, 221). This kind of active or iterative learning is also an important part of participatory design methods in ICT development. Kensing (2003) suggests that active participation is required in all stages of development, which includes negotiation of desired outcomes, evaluation and selection of technological components, design and prototyping of IT (information and technology) applications, and organizational implementation.

Merkel et al. (2004) observe that community networking studies have tended to focus on the need for ICTs to provide democratic access to community information and to facilitate civic engagement, whereas community informatics studies tend to "foreground the ways that information systems can be built to facilitate organizational goals" (1). Participatory Design approaches in the community context have produced research on how to engage community members in ICT-based projects (Merkel et al. 2005). However, this knowledge is somewhat tempered in light of the fact that participatory development approaches do not necessarily lead to changes in everyday practice (Boonstra and Vink 1996). In this chapter, we aim to shed light on the challenges CBOs face in designing and implementing an ICT initiative and, in particular, to identify and explore tensions that can emerge in attempting to meet the needs of various stakeholders: organizational, community members, and government funders.

OUR STUDY APPROACH

As is common with the case study as a methodological approach, in this study we triangulated three types of data sources: interviews, participant observation, and document review.

St. Chris was one of seven founding community partners in the CRACIN research alliance, a partnership of academic researchers, community networking practitioners, and government policy specialists funded by the Social Science and Humanities Research Council of Canada (SSHRC) from 2003 to 2007. Prior connections between researchers at the Faculty of Information Studies at the University of Toronto and St. Chris staff formed the basis of this case study research, in which good working relationships developed through earlier projects, the first starting in 2001 and studying everyday usage of Internet services (Viseu, Clement, and Aspinall 2004; Viseu et al. 2006), and then, as the CLN began development in 2002, a more collaborative project "to develop an evaluation framework that they would find useful in improving their ongoing practice as well as contribute to their accountability for their public funding" (Luke et al. 2004). St. Chris declined to pursue a full evaluation of the CLN project as originally envisioned.[3] However, the case study formally took shape when all parties agreed to focus on semi-structured interviews with select St. Chris staff. Furthermore, researchers combined participant observation and document review to triangulate with the interviews to assure strengthened validity in the study.

The focus on St. Chris staff, as opposed to volunteers and program participants more generally, was due to the phased nature of development and use that concentrated on the staff in the early stages. We indicated that we were interested in talking with a broad spectrum of staff, ranging from those making heaviest use of the CLN to light users, and across a variety of program areas. St. Chris management readily agreed and offered to contact staff on our behalf. We then drafted a series of questions designed to provide some insight into how the CLN is used and by whom, and in what ways the CLN does or does not reflect and support organizational values. In the spirit of participatory action research (PAR), we collaboratively refined the questions to be mutually beneficial.

A member of the St. Chris senior staff sent a written request for an interview to select staff members, which the interviewer, MacDonald, followed up with a phone call. Starting in early 2007, she began conducting semi-structured interviews with eleven (n = 11) St. Chris staff. Interviewees included five program coordinators, three program workers, and several managers. Interviewees were asked about the following:

1. Their current use of the CLN (e.g., Do you currently use the CLN? How do you use it? What tasks are you responsible for? Do you supervise anyone who uses it?)

2. Learning to use the CLN (e.g., How difficult or easy was it to learn to use? How did you overcome any of the difficulties that you encountered using the CLN? Did you receive enough training?)

3. Their involvement (if any) in the development process (e.g., What did you like or not like about the development process? What were your expectations as a result?)

4. Their hopes for future uses of the CLN (e.g., How would you like to see the CLN being used at St. Chris that it is currently not?)

Transcripts of the interviews were produced from audio recordings and analyzed for common patterns and themes. We asked senior managers at St. Chris to review drafts of this chapter to increase validity in the findings of our study.

In the early stage of the research, participant observation took place at several CLN advisory committee meetings that were designed to solicit feedback from St. Chris members on the various iterations of the software as it was being developed. Document review focused on materials produced about the St. Chris CLN, such as the "Blueprint for a Community Learning Network," produced by The Working Group (2003), the application (Terada 2001), and the final report produced by St. Chris to the funder, the Office of Learning Technologies (St. Christopher House 2005). In the following sections, we elaborate on the themes that emerged from the interviews, as informed by insights from participant observation over several years with St. Chris and documents reviewed.

THE ST. CHRISTOPHER HOUSE CLN

As a content management system (CMS), the St. Chris CLN is structured as a series of "rooms," or web pages, where content can be created and posted in either public or private spaces by any number of users. Prior to having their CLN, St. Chris had a fairly rudimentary website with a sparse amount of static, brochure-like content. Program information was limited to a short description of each program area on a single webpage. Furthermore, since St. Chris relied on an intermediary organization to post the content, the website was not regularly updated. Building a CMS has allowed individual program areas to develop their own web presence, putting some control in the hands of staff, program participants, and volunteers. The CLN home page (www.stchrishouse.org) is organized by program units and according to age groups (children and youth, adults, and older adults). Under "Older Adults," for example, there are links to almost twenty different programs, including Meals on Wheels, Friendly Visiting, and day programs for people with Alzheimer's. In contrast to the original website, the CLN is comprised of regularly updated individual web pages that are full of images (mostly photos), program and contact information, upcoming events, newsletters, and resources.

USE OF THE CLN BY ST. CHRIS HOUSE STAFF

Use of the CLN is defined with respect to staff as any of the following activities: accessing information, creating and or posting content, and use of the various features, including the communication tools, creating tutorials, or quizzes. The most active users at St. Chris tend to be people working in the program areas that use the CLN to recruit volunteers, but all of the St. Chris staff interviewed use the CLN to access information about St. Chris and the various program areas.

St. Chris relies on the participation of up to eight hundred active volunteers, so ongoing recruitment and outreach is tremendously important. Often potential volunteers are referred from specific program areas, such as Literacy, which relies heavily on volunteers (up to forty-five at any given time) to be tutors for one-on-one learning partnerships. While the Literacy web pages provide information in the form of answers to frequently asked questions (FAQs) for potential volunteer tutors, formal administrative processes to recruit volunteers are taken care of by the volunteer developer, who regularly posts volunteer opportunities to the CLN, along with instructions about the application process, photos, and stories written by St. Chris volunteers about their experiences. This is one example of how the coordination of recruitment across program areas within St. Chris is facilitated and improved by the formal administrative capacity of the CLN.

The Literacy program also uses the CLN to gather online information and resources that support teaching and learning for both tutors and learners. The CLN is a common point of reference for tutor-learner partnerships, providing resources or links to resources useful to both tutor and learner. In the case of learners, because the issue of adult literacy is often sensitive (in that often even the participant's family members are not aware that he or she is registered in the program), program materials and any online content produced by learners with their tutors are kept in a private, password-protected space on the CLN. Once participants are registered in the program, they have access to a calendar of events, information and resources about literacy, and the opportunity to create their own room (that is, web page) with the assistance of their tutor. Rather than reinvent the wheel, both learners and tutors access interactive learning tools that are in many cases created by other organizations.

Most of the staff interviewed do not create or post their own content, citing a lack of time or staffing. The majority, however, did express a desire to do so. For example, one interviewee ("A") said: "To be honest with you, I don't even have time to check email. I'm lucky if I can check it once a day . . . and I know I've been criticized for that. But the level of crisis for people here is more and more intense." She also reported that a volunteer had recently taken on the task of gathering content, such as photos, to post on the CLN.

However, some program units within St. Chris actively used technology long before the advent of the CLN. The Older Adult Centre (OAC), for example, had previously developed online interactive plays through the Health Action Theatre by Seniors (HATS) project. HATS uses theatre as an educational tool to help seniors learn how to problem solve. The plays, now accessible via the CLN, are used as teaching tools in group settings by St. Chris staff, and are shared with other agencies. Such prior experience with technology informed, to some degree, the understanding of one interviewee ("B") of the potential value of the CLN from its inception, when she actively participated in its development: "I was very involved in all aspects [of the CLN development]: the meetings, the steering committee, I was part of several working groups and I was the person who was to create a common vision [for the OAC]." Despite thinking of herself as a light user, she regularly publishes and archives a quarterly newsletter, but sees potential for more interactive uses of the CLN, including the internal use of the forums or discussion boards and maintenance of interorganizational relationships and contacts.

In general, however, CLN communication functionalities at the time of the interviews were somewhat underused by St. Chris staff, program participants, and volunteers. For example, in one program area, staff tried to use the CLN to support sharing and information exchange between volunteers. One interviewee ("C") notes that it is often difficult to find time for formal training opportunities since most volunteers have full-time jobs: "So we thought we'd try this online thing and [the volunteers] all thought that was a really good idea but then nobody is really using it."

Several program areas have experimented with the forums or discussion boards but have found little success in these efforts. For example, the Immigrant and Refugee services program began using the communication tools with some promise of success. A YouTube video and a link to the Immigrants' Integration Discussion Forum are featured prominently on the Immigrant and Refugee Services home page, where there are eighteen different discussion threads on various topics related to immigrants' experiences in Canada. However, most of the threads have only one or two postings, many of which were made in early 2007 when the forum was launched on the CLN. While some threads focus on online community resources or interagency sharing, a few appear to be posted by program participants or community members who presumably are recent immigrants. On 27 January 2007, under the subject heading *Something that works*, Saosen wrote: "Well, probably [what] we need is some kind of a combination of volunteering and training? Vocational education? Something to deal with the precious Canadian experience which is needed for work and [that] you can not get it unless you work. Yet, you got here because you are need[ed] in some kind of work . . . confusing, eh?" More recently, a senior manager observed that such low use by St. Chris's constituents is not surprising since there are so many options on the Internet now that St. Chris could never have anticipated.

Several interviewees see the CLN's communication tools as an area for future use and development at St. Chris. For example, one interviewee noted that the CLN is a place to publish research conducted by St. Chris, such as their recent report on modernizing income security. In terms of content development by users, St. Chris senior management readily express some disappointment. In particular, community participation was low, which is reflected in the number of CLN members (only a few hundred members of the public created user accounts), but the surge of Internet and social media use in St. Chris's various constituencies could not have been anticipated.

CLN DEVELOPMENT: NEW PRACTICES IN PARTICIPATION

As with many ambitious information systems initiatives, the development of the St. Chris CLN was fraught with difficulties—especially when initial enthusiasm that focused on needs assessment activities waned because of mismatched expectations. The development process included focus groups with staff and community members, and an intensive two-day needs assessment event in March 2003 facilitated by Cap Gemini Ernst and Young's Accelerated Solution Environments (ASE),[4] involving St. Chris staff and the software developers.

Following the ASE event, St. Chris and The Working Group (TWG), the software developer, agreed on a blue print document that constituted the software specifications. At this point communication between the St. Chris and TWG lessened considerably while the latter undertook the programming, periodically bringing provisional versions to a special St. Chris CLN advisory committee for testing. As is common in system development projects, deadlines slipped and costs far exceeded original estimates. However, St. Chris officially celebrated the public launch of the new CLN, replacing the old website, in February 2005.

The interviews revealed some ambivalence among St. Chris staff about their involvement in the participatory process. In one sense, participation was very important to many staff who felt the process reflected the values of the organization. One staff member (interviewee "D") suggested that even though "people expressed their concern that [the CLN] was unrealistic . . . there was still a lot of enthusiasm because we participated in the process." In another example, interviewee "E" stated:

> We all were [involved in the development process]; I have to give them [St. Chris senior management] credit for that. . . . Yes, we were all involved to some extent; some people more than others [depending on] personal interest. If I'm not mistaken there were several opportunities to join a working group, committees, discussions, there were interviews with all of us that took place to learn a little bit more about what we would like to see on the CLN. That was also [management's] style of work . . . to be really open and wanting to engage with people and get their feedback.

Interviewee "C" suggested that perhaps participation came at the wrong time: "I think the ASE [Accelerated Solutions Environment] should have been much later, after they had talked to different staff to find out what [they] wanted and then once there was a rudimentary structure have an ASE event and [ask] how can we use this and what can we add and tweak to make it more of a community development and learning tool?"

FIGURE 8.1 St. Chris House: Flipchart from the ASE needs assessment exercise

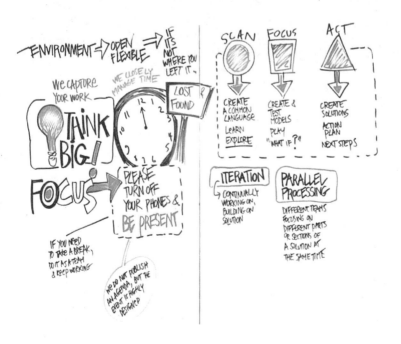

FIGURE 8.2 St. Chris House: Participants in the ASE needs assessment exercise

In another sense, some staff felt that the emphasis on participation caused the development of the CLN to shift in focus from community learning and organizing to more of an internal communication and administrative utility. One staff member who was involved in the early stages of development remarked that the original objectives outlined in the application to the funder narrowly targeted CLN adoption in select program areas. However, early in the development process a larger debate about inclusiveness and participation across the organization shifted the direction of the project to be what another senior manager called being "all things to all people." Interviewee "F" expressed frustration about the change in focus: "[The CLN is] just an office tool. That's an administrative thing . . . that's not a breakthrough about community learning together, because in fact when the staff are using the tool they're not doing it in a way that brings them together with other staff. . . . They're using it in order to get their tasks done and they're not necessarily looking to see what else is going on [in the organization]."

The emphasis on the CLN as an internal information sharing and administrative tool also drew attention to an underlying schism that emerged between hierarchical organizational structures and new participatory practices. Early in the development process, it was decided that explicit managerial controls were needed to ensure only web content appropriate for maintaining the good reputation of St. Chris should be presented to the public and, in particular, to funders. This approach conflicted somewhat with the participatory philosophy that underpins the entire initiative. Many interviewees raised concerns about the permissions process, and the delays incurred, to get content approved before it can be posted on the CLN. Some felt this hampers participation of staff, and consequently of program participants and community members. For example, one interviewee ("G") suggested that the permissions structures take away the potential for real community involvement and exchange: "If you have so many people to approve, approve, approve you're not having community involvement. Of course it's very hard because you have to know the content. You cannot have discriminatory stuff . . . especially when you consider [that] the agency is liable for the content. It's a virtual space but it's also under the St. Chris umbrella, which [makes it] very hard to create a learning network opportunity."

St. Chris managers felt they couldn't take the risk of offensive remarks tarnishing their long-standing, hard-earned reputation for integrity. This points to the uncomfortable dilemma that open-content contribution processes pose for organizations that depend so heavily on outside funding and donations. With the recent proliferation of social networking services, organizations can more easily distance themselves from potentially embarrassing postings, but when the CLN was being developed social networking sites were less common.

Another key aspect of participation was the involvement of a group of St. Chris volunteers, foreign-trained IT professionals known as the Community of Practice Understudy (CPU) group in the ongoing maintenance of the CLN. The CPU was positioned to take on the responsibility of maintaining the CLN once the software development was complete. The aim was to ensure the operational sustainability of the CLN, such that a continuous cycle of volunteers would be trained to maintain it and potentially to create new modules as needed. The CPU was thus structured to help ensure that CLN expertise stayed within the organization.[5] In practice, with the extended software development period, the original CPU lost momentum and was disbanded as volunteers moved on to other opportunities (such as jobs). However, a new CPU was started in 2006 with the goal of documenting the technical specifications of the CLN, which were not satisfactorily supplied by the software developer. One interviewee ("C") stated that the new CPU "are more focused on sustainability than the other group was and making sure that going forward there will be some documentation so whoever comes in and takes on the technical part of it will have something to go from." The new CPU has maintained a core of around four members who bring a range of PHP and Microsoft programming experience. It has made upgrades and fixes, such as making changes to the permissions structures. Rather than develop new capabilities within the main CLN system, the emphasis has been on incorporating connections to the growing number of freely available commercial services such as YouTube, Google Search, and Facebook. An indication of their success in maintaining the operational viability of the CLN is that following a recent internal evaluation in which alternative platforms such as Joomla were considered, St. Chris decided to continue with the CLN as their content management system.

Interviews with St. Chris staff also focused on their experiences with learning to use the CLN, which revealed in many cases a general discomfort with ICTs. Learning for staff began in the development stages of the CLN when, in the needs assessment activities, they were introduced to new concepts and new ways of working across the organization and with their clients. Interviewee "I" described her experience of taking part in a meeting at which the CLN project team were discussing the CLN: "For me it was like listening to a conversation in Russian. It didn't make sense, conceptually what they were talking about. 'CLN,' 'Learning Network,' 'Open Source'; I didn't know what open source was. So when I don't understand something, I just disconnect. [But] I see that it is very important, that it is the future. That [the CLN] has a lot of potential if you know *how* to do it."

Interviewee "F" suggested that many St. Chris staff did not understand the broader abstract implications of the CLN—how a CLN would both produce and support changes to the organization's structure. He stated: "The idea of a Community Learning Network as it was put together in our application was clearly too abstract for most people to understand because they didn't see the idea that somebody in their program would want to deal with anyone else and that their participants would actually care to be involved with other participants in another program." However, as we have learned from other interviewees, the CLN does in fact facilitate sharing of information across program areas for which volunteer recruitment is concerned.

Learning to use the CLN was a frustrating experience for some staff members who felt like "guinea pigs" when they were trained on early versions of the software riddled with bugs. In general, however, with the final release of the software, learning to use the CLN, although not particularly difficult, generally takes an investment of time many can not afford. Other more technologically savvy users described the CLN as non-intuitive or "clunky." One experienced computer user (interviewee "H") commented: "I don't think I found anything difficult about the CLN. I think I find it's restrictive and inconvenient in that it doesn't do exactly what we were hoping it would have done. . . . [Although] it does function in that it helps share information so everyone gets an account on the CLN, they log in, and they get access to a private site." Similarly, another staff member (interviewee "C") stated: "[The CLN] is very time consuming: there's an awful lot of clicking and it's not particularly intuitive. But once people have got used to it there aren't usually any problems."

In summary, the experience of learning how to use the CLN has been a frustrating experience for many St. Chris staff, which may partially account for its overall light use. Owing to their inexperience with ICTs in general, St.

Chris staff were unprepared to deal with an unfinished product, and it would seem that expectations had been unrealistically raised during the needs assessment phase of the project.

TRANSLATING ORGANIZATIONAL VALUES IN PRACTICE

The interviews with St. Chris staff shed light on how organizational values of participation and learning were being realized in the development and implementation stages of the CLN project. While staff participation in development was frustrating, it was also important because it reflected the organization's values. However, Luke et al. (2004, 12) concluded that because the development of the St. Chris CLN "was not informed directly by Participatory Design (PD) research and practice" that additional opportunities for participation and learning were lost. In particular, there was no use of mock-ups, prototyping, or others forms of in situ design activities that would have helped refine in practice the many ideas that came out of the ASE brainstorming exercise, while also helping fill the interactional hiatus that many in St. Chris found so discouraging. In its final report to the funder, St. Chris noted: "The number of software iterations was insufficient to meet the vast diversity of demands of our user base" (St. Christopher House 2005, section 9). Perhaps leadership with a more unified vision during the development and implementation stages would have helped staff find new ways to work together across the organization while using the CLN. One interviewee suggested that while loose overall coordination suited the style of the charismatic leader of the CLN project (who left the organization before the development phase was complete), a more cohesive vision would have been more effective, especially during implementation. She stated that leadership was needed from "someone who understands the organization, how the information flows, how the programs are connected, [and] programs staff needs to be involved in this process [of coordinating program areas to use the CLN]."

CONCLUSIONS

In many respects St. Chris was ahead of the curve when they embarked on this open source project. In the early 2000s, few off-the-shelf content management software products were available. While this is no longer the case, with several good options to choose from (Joomla, Mambo, or Drupal), the St. Chris experience in building their own CMS offers valuable lessons about participation and learning that might not otherwise have been learned. Some of the principal lessons are presented here, drawing on the recommendations of St. Chris staff.

Active user participation is a powerful approach to system development processes, and likely even essential in CBOS such as St. Chris. Without the commitment that active participation brought, it is doubtful that St. Chris could have pulled off its very ambitious development project. That the CLN remains central to St. Chris's internal and external communication is a remarkable achievement for an organization that had no prior background in major systems development. In effect, it designed and built its own bicycle (the CMS) without having ridden one. No small feat.

However vital, participation is no panacea and needs careful treatment. In this case, active involvement needed to be matched with the background and knowledge that members with widely varying degrees of interest and experience could bring. A more iterative approach, with shorter cycles of design, develop, test, and redesign, would likely have produced more satisfying results and reduced the frustrations experienced. One staff member (interviewee "B") made the following recommendation:

> Do not expose people to something that is not up to its potential yet because it's a very frustrating experience. If you invite people to test and if they know enough about it, I think that's wonderful. . . . But if you call it training, make sure you have a proper tool that will deliver and so people will see results and get enthusiastic and can see the potential. . . . Be creative, but realistic at the same time so people don't get disappointed. If you make it look like it will solve all the problems in the world and then people realize . . . it won't, its kind of a turn off. Always find ways of keeping people motivated.

Interviewee "C" recommended that other CBOS take on similar initiatives using a participatory approach, but

> on a smaller scale and maybe having more training before asking for input. . . . It was an impossible project in terms of what everyone wanted. I think once they've got . . . ready-made, off-the-shelf [software products] . . . then I think it's a lot easier to be participatory and say, OK, "What of these specific things [do you need]?" and, "This is what they do, and do you need that?" and "What do you use it for?" Then I think, yeah, [participation] would be really critical. Because I think . . . to do any kind of project in a community organization that is not participatory is not going to work very well.

Finally, a senior manager reflected on the fact that St. Chris did not meet its goal of reaching socially isolated community members. She stated:

> There [are] a number of people we work with who are pretty socially isolated. We thought giving them an online community would maybe open their community [and] their worldview up. . . . That's been one of our biggest disappointments with [the] CLN, that it still hasn't reached program participants

much less a broader community in a meaningful way because of the incredible delays we experienced [in the software development stages].

Furthermore, aspiring to link isolated individuals, she noted the success of CRACIN community partner K-Net, which connects over sixty geographically isolated First Nations communities in Northern Ontario (see chapter 13). Reaching those who are socially isolated is a particularly challenging goal, perhaps more so than reaching the geographically isolated, since there are increasingly robust wireless communications technologies to call upon. While new social networking technologies appear to hold promise, and there is evidence that they can be important ingredients in successfully connecting otherwise isolated individuals, new technologies alone can never produce desired results. With the growing availability and popularity of social networking services, St. Chris is becoming relieved of the need to take on major software development tasks, and can bring to bear its considerable talents in addressing the more fundamental social and learning issues.

It is ironic, then, that by treating the CLN development mainly as a construction project aimed at building ambitious e-learning applications, rather than principally as a learning project in its own right, St. Chris missed a number of other participation and learning opportunities along the way. In particular, there was potential, especially if a more iterative approach had been taken in the earlier stages of development, to learn more about new ways to work within the organization and with its constituents. In general, however, this reflects the pressure noted elsewhere in this volume (see chapter 19) for organizations to focus on more tangible project outcomes that satisfy funders.

This account of the challenges that St. Chris faced in undertaking a very ambitious community networking/learning project, and how in hindsight things might have been done differently, should not overshadow the substantial achievements. While the CLN did not achieve all that it set out to, it did much more than enhance the information infrastructure of the organization. The CLN played a vital role in developing the digital literacies of its staff, volunteers, and clients. The commitment to a free, open source approach to software development reflecting strongly held community values remains firm. The CLN has become deeply established in St. Chris, with several programs well embedded in Internet-based activities.

Furthermore, as with any major software project, learning and development continues after the initial implementation phase, and St. Chris is well positioned to tackle the emerging challenges. In this we hope that St. Chris's involvement in the CRACIN project to study this initiative may be helpful. At the very least, our investigations, and interviews in particular, show that St. Chris staff are dedicated to further shaping the CLN to meet organizational and community needs, and that they have valuable insights to offer in this ongoing process.

NOTES

1 See http://www.ic.gc.ca/eic/site/cap-pac.nsf/eng/home.
2 While the combination of CAP and CLN programs seemed well suited, a struggle to achieve financial sustainability for these ICT initiatives is ongoing. CAP has proved to be a highly unstable source of funding (Moll 2007), so organizations like St. Chris have learned not to rely on it. Further, as Rideout and Reddick (2005) observe, capital expenditures such as computer hardware and connectivity costs do not qualify under the CLN program as allowable expenses. Once the development funds for the CLN project were spent, computer training and support must come from the organization's core funding. In the case of St. Chris, this has meant that staff members juggle multiple jobs. See chapter 19 for a discussion of the challenges faced by organizations such as St. Chris in managing funds from different agencies each of which provide only partial funding for complex projects.
3 The reasons for this are several. The significant delays in the implementation of the CLN and the urgent need to focus on getting it working meant that the original timetable for a formative evaluation had to be scrapped. Also, the proposed evaluation approach, drawing on Outcome Mapping, would have required extensive participation by staff, volunteers, and program participants. These groups were expressing "evaluation fatigue" and not enthusiastic about this potential addition to their existing time burdens.
4 Toronto Accelerated Solutions Environment, 28 February–1 March 2003, http://www.stchrishouse.org/cooking/.
5 For more on the role that foreign-trained immigrants with ICT skills play in community networking initiatives, see chapter 9.

REFERENCES

Boonstra, Jaap J., and Maurits J. Vink. 1996. Technological and organizational innovation: A dilemma of fundamental change and participation. *European Journal of Work and Organizational Psychology* 5(3): 351–75.
Browning, Paul, and Mike Lowndes. 2001. JISC TechWatch report: Content management systems. http://www.jisc.ac.uk/whatwedo/services/techwatch/reports/horizon scanning/hs0102.aspx.
Choo, Chun Wei. 1998. *The knowing organization: How organizations use information to construct meaning, create knowledge, and make decisions.* New York: Oxford University Press.
Dabinett, Gordon. 2000. Regenerating communities in the UK: Getting plugged into the information society? *Community Development Journal* 35(2): 157–66.
Davenport, Thomas H. 1993. *Process innovation: Reengineering work through information technology.* Cambridge, MA: Harvard Business Press.
Elmholdt, Claus. 2003. Metaphors for learning: Acquisition versus social participation. *Scandinavian Journal of Educational Research* 47(2): 115–31.
Government of Canada. Office of Learning Technologies. 2003. Policy conversation on future directions for community learning networks. Ottawa: Human Resources and Skills Development Canada, Office of Learning Technologies.

Human Resources and Skills Development Canada. 2002. Summative evaluation of the Office of Learning Technologies. December.

Iivari, Juhani, and Magda Huisman. 2007. The relationship between organizational culture and the deployment of systems development methodologies. *MIS Quarterly* 31(1): 35–58.

Kensing, Finn. 2003. *Methods and practices in participatory design.* Copenhagen: IT-Universitetet Press.

Luke, Robert, Andrew Clement, Randall Terada, Dominic Bortolussi, Cameron Booth, Derek Brooks, and Darcy Christ. 2004. The promise and perils of a participatory approach to developing an open source community learning network. In *Proceedings of the eighth conference on Participatory Design: Artful integration—Interweaving media, materials and practices—Volume 1*, 11–19. New York: ACM. http://dl.acm.org/citation.cfm?id=1011873.

Merkel, Cecelia B., Mike Clitherow, Umer Farooq, Lu Xiao, Craig H. Ganoe, John M. Carroll, and Mary Beth Rosson. 2005. Sustaining computer use and learning in community computing contexts: Making technology part of who they are and what they do. *Journal of Community Informatics* 1(2): 158–74.

Merkel, Cecelia B., Lu Xiao, Umer Farooq, Craig. H. Ganoe, Roderick Lee, John M. Carroll, and Mary Beth Rosson. 2004. Participatory design in community computing contexts: Tales from the field. In *Proceedings of the eighth conference on Participatory Design: Artful integration—Interweaving media, materials and practices—Volume 1*, 1–10. New York: ACM.

Moll, Marita. 2007. Success doesn't compute for the federal Community Access Program. *The Monitor* (Ottawa) 14(2).

Rideout, Vanda N., and Andrew J. Reddick. 2005. Sustaining community access to technology: Who should pay and why. *Journal of Community Informatics* 1(2): 45–62.

Shillington, Richard. 2001. Community Undertaking Social Policy (CUSP): Final report. Tristat Resources and St. Christopher House. http://www.shillington.ca/stchrisreport.pdf.

Simpson, Lyn. 2005. Community informatics and sustainability: Why social capital matters. *Journal of Community Informatics* 1(2): 102–19.

St. Christopher House. 2005. *St. Christopher House, Community Learning Network, Office of Learning Technologies: Final report.*

Terada, Randall. 2001. Community Learning Networks Office of Learning Technologies (OLT) Funding Application: St. Christopher House.

Vaughan, Misha W., and Nancy Schwartz. 1999. Jumpstarting the information design for a community network. *Journal of the American Society for Information Science* 50(7): 588–97.

Venkatesh, Murali, and Mawaki Chango. 2007. Architecture, infrastructure, and broadband civic network design: An institutional view. *Computer Supported Cooperative Work* 16: 467–99.

Viseu, Ana, Andrew Clement, and Jane Aspinall. 2004. Situating privacy online: Complex perceptions and everyday practices. *Information, Communication and Society* 7(1): 92–114.

Viseu, Ana, Andrew Clement, Jane Aspinall, and Tracy L. M. Kennedy. 2006. The interplay of public and private spaces in Internet access. *Information, Communication and Society* 9(5): 633–56.

The Working Group. 2003. Blueprint for a Community Learning Network. Internal project report submitted to St. Christopher House.

9 VANCOUVER COMMUNITY NETWORK AS A SITE OF DIGITAL AND SOCIAL INCLUSION

Diane Dechief

Information and communication technologies (ICTs) are central to the shifts taking place within Canadian immigration; often used as a pre- and post-migration information source, ICTs also provide greater transnational communication opportunities, including access to cultural media such as on-line local newspapers in languages other than English or French, newsgroups, and chat rooms (Aizlewood and Doody 2002). Because of the increasing roles of ICTs in immigration and settlement activities, it is important to conduct research that explores the relationship between ICTs and social and economic inclusion for immigrants to Canada. The findings from this study suggest that urban community networks (CNs) can serve as sites of inclusion for newcomers. This chapter illuminates an unanticipated, socially beneficial outcome of a community-based technology initiative: the potential for an urban CN to contribute to newcomers' social networks, and to broaden the range of information newcomers can access. While many new immigrants become volunteers at Vancouver Community Network (VCN) as part of their search for employment, comments about the lasting impacts of their experiences suggest that volunteer activities at VCN helped to foster the development of a sense of community as well.

VANCOUVER COMMUNITY NETWORK:
THE RESEARCH SITE

VCN is an urban community network that offers a variety of free services to individuals and non-profit groups in Vancouver, including dial-up Internet service, public access computing space, computer software training, email accounts, website creation, and listserv and website hosting. In 2005, when this case study was conducted, 11,000 individual members and over 1,200 non-profit groups made use of VCN's services. The focus of VCN's initiatives is using ICTs to organize and empower marginalized individuals and groups. VCN works closely with community groups and community centres to equip and train staff and volunteers with computing resources, and to develop interactive websites to make their programs better known and more accessible to the local community. Significantly, VCN coordinates hundreds of public Internet access sites throughout the city, many of which are situated and designed to serve the poor, new immigrants, youth, and the homeless, including the residents of the city's Downtown Eastside neighbourhood, one of Canada's poorest. These sites exist in part because of support from the federal Community Access Program (CAP) and its Youth Initiative (CAP YI). Federal funding for both CAP and CAP YI has frequently been in danger of being terminated: in March 2010, coordinators of CAP sites received letters informing them that the funding had been cut, but a reprieve was granted in the same month, and the program continued for another year. In the Lower Mainland region, CAP sites succeed through partnerships between VCN and community organizations, including neighbourhood offices, public libraries, career centres, and settlement organizations. These sites are visited by a broad range of people who do not have regular access to the Internet, including a large number of recent immigrants to Canada (Moll and Fritz 2007).

Besides many recent migrants' use of CAP sites, the composition of VCN's volunteer base—nearly two-thirds of the volunteers immigrated to Canada within the past five years—exemplifies another way that a community network can meet some of the needs of its local community. In Vancouver, a city in which nearly half of the population was born outside of Canada (Statistics Canada 2010), many recent immigrants are looking for employment commensurate with their skills. Through its volunteer program, VCN provides an opportunity for civic participation, which many recent immigrants have found beneficial during their period of settlement.

While it is the volunteers' own efforts and initiative that bring them to VCN, their collective contributions are important to the success of VCN's Internet service provision and additional member services. Working toward these goals allows newcomers to experience civic participation and to enhance their skills and knowledge, particularly in relation to ICT work and related English language acquisition. Basing the study on qualitative and quantitative research completed in Vancouver during the spring and summer of 2005, I examine how the social inclusion of newcomers is influenced by VCN's volunteer program.

IMMIGRATION AND THE CANADIAN LABOUR MARKET

Many of VCN's volunteers have come to Canada as part of the Skilled Worker Class, defined by the Immigrant and Refugee Protection Act of 2002 as those applicants "who may become permanent residents on the basis of their ability to become economically established in Canada" (Tolley 2003, 1). Throughout the recent past, Vancouver's immigrant population has "grown at a considerably faster pace than its Canadian-born population" and consequently, in 2006, persons born outside of Canada and living in Vancouver, represented more than 45 percent of the city's population (Statistics Canada 2010). ·

In the past, when people migrated to and arrived in Canada, they faced challenges in getting established in the workforce. Given time, they overcame these difficulties and attained incomes on par with those of domestic-born workers (Schellenberg and Hou 2005, 49). Unfortunately, for people who migrated to Canada since the 1980s, this trend has not continued. Four related factors are thought to underlie immigrants' declining labour market outcomes (Schellenberg and Hou 2005, 49). First, there has been a marked shift in source countries from Western European nations to Asian ones. Currently, China, India, and the Philippines are the top three countries that newcomers emigrate from, and increased challenges exist due to differences in language and culture, as well as discrimination (Citizenship and Immigration Canada 2009). Second, declining returns to foreign experience and foreign education means that degrees and experience attained in the newer source countries are not recognized on the same basis as degrees and experience from Western countries. Third, during the 1980s and 1990s, all people looking for work in the Canadian job market—including young people, people returning to work, and recent immigrants—have found fewer attractive employment opportunities (Schellenberg and Hou 2005, 50). And last, the education levels of Canadian-born individuals have increased dramatically in the past twenty-five years. In this "competitive market, even marginal differences in educational quality, language or communication skills, or cultural norms could have an impact on employment outcomes" (Schellenberg and Hou 2005, 50).

The impacts of these and other factors are evident. Three-quarters of recent immigrants settled in the urban centres of Toronto, Montréal, and Vancouver. In 2001, in both Toronto and Vancouver, recent immigrants accounted for 17 percent of the total population, but composed 32 percent of the low-income population (Schellenberg and Hou 2005, 51). Between 1984 and 1999, the wealth of Canadian-born families increased by 37 percent, but for immigrant families who had been in Canada for less than a decade, wealth decreased by only 16 percent (51). Results of a survey of immigrants in Vancouver who had been in Canada since 1991 demonstrate that nearly 40 percent experienced problems entering the labour market (Hiebert 2003, 29).

Given these circumstances, what is a newcomer's best strategy for settlement? Acknowledging that most newcomers' key goal is to support themselves and their families, the findings described in this study suggest that time and effort devoted to civic participation and community formation may be vital for achieving economic success. For many newcomers with ICT expertise, VCN has provided opportunities to expand human capital in a Canadian context while building social capital in a culturally diverse setting.

THEORETICAL OVERVIEW

This study examines how recent immigrants consider volunteering as a means of increasing social inclusion; it considers some of the relationships between digital and social inclusion. Recent scholarship theorizes relationships between social capital, social inclusion, and the experiences of newcomers to Canada (Caidi and Allard 2005; Frith 2003; Justus 2004; Kunz 2003; Schellenberg and Hou 2005; Tolley 2003). This body of scholarship highlights the important role that civic participation and the development of social networks play in the settlement process. The field of community informatics provides further context to considerations of the relevance of recent-immigrant volunteers' in-person interactions at VCN. Community networks are one application of the field of community informatics, an "emerging interdisciplinary research field concerned with the study of enabling uses of information and communication technologies in communities" (Longford 2005, 6). Community informatics promotes a perspective beyond technical connectivity, which tends to focus on issues of access and digital divides. Gurstein's (2004) frame of "effective use" recognizes the importance of the "lived physical community" and interactions within it that involve ICTs. Through the lens of effective use it is possible to see recent immigrants as more than potential ICT *users*: their work and interactions at VCN—and perhaps other CNs—can be recognized in terms of contributing to social capital-building and increased social inclusion.

METHODOLOGY AND QUANTITATIVE FINDINGS

The case study approach of this project focused on VCN's volunteer programs. The project examined the influences of ICTs and community networks on settlement practices for people who had recently immigrated to Canada. The

use of ICTs by people who have migrated to Canada continues to gain attention (e.g., Caidi et al. 2008; Chien 2005; Dechief et al. 2010; Jansen, Jansen,
and Spink 2005; Veenhof 2006; Vertovec 2004; Zamaria and Fletcher 2007).
Using mixed methods to generate data provided a means of triangulating and
gaining multiple perspectives on VCN's volunteer program. For three weeks
in March 2005, I observed VCN's day-to-day goings-on as well as interviewing
nine of VCN's volunteers; I generated data through these interviews as well
as my ongoing conversations with VCN's coordinators. During individual
interviews with people who had immigrated to Canada in the past five years
and who were at that time current or past contributors to VCN, we discussed
their reasons for volunteering, the benefits of their volunteer experiences,
and their information-seeking strategies related to settlement activities and
employment seeking. An analysis of the data provided through the qualitative research component of this project is presented in the pages that follow.
I describe how civic participation at VCN has augmented human capital for
individual volunteers while it has simultaneously increased social capital
within Vancouver Community Network.

Completed in July 2005, the quantitative research component of this project contextualizes and demonstrates the pertinence of the insights gleaned
from the project's initial component. This second phase of fieldwork involved
collecting and perusing three data sources of varying sample size and time
periods:

1. Survey of current and past volunteers
2. Collection of volunteers' resumes
3. Database of online applications.

Each of these data sets provides evidence of how many people have been involved with VCN in a volunteer capacity, and how many of these people were
recent immigrants. These data sets provide multiple snapshots of VCN's diverse volunteer demographic.

On the basis of the quantitative data generated in 2005, more than 60
percent of VCN's volunteers are recent immigrants who have been in Canada
for five years or less.[1] Almost half of the volunteers were looking for work,
and they considered civic participation a means to becoming more employ-
able. They were selected to become volunteers at VCN because of their strong
ICT skills, gained through education and work experiences in their home (or
other) countries. In contrast with the findings at VCN, a 2003 survey completed by Statistics Canada found low levels of civic participation amongst
a broader immigrant demographic. People who immigrated to Canada after
1980 are less likely to be involved in even one organization than those who are
either Canadian-born or who immigrated to Canada in the 1970s or earlier

(Schellenberg 2004, 11). In particular, people aged 25 to 54 who came to Canada after 1990 were less likely than people who were born in Canada to have taken part in participatory activities such as signing a petition or attending a public meeting (Schellenberg 2004, 13).

In contrast to the minimal engagements reported in these general, pan-Canadian findings, at VCN the civic contributions of recent immigrants are vital. Reed and Selbee (2000) coined the term *civic core* to describe the "middle-aged, well-educated and affluent" people who are thought to take on the majority of the volunteer work accomplished in Canada (Schellenberg 2004). In some respects, the volunteers at VCN are atypical—VCN's "alternate civic core" *is* well educated: across the volunteer base 83 percent hold Master's or Bachelor's degrees, and within the recent immigrant demographic, 91 percent have these same levels of education, while the remaining 9 percent have computer-related technical diplomas. All of the recent immigrant volunteers have computer-related work experience from countries other than Canada, though 70.5 percent do not have any work experience in Canada.[2] With respect to age, VCN's volunteers tend to be younger than "middle-aged." The average age of volunteers determined by the July 2005 survey is 31, although the average age in the recent-immigrant volunteer demographic is slightly higher at 33.4. While there was no measure of wealth, or personal or family savings in this study, at the time of application 50 percent of VCN volunteers described their career status as "looking for work" and another 27 percent of VCN volunteers were students. Most VCN volunteers, therefore, share an employment situation that is not in concordance with that of Canada's civic core.

While VCN's volunteers have strong ICT skills, their absence of strong social networks is part of what makes VCN an attractive place to spend their time. The types of responsibilities the volunteers hold at VCN demonstrate their technical capabilities; they create language portals, work at the help desk, administer the network, and teach Internet skills to other network members. Language portal volunteers describe networking within language communities and choosing suitable web content as the most challenging tasks of portal creation. While the work of the language portal volunteers is largely independent and behind-the-scenes, help desk volunteers are VCN's "front-line" workers. Help desk volunteers must have strong technical skills to coach network members through establishing and troubleshooting dial-up connections, but strong social and language skills are also important, as these volunteers represent VCN to network members and to the public both over the phone and in person. Volunteers in the role of network administrators are experienced with hardware and servers and have the capabilities to maintain VCN's office networks. While liaising with help desk volunteers and VCN's coordinators, these volunteers also maintain and repair in-house and donated equipment that is then passed along to community groups. The final set of volunteers are Internet instructors who also combine their social skills with technical skills; they provide one-on-one Internet and software instruction to the network members who visit VCN's computer lab.

Given the strength of the volunteers' knowledge and technical skills—their access to, habitual use of, and expertise with the Internet—they can be described as "digitally included." Findings from one Statistics Canada report support the suggestion that many recent immigrants make regular use of their strong technical skills: "Immigrants who arrived in Canada since 1990 [are] more likely than others to use the Internet to communicate with their relatives. This is probably because the Internet [is] a cost-effective way for immigrants to communicate with family members in other countries, as well as because recent immigrants have, on average, higher levels of educational attainment than Canadian-born persons" (Schellenberg 2004, 16).

Although the volunteers are digitally included—more so than is common amongst longer-term residents of Canada—recent international relocation has resulted in these volunteers being less socially connected and more economically vulnerable than they were prior to emigration. This chapter's focus on a group of people who have strong technical skills and who are able to connect to information available online demonstrates that technical connectivity alone is not enough to ensure social well-being and economic security. Digital connections do not ensure social ones, and economic exclusion is often linked to social barriers.

QUALITATIVE FINDINGS

During interviews, people shared many different reasons for why VCN is a popular place to volunteer. The majority connected their choice to volunteer at VCN with a desire to increase their employability, by practicing English, gaining local experience, or getting a local work reference. Others mentioned VCN's central location and the ease of going there via public transportation. Contributing to the community and getting to know people was another common reason:

> [I volunteered to] do something for the community and also to practice computer skills. . . . [I want] to help others and . . . to better my communication skills because you know I am a new immigrant and my English is not good. (Volunteer 1)

> I came to VCN to improve my technical skills and to involve myself with more people. (Volunteer 7)

I liked that it is in Vancouver, not Surrey or Langley, so it is easy to come [here]. (Volunteer 2)

I think volunteers are serious because they can also benefit from this experience. After three months they can get a [work] reference, and they can practice their language skills and technical skills and communicate and learn things from others. Volunteers do get benefits from this. (Volunteer 3)

Each volunteer mentioned either job seeking or gaining work experience as a significant factor in his or her decision to volunteer at VCN. These volunteers are not unusual; according to the 2000 National Survey of Giving, Volunteering and Participating (NSGVP), 62 percent of unemployed volunteers "believed that volunteering would improve their job prospects" (McClintock 2004, 7). Also in concordance with the NSGVP, volunteers usually gave more than one reason for their civic participation, indicating that the reasons for and benefits of volunteerism amongst VCN's newcomer volunteers are multiple and overlapping (McClintock 2004, 7). While volunteers' initial attraction to VCN was the potential to establish a network of more or less instrumental relationships, or "weak ties" (Granovetter 1973), most volunteers reported that they valued the social benefits of volunteering at VCN more than the instrumental ones, particularly in terms of expanding their social networks, fostering a sense of community and, ultimately, easing their integration into the rest of Canadian society.

Social interactions are key to VCN's functions. VCN welcomes new volunteers who can contribute to the network's functions, and likewise there is great demand for the opportunity to volunteer in such a practical but specialized capacity. VCN's organizational strategies encourage personal initiative as well as relying on interactions between volunteers. A description of VCN's volunteer-training practices illustrates how this is achieved. Because the turnover of volunteers is high, new volunteers are trained by other, more experienced volunteers.[3] Each role is challenging and volunteers are required to learn quickly. The variety of questions asked of volunteers necessitates working together to respond to requests appropriately. One volunteer describes this positive learning experience as particular to non-profit organizations:

[At VCN] everybody shares information and that's interesting. In a company, everybody expects you to know everything. Here you feel free to say, "I don't know this part." (Volunteer 6)

In their official capacities at VCN, volunteers train one another, ask each other questions, and regularly come to other volunteers' aid. As an extension of these activities, volunteers also tend to feel comfortable sharing information that is more personally relevant. Conversation topics range from employment opportunities to educational programs, and even to the daily challenges of being a newcomer to Canada. Volunteers describe the exchange of information at VCN as free-flowing and non-hierarchical:

> I feel very comfortable with the volunteers at VCN. We are in the same position. We came from different countries to start work, to find something. (Volunteer 2)

> Basically it is an information exchange centre. You have so many people here [and] they all bring ideas and news to this place. (Volunteer 3)

> There are a lot of opportunities. When the volunteers come here, they exchange information about where there are jobs, and where there are interviews and which websites have a lot of postings. They tell each other about companies that are hiring people. That's the [kind of] information that is exchanged amongst volunteers. It's a cycle; it goes on and on. (Volunteer 7)

The interviews made it clear that information exchange is a necessary and regular part of the VCN volunteer program's functioning. Caidi and Allard (2005) explain the importance of information as an aspect of social inclusion. Citing Mwarigha (2002), they describe the information needs of recent immigrants in three stages:

Immediate includes essential matters such as where to find food and shelter, how to get around geographically, and ways of dealing with language barriers

Intermediate includes how to access and use various systems, such as municipal and legal services, long-term housing, employment, and health services

Integration needs are more diverse and individualized; meeting them contributes to social inclusion through cultural, political, and economic terms.

The current or past VCN volunteers who took part in interviews tend to be nearing the end of the second stage or are currently in the third stage of settlement. The then-current volunteers I spoke with were looking for work, completing contracts, or going to school—situations with limited economic security. Interviewees who were no longer volunteering were working full time in the ICT industry. All of the interview participants had been in Canada long enough to have found a reasonable place to live and have gained access to educational and health care services. They were volunteering at a stage of settlement when their information needs were not so general as to be easily located online, but required more personal interactions.

A social network provides important context for understanding cultur-ally specific information. One newcomer describes the importance of a social network for making sense of information:

> Other than using the Internet, I read Citizenship and Immigration Canada leaflets, and some information from other organizations. Because we get a lot of information like this, we don't know which is best, so a friend here helped me. (Volunteer 1)

Whether it is information provided about day-to-day events or knowledge gained over a series of interactions, VCN provides recent immigrants with opportunities to learn and exchange information in a broad social context. As well, VCN offers opportunities for civic participation at a later stage of settlement, when it may be particularly valuable. For newcomers in earlier stages of settlement, aid provided by CAP in the form of free access to com-puters and the Internet also proves helpful. According to Mwarigha's (2002) description of the information needs of recent immigrants, some newcomers' immediate information needs for sustenance, housing, and language may be aided by making use of a CAP site, but the final stage, integration—which in-volves more diverse and individualized needs—is more likely to be realized by becoming part of Canada's alternate civic core, as a volunteer at VCN or another community network.

The more information one has available, the easier it is to increase one's human capacities (abilities that allow an individual to gain human capital), and having greater human capacities creates access to even more information. For technically skilled recent immigrants, the civic participation that VCN offers provides a tangible means of stepping into this cycle. As volunteers in-crease their human and social capital—through improved English language skills, enlarged social networks and increased employability due to having local experience and a local employment reference—they also become more socially included. According to Frith (2003), "a real sense of belonging is cre-ated when newcomers can fulfill their potential—get and keep a job, transfer and apply previously acquired occupational skills and participate fully in Canadian institutions and community life" (36). Powell's (2006) research with a different population, technologically savvy but socially disengaged youth who volunteer with a Montréal-based community wireless group, also suggests that taking part in a volunteer-based, technology-enabling organ-ization serves as a gateway to community and civic participation (see also Dechief et al. 2008).

VCN AS A THIRD PLACE

All of the volunteers have the digital skills required to keep in touch with friends and family in their home countries and to find online information about living in Canada, but they are looking to connect with people in person. Although the volunteers are technically enabled and are aware of opportunities for online interaction, they choose to make face-to-face contact with other volunteers and network members on a regular basis. One volunteer describes the importance of regular interaction this way:

> Every Thursday [when I came to volunteer] there were a lot of new people, but I might see one or two people who I had already met. When you don't have a job or know a lot of people and don't have a very large social life it is good to know that every Thursday afternoon you will see these same people. (Volunteer 9)

One way of thinking about the relevance of recent-immigrant volunteers' in-person interactions at VCN is in terms of Oldenburg's (1989) concept of "third place." Third places tend to be casual hangouts such as coffee shops or pubs that "exist on natural ground and serve to level their guests to a condition of social equality" (42). They are "remarkably similar to a good home in the psychological comfort and support" they extend (42). In contrast to the casual interactions that take place at most third places, volunteers do come to VCN with the purpose of contributing to the organization's mandate, and once there, they follow an organized structure. However, the site suits many of the attributes of the third place including:

- nourishing relationships and a diversity of human contact
- helping to create a sense of place and community
- encouraging sociability instead of isolation
- furnishing a highly accessible place where a number of people regularly go.

Because a recent immigrant's home, or "first place," is a relatively new one, and his or her workplace, or "second place," is absent, as a third place VCN may be a key provider of much-needed social interaction and information exchanges. While all of the people who use VCN as an Internet service provider (ISP) gain information and opportunities for online interaction, contributing to the network *in person* (as a volunteer) may have significantly greater impacts. Werbin (2006, 13) reports similar findings: "The access that [foreign-trained professionals] really seem to value is access to in-person, physical communities that develop around initiatives like CAP sites, where work experience opportunities surface, and learning to be part of Canadian society is achieved face-to-face." (See also Dechief et al. 2008).

THE INTERRELATED CONCEPTS OF HUMAN CAPITAL, SOCIAL CAPITAL, AND SOCIAL INCLUSION

Throughout these interview excerpts, volunteers' experiences illustrate the concepts of human and social capital, and social inclusion. Human capital relates to the knowledge, education, skills, and experience held by an individual. Conversational English language capabilities are a significant aspect of human capital; research demonstrates that "proficiency in one of Canada's official languages is critical to effective integration" (Frith 2003, 35). Because English is the language spoken at VCN, every conversation is an opportunity for newcomers to practice conversational English and, in this small way, increase their human capital. Indeed, many volunteers say that improving their spoken English was a key reason for starting to volunteer at VCN. One volunteer describes his experiences this way:

> In China, I had little practice speaking in English, so it has improved a lot here. And now I talk to all kinds of people: seniors, men, [and] women. I talk with people from different places too. (Volunteer 5)

This same volunteer was just about to start a new job and explained how his interactions at VCN contributed to his employment success:

> Getting this job has benefitted a lot by my work experience at VCN. [At VCN I learned] how to talk with people, and even in the interview, how to answer their questions. Working at VCN gave me a lot of practice. (Volunteer 5)

Besides communication and language skills, volunteers' technical skills are kept up to date and broadened by their experiences at VCN:

> When I came here I learned to troubleshoot by going through this series of steps. I had to upgrade these [troubleshooting] skills. (Volunteer 7)

> I have learned about free software, and what kinds of software are used in Canada. I get to meet with other technical guys and learn and talk with them. (Volunteer 1)

> When you go for a [work] position it is good to show that you are still staying active in your field. (Volunteer 9)

Some of the activities at VCN are directly related to job seeking. One volunteer describes a seminar planned for this purpose:

> At the end of last year there [were] a couple of volunteers who got jobs and told us about how they did it—how they did the job search, how they did at the interviews. (Volunteer 3)

Even though the volunteers are already skilled and knowledgeable, gaining some experience with these skills in Canada seems to enhance their human capital and to benefit their job-seeking processes. Volunteer contributions to the network—while resulting in enhanced technical skills and practice with English language skills—also build social capital.

It is through interactions between volunteers and with network members at VCN that trust and social capital are built. Kunz (2003, 33) states: "Unlike human capital that is observable through diplomas and certificates, social capital is less tangible because it exists in the relations among individuals." Social capital is a "public good" created through social interactions. Putnam (2000, 21) defines it as "social networks and the associated norms of reciprocity." According to Kunz (2003, 33), "Success in the labour market depends as much on one's human capital as it does on the social capital one is able to accumulate." While one can often work on her human capital independently—through study, practice, and information searches—social capital can only be generated through social interactions and memberships.

Many people who would not otherwise have an opportunity to meet are able to connect and exchange information at VCN. For some volunteers, VCN provides a source of community other than one based on shared first-language or home-country cultures. Informally, it facilitates interaction amongst people from diverse cultural backgrounds, which in turn provides a means of learning about local or Canadian culture and other volunteers' home countries. Two volunteers describe their interactions in VCN's heterogeneous setting:

> Every week I meet people from many different origins. It's the most interesting. (Volunteer 9)

> It is already a year since I started, and I have found many friends here. I have friends from Yugoslavia, Germany, China, Austria, from France, from everywhere. Most of them have found jobs, but I keep in touch and sometimes we email. I like this place. (Volunteer 2)

Put in terms of social capital theory, Putnam differentiates between "bridging" and "bonding" social capital by describing social networks that include or *bridge* people of different races, ages, genders, religions, education, ideologies, geographies, and classes as useful for "getting ahead" (Putnam, quoting de Souza Briggs). According to Kunz (2003, 34), "bridging capital is . . . essential for immigrants to expand their networks beyond their own ethnic community and to acculturate into the receiving society." Conversely, social networks that *bond* members of a group to the exclusion of others are useful for "getting by" (Putnam 2000, 22). Kunz states (2003, 34) that "in terms of employment, [an] ethnic network is useful mainly in finding jobs with low human capital requirements." For those immigrants who are highly skilled and educated, it is bridging capital that enables economic and social advancement (Kunz 2003, 34).

The human and social capital building that occurs within VCN's offices is supported by a prevailing openness toward diversity. In accordance with its vision statement, VCN endeavours to be inclusive and multicultural in its efforts to provide access to electronic creativity and broad exchanges of ideas and knowledge (Kunz 2003). Breton (1997) suggests that "participation beyond ethnic or racial boundaries is partially a function of the openness of the associations, networks and structures of the host society." He adds: "The structure of opportunities for participation is crucial" (9).

How does social inclusion fit with human and social capital? Duncan (2003, 31) suggests that "a society that is socially inclusive is a society that grants access to everyone to the vehicles of the good life, as it is defined by that society." He goes on to note that "'the good life' is not a scarce resource, but one that grows as more people are involved." The quantity of "good life" available is "influenced by the extent to which people in a society, and this encompasses immigrants, are included in its workings and its decision-making." Because social capital is generated through social interactions and trust built through them, a more inclusive society "generates increased social capital" while an exclusive society reduces social capital.

As an inclusive, diverse network, VCN fosters social inclusion and social capital. Valuing diversity, providing opportunities for participation and personal development, recognizing competence, creating access to public places and opportunities for interaction, and belonging are some of the ways that VCN is socially inclusive (Shookner 2002, 1). Volunteers describe VCN as a place where they feel socially supported. In the absence of full-time work, volunteering is one way of being engaged and feeling useful, elements of being socially included. Interacting with others in the shared circumstances of job seeking and being a newcomer contributes to feelings of comfort and solidarity:

> You have to help each other. Because everyone is a foreigner here, it is easier if you help each other and get to know each other. That way you don't feel as depressed that you have left all of your friends behind. (Volunteer 8)

> When I came here, I met some other people who were volunteering as well. It was nice because you could talk to them and discuss your problems and get some idea of their problems. I felt a little bit better after I had a chance to meet people here and know that I am not alone in my situation. They have the same problems so we got to see our similarities. That was really good for me. (Volunteer 8)

Over time, volunteers' comfort levels increase and through their enhanced capabilities, they are more able to contribute to VCN's projects, as well as to access information beneficial to their own employment searches and skills development. These experiences are illustrations of Breton's (1997, 6) suggestion that "social participation can . . . sensitize group members to the fact that they are subject to the same economic, political, cultural or social conditions—such as immigrant status." He suggests that through "social involvement, people may realize that they share the same lot, are 'in the same boat' as others in certain respects." Newcomers can then "identify with a 'community of fate,' so that social expectations are based on the feeling of *interdependence*, involving mutual obligations, and the idea that co-operation may be generally advantageous." In this way, participation leads to increased social capital and inclusion.

The impacts of volunteering at VCN may continue for a lifetime, even though the actual stint of volunteerism may begin shortly after an immigrant arrives in Canada and end with the attainment of full-time employment. Lasting benefits of volunteerism include building a social network, gaining exposure to the operations of a not-for-profit organization, and attaining the technical or social skills required in each volunteer role. One obvious longer-term impact of volunteering at VCN is gaining local work-related experience, which may impact future economic stability.

Although this study's fieldwork was completed in 2005, its findings remain valid. As of spring 2010, VCN's volunteer program remains a sought after means of gaining "Canadian experience." Indeed the idea that volunteerism is a significant means of stepping into the Canadian job market has become further entrenched in the Canadian settlement landscape and is even recommended on the federally funded employment seeking website WorkinginCanada.com (Canada 2010, 11). As of 2010, at VCN's headquarters, the day-to-day volunteer roles and types of interactions remain similar to those in place in 2005, although a group of volunteers who work on Java programming projects now exists. Since 2005, the demand for dial-up Internet has generally decreased, which has resulted in fewer people making use of this service through VCN (and unfortunately annual individual donations to VCN have decreased as a result). However, the number of CAP sites resulting from partnerships with local community organizations, particularly in neighbourhood offices, has increased. These sites offer opportunities for their clients to receive basic computer and Internet training, as well as access to the Internet for purposes such as job seeking, settlement information, and free communication with friends and family in other countries. The benefits of these sites are significant; the potential termination of funding to this program would affect a great number of VCN's clients adversely.

CONCLUSIONS

The VCN, communities within the Lower Mainland, and the volunteers them-selves all benefit as interactions at the VCN contribute to newcomers' settlement processes. These contributions include involving recent immigrants in a not-for-profit organization, supplying training for volunteer roles, offering a space in which to interact and share information with others, and providing a means to gain "Canadian experience" by providing references for potential employers. At an individual level, each volunteer's human capital increases. Collectively, these interactions create social capital and enhance social inclu-sion at a community level.

Community networks, even smaller access points such as those funded by CAP, function as third places to provide information, social interaction, and support. Differing from pubs and coffee shops, CNs provide purposeful reasons for interaction. Arguably, VCN's volunteer program provides an or-ganizational structure for volunteers to act as vital sources of local economic development and innovation. The impacts of an ongoing opportunity for people from diverse cultural and socio-economic backgrounds to engage pur-posefully in civic participation should not be underestimated.

ACKNOWLEDGEMENTS

Having a curious researcher in the midst of VCN's operation required extra effort on the part of the coordinators and volunteers, and I thank each of them for their help. Thank you in particular to VCN's coordinators, Steven Chan and Peter Royce (who passed away in 2009), whose work allowed this study to exist. Heartfelt appreciation goes to the nine volunteers who—speaking English as their second, third, or fourth language—partici-pated in the sometimes challenging interviews. They remain nameless for anonymity's sake. Thanks to all of VCN's volunteers, past, current, and future!

I am grateful as well to the members of the Canadian Research Alliance for Com-munity Innovation and Networking (CRACIN) for their encouragement and support.

NOTES

1   This is not a situation that exists only at VCN. At St. Christopher House, in urban Toronto, the CN reports high numbers of recent immigrant volunteers. The online availability of a number of resources developed to aid volunteer coordinators who are working with recent immigrants also indicates that volunteering is a growing trend amongst newcomers. Examples of such resources include Volunteer Canada's *Career Information for New Immigrants and Refugees: Needs Assessment Research* (2004), Calgary Immigrant Aid Society's *Culturally Diverse Youth and Volunteerism: How to Recruit, Train and Retain Culturally Diverse Youth Volunteers* (2004), and the Canadian Centre for Philanthropy's *Understanding Canadian Volunteers: Using the National Sur-vey of Giving, Volunteering and Participating to Build Your Volunteer Program* (2004).

2   It is possible that a higher percentage of volunteers do have Canadian work experi-ence, but because it is not in their professional field, it is not listed on their résumés, which were the source for this figure.

3   Of VCN's volunteers who began their volunteer experience during the 20-month per-
    iod between 1 November 2003 and 30 June 2005, 80 percent also completed their
    duration within this time frame.

REFERENCES

Aizlewood, Amanda, and Maureen Doody. 2002. *Seeking community on the Internet: Ethnocultural use of information communication technology*. Hull, ON: Department of Heritage Canada.

Breton, Raymond. 1997. Social participation and social capital. *Immigrants and Civic Partici- pation: Contemporary Policy and Research Issues* (proceedings of the Second National Metroplis Conference), 4–11. Montreal: Department of Canadian Heritage. http:// canada.metropolis.net/events/civic/rbreton_e.html.

Caidi, Nadia, and Danielle Allard. 2005. Social inclusion of newcomers to Canada: An information problem? *Library and Information Science Research* 27(3): 302–24.

Caidi, Nadia, Danielle Allard, Diane Dechief, and Graham Longford. 2008. Canadian im- migration and social inclusion: What roles do ICTs play? Final report submitted to the Strategic Policy Research Directorate of Human Resources and Social Development Canada, 5 December.

Canada. 2010. Guide to working in Canada: A source of free and useful information for immigrants. http://www.workingincanada.gc.ca/guide_pdf/eng/complete_guide_ eng.pdf.

Chien, Elise. 2005. Informing and involving newcomers online: Users' perspectives of Settle- ment.Org. MA thesis, University of Toronto.

Citizenship and Immigration Canada. 2009. Facts and figures 2008—Immigration over- view: Permanent and temporary residents. http://www.cic.gc.ca/english/resources/ statistics/facts2008/permanent/10.asp

Dechief, Diane, Nadia Caidi, Danielle Allard, and Margaret Lam. 2010. Immigrants and the Internet: The information needs of Canadian immigrant job seekers and www.working inCanada.gc.ca. Final report submitted to the Foreign Credential Recognition Division of Human Resources and Social Development Canada, 31 March.

Dechief, Diane, Graham Longford, Alison Powell, and Kenneth Werbin. 2008. Enabling communities in the networked city: ICTs and civic participation among immigrants and youth in urban Canada. In *Augmented urban spaces*, ed. Alessandro Aurigi and Fiorella de Cindio, 155–70. Surrey, UK: Ashgate.

Duncan, Howard. 2003. Social inclusion, social capital and immigration. In *Canadian issues / thèmes canadiens: Immigration and the intersections of diversity*, ed. Meyer Burstein, 30–32. Montreal: Association for Canadian Studies.

Frith, Rosaline. 2003. Integration. In *Canadian issues / thèmes canadiens: Immigration and the intersections of diversity*, ed. Meyer Burstein, 35–36. Montreal: Association for Canadian Studies.

Granovetter, Mark. 1973. The strength of weak ties. *American Journal of Sociology* 78(6): 1360–80.

Gurstein, Michael. 2004. Effective use and the community informatics sector: Some thoughts on Canada's approach to community technology / community access. In *Seeking convergence in policy and practice: Communication in the public interest*, vol. 2, ed. Marita Moll and Leslie Regan Shade, 223–44. Ottawa: Canadian Centre for Policy Alternatives.

Hiebert, Daniel. 2003. Immigrant and minority enclaves in Canadian cities. In *Canadian issues / thèmes canadiens: Immigration and the intersections of diversity*, ed. Meyer Burstein, 27–29. Montreal: Association for Canadian Studies.

Jansen, Bernard J., Karen J. Jansen, and Amanda Spink. 2005. Using the Web to look for work: Implications for online job seeking and recruiting. *Internet Research* 15(1): 49–66.

Justus, Martha. 2004. Immigrants in Canada's cities. In *Our diverse cities*, no. 1 (Fall), ed. Caroline Andrew, 41–47. The Metropolis Project. http://canada.metropolis.net/ research-policy/cities/publication/diverse_cite_magazine_e.pdf.

Kunz, Jean L. 2003. Social capital: A key dimension of immigrant integration. In *Canadian issues / thèmes canadiens: Immigration and the intersections of diversity*, ed. Meyer Burstein, 33–34. Montreal: Association for Canadian Studies.

Longford, Graham. 2005. Community networking and civic participation in Canada: A background paper. http://archive.iprp.ischool.utoronto.ca/cracin/publications/pdfs/ WorkingPapers/CRACIN%20Working%20Paper%20No%202.pdf.

McClintock, N. 2004. *Understanding Canadian volunteers: Using the National Survey of Giving, Volunteering and Participation to build your volunteer program.* Toronto: Canadian Centre for Philanthropy.

Moll, Marita, and Melissa Fritz. 2007. Community networks and Canadian public policy: Preliminary report on the CRACIN survey of community networks. http://archive.iprp. ischool.utoronto.ca/cracin/Moll_Fritz_Info-incan.pdf.

Mwarigha, M. S. 2002. *Towards a framework for local responsibility: Taking action to end the current limbo in immigrant settlement, Toronto.* Toronto: Maytree Foundation. http://maytree.com/PDF_Files/SummaryTowardsAFrameworkForLocalResponsibility MwarighaMS2002.pdf.

Oldenburg, Ray. 1989. *The great good place: Cafés, coffee shops, community centers, beauty parlors, general stores, bars, hangouts, and how they get you through the day.* New York: Paragon House.

Powell, Alison, and Leslie Regan Shade. 2006. Going Wi-Fi in Canada: Municipal and community initiatives. *Government Information Quarterly* 23: 381–403.

Putnam, Robert. 2000. *Bowling alone: The collapse and revival of American community.* New York: Simon and Shuster.

Reed, Paul B., and L. Kevin Selbee. 2000. Patterns of civic participation and the civic core in Canada. Research paper. Statistics Canada. Originally presented at the 29th ARNOVA Annual Conference, New Orleans, Louisiana, 16–18 November. http://publications. gc.ca/collections/Collection/CS75-0048-3E.pdf.

Schellenberg, Grant. 2004. 2003 General Social Survey on Social Engagement, cycle 17: An overview of findings. Ottawa: Minister of Industry. http://www.statcan.gc.ca/ pub/89-598-x/2003001/4067781-eng.htm.

Schellenberg, Grant, and Feng Hou. 2005. The economic well-being of recent immigrants to Canada. In *Canadian issues / thèmes canadiens: Immigration and the intersections of diversity* (Spring), ed. Myer Siemiatycki, 49–52. Montreal: Association for Canadian Studies.

Shookner, Malcolm. 2002. *An inclusion lens: Workbook for looking at social and economic inclusion and exclusion.* Halifax: Population and Public Health Branch, Health Canada.

Statistics Canada. 2010. 2006 Community profile: Vancouver, City. http://www12.statcan. ca/census-recensement/2006/dp-pd/prof/92-591/details/page.cfm?Lang=E&Geo1=C MA&Code1=933&Geo2=PR&Code2=59&Data=Count&SearchText=Vancouver&Sea rchType=Begins&SearchPR=01&B1=All&GeoLevel=PR&GeoCode=933.

Tolley, Erin. 2003. The skilled worker class: Selection criteria in the Immigration and Refugee Protection Act. Metropolis policy brief no. 1 (January). In *Canadian issues / thèmes canadiens: Immigration and the intersections of diversity*, ed. Meyer Burstein, 1–8. Montreal: Association for Canadian Studies.

Veenhof, Ben. 2006. *Determinants and outcomes of heavy computer use: An international and interprovincial comparison*. A presentation at the Statistics Canada Socioeconomic Conference, Gatineau, Québec, 15 May.

Vertovec, Steven. 2004. Cheap calls: The social glue of migrant transnationalism. *Global Networks* 4(2): 219–24.

Werbin, Kenneth C. 2006. Where is the "community" in community networking initiatives? Stories from the "third spaces" of Connecting Canadians. CRACIN Working Paper no. 11. February. Toronto: Canadian Research Alliance for Community Innovation and Networking. http://archive.iprp.ischool.utoronto.ca/cracin/publications/pdfs/ WorkingPapers/CRACIN%20Working%20Paper%20No%2011.pdf.

Zamaria, Charles, and Fred Fletcher. 2007. *Canadian Internet Project: 2007 Results, Canada Online!* Toronto: Canadian Internet Project.

PART IV

Community Innovation II: Wireless Networking

10 COMMUNITY AND MUNICIPAL WI-FI INITIATIVES IN CANADA
Evolutions in Community Participation

Alison Powell, Leslie Regan Shade

The increase of wireless (Wi-Fi) Internet access projects in cities and towns across the United States and Canada in the early to mid-2000s focused attention on Wi-Fi technology as an inexpensive means of accessing the Internet. Given the excitement surrounding these developments, questions have been posed regarding the material and socio-political potential of Wi-Fi; for instance, what practices, policies, and innovative technical developments could influence its trajectory? Now, after several years, with many projects firmly established, questions remain about sustainable funding models for community and municipal Wi-Fi initiatives.

Compared to earlier developments in the United States, Canadian municipal and community Wi-Fi projects evolved more slowly. Due to the widespread deployment of DSL and cable modems in Canada, most major Canadian cities have broadband access; OECD (Organisation for Economic Co-operation and Development) statistics for June 2007 indicated that there were twenty-five subscribers per hundred inhabitants, placing Canada eighth in terms of OECD countries (OECD 2007). Three years later, Canada's broadband performance had slipped, according to figures released by Harvard University's Berkman Center on Internet and Society, with lower penetration rates, higher prices, and slower speeds than other countries, placing Canada's ranking at nineteenth place worldwide, from its 2002 rank of second place (Benkler 2010). As in US cities, several Canadian cities initiated private Wi-Fi ventures whose objectives were to provide wireless connectivity in commercial establishments. Alongside these business ventures, which primarily provide Wi-Fi connectivity in publicly accessible locations such as hotel lobbies and airports, municipal governments have planned large-scale Wi-Fi coverage projects, and some non-profit groups and co-operatives have also formed among people interested in non-commercial Wi-Fi development. These groups support, through dedicated volunteers, the development or deployment of Wi-Fi services in regional community spaces. Often, the groups also develop and refine software intended to facilitate local communities in creating and displaying art and local content over Wi-Fi networks.

In this chapter we introduce community Wi-Fi projects as forms of community infrastructure. Responding to the themes introduced by Sandvig in chapter 7 of this volume, we position the context for the development of this infrastructure as a form of community network, as a learning community, and as a mode of Internet access infrastructure. We first present a brief discussion of various Wi-Fi networking models and the state of Canadian spectrum policy. We then explore how Wi-Fi development and innovation is occurring within urban Canadian communities, situated within municipal government projects and grassroots community technology initiatives. We conclude with a reflection on the relationships between community Wi-Fi and other forms of community networking, as well as the policy challenges raised by community wireless Internet development.

NETWORKING WIRELESS TECHNOLOGIES

Wireless Internet technologies are often adopted by community and municipal groups as inexpensive means of extending broadband Internet to citizens. Wireless systems either use licensed parts of the radio spectrum (most often using the public safety frequencies at 4.9 GHz) or they transmit signals over the license-exempt portions of the radio spectrum at 2.4 GHz. Many devices, including garage door openers and commercial wireless equipment, use the latter portion of the spectrum. Other systems, including emergency services and specific data transfer services such as automated utility meter reading, operate on spectrum that is licensed for a particular use and often require specialized receivers for users. Open wireless, which operates on license-exempt radio spectrum, has a much lower signal strength than fixed wireless using licensed spectrum, and as the license-exempt band fills up, transmission speeds can diminish. However, open wireless has become increasingly popular as a last-mile solution for homes and neighbourhoods because there is no license fee for the radio spectrum and because all commercial systems use the same standard for wireless transmission; devices are thus easily interoperable. While there are numerous potential technical configurations for wireless Internet projects, municipal, and community projects tend to organize their networks on at least one of several potential network configurations: hotspots, either individually connected to the Internet or linked by a meshed network; hub-and-spoke systems that broadcast coverage to many devices; or dynamic mesh networks that configure network nodes as both senders and receivers of data. Meshed networks enable the sharing of one Internet connection amongst many distant nodes by routing the traffic around damage or interference. The choice to use one type of networking model over another depends upon network goals. While networks can serve local needs without connecting to the Internet (as commonly occurs with mesh networks), Internet connectivity also requires a consistent and reliable source of bandwidth. In hotspot models, this bandwidth is provided at each individual access point. In hub-and-spoke models the bandwidth (often a higher-throughput fibre connection) is located at the hub. In mesh networks, any node can connect to the Internet and share this connectivity across the whole network. The more mesh nodes in a network are connected to the Internet, the higher the average speed of connectivity over the network as a whole.

NETWORKING MODELS

Hotspots (Also Called Access Points). Hotspots are points at which broadband Internet signals are broadcast wirelessly to the immediate geographical area. Coverage normally extends out to a maximum three hundred meters from the source signal, although it can be more limited indoors. The community Wi-Fi groups Île Sans Fil and Wireless Toronto use hotspots to provide a simple way for local businesses and organizations to share bandwidth, and to display local art and encourage the development of local community content production. Each hotspot provides its own connection to the Internet.

Hub-and-Spoke Systems. In isolated areas, a single high-powered antenna can broadcast a signal from, for example, a hill to the homes in a valley below. Hub-and-spoke systems are often used in fixed wireless installations in which wireless is used to disseminate a signal in areas where fibre-optic cable cannot be laid due to geographic or economic limitations. Often hub-and-spoke systems distribute Internet signals using licensed spectrum between hubs connected to backhaul bandwidth and receivers equipped with specialized receivers. The municipal Fredericton Fred eZone uses a combination of hotspots and high-powered hub-and-spoke systems. The latter function best when the community can purchase and distribute adequate bandwidth and purchase the licenses often required to use the less cluttered proprietary spectrum.

Dynamic Mesh. Interconnected nodes in a neighbourhood share bandwidth drawn from one or more links to the Internet. Each of the nodes can communicate with other nodes as well as the Internet, providing the possibility for creating robust local area networks. Deploying mesh networks with Internet connectivity necessitates a certain number of individuals or organizations that are willing to share their Internet backbone. When mesh networks function well, communication between nodes is as important as communication with the Internet. Robust and flexible software for developing community mesh networks has been produced by a range of community and non-profit actors, including CUWin, the Champaign-Urbana, Illinois, community wireless network, GuiFi, a community network from Catalonia, and an international project begun by the founders of the Freifunk network in Berlin. Commercial providers such as Meraki also produce self-configuring mesh networking nodes. Canadian wireless projects make decisions about their network configurations based on their social and political goals, as well as the availability of Internet bandwidth (Meinrath 2004).

CANADIAN WIRELESS POLICY

Canada's spectrum policy is established by Industry Canada under the Radiocommunication Act and the Department of Industry Act. Domestic spectrum policy is set out in the Telecommunications Act and in coordination with other countries and international bodies. Canada has provided spectrum for wireless broadband in several frequency bands with plans to create additional spectrum. The 2500 MHz band is currently licensed for multipoint distribution system (MDS) and wireless Internet multipoint communication system (MCS) services. In the 2001 public consultation on opening the 3500 MHz band for fixed wireless access (FWA) and wireless communications services (WCS) in the 2300 MHz range, Industry Canada allowed that up to 200 MHz for FWA and 30 MHz for WCS could be opened in the 3500 MHz band.

Industry Canada (2005) undertook a review of the use of spectrum in the 3 to 30 GHz range; the May 2005 *Consultation on a Renewed Spectrum Policy Framework for Canada and Continued Advancements in Spectrum Management* contained a set of core objectives and policy guidelines for public consultation in modernizing Canada's spectrum program. Four broad themes for policy development were identified: (1) facilitating access to spectrum, (2) providing spectrum availability for priority requirements and societal needs, (3) improving the utilization of spectrum resources, and (4) delivering the

Canadian Spectrum Management Program. Industry Canada's intent was to also facilitate access to spectrum for licensed and license-exempt application, give priority to spectrum usage for national security and public safety needs, provide a degree of international harmonization, and allow for flexibility in the application of frequency allocations.

In the final report of Industry Canada's Telecommunications Policy Review Panel (TPRP), whose mandate was to review Canada's telecommunications policy and regulatory framework, the panel recommended that Industry Canada release additional spectrum so as to encourage new entrants and foster greater competition in the burgeoning wireless services markets, ostensibly as a mechanism to improve services to consumers and to lower prices. The TPRP also called for spectrum reform that would further entrench market forces toward a property rights model (Telecommunications Policy Review Panel 2006). Longford (2008) commenting on the politics of spectrum allocation and licensing in Canada and in the United States, argues that the processes have only "led to the concentration of spectrum in the hands of a few deep-pocketed firms," thus "threaten[ing] to place it further beyond the reach of Canada's citizens and communities. These and other developments constitute a regulatory clearing of the spectrum commons, an enclosure and expropriation of the public airwaves for private gain that ignores the interests of consumers and undermines public rights to the airwaves" (99). Spectrum auctions in Canada in 2004 and 2005 resulted in "the issue of over 800 licenses, 458 of which were won by Bell, Rogers, and Telus alone. Together, these three firms spent $56 million for spectrum licenses, over five times more than all 28 other license winners combined" (101). And, as Longford, Moll, and Shade note in chapter 21 of this volume, with the transition to DTV (digital television), the forthcoming 700 MHZ spectrum auction should prove to be an important site for reclaiming the spectrum commons.

Given these ongoing and future telecommunication reforms, several aspects of community wireless development require policy attention, particularly with regard to a possible reform of spectrum allocation policy. Most community wireless projects use the license-exempt section of the radio spectrum, at 2.4GHZ. As time passes and more and more devices use this section of the spectrum, interference will undoubtedly increase and data transfer will become more difficult. Policy-makers need to be aware that providing more unlicensed spectrum may not only provide more affordable last mile communications potential but could also expand the ability for community Wi-Fi groups to develop creative local applications. Policies that promote the opening of more unlicensed or license-exempt spectrum, or which help to prioritize signals sharing the currently license-exempt spectrum, would permit communities more options for serving their local communication needs, which could include static or meshed wireless networks. The unlicensed portion of radio spectrum is a major site of innovation, since community Wi-Fi groups and others can develop applications without paying for expensive proprietary licenses. Unlicensed spectrum leaves a space for citizen involvement in technology development.

MUNICIPAL WI-FI PROJECTS

Municipal wireless in Canada has expanded from demonstration projects such as the WirelessCity project, which created four free access zones in downtown Calgary in 2003. In 2004, Fredericton, a small city of 50,000 people, connected its Fred E-zone Wi-Fi hotspots located on city-owned property and in public spaces such as cafés, restaurants, and shopping malls to a municipally owned fibre network. The resulting network provides free Internet access to citizens and visitors. Supported by the Government of Saskatchewan and the province's post-secondary institutions, the Saskatchewan! Connected $1.3 million wireless network provides free basic Internet service outdoors and indoors on post-secondary campuses and in the downtown business districts in Regina, Saskatoon, Prince Albert, and Moose Jaw. In Toronto, Cogeco (formerly Toronto Hydro Telecom) sells subscriptions to its high-speed wireless network over the business district for $30 per month. These networks vary in terms of expected service level, cost, and coverage. They are similar to community networks in that they aim to connect localities, but the process of creating community engagement through technology is less important than the product of a relatively robust network that can be used by subscribers, residents, or visitors.

COMMUNITY WI-FI: THE FRONTIERS
OF COMMUNITY NETWORKING?

Community groups working with wireless Internet technologies have sprung up in cities across Canada since 2004. These groups developed either independently or from existing community networks, focusing on the relatively flexible nature of commercially available Wi-Fi technology—that is, the interoperability of devices operating in license-exempt spectrum. Open-source software enthusiasts are active in the community Wi-Fi movement, attracted by the challenge of developing new functionalities and expanding connectivity. Common to all community wireless groups is the desire to keep certain parts of the wireless spectrum unlicensed and to provide free and open possibilities for computers to connect with each other and with the Internet.

However, all community-based wireless groups are not created equal. The objectives and missions of these organizations vary, from providing a space for discussion of new technological developments by enthusiasts to creating a mesh network of Wi-Fi nodes to permit the development of an alternative "intranet" network, not necessarily connected to the Internet. Some groups dedicate themselves to opening hotspots, while others are concerned with the social and community aspects of wireless technology.

The best-known, earliest community wireless groups are Seattle Wireless, which started in 2000 (http://seattlewireless.net/); CUWin in Champaign-Urbana, Illinois, an initiative of the Urbana-Champaign Independent Media Centre, and now in hiatus; NYCWireless in New York City (http://www.nycwireless.net/); and the Freifunk meshed wireless projects that have expanded across Germany (http://start.freifunk.net/). Catalonia, in northern Spain, also has a very active community Wi-Fi movement (http://www.guifi.net). As Wi-Fi technology has become more widespread and simpler to operate, some community Wi-Fi groups such as Wireless London (made up of several distinct smaller groups), and Paris Sans-Fil have become inactive: their mandates of expanding Wi-Fi access having largely been fulfilled by commercial offerings. Others, such as GuiFi and the Djursland wireless network in rural Denmark, operate networks in areas of market failure. In well-served communications markets, community groups still in operation have moved away from their initial goal of primarily providing wireless Internet access toward broader community goals. For instance, CUWin released software that could easily be used in any context to create a municipal mesh network (see http://cuwireless.net/news); Île Sans Fil, Ottawa-Gatineau (OGWi-Fi), and the Zone d'Accès Public (ZAP) projects focus on providing access to community media and local information at their hotspots.

Similar to the first community networking experiments in the early 1990s (Schuler 1995), the interests of wireless groups depend on the interests and ideals of their mostly voluntary members. Sandvig (2005) argued that the primary missions of the first wave of North American and European wireless community groups did not necessarily offer significant challenges to dominant telecommunications policy or delivery mechanisms, depending on "accidental sharing." However, as wireless technology becomes more ubiquitous, and as private companies and municipalities develop high-level and potentially expensive wireless Internet services, wireless groups have also worked to develop a community focus that could permit the development of local content and civic participation.

Coming after more established North American Wi-Fi projects, Canadian wireless projects are considered to be the "second wave" of community wireless innovation. Aware of the achievements of more established groups in the United States and Europe through their participation in conferences and online forums, Canadian community wireless groups active in the early 2000s adopted goals addressing a range of issues beyond simple wireless access. These goals often evoke community, economic, or social development, facilitated by the process of constructing community Wi-Fi networks, or through the media, delivered using Wi-Fi hotspots as platforms. This suggests there are shared goals between community networks and community Wi-Fi. However, while current Canadian community networks share some characteristics with the previous generation of community networks, the current networks do not, as the early free-nets did, necessarily explicitly aim to address the digital divide or to promote local communities through the provision of locally produced community content. In fact, the relatively restrained hotspot models of the ZAP projects, which define home use as potential abuse, explicitly frame community Wi-Fi as a form of public connectivity, or possibly even public media.

All of Canada's community wireless groups attempt to respond to their specific local circumstance. At the same time, though, community wireless networks came about as a product of a specific socio-technical moment; in Canada, while computing and Internet access were becoming ubiquitous, government-funded Canadian public Internet access (as Moll and Fritz detail in chapter 3), was suffering from a withdrawal of public funding (see also Rideout and Reddick 2005).

Table 10.1 summarizes municipal and community wireless networking projects in Canada. Of these examples, the Fred-eZone and the Saskatchewan! Connected network come closest to establishing public infrastructure, since they use public funds to create freely accessible telecommunications services. Both projects occur in contexts in which governments have already invested in broadband connectivity. In Saskatchewan, the government-owned telecom operator, SaskTel, laid fibre throughout the 1990s that provides broadband access to residents of most large communities. The Community Network project extended broadband connectivity to remote communities via satellite and fixed wireless. Eighty-six percent of Saskatchewan residents now have access to broadband services, and the broadband network facilitates the distribution of wireless signals in urban centres.

In New Brunswick, a duopolistic broadband market compelled municipal leaders to set up their own non-profit company to become a non-dominant carrier. In 1999, the government invested in a municipal fibre-optic network backbone, and in 2001 added a wireless connection to the airport. A city-owned company, e-Novations, runs the fibre network and is licensed as a CRTC (Canadian Radio-television and Telecommunications Commission) non-dominant carrier. Local business and universities support its co-op model. Fredericton's project uses a variety of high-powered transmitters fixed to antennas, bridges, and other structures to broadcast strong Internet signals over the downtown business district, municipal parks, local arenas, hotels, Kings Place Mall, and the Fredericton Mall. While the project has stopped short of its original goal of providing Wi-Fi over all of Fredericton's business corridors, it has provided basic wireless signals to citizens and visiting business travellers. The Wi-Fi network is integrated into a business development strategy that hopes to brand Fredericton as an innovative knowledge hub within its region.

The municipal and provincial investment in connectivity in the E-zone and Saskatchewan! Connected projects can be considered illustrative examples of public broadband development. In terms of their public investment, they challenge regulations (Tapia and Ortiz 2006) that suggest that governments should not provide telecommunications services. Still, these networks provide neither home connectivity nor any speeds above "basic" Internet service appropriate for checking email or visiting non-multimedia web pages, and the Fredericton project provides "best effort" service that is designed with visiting business people in mind. Neither project explicitly aims to cover residential areas, although some parts of the Saskatchewan network cover areas where many university students live. However, three years after being launched, coverage in the city was found to be spotty, and the province now has no immediate goals to expand its coverage within the city, with their focus instead on connecting rural and remote regions (Hutton 2010). This restriction of the public networks may suggest that municipalities are not willing to directly compete with ISPs offering residential services. The difficulties experienced by Toronto's now-defunct Wireless Nomad testify to this: many subscribers were not willing to switch to a small Internet service provider, even if the price was lower than that offered by commercial operators and regardless of whether the subscription provided access to free Wi-Fi. (See chapter 12 in this volume.) However, in rural areas without other connectivity options, such as the Northern Ontario Lac Seul communities, the situation is different: community wireless networks provide access to the Internet that would otherwise not be available.

Dumais (2005) has suggested that municipalities could partner with community groups instead of public partners to provide wireless services, a public-community model that seems to be emerging in Québec. In 2007 Montréal's Île Sans Fil presented a proposal to the City of Montréal government for a public-community partnership model for creating and maintaining a network of publicly accessible hotspots. The municipal government would contribute funding for staff who would manage volunteers and low-cost equipment. The ZAP Sherbrooke project has recruited partners from the public and community sectors to act as hosts of hotspots, drawing organizational and financial support from the University of Sherbrooke and Bishop's University. Like the E-zone, these public/community partnerships

TABLE 10.1 Municipal and community wireless networking projects

Municipal WiFi networks	Technology	Network model
Fred-eZone (Fredericton, NB) http://www.fred-ezone.ca Fibre network initiated in 1999; Wi-Fi network initiated in 2003	IEEE 802.11g; 22 km city-owned fibre backbone, hub-and-spoke system fixed wireless to some areas, combined with hot zones	Municipally owned non-profit corporation (e-Novations), with basic access provided free in public areas
K-Net (Lac Seul First Nations) http://www.knet.ca Lac Seul communities own Wi-Fi network managed by non-profit K-Net network.	IEEE 802.11g technologies using unlicensed spectrum, combined with licensed spectrum at 3.5 GHz	Not-for-profit public infrastructure: community services have access to 3.5 GHz transmitters/receivers; unlicensed Wi-Fi provided to residents and businesses (line-of-sight and equipment required).
One Zone http://www.onezone.ca/ (Originally Toronto Hydro Telecom One Zone, http://www.thtelecom.ca/onezone)	IEEE 802.11g; Bel Air direct outdoor transmitters	$29.00 + taxes/monthly subscription fee for Wi-Fi services. $9.99/day for daily services, $4.99/hour for hourly service. iPass and Boingo subscribers can access One Zone.
Saskatchewan! Connected (Saskatoon, Regina, Prince Albert, Moose Jaw) http://www.ito.gov.sk.ca/wireless-Internet/ Initiated in 2007	Cisco outdoor wireless mesh	Provincially financed basic public Internet connectivity working indoors and outdoors
Wireless City (Calgary) http://www.witec.ca/wireless/bins/index.asp	IEEE 802.11b; Cisco access points; multiple WISPs connected in access zones, backhauled by Wi-LAN, network management	Demonstration project to raise profile of local technology development
BCWireless http://www.bcwireless.net/ Initiated in 2001. Not-for-profit grassroots organization that helps BC communities set up local Wi-Fi networks	IEEE 802.11b; experiments in extending range and power of signal, new work on hotspots	Bandwidth sharing within group; mesh networking experiments; policy advocacy

Partners/funders	Mission	Uses/users	Notes
City of Fredericton Team Fredericton Cisco Systems Motorola 3D Datacomm Eastern Wireless Several other local vendors	To create a municipal area network (MAN) and provide free wireless access in public places (city-owned property and downtown core)	Support forums suggest that users are pleased but would like this municipal network to provide stable home connectivity.	Bandwidth draws on public fibre network whose core tenant is the City of Fredericton. Excess bandwidth shared through Wi-Fi network.
Industry Canada FedNor Tbaytel (Thunder Bay) K-Net services Ownership by the local community	To provide a shared network of high-quality bandwidth for the First Nations organizations interested in being connected to broadband services	Video conference units provided in band offices; unlicensed Wi-Fi used for email and chat by residents	Equipment in band offices is provided by FedNor; individuals must purchase their own Wi-Fi receivers; public access centre available
A project first mounted by Toronto Hydro Telecom, a subsidiary of Toronto Hydro, which owns a 450 km fibre optic network. Billing and authentication provided by Siemens Canada. In 2008 Toronto Hydro Telecom was bought out by Cogeco Cable Inc. and now operates as Cogeco Data Services.	Claims to be the highest-speed wireless network in North America	Covers downtown business district with outdoor coverage; indoor home or office connectivity possible with use of router to amplify signal	
University of Regina University of Saskatchewan SIAST (Saskatchewan Institute of Applied Science and Technology) SaskTel	To provide basic Internet connectivity in downtowns and on university campuses	Network covers downtowns and post-secondary campuses in four cities	Built as a response to the 2007 Youth Summit, where youth described connectivity as important
Cisco Systems Fringe Solutions Inc. Guest-tek Wi-LAN Inc. City of Calgary W. R. Castell Central Library Calgary Parking Authority NetWireless TELUS Mobility	To raise the profile of Calgary and identify Calgary as a world technology leader	Limited to one free hour per person per day	Initiated as a demonstration project in 2003 and now a project of WiTec Alberta, an industry association focusing on Alberta wireless and telecom industries
Equipment donated by partners; some tests done in partnership with Environment Canada	To promote free networking using wireless technology	Mesh nodes do not have many users; new community wireless project, Free the Net, hopes to be "less geeky"	

TABLE 10.1 (cont'd)

Municipal WiFi networks	Technology	Network model
Free the Net (Vancouver) http://www.freethenet.ca Initiated in 2006 and run as a legal co-op	Meraki mesh nodes	Individuals attach Meraki nodes to their home wireless connection, sharing some bandwidth to passersby or over the mesh network. $5/month for membership in VONIC (Vancouver Open Network Initiatives Cooperative)
Île Sans Fil www.ilesansfil.org Initiated in 2003	IEEE 802.11b and g; WiFiDog authentication software installed on on commercial equipment	Cafés and other public spaces share their Internet bandwidth with clients
Ottawa-Gatineau WiFi http://ogwifi.ca Initiated in 2005	IEEE 802.11b; WiFiDog	Hotspot model with bandwidth donated by participants
Wireless Toronto http://wirelesstoronto.ca/ Initiated in 2005 as a not-for-profit community group	Linksys wireless router	Parks and large public spaces covered with Wi-Fi drawing on donated bandwidth
Wireless Nomad http://www.wirelessnomad.com/ Initiated in 2005; in 2008 turned its DSL connections over to small private ISP TekSavvy; all Wi-Fi nodes have been shut down	IEEE 802.11b; modified Linksys routers running Chillispot authentication server, open VPN	Non-profit cooperative ISP that required its members to share Wi-Fi; provided low-bandwidth Wi-Fi access free at subscriber locations and from one antenna location
ZAP Québec (Zone d'Accès Public) (Québec City) http://www.zapquebec.org	IEEE 802.11b; modified Linksys routers, WiFiDog software	Hotspot hosts share bandwidth
ZAP Sherbrooke www.zapsherbrooke.org	IEEE 802.11b; modified Linksys routers, WiFiDog software	Hotspots hosted by universities, businesses, and community organizations

Partners/funders	Mission	Uses/users	Notes
Equipment purchased by participants, depending on specific needs for routers or antennas.	To extend free wireless Internet across downtown Vancouver.	Individual users with individual hotspots	Extension of Meraki-instigated project Free the Net in California
Mobile Digital Commons Network (Heritage Canada), téliPhone (VoIP telephone company), Canada Council for the Arts (through Terminus1525); current partners include La Société des arts technologiques (SAT), Communautique, Taste of Blue, Mikimya.com, Digital Days.	To provide wireless Internet access in public spaces and create community through unique applications		Developed location-based social software application and custom portal page for each hotspot, managed through WiFiDog. Currently developing a new authorization server system.
Received some funding through Terminus1525	To build a community communication infrastructure to bridge the public and private spaces of our cities		
Kijiji online classifieds Toronto Public Space Terminus1525	To bring no-fee Internet access to Toronto	Cafés, restaurants, public markets, cooperative work spaces	Focus on cultural aspects of connectivity
Co-operatively funded by its founders	To allow subscribers to control their own Internet access and to connect and empower the community for a fair price	Primarily home subscribers paying $36.95 per month; free accounts were limited	Was a co-op ISP that required sharing bandwidth. One hundred subscriber locations, most in private homes. Little indication of uses.
Canadian Heritage, through the Terminus1525 project. Current partners include Ville de Québec, Québec government, Ici pour vous, Forum jeunesse	To develop, install, and maintain free wireless hotspots as a means of making Québec a dynamic and pleasant city		
Created through Pôle Universitaire Léonard de Vinci; partners include universities, chamber of commerce, Québec economic development	To promote free wireless Internet access points	140 hotspots	

(discussed in more detail later in this chapter) provide Internet access in publicly accessible places, not in homes or offices. The terms and conditions of ZAP Sherbrooke and Île Sans Fil state that the service is meant to be "mobile and temporary" and sustained use is considered to be abuse. As more of these public-community partnerships are proposed, now is an appropriate time to reflect on the nature of explicitly *community* wireless networking initiatives in comparison to municipal networks. This requires thinking about community wireless networking as a form of community network.

TOWARD SUSTAINABLE MODELS FOR COMMUNITY AND MUNICIPAL WI-FI

When community Wi-Fi initiatives first transpired, Canada's funding initiatives were increasingly designed to promote the development of new initiatives in the social economy: the entrepreneurial, not-for-profit sector whose objectives include enhancing the social, economic, and environmental conditions of communities. The social economy, which received policy attention in the February 2004 Speech from the Throne (Canada 2004), when the Liberal Party's Paul Martin was prime minister, aimed to create economically viable businesses that provided important social services; for example, day care services were considered social economy enterprises. The emergence of public-community models that sought to develop community infrastructure and community media could perhaps be considered a form of social economy of media and communications.

Québec networks have been able to continue the social economy model via hybrid community partnerships, a potentially salient example of a model for sustainability. In Québec, the new institutional form of the public community partnership has been successfully adopted as a means of easily and inexpensively developing local communications infrastructure. As discussed in Tapia, Powell, and Ortiz (2009), between 2006 and 2008, Québec City, Sherbrooke, Drummondville, and the Montérégie region of Québec all began Wi-Fi projects, adopting a model similar to that of ISF but more broadly directed at hotspots sponsored by businesses and community organizations. In Québec City, the local Wi-Fi project was named Zone d'Accès Public, or ZAP, helping its volunteer founders to attract funding from government and other sources. In Sherbrooke, the Pôle Universitaire, a strategic alliance between the area's postsecondary institutions, applied for funding from Innovation et Exportation du Québec, and received $70,000 to build a network of 150 hotspots that was completed in January 2008. The project began with hotspots at universities and then expanded to commercial properties through a partnership with the Chamber of Commerce, and the final pillar of development aims to connect more hotspots within the community sector. The project adopted ISF's hardware and developed the ZAP brand in the local context. ZAP Sherbrooke has no employees. Volunteers cold call businesses and distribute promotional materials, while local companies install and maintain the network. More than one third of ZAP sites are in universities, libraries, or community centres where connectivity is supported by the City of Sherbrooke, and other strategic alliances integrate Wi-Fi into other social service contexts. Bruno Lacasse, one of the members of the Pôle Universitaire in Sherbrooke, remarks that the ZAP model for providing "secondary" Internet access is "the best of both worlds" because it provides inexpensive Wi-Fi to universities and community organizations and establishes a non-profit model that could become the basis for a future co-operative telecommunications operator managed by the municipal government and the Pôle Universitaire.

Institutional support for community-based networks has been extended to other Québec networks, which have formed a provincial alliance of community networks. New networks have opened in the centre of the Québec region, also based on the ZAP model, and a volunteer group has formed in the Bas-St-Laurent region. OGWi-Fi, the Ottawa network, continues to form part of the alliance as well. Many of the Québec projects have been funded by the provincial government's APSI program, "assistance au passage à la société de l'information." This fund supports projects that open up access to the Internet or who facilitate integration into the information society. In particular, the funding supports tangible strategies for achieving this integration and for providing alternate means of accessing e-government services.

Local funding from electoral councils, youth participation strategies, and local economic development authorities also support community networking efforts, particularly the mobile broadband hotspot developed in Québec City for use outdoors during the summer festival season.

The more stable funding situation for the Québec organizations has allowed them to better work together. After several years of using the same hotspot authentication software, the alliance members have invested in developing new software from scratch, leaving behind the prosaically named Wi-FiDog to invest in software that is better suited to managing authentication and bandwidth management in higher-traffic contexts.

In Toronto, Wireless Toronto has continued to focus on the intersection of art, technology, and space. In 2009 it hosted an expansion of the Insite local art project, which saw new works commissioned specifically for presentation at Wi-Fi hotspots. The project was funded by the Canada Council for the Arts.

CONCLUSION

Returning again to Sandvig's questions regarding infrastructure, in this chapter we have sought to elucidate how Canadian Wi-Fi projects are situated within the ecology of Internet access, how community Wi-Fi projects relate to other forms of community networking and municipal initiatives, and their implication in telecommunication policy shifts. Now we would like to conclude by addressing Sandvig's final questions about the prospects for community Wi-Fi initiatives and the factors that are likely to be important for their future.

Although community Wi-Fi projects share many of the same goals as their predecessors in the guise of "free-nets," and groups such as ISF were initially fuelled by the exuberant energy of committed volunteers, the sustainability of these initiatives is fraught. Users of public Wi-Fi are likely to be opportunistic or indeed to be using mobile devices that they carry with the expectation of free Wi-Fi connectivity. Providing citizens who are not part of this elite group of technology users may require more partnerships, education, and support. Synergies with municipalities might be a powerful incentive to develop diverse community Wi-Fi initiatives, allowing content to go beyond what is provided by municipal services.

Fuentes-Bautista and Inagaki (2006), in their study on the multiple dynamics and stakeholders configuring Wi-Fi access in Austin, Texas, pointed out "wireless divides" wherein service is limited in areas where ethnic minority and low-income citizens live: "Austin's public Wi-Fi initiatives as a whole have failed so far to turn the opportunity provided by the unlicensed spectrum into a program attending to the issue of digital inequalities in the city" (33). They thus challenge Wi-Fi providers, local governments, and policy makers to attend to creative efforts to "deliver the promise of universal broadband access through the unlicensed spectrum" (33). These challenges apply equally to Canadian Wi-Fi projects, especially in urban areas. The adoption of certain aspects of the Île Sans Fil model by the ZAP networks in Québec indicates that the concept of the "social partnership" for providing Internet hotspots can be a viable model for hotspot management. Hotspot companies target business customers; cafés and community centres want to offer Wi-Fi without getting too concerned about technical management. The ISF/ZAP model provides a way to use volunteers as well as public and private partners to facilitate this service. However, this model draws from existing broadband subscriptions, and thus does not provide a true competitor to telecommunications companies. Nor does it recognize the public utility nature of Wi-Fi. Rick Bunt, chief information officer at the University of Saskatchewan, who runs Saskatchewan! Connected, has commented that Wi-Fi needs to be treated as a public good which requires constant attention to fix technical slippages: "With roads, if people find potholes the Highways department will come and fix them, so if people find a hole in the coverage a repair man needs to be sent out" (quoted in Hutton 2010).

Middleton and Crow (2008), in their research on three Wi-Fi communities in Canada—ISF, Fred-eZone, and Lac Seul—argue that the model of a public information utility is a useful lens for examination. Public information utilities enable local communities through prioritizing local content, information, and resources. Successful sustainability measures include a core group of dedicated volunteers and community champions ensuring user integration across the network. Challenges for the continued innovation of community Wi-Fi applications identified by Middleton and Crow include resilient quality of service, a policy framework for license-exempt spectrum, and integration into the now increasingly pervasive mobile media infrastructure.

Likewise, Tapia, Powell, and Ortiz (2009) argue that hybrid public networks, such as the Québec models discussed above, can promote sustainability for community and municipal Wi-Fi. They recommend that policy be developed

> to design, build, and deploy broadband service as reliable as the other common utilities, such as water, power, and the telephone, with clear performance standards established. The policy should also encourage these hybrids to build and deploy broadband service coverage, which would include every household, business, organization, public space, and public transit corridor in the communities' coverage area. This policy should also encourage these hybrids to charge for the broadband service prices that are affordable, nondiscriminatory, and universally available in order to ensure universal access for all. (370)

Canadian municipalities should also still monitor the consequences of laws being passed in some US jurisdictions that forbid public-community partnerships. These laws are based on a presupposition that government-supported, universal access to information infrastructure is inherently dangerous for competitive telecom development. An adoption of this type of law in Canada would contradict a policy position that telecommunications are a public good and would undermine the ongoing developments of public-community partnerships.

Meanwhile, continued research needs to be undertaken to investigate the developing community wireless experience in Canada (see, for instance, the work of Cho [2008] on Wireless Toronto, and the work of Middleton and the Community Wireless Infrastructure Research Project [2008]) and its integration into the mobile media infrastructure. If, over time, wireless devices become more affordable and portable, will the uses of community-based wireless services change? Or will the development of this technology follow that of Canada's original community networks? We could do well to heed the advice of Meinrath (2005, 236) who admonishes us to become technically savvy and engaged with these technologies: "The challenge then is for an engaged public to build these cost-effective alternatives and become active agents in determining the future of the wireless telecommunication infrastructure."

REFERENCES

Benkler, Yochai. 2010. *Next generation connectivity: A review of broadband Internet transitions and policy from around the world*. Final report, February. Cambridge, MA: Berkman Center for Internet and Society, Harvard University. http://cyber.law.harvard.edu/pubrelease/broadband/.

Canada. Privy Council Office. 2004. Speech from the Throne to open the third session of the 37th Parliament of Canada. 2 February. http://www.pco-bcp.gc.ca/index.asp?lang=eng&page=information&sub=publications&doc=aarchives/sft-ddt/2004_1-eng.htm.

Cho, Hanna Hye-Na. 2008. Towards place-peer community and civic bandwidth: A case study in community wireless networking. *Journal of Community Informatics* 4(1). http://www.ci-journal.net/index.php/ciej/article/view/428/396.

Dumais, Michel. 2005. Technologie: Le boulevard St-Laurent à l'heure du sans-fil. *Le Devoir*, 31 January. http://www.ledevoir.com/societe/science-et-technologie/73763/technologie-le-boulevard-saint-laurent-a-l-heure-du-sans-fil.

Fuentes-Bautista, Martha, and Nobuya Inagaki. 2006. Reconfiguring public Internet access in Austin, TX: Wi-Fi's promise and broadband divides. *Government Information Quarterly* 23(2): 404–34.

Hutton, David. 2010. Holes in city's Wi-Fi blanket. *The Star Phoenix*, (Saskatoon), 22 April.

Industry Canada. 2005. Consultation on a renewed spectrum policy framework for Canada and continued advancements in spectrum management. Gazette Notice DGTP-001-05. May. http://www.ic.gc.ca/eic/site/smt-gst.nsf/eng/sf08383.html.

Longford, Graham. 2008. Spectrum matters: Clearing and reclaiming the spectrum commons. In *For sale to the highest bidder: Telecom policy in Canada*, ed. Marita Moll and Leslie Regan Shade, 95–107. Ottawa: Canadian Centre for Policy Alternatives.

Meinrath, Sascha. 2004. The Champaign-Urbana Community Wireless Network. *Community Technology Review* (Winter), http://comtechreview.org/winter-2004-2005/000259.html.

———. 2005. Wirelessing the world: The battle over (community) wireless networks. In *The future of the media: Resistance and reform in the 21st century*, ed. Robert McChesney, Russell Newman, and Ben Scott, 219–42. New York: Seven Stories Press.

Middleton, Catherine, and the Community Wireless Infrastructure Research Project (CWIRP). 2008. *ICT infrastructure as public infrastructure: Connecting communities to the knowledge-based economy and society*. Final report, October http://www.cwirp.ca/files/CWIRP_Final_report.pdf.

Middleton, Catherine, and Barbara Crow. 2008. Building Wi-Fi networks for communities: Three Canadian cases. *Canadian Journal of Communication* 33(3): 419–41.

OECD. 2007. OECD Broadband Portal. http://www.oecd.org/sti/ict/broadband.

Rideout, Vanda N., and Andrew J. Reddick. 2005. Sustaining community access to technology: Who should pay and why. *Journal of Community Informatics* 1(2), Special Issue: Sustainability and Community ICTs. http://www.ci-journal.net/index.php/ciej/article/viewArticle/202.

Sandvig, Christian. 2005. An initial assessment of cooperative action in Wi-Fi networking. *Telecommunications Policy* 28(7–8): 579–602.

Schuler, Douglas. 1995. *New community networks: Wired for change*. Reading, MA: Addison-Wesley.

Tapia, Andrea H., and Julio Angel Ortiz. 2006. Municipal responses to state-level broadband policy. Paper presented at 34th Annual Telecommunications Policy Research Conference on Communication, Information, and Internet Policy, Arlington, Virginia, USA, 28 September–1 October.

Tapia, Andrea H., Alison Powell, and Julio Angel Ortiz. 2009. Reforming policy to promote local broadband networks. *Journal of Communicative Inquiry* 33(4): 354–75.

Telecommunications Policy Review Panel. 2006. *Telecommunications Policy Review Panel Final Report, 2006* (March). Ottawa: Minister of Industry. http://www.ic.gc.ca/eic/site/smt-gst.nsf/vwapj/tprp-final-report-2006.pdf/$FILE/tprp-final-report-2006.pdf.

11 WI-FI PUBLICS Defining Community and Technology at Montréal's Île Sans Fil

Alison Powell

In August 2004, I walked into an organic, vegetarian co-op bar to meet Montréal's community Wi-Fi activists, a group known as Île Sans Fil (ISF), or "wireless island." Over pitchers of beer, they told me about their volunteer technology project: they were setting up free wireless connections to the Internet in parks and cafés, funded by a small arts grant. The young men and women I met that night talked about covering the city with Wi-Fi to create an alternative communications infrastructure that anyone could use to access the Internet, which would also provide platforms for new media art projects. They felt that this infrastructure could connect local community organizations to one another, allowing them to exchange information without having to pay for expensive, commercialized Internet services. With intelligence and passion, they described how the technical flexibility of Wi-Fi would make it possible to create such a community-based infrastructure. They debated ways to organize among themselves to solve the technical and political challenges of this project as a "community" rather than a large hierarchical organization.

Three years later, some of the people I met that night voted to restructure their organization in order to create a more conventional non-profit administration structure, complete with a board of directors charged with making most financial and strategic decisions. In March 2007, I sat in an oak and leather chair in the marble meeting room of the Montréal city hall and listened to the president of this council present a partnership project with the city of Montréal. The evolution of this Wi-Fi group suggests an important shift in the representation and impact of "community Wi-Fi" projects, as wireless Internet becomes viewed as a public service. What can the history of ISF indicate about the relationship between community networks (CNs) and public networks?

In this chapter, I take a more theoretical perspective on the ISF case, drawing out the tensions between the "geek" community created through participation in the ISF project and the broader Montréal community that would be served by a partnership with city hall. It specifically considers how "Wi-Fi geeks" became engaged in their community through the ISF project. I then consider the tensions that emerged along the path leading from the bar to the city hall. I finish with an assessment of the future role for initiatives such as ISF.

ACADEMIC ASSESSMENTS OF WI-FI PROJECTS

When I walked into the bar in 2004, theorists and proponents of Wi-Fi had been describing Wi-Fi as a disruptive technology associated with decentralized, local projects undertaken by small-scale organizations: neighbourhoods, community organizations, and municipal governments (Bar and Galperin 2004). Like first interpretations of the Internet (Abbate 1999), cable television system (de Sola Pool 1977), and radio (Douglas 1987; Haring 2006), this theorization of Wi-Fi focused on the technology's flexibility, interoperability, and the fact that many innovative experiments with Wi-Fi were emerging from community groups such as ISF. The first assessments of these projects (Auray, Charbit, and Fernandez 2003; Sandvig 2004) focused on the explicitly technical focus of these first Wi-Fi communities and argued that perhaps Wi-Fi was a particularly appropriate technology for small-scale, local endeavours. In the intervening years, activists, theorists, technologists, and the mass media have begun to represent Wi-Fi and other wireless technologies as means of providing Internet connectivity cheaply to broad areas. As the discussion in chapter 10 of this volume demonstrates, municipal Wi-Fi initiatives have boomed and busted across Canada and the United States. In this chapter I take a different perspective, asking not how to maintain public Wi-Fi but what Wi-Fi projects might tell us about the relationship between community and technology.

FRAMING WI-FI COMMUNITIES

I argue here that local community Wi-Fi experiments are attempts to reestablish the community as an appropriate site for political and social action. As is the case for immigrant professionals gaining skills at community networking (CN) sites (see chapter 9) or free and open source software advocates working with community organizations (see chapter 5), the community emerges in unexpected ways and in new kinds of social sites. In community Wi-Fi, *community* refers both to the members of the community group who modify and develop the Wi-Fi technology, as well as to the local geographic community around them. Because building Wi-Fi networks implies a process of debate and the creation of a shared space—the same kind of shared space that local democracy creates—we can refer to both of these communities as publics. In contrast to chapter 10, which focuses on the organizational innovations produced by ISF and their impact on the delivery of Wi-Fi in Canada, and chapter 6, which reflects on the gendered elements of voluntary labour at ISF, in this chapter I concentrate on the theoretical terrain of this project. Specifically, I investigate the extent to which the ISF project (and, by extension, other non-formal community informatics projects) establishes more robustly public information and communication spaces.

METHODS: TECHNOLOGY AS SOCIAL AND TECHNICAL

This chapter is based on an ethnography of the ISF project conducted between August 2004 and May 2007. Drawing from methodological approaches in participatory action research (PAR) (see Lennie and Hearn 1999; Pinkett 2003), my research strategy included observation of administrative council meetings, observation of and participation in general meetings, monitoring of the group's mailing list, and other types of active participation, including the supervision of an undergraduate intern and participation in several conference presentations along with other members of ISF. Throughout, I produced daily and weekly field notes, research reports, interview transcripts, and a media file. Fifteen formal interviews with core members of ISF were conducted, as well as numerous informal interviews. In addition, I interviewed ISF's core collaborators, including one of the city councillors involved in the partnership bid.

In this context, my research activities certainly contributed to the construction, definition, and promotion of ISF. I consistently presented research results to ISF general meetings, and distributed reports and articles produced for general readers to group members. For a period of two years I maintained this participatory stance, conducting regular meetings with core group members, especially Michael Lenczner, who had originally invited me to work with ISF. These privileged informants provided their perspective on the organization of the group, its technical choices, and their sense of its trajectory. I interviewed these core members several times over the two years of participatory research, and again one year later as fieldwork concluded. During the period of participatory research I was offered but declined a position on the board of the organization, although I did attempt to contribute as much expertise as possible to describing the group's activities in a manner that would assist ISF in obtaining funding or developing a sustainable structure.

The main differences between the methodology described in this chapter and classical ethnography as described by Hammersley and Atkinson (1995) are the participatory element and the inclusion of the Wi-Fi technology itself as part of the object of study. The participatory nature of my fieldwork required a reflexive engagement with the structures, processes, and consequences that I observed and influenced (for more on the nature of this engagement, see chapter 6). The research concentrated not only on the self-organizing social structures of the ISF project, but also on the potential of the group's wireless Internet technology to create an alternative form of community media. Thus, the technology's structure and materiality were also important. Drawing from actor-network theory as outlined by Latour (2005), I also paid attention to the role the wireless technologies themselves played in defining "community" or "public" Wi-Fi.

FROM COMMUNITY TO PUBLIC

Mackenzie (2005, 207) writes: "The constant appearance of new gadgets, devices, and practices that modify, alter, or hybridize Wi-Fi suggests that hopes for other forms of sociality and openness associated with communication technology still persist. That hopefulness is conditioned by the recent history of new media, particularly by a consciousness of the almost total commercial ownership and control of Internet and communications infrastructure." In a turn away from the globally scaled visions of the Internet as a democratic public sphere (Papacharissi 2002), the claims for the success of Wi-Fi are made primarily with reference to the local scale. The membership and values of these groups create a community—or perhaps even a public—in and of itself.

Both Taylor (2002) and Warner (2002) define a public as a social imaginary constituted through its discourse about itself. That is, a public is formed by its deliberations about ideas of shared interest, particularly those that are also concerned with some broader social good. Taylor (2002) claims that the precondition of a public is a "social imaginary" that includes the "ways in which people imagine their social existence, how they fit together with others, how things go on between them and their fellows, the expectations that are normally met, and the deeper normative notions and images that underlie these expectations" (Taylor 2002, 106). When these expectations and normative notions are constructed through discourse that is reproduced and circulated among people, a public forms. I argue that there are at least two publics invoked by the imagination of community Wi-Fi in Montréal: one, a "geek public" that volunteers aspire to become part of, and another, a "community public," whose existence helps to define the purpose of community Wi-Fi endeavours.

COMMUNITY WI-FI IN MONTRÉAL: ÎLE SANS FIL'S ACTIVITIES

Île Sans Fil helped to define and develop a set of discourses and practices (technical, organizational, and symbolic) that define community Wi-Fi. Its approach has influenced discussions on wireless applications for local communities in the national and international context. The original vision of ISF was to "use new technology, especially wireless technology, to empower individuals and to foster a sense of community."[1] This mission statement established normative expectations that community could—and should—be created through technology.

During the course of my fieldwork, ISF members undertook two main technical activities: they installed Wi-Fi hotspots and built software, and they formed partnerships with other individuals and groups. Installing hotspots was initially a response to a feeling among ISF members that Montréal did not have enough free Wi-Fi. Hotspots were (and are) located in places open to the public, though not, strictly speaking, always public places: parks, cafés, bars, restaurants, and artist and community centres. While some hotspots have been sponsored by business development associations, most have been installed by volunteers in places that they themselves visited. The group's meetings are held every two weeks at one of the hotspots, where group members discuss priorities, plan software development, order food and drinks, and access the ISF network using their laptops and PDA devices.

ISF members also developed WiFiDog, an open-source software program that transforms off-the-shelf Wi-Fi modems into nodes in the group's network that display a unique opening page (the portal page). Members of ISF instigated this project in 2003. The software was meant to provide a unique media environment for each of the group's hotspots. Each modem equipped with this software connects users to a central server, where their access is authenticated, and displays a portal page containing specific content related to the location. The portal page is meant to host local news, artwork, and community content, and to deliver social networking tools that will contribute to the culture of the hotspot. Its visual identity has been a source of intense debate within ISF, with the results of this debate played out in a series of different portal page designs.

In 2005, ISF developed a social software application for WiFiDog, as well as an associated multimedia distribution project, Hub des Artistes Locaux, that hoped to establish Wi-Fi hotspots as unique social and cultural spaces.[2] This social software was one in a series of projects that attempted to use

Wi-Fi hotspots as community media sites. Inspired by a volunteer who had experience as a new media curator, ISF launched a series of interventions on the portal page: first, a series of curated location-specific art projects, then a distribution of emerging Canadian artists funded by Heritage Canada's Terminus1525 program, and finally an aggregation of political information in the weeks leading up to the Québec provincial election. Some ISF members interviewed during my fieldwork saw these projects as their real contribution to community Wi-Fi—interventions in and explorations of using technology to achieve social goals. These members have always envisioned Wi-Fi as providing another way to be in a place with other people.

ISF also created partnerships with universities, research groups, and other community organizations. In addition to my own involvement through the CRACIN project, ISF partnered with the Mobile Digital Commons Network, which funded the development of ISF's first fifteen hotspots. ISF subsequently won funding from Heritage Canada for the Terminus1525 project. In exchange for Wi-Fi installations, the group has office space at Centre St-Pierre, a host site for community and religious organizations. Its relationships with established CN organizations such as Communautique have been more tenuous: although ISF was recognized by Communautique as a winner of the Prix d'Innovation Sociale in 2005, its official partnerships with Communautique have been few. ISF provides Wi-Fi in Communautique's offices, and Communautique's director general was on ISF's board of directors in 2009. Notwithstanding these external links with other organizations, for many ISF volunteers meeting every two weeks and discussing Wi-Fi technology and its social impact has provided the most significant social value. For some, it has provided a way of feeling part of a larger process, one that draws from and valorizes technical skills. One ISF group member wrote on the group's mailing list: "I'm very happy at how Wireless Internet has taken me away from my indoor computer to the outside world. Today I meet many people, discuss how this technology can help communities, develop new potentials for people" (list posting February 2005).

GEEKS: TECHNICAL EXPERTS WITH SOCIAL STATUS

The volunteer quoted above expressed how being part of ISF provided him with an identity, made him part of something. As Dechief notes in chapter 9, volunteering provides a means of defining one's identity as part of a community. Volunteers at ISF are students, professionals, or retirees. Since 2003, there have been over a hundred volunteers, some involved for months, others for years. They express different kinds of interest in Wi-Fi. For some, it is a medium for artistic interventions reflecting on nomadic work and everyday mobility; for others it is a practical service lacking in Montréal; for still others it can act as a means of engaging citizens in the life of their local community. This range of interests made ISF a dynamic, if chaotic, organization throughout the period of my fieldwork, provoking intense debates about the relative importance of software development, network expansion, or development of art and community context.

Yet all volunteers, regardless of their interest in Wi-Fi, described their involvement in ISF with relation to the term *geek*. Kelty defines geeks as "technically competent individuals concerned with and engaged in defining, developing, and debating the technical and legal structures of the Internet and other computer networks" (Kelty 2005, 185). Volunteers at ISF all seemed to be aspiring to achieve the status of "geek," a status signifying a technical expert with some social influence. One female ISF member, whom I interviewed in 2005, described herself as "lacking any geeky skills" before outlining the contribution she hoped to make in using Wi-Fi hotspots as diffusion sites for artistic content. Within the context of a volunteer organization developing a new technology with potentially broad social implications, geeks are imagined as playing an influential role. Becoming a Wi-Fi geek means developing this identity and the social capital that accompanies it. The development of a geek public at ISF created not only a set of debates about Wi-Fi technology and the construction of new Wi-Fi tools, but also led to collaborations between artists and members of community organizations, and to political lobbying and other forms of civic engagement.[3] These collaborations invoke another kind of public: a "community public" broader than the expert group of geeks.

Kelty (2005) calls geeks a "recursive public" because they are concerned with the production of their own means of communication and self-definition. This includes not only talking and writing about the Internet, as Warner's (2002) definition of *public* implies, but also "hacking, coding, and compiling" (Kelty 2005, 203) the technical platform upon which geeks' shared engagement depends. Wi-Fi geeks hack hardware and software in an attempt to change the way that Wi-Fi operates, so that the technology can become open. This hacking implies talk, collaboration, and modification of hardware and software. While it serves to reinforce the recursive geek public, its stated goal is to expand access to Wi-Fi and promote its use.

DEFINING AND BUILDING WI-FI PUBLIC SPHERES

When they get together to talk about and build networks, Wi-Fi geeks are participating in the construction of their own public sphere of communication. Utopian public spheres proliferate in physical or mediated spaces, from Habermas's (1989) ideal public sphere, based in the bourgeois café (but inaccessible to women or to the poor [Fraser 1992]) to Dewey's (1964) newspaper containing the perfect information that would inspire democratic communication. As Mosco (2004) argues, the Internet has also represented the promise of a public sphere, one that could transcend a declining urban public space no longer capable of acting as a democratic public sphere. Community Wi-Fi promises this transcendence through the distribution of free Wi-Fi across the city to the community public. The imagined means to achieving this alternative infrastructure and a more democratic community public is through the creation of a geek public of experts motivated by progressive social values.

These two imagined purposes—to create a space for communication and debate between experts, and to extend a communication infrastructure to a more generalized public—capture one of the rhetorical and practical tensions between different interpretations of community in Wi-Fi projects. When I posed the question, *Who is community Wi-Fi for?* to ISF volunteers during interviews conducted in November 2005 and February 2006, I received a variety of answers: "For us, for people like us," "For community organizations," "For artists," "For everyone." Geeks working on community Wi-Fi projects presume that increased access to the Internet is desirable, not just for them, but for everyone, and they often first imagine themselves as "everyone"—thus the first hotspots established in locations where volunteers already visited. Their "building, coding, and compiling" (Kelty 2005) is intended not only for the benefit of their recursive public, but also for a greater Internet-enabled public in Montréal. How are these balanced? What are their impacts?

WI-FI COMMUNITIES AS PUBLICS

The tensions between recursive geek publics and community publics have been thoroughly discussed in previous work on community Wi-Fi. Sandvig (2004) argued that the first wave of European and American community Wi-Fi projects, begun around 2000, did not offer real policy or technical challenges to the structure or function of the Internet. Subsequently, Wi-Fi technology has become more ubiquitous and commercialized, and a second wave of Wi-Fi communities (sometimes called community wireless networks, or CWNs), described by Meinrath (2005), Powell and Shade (2006), and Cho (2006), developed a discourse and practice of community Wi-Fi. These projects later included a contextualization and politicization of Wi-Fi as an open network built by and for citizens. Many Wi-Fi communities were initially organized around the idea that they could provide an infrastructure alternative to that of the increasingly commercialized Internet: their design of independent meshed networks enabled the sharing of community and neighbourly information.[4] These projects, common to many of the second-wave CWNs, are similar to the original community networking (CN) projects (Schuler 1996) that envisioned computer networking as a platform for reinforcing local communities.

Like CNs, current community Wi-Fi projects link social goals to what have generally been considered inward-looking technical tasks. Some of the normative themes that O'Neil (2002, 79–82) describes as central to the CN movement—(1) "strong" democracy, (2) social capital, (3) individual empowerment, (4) sense of community, and (5) opportunities for economic development—are articulated in current CWN projects, suggesting that the oppositional, do-it-yourself ideologies of the first-generation Wi-Fi communities may be tempered. Historically, CN projects attempted to work with these themes by advocating for universal Internet access and computer literacy (Clement and Shade 2000) and by integrating computing and information tools into the local community, for example, at neighbourhood centres, libraries, or language schools. In short, CNs attempted to mobilize existing community publics by improving access to networked communication.

If the CN movement was characterized by the development of community (networking) publics, current Wi-Fi communities are embedded in a more ambivalent production of both geek publics and community publics. CWNs, like some early CN projects such as the Berkeley Community Memory project, are closely connected to free, libre, and open source software development, known as the FLOSS movement, and to the "hacker ethic" of technical experimentation, described by Levy (1984). Non-hierarchical, action-oriented, and meritocratic, this culture has roots in an ethic that valorizes decentralization and what's called conspicuous contribution. This, combined with an interest by some CWNs in resisting corporate structures, has meant that CWNs have attempted to do their work within non-hierarchical, consensus-based organizational forms.

ORGANIZING A CWN: STRUCTURAL TRANSFORMATIONS

In 2004, ISF presented itself as an organization inspired by open source values. Rejecting standard organizational structures including the use of protocols for running meetings, general meetings in 2004 and 2005 were held at a local bar, and all decisions were made based on consensus. Anyone could join as a member after attending three meetings. The innovation structure was open: any new idea was accepted if it was presented as a convincing improvement on another idea. In practice, this meant flame wars on the group mailing list, and three-hour long face-to-face meetings.

This open structure attracted highly skilled volunteers from many different backgrounds whose various positions and demands formed a heterarchy (see Stark 2001), with different actors impassioned by different aspects of ISF. Some wanted a more robust network. Others wanted to use Wi-Fi hotspots to create network art. Still others wanted to build software.

HETERARCHY TO HIERARCHY

Throughout the fieldwork period, as ISF's projects attracted more media attention, and as they renewed partnerships with the Mobile Digital Commons Network and CRACIN, both the hotspot network and the WiFiDog software required more stability. The release of WiFiDog as an open source project with its own website separated the WiFiDog developer community from ISF, and the group introduced a more hierarchical management structure in which the board made most decisions. This structure made possible several successful grant applications because it facilitated drafting and commenting on work in progress. As one volunteer explained, ISF also made a concerted effort to present a positive image to media and funders in 2006, closing the wiki on its website because the messy works-in-progress looked unprofessional. Still, ISF's organizational structure remained in a liminal space between that of an open-source software group and that of a community network. This liminal structure provided different challenges. One artistic collaborator, whom I interviewed in July 2007, remarked that although ISF was very open to partnerships, decision making took a long time because the main ISF contact would say, "'I have to go back and talk to the board, and I have to talk to this person who is in charge of this.' And in another kind of environment that probably could have happened in a week, but in a loosely coupled environment like ISF, sometimes it would take a month or something like that." Meanwhile, a long-time member of ISF, also interviewed in 2007, found that the group had gone from being "geek friendly to geek unfriendly" because of the emphasis on maintaining a positive media image at the expense of maintaining records of ongoing or past projects.

The partnership with the city of Montréal, framed by city decision-makers as responding to media coverage of ISF's activities and its "mind-share" with the public, attempted to retain a volunteer structure with the paid support of a director general. Volunteers would still create and maintain ISF hotspots (one hundred of them in city parks) and would be encouraged to work on more software projects. As of 2010, this promised partnership has yet to materialize, suggesting that the attempts by ISF's geeks to make their community Wi-Fi project relevant outside of the geek public is more complex than expected. This insight in turn suggests that the difficulty of broadening communities of practice such as ISF may be a central challenge for community informatics. As indicated in chapter 6 of this volume, numerous cultural (as well as organizational) factors combine to restrain, rather than expand, community networks.

EVOKING LOCAL COMMUNITY

The actions of producing a geek public—constructing, debating, and modifying the structures of communication—can result in the creation of a collective identity providing legitimacy and social capital. This process can be compared to the process of legitimating electricians that Marvin (1988) describes: by establishing a discourse that separated electricians from non-electricians, early electric practitioners legitimated their activities and created a new profession. In some ways, community Wi-Fi in Montréal looks like it could be explained primarily in terms of social capital production. However, the Wi-Fi geeks in Montréal are proud of the fact that they are "do-ers, not talkers." What they do, is provide Wi-Fi in public places, to a community wider than their group.

Escobar (1994, 185) writes: "Any technology represents a cultural invention, in the sense that it brings forth a world; it emerges out of particular cultural conditions and in turn helps to create new ones." ISF's efforts resonate with a culture of community action and grassroots projects in Montréal. The city has a long tradition of grassroots organizing and mutual aid, extending back to the organizing efforts of the Catholic religious colonists. More recently, decades of Québec leftist governments have solidified in citizens the concept of a shared good, and a connection between radical politics and community media (Raboy 1984). Therefore, the idea of a community group providing a technical service is culturally resonant, and ISF's contribution to the community public resonates with Montréal's local history and culture.

The group's organizational transformations suggest that, over time, ISF aligned itself more and more with the image of the community public. The oppositional hacker ethic that originally evoked a geek identity made it difficult for ISF to collaborate with more conventionally structured organizations. But outside of these collaborations, what kind of impact has this hacking had on the development of a wider Wi-Fi public in Montréal through the use of the ISF network?

NEW PUBLICS: NON-GEEK "USERS" OF THE ISF NETWORK

ISF's community wireless network had over 110,000 registered users at the conclusion of fieldwork.[5] Survey data from online surveys conducted in January and April of 2006 suggested that, at the time, about two-thirds of these users were men and that they primarily used ISF hotspots at cafés and restaurants, surfing the Web and sending email.[6] While the users surveyed said that they would seek out locations where free Wi-Fi was provided, they also indicated that they used free Wi-Fi wherever it was available, not necessarily only at ISF hotspots. The fact that the service was "free"—as in, free of charge to the user—was considered more important than the facts that ISF's network was freely open to submissions of content and to interactions between users and that its technical and social structure were open to participation.

My fieldwork suggested that the users of the network did not have the same goals as ISF members. Observations and interviews conducted in November 2005 and May 2007 with people using ISF hotspots indicated that while the discourse of community is important to users, some user practices opposed ISF's social goals. ISF users primarily want to gain access to the Internet freely—one user described himself as "opportunistic—but aren't we all?" (interview with M, 2005). These opportunistic users picking up wireless signals are more interested in connectivity to the Internet than in socializing with people sitting nearby in a café. Viewing local content on the portal pages is perceived as a necessary impediment to connecting to the Internet to send email or surf the Web. Despite the fact that WiFiDog provided the ability to see which users were online and where, and to create a personal profile accessible to other people online at the same hotspot, most users interviewed said that they did not use profiles, and some were opposed to the idea of putting personal information online where it would be visible to people in the same location. One person explained that he used the number of user names appearing on a hotspot's page as a gauge for the amount of bandwidth available, and avoided locations with too many people online.

The activities of these users suggest that the ISF model did to a certain extent politicize Internet infrastructure. However, users seemed ambivalent at best about the group's social goals, and seemed most interested in getting free Wi-Fi, not in participating in a mediated version of café society. Like Habermas's eighteenth-century bourgeois public sphere composed of men encountering one another in cafés, the recursive geek public in Montréal reinforces its own social connections in public spaces. ISF members "adopt" hotspots where they maintain the access point, and many hotspots were established in places that ISF geeks liked to go. The geeks are in cafés, but the users may be elsewhere. Crow, Powell, and Miller (2007) suggested that a significant number of ISF users were accessing the Internet from adjacent office buildings, restaurants, or homes. In addition, many of the people I interviewed would prefer to access the Wi-Fi network anonymously, without having to register using an email address to provide authentication. The users of ISF are beginning to expect Wi-Fi to be an infrastructure. From this perspective, community Wi-Fi is playing the role described by Fischer (1992) in his social history of the early adoption of the telephone in the United States, whereby telephone connectivity provided by local co-ops compensated for the lack of provision by established telephone companies. In this case, an alternative infrastructure replaces a missing service: ISF continues to provide the majority of free Wi-Fi hotspots in Montréal. However, the continuing role of geeks in creating this infrastructure, at least in Montréal, evokes a more complex relationship. The fact that ISF maintains hotspots where access to the Internet is free of charge introduces a tension between the development of Wi-Fi as a means for geeks to get together in person and develop their expertise, and its use as a communication tool for a larger community public who would prefer anonymity and ubiquity. Where ISF set out to establish Wi-Fi as a community media, its success has been, in the words of Michael Lenczner (interview, 2007), "domesticating free Wi-Fi in Montréal."

In November 2007, I spoke with one of the members of the city of Montréal's committee on economic development. He was trying to understand how the city could support an expansion of the ISF network. In our conversation, he referred to ISF as "a group of geeks," and felt that the city's partnership with ISF should support, not replace, what he saw as a fragile organizational form that contributed to Montréal's culture. Negotiations have since continued, without any formal agreement between ISF and the city of Montréal. The funding programs that have supported other community networking organizations, discussed in chapter 10 of this volume, have not supported ISF. Instead, the group is continuing to cover its costs through the annual fees that it charges its hotspot partners. To keep geek volunteers motivated, the group has been focusing on mobile application development, particularly applications that help to find free or open Wi-Fi hotspots, and on replacing the WiFiDog authorization server software with new software that allows more precise network management. Considering the tension between the geek public that evolved in Montréal and the idealized (or desired) community public, these decisions are significant. Continuing opportunities for technical development provide more opportunities for the development of a geek public concerned with building the technology that facilitates its own interactions, but do not necessarily restructure public provision of communications access.

CONCLUSION

The energy I felt in 2004 upon first meeting Montréal's Wi-Fi geeks convinced me that this group could potentially redefine local culture and communications. However, the tension that emerged at ISF between the geek public—who built social capital and skills through their engagement with each other—and the community public, solidified through access to robust communications infrastructure, suggested purposes at odds with each other. In the terms that Sandvig presents in chapter 7 of this volume, ISF is simultaneously defining Wi-Fi geeks as legitimate social and political actors (as per Marvin 1988), and filling an infrastructural gap (as per Fischer 1992). I would argue that these two purposes, and the two publics that they have evoked, create part of the dynamism of projects such as ISF. Maintaining this dynamism is difficult and may be one of the reasons that projects based on innovation and experimentation, rather than service delivery, do not have very long lifespans.

Within the tensions between geek publics and community publics and the expression of differing purposes for community Wi-Fi may lie a lesson for the future of social action embedded in technology. The difficulty in balancing the development of a geek public and a community public may result from the fact that contemporary politics no longer operate on a scale in which mass publics have influence (Dean 2003). While Dean advocates the creation of "issue networks" to connect people together to work on specific issues, without the actors being reduced to groups of consumers, the community Wi-Fi phenomenon suggests that the local community may also act as a locus of resistance. Mobilizing such resistance means creating opportunities for members of geek publics to leverage their interest in technical development for greater engagement in their local community. In Warner's (2002) terms, none of the Wi-Fi communities discussed here are currently expanding their publics. In fact, all of them risk turning their discourse and practice inward. Recent attempts to form a global community wireless "movement" testify to the difficulties of connecting locally based community Wi-Fi projects: despite the fact that such local projects use similar technologies and are created by people with similar values, the particularity of each local project prevents a unified approach to community Wi-Fi networking.

Wi-Fi communities may be part of a new generation of projects that politicize communication technology. Their challenges should encourage us to ask questions about culture, and about change. If geek publics can assist their communities in creating appropriate technical systems, we must develop ways to encourage them to make their hacking relevant and useful to their local communities. However, we must also remain realistic about the limits of this hacking as a form of social justice.

ACKNOWLEDGEMENTS

The ethnography described in this paper was supported by the Canadian Research Alliance for Community Innovation and Networking (CRACIN) and by the Laboratoire de Communication Médiatisée par Ordinateur at the Université du Québec à Montréal. Both of these projects are funded by the Social Sciences and Humanities Research Council of Canada. Some of the data presented here were also collected as part of the Community Wireless Infrastructure Research Project (CWIRP), funded by Infrastructure Canada. Thank you to the leaders and team members on all of these projects for supporting and contributing to my work. I would also like to thank Professor Leslie Regan Shade for advice, guidance, and helpful comments. Finally, thank you to my geek friends and colleagues at ISF, especially Michael Lenczner and Benoît Grégoire.

NOTES

1   This statement appeared on the ISF website (www.ilesansfils.org) in 2007. It was later revised to: "We believe that technology can be used to bring people together and foster a sense of community. In pursuit of that goal, Île Sans Fil uses its free public

access points to promote interaction between users, show new media art, and provide geographically—and community—relevant information."

2 Hub des Artistes Locaux was a partnership among Île Sans Fil, a community radio station, and the campus television station of Concordia University. The project used ISF hotspots to host music and video servers that broadcast music and video content curated so as to relate to the specific culture of the hotspot.

3 In this context, civic engagement is defined as an active contribution to the creation of a meaningful civic life. It is not limited to politics and is oriented toward improving the democratic or cultural lives of citizens in a local area.

4 A meshed network is a wireless network in which each node acts as both a sender and a receiver of data. This allows the network to automatically route around damage or interference. Meshed networks are meant to be non-hierarchical.

5 As of July 2009. See: http://www.ilesansfil.org/message/110000-un-nouveau-record-pour-ile-sans-fil/.

6 The survey was developed and deployed in partnership with Laura Forlano, then a PhD candidate in the Communications program at Columbia University. The full results appeared in Forlano's dissertation, "When Code Meets Place: Collboration and Innovation at WiFi Hotspots" (2008).

REFERENCES

Abbate, Janet. 1999. *Inventing the Internet*. Cambridge, MA: MIT Press.

Auray, Nicolas, Godefroy Beauvallet, Carole Charbit, and Valérie Fernandez. 2003. WiFi: An emerging information society infrastructure. In *Socio-economic trends assessment for the digital revolution*. Issue Report no. 40 (September). Milan: STAR Project, IST Programme, European Commission. http://ses.telecom-paristech.fr/auray/Auray%20Beauvallet%20Charbit%20Fernandez.pdf.

Bar, François, and Hernán Galperin. 2004. Building the wireless Internet infrastructure: From cordless Ethernet archipelagos to wireless grids. *Communications and Strategies* 54 (2nd quarter): 45–67. http://www.idate.fr/fic/revue_telech/348/CS54_BAR_GALPERIN.pdf.

Cho, Hanna. 2006. Explorations in community and civic bandwidth: A case study in community wireless networking, communication and culture. MA thesis, Ryerson University and York University, Toronto.

Clement, Andrew, and Leslie Regan Shade. 2000. The access rainbow: Conceptualizing universal access to the information/communications infrastructure. In *Community informatics: Enabling communities with information and communications technology*, ed. Michael Gurstein, 32–51. Hershey, PA: Idea Group Publishing.

Crow, Barbara, Alison Powell, and Tammy Miller. 2007. Examining Wi-Fi network infrastructure: Insights from Canadian case studies. Paper presented at the annual conference of the Canadian Communication Association, Saskatoon, SK, May.

Dean, Jodi. 2003. Why the Net is not a public sphere. *Constellations* 10(1): 95–112.

de Sola Pool, Ithiel. 1977. *The social impact of the telephone*. Cambridge, MA: MIT Press.

Dewey, John. 1964. *Democracy and education*. New York: Macmillan.

Douglas, Susan. 1987. *Inventing American broadcasting, 1899–1922*. Baltimore: Johns Hopkins University Press.

Escobar, Arturo. 1994. Welcome to Cyberia: Notes on the anthropology of cyberculture. *Current Anthropology* 35(4): 211–31.

Fischer, Claude. 1992. *America calling: A social history of the telephone to 1940*. Berkeley: University of California Press.

Fraser, Nancy. 1992. Rethinking the public sphere: A contribution to the critique of actually existing democracy. In *Habermas and the public sphere*, ed. Craig Calhoun, 109–42. Cambridge, MA: MIT Press.

Habermas, Jürgen. 1989. *Structural transformations of the public sphere: An inquiry into a category of a bourgeois society*. Translated by Thomas Burger and Frederick Lawrence. Cambridge, MA: MIT Press.

Hammersley, Martyn, and Paul Atkinson. 1995. *Ethnography: Principles in practice*. London: Routledge.

Haring, Kristin. 2006. *Ham radio's technical culture*. Cambridge, MA: MIT Press.

Kelty, Christopher. 2005. Geeks, social imaginaries, and recursive publics. *Cultural Anthropology* 20(2): 185–214.

Latour, Bruno. 2005. *Reassembling the social: An introduction to actor-network theory*. New York: Oxford University Press.

Lennie, Jennifer, and Greg Hearn. 2003. The potential of PAR and participatory evaluation for increasing the sustainability and success of community development initiatives using new communication technologies. Paper presented at the Action Learning, Action Research and Process Management and Participatory Action Research Congress, University of Pretoria, South Africa, September.

Levy, Steven. 1984. *Hackers*. Garden City, NY: Doubleday.

Mackenzie, Adrian. 2005. Untangling the unwired: Wi-Fi and the cultural inversion of infrastructure. *Space and Culture* 8(3): 269–85.

Marvin, Carolyn. 1988. *When old technologies were new*. Cambridge, MA: Harvard University Press.

Meinrath, Sascha. 2005. Wirelessing the world: The battle over (community) wireless networks. In *The future of the media: Resistance and reform in the 21st century*, ed. R. McChesney, 219–42. New York: Seven Stories Press.

Mosco, Vincent. 2004. *The digital sublime: Myth, power, and cyberspace*. Cambridge, MA: MIT Press.

O'Neil, Dara. 2002. Assessing community informatics: A review of methodological approaches for evaluating community networks and community technology centres. *Internet Research: Electronic Networking Applications and Policy* 12(1): 76–102.

Papacharissi, Zizi. 2002. The virtual sphere: The Internet as a public sphere. *New Media and Society* 4(1): 9–27.

Pinkett, Randall. 2003. Community technology and community building: Early results from the Creating Community Connections project. *The Information Society* 19(3): 365–79.

Powell, Alison, and Leslie Regan Shade. 2006. Going Wi-Fi in Canada: Municipal and community initiatives. *Government Information Quarterly* 23: 381–403.

Raboy, Mark. 1984. *Movements and messages: Media and radical politics in Quebec*. Toronto: Between the Lines.

Sandvig, Christian. 2004. An initial assessment of cooperative action in Wi-Fi networking. *Telecommunications Policy* 28(7/8): 579–602.

Schuler, Douglas. 1996. *New community networks: Wired for change*. New York: Addison-Wesley.

Stark, David. 2001. Ambiguous assets for uncertain environments: Heterarchy in postsocialist firms. In *The twenty-first-century firm: Changing economic organization in international perspective*, ed. Paul DiMaggio, 69–104. Princeton: Princeton University Press.

Taylor, Charles. 2002. Modern social imaginaries. *Public Culture* 14(1): 91–124.

Warner, Michael. 2002. *Publics and counterpublics*. New York: Zone Books.

12 WIRELESS BROADBAND FROM INDIVIDUAL BACKHAUL TO COMMUNITY SERVICE Co-operative Provision and Related Models of Local Signal Access

Matthew Wong

For many cities, the current availability of broadband Internet, coupled with affordable wireless networking technology, creates an environment of great community broadband potential. With many homes and businesses connecting to the Internet via high bandwidth broadband services and using standard wireless technologies, it is now common to detect multiple wireless signals in public and private spaces. While many wireless signals are often protected to block unauthorized access, others are left in an unprotected or "open" state. Whether intentional or not, this creates an abundance of disorganized but accessible high-speed wireless connections that blanket parts of these urban areas. A variety of different wireless groups have recognized the potential for this broadband "backhaul" to be transformed into some form of community service. These groups typically differ from each other in their vision for what these services could be, how they might be organized, and what philosophies drive their work. However, these groups are unified in their goals for value-added access and infrastructure for individuals and communities.

This chapter explores the theme of converting existing wireless broadband backhaul into services designed to benefit communities. This work is primarily based on case study research conducted on Wireless Nomad, a Toronto-based

Internet service provider (ISP). In addition to Wireless Nomad, Île Sans Fil and Wireless Toronto, two similar Canadian community groups, as well as FON, a worldwide personal Internet sharing organization, will also be explored. These wireless networking organizations will be discussed in relation to their various approaches to transforming wireless broadband backhaul into community-oriented services. This discussion will also consider the ways in which these organized possibilities for signal sharing can be further explored for greater infrastructure potential, decreased cost, greater accessibility, and reliability.

BROADBAND SERVICE AND INTERNET CLOUDS

Over the past decade, Internet use in countries around the world has grown dramatically, particularly in large Canadian cities. Canada is widely acknowledged as having strong broadband penetration rates (Ngini, Furnell, and Ghita 2002; Frieden 2005; Wu 2004), and the statistics available from Canadian census data suggest Internet growth across the country. Internet use in Canada continues to rise, with Statistics Canada reporting increases in usage in the most recent Canadian Internet Use Survey (Statistics Canada 2008). At that time, the national average rate of Internet use in Canada was 73 percent, with British Columbia, Alberta, and Ontario all above the national average. Major census metropolitan areas, such as Calgary (85%), Victoria (83%), Vancouver, Edmonton, and Québec City (each 78%), demonstrated Internet usage rates for people aged 16 or older that were higher than the national average. Users are increasingly relying on the Internet in connection with many facets of their lives, including communication, entertainment, commerce, education, and information seeking, to name but a few popular uses.

One influence in the growing use of Internet services is the standardization of wireless Internet technology, or Wi-Fi. Wi-Fi uses radio technology coupled with sophisticated software and hardware transmission protocols in order to transmit data that computers can quickly and easily send and receive. These transmission protocols fall under a family of standards known as the *802.11* standards, as devised and regulated by the Institute of Electrical and Electronics Engineers (IEEE). Wireless networking is being used as a way to provide access in new places and the effect that this growth has had around the world is striking. It is roughly estimated that some 200 million Wi-Fi chipsets had been sold in 2005 (Shah and Sandvig 2005, 7). With wireless, individuals can now create opportunities for Internet use without being tethered to a wired location. Wireless signals, being radio waves, often overlap one another and create dense "clouds" of wireless coverage.[1] When left in an open state, wireless devices can detect a signal and use it to access the Internet. Alternatively, shared access can be granted by providing users of the signal with the requisite security key[2] that corresponds to the particular Service Set Identifier (SSID). Another form of intentional sharing uses captive portal technology, which redirects users to a log-in page requiring a password. Both of these approaches have been employed by individuals and organizations in order to explore opportunities for sharing. However, by and large, these wireless signals, while overlapping, remain discrete and disconnected from the other signals that surround them. These disparate network nodes have been described as "islands," an accurate moniker despite their collective connection to the Internet (Sandvig, Young, and Meinrath 2004).

Indeed, many of these so-called islands are likely to remain separated, as Wi-Fi signal sharing is often the result of networks being *inadvertently* left open, as opposed to intentionally so. Users are often cautioned about leaving their networks unprotected for fear of hacking, privacy invasion, or unauthorized use (Shah and Sandvig 2005). A CRACIN study of wireless Internet users confirmed these concerns, as well as demonstrating the contradictory attitude of some respondents to freely use other people's unprotected wireless signals, while being opposed to others using their signal over concerns about over-use and security (Wong and Clement 2007). Thus, in this environment of wariness toward sharing and presumed unwanted contact, promoting sharing as a viable form of service can be daunting. Sharing one's connection with others when fair access, usage, and payment may all be in question can present an unappealing proposition. Furthermore, since 802.11 networks operate in the crowded, license-exempt 2.4 GHZ industrial, scientific, and medical (ISM) band, interference often creates signal reliability issues that reduce the appeal of longer-ranged Wi-Fi connections. With the potential for a multitude of commercial devices (such as microwave ovens) to disrupt signals, interference can often pose a serious problem. However, with the abundance of wireless signals carrying high-bandwidth broadband, and the motivation by dedicated wireless interest groups to create something better for the people under these wireless clouds, there is a clear potential for uniting even some of these signals into greater Internet projects, thereby creating a network that is more than the sum of the individual, disparate parts (see chapter 11 in this volume, "Wi-Fi Publics," for a broader analysis of producing community with Wi-Fi). Andersen (2003) described this evolving ubiquitous use of wireless networks as a new paradigm and speculated that "the future belongs to small, connected devices that will wirelessly allow the user—and the technology—to self-organize, creating something smart out of many small and simple nodes and connections."

Toward creating these new networks, numerous organizations have sprung up in recent years, trying to tap into the potential of wireless networks. Sandvig (2004) noted that in 2003, there were dozens of Wi-Fi co-operatives in the world. Tapia and Ortiz (2006) identified nearly 360 municipal wireless projects in the United States alone. There are probably many smaller, less formalized, grassroots community initiatives as well. The interests and objectives of community and municipal wireless Internet projects can be loosely grouped into two broad goals: improving access through wider availability and lower costs, and improving democratic ownership over public goods, in part by gaining control of communications infrastructure that would otherwise be in the hands of private telecommunications companies (Gibbons and Ruth 2006; Goth 2005; Lentz 1998; Wong 2006). However, not all groups interested in utilizing Wi-Fi are the same, with the presence of distinctions between even broad categories of description. For example, there are differences between projects of large-scale municipal governments and small, neighbourhood ones, and differences between urban and rural networks. There are also groups interested in opening hotspots, as well as those interested in social and community technology (Powell and Shade 2005, 6).

APPROACHES TO CONVERTING WIRELESS BROADBAND INTO COMMUNITY SERVICE

The following sections present three examples of organizations attempting to transform existing individual wireless broadband connections into some form of community service. The first example details the case of Wireless Nomad Co-operative, a Toronto-based ISP. Wireless Nomad is discussed in more detail than the other examples, given my long-term working experience with the organization. From 2005 to 2007, I maintained a volunteer working relationship with the Wireless Nomad team, studying their planning and approach, and helping with network installation. Wireless Nomad was a community partner in Toronto for the CRACIN project, and they met with the CRACIN researchers numerous times during the life of the project. CRACIN also provided a small funding grant to the Wireless Nomad team to help develop their open-source software and pilot test some of their technology. I formally interviewed the two principle members of the Wireless Nomad team twice, once near the beginning of the project in 2005, and later in 2007. Furthermore, throughout the two years spent working with Wireless Nomad, significant supplemental field notes were also taken. Wireless Nomad's approach combined a residential monthly-subscription service with a free wireless access component, and was administered as a co-operative.

The second example looks at FON, a Spain-based worldwide wireless network company. In many respects, FON can be seen as a vastly scaled-up version of Wireless Nomad's access model. This applies not just to FON's international reach, but also by its significant financial backing and technology. Finally, the approaches of Île Sans Fil, a Montréal-based community networking group, and its companion organization, Wireless Toronto, are examined. Their approaches are technically hotspot models; however, their vision is to do much more than just provide Internet connectivity for the community.

Wireless Nomad Co-operative

Wireless Nomad (wn), was a Toronto-based isp that began in early 2005 as the collective idea of founders Damien Fox and Steve Wilton.[3] Damien and Steve originally met in late 2004, at a Wi-Fi meet-up group in Toronto. Steve, who had spent some time working as a network administrator, and Damien, a law student with an interest in Internet law, shared an attraction to wireless networking and its potential for experimental customization in connectivity and signal sharing. With guidance and advice from a local business development centre, Steve began working on a business plan for a wireless Internet company and came up with the name Wireless Nomad. In January 2005, the two incorporated Wireless Nomad Co-operative. Originally, there were to be two business streams: a residential DSL service at 1 Mbps, and Hot Wireless, the brand name for their business DSL service. Some of the original premises for the co-op were:

- There would be full user access, such as the ability to run servers (commonly prohibited by ISPs) and not blocking ports (e.g., email protocol ports).
- There would be free accounts for wireless access within the network.
- Revenue would be reinvested in the co-operative and the network.

Their slogan was "Internet done right," representing their interests in a more accessible Internet for their subscribers and also in providing free access for other users. However, they were careful to throttle the connection speed of free accounts to 128 kbps, since those connections were using the bandwidth paid for by subscribers. They did not want to impair or associate their brand with slow speed.

Their original plan called for providing customized wireless hardware that would run wn's software. Linksys WRT54G routers would be reprogrammed to use the OpenWRT Linux-based software platform. These customized routers would then be enclosed in all-weather housings to be mounted outside the subscriber's homes for increased signal accessibility. The equipment setup would also include a DSL modem. The original subscription model would have subscribers pay a CAD $150 fee for ownership of the equipment.[4]

It was not until September 2005 that wn started to sign up their first customers for one Mbps DSL service. The original rate they charged for this service was $30 per month. Even at this early stage of the co-op's life, it was evident that the business plan was flawed in a number of ways. For one, they realized that the people in the business development centre that they had relied on for input lacked experience in the Internet provider market. As a result, some of the approaches they had implemented, such as door-to-door sales and putting up posters in the neighbourhood, were not very effective. Damien noted that the business development planners they spoke with probably had more experience with individuals setting up small bricks-and-mortar businesses for arts, crafts, and similar goods, as opposed to Internet service. Furthermore, their original plan to sell their equipment as a one-time $150 equipment cost was ill conceived. Even their friends were reluctant to get involved with the project with costs for the equipment being that high, in addition to a monthly fee that was very similar to existing incumbent service providers. Exacerbating this problem was the sharing aspect, which users did not perceive to be much of an advantage. WN quickly changed the equipment sale to a deposit and started investigating the use of mesh network technology in order to broaden their network, while reducing some of the expensive DSL connection costs. In October 2005, they ended up dropping the Hot Wireless business connection side of their operation altogether, after experiencing little success with it.

In late 2005, after some experimentation with modified, two-radio routers, WN deployed an experimental mesh network in the neighbourhood located around Damien's house. (For more on mesh networking, see O'Brien [2003] and Xue and Ganz [2002].) In the first quarter of 2006, more nodes were deployed until eventually a peak of seven mesh nodes were operating with five DSL connections as backhaul. Unfortunately, despite this initial successful foray into mesh networking, two things eventually doomed the mesh project. Firstly, a combination of people moving away or abandoning the service dropped the number of active nodes to only three, including two at Damien's own house. Secondly, outdoor deployment of the routers started to become a problem due to inclement weather, the necessity of having a vehicle for the installations, and the placement of the drilled holes in the house (i.e., the location of the hole was not necessarily aesthetically compatible with the best signal position). In fact, since this was a problem with the regular routers as well as the mesh routers, WN also discontinued outdoor deployment altogether during this period. Damien and Steve were both quite disappointed with this outcome, particularly as they had had some success in a neighbourhood where they had not anticipated it. By March 2006, things were looking bleak for WN. They looked at different ways to change the organization and decided on three major alterations. First, they increased the price of the service to $33 per month. Second, they got rid of the deposit system, which was a problem when people moved and the equipment needed to be recovered, and switched back to selling the equipment, albeit at a lower price. Third, they stopped renting the small office at a business development centre they had been using at a cost of $600 per month. Finally, they cut what little advertising they had been doing.

In May 2006, the co-operative was surviving, but Damien and Steve were looking at alternative ways to generate new business. While both were gaining tremendous experience with running an Internet business and interacting with their co-operative members, they were still accumulating debt on high bandwidth costs. They identified two specific areas where they could find new subscribers. One was providing service to people who did not own a landline phone but still wanted an Internet connection. The other was for "budget retail" locations, such as the small businesses in their neighbourhoods. These businesses might not be able to spend $100 per month for a typical business connection, but might be interested in paying $10 to $20 per month for lower-speed wireless access. Unfortunately, neither prospective plan worked. Individuals without a phone line turned out to be a non-starter since they primarily seemed to be students who were only looking for limited, short-term connections. Furthermore, Bell, the owner of the lines, would charge an additional $10 per month to maintain the "dry-line" (the DSL connection without an accompanying phone service). As for the wireless service for the budget retail locations, Damien (pers. comm., 15 April 2007) admitted: "In the end, I think we had some really good ideas and the technology, I think, would have worked. But there was no way to prove it, and without a very good degree of certainty there was no way I was going to try and get money from people and there was no way I was going to spend another six months on it. You know, I think it had a shot, but it wasn't a sure enough thing for us to continue on with that." Late in May 2006, Damien met again with researchers associated with CRACIN, including me. Damien sadly noted that WN had seemed to have run its course. It was becoming increasingly too much work for the pair of them to continue operations with very little payoff (they were in considerable debt at this point). However, they did not want to strand their current subscribers, which at this point numbered somewhere around fifty to sixty. As a result, Damien and Steve tried to find alternative providers, such as the Toronto Free Net (a philosophically similar DSL provider), that they could shift their subscribers over to.

Surprisingly, in what Damien considered a series of miracles, WN's fortunes seemed to turn around. Despite a higher price and being required to buy the equipment once again, people kept signing up for the service. Also, in a major improvement, they switched their bandwidth wholesaler to a different company. Previously they were being charged $23/month per DSL circuit (one per subscriber) plus an additional $2/gigabyte of transfer. This pricing plan was considered prohibitively expensive. Their new wholesaler was instead charging $26/month per circuit plus the first ten gigabytes of transfer were free and pooled. This meant that they collectively had a pool of ten gigabytes per month per circuit that they could draw from, meaning that high-capacity users were balanced out by lower-capacity ones. While they still owed thousands of dollars to the old wholesaler, WN felt that at least under the new plan their business had a chance. For the next several months, until November 2006, the co-operative remained afloat. However, things were getting so tenuous financially that Damien and Steve both found full-time jobs and switched to running WN on the side.

In December 2006, disaster struck when a massive server failure severely affected WN's service. Users lost the ability to log in because the authentication server was down, and voicemail and email services stopped functioning. To make matters worse, Steve was out of the country during this time and even when he returned, he did not have reliable Internet access to interface and repair the server. After many days of no service, subscribers started to leave, and by January 2007, Damien and Steve thought that WN was finished. However, the problems were eventually resolved as Steve was able to find some time to work with the server. WN did stop signing up new subscribers though. The following month they had a meeting with their co-operative members in order to discuss the future of WN. Much to Steve and Damien's surprise, the meeting was well attended and suggestions were offered by the members. They decided to raise the price to $36.95/month for the now up-to-3 Mbps connection and contract the bandwidth wholesaler to also provide technical support from 9 a.m. to 9 p.m.. Previously Steve had been answering all technical support calls on his cell phone. WN also began to finally collect on some of the previous outstanding bills they were owed. Due to billing errors, some individuals had not been charged for various legitimate fees for months at a time. For just over two years, the co-operative continued to remain operational, although new subscriptions stayed offline while they fine tuned their billing services (e.g., switching to online billing, using credit card only transactions, etc.). However, by early 2009, it seemed again that WN had run its course. With declining membership and the co-operative never regaining the number of subscribers it had in its early years, Damien and Steve decided to end WN. In March, 2009, WN shut its doors and transferred their remaining customers over to TekSavvy, another Toronto-based ISP and the bandwidth wholesaler whom they had partnered with in 2006.

While WN ceased operations, through their connection with their members and the broader Wi-Fi community, the philosophy of WN lives on. Damien summed up the general ideology of the organization as "user empowerment first": their typically more-sophisticated users could control their Internet resource, meaning that they could run a server, not have ports blocked, and have their privacy and legal rights protected as much as possible. When asked about the co-op's feelings toward sharing, which was mandatory, Damien added: "Selfish user aims are being denied, whereas user aims that contribute towards [the co-op are promoted] . . . it's sort of trying to avoid the prisoner's dilemma situation. No one is allowed to rat out, no one is allowed to not share. Because if everybody else shares and I don't, I'm ahead. I [benefit from] this sharing but I don't have to deal with sharing [back]. We don't allow that. Everybody has got to contribute back." This perspective highlighted wn's philosophy toward forced sharing, in that they recognized that if provided, in an opportunity to not share but still reap the benefits of a shared network, there would be no incentive for anyone to participate. To avoid this problem, everyone was required to participate in the sharing network. In terms of having the free accounts, Damien's reasons for that were quite pragmatic, if not altruistic. He stated that "free accounts are important to us because if you don't have that [then] people who aren't willing to pay are shut out and letting them in doesn't cost anything . . . so why not let that happen?" Consistent with this notion of fairness to others, Damien believed that it was fair to charge users a fee if they were going above and beyond occasionally checking email using one of their free accounts. He suggested that there needed to be an acknowledgment that the service incurred costs that someone has to pay. Damien succinctly noted that "some philosophical commitment to free Internet is not going to change [the costs] . . . someone has to lay a cable, someone has to pay guys like Steve to run servers . . . and you want people who are good at it, or else what happens is that half the time [the network] doesn't work." However, Damien was quick to point out that there was some middle ground between having a service that maximized profit and a service that tries to make the offering entirely free. This is what Damien considered their "fair and reasonable" philosophy, in that there are kinds of services that are free but there are also kinds of services worth paying for.

FON

FON is a worldwide organization operating primarily throughout Europe, although they are expanding into North America and Asia. FON is one of the largest of the community groups examined here, and certainly the most well funded. After receiving USD$22 million from Google, Skype, and various venture capital firms, FON went live in November 2006 (BBC News 2006a). In June 2006, BBC News (2006b) reported that FON had some 54,000 people signed up worldwide, primarily in cities. The same article quoted the general manager of FON North America as aiming to have 50,000 hotspots by September 2006, 150,000 by year's end, and one million by the end of 2007.[5] According to the founder of FON, Martin Varsavsky, one of FON's dreams is "a unified global broadband wireless signal" (BBC News 2006a). In October 2007, FON partnered with British Telecom to expand FON's community to include existing British Telecom Wi-Fi broadband customers, a reported three million users (BBC News 2007).

FON's service comes in two configurations. In the first, a user already subscribing to another ISP's service purchases a specialized FON router called La Fonera for approximately $40 USD.[6] This individual is called a "Fonero" and may choose between one of two different paths. By becoming a "Linus," Foneros freely share their connection with other members of the FON network. In exchange, they may freely access any other FON node that they can detect. Alternatively, a Fonero may become a "Bill," so access to their wireless node costs money to external users (administered by the FON network). In exchange, they receive 50 percent of the money generated from use of their node. However, unlike Linuses, Bills must pay for any use of the FON network beyond their own node. Bills and Linuses are able to restrict the amount of bandwidth available for communal connections. In June 2007, the model was changed such that Bills and Linuses both got free access and part of the proceeds. The second service configuration creates individuals known as "Aliens," or external users, who are free-floating pay-as-you-go users. FON service is similar to WN in that sharing is promoted through the use of one's own network connection. Also like WN, roaming users are able to connect to network nodes wherever they can find them, which would likely be near residential homes (FON makes use of existing broadband connections, after all). However, in both cases, there is a strong requirement for a large, extensive network in order for the roaming service to have maximum usefulness. Clearly, the goal of the FON network is to continuously build the network, in order to not only provide greater access, but to also encourage more users.

The FON business model is based on piggybacking off of existing ISPs' bandwidths and connections. FON generates revenue from its pay-as-you-go customers as well as from the sale of their equipment. However, much to their advantage, since FON does not own or maintain the backhaul network equipment, their obligations and responsibilities from a financial perspective are rather limited compared to those of most other ISPs. The general manager of FON North America described this as "changing the economics of Wi-Fi" (BBC News 2006b). This can be problematic because many ISPs prohibit individuals from reselling their Internet connections or sharing it without authorization. Indeed, as one analyst described it, FON is "treating Wi-Fi as communal property when it is not" (BBC News 2006a). FON's response has been to seek explicit authorization from local ISPs but otherwise suggest that Foneros check and comply with their ISP's terms and conditions. FON believes that they can create workable relationships with ISPs:

a FON France representative said: "We tell the ISP . . . basically 'come with us, let's strike a deal . . . because you, as an ISP, can benefit from something you never thought of'" (Reid 2006).

FON considers itself a community as well as a social movement. However, it is unique as a movement because while its prime motivation is to possess a widespread sharing network, it sells itself to potential members by catering to individual interests. For example, one FON executive said: "When we are trying to sell the idea of FON, we are not telling people 'share your Wi-Fi because it is good for your community, it is good for your neighbourhood, it is good for your country' . . . we are saying 'share your Wi-Fi because it is good for you because, when you're going to move around, when you're going to leave your home and you want to connect to the Internet, you can'" (Reid 2006).

This is an interesting way to promote the service because it specifically addresses a very powerful motivator in Internet use: personal gain. However, in terms of community motives, it is a bit suspect to promote socially progressive notions based primarily on selfish aims. While FON describes itself in terms of a community approach as well as calling its participants "members," it is unclear whether or not the members have much say in the operations of the greater FON network. However, it is true that Foneros retain elements of control over their own connections, such as limiting the bandwidth. Otherwise, FON appears to operate much like a regular ISP in that they sell the hardware as well as administer the network, particularly the payment schemes.

Wireless Toronto and Île Sans Fil

Wireless Toronto (WT) and Île Sans Fil (ISF) are two similar, community wireless networking organizations based in Toronto, Ontario and Montréal, Québec, respectively. Since in many ways, WT is based on the ISF model and approach to wireless, it is useful to describe these projects together (see chapter 10 in this volume, "Community and Municipal Wi-Fi Initiatives in Canada," for a more in-depth review of ISF). Wireless Toronto (WT) is another wireless networking group in Toronto that operates within the city, although moreso in the urban core as opposed to the suburban extremities. It was founded in April 2005 as an all-volunteer, not-for-profit community group. Like WN, WT formed as a result of an initial meeting among interested parties, in this case, at Social Tech Brewing, a forum promoting communities and technology. At this particular meeting, one of the co-founders of ISF was present, and explained how this community organization worked and how a similar one might operate in Toronto (Cho 2006, 15). Soon after, WT was formed. Both ISF and WT operate on a hotspot model of access at local cafés and other venues, which provide the broadband backhaul to the wireless equipment set up by

ISF or WT volunteers. In addition to Internet access, ISF and WT also provide a number of other artistic and community services that host and promote various projects such as artwork, music, virtual space, and information. In contrast to WN and FON, ISF and WT are not residential services and do not promote their network nodes for homes.

Ideology plays a large role in both the ISF and WT projects, as both share strong goals and values when it comes to community wireless networking and access. For example, one of WT's goals is "to facilitate public awareness over the social and economic benefits of non-commercial, community-based provision of wireless Internet, as well as encourage new and innovative approaches to building community with the technology" (Cho 2006,16). Similarly, as Powell (2006, 8) wrote, ISF's goals include creating "wireless Internet access points accessible free of charge in public places, and . . . [using] emerging technologies to build communities." These goals clearly suggest a strong allegiance to promoting communities, and to this end, both groups work hard to incorporate local interests, arts, and media in their projects. Also, the commitment to free access is very important to both groups. For example, hotspot owners are required to sign a social contract with ISF or WT, which "codifies the relationship between the host, ISF [or WT], and the end users as social rather than commercial" (Powell 2006, 8). This contract also specifies that the hotspot owner cannot run ads on the router. In order to maintain the principle of free access, hotspot owners are also not allowed to charge users for Internet use. That is, presumably not more than the cost of a cup of coffee or a snack.

REVIEWING THE DIFFERENT APPROACHES TO COMMUNITY WIRELESS

The preceding review briefly highlighted a number of community wireless groups and their various approaches to transforming Internet backhaul into a community service. In the case of WN and FON, the approach relied on sharing to transform what would otherwise be personal or business broadband access into a service that others could use. This approach presented opportunities and challenges for both providers. One significant hurdle, and one that WN clearly experienced, is that any network of this type has a benefit for users proportional to the density of the network. In other words, both services would need to achieve a critical mass of users and network nodes. It does no good for a WN or FON customer to have access to a network that is limited to a few sporadic houses in locations all over a city. Furthermore, there is the added concern that if you happen to be the node located in a popular location—for example near a downtown square or café—you could very well be overwhelmed with connection requests. Another challenge is the ownership of the network connection. WN became the ISP to address this challenge, while FON relied on "donated" bandwidth from Foneros's pre-existing broadband subscriptions. It is unclear whether this is sustainable from a legal perspective as well as an industry perspective. That is, until explicit arrangements are made between ISPs and FON, it is unclear whether it is legal to resell or share a wireless connection in such a systematic way. FON's partnership with British Telecom, however, would seem to suggest that FON has been able to successfully enter into co-operative agreements with major ISPs.

A sharing approach does present several opportunities for success, however. First, in WN's case, by forcing sharing on users, the playing field between subscribers is levelled, in that everyone has to share. Requiring everyone to share or providing a strong incentive to share may be the only ways to ensure sharing between participants and the growth of a shared network when participants might otherwise elect not to. Second, an administrated shared network addresses many of the concerns individuals may have with sharing, such as addressing security and privacy (mandatory authentication), fair usage (controlled communal bandwidth), cost sharing, and access to a wider network of coverage. In fact, many commercial providers in both Internet and cellular access already share connections; they merely hide this from the consumer. FON may have also had the right idea about market sharing—that it is good for the user. This might be the best way to build critical mass, as it is likely an ideology that people can identify with. WN's pragmatic approach, as indicated by Damien, as to what is fair and worth paying for might also resonate with individuals, particularly those already paying for Internet.

In comparison, the approaches by ISF and WT, while technically hotspot oriented, but socially more progressive and less commercial, present a different perspective. There is a notable distinction in that these groups are not aiming for residential access, but rather to improve Internet accessibility in public locations and the content available there. In fact, the distinction that these groups aim to provide not just access but community-relevant content is an important one. Whereas FON and WN would likely be best described as access providers, ISF and WT probably prefer to be considered more as community development enablers. ISF and WT are very ideologically driven, with commitments to both free wireless and promoting local interests in the arts, media, and information. (WN and FON are also ideologically driven, albeit by a different ideology.) As Powell (2006) found in studies, for many of these community groups, it is more than just providing an opportunity for people to surf and check email, but rather an emerging form of civic participation. However, it is possible that this ideology might be less appealing for some, particularly with wariness surrounding "free" wireless. Other CRACIN research found less interest in the community aspects of wireless compared to the individual benefits (Wong 2006). However, this is not to suggest that community aspects are problematic or even off-putting, but rather, that it is relevant to consider whether some of the strong messages of community growth may fall on deaf ears. This is particularly important for non-profit and volunteer groups, such as ISF and WT, that rely on community support for their sustainability. Then again, since many of these groups are located in large urban environments such as Toronto and Montréal, it is more than likely that there are enough interested individuals whom these messages inspire and excite. Certainly this suggests that it is possible for both personal-benefit and community-oriented organizations to co-exist in the same locations.

Considering Sandvig's discussion in chapter 7 of this volume on what community networks are an example of, all of these cases might be seen as an example of "revolutionary infrastructure creation" in that they take an existing form of network infrastructure—individual broadband Internet—and through the use of wireless technology, alter it to serve the community. This concept is revolutionary in the sense that what would otherwise be disconnected, disparate networks are linked into one overarching network. It is also revolutionary in that the goal is to share connectivity rather than hoard it or make it exclusive, to varying extents. In fact, some of these networks might also be viewed as an example of user autonomy and protest. WN, in particular, sought to bring features to their users that conventional ISPs prevented, such as running personal servers.

Applying Sawhney's (1992) infrastructure development model, these Wi-Fi networks may find themselves somewhere between stages three and five of development. Stage three is characterized by the new infrastructure being encouraged by the old system. In this case, the old system would be individualized, home broadband connectivity. The familiarity and expectation of high-speed broadband encourages the use of wireless for greater mobility and locations of access. Stage four is characterized by long-distance capabilities and system formation. While Wi-Fi as a technology is not necessarily conducive to long-range transmission, given interference and power limitations, things such as mesh technology can theoretically help to mitigate these problems and extend transmission range. Stage four is also noted for the process of isolated bits of the new technology becoming interconnected with one another. Stage five is characterized by the outright competition of the new system with the old system. In this stage, Sawhney (1992, 543) highlights the "need to protect the franchises of the old system" and how "emerging competition is depicted as wasteful." This might be consistent with the recent debates over wireless spectrum and the use of legislation to prevent municipal wireless networks from developing. It is unclear whether or not these emerging community networks will see the development model through to completion, when Wi-Fi networks would subordinate traditional landline networks until a newer technology in turn replaces them. In fact, given Wi-Fi's dependency on backhaul connectivity somewhere in the infrastructure, it is more likely landline and Wi-Fi networks will remain complementary services. However, it is clear that Wi-Fi networks, which are altering the existing model of individualized, personal broadband into more community-oriented services that help to reduce costs, improve access, and create local Internet awareness and content, have the potential to change and complement this existing system for the better, over time.

CONCLUSION AND FUTURE PROSPECTS

I began by exploring the concept of urban wireless Internet clouds of access, the result of many individual wireless nodes broadcasting broadband connections in wide areas throughout cities. These clouds of access are a source of great potential for a number of wireless community groups who seek to turn this broadband backhaul into community services. Both the successes of and the challenges facing the groups described above suggest that, while wireless Internet is here to stay, what individuals have come to expect from it and what they wish to do with it are still in flux. This is fitting, given that this is still a formative period of infrastructure development for wireless Internet.

Still, there are unanswered questions about how people perceive their wireless connections in terms of ownership and sharing. For example, is one's home Internet connection an extension of one's personal property? Is connectivity perceived as a home service much like phone or television access? In the latter case, how much appeal might sharing have? Extending sharing to public spaces, what is the value to users beyond the ability to have access? Do individuals expect or want more from their connection than just access? Or do community and local content really resonate with the users? The groups reviewed here, among many others, seek to answer just those questions as they aim to transform some of these perceptions of Internet access into their own vision of community service. With a variety of different approaches and motivations available, it seems likely that the project of transformation will succeed to varying degrees if certain conditions are met. These might include addressing individual concerns about sharing, reducing costs collectively as individual costs rise, promoting interesting and valuable local content, and improving the stability and reliability of the networks.

ACKNOWLEDGMENTS

I would like to thank professors Andrew Clement and Catherine Middleton and the CRACIN and Canadian Wireless Infrastructure Research Project (CWIRP) teams for their help and assistance. My thanks as well to Alison Powell and Hanna Cho and to the Social Sciences and Humanities Research Council of Canada and Infrastructure Canada. I am especially grateful to Damien Fox and Steve Wilton, of Wireless Nomad, for their insight and support over the years.

NOTES

1 Sandvig (2004, 583) also uses the term *cloud* in this sense, suggesting that these clouds are composed of "heterogeneous networks that interoperate by accident as often as by intent."
2 Currently either Wired Equivalent Privacy (WEP) or Wi-Fi Protected Access (WPA).
3 Names used with permission.
4 Unless indicated otherwise, all subsequent dollar amounts are in Canadian currency.
5 It was not possible to determine the precise number of Foneros and nodes in existence at the time this chapter was written.
6 As of April 2010, converting €29.95.

REFERENCES

Andersen, Espen. 2003. Genesis of an anthill: Wireless technology and self-organizing systems. *Ubiquity* 3 (February): 1. http://ubiquity.acm.org/article.cfm?id=764006.
BBC News. 2006a. Global Wi-Fi plan gets $22m boost. 7 February, online edition. http://news.bbc.co.uk/2/hi/technology/4686914.stm.
———. 2006b. Wi-Fi pioneers offer cheap router. 27 June, online edition. http://news.bbc.co.uk/2/hi/technology/5116960.stm.
———. 2007. Wi-Fi sharing plan launched in UK. 4 October, online edition. http://news.bbc.co.uk/2/hi/technology/7027871.stm.
Cho, Hanna. 2006. Explorations in community and civic bandwidth: A case study in community wireless networking. MA thesis, Ryerson University and York University, Toronto, Canada.
Frieden, Rob. 2005. Lessons from broadband development in Canada, Japan, Korea and the United States. *Telecommunications Policy* 29(8): 595–613.
Gibbons, James, and Steve Ruth. 2006. Municipal Wi-Fi: Big wave or wipeout? *IEEE Internet Computing* 10(3): 52–57
Goth, Greg. 2005. Municipal wireless networks open new access and old debates. *IEEE Internet Computing* 9(3): 8–11.
Lentz, R.G. 1998. Corporations vs. communities: Evolution of wireless services in the US and the devolution of local control. *Telecommunications Policy* 22(10): 791–95.
Ngini, Chukwuma U., Steven M. Furnell, and Bogdan V. Ghita. 2002. Assessing the global accessibility of the Internet. *Internet Research: Electronic Networking Applications and Policy* 12(4): 329–38.
O'Brien, Danny. 2003. Rebel network: Why pay a fortune to get wired up to broadband when you could join an anarchic wireless network that does the job. *New Scientist* 180 (October): 26.
Powell, Alison. 2006. "Last mile" or local innovation? Canadian perspectives on community Wireless networking as civic participation. Paper presented at the 34th Annual

Telecommunications Policy Research Conference on Communication, Information, and Internet Policy, Arlington, Virginia, USA, 28 September–1 October.

Powell, Alison, and Leslie Regan Shade. 2005. Going Wi-Fi in Canada: Municipal and community initiatives. CRACIN Working Paper no. 6. June. Toronto: Canadian Research Alliance for Community Innovation and Networking. http://archive.iprp.ischool. utoronto.ca/cracin/publications/pdfs/WorkingPapers/CRACIN%20Working%20Paper%20No%206.pdf.

Reid, David. 2006. Wi-Fi sharing could be the future. BBC News, 29 September, online edition. http://news.bbc.co.uk/2/hi/programmes/click_online/5371320.stm.

Sandvig, Christian. 2004. An initial assessment of cooperative action in Wi-Fi networking. *Telecommunications Policy* 28(7–8): 579–602.

Sandvig, Christian, David Young, and Sascha Meinrath. 2004. Hidden interfaces to "ownerless" networks. Paper presented at the 32nd Annual Telecommunications Policy Research Conference on Communication, Information, and Internet Policy, Arlington, Virginia, USA, September. http://www.saschameinrath.com/downloads/hidden interfaces.pdf.

Sawhney, Harmeet. 1992. The public telephone network: Stages in infrastructure development. *Telecommunications Policy* 16(7): 538–52.

Shah, Rajiv C., and Christian Sandvig. 2005. Software defaults as de facto regulation: The case of wireless APs. Paper presented to the 33rd Annual Telecommunications Policy Research Conference on Communication, Information and Internet Policy, Arlington, Virginia, USA, 23 September.

Statistics Canada. 2008. *The Daily: Canadian Internet Use Survey.* http://www.statcan.gc.ca/daily-quotidien/080612/dq080612b-eng.htm.

Tapia, Andrea H., and Julio Angel Ortiz. 2006. Municipal responses to state-level broadband Internet policy. Paper presented at the 34th Annual Telecommunications Policy Research Conference on Communication, Information and Internet Policy, Arlington, Virginia, USA, 28 September–1 October.

Wong, Matthew. 2006. Sharing wireless Internet in urban neighbourhoods. MA thesis, University of Toronto.

Wong, Matthew, and Andrew Clement. 2007. Sharing wireless Internet in urban neighbourhoods. Paper presented at the 3rd International Conference on Communities and Technologies, East Lansing, Michigan, USA.

Wu, Irene. 2004. Canada, South Korea, Netherlands and Sweden: Regulatory implications of the convergence of telecommunications, broadcasting and Internet services. *Telecommunications Policy* 28(1): 79–96.

Xue, Qi, and Aura Ganz. 2002. QoS routing for mesh-based wireless LANs. *International Journal of Wireless Information Networks* 9(3): 179–90.

PART V

Rural and Remote Broadband

13 "WE WERE ON THE OUTSIDE LOOKING IN" MyKnet.org — A First Nations Online Social Environment in Northern Ontario

Brandi L. Bell, Philipp Budka, Adam Fiser

In 2000, one of Canada's leading Aboriginal community networks, the Kuh-ke-nah Network, or K-Net, was on the verge of expanding into broadband services. (For more on K-Net, see chapter 14.) K-Net's management organization, Keewaytinook Okimakanak Tribal Council, had acquired funding and resources to become one of Industry Canada's Smart Communities demonstration projects. Among the innovative services that K-Net introduced at the time was MyKnet. org, a system of personal home pages intended for remote First Nations users in a region of Northern Ontario where numerous communities have lived without adequate residential telecom service well into the millennium (Fiser, Clement, and Walmark 2006; Ramírez et al. 2003). Shortly thereafter, and through K-Net's community-based Internet infrastructure, this free-of-charge, free-of-advertising, locally supported, online social environment grew from its core constituency of remote First Nations communities to host over 30,000 registered user accounts (of which approximately 20,000 represent active home pages). The numbers are notable given that the system primarily serves members of Northern Ontario's over fifty First Nations communities, whose combined population totals approximately 45,000, occupying a geographic area roughly the size of France. Equally significant is that over half of this population is under the age of 25, making MyKnet.org primarily a youth-driven online social environment.

In this chapter we report on a study investigating the development of MyK-net.org and its embeddedness within the particular rural/remote First Nations context of Northern Ontario. We postulate that MyKnet.org has become a vibrant medium for Northern Ontario First Nations in part as a result of its historical connections with K-Net's broader "computerization movement" and older Indigenous media practices in Northern Ontario. We explore both how MyKnet.org grew out of a drive for broadband telecom service in the region and how it currently plays an important socio-cultural role by enabling First Nations individuals and communities to shape web space and extend their social ties online.

A number of scholars (see, for example, Forte 2006; Landzelius 2006a; Srinivasan 2006) have discussed the potential of new media technologies for Indigenous peoples, particularly for sharing knowledge, constructing identities, and communicating across distances and borders. According to Srinivasan (2006), the challenge for Indigenous communities and their collaborators is to tailor new media and information systems to specific local cultural needs. We believe that, as an Indigenous-controlled online medium, MyKnet.org meets this challenge. The success of MyKnet.org extends the observation made by Anderson (1991) and others that older media such as print and radio have played a role in the social construction of community and concepts such as Indigenousness and nationhood.

RESEARCH CONTEXT

We use the term *First Nation* to designate an Indian band registered with Indian and Northern Affairs Canada, in accordance with the Indian Act (R.S., 1985).[1] Each First Nations community occupies its own reserve and participates in local governance through the auspices of a band office directed by an elected chief and council. At the time of the 2006 census, there were an estimated 698,025 First Nations people in Canada and 615 First Nations bands, representing fifty-two distinct cultural-territorial groups (Cree, Haida, Mohawk, Ojibwe, etc.). In Ontario, where this study took place, there were approximately 158,395 First Nations people, many of them living in rural or remote environments, and a total of 134 First Nations communities (Statistics Canada 2006).

MyKnet.org is particularly significant in the lives of First Nations individuals in Northern Ontario who occupy land apportioned by Treaties 9 and 5. This land corresponds to a political territory known as Nishnawbe Aski Nation (NAN), which is home to over fifty First Nations communities. Communities in and around NAN are remote: they have no year-round road access and are generally located north of the 50th parallel and/or over 50 kilometres from the nearest service centre. Most are fly-in communities, although some have devised temporary winter roads (constructed across frozen lakes) to link into a southern supply corridor during the months of February and March. In the absence of such roads, it costs anywhere from CAD$400 to $4,000 for a one-way trip by scheduled aircraft to the nearest town, Sioux Lookout (in Ontario), or the larger proximate cities of Thunder Bay, Ontario, and Winnipeg. Under such conditions, personal mobility is severely restricted for most of the region's inhabitants.

Our research draws from three years of community-based research, initiated with Northern Ontario First Nations under a partnership between Keewaytinook Okimakanak (the tribal council that manages K-Net) and the Canadian Research Alliance for Community Innovation and Networking (CRACIN). With guidance from staff at K-Net and the Keewaytinook Okimakanak Research Institute,[2] we designed our research plan to establish community participation and community control over data collection. Under this research plan, Budka and Fiser visited more than twenty First Nation communities, and numerous fieldwork activities were undertaken. These included visits to schools and public Internet-access points, such as e-centres in local communities,[3] and individual and group discussions with youth and adults (both offline and online), as well as researcher participation in youth training and employment programs and video conference discussions. This fieldwork provided us with important foundational information regarding the region, its communities, and their development and use of media technologies, in addition to establishing working relationships with people in the region.

In order to gain a more thorough understanding of MyKnet.org, online and telephone interviews were conducted with the explicit goal of exploring the development, uses, and meanings of MyKnet.org. Initially, we sought the perspectives of administrators, early innovators, casual users, and non-users. However, following input from this community, we broadened our scope to include respondents who could help us compare MyKnet.org with other media in the First Nations (particularly community radio and satellite television) and who could help us explore the traditional and popular cultural context of First Nations individuals' media usage.

Our resulting sample for this particular research included ten interviews completed by teleconference, as well as numerous online encounters with users via email and an open online meeting platform. Our data collection activities were conducted with the participation of all three researchers, as appropriate and possible.[4] This sample is biased toward long-standing users, who had at least four years of experience with MyKnet.org, and toward non-users who make use of computer-mediated communications and have participated in other K-Net initiatives. The mean age of our combined respondents (28 years) also exceeds the mean age of the communities. This sample is therefore not meant to be representative of the general population of MyKnet.org users or non-users but is instead made up of "key informants" (Millen 2000) who possess an *emic* understanding of their socio-cultural milieu, in this case K-Net initiatives and/orMyKnet.org and its embeddedness in the context of Northern Ontario First Nations life.

Concurrent with data collection activities, and more extensively once data collection was completed, we independently reviewed interview notes in order to summarize themes and findings, while also taking into account the existing knowledge gained from previous fieldwork, interviews, or community interactions. Adopting an iterative process of analysis, we identified themes in order to "bring together components or fragments of ideas or experiences, which often are meaningless when viewed alone" (Leininger 1985, 60). We also engaged with new questions and issues that emerged so that these might guide ongoing data collection (Miles and Huberman 1994). This process led us to expand our reach in interviews, as described above. As we met repeatedly to further review and refine our findings, we also returned to interviewees or other community members, as needed, to check our understandings and interpretations of the data.

TOWARD A FRAMEWORK FOR STUDYING MYKNET.ORG

As we set out to examine MyKnet.org, we felt it was important to situate our work within an historical appreciation of Aboriginal and First Nations media. As our research proceeded, this grounding proved valuable in helping us explore MyKnet.org's embeddedness. While writings on Aboriginal media helped us understand the cultural aspects of MyKnet.org and its uses, as well as the desire of First Nations individuals to develop their online social environment, the practicalities of such development were left unexplained. In an effort to better understand how such an online social environment came to exist within its specific contexts, we therefore draw upon the notion of a computerization movement.

MyKnet.org as a Computerization Movement

According to Kling and Iacono (1988, 228), the concept of a computerization movement refers to efforts to use "computer-based systems as instruments to bring about a new social order." They argue that "computerization movements are based upon collaborations of participants with diverse interests" (229). Our account of MyKnet.org's development considers it to be part of a computerization movement that connects local and national interests.

The phase in which MyKnet.org emerged, when much of K-Net's core broadband network infrastructure was being built, coincided with the

Canadian government's national focus on "Connecting Canadians" to the Internet. (See Fiser and Clement's historical account in chapter 14.) Most of the initiatives that K-Net's alliance of First Nations undertook to develop their network infrastructure and applications benefitted from federal investments in provincial, regional, and local computerization movements, to implement computer technology as a means of bridging social and technological divides in Canada (Fiser, Clement, and Walmark 2006). A central component of any computerization movement concerns the many decisions that are made about control and use of technology during the development process (Kling and Iacono 1988). At each step of K-Net and MyKnet. org's development, choices about appropriate investment and control over equipment and expertise were made within the communities. As such, on a regional level the development of K-Net and MyKnet.org can be seen as part of an Indigenous computerization movement lead by local leaders in the First Nations communities. These leaders—from First Nations councils, economic development agencies, education and health authorities, and civic groups—collaborated with the intent not only to implement computer technology but also to adopt and adapt that technology to the local needs of their communities. For example, as we discuss below, they focused youth training and educational opportunities to complement the physical network infrastructure's development. Thus, counter to arguments that view computerization in terms of a simple market formula of "cost-effective computing tools," Kling and Iacono (1988) and the experiences of Keewaytinook Okimakanak (KO) Tribal Council and its collaborators suggest that the acquisition, installation, and adoption of computers and information and communication technologies (ICTs) depend on an equally important array of non-economic choices.

MyKnet.org as a Community-Driven Online Social Environment

While we interpret MyKnet.org's development as part of an Indigenous computerization movement with strong ties to both local and national interests, we also recognize that MyKnet.org is a unique online social environment that has been directly shaped by the interactions of its individual users, who extend their social ties online.

One of the common reasons that prompt Indigenous peoples, groups, and organizations to create an online presence is "to provide information from a viewpoint that may not have found a voice in the mainstream media" (Cisler 1997). Indigenous communities have made early inroads on the World Wide Web. The Oneida First Nation of New York state, for instance, mounted the first Indigenous-owned website in spring 1994, well before the home page of the White House went online (Polly 1997), and the Blackfeet Confederacy in Alberta established the first Aboriginal Canadian web presence one year later (Prins 2002).

The individual contributions that shape these online social environments may take a variety of forms. Landzelius (2003, 2006a) refers to the "self-authored engagements" of Indigenous peoples online as "Indigenous cyberactivism" and distinguishes between "outreach" and "inreach" activities. In this case cyberactivism may not only encompass but also transcend narrowly political communications. Indigenous outreach initiatives include public relations and tourism management, sovereignty campaigns, liberation movements, and common-cause partnerships between Indigenous and non-Indigenous groups. However, we have found that MyKnet.org focuses more heavily on Indigenous inreach activities, which are oriented toward an internal public and include activities such as public services (e-health and e-learning, for example), as well as personalized social networking practices such as communications directed between families and friends. As we elaborate in our discussion below, this inreach focus points to the importance of MyKnet.org as a locally developed and owned online social environment, which stands in contrast to mainstream online social network sites such as Facebook.

MyKnet.org as an Extension of Indigenous Media Production in Northern Ontario

The First Nations' use of Internet technologies, though a development of new media corresponding to Landzelius's concept of cyberactivism, resonates with older media practices within the greater context of Indigenous media production. During the 1970s, several First Nations newspapers and newsletters came into existence across Canada, following the release of the 1969 White Paper on Indian policy. In Northern Ontario, the multilingual *Wawatay News* was published for the first time in 1973, providing the First Nations communities of the region with news in English, Ojibwe, Oji-Cree, and Cree syllabics.

Most of the money for media production came from the federal Native Communication Program, which was also established in 1973 (see Avison and Meadows 2000). However, when the Canadian government cut funding in 1990, some newspapers were forced to cease publishing, while others, such as *Wawatay News*, became more commercial and now include advertisements at the cost of other content (Demay 1993).

Together with *Wawatay News*, the Wawatay Native Communications Society established a community radio system for Northern Ontario's First Nations. The first community radio station was established in 1974, and, in 1986, the Canadian Radio-television and Telecommunications Commission (CRTC) licensed the Wawatay Radio Network, which provides programming in Oji-Cree and Cree language. Particularly in the northernmost communities, where Native languages continue to be spoken by a majority of residents, the radio network's programs have reached up to 80 percent of local populations (Karam and Zuckernick 1992). However, community radio broadcasts now compete with satellite television and the Internet, which are particularly dominated by the English language, and there are fears that audiences have diminished.

Following the launch of the Anik satellites at the end of the 1970s, several Aboriginal broadcasters, such as the Inuit Broadcasting Corporation, started to provide Native-language programming (see, for example, Baltruschat 2004; Roth 2005). In 1983, the Northern Broadcasting Policy and the Northern Native Broadcast Program created the basis for a northern satellite distribution system, which eventually resulted in the launch of Television Northern Canada (TVNC) in 1991. In 1999, the Aboriginal Peoples Television Network (APTN) was launched, after TVCN was approved for a national broadcast license. APTN blends multilingual programming on Aboriginal cultures, lives, traditions, and histories with news and public affairs in a mainstream broadcasting style. It also depends on local and regional Aboriginal media producers, such as Wawatay, for content. Despite the existence of this vital network, approximately 35 percent of Aboriginal people living on reserves, particularly in the North, still do not receive APTN programming (Roth 2005). At the same time, APTN, while Aboriginal-controlled and Aboriginal-focused, must attempt to represent Canada's vast Aboriginal experience, thus diluting the potential for locally controlled and community-focused media.

Following the inroads of Indigenous newsprint, radio, and television up to the mid-1990s, Canadian Indigenous groups began to mobilize for improved access to telecommunications facilities and the establishment of Internet infrastructure. In Northern Ontario, Wawatay and KO Tribal Council's K-Net Services spearheaded a movement for improved telecom services that paved the way for K-Net's introduction of broadband services in 2000 (see chapter 14). First Nations across Northern Ontario had input into Wawatay and the KO Tribal Council's regional campaign, and awareness was raised around the feasibility and usefulness of Internet applications such as email and personal home pages. This legacy directly shaped MyKnet.org's online social environment when it appeared on the Web in 2000.

DEVELOPMENT OF MYKNET.ORG: AN INDIGENOUS COMPUTERIZATION MOVEMENT

In 1994, staff members of the Keewaytinook Okimakanak Tribal Council, which represented seven (later to become six) remote fly-in First Nations, organized an experimental bulletin board system (BBS) for their communities.[5] This was the beginning of the Kuh-ke-nah Network (K-Net), an amalgam of

Oji-Cree and English meaning "everybody's network." As part of its nascent computerization movement, KO configured the K-Net BBS to support a Stay in School project in the First Nations. The goal of the movement was to create a computer-mediated communications link between the First Nations and their high-school-aged youth who, in seeking higher education, had to board in Pelican Falls, a residential school for First Nations near the town and service-hub of Sioux Lookout. The BBS presented an innovative solution to a serious telecommunications problem: some communities only had one public payphone, placed outside the community's band office. Others had to rely on trail radio for communications. Few, if any, had access to computers.

The KO communities are among over fifty First Nations in a territory that the CRTC designates as a high-cost serving area, and market forces alone have failed to support their telecommunications needs (Fiser, Clement, and Walmark 2006). Similarly, the diffusion of computers and related ICTs in the territory depends on grassroots initiatives and public-private sector partnerships. To establish the BBS as a communications link between the First Nations, Pelican Falls, and Sioux Lookout, the KO Tribal Council had to build a computer-communications infrastructure from the ground up. They thus constituted a localized computerization movement, focused on finding ways to use technology to support and meet the needs of the local communities.

The experiences of the KO Tribal Council and its collaborators reflect the argument of Kling and Iacono (1988) that the acquisition, installation, and adoption of computers and ICTs depends on an array of non-economic forces, rather than simply cost-effectiveness. With K-Net, a core group of community leaders worked with First Nations members and interested parties from local education, health, and community service fields to build a business case for Internet access and later broadband. As more and more local interests came to share their vision of an Indigenous network, the KO Tribal Council and its allies brokered public-private sector partnerships to develop their network, built around the principles of a not-for-profit organization and co-operative enterprise. Notably, education has been a major component of the network. K-Net staff have worked hard to impart a technology curriculum, or culture of use, in the communities (Beaton, Fiddler, and Rowlandson 2004) by providing workshops for users to experiment with computers and by supporting individual community champions to manage and organize public access to computing through local institutions such as band offices, e-centres, and schools. By 1996, 730 users in twenty-one First Nations communities of Northwestern Ontario had access to the K-Net BBS. What was initially the Stay in School project rapidly became a regional communications medium for adults and youth alike, despite being limited by a text-based, low-bandwidth device.

There was no access to the World Wide Web offered by K-Net during this period, and all of the online connections went through dial-up. Despite slow download speeds, users were creating and linking personal profiles, sharing messages, writing stories and jokes, discussing current events, posting notices and ads, learning about computing, and more. Some of the very remote communities that participated, such as North Spirit Lake and Keewaywin, had no direct access to K-Net, but they acquired computers, and KO periodically airmailed floppy disks between the communities and the BBS server to update the messages, demonstrating the commitment organizers had to serving local communities and using technology to facilitate community development and communication.

Reflecting the K-Net computerization movement as a broad-based initiative driven by community needs, as well as its connection to a broader national computerization movement, from 1997 to 2000 KO partnered with Industry Canada's First Nations SchoolNet, Telesat Canada, and the Stentor Alliance to install DirecPC technology in First Nations elementary schools and some off-reserve high schools (Fiser 2004). In 1997, KO also began to receive support from Industry Canada's Community Access Program (CAP) to establish public access sites in K-Net communities across Northwestern Ontario. Coupled with the SchoolNet program and support from regional and provincial partners, CAP enabled K-Net communities to leverage school connectivity for public access and hire local coordinators. As KO facilitated the SchoolNet initiative and the development of CAP sites in each community, its staff members travelled around Northern Ontario to deliver workshops on computing, web page development, and basic Internet skills (from 1997 to 1999), as well as providing ongoing online training and support over the K-Net BBS, thereby building local capacities.

It was during this period that MyKnet.org's web-based precursors emerged. The web-based graphical interface of the BBS (as it existed in 1998) enabled K-Net to serve community portals and home pages. The earliest home pages were strictly HTML and service oriented. KO staff created initial templates and embedded them within a tutorial designed to facilitate self-directed learning. Most learning was undertaken by community members on their own initiative, online, at the public access sites. To this end, KO staff dedicated much personal effort to building online support systems, chat rooms, tutorials, bulletin boards, listservs, and so on.

In 2001, K-Net became one of Industry Canada's SMART demonstration projects (see Ramírez et al. 2003). This project would catalyze K-Net's evolution into a regional wide area network (WAN) and Internet service provider. Support leveraged from project partners, including Industry Canada, FedNor, and the Northern Ontario Heritage Fund, enabled KO to order T1 services (1.544Mbps) for four of the KO communities and to establish a shared, high-speed satellite service for its most remote community, Fort Severn. The K-Net BBS was retired, and MyKnet.org acquired its own domain name and dedicated server.

A year later, the Fort Severn satellite initiative led KO to partner with Telesat Canada R&D and Industry Canada to initiate the C-Band Public Benefits Transponder agreement (Keewaytinook Okimakanak Research Institute 2005). A logical complement to the SMART initiative, the C-Band satellite service would help deliver broadband applications in twelve remote First Nations in Northern Ontario that could not otherwise acquire network services. With broadband, residential Internet access finally became a feasible project in the region, although public access e-centres and schools continue to be the primary access points for MyKnet.org end-users in the region. The ensuing years, up to the present, have seen K-Net expand broadband services in partnership with forty other remote communities.

Owing to the high cost of network services in remote areas, limited bandwidth is an ongoing management issue, especially for users over K-Net's satellite network, which services forty-four communities. As part of a community-based network, MyKnet.org users have to negotiate uptime with regularly scheduled high-capacity applications such as video conferencing and telemedicine. The increasing use of audio and video on MyKnet.org home pages led to a 2006 decision by K-Net staff to institute a daily quota, in order to manage community bandwidth. Other than to support higher-capacity community-based applications, K-Net does not regulate the type of content created on the MyKnet.org server. However, to ensure that MyKnet.org does not disrupt services such as video conferencing and telemedicine, especially in the K-Net satellite communities, staff evaluate pages and disk usage and temporarily suspend high-bandwidth-consuming pages until services are rendered.

It is important to recognize that MyKnet.org emerged out of a national computerization movement on the part of the Canadian government, which provided programs and funding for much of the technological implementation in the region. However, its development within a *local* computerization movement in the region that was (and is) focused on local education, local ownership and control of media, and the development of local capacities, particularly among youth, is central to its understanding by users and community members. MyKnet.org is seen as belonging to the community and, as the discussion below highlights, is used in various ways as a means of supporting local communication, networking, and community building.

MYKNET.ORG AND ONLINE SOCIAL NETWORKING

Social networking websites, typically defined as websites on which users create personal profiles and network with others through online tools (Barnes 2006; Ellison, Steinfield, and Lampe 2006), have become increasingly popular in recent years, with large commercial websites attracting interest in popular media (Lewis 2006; Rawe 2006) and the most popular websites boasting millions of users (Stone 2005). However, as scholars have noted, the networking aspects of such websites are not new, and other forms of Internet communication, including instant messaging, home pages, and blogs, involve aspects of social networking (boyd 2004; Ellison, Steinfield, and Lampe 2006). Although MyKnet.org does not technically resemble popular social networking websites, most notably because it is made up of interlinked home pages and does not formally encourage users to create networks of "friends," it is similar in many ways, particularly in its function and use. MyKnet.org is, for many First Nations members of the NAN communities, an important tool for presenting oneself and communicating with others in locally meaningful ways.

While literature on Internet communication has extensively explored the ways in which various online tools and environments facilitate (or complicate) social networking among peers and strangers (see, for example, Wellman and Haythornthwaite 2002), literature on social networking websites has tended to emphasize popular commercial enterprises, such as MySpace and Facebook. MyKnet.org is, in contrast, locally developed and locally controlled and operates on a not-for-profit basis, and its development in many ways prefigured the growth of popular social networking websites. Unlike those websites, however, the focus of MyKnet.org on building and strengthening particular kinship and community ties is central to its existence and use.

MYKNET.ORG AS COMMUNITY-BASED AND COMMUNITY-FOCUSED MEDIA TECHNOLOGY

The relationship between media and community is closely connected to the development and diffusion of communication technologies. From newspaper to the Internet, every new medium has been credited with the "possibility of regenerating community through mediated forms of communication" (Jankowski 2006, 55). Research into community media can be traced back to the beginning of the twentieth century, when newspapers and radio were analyzed for their contributions to community building. In the 1970s and 1980s, case studies focusing on new electronic media, such as video and cable television, investigated the potential of community media for political and cultural activism as well as their interrelations with social capital (see Jankowski 2006 for a review of the literature). Community media studies turned to the Internet in the 1990s. Almost every published volume on the socio-cultural aspects of the Internet discussed community construction, often in connection to identity formation in and through new media technology (Benedikt 1991; Jones 1995, 1997; Rheingold 1993; Smith and Kollock 1999). While the bulk of this literature has concentrated on online communities and their characteristics, other projects have investigated what has been termed the digital divide. Referring to the unequally distributed access to ICTs, this concept is epistemologically linked to the concept of haves and have-nots. This is why community informatics, for instance, focuses on what Gurstein (2003) calls "the effective use" of ICTs, including their implementation and use in specific geographically based community contexts (see also Gurstein 2000 and the introduction to the present volume). As recent studies on ICTs and community (see, for example, Haythornthwaite and Kendall 2010) indicate, information technologies such as the Internet can be used to reinforce and regenerate geographically based communities and identities.

In the remote First Nations communities of Northern Ontario, media services develop more slowly, but, as our respondents stated, any new medium that is made available will be used provided community members have enough control to make it work for their purposes. MyKnet.org is taking its place among other community media in the region, in some ways acting as a substitute for the telephone, which was, owing to a lack of infrastructure, never widely used among the communities. In other ways, MyKnet.org functions like community radio—present in the region since the 1970s—but with a younger audience and user group at the helm. Community radio broadcasts mainly in Native languages (Cree, Oji-Cree, and Ojibwe), and its audience consists primarily of older community members (those over 40 years of age), whereas younger people in many of the communities do not speak these languages as fluently as their elders and thus find English-language media more accessible. Some respondents compared MyKnet.org to community radio, particularly as both are locally driven and locally operated initiatives, and both provide access for individual community members to participate and make their voices heard. While access and language issues caused our respondents to be cautious about claiming that MyKnet.org is *as* broadly accessible to First Nations as community radio, they made it clear that both media are important to community members specifically because they are considered to be owned and shaped by the communities themselves (unlike satellite television, for example).

Like community radio, MyKnet.org connects individuals within communities, but it also enables connections across communities. We heard a number of stories about the possibilities for communication among frequent MyKnet.org users. We were told particularly of parents who use MyKnet.org to locate their children when they travel abroad, or even within the local communities. In one story we heard, parents asked their older daughter where her sister was going to be that night, and the older daughter went onto her sister's MyKnet.org home page to discover her location. Our respondents told us that these were not uncommon patterns of use.

Such purposeful searches of MyKnet.org are facilitated by daily patterns of home page use (updating and reading), supported by a K-Net policy that requires MyKnet.org users to register accounts under their surname and given names. Coupled with this policy, the uniqueness of surnames in Northern Ontario First Nations turns MyKnet.org into a dynamic map of kinship ties in the region. We were told that Native users who understand the correspondences between surnames, territories, and communities can use MyKnet.org to follow the movements of their peers and relations across the region. We also heard stories about distant family relations becoming reunited through MyKnet.org, including estranged family members scattered across provinces and remote/urban divides. As Arnold and Plymire (2004) have argued, Aboriginal online activities can be important means for cultural communities to keep in touch and to maintain a sense of community despite changing geographic locations. In its uses by community members, MyKnet.org is playing just such a role, as home pages are used extensively to keep in touch with friends, family, and colleagues (Budka 2009).

MyKnet.org home pages cover the entire community lifecycle, announcing births, graduations, marriages, separations, and deaths. MyKnet.org communities post their own home pages to advertise local events, and local programs, associations, and sports teams create pages to keep the public informed about their activities.[6] Aside from personal miscellany, individuals use home pages to promote business, arts, spiritual beliefs, and teachings from the land.[7]

Unforeseen events also become woven into the fabric of MyKnet.org. One of our respondents told us of the time she learned of a fire in a neighbouring community by reading a friend's home page. News of the fire spread across MyKnet.org, and within a few days there was a movement, coordinated largely over MyKnet.org, to provide relief to the effected community. Other disasters, such as teen suicides, have led to memorials and public information bulletins on MyKnet.org. Respondents told us that some community members have been known to monitor their local youths' home pages for signs of depression and have staged interventions on a number of occasions. In such ways, MyKnet.org fulfills an important role not only in strengthening familial and friendship ties but also in facilitating intercommunity communication, civic action, and other interpersonal connections. Uses of MyKnet.org that focus on connecting communities and community members by advertising events or providing information on local organizations, for example, reflect the important inreach activities described by Landzelius (2003, 2006a).

Another part of the community-based and community-focused aspect of MyKnet.org is its non-commercial nature. While mainstream online social network sites, such as Facebook, Beebo, and MySpace, have seen increasing amounts of marketing and advertising on their pages, from marketers gleaning information from profiles to celebrities using the networks for promotion (Barnes 2006), MyKnet.org remains non-commercial and locally focused. On MyKnet.org there is no fear of marketers seeking users online, and the promotion that does take place is by local artisans, musicians, or organizations through their respective home pages.

As a community-based and community-focused medium, MyKnet.org provides an alternative to mainstream commercial online social network sites. The uniqueness of its user pool, along with the kinship and community ties it represents, provides MyKnet.org with an advantage that any competing commercial network would not presently be able to meet. This advantage however, is predicated on sustainable public infrastructure. As Fiser and Clement point out in chapter 14, applications such as MyKnet.org can be free of charge and community based because K-Net has a system of resource sharing and co-operation in place between First Nations, telecom service providers, regional organizations, the Province of Ontario, and the Government of Canada. Given a fiscal climate in which community-focused funding programs, such as the federal Community Access Program and First Nations SchoolNet, have steadily declined in scope, innovative community-based applications such as MyKnet.org are at risk of being undervalued. Nevertheless, our research indicates that local demand for MyKnet.org's community-based media continues to thrive.

Respondents told us that they identify K-Net and MyKnet.org as part of their community experience, in contrast to other websites and online social environments that they may visit and use. MyKnet.org users are intimately enveloped by the cultural experience of a computerization movement in the Northern Ontario First Nations, such that there is more to MyKnet.org's appeal than simple communications.

CONCLUSION

This exploratory study of MyKnet.org aims to draw a preliminary map of this rich and fascinating online environment, focusing particularly on the importance of the community-based nature of the network's development and uses. We encountered much that is worth celebrating in terms of the vitality of Northern Ontario's remote First Nations and also discovered some particular areas of caution and uncertainty. While there are many other stories to be told about MyKnet.org, this particular account drew its interpretations from a selected group of key informants: administrators, early innovators, casual users, and non-users who have been actively thinking about what makes MyKnet.org a social networking environment and cultural milieu. Their stories revealed the many ways in which the network is used to build and maintain familial, friendship, and community relationships and how these relationships are structured within and through the realities of the geographical location and demographic makeup of the Northern Ontario First Nations, particularly the peoples of Nishnawbe Aski Nation.

Within the framework of Aboriginal media, MyKnet.org stands out in many ways. Those we spoke to suggest that MyKnet.org is a vibrant social networking site, not by virtue of a narrowly configured web server but by virtue of the practices of its users. No one knows who created the first "shout out" or the first interactive guest book on MyKnet.org, nor can our respondents say for certain who started the first daily blog or listing of community events or who created the first tribute to a deceased loved one, and so forth. What they know is that such functions are now integral to users' MyKnet.org experience and contribute to their community life. For observers of MyKnet.org it is clear that local experiences of life in the First Nations contribute to shaping and connecting the MyKnet.org home pages (see Miller and Slater 2002).

Moreover, within the context of global Indigenous Internet usage, MyKnet.org and its many creators and users demonstrate that "historically marginalized peoples are not only taking roles, but in certain respects taking the lead, as savvy, technoscientific actors themselves 'colonizing' global media channels and converting them into fertile habitats for the exercise of identity and voice across distance" (Landzelius 2006b, 300). The passion of local leaders and their ability to develop a local computerization movement within a national movement to "connect Canadians" clearly drove the implementation of computer technology in the region and helped to shape the uses of the technology that facilitate intercommunity communication as well as personal development.

ACKNOWLEDGEMENTS
We would like to acknowledge the financial support of the Canadian Research Alliance for Community Innovation and Networking (CRACIN) and the University of Vienna, as well as the research support provided by K-Net and the Keewaytinook Okimakanak Research Institute. Sincere thanks to all of our research participants for sharing their insights and stories.

NOTES

1 See section 2 of the Indian Act, R.S., 1985, c. 1–5, http://laws-lois.justice.gc.ca/eng/
   acts/I-5/page-1.html. The term *First Nation* is not synonymous with *Aboriginal*.
   Canada's Aboriginal population also includes the Inuit and the Métis.
2 We were guided by a draft of KORI's Community Consultation Standards, available
   at the time at http://research.knet.ca/?q=system/files/07-06-08_Community%20
   Consultation%20Guidelines_0.pdf, although this document has since been taken
   down. For current information, see http://www.ccednet-rcdec.ca/en/node/9535.
3 E-centres are local public-access facilities, usually housed in or near a community Band
   Office or school, that provide multimedia PCs and Internet access free of charge to
   residents and visitors. Periodically, staff members offer relevant workshops.
4 In respect of our participants' privacy, we have chosen to keep our discussions
   anonymous.
5 The communities are Deer Lake, Fort Severn, Kasabonika, Keewaywin, North Spirit
   Lake, and Poplar Hill. A seventh community, McDowell Lake (population 51) is a
   seasonal settlement without a school. Kasabonika left the tribal council in 1998.
6 See, for example, http://sandylakerecreation.myknet.org/, http://sandylakefiredept.
   myknet.org/, and http://littlebandshockey.myknet.org/.
7 See, for example, http://ronniebeaver.myknet.org/, http://josephsutherland.myknet.
   org/, http://leonakakepetum.myknet.org, http://calkenny.myknet.org, and http://
   dokodesigns.myknet.org.

REFERENCES

Anderson, Benedict. 1991. *Imagined communities: Reflections on the origin and spread of
   nationalism*. London: Verso.
Arnold, Ellen, and Darcy Plymire. 2004. Continuity within change: The Cherokee Indians
   and the Internet. In *Web.Studies*, 2nd ed., ed. David Gauntlett and Ross Horsley, 254–
   64. London: Arnold.
Avison, Shannon, and Michael Meadows. 2000. Speaking and hearing: Aboriginal newspapers and the public sphere in Canada and Australia. *Canadian Journal of Communication* 25(3). http://www.cjc-online.ca/viewarticle.php?id=586&layout=html.
Baltruschat, Doris. 2004. Television and Canada's Aboriginal communities: Seeking oppor-
   tunities through traditional storytelling and digital technologies. *Canadian Journal of
   Communication* 29(1). http://www.cjc-online.ca/viewarticle.php?id=858&layout=html.
Barnes, Susan B. 2006. A privacy paradox: Social networking in the United States. *First
   Monday* 11(9). http://firstmonday.org/htbin/cgiwrap/bin/ojs/index.php/fm/article/
   view/1394/1312.
Beaton, Brian, Jesse Fiddler, and John Rowlandson. 2004. Living smart in two worlds:
   Maintaining and protecting First Nation culture for future generations. In *Seeking
   Convergence*, ed. Marita Moll and Leslie Regan Shade, 283–98. Ottawa: Canadian
   Centre for Policy Alternatives.
Benedikt, Michael, ed. 1991. *Cyberspace: First steps*. Cambridge, MA: MIT Press.
boyd, danah michele. 2004. Friendster and publicly articulated social networks. Paper pre-
   sented at the *Conference on Human Factors and Computing Systems*, Vienna, Austria,
   24–29 April. http://www.danah.org/papers/CHI2004Friendster.pdf.
Budka, Philipp. 2009. Indigenous media technology production in Northern Ontario,
   Canada. In *Canada in Grainau / Le Canada à Grainau: A multidisciplinary survey of*

Canadian Studies after 30 years, ed. Klaus-Dieter Ertler and Hartmut Lutz, 63–74. Frankfurt am Main: Peter Lang.

Cisler, Steve. 1997. The Internet and Indigenous groups: An introduction. *Cultural Survival Quarterly* 24(1). http://www.culturalsurvival.org/publications/cultural-survival-quarterly/none/introduction-internet-and-indigenous-groups.

Demay, Joël. 1993. The persistence and creativity of Canadian Aboriginal newspapers. *Canadian Journal of Communication* 18(1). http://www.cjc-online.ca/viewarticle. php?id=143&layout=html.

Ellison, Nicole, Charles Steinfield, and Cliff Lampe. 2006. Spatially bounded online social networks and social capital: The role of Facebook. Paper presented at the Annual Conference of the International Communication Association (ICA), Dresden, Germany, 19–23 June.

Fiser, Adam. 2004. First Nations SchoolNet Regional Management Organization (RMO) Backgrounder. CRACIN Working Paper no. 1. Toronto: Canadian Research Alliance for Community Innovation and Networking. http://archive.iprp.ischool.utoronto. ca/cracin/publications/pdfs/WorkingPapers/CRACIN%20Working%20Paper%20No %201.pdf.

Fiser, Adam, Andrew Clement, and Brian Walmark. 2006. The K-Net development process: A model for First Nations broadband community networks. CRACIN Working Paper no. 12. February. Toronto: Canadian Research Alliance for Community Innovation and Networking. http://archive.iprp.ischool.utoronto.ca/cracin/publications/pdfs/Working Papers/CRACIN%20Working%20Paper%20No%2012.pdf.

Forte, Maximilian C. 2006. Amerindian@Caribbean: Internet indigeneity in the electronic generation of Carib and Taino identities. In *Native on the Net: Indigenous and diasporic peoples in the virtual age*, ed. Kyra Landzelius, 132–51. London and New York: Routledge.

Gurstein, Michael. 2000. *Community informatics: Enabling communities with information and communication technologies*. Hershey, PA: Idea Group.

——. 2003. Effective use: A community informatics strategy beyond the digital divide. *First Monday* 8(12). http://firstmonday.org/htbin/cgiwrap/bin/ojs/index.php/fm/ article/view/1107/1027.

Haythornthwaite, Caroline, and Lori Kendall. 2010. Internet and community. *American Behavioral Scientist* 53/8: 1083–94.

Jankowski, Nicholas W. 2006. Creating community with media: History, theories and scientific investigation. In *Handbook of new media: Social shaping and social consequences of ICTs*, Updated student edition, ed. Leah A. Lievrouw and Sonia Livingtone, 55–74. London, UK, Thousand Oaks, CA, and New Delhi: Sage.

Jones, Steven G., ed. 1995. *Cybersociety: Computer-mediated communication and community.* Thousand Oaks, CA: Sage.

——, ed. 1997. *Virtual culture: Identity and communication in cybersociety.* Thousand Oaks, CA: Sage.

Karam, Robert, and Arlene Zuckernick. 1992. *A study of audiences for Aboriginal community radio: A profile of four Northern Ontario communities.* Toronto: Queen's Printer for Ontario.

Keewaytinook Okimakanak Research Institute. 2005. Assisting remote communities across Canada to access and use c-band public benefit, draft report. Keewaytinook Okimakanak. http://research.knet.ca.

Kling, Rob, and Suzanne Iacono. 1988. The mobilization of support for computerization: The role of computerization movements. *Social Problems* 35(3): 226–43.

Landzelius, Kyra. 2003. Paths of Indigenous cyber-activism. *Indigenous Affairs* 2(3): 6–13.

———. 2006a. Introduction: Native on the Net. In *Native on the Net: Indigenous and diasporic peoples in the virtual age*, ed. K. Landzelius, 1–42. London and New York: Routledge.

———. 2006b. Postscript: *Vox populi* for the Margins? In *Native on the Net: Indigenous and diasporic peoples in the virtual age*, ed. K. Landzelius, 292–304. London and New York: Routledge.

Leininger, Madeleine M. 1985. Ethnography and ethnonursing: Models and modes of qualitative data analysis. In *Qualitative research methods in nursing*, ed. Madeleine M. Leininger, 33–72. Orlando, FL: Grune and Stratton.

Lewis, N. 2006. MySpace proves to be a big marketing tool for artists. 2 September, *CanWest News*.

Miles, Matthew B., and A. Michael Huberman. 1994. *Qualitative data analysis*, 2nd ed. Thousand Oaks, CA: Sage.

Millen, David R. 2000. Rapid ethnography: Time deepening strategies for HCI field research. In *Proceedings of the Conference on Designing Interactive Systems: Processes, Practices, Methods, and Techniques*, ed. Daniel Boyarski, 280–86. New York: ACM Press.

Miller, Don, and Daniel Slater. 2002. Ethnography and the extreme Internet. In *Globalisation: Studies in anthropology*, ed. Thomas H. Eriksen, 39–57. London: Pluto Press.

Polly, Jean Armour. 1997. Standing stones in cyberspace: The Oneida Indian Nation's Territory on the web. *Cultural Survival Quarterly* 21(4). http://www.culturalsurvival.org/ourpublications/csq/article/standing-stones-cyberspace-the-oneida-indian-nations-territory-web.

Prins, Harald E. L. 2002. Visual media and the primitivist perplex: Colonial fantasies, Indigenous imagination, and advocacy in North America. In *Media worlds: Anthropology on new terrain*, ed. Faye D. Ginsburg, Lila Abu-Lughod, and Brian Larkin, 58–74. Berkeley: University of California Press.

Ramírez, Ricardo, Helen Aitkin, Rebekah Jamieson, and Don Richardson. 2003. Harnessing ICTs: A Canadian First Nations experience—Introduction to K-Net. Institute for Connectivity in the Americas. Ottawa: IDRC. http://www.idrc.ca/en/ev-106936-201-1-DO_TOPIC.html.

Rawe, Julie. 2006. How safe is MySpace? *Time*, Canadian edition, 3 July.

Rheingold, Howard. 1993. *The virtual community: Homesteading on the electronic frontier*. Reading, MA: Addison-Wesley.

Roth, Lorna. 2005. *Something new in the air: The story of First Peoples television broadcasting in Canada*. Montreal and Kingston: McGill-Queen's University Press.

Smith Marc A., and Peter Kollock, eds. 1999. *Communities in cyberspace*. London and New York: Routledge.

Srinivasan, Ramesh. 2006. Indigenous, ethnic and cultural articulations of new media. *International Journal of Cultural Studies* 9(4): 497–518.

Statistics Canada. 2006. Aboriginal peoples. Ottawa: Statistics Canada. http://www12.statcan.gc.ca/census-recensement/2006/rt-td/ap-pa-eng.cfm.

Stone, Brad. 2005. The MySpace.com guys: Their social networking site is busier than Google. *Newsweek*, US edition, 26 December.

Wellman, Barry, and Caroline Haythornthwaite, eds. 2002. *The Internet in everyday life*. Malden, MA: Blackwell Publishers Ltd.

14 A HISTORICAL ACCOUNT OF THE KUH-KE-NAH NETWORK Broadband Deployment in a Remote Canadian Aboriginal Telecommunications Context

Adam Fiser, Andrew Clement

In this chapter we describe the Kuh-ke-nah Network (K-Net), an example of broadband deployment in telecom high-cost serving areas (HCSAs) that emerged to address the telecommunications and computer service needs of remote First Nations in Northwestern Ontario. Our account is based on four years of work with Keewaytinook Okimakanak (KO) Tribal Council, the not-for-profit organization responsible for K-Net's overall management and development. KO was an original research partner of the Canadian Research Alliance for Community Innovation and Networking (CRACIN), and has supported field visits to Northwestern Ontario First Nations by CRACIN researchers in 2003, 2004, 2005, and 2006. Our research has been participatory, pairing CRACIN researchers with First Nations community representatives to pursue an inquiry into how K-Net developed up to its first phase of broadband deployment, between 1994 and 2006. In the process we have also examined how K-Net's organization operated as a technical, economic, and socio-political network during this time period. There is much to yet learn and discover as K-Net and its environment continue to transform. As of 2011, several CRACIN-associated researchers continue to collaborate with K-Net members on applications and research (Beaton et al. 2010; Caidi, Fiser, and Lam 2009; Fiser 2010; O'Donnell, Walmark, and Hancock 2010).

In this chapter we focus on K-Net's early historical development as a reflection of Northwestern Ontario's economic and socio-political context.[1] With its inception in 1994, as a 14.4 baud bulletin board system, K-Net served as one of the oldest examples of community networking that CRACIN studied. In terms of its technical size, K-Net comprises over a hundred community broadband points of presence (POPs). This includes Aboriginal communities and related organizations across Ontario. K-Net Services, KO's network management organization, also provides support to northern satellite-served communities in Manitoba and Québec.

As a distinguishing feature, K-Net POPs enable small remote First Nations to develop and control local Internet services, while participating in a regional network of broadband applications that includes video conferencing, the voice-over Internet protocol (VOIP), and IP-cellular telephony, as well as services such as KO Telemedicine, and the Keewaytinook Internet High School (Fiser, Clement, and Walmark 2006). In this chapter, we seek economic and socio-political explanations for K-Net's rapid growth and technical achievements as a community network. We identify a historical series of economic and socio-political partnerships that paralleled K-Net's technological evolution and advanced its development. In short, K-Net's evolution was greatly accelerated by KO Tribal Council's active participation in the national Connecting Canadians agenda, and related Industry Canada initiatives, circa 1994 to 2004.

As an object of policy, K-Net has been a vehicle for nearly all of Industry Canada's major community connectivity programs, including First Nations SchoolNet and the Community Access Program (CAP), as well as broadband- and spectrum-related projects under the Smart program, C-Band Public Benefits initiative, and National Satellite Initiative. It is our thesis that KO Tribal Council leveraged socio-political relationships, particularly under Connecting Canadians, to reinforce local community networks and demonstrate the efficacy of K-Net's decentralized approach. Nevertheless K-Net's interplay of efficacy and socio-politics is dynamic and part of a dense constellation of interests that are outside KO's locus of control. Our account of K-Net's past achievements does not therefore predict its future state in an uncertain policy environment.

EARLY TELECOMMUNICATIONS IN REMOTE REGIONS: COSTS VERSUS NEEDS

Large-scale telecommunications development in the remote regions of Canada is encumbered by higher-than-average costs owing to the low population density of these regions with respect to the vast distances that separate their respective settlements. In Northwestern Ontario, the average distance between the twenty-four resident First Nations communities and their nearest town service centre is approximately 300 kilometres by air. The region is around 385,000 square kilometres, with a total population of less than 30,000, including the populations of the two nearest towns, Red Lake/Balmertown and Sioux Lookout (see figure 14.1). These conditions severely hamper the growth of a competitively viable broadband telecommunications industry for the region.

FIGURE 14.1 Map of Keewaytinook Okimakanak First Nations in Northwestern Ontario. Courtesy of the Keewaytinook Okimakanak Tribal Council.

As demand in high-density markets feeds competition and innovation in telecom, companies in remote regions do not readily have a critical mass of subscribers to help them recover the costs of physical infrastructure development. Risk on investment is high, and partnerships between industry, government, and consumer interest groups are particularly important for providing incentives to business and to develop supply. In the remote environment, public procurement may be the most profitable contractual arrangement for ISPs. The disposable incomes of residents in small remote communities is typically less than the national average, while the public organizations that serve residents, such as schools and hospitals, have a regional and federal tax base that can support large capital projects for communications infrastructure.

Public organizations can play an important role in shaping the economies of remote regions. This is especially the case in Northwestern Ontario's remote First Nations, where federal government departments, such as Indian and Northern Affairs Canada (INAC) and Health Canada, provide core funding for community infrastructure and social services as part of the federal government's treaty-based fiduciary obligations to First Nations' members. In this context of federal-Aboriginal jurisdiction, the provincial government of Ontario plays a secondary supportive role, while also being implicated to varying degrees in the delivery of essential services such as medical care, transportation systems, employment training, and even education.

As for the role of private sector entities, whereas market discipline can be a valuable driver of telecom innovation in high-density urban sectors, high-cost, low-density markets are usually on the fringes of a monopoly incumbent local exchange carrier's (ILEC) territory. Here the ILEC has little to no threat of entry by companies of comparable size. In Northwestern Ontario (north of the 51st parallel), Bell Canada (now Bell Aliant) has been the monopoly ILEC since the mid-1970s, and its only terrestrial threats have been local municipally focused independent operators, such as the Thunder Bay Telephone Company. Bell's competitors have so far had little impact on its monopoly over the First Nations' terrestrial telecommunications option, one of the reasons being that these independent operators have a substantial cost disadvantage compared to Bell's already established infrastructure.

Public subsidy has dominated telecommunications development in Northwestern Ontario. Bell's entry in the 1970s was stimulated by strategic investments on the part of Ontario's Ministry of Transportation and Communication. At the time, the incumbent's strongest customer base in the Northwestern Ontario First Nations consisted of Health Canada-funded nursing stations. In need of a communications network between community nursing stations and the Sioux Lookout District Zone hospital, the department first bulk-purchased high frequency (HF) radios and later acquired telephone links for nursing stations in the most populous communities (Dunn et al. 1980; Conrath, Dunn, and Higgings 1983). These stations have traditionally served as community health centres and hubs for the local populations and smaller surrounding neighbours. Notwithstanding the clinical context, residents perceived their emerging communications network as part of a First Nations community communications infrastructure (see Fiser and Luke 2008).

Conrath, Dunn, and Higgings (1983) report that nursing stations did not consider HF radio—or "trail radio," as it was called—to be a reliable communications device and opted for access to the public switched telephone network (PSTN) where it was available. Local residents, however, formed the Wawatay Native Communications Society, which helped First Nations members produce local media and actively promoted their use of trail radio for interpersonal communications. With Wawatay's support, trail radio became a channel to maintain ad hoc community networks between settlements and outlying family camps, traplines, and hunting lodges "on the land."

As technical options for community media improved throughout the 1970s and 1980s, local residential demand expanded and Wawatay became a champion and resource centre for the local uptake of First Nations communications technology. Among its achievements, Wawatay successfully established a bilingual newspaper featuring northern Ontario news in Oji-Cree and English, as well as a northern Ontario Aboriginal radio station, in partnership with the Canadian Broadcasting Corporation (Hudson 1977; Mohr 2001). Wawatay also introduced video production in the mid-1980s, and later joined the Aboriginal Peoples Television Network (APTN) in 1999. These facets of its regional communications strategy continue to enrich northern Ontario (see http://wawatay.on.ca).

As an immediate historical predecessor to K-Net, Wawatay represents the important strategy of community relationship building to aggregate local consumer demand and build local capacities for technology deployment and management. Wawatay successfully diffused new communication technologies to First Nations community members, and it developed local awareness and technical capabilities to support community media that reflected First Nations needs and desires (Mohr 2001). As a community network, K-Net would later build upon the same strategy and tactics. However, Wawatay's historical milieu lacked federal and provincial partnership opportunities to help it make deeper connections to telecom service provision. Indeed, by the early 1990s, Wawatay and Canada's other forty or so Native Communications Societies suffered drastic cutbacks in federal support (Mohr 2001), just as the federal government started to seek out new partnerships for the emerging information highway initiatives that would become Connecting Canadians.

In this period of Northwestern Ontario's history, leading up to K-Net's emergence and first experiments with computer-mediated communications (1970s to mid-1990s), Health Canada and Indian and Northern Affairs Canada (INAC) were the largest consumers of available bandwidth. As such, it was the public sector and its administrative needs that primarily shaped pathways for innovation in Northwestern Ontario's telecom infrastructure. Without public sector interest and financial backing, the comparatively resource-poor, mainly residential consumers in the First Nations were left to adapt what technologies they could salvage (such as HF radios). Moreover, the absence of more than one or two telephone access points in the remote communities severely restricted bandwidth and impeded opportunities to experiment locally.

FIGURE 14.2 Two K-Net Services staff members playfully demonstrate the inadequacy of public telephone infrastructure in KO First Nations, circa 2000. Photograph courtesy of the Keewaytinook Okimakanak Tribal Council.

IN PURSUIT OF A BROADBAND DEPLOYMENT OPTION

In Northwestern Ontario, the First Nations' telecom infrastructure has been based around two Bell-owned/controlled microwave backhaul systems, one north of Red Lake and the second north of Pickle Lake. These were the systems that Bell had developed in partnership with Ontario's Ministry of Transportation and Communications between 1975 and 1979 under an initiative known as the Rhodes agreement. Total capital expenditure on the original analog systems was approximately CAD$15 million (circa 1979), largely paid for by the ministry under a mandate to invest in Northern Ontario Remote Area Communications and Transportation (NORACT).

Change crept slowly after this. Twenty years later, the digital upgrades to Bell's analog infrastructure cost over CAD$20 million (circa 2000). The upgrades created a broadband deployment option and were undertaken between 1998 and 2000, this time by Bell, participating First Nations, federal partners (Industry Canada, INAC, and Human Resources Development Canada), and the province's Northern Ontario Heritage Fund Corporation. By itself, the First Nations' regional leadership could not afford to entice Bell to pursue a broadband deployment option. Bell had no internal incentive to make digital upgrades, nor were the First Nations' largest public sector organizations, Health Canada and INAC, prepared to be sole or majority investors in an eventual broadband solution. How the digital upgrades came about, and how they came to be partially community based under K-Net, can best be explained by an examination of the historical emergence of new public sector investors, particularly Industry Canada, under the federal Connecting Canadians agenda.

1994 to 1999: A New Internal Coalition and a New External Investor

In the mid-1990s, Health Canada conducted experiments with broadband satellite on a limited trial period to support clinical video conferencing between two community nursing stations (Kitchenuhmaykoosib Inninuwug and Webequie), the Sioux Lookout District Zone hospital, and the Indian Health Services Regional Office in Ottawa. It concluded that the experiments (dubbed Merlin) were too costly to extend as services. The other major public sector player, Indian and Northern Affairs Canada (INAC), had no specific mandate for broadband, and in some small, very remote communities it had no mandate to support plain old telephony. Since the 1970s, INAC had become heavily invested in other costly forms of community infrastructure, such as sewage, water treatment, electrification, and improvements to community buildings and housing (Fiser 2004).[2] Yet, in the 1990s, its regional managers were willing to support special projects and follow the lead of seed investors.

For their part, the Northwestern Ontario First Nations, and their respective regional service organizations from the hub towns of Sioux Lookout and Red Lake/Balmertown, were exploring options to work around Bell's analog telecommunications system. Their coalition reached out to external players such as Industry Canada and the Province of Ontario. They also lobbied Canada's national regulator, the Canadian Radio-television and Telecommunications Commission (CRTC), as it was undertaking a national review of the rules of telecom business in Canada's high-cost serving areas. In both cases, they researched local consumer needs and challenges, and tapped industry contacts to study the technical and economic feasibility of alternate communications technologies such as MSAT satellite phones (K-Net Services 2001).

Calling itself the Northern Ontario Telecommunications Working Group, the coalition originally followed the lead of Wawatay Native Communications Society, and consisted of important regional service organizations such as the Sioux Lookout Aboriginal Area Management Board (SLAAMB), Nishnawbe Aski Development Fund (NADF), Nishnawbe Native Education Council (NNEC), the Sioux Lookout First Nations Health Authority, the Sioux

Lookout District Zone hospital, Nishnawbe Aski Police Services, Nishnawbe Aski Legal Services, Nishnawbe Aski Nation, and tribal councils such as Keewaytinook Okimakanak (KO), Shibogama, Windigo, Matawa, Wabun, the Independent First Nations Alliance (IFNA), and Mushkegowuk (in the eastern part of the region) (K-Net Services 2001).

Most of the regional service organizations joined the coalition to fulfill particular institutional mandates, such as to improve the delivery of healthcare, education, or policing. Their representatives hoped that together, their aggregate regional demand would help drive a common community access solution for improved telecom infrastructure. Some regional entities, such as SLAAMB and the NADF, had broader mandates to invest in First Nations community economic development, and were less restricted by an expectation of what broadband should do in terms of public service delivery. The coalition hoped that their respective focus on development would help stimulate job growth and new industries by way of local capital projects, as well as employment training for First Nations computer technicians, network administrators, and applications developers.

As for the organizations that directly represented interested First Nations, Nishnawbe Aski Nation, the tribal councils, and First Nations leaders had an immediate interest in improving communications and services for community constituents. The coalition decided that it was in its members' best interest to develop a shared telecom system that was reliable, affordable, and scalable. In terms of its overall direction, the coalition was fairly consistent in its mission throughout the 1990s, although Wawatay suffered an organizational upheaval brought on by diminished resources (from federal cutbacks to Native Communications Societies) and in 1998 transferred its leadership role to KO Tribal Council's K-Net Services branch.

KO Tribal Council, K-Net's founding partner and management organization, had a special interest in changing the analog telecommunication system as it existed since the 1970s' Rhodes agreement. KO represented six First Nations communities: Deer Lake, Fort Severn, Keewaywin, McDowell Lake, North Spirit Lake, and Poplar Hill (see figure 14.1). Two of these communities had no direct telephone access. Another (Fort Severn) was Ontario's most northern community, with limited telephone access and little hope for terrestrial broadband access. Another depended almost entirely on access to the town of Red Lake/Balmertown for services.

The elected chiefs of these First Nations thus felt the pressure of concerned constituents and made telecom a policy priority. KO also had two education program staff members, Margaret Fiddler and Brian Beaton, who had initiated and implemented Wahsa, one of northern Ontario's success stories in distance education (McMullen and Rohrbach 2003). Beginning in 1991, Wahsa combined radio broadcasts, paper-based course packs, periodic community visits, telephone follow-ups, and even faxes where available. With their backgrounds in education, their strategic use of multimedia, and a mandate from the KO chiefs to improve learning opportunities for First Nations youth, Fiddler and Beaton set out to explore computer-mediated communications over the analog telephone system (see Beaton and Fiddler 1999). K-Net Services appeared in 1995 after a year of planning and small-scale pilots. (For a closer look at these formative projects, see chapter 13.)

In its historical milieu, KO was a relatively young tribal council, having been incorporated in 1992. Other Sioux Lookout District councils, such as Windigo and Shibogama, had already made significant changes for member First Nations. They had paved the way for winter roads, electrification, and air transport in the 1970s and 80s, and though not every small First Nation shared in such amenities, these councils helped to modernize development and were already legacy keepers by the time KO appeared. In terms of positioning the KO communities in this regional economic landscape, KO's chiefs had found a relatively unoccupied operating niche to cultivate, as well as an important source of symbolic capital in the emerging computer services and telecommunications fields of the 1990s.[3] Through the work of its K-Net Services branch, KO rapidly became a recognized leader in northern Ontario, legitimated by the endorsements of area First Nations and councils within the regional sociopolitical forum of the Nishnawbe Aski Nation (Kakekaspan and Beck 2003).

KO built its reputation early by coupling technology development with local employment training initiatives. From 1995 to 1999 KO's K-Net Services worked with the Sioux Lookout Aboriginal Area Management Board (SLAAMB) on a series of human resource development initiatives to deliver computers and computer skills training to the twenty-four Sioux Lookout District First Nations. With initial support from SLAAMB and INAC's regional office they developed a K-Net bulletin board system (BBS) with modems over the existing analog telephone infrastructure. The BBS was originally conceived to allow email between the First Nations and the local boarding school Pelican Falls, where their youth attended high school. From that application it evolved to become a platform for delivery of training courses and to host virtual conferences on behalf of the First Nations and regional service organizations (particularly in education). As the K-Net BBS expanded across the region in 1996, four of the twenty-four First Nations still had no access to the analog telephone system, and KO couriered floppy disks back and forth to enable their participation "online." None of the member First Nations could access the Internet through the K-Net BBS, but owing to parallel developments by a group at Thunder Bay's Lakehead University, an ISP, LU-Net, was established in the town of Sioux Lookout and several neighbouring communities.

First Nations with access to K-Net BBS and/or dial-up Internet via LU-Net experienced frequent data transmission failures and paid long distance charges as high as CAD$25 per hour. There was little to no residential access outside the towns, and users in the remote First Nations frequented community access sites, usually a computer terminal within an INAC-funded school or band office (administrative centre). However, in 1996, K-Net Services received a substantial boost after it won a contract to become a helpdesk for Ontario's 144 First Nations schools under Industry Canada's newly created First Nations SchoolNet program. This was the beginning of a radically new technology partnership for the Northwestern Ontario First Nations.

SchoolNet had emerged in 1993 as part of the first federal information highway mandate, and it grew to prominence under Industry Canada's Connecting Canadians agenda (circa 1998). Industry Canada, largely an outsider to the First Nations' public sector economy, had a mandate to subsidize community Internet access points, to deliver computers for schools, and to build up Canada's connectivity profile on the world stage. Although SchoolNet was its national showcase, Industry Canada also instituted the Community Access Program (CAP), a refurbished computer delivery program called Computers for Schools, as well as a web content creation initiative called Canada's Digital Collections, to promote wider public uptake of computers and the Internet. KO's K-Net Services coordinated grant submissions with all of the Sioux Lookout District's tribal councils to lever each of these funding programs, and through their joint initiative with Industry Canada, by 2000 they had built an Internet-accessible community computing infrastructure in at least seventeen of the twenty-four First Nations, with thirty-five Ontario First Nations in total having public Internet access through a K-Net Services–supported SchoolNet connection.

Although dependent on short-term grants for capital and operating funds, this infrastructure became community owned through the care of local (K-Net Services and SLAAMB trained) band technicians, school staff, and volunteers, who together with KO and its government partners, offered K-Net to individual consumers and civil society as their First Nations version of the information highway.

Riding a wave of federal program investments that the Connecting Canadians agenda had stimulated, K-Net Services helped the national First Nations SchoolNet program equip First Nations schools with DirecPC satellite connections, from 1996 to 1998, which Bell Canada and the now-defunct Stentor Alliance of telecommunications companies (including Telesat) had donated, in part, to compensate for their poor terrestrial services in high-cost serving areas. In 1998, Industry Canada's mandate expanded in scope under the federal Connecting Canadians agenda, which enlarged the purse of its Information

Highway Applications Branch and redirected its focus toward more ambitious projects, such as overall community connectivity for broadband deployment, at a target inbound bit rate of 1.544 Mbps following the recommendations of Industry Canada's Communications Research Centre and the National Broadband Taskforce.

Yet it appeared that so long as the First Nations had no control over the points of presence (POPs) and local loop infrastructure that distributed the ILEC Bell's terrestrial bandwidth, they and their allies would have little chance to create affordable shared broadband connections for individual consumers and civil society. This diagnosis pertains to the coalitions' observation that Bell would not (and given a per-community capital expenditure of between $400,000 and $1.5 million probably could not) make a business case for residential connectivity without bold public sector support.[4]

At times, the Northwestern Ontario public sector's regional service organizations had difficulty following KO's tribal council lead. Their important service mandates for health, education, and policing meant that they had to answer to the federal and provincial government departments that funded them, such as INAC and Health Canada. K-Net was becoming the region's showcase technology, a simultaneous revelation of the analog telecom system's inadequacies and a demonstration of the possibilities that could be harnessed if broadband Internet infrastructure was in place throughout the Sioux Lookout District and greater territory of Nishnawbe Aski Nation (K-Net Services 2001). K-Net also represented the public sector organizations' likely future orientation, particularly in terms of their evolving data-communications needs and the partial transformation of their services into broadband e-services.

The disjuncture between partial visions and realities thus created uncertainty within K-Net's coalition of regional allies, particularly around the question of how to steer K-Net's development beyond the millennium. Members had to find a balance between KO's leadership role and its emphasis on the decentralized community ownership of POPs and community networks, with their more centralizing policy pressures to maintain regional, as well as federal and provincial, standards for service delivery in healthcare, education, and policing.

In the 1990s, some members of the public sector, particularly staff at the Nishnawbe Native Education Council (NNEC), which disbursed INAC education funds, openly wondered whether K-Net should remain a KO Tribal Council initiative and not become absorbed into a regional service organization such as NNEC. The rationale was that KO officially represented only six of the twenty-four Sioux Lookout District First Nations that the NNEC represented, notwithstanding the more than twenty other First Nations in the larger Nishnawbe Aski Nation of northern Ontario. KO's chiefs were directly answerable to their community constituents (who elected them) and were not specifically responsible for any of the other communities or services that K-Net involved. However, setting aside those perceptions, KO's leadership role ran deeper than the politics of representation, for it was KO's chiefs who had identified the opportunity to develop a competitive advantage in the field of telecommunications, and now its staff had the capabilities and robust federal program ties to make broadband deployment a regional economic reality. No other organization in the region had the capability during the specific period when the Connecting Canadians agenda was prepared to take off into further rounds of investment in telecom high-cost serving areas. Given the momentum that was behind KO/K-Net Service's capabilities at the time (circa 1998–2000), it is difficult to envision feasible alternatives for rallying partnerships and organizing a broadband solution for Northwestern Ontario's First Nations.

By contrast, the public sector's regional service organizations, such as the NNEC, the Sioux Lookout First Nations Health Authority, or Nishnawbe Aski Police Services, were in no position to fund the capital costs of infrastructure development out of their own budgets, let alone support the ongoing operating expenditures of K-Net, without additional assistance from federal and provincial programs. At this time, their core mandates were not aligned with any concrete connectivity policy, and thus, they, alongside the local First Nations bands and councils, followed KO's appeals to Industry Canada in support of K-Net's community computing infrastructure strategy, simply to enable Internet access for their staff operating in the First Nations. The health organizations for example, were severely restricted by Health Canada, which would not commit to K-Net until 2002, after KO and several health service organizations undertook a series of pilot projects and delivered an extensively researched regional proposal for community-based telemedicine (Rowlandson 2005). Similarly, in education, and despite some of the NNEC staff's reservations about K-Net's tribal council leadership, the NNEC had few funds in its education mandate to commit to connectivity, and its managers were dependent on KO's ability to draw connectivity funding from First Nations SchoolNet and similar Industry Canada initiatives. Administrative differences had to be set aside if K-Net's transformation was to continue in a positive direction for Northwestern Ontario.

1997 to 1999: An Opportunity to Change the Course of Development

Industry Canada's partnership with KO and K-Net's coalition of regional allies was a major force for regional change, but the catalyst for systemic change was a national regulatory review of the state of telecommunications high-cost serving areas by the Canadian Radio-television and Telecommunications Commission, begun in 1997 (see CRTC 1997). In itself, the regulatory review accomplished little to compel incumbent service providers such as Bell to deploy broadband; but it established a policy arena for consumer groups to find common ground, voice their concerns nationally, and confront service providers with their concerns. For Northwestern Ontario, the CRTC review was fortuitous, as it coincided with the K-Net coalition's gathering strength under Industry Canada's Connecting Canadians agenda. Through Wawatay, the coalition had earlier appealed to Industry Canada FedNor, the federal economic development initiative for northern Ontario, which gave members a grant to study local telecom access conditions and survey market demand before appearing at the CRTC proceedings. KO's K-Net Services levered this research process into a regional networking strategy.

In 1995, FedNor had funded an Aboriginal Working Group to advise on regional telecom policy, as well as a study of forty-eight First Nations across Northern Ontario, in order to assess their telecommunications and computing needs against the prevailing realities of the telecommunications systems in place. It concluded that extensive investment in infrastructure would be required if broadband was to become feasible in the remote regions. By 1998 FedNor was prepared to become a seed investor for the digital upgrades to Bell's analog systems. In the 1990s, FedNor was investing approximately CAD$50 million annually in diverse northern Ontario municipal, Aboriginal, not-for-profit, and private-sector economic initiatives. The development of telecommunications and information technology had been one of its specific mandates (as part of Industry Canada). FedNor's interests dovetailed well with the interests of Wawatay, KO's K-Net Services, and coalition allies. It also had no interest in managing infrastructure (or some layer of service within) but was open to supporting a First Nations-controlled broadband deployment model, provided that the K-Net model could work with the incumbent telephone companies to promote the industrial sector and fulfill public sector requirements for service delivery and quality of service.

WHAT K-NET ACHIEVED

At the heart of the CRTC hearings was the question of what incumbent local exchange carriers such as Bell owed to their customers in high-cost serving areas. Although Wawatay and KO's K-Net Services lobbied valiantly for the CRTC to include a broadband-service option in its bundle of essential services to high-cost serving areas, their proposals were overwhelmed by the reluctance of the incumbent local exchange carriers. The CRTC concluded that broadband was not an essential service, at least not one it would support through the national system of subsidy it managed to help ILECs defray telecom costs in high-cost serving areas.

Nevertheless, the coalition from Northwestern Ontario and allied consumer groups from high-cost serving areas across Canada did gain ground on a number of important service issues, including the elimination of long-distance charges for dial-up Internet (CAD$25/hour in some Northwestern Ontario communities), and the implementation of single-line touchtone service, operator and directory assistance services, and 911 emergency call services. Moreover, the CRTC's commissioners called for a broadband service debate to continue and acknowledged the value of innovation in telecom and a need for new public-private partnerships, such as those that Industry Canada FedNor was prepared to make. In response, KO's K-Net Services and the coalition continued their mission, hopeful that FedNor and other public sector programs were ready to support broadband deployment as part of a shared services model.

From 1998 to 1999, KO worked on a grant proposal to establish a wide area network (WAN) between its six member First Nations and offices in Sioux Lookout and Red Lake/Balmertown. FedNor was a seed investor, as was its provincial counterpart, the Northern Ontario Heritage Fund Corporation (NOHFC), a crown corporation with a similar economic development mandate. The vision that was to be realized in this next iteration of K-Net[5] was of a First Nations-controlled IP network that would ride atop leased terrestrial and satellite carrier infrastructure from Bell, and Telesat Canada, which Bell owned at the time. This vision acquired further legitimacy after KO successfully bid to become one of Industry Canada's Smart Community demonstration projects and acquired a purse of CAD$5 million in 2000, after two years of proposal work, based on its designs for a community-based WAN to augment the community computing infrastructure it had developed through First Nations SchoolNet and CAP (Ramírez et al. 2003).

Yet, during the period between 1999 and 2000, two major economic and technological obstacles stood in K-Net's way: (1) carrier backhauls had to be upgraded or, in the case of satellite, be established, and (2) community local loops had to be upgraded and/or built to accommodate shared Internet connections in participating First Nations.

Between 1999 and 2000, the ILEC Bell spent approximately CAD$20 million in capital expenditures to upgrade its northern Ontario systems to digital service infrastructure. Bell had made this decision to invest based on its reading of the climate for public-private partnerships and the joint federal-provincial commitment to growing broadband services, particularly in public sectors of the high-cost serving areas. In Northwestern Ontario, Bell invested approximately CAD$8 million in upgrades to its Central Offices, with about CAD$1 million of additional support from FedNor. In addition, FedNor, the NOHFC, and public sector partners such as INAC and Human Resources Development

Canada, invested in the First Nations' local loops, for a combined investment of approximately CAD$3.2 million (K-Net Services 2001). This series of concentrated public-private partnerships substantially reconfigured the ailing analog telecom system, which resulted in the availability of shared terrestrial broadband POPs in thirteen of the area First Nations and spurred the development of a special not-for-profit satellite arrangement for the remaining eleven First Nations (and allied communities in Québec and Manitoba), also with substantial support from Industry Canada FedNor.

Backhauls and Points of Presence

Since 2000, terrestrial broadband POPs in Northwestern Ontario have entailed T1 connections, at 1.544 Mbps, leased from the ILEC Bell (now Bell Aliant). Our research with K-Net has found that the price of a T1 connection (1.544 Mbps) to remote communities of Northwestern Ontario has been as high as eight times the price offered to communities in large metropolitan areas such as Toronto (e.g., CAD$8,000:1000/month). In this case the prices are set by Bell's rate band system, largely on the basis of population density. With ongoing technological change and government subsidy, particularly from FedNor and its Ontario counterpart, the NOHFC, the T1 price gap has narrowed to approximately four times the high-density urban price (CAD $1,270:350/month). However, other significant differences remain between the quality of service offered to remote communities and their high-density urban counterparts. Connections to remote regions come with minimal service guarantees largely owing to the distance of the communities from the nearest telephone company's service depot. This means that remote customers may wait longer for repairs, and have to devise local technical capabilities and human resource strategies to enable effective monitoring and repair of local telecom equipment, particularly in terms of local loop infrastructure and customer premises equipment (CPE) owned by the communities' vested authority and customers.

In K-Net's historical milieu, Wawatay had experienced similar human resource challenges during its early HF radio days in the 1970s and with the maintenance of its community-based radio network (Mohr 2001). KO's K-Net Services had also experienced this human resource challenge in the 1990s as its two-person staff worked with over fifty First Nations to establish DirecPC satellite connections under First Nations SchoolNet and earlier, during K-Net's BBS days. From the beginning of its career in computer-mediated communications, KO had worked with the regional Sioux Lookout Aboriginal Area Management Board (SLAAMB) to establish the knowledge that local First Nations technicians would require to maintain computers, modems, and later Internet access points, Ethernet local area networks (LANs), and wireless area networks.

Pushing necessary knowledge and skills to the edges of K-Net's emerging network, out of the need for survival, also led to local innovations. KO and several of K-Net's most remote partners worked with Industry Canada FedNor, for example, to devise an alternate MSAT phone solution that made DirecPC feasible in remote communities that lacked the infrastructure for a dial-up uplink (as required by the technology). Such learning experiences (over a span of five years) prepared KO and its coalition of allies to negotiate the feasibility of community-owned broadband local loops (access networks) with the ILEC Bell and government partners.

The technical prowess of KO and its allies convinced FedNor and other public sector partners that local First Nations ownership and co-operative network management, rather than centralized public or private sector ownership, were the proper pathways for broadband deployment in remote Northwestern Ontario.

With FedNor onside, as a complementary regional/federal advocate based in the "metropolitan" area of Thunder Bay, in Northwestern Ontario, it was easier for KO and K-Net's coalition of allies to communicate their interests before other government players and the incumbent Bell (now Bell Aliant). Thus KO's WAN project was implemented and became a prototype for broadband infrastructure development across the twenty-four Northwestern Ontario First Nations (gradually and with multiple investors between 2000 and 2005). Yet between 2000 and 2002, the missing link in Northwestern Ontario was a broadband option for eleven of the First Nations, which were not slated to benefit from the upgrades to Bell's infrastructure and/or had no direct access to the telephone system due to their extreme remoteness and small size.

The provision of satellite infrastructure was critical in bringing these First Nations online, and it depended on the viability of a not-for-profit service contract. The solution emerged through an opportune moment that KO capitalized on while working in 2000 on a satellite solution for its member First Nation of Fort Severn, Ontario's northernmost community. K-Net had just been awarded demonstration project status with Industry Canada's Smart Communities and KO now had a relatively substantial purse to invest in telecommunications and computer infrastructure for its six member communities (Ramírez et al. 2003). Bell and Telesat (which Bell owned at the time) were working with KO on a series of satellite trials for Fort Severn. However, the devised solution proved to be unaffordable if undertaken through Bell's commercial line (Fiser and Clement 2007). Although KO had no hope for a commercial satellite solution, Telesat's R&D department, impressed by how K-Net Services' technicians managed Fort Severn's satellite solution, intervened and allowed the network to continue to experiment with a portion of the R&D transponder on a trial basis.

Then in 2001, Telesat made a game-changing deal with Industry Canada. In exchange for orbital space, it would reserve 30 Mhz, or one transponder, on its Anik E satellite for public benefits, to be determined by Industry Canada. Noticing that Industry Canada had no immediate plans for the public benefits transponder, Telesat's vice-president Paul Bush, knowing of K-Net's reputation, contacted KO's Brian Beaton, now K-Net Services Coordinator, to inform him of a possible not-for-profit solution for remote First Nations to gain improved satellite access. With federal support from FedNor, School-Net, and the management team at the Smart Communities program, as well as private support from Telesat R&D, KO then lobbied Industry Canada's Spectrum division to dedicate a portion of the public benefits resource to K-Net's underserved First Nations partners (Fiser and Clement 2007). What apparently secured the deal was an audience (at the deputy minister's level of Industry Canada) that appreciated K-Net's achievements and approach to local infrastructure ownership and control, largely informed by KO's direct participation in the family of mid-to-late 1990s' Industry Canada programs.

Though it worked in collaboration with Industry Canada and Telesat, the organizations responsible for Anik E's Public Benefits, KO proved that it could manage its portion of the satellite resource. K-Net Services became the satellite network manager and implemented a protocol to dynamically allocate about 15 Mhz of public benefits bandwidth for broadband e-services in eleven First Nations communities. That translated to approximately 780 kbps for each POP, but under the protocol this could be augmented to bursts of up to 2 Mbps concentrated in any one POP to support video conferencing and telemedicine.

K-Net's acquisition of the satellite resource had broader socio-political and economic linkages, as it augmented the organization's goal to extend and share the public benefits of broadband (that is, bandwidth) with Aboriginal groups throughout and beyond northern Ontario, thus creating a stronger interregional network of communities upon which to establish further public sector innovation and investment. Other groups became interested by the public benefits project and lobbied Industry Canada for a portion of the transponder. The Northwest Territories and Nunavut took their portions in 2002, leaving KO with 15 Mhz, and chose not to work with K-Net and pool their resources under its co-operative scheme.

In 2004, an additional transponder was allocated to the public benefits project and KO convinced the Kativik Regional Government of northern Québec and Keewatin Tribal Council of northern Manitoba to pool their allocated resources with K-Net Services, thus creating 30 Mhz of shared bandwidth. Then in 2007, K-Net and its Québec and Manitoba partners received additional transponder space through the federal National Satellite Initiative, thus creating a shared resource of 90 Mhz, which dramatically expanded the range of broadband applications that these satellite communities can develop. Presently, their not-for-profit partnership has configured the shared resource into voice, video, and data applications that each of the partner networks manages independently to serve their respective regions and communities (Fiser 2010).

Throughout K-Net's historical evolution, what appears consistent is the role of local technical knowledge and endogenous capability as empowerments of community level interests and bridges to the interests and standards of external partners. From a project investment standpoint, local knowledge and endogenous technical capability, both within K-Net Services and in First Nations partners, help to convince external investors that decentralized community ownership of systems is feasible, reliable, and cost effective compared to more centralized technology solutions. From a community development standpoint, these empowerments represent critical investments in local human resources that enable individual community members to take up and apply the tools of their local networks and the Internet. K-Net Services staff has called their strategy to seed these empowerments "walking the talk." In building the network, they demonstrate that First Nations partners can participate in local ownership and control. It is a recurring perspective among several CRACIN case study partners. As Gurstein explains in chapter 2 of this volume, the focus on matters of local knowledge and endogenous technical capability strategically shifts the problem of community networking from issues of simple access across digital divides to more complicated (yet substantial) issues of effective ICT use. Gurstein succinctly pinpoints the overarching goal of this perspective as "how to manage and control the tools and opportunities presented by ICTs to realize meaningful benefits for individuals and communities both distant geographically and culturally from the central, dominant drivers of the primary networks of which the information society in Canada is constituted" (38).

Moreover, as with the satellite network management case, K-Net's endogenous technical capability persuaded investors and the dominant commercial carriers to relinquish partial control over their regional and national systems to support not-for-profit community organizations such as KO's K-Net Services and its partners in Québec and Manitoba. Without this endogenous technical capability to demonstrate K-Net's viability in places such as Fort Severn or Cat Lake, K-Net Services would only be left with advocacy tactics. As we have seen earlier, the Northern Ontario Telecommunications Working Group had undertaken to lobby for ICTs with mixed results in the telecom domain, having made few inroads with industry at the CRTC hearings on high-cost serving areas, but gaining local ground in terms of rallying service organizations and Aboriginal groups together. Frank Winter's study of the Keewatin Career Development Corporation's struggles to survive (see chapter 16) echoes similar tensions between the community networks' needs to develop local capabilities, their ongoing needs to secure uncertain project funding, and the pressures to maintain working ties with industry and telecom incumbents. As these forces are not necessarily aligned to benefit all parties, their resulting tension can threaten a community network's survival.

As Wawatay had discovered in K-Net's prehistory, technology is part of a constellation of strategic focal points. If, among those focal points, the socio-political and economic arrangements between public and private sector partners establish undesirable parameters for capital investment, the communities' endogenous technical capabilities will be insufficient to guide technological change. Thus KO's multi-faceted and parallel partnerships with Industry Canada enabled it to achieve a level of community network access that had seemed impossible before Connecting Canadians.

Compared to the other CRACIN case study sites of comparable age and scope, KO's career as an Industry Canada partner appears to be an outlier. As Winter's analysis in chapter 16 of the Keewatin Career Development Corporation suggests, community-based organizations such as KO are rarely so well positioned to ride successive waves of government funding. Similarly, as Katrina Peddle indicates in her discussion of community networking in Atlantic Canada (see chapter 15), there can be many onerous obligations attached to government funding, while stovepipe public agendas and limited program funds for community networks can seed intersectoral rivalries between potential allies. As Peddle explains, such forces may simultaneously hamper and divide community partners despite their communities' demonstrable capacity to benefit local learning, capacity building, connectivity, and human resources development.

While K-Net's community partners were able to work through their substantive differences and successfully navigate the federal and provincial funding landscape that was Connecting Canadians, many other community networks have succumbed to the vicissitudes of regional socio-politics and a downgraded federal ICT policy (see chapter 19 and the appendixes in this volume).

Community Ownership and Local Loops

The efforts of K-Net's coalition partners led to substantial gains in local communications access, ownership, and control. For K-Net communities, ownership and control over the decentralized community network depends on access network conditions at the local loop. While local loop options from the incumbent telephone company have traditionally been copper wire, remote First Nations in Northwestern Ontario have been fortunate to have had FedNor, the NOHFC, and other partners co-invest in local community cable and/or wireless infrastructure, which can be used to internetwork and/or distribute broadband POPs to serve multiple locations within a single community, independently of the telecom service provider that provisions backhaul. In terms of services, this arrangement can lead to structural separation. At the local loop each participating First Nations' government or an appointed SME (small or medium-sized enterprise), such as a community cable company, can retain some measure of control over local bandwidth, and consumers (institutional, residential, etc.) do not have to individually subscribe to the ILEC, but rather may share the costs and bandwidth of a single or multiple POP(s). K-Net coalition members call this their Indigenous Broadband Community Network Model.

Shared broadband becomes technically and economically feasible because, by pooling resources, consumers can support the employment and training of a community technician with additional support from KO's K-Net Services and its public sector partners. (This funding base supports what Gurstein calls "effective use," through the cultivation of local knowledge and endogenous technical capability: see Gurstein 2004, as well as chapter 2 in this volume.) Community support for human resources is also further augmented by investments from economic development projects such as those KO and SLAAMB undertook with First Nations throughout the 1990s. By working under a coalition structure such as K-Net's, the communities may also take advantage of bulk rates for commodity bandwidth that KO can procure from the ILEC and other internetworked telecom service providers, on account of K-Net's procurement of multiple POPs versus a single-buyer or single-purpose public-sector buyer (such as Health Canada). Moreover, because K-Net is an IP overlay network, which is logically separated from satellite and terrestrial carrier systems, the communities take part in community-driven IP applications that KO and K-Net First Nations support by virtue of their local knowledge, endogenous technical capabilities, and community-driven policies (Fiser and Clement 2008).

These community-driven applications include residential Internet, public video conferencing, and residential voice-over IP and IP cellular telephony, among others. These are community services managed by the First Nations government or an appointed SME, and are funded by individual consumers in each First Nation.

CONCLUSION: THE POWER OF K-NET'S COALITION

To build and maintain telecom infrastructure in the remote regions that K-Net represents, particularly in the form of backhauls and regional backbones, an ILEC such as Bell Aliant insists on subsidy from the national regulator and public-sector interests. Yet even after public-private partnerships cover capital expenditures, the ILEC's monopoly may still lack a viable consumer base from which to recover the ongoing costs of operation and maintenance, let alone to make a profit that will attract shareholders to a remote market. Residential subscribers, a major source of revenue for service providers in high-density markets, are not enough of a force to break the economic constraints of high-cost serving areas, whose low density is equally matched by the paucity of remote business subscribers that would normally feed innovation in higher-bandwidth applications such as video conferencing or enterprise resource planning. Remote businesses are typically SMEs, and their voice, video, and data-switching needs are significantly smaller in scale than what the sales offices of ILECs recognize or cater to in their focal urban environments. The pockets of residential and business consumers in remote regions represent diminutive sources of revenue compared to the ILEC's urban business lines, and, as in the case of Northwestern Ontario, these consumers usually have little to no influence over how the ILEC and other large telecom service providers allocate internal resources to innovate new applications for consumers. We would advise any readers who harbour significant doubts of this fact to review the Canadian Radio-television and Telecommunications Commission's proceedings on High-Cost Serving Areas (CRTC 1997).

As the histories of K-Net and its forebearer Wawatay have equally shown, a regional coalition of consumers that involves residents (including local SMEs), and relevant public sector organizations, can mobilize constituents to influence the monopoly ILEC's prevailing business strategy. However, even a coalition of remote regions and local players, acting on its own, may not be enough to pay down the capital development costs that fundamental improvements to carrier infrastructure require. Regional policies and local campaigns may have to intersect with the higher-level funding circuits of federal and provincial public policy.

Consumers in remote regions (i.e., high-cost serving areas) cannot appeal to the ILEC's profit motive. They depend on a public goods justification for telecom service. For Canada's First Nations, such a justification requires federal support and buy-in from industry. Without acknowledgement by the various players involved in remote telecom that shared-access networks for Internet and broadband deployment can address community needs without jeopardizing industry, there is very little that can be done to include the residents of those communities. Moreover, without a strategy for infrastructure development that exceeds a profit motive for service delivery, the ongoing capital and operational costs of remote telecom will be difficult to address for the long term. In that respect, the decentralized, coalition-based approach to community networking that K-Net represents may be better suited to operationalize service, given the unique business constraints of remote regions and the needs of their communities and regional service organizations. Such an approach does not preclude the ILEC and other private sector operators from delivering services (and recovering costs), but it places a community-oriented, not-for-profit organization such as KO at the head of an interdependent coalition of public and private partners. The private corporate sector is not necessarily diminished by the not-for-profit orientation. Indeed, our CRACIN research found that the ILEC Bell Aliant absorbed approximately 75 percent of the annual revenue generated by K-Net's terrestrial POPS (circa 2007), notwithstanding K-Net's arrangement of local First Nations ownership and control. This annual revenue may not impress Bell Aliant shareholders, but it does provide a dimension of social responsibility that establishes K-Net's core sustainability of services.

From studying K-Net we have learned that a not-for-profit driver such as KO can take some of the risk away from the private sector, can improve local monitoring, operations, and maintenance, and build effective consumer demand by responsively aggregating the purchasing power of remote businesses, residential subscribers, and public sector organizations. It co-operates with large public and private sector partners without alienating more vulnerable, resource-poor residents, and nurtures individual appropriations of technology as it supports the particular service mandates of regional and federal institutions. This ability to balance multiple interests and responsibilities within a complex technical system complements a complicated socio-political environment that Dutton and other scholars have described an as "ecology of games." As Dutton, Schneider, and Vedel (2008, 21) explain, the concept of an ecology of games "emphasizes the complexity of social and political conflict within nested (public and private) decision-making processes that relate to social and technical interdependencies. Governance of the Internet can then be understood as the outcome of a variety of choices made by many different players involved in many separate but interdependent policy games or areas of activity." We would add that "K-Net" could be substituted for "Internet" here.

In chapter 16, Frank Winter reflects on the challenge that community networking organizations face in maintaining a diverse repertoire of tactics and alliances to manage socio-political conflicts and weather extreme policy changes. Unlike community networking organizations that learn to concentrate on a narrow application area or survive off of a single source of program funding, K-Net's coalition established a holistic, multi-faceted strategy that harnessed lessons from past campaigns and multiplied the strengths of local, regional, and federal players in education, healthcare, justice, information technology, and telecommunications, to build and sustain a network infrastructure that could serve their communities' separate but interdependent needs.

EPILOGUE: ONLY A BEGINNING

In this chapter, we set out to explain the origins of K-Net by situating its emergence against a historical context of communications development in and around Northwestern Ontario. The similarities and differences between Wawatay in the 1970s and K-Net in the 1990s should inform practitioners and policy makers to look beyond the current hype of broadband and heed the lessons of earlier eras, such as the now out-of-vogue information highway policy and its legacy, Connecting Canadians. We believe that the new digital economy of 2010 and beyond is very much predicated on the legacies of the old economy. In terms of similarities, K-Net and Wawatay both demonstrated that geographically isolated and economically marginalized communities can unite over great distances to effectively mobilize regional policy for investment in community media. KO Tribal Council's support of early broadband and First Nations Internet echoes Wawatay's support of early ad hoc trail radio networks and community media in the 1970s. Both organizations trained local First Nations technicians for new professions, and enabled a regional First Nations economy around the regular management and repair of their respective communications systems. Both Wawatay and K-Net also provided alternatives to the narrowly administrative government approaches to communications that dominated the remote First Nations economies and had left residents with inadequate telecommunications options.

In different ways, Wawatay and K-Net also clearly demonstrated that regional policy by itself may not be sufficient to mobilize the capital required to move voice and/or data traffic beyond local ad hoc community networks. In Wawatay's historical milieu, the mission to interconnect the Sioux Lookout District First Nation with facilities beyond the scope of trail radio required a public switched telephone network (PSTN). A PSTN is a substantial undertaking for any region. In remote high-cost serving areas (HCSAS), a PSTN depends upon the resources of heteronomous entities outside the purview of locally autonomous communities: in this chapter, we juxtapose community relationship building with Bell's regional monopoly, federal public programming, and the CRTC's national regulatory oversight.

As we see in K-Net's historical milieu, to transform the Sioux Lookout District's analog PSTN into a digital infrastructure capable of supporting Internet and 1.544 Mbps traffic required significant capital and partnerships. Since 1994 to 1996, when K-Net was a text-based bulletin board system connecting to First Nations communities at 14.4 baud, KO's mission has been to establish connectivity within the parameters of local community ownership and co-operative community control because that is what the First Nations have historically wanted. Such an ethos traces back at least as far as HF trail radio in the early 1970s, when the Wawatay Native Communications Society began to ask regional Aboriginal policy questions about locally relevant community media and communications technology. The PSTN of Wawatay's trail radio era became the legacy analog infrastructure of K-Net's 1990s emergence and eventual broadband deployment beyond 2000.

Throughout its historical mission, KO has always had to work with the monopoly ILEC Bell to develop its services, while striving to secure infrastructure that the First Nations could recognize as something they too owned. KO's mission achieved a good measure of success in the 1990s, through successive iterations of development, only after the regional coalition of consumers that K-Net represents met the federal investment capability of Industry Canada, particularly through the offices of FedNor and First Nations SchoolNet. Without the co-operation of these regional and federal forces, to keep the ILEC onside there would likely have been no K-Net to speak of. In this way, K-Net and its regional and federal allies enabled the first phase of broadband deployment for remote Northwestern Ontario First Nations. But their fate has been subject to a constellation of socio-political and economic forces outside their locus of control.

The historical and institutional profile we have captured only marks the beginning of a possible broadband-enabled First Nations information society in Northwestern Ontario. In 2010, the situation was equally full of promise and uncertainty. On its technical side, K-Net's broadband capabilities continue to develop unevenly across the network. While some terrestrially served First Nations communities and peri-urban hubs have access to 10 or even 100 Mbps POPs, many of K-Net's remote First Nations community networks still make the most of shared bandwidth equivalent to 1.544 Mbps or less.

In 2009, advertised rates for K-Net community ISPs averaged CAD$40 per month, at 384 kbps (inbound), which is significantly above reported provincial averages for ISP offerings to Canadian First Nations residents (Fiser 2010). Moreover, without further upgrades to Bell Aliant's PSTN, pooled and dynamically allocated bandwidth resources translate to less than 256 kbps (inbound) for residential applications, particularly during peak operations, for K-Net community services such as telemedicine or video conferencing.

Since 2009, the KO Tribal Council has been in negotiations with Bell Aliant to upgrade member POPs in the Sioux Lookout District to 10-plus Mbps. These negotiations involve prospective partnerships with FedNor, the Government of Ontario's Northern Ontario Heritage Fund Corporation, and contributions from Bell Aliant and the First Nations. Based largely on fibre deployment, the proposed upgrades could cost as much as CAD$105 million. If such a proposal were to pass, it would significantly change access conditions for Northwestern Ontario's First Nations, increasing shared 1.544 Mbps or less to 10-plus Mbps. Presently, there is no clear indication that the negotiations will conclude. A decision very much depends on the fate of K-Net's evolving public sector partnerships.

Since 2006, critical players from the 1990s and early 2000s, particularly programs within Industry Canada, have significantly declined in influence as K-Net passed its first phase of broadband deployment. What were once guiding forces in K-Net's development, such as Industry Canada's Community Access Program, no longer provide catalysis for next-generation innovation. The services and applications that will shape K-Net over the next ten years, beyond 2010, fall under the purview of more traditional First Nation-Federal government programming. As they were before Connecting Canadians and the 1990s' information highway, Indian and Northern Affairs Canada (INAC) and Health Canada are the First Nations' focal public partners for next-generation network development and core sustainability.

The broadband services that core INAC programs require are currently in a fledgling state and subject to a policy environment that is more conservative about ICT investments than was Industry Canada under Connecting Canadians (Fiser 2004). In 2006, First Nations SchoolNet became a part of INAC's Education Branch. Since then it has received approximately one fifth of the budget it had in 2002. In 2011, First Nations SchoolNet's mandate is up for renewal, and there is no clear indication that the program will continue to support community networks such as K-Net. Nevertheless, INAC programs are turning toward more intensive uses for data networks, resource planning, and information management services. New standards and possible partnerships are on the horizon for electronically managed fiscal transfers, First Nations identities (e.g., Indian status cards), administrative records, program performance outcomes, and more, across a spectrum of services in education, public works, and financial administration. INAC's counterparts in Health Canada and at the Ontario Ministry of Health and Long-Term Care are similarly redefining their information communications technology (ICT) mandates, and consulting with coalition groups such as K-Net, to define standards for electronic public health records, the adequacy of telemedicine, and the secure transfer of medical information, among other critical issues in the domains of public health, medicine, and pharmacy.

The future for K-Net is therefore pregnant with possibility, and the community networking practices that the KO Tribal Council and allies inherited from Wawatay, and deepened under Connecting Canadians, will be tested anew. Though difficult to predict, there will be new pathways for Northwestern Ontario's First Nations to navigate, with new lessons from history in store. Nevertheless, what must remain constant for the K-Net model to continue to thrive in this changing landscape of technology, policy, and investment is the First Nations' participation in ownership and control of their local and regional networks. With that, the vow of determination made by Matthew Coon Come, then national chief of the Assembly of First Nations, in 2001 will continue to ring out in regions such as remote Northwestern Ontario:

> We can use technology. With access to new Internet infrastructure that can be applied with the best networking capacities that are there, we can connect our communities, our hospitals, and our schools. . . . We missed the Industrial Revolution; we will not miss the information technology revolution. (Coon Come 2001)

NOTES

1 Readers interested in the network's technical arrangements may refer to Fiser and Clement (2008). Readers interested in the evolution of K-Net's organizational arrangements may refer to Fiser (2004), Fiser, Clement, and Walmark (2006), and Fiser and Clement (2007), as well as the case studies of Ramírez (2000) and Ramírez et al. (2003), which examine K-Net in terms of information communications technology for development. Finally, KO and partners have issued a number of important documents discussing the First Nations' local goals and regional strategies for K-Net's development. In particular, we refer readers to K-Net's online information portal at http://knet.ca and KO's research branch, http://research.knet.ca, and recommend the work of Beaton et al. (1999) and Rowlandson (2005).

2 This information is derived from CRACIN research interviews with former SchoolNet and INAC managers undertaken in 2004.

3 Following Bourdieu (1989), we use *symbolic capital* to evoke the intangible benefits (and sources of power) that accrue from a position of respect, recognized authority, leadership, and so forth.

4 The dollar amounts are based on Bell's estimates from 1998, in response to questions from the Northern Ontario Telecommunications Working Group before the CRTC's hearings on high-cost serving areas.

5 The first two iterations were 1994–1996, K-Net BBS, modem over Plain Old Telephone Service (POTS), and 1996–2000, K-Net BBS, DirecPC/MSAT and modem over POTS.

REFERENCES

Beaton, Brian, and Jesse Fiddler. 1999. Living smart in two worlds: Maintaining and protecting First Nation culture for future generations. Paper presented at the Local Knowledge / Global Challenge: Smart Community Development conference, 13–16 October, Summerside, Prince Edward Island, Canada.

Beaton, Brian, Susan O'Donnell, Adam Fiser, and Brian Walmark. 2010. CI and Indigenous communities in Canada—The K-Net (Keewaytinook Okimakanak's Kuhkenah Network) experience. *Journal of Community Informatics* 5(2) (special issue). http://ci-journal.net/index.php/ciej/article/view/583/452.

Bourdieu, Pierre. 1989. Social space and symbolic power. *Sociology Today* 7(1) (Spring): 14–25.

Caidi, Nadia, Adam Fiser, and Margaret Lam. 2009. Trial by fire: Teaching community engagement. Paper presented at the annual meeting of the American Society for Information Science and Technology, 6–11 November, Vancouver, British Columbia, Canada.

Canadian Radio-television and Telecommunications Commission (CRTC). 1997. Telecom Public Notice 97-42: Service to High-Cost Serving Areas, File no. 8665-C12-14/97.

Coon Come, Matthew. 2001. Opening remarks. Indigenous Peoples Summit of the Americas. 29 March. Ottawa. http://www.dialoguebetweennations.com/OASdeclaration/english/MatthewCoonCome.htm.

Conrath, David W., Earl V. Dunn, and Christopher A. Higgings. 1983. *Evaluating telecommunications technology in medicine.* Dedham, MA: Artech House.

Dunn, Earl, David Conrath, Helen Acton, Chris Higgins, and Harry Bain. 1980. Telemedicine links patients in Sioux Lookout with doctors in Toronto. *Canadian Medical Association Journal* 122 (23 February): 484–87.

Dutton, William H., Volker Schneider, and Thierry Vedel. 2008. Large technical systems as ecologies of games: Cases from telecommunications to the Internet. Paper presented at the Complexity and Large Technical Systems Conference, 30–31 May, Meersburg, Germany.

Fiser, Adam. 2004. First Nations SchoolNet Regional Management Organization (RMO) Backgrounder. CRACIN Working Paper no. 1. August. Toronto: Canadian Research Alliance for Community Innovation and Networking. http://archive.iprp.ischool.utoronto.ca/cracin/publications/pdfs/WorkingPapers/CRACIN%20Working%20Paper%20No%201.pdf.

Fiser, Adam. 2010. A map of broadband availability in Canada's Indigenous and Northern communities: Access, management models, and digital divides. *Communication Politics and Culture* 43(1): 7–47.

Fiser, Adam, and Andrew Clement. 2007. The K-Net broadband deployment model: How a community-based network integrates public, private and not-for-profit sectors to support remote and under-served communities in Ontario. Information Policy Research Program, Faculty of Information Studies, University of Toronto, May.

Fiser, Adam, and Andrew Clement. 2008. The K-Net broadband deployment model: Enabling Canadian Aboriginal community control of telecom infrastructure through relationship building and heterogeneous engineering. Presented at IEEE International Symposium on Technology and Society Fredericton, 26–28 June, New Brunswick, Canada.

Fiser, Adam, Andrew Clement, and Brian Walmark. 2006. The K-Net development process: A model for First Nations broadband community networks. CRACIN Working Paper no. 12. February. Toronto: Canadian Research Alliance for Community Innovation and Networking. http://archive.iprp.ischool.utoronto.ca/cracin/publications/pdfs/WorkingPapers/CRACIN%20Working%20Paper%20No%2012.pdf.

Fiser, Adam, and Robert Luke. 2008. Between the clinic and the community: Pathways for an emerging e-health policy in the remote First Nations of Northwestern Ontario. In *Mediating health information: The go-betweens in a changing socio-technical landscape,* ed. C. Nadine Wathen, Sally Wyatt, and Roma Harris, 128–49. New York: Palgrave Macmillan.

Hudson, Heather. 1977. The role of radio in the far North. *Journal of Communication* 27(4) (Autumn): 130–40.

Kakekaspan, George, and Ernest C. Beck. 2003. Resolution 03/49: Support for the Development of the Nishnawbe Aski Nation Broadband Regional Network for First Nations, Passed on February 27, in Thunder Bay, Ontario, Canada.

K-Net Services. 2001. From potential to practice: Telecommunications and development in the Nishnawbe-Aski Nation, K-Net Services report to Industry Canada FedNor. 21 March. http://knet.ca/NAN-wide.pdf.

McMullen, Bill, and Andreas Rohrbach. 2003. *Distance education in remote Aboriginal communities: Barriers, learning styles, and best practices.* Prince George, BC: College of New Caledonia Press.

Mohr, Lavinia. 2001. To tell the people: Wawatay Radio Network. In *A passion for radio: Radio waves and community,* ed. Bruce Girard, 17–28. Toronto: Communica.

O'Donnell, Susan, Brian Walmark, and Brecken Rose Hancock. 2010. Video conferencing in remote and rural First Nations communities. In *Learning, technology, and traditions,* Vol. 6 of *Aboriginal policy research,* ed. Jerry P. White, Julie Peters, Dan Beavon, and Peter Dinsdale, 128–39. Toronto: Thompson Educational Publishing.

Ramírez, Ricardo, and Don Richardson. 2000. PACTS for rural and remote Ontario: Partnerships, accessibility, connectivity transformation strategies (Research Project Report, Year 1). School of Rural Extension Studies, Guelph, ON: University of Guelph. ftp://storage.knet.ca/pub/Brian/A1-SMART/PR-Marketing%20Info/PACTS/Report.pdf.

Ramírez, Ricardo, Helen Aitkin, Rebekah Jamieson, and Don Richardson. 2003. Harnessing ICTS: A Canadian First Nations experience: Introduction to K-Net. Institute for Connectivity in the Americas, Ottawa: International Development Research Centre.

Rowlandson, John. 2005. Position paper: Turning the corner with First Nations telehealth, Keewaytinook Okimakanak. May. http://ci-journal.net/index.php/ciej/article/viewFile/260/217.

15 ATLANTIC CANADIAN COMMUNITY INFORMATICS The Case of the WVDA and SmartLabrador

Katrina Peddle

Throughout the course of the CRACIN project, researchers have attempted to map and better understand how communities are using technology for their own purposes. In this chapter, I explore fieldwork conducted at two grassroots community informatics organizations in rural and remote Atlantic Canada—the Western Valley Development Agency, and SmartLabrador—to illuminate how they engaged with community technology to secure access to information and communication technologies (ICTs) in their regions. I examine each organization in relation to their participation in federal connectivity programs funded by Industry Canada. The analysis of rural and remote experiences with Industry Canada programs and community technology is pertinent to discussions of community informatics and policy given the opportunities that such programs were alleged to provide in rural and remote communities (e.g., e-business, telehealth, and distance education).

Specifically, I elaborate upon the role of local knowledge and learning as qualitative project outcomes in community informatics. I also focus on the role of public and private partnerships in community informatics efforts, and demonstrate how these two grassroots technology organizations serve as catalysts for community development and the "effective use" of ICTs (Gurstein 2004), while recognizing that mediated communication is often leveraged by communities for purposes that are very connected to their geographic, face-to-face community (Collins and Wellman 2010). This illuminates how community informatics organizations are using technology as tools for community development and enhancing community autonomy. It also underlines the importance of state support in community informatics initiatives, and the need for a dynamic relationship between federal programs and the local context.

The first case site, the Western Valley Development Agency (WVDA), was one of Nova Scotia's thirteen regional development authorities (RDAs) created to stimulate and champion community development. While it operated as a broad-based development organization, it participated in several large Industry Canada programs and focused its work largely on connectivity projects. The second case site, SmartLabrador, was created as the result of an Industry Canada Smart Community grant. It emerged from the Labrador Information Technology Initiative (LITI), a grassroots community technology project that was created in 1997 as a joint partnership in local development. Over the decade of the 2000s, SmartLabrador/LITI has participated in many Industry Canada programs.

As Moll and Shade (2001) and McDowell and Buchwald (1997) have demonstrated, there is a long-standing, public-interest social movement around the use of ICTs in Canada. While many community technology centres were started with small seed grants to build local ICT capacity and remained small, WVDA and SmartLabrador were chosen largely due to their participation in the federal Smart Community program. Smart Community was created under the umbrella of the Connecting Canadians agenda administered by Industry Canada. While Smart Community was the largest funding envelope either organization had ever received, both the SmartLabrador (via its predecessor the LITI) and WVDA had long been active in making ICTs accessible and useful to residents of their respective areas.

Indeed, there are many parallels between the WVDA case study and the experiences of SmartLabrador. There are, however, notable demographic and geographic differences. The Western Valley is a rural area just a few hours from the provincial capital, while many Labrador communities are not connected by roads and have a much smaller population. In this chapter, I compare how each organization interacted with issues of partnership and community learning, and elaborate upon how these organizations have worked to facilitate ICT access within the Connecting Canadians framework in the early millennium. The experiences of these two organizations in negotiating local involvement and outcomes, relationships with different levels of government, and competing public/private priorities demonstrate the importance of recognizing community-based outcomes when evaluating federal connectivity programs.

METHODOLOGY

As mentioned above, in this chapter I draw on fieldwork done with both the WVDA and SmartLabrador. Yin (2008, 11) argues that case studies such as the ones discussed here are well suited to questions of *how* and *why* and that "the case study's unique strength is its ability to deal with a full variety of evidence—documents, artifacts, interviews, and observations." In this research I was concerned with how rural and remote communities were using community informatics to meet their technology needs and why they chose the areas of focus that they did. In the WVDA case, I also looked at why using community informatics for individual capacity building was understood as a low priority by municipal politicians but was of considerable importance to local development workers (see also chapter 6). When presented with the opportunity to conduct field studies with the WVDA and SmartLabrador, Yin's work, in addition to discussions with community partners, guided the decision to use two major methods: interviews and participant observation.

Interviews were conducted in Nova Scotia in 2005 during a one-month field study and, in Labrador, over the course of a three-month study during the fall of 2006. I relied heavily on snowballing methods for my interview sample as this allowed for the targeting of specific individuals who were active in community informatics (for both the SmartLabrador and WVDA cases) and municipal politics (the WVDA alone) (King and Horrocks 2009). Participant observation likewise took place over one month in Nova Scotia and three months in Labrador. I worked as an embedded researcher with both organizations, and many observations emerged not only from specific interviews but also from insights garnered from lunch conversations, municipal council meetings, board meetings, and a variety of other interactions in the community. I engaged in the qualitative journaling method to ensure adequate notes for later coding of data (Creswell 2007).

Berg (2001, 139–40) argues that the researcher's attitude is a key part of the eventual results of the project and cites Matza (1969) in saying that it is important to "enter appreciating the situations rather than intending to correct them." He discusses the importance of empathy and the need to understand what is happening in the research environment instead of simply advocating for or critiquing it. This was especially important in updating the Nova Scotia case, as the precursors to the WVDA's closure occurred during data collection in 2005. Wanting to put assumptions aside as much as possible while acknowledging the impossibility of navigating any situation unbiased, I used a grounded theory approach to analyze the data. I used open coding for the data set, based on themes that became evident in interviews and throughout participant observation. Strauss and Corbin (2008, 195) define open coding as an analytic process of identifying concepts in data that takes place by "delineating concepts to stand for blocks of raw data." The open categories were then cross-referenced for commonalities and differences (what Strauss and Corbin refer to as axial coding). Interviews were coded and cross-referenced using NVivo coding for common and divergent themes. This provided a better picture of the community informatics initiatives in both case sites.

A total of thirty-four interviews from both case sites inform this research, along with countless informal conversations with community informatics workers whose perspectives provided invaluable insights into the rural and remote community-oriented ICT context. Understanding the interviews as a series of stories being told to me by interviewees, I drew extensively from Mishler's (1986) narrative approach in data analysis.

HISTORY AND BACKGROUND

The Western Valley Development Agency

In this section I discuss the history of the WVDA, highlighting the local context and the experiences of the organization in terms of participation in Industry Canada programs and in community informatics initiatives. I reflect on how the closure of the organization impacted the effective use of technology in the area, and analyze the shift from the WVDA to the new regional development authority (RDA), the Annapolis Digby Economic Development Agency (ADEDA), in terms of community technology and government funding.

The WVDA was formed in 1994 during a period of intense change precipitated by an economic crisis in the Western Valley of Nova Scotia. The ground fishery collapsed in 1992, and with it thousands of jobs in the area also disappeared. Additionally, in 1994 the federal government announced the closure of CFB Cornwallis, a military base that employed over 700 people. Clearly, the WVDA was facing an uphill battle of community economic development in a context of high unemployment. A decade later, the economy of the Western Valley had diversified, and the former CFB Cornwallis has been transformed into a business park employing over 900 people (MacNeil 2004). There was also a vibrant arts and culture community in the area, which several interviewees described as an important factor in their decisions to live in the region. While the WVDA did not claim exclusive credit for this shift toward a rejuvenated and diverse rural economy, it prided itself on stimulating community-based innovation.[1] Currently, the area continues to evolve economically as the resource-based economic sectors shrink (Annapolis Digby Economic Development Agency 33, pers. comm.).

The WVDA, Connecting Canadians, and the Challenge
of Sustaining Community Informatics

Here I elaborate on the WVDA's participation in Industry Canada programs, and highlight the shifts in thinking around the use of Western Valley's community-owned dark fibre network, and the of use of government project funding. The WVDA participated in several major initiatives available under the Industry Canada Connecting Canadians umbrella, including the Community Access Program (CAP), the Smart Community Program, and the Broadband for Rural and Northern Development Program (BRAND). The WVDA thus provided an interesting lens through which to examine implications of this policy agenda for the role of ICTs and community development in the rural Canadian context. The WVDA's activities focused on community economic development across all areas of the local economy, including tourism development and small business training. The organization's activities often involved ICT projects, with its largest being Nova Scotia's Smart Community.

As a key partner in the FUNDYweb Broadband Project, the WVDA worked with local municipalities, the Nova Scotia Community College (NSCC), and two small private telecommunications providers to bring broadband into the area. As the only community-owned high-speed network of its kind in Canada, the FUNDYweb broadband network provided high-speed Internet access to community members as well as major employers such as Convergys, a large call centre that employed 500 people.[2]

The WVDA closed as its municipal funders grew increasingly frustrated with the organization's capacity building, which was seen by several municipal councillors as coming at the expense of business development. (For a more in-depth analysis, see chapter 6.) The WVDA's closure left a serious gap in human resources necessary to help facilitate its ongoing operation and effective use. As community champions are an important element of integrating new technologies into a given community, the dissolution of the WVDA just as FUNDYweb began operating marked a serious gap in the face-to-face community championing that would encourage network use in areas of education and health care and promote the effective use of technology (WVDA staff 8, pers. comm.; Gurstein 2004). Despite this, the mere existence of a community-owned dark fibre network is an interesting example of leveraging federal funds to meet community needs. FUNDYweb remains a unique network that could still serve as a model of community-owned technology in rural areas.

Annapolis Digby Economic Development Agency (ADEDA) was the new RDA created two years later to replace the WVDA. With an executive director starting in February 2007, the organization is focusing largely on economic development (Sloan 2007). ADEDA has not participated in other Industry Canada connectivity programs, but uses the established broadband network to attract businesses to the region (ADEDA executive director 33, pers. comm. 2010). Despite the move away from supporting grassroots capacity building to a focus on business attraction and retention, the agency still sees technology as an important element of local development. ADEDA is focused on nurturing the growth of local technology companies, notably hosting monthly "tech socials" at a local pub where a business owner can present his or her enterprise and have a chance to connect with people in the community. Broadband is considered to be an essential element of the region's infrastructure, but activities related to using ICTs are framed more in terms of business development than capacity building, reflecting the changing municipal priorities laid out in 2005 when the fieldwork was conducted. The region still benefits from the broadband network established via Industry Canada partnerships, but now has a focus on being less dependent on government funding, a move that was articulated by the executive director as being motivated by the many strings that come attached to government funding. ADEDA is instead encouraging local development to happen in ways that are self-sufficient. However, there would be a higher return on investment from earlier Industry Canada programs if there were more resources to in some capacity continue the work undertaken by previous connectivity programs such as BRAND and Smart Community (ADEDA staff member 33, pers. comm. 2010). Moving from large government grants for connectivity to focusing on local sustainability was a key shift between the WVDA and its successor. This reflects decreased state involvement in community technology initiatives, and the increased expectation that community organizations become able to sustain their activities without federal project support.

SmartLabrador

Here I discuss the history of SmartLabrador, highlighting the local context and the experiences of the organization in terms of participation in Industry Canada programs and in community informatics initiatives. I demonstrate how the community technology organization has been forced to work under a business model in order to stay afloat, and reflect on how the unregulated monopoly existing in this remote environment made it extremely difficult to negotiate with the incumbent telecommunications company.

Labrador is one of the most rural and remote regions in the province of Newfoundland and Labrador. Covering a huge geographic area, Labrador is larger than the Maritime Provinces of Nova Scotia, Prince Edward Island, and New Brunswick combined. Labrador faces many challenges to communication, including limited transportation links between communities (see chapter 4 in this volume). With a total population of fewer than 30,000 people, connecting these communities with road access is often prohibitively expensive.

Given significant Inuit, Innu, Métis and Settler populations, the situated use of community technology requires attention to a very diverse set of social, cultural and educational contexts (Suchman 2007).

The limited resources available to service the region have long motivated partnerships between different Labrador regions and organizations. Building on this history of partnership, the Labrador Information Technology Initiative (LITI) was founded in 1997 as part of a co-operative strategy between Labrador's five economic development corporations. Recognizing that there was no organization dedicated to championing the use and development of ICTs in Labrador, the LITI was founded with four primary focuses: awareness, equal access, skills development, and business development. The LITI has managed major investments in infrastructure and service development, the largest of which was the Smart Community demonstration project, which developed a now dismantled broadband satellite network and accompanying applications.

Following from its long history in ICT skills development, SmartLabrador is currently focused on applications development in learning experiences, preserving cultural knowledge for tourism development, and communication across Northern communities within Labrador and along the North Atlantic rim. They have invested in developing partnerships with Northern communities in Iceland, Greenland, and the Faroe Islands as a means of addressing similar challenges facing remote northern areas.

Having been funded largely by the federal and provincial governments, SmartLabrador works on a very limited budget with two full-time staff. SmartLabrador was created with extensive community consultation and, as such, relies heavily on having the support and contribution of its local partners. This demonstrates the importance of integrated local participation in community informatics initiatives. However, with the funding once available via Connecting Canadians now finished, SmartLabrador has been forced to charge for its services and run under a business model. While this was not the initial vision of providing community access to technology, it has been necessary to ensure the organization's survival (SmartLabrador director 34, pers. comm. 2010). Like the WVDA, SmartLabrador has found that developing local and international partnerships proved more useful over time than accessing Industry Canada funding, which is too often earmarked for working with Bell Aliant, which enjoyed an unregulated monopoly in the Labrador telecommunications market. The challenge of working with an unregulated incumbent is examined below. SmartLabrador found that the relationship with Bell Aliant required by BRAND to be unfruitful and financially exploitive, and that they had little negotiating power. The organization then began partnering with rural communities along the North Atlantic rim that are facing similar challenges in sustaining their communities and ensuring access to appropriate technology to help them flourish in a shifting economy. The mutual interest of creating community-based solutions for rural and remote areas has been key to these partnerships.

In the following sections I analyze the themes that emerged from the data in terms of local knowledge, partnership development, the problems with public/private partnerships under the Connecting Canadians umbrella, local learning and community innovation, and community-based outcomes.

LOCAL KNOWLEDGE: CAPACITY AND COMMUNITY BUILDING

Community-based technology centres have often been framed as places of learning. Traditionally, however, solutions for community problems have been often sought by consulting with some kind of outside "expert." This approach has been heavily critiqued for its disempowering impact and its tendency to limit the capacity of communities to make decisions directing their own futures, rather than cultivating the community's capacity to act in its own interests (Laverack 2007). Having learned through experience that such a top-down approach does not tend toward participation and empowerment, a grassroots focus on learning is thus important to many community informatics organizations (Cook and Smith 2004; Devins, Darlow, and Smith 2002; Kaiser 2005). Community learning happens at multiple levels, and includes community members, community development workers, community champions, board members, and others. Both SmartLabrador and the wvda have challenged the assumptions implicit in many federal connectivity programs and have a strong history of working "outside the box." Southern Labrador has long made a habit out of challenging the status quo.[3]

Rather than situating telecentre users as people who do not have preexisting skills and experience, SmartLabrador's work is predicated on building upon local knowledge and strengths within the community, an approach that is appropriate in many contexts in which people are facing a new challenge (Bartle 2008). Their commitment to focusing on strengths has been demonstrated through several learning initiatives that have been undertaken over the past several years.

SmartLabrador has used its experience in ICTs and community development to create a model for capturing local knowledge, in the creation of heritage tourism. They have created a toolkit to prevent the disappearance of traditional knowledge due to young people not performing the same kinds of work that their parents and grandparents have done. SmartLabrador has also recognized that this traditional knowledge had an economic value in terms of heritage tourism, a market that the region wishes to tap as it grows its tourism sector. Boatbuilding and the making of hooked mats were formerly skills that many Labradorians possessed. In an attempt to preserve these skills, SmartLabrador developed the Coastal Heritage Experience as a prototype for how to engage with technology at the service of sustainable, locally controlled tourism.

The WVDA was also involved in many initiatives that support the development of local skills, and the organization's commitment to learning was both inwardly and outwardly focused.

The WVDA was a long-term participant in the Community Access Program (CAP), a program discussed in more detail by Longford, Moll, and Shade in chapter 21 of this volume. Addressing its mandate of broad-based community development, the WVDA also created spaces for community learning not limited to ICTs. For example, the WVDA participated in the national Learn$ave pilot project, which was developed to examine how people with low incomes can improve their ability to plan their finances. A clear element of the WVDA message focused on building on the strength of the region in several areas, and how to best utilize ICTs for this purpose. Certainly, the creation of a community-owned fibre network makes a significant contribution to daily life in the Western Valley. One local artist reported that having broadband access dramatically changed her work life, as she could now download large image files quickly and interact more easily with customers in larger centres such as Halifax, and beyond (artist 12, pers. comm.). The WVDA also focused on experiential learning for its staff. A WVDA staff member (WVDA staff 19, pers. comm. 2005) recounted his experience in "doing ICT": "[I] love it! Like I said, I've been here for eight years. I started out as administrative assistant, assistant to Janet [Larkman, WVDA executive director]. I was on the phones, I was her secretary . . . worked my way into the techie . . . just by learning along the way."

The above examples highlight the centrality of experiential learning to the WVDA's working philosophy. Valuing local knowledge and engaging community learning are important to community development and indeed community informatics, but it must be recognized that local knowledge is increasingly negotiated in relation to technological change (Murray and Neis 2006). Both SmartLabrador and the WVDA embraced local knowledge and ICTs as means of growing knowledge in their communities. This does not mean, however, that local knowledge should not be open to debate and that different versions of local knowledge do not exist. Indeed, this knowledge should not only be valued, but also regarded with the same principles of critical review expected of other sources.[4]

PARTNERSHIP DEVELOPMENT SKILLS IN
LABRADOR AND THE WESTERN VALLEY

A history of community informatics in Atlantic Canada reveals a complex network of partnerships at the local, provincial, and federal levels. In the following sections I delineate these partnerships, and demonstrate that attention to the local context is crucial for partnership success in community informatics. An in-depth analysis of the Connecting Canadians agenda requires investigation of how public-private partnerships worked at the community level. While each site was proud to have won the large Smart Community demonstration project, it is clear that a project of this scope created great expectations in Labrador and in the Western Valley, especially given the historical context of the projects having been awarded before the burst of the dot-com bubble in the late 1990s.

Partnerships: The Western Valley Experience

The WVDA had great success in its partnerships with public sector institutions during the Smart Community demonstration project. For example, its partnership with the local library resulted in the creation of an online catalogue accessible to local residents from their homes. Library usage increased dramatically following the creation of the catalogue, which reflects the nature of the rural environment in which the WVDA was situated, often requiring individuals to travel several kilometres to physically access library services (Nova Scotia librarian 21, pers. comm.). The Smart Community project did not result in the creation of a broadband network in the Western Valley during the project. The WVDA's Smart Community public partners were micro in scale and were not required to make capital investments in order to participate in the project past the demonstration phase of the Smart Community. The WVDA's most successful public partnership was negotiated following the end of the Smart Community demonstration project. Private partnerships during the course of the project were unproductive and frustrating for the WVDA, and staff members often noted the importance of planning and negotiation with private partners. Following the end of Smart Community funding, the WVDA, via a funding partnership with the Atlantic Canada Opportunities Agency that was eventually considered a BRAND project, partnered with Nova Scotia Community College (NSCC), which made a one-time capital investment in the FUNDYweb broadband network to purchase a major server that is housed at NSCC's campus in the Western Valley. This investment matched the college's needs as well, as they required broadband access for the provision of several post-secondary programs, and was key to creating the network (FUNDYweb Broadband Board [FBB] member 2, pers. comm.).

The FUNDY web broadband network involved partnering with two private telecommunications companies in order to secure access to the fibre network and to have the capacity to administer residential accounts; understandably, the WVDA did not want to become involved in billing or administering home Internet services. This negotiation took place without a binding government program, and the community partners were satisfied with the technical and business competencies that Rush Communications and Eastlink (two telcos) brought to the table.[5] This case demonstrates that a partnership between a community informatics organization and small telecommunication companies in a non-monopoly context can be a useful means of providing broadband services in a rural environment.

The WVDA demonstrated its skills in working around the restrictions of government funding mechanisms by obtaining funding for its community-owned network without meeting the conditions of the BRAND program, although they were acknowledged on the BRAND website as having received BRAND funding despite having twice been rejected (WVDA staff 8, pers. comm. 2005). The WVDA's leveraging of federal funds for a community-owned infrastructure is an exceptional case of negotiating strict program criteria in order to create community owned infrastructure; indeed, the SmartLabrador experience with BRAND discussed later in this chapter demonstrates the many restrictive elements of the program, including the hasty signing of agreements and the limited follow-through on behalf of the incumbent telecommunication provider. Such leveraging of funds also speaks to the WVDA's ability to adapt largely inflexible programs to community needs.

SmartLabrador: The Lack of Public Institutional Support for the Community-Owned Network

Given its lack of core funding, SmartLabrador has proved resourceful in its ability to outlive many other Smart Community projects. SmartLabrador has leveraged longer-term contributions from a variety of sources, notably the provincial government and the International Grenfell Association (IGA), a charitable organization that funds community projects throughout Labrador.

Like the WVDA, SmartLabrador had a long history of working in partnership with a variety of organizations. This history was evident in the support the organization received during the Smart Community demonstration project. One SmartLabrador board member (SmartLabrador board member 31, pers. comm. 2006) noted: "There were all kinds of partnerships. . . . We got $5 million but we had to raise $5 million. And some of that was in kind and some of that was real money, real dollars. We were fortunate that we raised this money. That was the hard work side of it, that was the part that was tough."

SmartLabrador engaged in successful public partnerships, notably with the development of a strong partnership with the Newfoundland and Labrador Department of Justice. SmartLabrador's video conferencing services were often used by the Department of Justice to avoid the expenses of having an individual flown from a small community to the larger community of Goose Bay, where the courthouse is located. These partnerships enhanced the services offered by these provincial governmental partners without forcing them to incur a significant cost. It is also worth noting that while the Department of Justice was happy to participate during the pilot phase (when all video conferencing services were free of charge), it was less eager to participate once a fee-for-service model was introduced (Peddle 2004).

SmartLabrador encountered significant challenges in working with other larger public organizations. The SmartLabrador broadband network was created with the intention that larger institutions such as health, education, and social services would use it, thus creating enough traffic to support network operations while enabling connectivity to individual homes for a price competitive with urban areas in Canada. For example, extensive network use was anticipated by the regional health board for video conferencing services for administrative and clinical purposes. Given the challenges of providing health services to such a small and dispersed population, delivering health services over video conferencing was strongly supported in public consultations when the LITI was applying for Smart Community funding to create the SmartLabrador network.

SmartLabrador staff reflected on the importance of technical partnerships and planning in relation to community technology initiatives, noting that some technical expertise was lacking at the planning phase of the Smart Community project. This lack of sufficient technical partnerships, along with the short timeline allotted for completing the project, meant that certain elements of the network were put together very quickly. Indeed, SmartLabrador immediately set about the creation of a hybrid network upon receiving Smart Community funding.

A SmartLabrador technician (SmartLabrador technician 32, pers. comm. 2006) elaborated on the lessons learned around technical planning:

> It was something that we talked about later in the game, about how the whole technical aspect was introduced. There was a lot of planning and human resource planning and deployment that happened, and then the project moved into the technical side and putting the equipment out there and doing things. In hindsight, that kind of technical stuff needed to happen much earlier, because there was a lot of catch-up to be done. It was a bigger job than anybody foresaw in this. With 44 sites in 20-odd communities, that's a lot.

Initially, SmartLabrador had negotiated in-kind contributions from public partners such as provincial departments of health and justice, and the paid use of the network was a cornerstone of the SmartLabrador sustainability plan following the end of Industry Canada funding. There were many factors that influenced why the institutional support anticipated in the Labrador region did not come through in the form of network service usage beyond the pilot phase. When this public partnership did not bridge into a fee-for-service investment, the result was a lack of network traffic and a serious sustainability problem for the community-based technology network.

PROBLEMS WITH PRIVATE PARTNERSHIPS

SmartLabrador community workers noted that some of their Smart Community private technical advisors charged large consulting fees with limited outputs. Over time, it was understood that technical partners saw SmartLabrador as a "cash cow." SmartLabrador eventually changed its budget in reaction to these limited outputs, redirecting monies to other parts of the project.

Following the end of Smart Community funding, SmartLabrador sought funding through the next large Connecting Canadians program, the Broadband for Rural and Northern Development Program (BRAND). Working directly within BRAND's structure dealt a significantly different hand for SmartLabrador than the WVDA. SmartLabrador operated in a context in which existed a hybrid community network, some governmental connectivity, and an incumbent active in major centres such as Goose Bay. As a result, the BRAND program required SmartLabrador to engage in a private partnership with Bell Aliant. This partnership was marked by high costs and a lack of commitment to making things happen at a community level (SmartLabrador staff 30, pers. comm.). SmartLabrador representatives also noted feeling a great deal of pressure from Industry Canada to "sign on the dotted line" in their agreement with Bell Aliant, which provided services to SmartLabrador at a huge expense.

WRESTLING WITH AN ELEPHANT? THE PARTICIPATION OF PROVINCIAL INSTITUTIONS IN COMMUNITY-OWNED INFRASTRUCTURE

In this section I analyze the different forms of partnerships engaged in by each organization. While both organizations experienced similar success in smaller-scale public partnerships, the sites differed in their experience with larger public partnerships.

SmartLabrador had limited success in enticing provincial institutions to use the network for their broadband needs. Several factors, including a lack of provincial telehealth policy at the time that the network was created, the challenges of working between non-unionized and unionized organizations, and fiscal constraints at the health board level, contributed to a lack of uptake of video conference services in the health sector, which would have supplied a central element of funding for the SmartLabrador network (for an expanded analysis, see Peddle 2004). This lack of uptake severely hampered SmartLabrador's attempts to remain sustainable following the end of Smart Community funding.[6]

Regardless of the how a group intends a technology (for example, video conferencing) to be used, it is often adopted in different and unpredictable ways in a situated community context in which different factors (such as cash flow and privacy concerns) impact how it is incorporated into a new environment. What is clear from both the wvda and SmartLabrador experiences is the need for larger institutional participation at the provincial level (e.g., departments of education, justice, and health) to ensure adequate usage levels in a rural environment with a relatively small population. Partnerships with provincial institutions can provide key support by creating traffic (and hence cash flow) on a given network.

In the SmartLabrador case, the lack of participation by several provincial institutions is related to the duplication of broadband infrastructure and overlapping federal programs. For example, the education system in Newfoundland and Labrador also created a dedicated network to meet its needs in distance education at the secondary level. This huge amount of traffic, which could have been directed via the SmartLabrador network, is instead being vetted through a network dedicated solely to Department of Education traffic. This network was funded through the Canadian Strategic Infrastructure Fund's Broadband Access to Rural and Remote Schools and Communities project (Infrastructure Canada 2005). Overlapping networks in areas of market failure create a disincentive for provincial actors to use a community network. At the same time, as several networks are active across a sparsely populated region, SmartLabrador was working at a grassroots level to find a solution for the eleven Labrador communities that still did not have broadband access. This demonstrates how community champions find-last mile solutions in partnership with remote citizens regarding their technology needs. This, however, does not necessarily translate into larger-scale institutional support, as federal and provincial monies dedicated to creating duplicate networks minimize the likelihood that larger public organizations will decide to use a community-owned network in lieu of developing their own. SmartLabrador's sustainability plan was predicated on a shared network with institutional support. This is also indicative of a lack of support at the federal level in aiding the small community organizations that received these grants, to negotiate with provincial actors in the public sector.

The Smart Community project laid the groundwork in the Western Valley for the creation of the FUNDYweb broadband network. Know-how and experience gained through the Smart Community pilot project enhanced the strengths of the WVDA in mobilizing local actors in the network's development, and the WVDA conducted a large amount of research on creating such a network over a year before approaching local partners (WVDA staff 8, pers. comm.). Notably, their work was situated in a competitive telecommunications market in a region where a major post-secondary institution did not yet have broadband access. This speaks to their diligence as community champions and their extensive experience in community informatics, and points to the ability of a community network to handle large amounts of institutional traffic when there are no other broadband options.

The question of public-private partnerships is complicated in relation to ICTs. Fibre networks often require large capital investments that are simply beyond the reach of small community informatics organizations. The ability of the WVDA to obtain infrastructure funding without having to work within the constraints of the BRAND program enabled it to leverage funds while maintaining autonomy when negotiating terms of service with project partners. SmartLabrador also has a great deal of experience working with federal partners and negotiating as much of a local fit as possible. Despite their expertise, it proved difficult to negotiate outside the parameters of Connecting Canadians programs. These two cases illustrate that while partnership with a private telecommunications provider can be a means of securing broadband access, community organizations must have negotiating power and governmental support to do so. They also demonstrate that private partnerships work better in a competitive telecommunications market than in an unregulated monopoly situation. Indeed, the BRAND program functioned much like a federal telecommunications subsidy, vetted through the guise of community technology.

The SmartLabrador case reflects the need for government programs to be adaptable to the specifics of the market in question, such as a small competitive telecommunications market in the WVDA case and an unregulated monopoly in the case of SmartLabrador. Indeed, this reflects the problematic policy move in telecommunications away from the regulation of monopolies and the provision of universal service (Winseck 1998).

SUSTAINABILITY AND FUNDING IN RURAL COMMUNITY INFORMATICS

The WVDA functioned for a decade as a relatively stable, core-funded organization. Despite this core funding, the WVDA eventually lost the support of their municipal partners, reflecting that core funding is only one element of an organization's sustainability. The cases of the wvda and SmartLabrador demonstrate the importance of support at the local (e.g., board of governors), provincial (e.g., large public institutions), and federal (e.g., policy and funding) levels. Indeed, the federal partnership in connectivity projects is typically finite in scope, which leaves community informatics groups without an obvious route to sustainability. Recognizing the need for a broad base of funding sources acknowledges the role of provincial and non-governmental actors in the history of connectivity in Labrador, and community champions were quick to note that their continued existence hinged largely on these contributions. These networks of partners demonstrate that the investments in community informatics go far beyond federal infrastructure dollars and include vital contributions from partner organizations. These public partnerships are predicated on trust and long-term activity in the community. Indeed, social and professional networks at the local and regional levels played key roles in the demonstration projects, a contribution that is often invisible in terms of project inputs. Not surprisingly, these partnerships were among the most fruitful elements of the two projects.

PARTNERSHIPS AND INVISIBLE OUTPUTS

Although SmartLabrador received provisional funding from the provincial government to continue network operations, these funds were eventually exhausted and the network was shut down. Sticking to their mandate that it is *people,* not *technology,* that are the lifeblood of SmartLabrador, the organization continues to operate with two staff members: an executive director and technician. These two people work as "jack and jill of all trades" to ensure there is a community technology presence in Labrador. This has presented a significant challenge, given the geography and amount of work to be done. However, SmartLabrador's commitment to hire and train local people throughout the Smart Community project has meant that ict skills remain in communities throughout the region long beyond the scope of the project. For example, a former fieldworker from the Smart Community project in the coastal community of Port Hope Simpson was still volunteering in 2010 with SmartLabrador in their continued work in community Internet radio. The volunteer is also a community technology champion who shares his skills with many people who see him as a "go to" person for technical support (SmartLabrador technician 32, pers. comm.).

Despite these successes, the organization deals with the constant instability of funding in project planning. Certainly, a key challenge for SmartLabrador in the past several years is to obtain adequate project funding to ensure the organization's continued existence. Funding sources following the end of the Smart Community project were difficult to secure, and although the organization still receives an annual CAP grant for $5,000, this small amount of funds is generally not earmarked for the human resources that are necessary for community informatics organizations to exist.

However, SmartLabrador has maintained itself by pursuing other partnerships and adapting its service model. By developing the Coastal Heritage Experience discussed above as a prototype for use in other areas, Smart-Labrador enhanced its sustainability by offering its niche skills in ICTs and heritage preservation on a contract basis to other rural areas. Additionally, it is currently using its experience in Northern communications to provide a platform for the creation of a Northern Knowledge Network, designed for knowledge sharing across communities in the North Atlantic, many of whom face similar challenges in accessing ICTs and adapting to changing resource-based economies. This being the case, SmartLabrador is partnering with similar regions in other countries—namely Iceland, Greenland, and the Faroe Islands—to stimulate economic development throughout Labrador and to share community-based knowledge (see chapter 2 in this volume). The focus of the SmartLabrador project is on capturing traditional forms of knowledge that are devalued and disappearing. In order to become sustainable over the past few years, it adopted a business model in which it charges for its services. While this was not the desired approach to community technology, the organization had no other choice in order to keep its doors open (SmartLabrador director 34, pers. comm.). This organizational change marked a commitment to looking inward for creative solutions in community development, rather than having a lack of government funding force SmartLabrador's closure. It also reflects the importance of leadership and entrepreneurship in creative Northern communities (Petrov 2008).

SMALL IS BEAUTIFUL: COMMUNITY-BASED OUTCOMES AND EFFECTIVE USE OF ICTS

Community informatics focuses largely on the potential of ICTs to enable meaningful contributions to community life (Gurstein 2004). It is thus important to consider what community-based outcomes exist from the two case studies presented here. Both the WVDA and SmartLabrador can be seen as models for experiential learning on the job. Each organization has enabled its staff to learn new skills and perform work that typically has only been available to people with specific training that is often unavailable in rural areas (acknowledging that proximity to a college is just one element of post-secondary training).

Focusing my analysis on small-scale community development illustrates how community development efforts interface with the daily lives of people in the two respective regions. The value of such initiatives is often hard to capture in a quantitative format, and as such does not match well with federal accounting mechanisms that often seek quantifiably measurable outputs (Ramírez 2007). Despite being slippery to measure, the qualitative changes in people's daily lives are important elements of community development that must be taken into consideration when assessing outcomes in relation to community informatics.

Local Learning: Building a Geographically Stable Knowledge Base

A major part of both organizations' community technology efforts focused on learning; they demonstrate how community informatics initiatives do not take place in a vacuum but are situated within a broader spectrum of community development activities. These activities range from helping individuals gain skills in ICTs, from the basics of word processing to e-business support at the WVDA, to working with local people to ensure that cultural knowledge is recorded and preserved, including capturing stories and running an Internet radio station at SmartLabrador. This preservation of local knowledge serves a dual purpose. First, local citizens are encouraged to value the traditional skills and knowledge that they possess. Second, this knowledge can then be used to develop locally controlled heritage tourism. In these instances, community informatics builds a bridge between traditional knowledge and ICTs. SmartLabrador prided itself on hiring all its technicians locally, with a commitment to train them with any new skills required to do their jobs.

Innovation and Community Informatics: Community Technology Champions

Community technology centres have long been documented as being about more than just technology training (Gurstein 2004; Huggins and Izushi 2002; Pigg 2001). Both the WVDA and SmartLabrador predicated themselves on being centres for innovation and development in their regions, with a focus on the social side of development. Framed as a "one-stop shop" for local businesses, the WVDA prided itself upon assisting local businesses and entrepreneurs in the region. Indeed, as an RDA with a broad mandate beyond community informatics, the WVDA was engaged in many development-oriented activities, including ongoing e-business support with workshop series and guest speakers.

Building Community Strengths

Comparatively, SmartLabrador often works with other community groups to write funding proposals, which range from community development to larger-scale business development. Key to SmartLabrador's engagement is not the technology employed, which will inevitably need to be replaced, but how bringing people together to build new skills and reflect on the ones they already possess provides communities with leverage to act in their own best interests. This again demonstrates their commitment to promoting community self-reliance. The integral element of the work of both the WVDA and Smart-Labrador involved the creation of a space in which people can gather to talk about ideas and brainstorm about important future projects. This catalytic role played by both organizations is important in community development, especially in rural areas where government services and other forms of institutional support are sparse. The champion role also extended into an advocacy position as each organization fought to bring resources to their regions.

Innovation in Local Infrastructure

The WVDA and SmartLabrador also each demonstrate innovation in terms of deploying infrastructure. The original impetus for community-owned infrastructure emerged from a lack of broadband services in both regions, where the incumbent telecommunications provider (Bell Aliant, owned by Bell Canada Enterprises [BCE]) refused to provide broadband services due to reasons of market failure (WVDA staff member 8, pers. comm.; municipal councillor 30, pers. comm.). This desire for local ownership is also reflected in research on ICTs in rural Australia, where citizens have expressed that they feel community-owned telecommunications will be more accountable to them (Goggin 2003). Aliant is now active in both areas following large federal infrastructure investments, especially, in the Labrador case, made via the BRAND program. One member (FBB member 2, pers. comm. 2005) of the FBB recalls:

> The major telecommunications in this province is a division of Bell Canada—Aliant. And Aliant have fibre throughout the province, they laid the fibre years ago, before it became fashionable. And, anyway, when we started this project, the initial idea was to go to Aliant and say, "Let us use some of that fibre space that you have for this project." And Aliant initially said "No," and then said, "Yeah, maybe, but we want several million dollars for that." And that was when we said, "You know, we could probably do this—there is probably another way to approach this" . . . 'cause it is all about building capacity in rural Canada and rural Nova Scotia. So we decided that we will build our own.

Thus community informatics groups often work around the constraints of market failure to provide workable solutions at the grassroots level, and community-owned broadband is an effective means of providing services in rural and remote areas where they otherwise would not exist.

Conclusion

This chapter serves to outline the experiences of two community informatics organizations in Atlantic Canada, highlighting their engagement with Industry

Canada connectivity initiatives. While the Western Valley and Labrador have significantly different geographies and local contexts, they share several commonalities in relation to community informatics in rural and remote environments. Both organizations had positive experiences in partnerships with public organizations. Outputs at the community level were significant in both cases, with enhanced access to library services, community knowledge, and actual broadband infrastructure. There are key differences in how each site rolled out their Smart Community project, including the types of public partnerships in which each project engaged.

That granted, both organizations had greater success partnering with public institutions than with private ones. The WVDA, however, had more success in having a public partner make a large financial investment in its broadband network and engaging with private telecommunications in building a network. This is largely linked to the significant educational needs in the region, where the costs of setting up infrastructure made the provincial incumbent reticent to become a service provider. It also reflects the lack of dedicated networks available for provincial institutions in the Western Valley of Nova Scotia.

Many partnerships engaged in with private companies during the Smart Community project did not have long-term results or did not obtain project goals for both cases examined here. This demonstrates the rapid change in the IT sector, and the different goals of community informatics (e.g., community development) versus private industry (e.g., cash flow). Nonetheless, the WVDA and SmartLabrador Smart Community projects are also strong examples of how small communities are making technology work for their own interests, despite the continual search for funding and the limits of program constraints on their organizations.

Examining Atlantic Canadian community informatics offers several insights for policy. First, there is a need to coordinate connectivity projects at the federal and provincial levels in order to avoid network duplication and ensure that all communities have access to ICTs, regardless of size or geography. Second, it is clear that there is no single level of funding that provides the lynchpin to sustaining community informatics. Support is required from local, provincial, and federal levels. Provincial support is essential, as provincially administered institutions, such as those in the health and education sectors, make up a great deal of the network traffic that can make rural and remote community networks viable. In the Labrador case, a kind of intersectoral competition is taking place, in which different governmental institutions (notably health and education) are building separate networks that will coexist in the same remote region. This is problematic, given the intensive costs associated with building each network and the possibilities of sharing a network with bigger capacity to ensure universal coverage throughout the region.

Each case study demonstrates how rural and remote community informatics organizations are innovators that serve a catalytic role in community economic development. From ensuring access to infrastructure via community-owned models to engaging communities in local knowledge to create an alternative tourism sector, the WVDA and SmartLabrador show how locally controlled ICT initiatives contribute to building strong communities outside Canada's urban spaces. As such, it is vital that policy makers take the qualitative nature of community development work into account when designing outcome measures for evaluating community projects. Looking broadly at the overlapping ways in which different areas of community development (e.g., literacy and community informatics) contribute to the life of a rural or remote community reveals much more than quantitative measures that do not capture the complex and often invisible ways that community development happens.

Community-based technology generally requires state support in order to exist, and the federal policy move away from funding these small organizations seriously threatens their survival, and pushes them toward business models. Both cases here have expressed repeated frustration with the many strings attached to government funding, and the ways in which the organizations felt their hands were tied due to the nature of the funding. Yet both case studies demonstrate the capacity of community informatics to benefit local learning, capacity building, connectivity, and human resource retention in rural and remote areas of Atlantic Canada. It is incumbent upon policy makers, then, to use a qualitative evaluation to understand the impacts of community informatics on rural areas. Doing so will reveal the many overlapping contributions it continues to make in rural and remote communities.

NOTES

1   This information is drawn from the Western Valley Development Authority Business Plan 2004–2005, from a now-defunct WDVA website, last accessed by the author on 15 August 2005.

2   For a critique of call centres, see Scott-Dixon (2005). In addition, I have laid out the problematic relationship between call centres and a "knowledge-based economy" in Peddle (2007).

3   For example, following the closure of the ground fishery, the federal government offered massive adult basic education training to "retrain" former fishery workers to work in other business sectors, many of which did not exist in the local area, nor did these areas have the population to support many of the professions for which people received training. The cookie-cutter approach to education that was adopted to deal with the training needs of the thousands of displaced fishery workers demonstrated to community development workers—many of whom engaged with SmartLabrador—to recognize that requiring participants to sit in a classroom for 25 hours each week was not an appropriate strategy for adult education.

4   This strength-based approach engages a community with what it already knows in order to better interface with the possibilities of community development. DeFillipis (2001, 789) notes, "no place (a community, a region, or whatever) is solely a function of the internal attributes of the people living and working there. If communities are outcomes, they are not simply outcomes of the characteristics of those within them, they are also outcomes of a complex set of power relationships—both internally, within the communities, and externally, between actors in the communities and the rest of the world."

5   Rush Communications Ltd. was bought out by Eastlink in September 2007.

6   Despite this, large public institutions did not make use of the network in the ways anticipated during its design, which reflects Suchman's (2007) differentiation between plans and situated actions in technology uptake and use. For more on the situational challenges faced in telehealth, see Jennett et al. (2005).

REFERENCES

Bartle, Phil. 2008. The human factor and community empowerment. *Review of Human Factor Studies* 14(1): 99–122.

Berg, Bruce L. 2001. *Qualitative research methods for the social sciences*, 4th ed. Toronto: Allyn and Bacon.

Collins, Jessica L., and Barry Wellman. 2010. Small town in the Internet society: Chapleau is no longer an island. *American Behavioural Scientist* 53(9): 1344–66.

Cook, John, and Matt Smith. 2004. Beyond formal learning: Informal community eLearning. *Computers and Education* 43(1–2): 35–47.

Creswell, John W. 2007. *Qualitative inquiry and research design: Choosing among five approaches.* Thousand Oaks, CA: Sage.

DeFilippis, James. 2001. The myth of social capital in community development. *Housing Policy Debate* 12(4): 781–806.

Devins, David, Alison Darlow, and Vicki Smith. 2002. Lifelong learning and digital exclusion: Lessons from the evaluation of an ICT learning centre and an emerging research agenda. *Regional Studies* 36(8): 941–45.

Goggin, Gerald. 2003. *Rural communities online: Networking to link consumers to providers.* Melbourne: Telstra Consumer Consultative Council.

Gurstein, Michael. 2004. Effective use and the community informatics sector: Some thoughts on Canada's approach to community technology / community access. In *Seeking convergence in policy and practice: Communications in the public interest*, vol. 2, ed. Marita Moll and Leslie Regan Shade. Ottawa: Canadian Centre for Policy Alternatives.

Huggins, Robert, and Hiro Izushi. 2002. The digital divide and ICT learning in rural communities: Examples of good practice service delivery. *Local Economy* 17(2): 111–22.

Infrastructure Canada. 2005. Agreement Brings Broadband Access to Rural and Remote Schools and Communities in Newfoundland and Labrador. 15 September. http://www.infc.gc.ca/media/news-nouvelles/csif-fcis/2005/20050915stjohns-eng.html.

Jennett, Penny, Andora Jackson, Kendall Ho, Theresa Healy, Arminee Kazanjian, Robert Woollard, Susan Haydt, and Joanna Bates. 2005. The essence of Telehealth readiness in rural communities: An organizational perspective. *Journal of Telemedicine and E-Health* 11(2): 137–45.

Kaiser, Scott. 2005. Community technology centers and bridging the digital divide. *Knowledge, Technology and Policy* 18(2): 83–100.

King, Nigel, and Christine Horrocks. 2009. *Interviews in qualitative research*. Thousand Oaks, CA: Sage.

Laverack, Glenn. 2007. *Health promotion practice: Building empowered communities*. New York: Open University Press.

MacNeil, Ryan. 2004. *Information and communication technologies and community economic development: Lessons for governance at the Western Valley Development Agency*. Cornwallis Park, NS: Canadian Research Alliance for Community Innovation and Networking.

Matza, David. 1969. *Becoming deviant*. Englewood Cliffs, NJ: Prentice Hall.

McDowell, Stephen D., and Cheryl Cowan Buchwald. 1997. Public interest groups and the Canadian information highway. *Telecommunications Policy* 21(8): 710.

Mishler, Elliott G. 1986. *Research interviewing: Context and narrative*. Cambridge, MA: Harvard University Press.

Moll, Marita, and Leslie Regan Shade, eds. 2001. *E-commerce vs. e-commons*, vol. 1 of *Communications in the public interest*. Ottawa: Canadian Centre for Policy Alternatives.

Murray, Grant, Barbara Neis, and Jahn Petter Johnsen. 2006. Lessons learned from reconstructing interactions between local ecological knowledge, fisheries science, and fisheries management in the commercial fisheries of Newfoundland and Labrador, Canada. *Human Ecology* 34(4): 549–71.

Peddle, Katrina. 2004. The nurse on the roof with the satellite dish: A critical study of telehealth in a Smart Community. MA thesis, Simon Fraser University.

——. 2007. Smart community, community informatics, ideology, and governance: The experience of the Western Valley Development Agency. CRACIN Working Paper no. 20. February. Toronto: Canadian Research Alliance for Community Innovation and Networking. http://archive.iprp.ischool.utoronto.ca/cracin/publications/pdfs/WorkingPapers/CRACIN%20Working%20Paper%20No.%2020.pdf.

Petrov, Andrey N. 2008. Talent in the cold? Creative capital and the economic future of the Canadian North. *Arctic* 61(2): 162–76.

Pigg, Kenneth E. 2001. Applications of community informatics for building community and enhancing civic society. *Information, Communication and Society* 4(4): 507–27.

Ramírez, Ricardo. 2007. Appreciating the contribution of broadband ICT with rural and remote communities: Stepping stones toward an alternative paradigm. *The Information Society* 23: 85–94.

Scott-Dixon, Krista. 2005. From digital binary to analogue continuum: Measuring gendered labour—notes toward multidimentional methodologies. *Frontiers* 26(1): 24–42.

Sloan, Carolyn. 2007. Michael Gushue executive director of new RDA: First order of business is to listen. *The Spectator*, 17 February. http://www.novanewsnow.com/Employment/2007-02-13/article-591683/Michael-Gushue-executive-director-of-new-RDA/1.

Strauss, Anselm, and Juliet Corbin. 2008. *Basics of qualitative research: Grounded theory procedures and techniques*, 3rd ed. Thousand Oaks, CA: Sage.

Suchman, Lucy. 2007. *Human-machine reconfigurations: Plans and situated actions*. New York: Cambridge University Press.

Winseck, Dwayne. 1998. *Reconvergence: A political economy of telecommunications in Canada*. Creskill, NJ: Hampton Press.

Yin, Robert K. 2008. *Case study research: Design and methods*, 4th ed. Thousand Oaks, CA: Sage.

16 REVERSE ENGLISH Strategies of the Keewatin Career Development Corporation in Discourse Surrounding the Knowledge-Based Economy and Society

Frank Winter

Ensuring that rural and remote areas in Canada have access to reasonably affordable telecommunications has been a long-standing governmental objective that can be traced back to policies regarding universal access policies for telephony. The early 2000s saw a burst of federal and provincial programs aimed at extending affordable Internet service to such areas. In January 2001, Brian Tobin, the federal minister of Industry at the time, established the National Broadband Task Force (NBTF), the principal mission of which was "to map out a strategy for achieving the Government of Canada's goal of ensuring that broadband services are available to businesses and residents in every Canadian community by 2004" (National Broadband Task Force 2001, 1).

The NBTF's report, *The New National Dream: Networking the Nation for Broadband Access*, opened with lofty promises of the sweeping social transformations that would follow in the wake of broadband. The following passage, from the report's executive summary, is typical of the rhetoric employed throughout:

> The Task Force is convinced that, over the next 10 or 20 years, the development of broadband networks, services and applications will have a profound effect on all aspects of Canadian life. Broadband will transform the way we learn, the way we work, the way we use our leisure, the way we govern ourselves,

the way we communicate, the way we express ourselves and the way we care for each other.

It is no exaggeration to say that over time, the impact of broadband communications on Canadian life will be at least as great as the impact of railways, highways, airlines, traditional telecommunications and broadcasting. (National Broadband Task Force 2001, 3)

Although this upbeat rhetoric was widely supported at the time, there were specific challenges from some quarters with respect to who would underwrite the costs of this ambitious vision.[1] Questions also arose concerning representation on the task force. As in the case of the earlier Information Highway Advisory Council, there had been limited opportunity for public input into the work of the task force, and NBTF membership was heavily weighted toward executives from telecommunications companies. Despite the report's recommendation that priority be given to First Nations, Inuit, and rural and remote communities, groups representing specific communities, including Aboriginal groups, wondered how far the report's recommendations would, in practice, address their interests and concerns. (See, for example, Assembly of First Nations 2001b.) There were worries that other considerations—such as the goal of universal access, the need to address the sustainability of proposed programs, humanistic objectives (for example, the need for people to be connected to a community in order to feel a sense of belonging), and concerns about civic participation (that is, the need to ensure that citizens in an online world will be able to fully exercise their civic rights)—had been subordinated to the government's overarching agenda, which was fundamentally an economic one. These concerns were articulated through briefs and presentations to government policy groups such as the NBTF, in newsletters and on websites, and in academic research. But these expressions of concern were largely overlooked in national media outlets, and they had little impact on the NBTF report itself.

In 2002, a pilot program, Broadband for Rural and Northern Development (BRAND), was set up, albeit on a more modest scale than that proposed by Tobin and the NBTF. The goal of BRAND was to assist rural, Northern, and First Nations communities in improving access to broadband telecommunications in support of educational, health, and economic opportunities.[2] A call for applications to the program was then issued.

Among the successful applicants was the Northern Broadband Network (NBN), a non-profit Saskatchewan corporation consisting of three partners: the Meadow Lake Tribal Council, the Prince Albert Grand Council, and New North, an umbrella organization of communities in northern Saskatchewan. Each had submitted unsuccessful applications to the first round of the BRAND competition but had been encouraged to resubmit as a combined group. The Keewatin Career Development Corporation—a community-based organization (CBO) located in La Ronge—provided technical advice regarding both rounds of applications, as well as management services later on, while the NBN project was being implemented.[3] The NBN chose SaskTel, the crown corporation responsible for telecommunications in the province, to do the actual work of installing cables and equipment. The plan called for the NBN to be dissolved when the project was complete, following which SaskTel would operate the new network as part of its provincial network, CommunityNet.

This chapter describes how the Keewatin Career Development Corporation (KCDC) came to be so involved in telecommunications. I examine how far the KCDC was able to ensure that programs such as BRAND met the needs of its community and to what extent it was forced to abide by rules established by more powerful actors that worked to the detriment of the community. Are there lessons to be learned from the KCDC's experiences, both in their own right and in comparison with the experience of other organizations, such as K-Net, the Western Valley Development Agency (WVDA), and SmartLabrador (see chapters 14 and 15), that likewise participated in Industry Canada programs? The stakes for the KCDC were high. Surviving on short-term fees from government programs, it struggled to deliver skills training and network support for specific geographic areas and local communities. At the same time, its circumstances prevented it from becoming as fully embedded in its local community as, for example, K-Net was (and still is). Unlike K-Net, the KCDC is not formally affiliated with a First Nations tribal council (although it serves a primarily Aboriginal population), nor is it involved in the delivery of health care services, again in contrast to K-Net, which receives significant funding from Health Canada. Without successful project applications and/or the development of another source of sustaining revenue, the KCDC would not be able to support itself. In such precarious circumstances, the KCDC might ultimately have been reduced to a shadow organization, as in the case of SmartLabrador. Or, as was the case with WVDA, it might simply have ceased to exist. Either outcome would have been a setback for its community.

THE KEEWATIN CAREER DEVELOPMENT CORPORATION

The KCDC was founded in 1996, with the goal of delivering networked and multimedia career services to career counsellors and teachers in northern Saskatchewan. The organization is a partnership of fourteen career and educational service-providing agencies, variously associated with schools (K–12 and post-secondary), Métis training organizations, First Nations tribal councils, and the provincial government. Its broad mission was, and remains, to use information and communication technologies (ICTs) for the social and economic benefit of the residents of northern Saskatchewan, including First Nations, Métis, rural, and remote communities. During the period covered in this study, the KCDC's website slogan was "Bringing technology to the north." A non-profit organization, still based in La Ronge, the KCDC funds its operations through grants and service fees. Each member agency appoints one individual to the board of directors, which provides corporate direction. The KCDC also has ex officio board members, representing government departments such as Industry Canada, with whom it interacts in connection with various public programs in which it is involved. Its operations are overseen by a general manager and carried out by paid staff.

As one of six First Nations SchoolNet regional management organizations (RMOs) in Canada, the KCDC also develops and maintains Internet and video conferencing services for eighty-three First Nations schools in Saskatchewan and, until 2009, did the same for seventy-three First Nations schools in Alberta. Northern Saskatchewan is, however, the KCDC's primary service area. Although Saskatchewan's Northern Administration District (see figure 16.1) encompasses approximately half of the province's land area, it has only about 37,000 residents. About 80 percent of those residents are Aboriginal (Cree, Dene, and Métis), and two-thirds are under the age of 35.[4] The region's chief economic driver is mining.

The KCDC's history can be divided into four phases. During its initial period of growth, from 1996 to 2001, the KCDC participated in a number of federal and provincial programs. It proposed and implemented a project for the development and support of networked career services in northern Saskatchewan. In a hotly competitive contest, it also bid successfully to become the Saskatchewan demonstration site for Industry Canada's Smart Communities initiative. The KCDC was justifiably proud of being a small Northern group that won a very large and prestigious competition. Its Smart Communities project, called Headwaters, ran from 2000 to 2004 and had several components, including an online technology training program delivered to over five hundred teachers. Headwaterstech, a for-profit vendor of hardware and software products for individuals, businesses, and First Nations schools in northern Saskatchewan, was established in a storefront in La Ronge's business district. In addition, a youth IT training program was set up.

At the peak of its activities, from 2002 to 2006, the KCDC successfully competed to become the First Nations SchoolNet RMO for Saskatchewan and Alberta, while also implementing its Headwaters project and participating in the BRAND, Saskatchewan CommunityNet, and Alberta SuperNet projects.[5] The youth IT training program grew significantly both in size and formality through its partnership with the Cisco Networking Academy. Drawing

FIGURE 16.1 Northern Administration District, Saskatchewan (2010).
Courtesy of Saskatchewan Ministry of First Nations and Métis Relations.

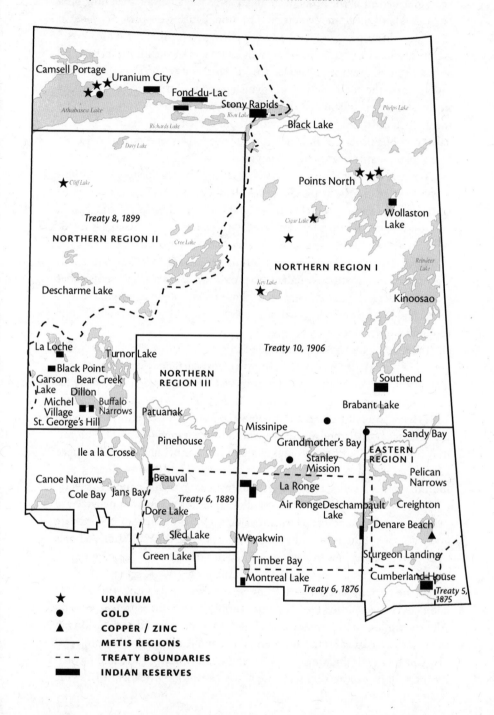

Camsell Portage
Uranium City
Fond-du-Lac
Stony Rapids
Black Lake
Athabasca Lake
Riou Lake
Richards Lake
Phelps Lake
Davy Lake
Cliff Lake
Points North
Wollaston Lake
Treaty 8, 1899
Cigar Lake
NORTHERN REGION II
Cree Lake
NORTHERN REGION I
Reindeer Lake
Descharme Lake
Key Lake
Kinoosao
La Loche
Turnor Lake
Treaty 10, 1906
Black Point
Garson Lake
Bear Creek
Dillon
NORTHERN REGION III
Southend
Michel Village
Buffalo Narrows
Patuanak
Brabant Lake
St. George's Hill
Missinipe
Sandy Bay
Pinehouse
Grandmother's Bay
EASTERN REGION I
Ile a la Crosse
Stanley Mission
Pelican Narrows
Canoe Narrows
Beauval
La Ronge
Creighton
Cole Bay
Jans Bay
Treaty 6, 1889
Air Ronge
Deschambault Lake
Dore Lake
Denare Beach
Sled Lake
Weyakwin
Sturgeon Landing
Green Lake
Timber Bay
Cumberland House
Montreal Lake
Treaty 6, 1876
Treaty 5, 1875

★ URANIUM
● GOLD
▲ COPPER / ZINC
— METIS REGIONS
- - - TREATY BOUNDARIES
■ INDIAN RESERVES

on funds from several federal government sources, this program gave Aboriginal youth practical and accredited experience and training in computer repair and networking. In addition, in 2005 the KCDC submitted a proposal to the Workplace Skills Initiative of Human Resources and Skills Development Canada (HRSDC), which would build upon the KCDC's skills training and video teleconferencing expertise to provide training support for various enterprises (both public and private sector) in northern Saskatchewan and northern Alberta (see Keewatin Career Development Corporation 2005). During this period, the KCDC had approximately twenty paid employees and about twenty youth IT trainees each year.

The third period—the year 2006—was one of struggle. During this time, the Headwaters and BRAND projects came to an end, as planned. As First Nations SchoolNet RMO, the KCDC was partnering with Saskatchewan CommunityNet, but there was concern that SaskTel would lose interest in CommunityNet once the subsidies from the provincial government had been used up. Moreover, the First Nations SchoolNet RMOs went through a period of great uncertainty that was only somewhat resolved by the transfer of the SchoolNet program from Industry Canada to Indian and Northern Affairs Canada (INAC). In addition, the KCDC's application to the Workplace Skills Initiative was unsuccessful. Half of the KCDC's staff members were laid off.

Most recently, the KCDC has managed to recover to a considerable extent, although there is a constant struggle for revenue. After the First Nations SchoolNet program moved to INAC, the RMOs were guaranteed funding for only two more years. Funding was extended in 2009 for an additional three years, albeit at a significantly reduced level (Indian and Northern Affairs Canada 2009). Other activities continued, however, and even grew. An innovative online video career counselling program, Breaking Barriers, was a success. The program evolved, in part, out of the unsuccessful Workplace Skills Initiative proposal, but in the case of Breaking Barriers the KCDC instead turned to the private sector for funding and was able to attract significant sponsorship from Cameco, a major mining company. The KCDC's expertise in multicast video conferencing has gained the organization considerable recognition, and the KCDC has also established a lucrative working relationship with SaskTel. The KCDC is now a very successful SaskTel Authorized High-Speed Internet Dealer, repeatedly winning SaskTel's Rural Dealer of the Year award. The income from this commercial enterprise has become a very important part of the KCDC's budget, as public funding from community development initiatives has declined.

The theme of training and skills development runs through all of the KCDC's activities over the years, reflecting its origins and mission. In particular, the creation of a local workforce skilled in ICTs was critical not only to the success of the initial NBN project but also to the KCDC's evolution from a CBO into an organization tied more closely to the private sector.

CANADA AS A KNOWLEDGE-BASED ECONOMY AND SOCIETY

In the course of its involvement in federal programs, the KCDC inevitably had to interact with the government's own agenda regarding "connectivity" and telecommunications. In promoting this agenda, the government has relied heavily on the concept of a knowledge-based economy and society (KBES), a concept frequently invoked in a wide variety of publications and presentations. Rooney et al. (2003) define a "knowledge economy" as one that creates value primarily through intellectual activity. A "knowledge-based economy" is, accordingly, an economy in which knowledge is the most important productive factor (see, for example, Jessop 2005). The concept of a "knowledge-based society" encompasses a broader range of socio-cultural activities, extending beyond economic, commercial, or industrial interests. In any KBES, technology—especially ICTs—necessarily plays a central role, as the means by which knowledge is created and disseminated.

In the discourse surrounding Canada as a KBES, the digital divide—defined most simply as the divide between those individuals who have Internet access and those who don't—is presented as a problem that must be corrected so that all individual Canadians can participate fully in the economic and social affairs of the country.[6] The reasons that make it important for individuals to be able to participate are, however, rooted firmly in the government's desire to ensure that Canada will be able to compete effectively in the global KBES—an ability on which Canada's future economic prosperity is said to depend. Little weight is given to other possible objectives, such as supporting and expanding citizens' opportunities to participate meaningfully in the democratic governance of their country or fostering individual growth in terms of human capabilities and interests.

The actual changes implemented under the rubric of Canada as a KBES, notably increased privatization and cutbacks in funding for a broad array of social programs, have had far-reaching impacts in all areas of activity that are characterized by a high degree of government involvement, such as education (Moll 1997; Taylor 1997), (un)employment programs and job training (McBride 2000; Russell 2000), and welfare (Ilcan and Basok, 2004), as well as on basic telecommunication services. Many of these changes have in turn affected other areas, including the policy options that the federal government has pursued in an effort to address the digital divide (Rideout and Reddick 2005).

CBOs have been expected to fill the gap left when the government withdraws from the direct provision of community services, but typically they lack the resources necessary to do a good job. Rideout and her colleagues, using data gathered in a large-scale survey of Canadian CBOs, present a general picture of overworked, underpaid—if paid at all—and burnt-out staff members struggling to deliver the services that various government agencies now rely on them to provide (Gibson, O'Donnell, and Rideout 2007; Rideout 2007; Rideout et al. 2006; see also chapter 19 in this volume). Staff members are far too busy applying for project money and keeping up with the administrative and reporting requirements of the various programs for which they are responsible to have time to function as community advocates.

COMPETING DISCOURSES

In what follows, I will seek to describe how specific local actors—the Province of Saskatchewan, First Nations groups, and the KCDC—sought at once to engage with and to resist the dominant federal discourse, with its vision of Canada as a KBES, by developing their own modes of discourse. In so doing, I will draw in part on the methods of critical discourse analysis (see, especially, Fairclough 1995; Hardy and Phillips 2004). This approach enables a researcher to identify key texts that suggest competing discourses and to identify discourses that may have been forced into position of subordination by the dominant discourse, as well as to identify strategies that those who participate in alternative discourses employ in an effort to modify the dominant discourse so as to better represent their own interests.

The evidence employed in this analysis has been culled from a large corpus of texts, including publicly available official documents (speeches, presentations, reports, press releases, and the like), internal working documents, and other texts such as newspaper articles. The written corpus has been enriched by visits to the KCDC's headquarters in La Ronge and interviews with individuals from Industry Canada, the Province of Saskatchewan, SaskTel, and the KCDC. I will begin by examining the texts produced by each of the four primary actors separately, in order to identify their respective discursive positions. These discursive positions will then be analyzed in the context of the NBN application to the BRAND program.

The Federal Discourse: A Connected Canada

At least with respect to BRAND, it is the vision of the KBES manifested in texts produced by Industry Canada that constitutes the dominant discourse. For the purposes of this analysis, four PowerPoint slides taken from presentations delivered by senior Industry Canada personnel (Lynch 1999; Hull 2000; Binder 2003, 2005) can serve to illustrate the chief features of this discourse.

FIGURE 16.2a The federal discourse of the KBES. A graph taken from a presentation by Kevin Lynch, 1999.

Why should we focus on an Information Economy/Society agenda?

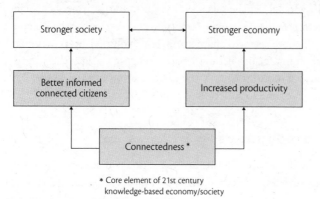

* Core element of 21st century
knowledge-based economy/society

FIGURE 16.2b The federal discourse of the KBES. A graph taken from a presentation by Douglas Hall, 2000.

Why connect Canadians?

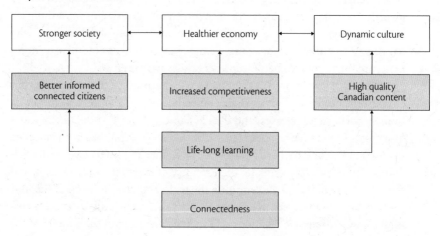

FIGURE 16.2c The federal discourse of the KBES. A graph taken from a presentation by Michael Binder, 2003.

Broadband is the Platform

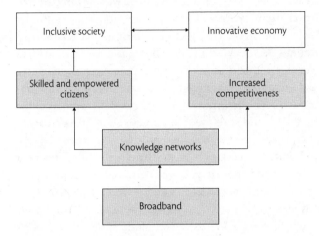

FIGURE 16.2d The federal discourse of the KBES. A graph taken from a presentation by Michael Binder, 2005.

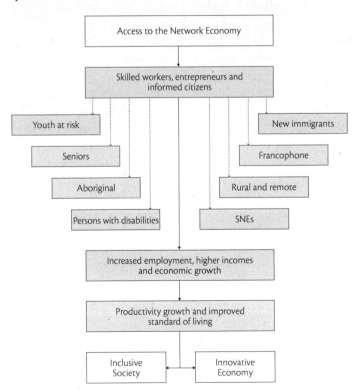

For several reasons, these slides can be viewed as offering a definitive summary of the government's agenda. Each of the presenters held a senior position in Industry Canada. The first presentation was made by Kevin Lynch, at the time the deputy minister of Industry Canada. Doug Hull was the director general of the Information Highway Applications Branch, and Michael Binder was the assistant deputy minister of the Spectrum, Information Technology, and Telecommunications Sector. All three thus had significant authority in the areas of management and telecommunications policy development. In addition, all four presentations took place before large and politically important audiences. Lynch's 1999 presentation was directed to members of the SchoolNet Advisory Board, and Hull's presentation in 2000 formed part of a "North American Day" conference on e-government, which included representatives from the United States and Mexico. The talk that Binder gave at the Information Highway Conference in 2003 was delivered, with only minor variations, more than twenty times in 2003 and 2004 to a wide variety of industry, governmental, and public audiences worldwide. His second presentation, in 2005, took place at the Wireless Communications Association's Global Harmonization and Regulatory Summit, an international conference held in Washington DC. All four presentations thus constituted explicit public statements regarding Canada's perspective on telecommunications.[7]

The federal government's economic agenda is most clearly visible in the slides used by Lynch and Binder (figures 16.2a and b). There is an assumed causality in Lynch's presentation, which begins with "connectedness," described as a "core element" of the twenty-first century KBES. Connectedness leads, on the one hand, to "better informed, connected citizens" and thus to a "stronger society" and, on the other, to "increased productivity" and thus to a "stronger economy." The same basic linkage is visible in Binder's 2003 slide, albeit with certain variations in wording: "knowledge networks" now produce "skilled and empowered citizens" and ultimately an "inclusive society," while "increased competitiveness" leads to an "innovative economy." Binder's 2005 slide (figure 16.2c) makes it clear that various marginalized groups (including Aboriginals) are included among "skilled workers, entrepreneurs, and informed citizens"—who, as participants in the "network economy," will enjoy "higher incomes" and an "improved standard of living." In these slides, one can trace the evolution of the Innovation Agenda, which was Industry Canada's science and technology policy in the early 2000s. Only in Hull's 2000 presentation to the e-government conference (figure 16.2d) do we find references to factors such as personal development ("life-long learning") and the dissemination of culture ("high-quality Canadian content").

I asked several of the people I interviewed to comment on these slides. A senior manager in Industry Canada's telecommunications division suggested that Lynch's presentation "was really a messaging text: 'There's something new here. We should all get behind it. We should all support it because it's an engine of change.'" In his interpretation, although the message that connectivity is necessary to a stronger economy remained consistent throughout the slides, the later slides began to highlight specific applications as the initial message was absorbed and new priorities emerged.

He also acknowledged that the government's new agenda had initially met with some resistance. Regarding Lynch's 1999 presentation to the SchoolNet Advisory Board, he commented:

> When [we] started promoting SchoolNet, guess who were the ones to oppose us? Schools. School boards, teachers . . . We used to come to the SchoolNet Advisory Board, and [one teacher] used to say, "You want to invest in education? Hire more teachers." And you know, we snuck up on schools. We started in libraries because librarians were the most advanced knowledge-based managers in the school system.

He expanded on the theme of resistance to Industry Canada's vision of a connected Canada with regard to the later slides:

> We are now into pitching productivity. And so we're trying to get productivity as our new password . . . only we're running into huge difficulties. Ministers are scared of the word because in many, many fora, productivity is viewed as less pay for more work. . . . And unions don't like the P word, even though economists love this. Politically it's a very, very tough sell.

As his use of the word "pitching" suggests, these slides serve a promotional purpose. As so often in PowerPoint slides, arrows substitute for a detailed analysis of cause-and-effect relationships.

The Saskatchewan Discourse: Equitable and Affordable Telecommunications

The Saskatchewan government has had a long-standing policy objective of providing affordable basic telecommunications services to all the province's residents (Pike 1998). For many decades, SaskTel worked to achieve this objective by the commonly used strategy of cross-subsidizing the rural and remote telephone system by increasing its rates in urban areas. Changes in the regulation of the telephone system in the 1990s ended that ability to cross-subsidize (Wilson 2000). In addition, as the result of a Supreme Court of Canada decision in 1989, SaskTel was brought under the control of the Canadian Radio-television Telecommunications Commission (CRTC) as of the year 2000, at which point SaskTel had to comply with the CRTC's rulings and tariffs.

One product of the province's objective of equitable and affordable telecommunications for all is CommunityNet—an initiative to deploy broadband throughout Saskatchewan. Planned in 2000 and implemented starting in 2001, CommunityNet was the earliest of numerous programs with similar objectives that would come to exist in almost every Canadian province or territory (Canadian Radio-television Telecommunications Commission 2003). CommunityNet works on the model of aggregating the telecommunication needs and uses of public sector units, such as schools, health facilities, libraries, and government offices, including those located in rural and remote communities. Gathering these individual facilities under the umbrella of a single anchor tenant—the Province of Saskatechewan—allowed SaskTel to submit a single bill to the Saskatchewan Information Technology Office, which resulted in considerable administrative savings. During CommunityNet's initial phase (from 2001 to 2003), the savings produced by this aggregation, combined with a subsidy from the provincial government and Western Economic Diversification Canada, enabled SaskTel to improve its rural and remote service by installing backbone lines, switches, and other core networking equipment in smaller communities. Although at the outset CommunityNet was available only to the public sector units affiliated with the anchor tenant, SaskTel was able to use its upgraded core facilities to market its Internet services to individuals, privately owned businesses, and other organizations located in smaller communities at prices roughly comparable to those available in larger cities (Himmelsbach 2000; Murray 2002).

Implicit in the anchor tenant approach is a significant challenge of scale. Government offices and major health facilities tend to be concentrated in larger cities and towns, but schools and libraries are located in many more, and much smaller, locations, scattered across a large territory. The CommunityNet plan to link them all to the Internet was thus very ambitious. As of 2008, CommunityNet had connected most of the province's schools, including all eighty-five First Nations schools, and the regional colleges, as well as health facilities, government offices, and public libraries. High-speed broadband of at least 1.5 Mbps was available to 366 communities (some with as few as three hundred residents), and the number of communities being connected has continued to grow.[8]

During the period when CommunityNet was first being designed and implemented, the Province of Saskatchewan was actively engaged in trying to shape the national telecommunications policy environment in a manner that would enable the province to achieve its goals. Saskatchewan was an active participant in the CRTC Service to High-Cost Serving Areas hearings that began in 1997. The province, together with many other participants in the hearings, advocated the establishment of national standards of telephone service and the creation of a Universal Service Fund, which would have provided residents of rural and remote communities with basic telephone service at affordable rates. When the CRTC rejected the call for a Universal Service Fund, Saskatchewan, together with Manitoba (although that province later withdrew as a result of the privatization of Manitoba Tel), appealed the decision to the federal cabinet. The federal cabinet supported the CRTC's objections to the idea of a Universal Service Fund and rejected the appeal, but it did acknowledge the importance of the issue of equity by ordering the CRTC to monitor telephone companies' deployment of telecommunication services to underserved areas by having companies file annual Service Improvement Plans (Sanders 2000). Importantly, however, the CRTC's decision pertained only to basic telephone service, not to the additional equipment and services needed to support Internet access. In its submissions in 2005 to Industry Canada's Telecommunications Policy Review Panel (Saskatchewan 2005; Hersche 2005) and again in 2010, in connection with CRTC consultations regarding basic telecommunications services (Saskatchewan 2010; Fiske 2010), the province has continued to press its objective of providing affordable telecommunications services to all residents. It insists that it is the federal government's responsibility to provide a sustainable national solution to the problem of servicing rural and remote areas, in which the potential for market failure makes a private sector solution unlikely.

The province's statements regarding the need for affordable and equitable telecommunications, along with its arguments in support of CommunityNet, together form a consistent discourse that is distinct from that of the federal government. This competing discourse promotes an activist role for the provincial government and insists that an ongoing subsidy is necessary to compensate for persistent market failure in rural and remote areas. The discourse adopted by the Province of Saskatchewan has, in turn, had an impact on the KCDC in its actions as a CBO facilitating the penetration of broadband telecommunications services to northern Saskatchewan.

When questioned about the province's consistency of purpose regarding universal access, a SaskTel executive—someone who had considerable prior experience as a civil servant responsible for a variety of telecommunications activities—commented: "There is consistency in [the] desire to do that because rural people want it: it's not a political statement of just Conservatives versus NDP. This government listened to that. The previous government listened to that. That's why CommunityNet got built, but we started some of CommunityNet under Gary Lane." [9] He went on to list an unbroken sequence of cabinet ministers from the Conservative, New Democratic, and Saskatchewan parties who had supported CommunityNet and the goal of affordable and equitable telecommunications. For him, the only real variation had to do with how much funding the province was able to afford or willing to invest at a given time in order to advance this goal. Some times were better than others, to be sure, but there was never any wavering from the overarching objective.

He also took considerable pride in Saskatchewan's accomplishments in this area, especially in view of what he viewed as the disproportionate attention given to Alberta's SuperNet project in venues such as the *Globe and Mail* and the *National Post*. As he noted, the relative lack of attention to Saskatchewan's achievements "was part of the province's not having any money. When I was going to the feds, we were talking about CommunityNet, and Alberta was coming on with SuperNet. Well, they had $2 million just for PR. I had nothing. I had me. So they had full videos and whatever of all the things that they were going to do, and I had me."

I also spoke with a Saskatchewan civil servant who had managerial and policy responsibility for the province's telecommunications strategy and operations. He, too, described how proud the province was of CommunityNet, particularly because its success demonstrated to SaskTel that there was a market for residential and business broadband services in smaller communities:

> I always remember back in 1999 the view even from the telco was sort of, "Well, you know, we've done a business case, and we've identified sixteen communities where clearly broadband high-speed Internet will be a seller, but the rest, probably not." It's almost a leap of faith, right, because then suddenly we're at 366 communities and it's selling like hotcakes and everybody's on it and everybody wants it. So sometimes it's not a business case, and/or the business case is not readily apparent.

Both he and the SaskTel official not only recognized the difference in outlook between the federal and the provincial governments but also appreciated the reasons for it. In response to a question about whether the Province of Saskatchewan and the federal government differed in their objectives with respect to extending broadband to rural and remote areas, the SaskTel official responded: "What we would like to see is exactly the same. We would like to see rural people with access. We would like to see that." But he went on to point out that the provincial government had a "different methodology" and that Industry Canada had other issues to address—"circumstances in Canada that I don't have to deal with in Saskatchewan." As he saw it, certain features of the BRAND program were not particularly well suited to the situation in some of Saskatchewan's smaller communities. The BRAND program was designed on a community aggregator model in which each community was represented by a community champion. If a community could not find a champion, it could not apply to the program. The program's tight timelines for initial applications, as well as its sustainability requirements, also placed communities that were very small and/or beset by poverty and social problems at a disadvantage. Moreover, under the BRAND program, only communities that were not served at all by publicly available broadband were eligible to receive a subsidy. Underserved communities, which might be adjacent to unserved ones, were not eligible. The Saskatchewan preference was clearly to install broadband over as large a contiguous region as possible, to include not only communities that were underserved or had no service at all but also communities that might otherwise be regarded as too small or too "backward" to be ready for broadband. In addition, the BRAND program favoured private sector telecommunications companies (Ritter 2006), whereas SaskTel, as a crown corporation, was a public sector company.

For him, the solution was to ensure that federal programs could accommodate differences among the provinces. He described how the BRAND program had been modified to fit the circumstances in Saskatchewan, in an effort to address the interests of the assorted staekholders: "We did work this out. We fought very hard. I worked with the PA [Prince Albert] Grand Council and the Meadow Lake Council and New North, which was KCDC for all intents and purposes. And the feds wanted to divide this BRAND program up, so only the guys in Meadow Lake or PAGC would win, or the New North. Luckily, we had solidarity." He also noted that SaskTel has only one shareholder, the Province of Saskatchewan. This very direct relationship means that the company's policy objectives are closely connected to those of the province. In contrast, private sector competitors have many shareholders whose fundamental goal is to maximize their profit, not to subsidize services to remote and rural users.

In addition, I spoke with a KCDC manager who had considerable expertise in and responsibility for computer applications and telecommunications and who was involved with the BRAND applications. He used the word "aggressive" to characterize SaskTel's interest in the Northern Broadband Network: "SaskTel was incredibly aggressive about pursuing it. They wanted it, and in fact they were . . . at times almost stepping on our toes in terms of trying to take ownership of the project, even though technically it was our project and they were our vendors." I also talked to an Industry Canada policy analyst who had extensive experience with the department's programs in Saskatchewan. Regarding SaskTel and its working relationship with Industry Canada, she commented:

> It's a love/hate relationship. You love them because they are the only ones who are here and who always come to the table and indicate an interest, and you hate them because they're the only ones here. . . . They are a crown corporation, and they are very protective of their territory. As a business they do what they have to do as a business.

But she also described SaskTel as "good corporate sponsors": "They contribute to events. They contribute significantly to the Computers with Schools partnership with Industry Canada. If it wasn't for the SaskTel Telephone Pioneers in Saskatchewan, we'd be very hard pressed."

SaskTel's involvement in the NBN project demonstrates how the province's discourse succeeded in influencing the implementation of a federal program, namely, BRAND. The SaskTel executive, the KCDC manager, and the Industry Canada policy analyst all provide interesting insights into the interactions that went on in the course of the initial applications to BRAND and the development of the NBN's business case. SaskTel's expertise, its existing network infrastructure, and the financial resources the crown corporation could bring to bear, not only on the BRAND requirement of a 50 percent matching contribution from the applicants but also a five-year commitment to sustaining the network, meant that it could play a dominant role in the implementation of the NBN. Employing these advantages, SaskTel was able to ensure that BRAND's support for the NBN also supported the province's discourse of affordable and equitable telecommunications.

The Aboriginal Discourse: Ownership, Control, Access, and Possession

Matthew Coon Come, national chief of the Assembly of First Nations, endorsed the recommendations of the National Broadband Task Force immediately upon the release of its report. His comments established the priorities of economic development, health care, education, and autonomy, themes that would be repeated consistently:

> The establishment of a network that will link all of our communities to the communications network will be a major benefit to all of our communities. It will improve the strength and productivity of the First Nations economy, will improve the quality of the First Nations health care system and ensure that all of our citizens have access to learning opportunities. As we move to assume control of our own affairs, this will be a major tool in achieving this goal.

He noted that the Assembly of First Nations, in anticipation of the report, had entered into discussions with major telecommunications companies about potential partnerships in order to take advantage of the opportunities to come. "We missed the Industrial Revolution; we will not miss the information technology revolution," he declared (quoted in Assembly of First Nations 2001a).

The needs of the Aboriginal community in this area were acknowledged by the federal government in the 2001 Speech from the Throne (Canada 2001), which recognized "the critical goal of making broadband access widely available to citizens, businesses, public institutions and to all communities in Canada by 2004" and made explicit reference to Aboriginal communities. As noted earlier, when the BRAND pilot program was announced in 2002, priority was to be given to unserved First Nations, Inuit, and remote and rural communities. A flurry of activity ensued over the following year, with reports, resolutions, and proposals produced by many groups at levels ranging from local to national. An analysis of these texts, including the unsuccessful applications of the Meadow Lake Tribal Council and the Prince Albert Grand Council to the first round of the BRAND program and the successful application of the Northern Broadband Network, reveals the discursive position of Aboriginal communities in relation to telecommunications.[10]

Two of the three applicants for the first round of BRAND funding were the Meadow Lake Tribal Council and the Prince Albert Grand Council. Tribal councils represent the interests of the individual bands that make up their membership. They were initially responsible for managing the various social welfare programs whose administration had devolved to local organizations, but their activities have expanded over the years in accordance with specific circumstances. In particular, they have become quite prominent as a vehicle for economic development.

The Meadow Lake Tribal Council, which originated in 1981, represents nine First Nations bands located in the northwestern section of Saskatchewan. It manages several educational and social welfare programs on behalf of its members and has also been notably successful in the area of economic development, with a strong presence in the forestry sector through its share of ownership in several forestry enterprises. More recently, as the forestry sector has languished, the council has embarked on commercial partnerships and joint ventures in the emerging oil and gas sector in that part of the province. The Prince Albert Grand Council, which dates back to 1977, represents twelve First Nations bands in central and northern Saskatchewan. Like the Meadow Lake council, it has a very active and successful record of economic development. Until recently, it was principally involved with businesses such as hotels and gas bars in urban areas, although its activities are diversifying. In the area of economic development, both the Meadow Lake Tribal Council and the Prince Albert Grand Council are well established, knowledgeable, and notably successful, with extensive experience in partnering with other companies.

The initial BRAND applications from the Meadow Lake Tribal Council and the Prince Albert Grand Council originated from their economic development offices. During the 1990s, Robert Anderson carried out research on Saskatchewan tribal councils and their economic development activities, and his ideas provided a helpful tool for analyzing the discourse of the Meadow Lake and Prince Albert councils in relation to the NBN. Anderson (1999) argues that Aboriginal engagement with the global economy can provoke a variety of responses, ranging from various forms of opting out—whether passively, through isolation, or actively, through open resistance or even violence—to various modes of engagement, which can again be active or passive. Within this analytical framework, the actions of Aboriginal peoples in Canada in the area of economic development have been characterized by active engagement, but on their own terms (Anderson, Dana, and Dana 2006).

Anderson (1999, 13) describes the Aboriginal approach to economic development as:

1. A predominantly collective one centred on the community or "nation"
2. For the purposes of:
   - Attaining economic self-sufficiency as a necessary condition for the realization of self-government
   - Improving the socioeconomic circumstances of Aboriginal people
   - Preserving and strengthening traditional culture, values and languages (and reflecting the same in development activities)
3. Involving the following processes:
   - Creating and operating businesses to exercise control over the economic development process
   - Creating and operating businesses that can compete profitably over the long run in the global economy, to build the economy necessary to support self-government and improve socioeconomic conditions
   - Forming alliances and joint ventures among themselves and with non-Aboriginal partners to create businesses that can compete profitably in the global economy
   - Building capacity for economic development through (i) education, training and institution building and (ii) the realization of the treaty and Aboriginal rights to land and resources
   - Strengthening bonding and bridging social capital.

As Anderson's analysis might suggest, the terms *ownership* and *control* figure prominently in the discursive strategy of Aboriginal peoples, as does the fact of their collective ownership of the land awarded them by treaty. The phrase "ownership, control, access, and possession," which I chose to describe the competing discourse offered by Aboriginal groups, derives from an influential article by Brian Schnarch, who elaborates on these four principles in relation to research by and with First Nations, with particular reference to the concept of self-determination. According to Schnarch (2004, 80), "ownership, control, access, and possession" can be understood as "a political response to tenacious colonial approaches to research and information management." Clear parallels exist between Schnarch's summary of these principles as they pertain to information management and Anderson's analysis of Aboriginal economic development (see table 16.1).

TABLE 16.1 Principles articulated in Aboriginal discourse

	Schnarch (2004, 81)	Anderson (1999, 13)
Ownership	"A community or group owns information collectively."	The community has collective ownership of economic enterprises.
Control	First Nations peoples "control all aspects of the research and information management processes that impact them."	*Control* refers not only to ownership but also to the strategies of partnerships and joint ventures by which ownership is exercised.
Access	"First Nations peoples must have access to information and data about themselves and their communities regardless of where it is currently held."	Access to the First Nations lands is one of the most powerful levers that First Nations can use to achieve their economic development goals.
Possession	Possession is a "mechanism by which ownership can be asserted and protected."	Ownership and joint ventures provide access to the operating details of various enterprises in a manner that promotes trust and confidence.

Ownership of the NBN was initially a high priority of the two tribal councils. The SaskTel official whom I interviewed had been actively involved in the company's response to the Request for Proposal (RFP) issued by the NBN. In answer to a question about whether the Meadow Lake Tribal Council and the Prince Albert Grand Council viewed the project slightly differently than did Industry Canada and SaskTel, he commented: "Yes. When they started . . . they looked at it as a business opportunity. So they said, when we first got started, 'I want to own it.'" To the same question, the KCDC manager and telecommunications expert, who was likewise closely involved with the preparation of the applications to BRAND, responded:

> The perspective was there, from the Northern Broadband Network side, that there would be some type of ownership of the network at the end of the day, and SaskTel didn't want to do that. . . . There was going to be some discussion about business opportunities, etc. etc., which never really came to a whole lot. There was no network ownership. . . . No other sort of businesses started between SaskTel and the tribal councils to take advantage of that.

A senior KCDC staff member, who was also closely involved with the NBN application as it was developed, made a similar comment: "The philosophy for the First Nations side was that the money came to them from the federal government and that they should be able to leverage some of that into some ownership of the network," although, as he went on to note, "even within the tribal council[s] there was the alternate opinion that ownership of the network would include risk."

SaskTel was opposed to joint ownership of the NBN. In interacting with the tribal councils, their strategy was to call attention to the considerable ongoing costs and risks involved in running a broadband telecommunications network. These included the financial risk of extending service to small, remote, and geographically scattered areas, as well as the costs of maintaining and upgrading equipment. SaskTel also highlighted the risk of having to cut off delinquent customers who might be members of one of the First Nations bands represented by the tribal councils who co-owned the network. As the senior KCDC staff member's comment indicates, at least some members of the tribal councils recognized these risks.

It is evident from this analysis that the approach taken by the Meadow Lake Tribal Council and Prince Albert Grand Council illustrates the pattern of active engagement, but on their own terms, that Anderson sees as characteristic of the approach of Canadian Aboriginal groups to economic development. Their interest in establishing ownership of the NBN also illustrates several of the processes of economic development that Anderson lists, among them "forming alliances and joint ventures among themselves and with non-Aboriginal partners to create businesses that can compete profitably in the global economy" and "creating and operating businesses to exercise control over the economic development process." This was the immediate goal of the discourse of ownership, control, access, and possession. Also apparent, however, is the existence of a pragmatic element that recognizes, on a case-by-case basis, when that discourse might not be appropriate, as was the case with the NBN in its final form—a not-for-profit corporation formed solely for the purpose of administering the BRAND proposal.

The KCDC Discourse: Land, Health, and Jobs

Conversations with staff members at the KCDC during site visits and interviews made it clear that they see a distinction between the values and interests of northern Saskatchewan and those of Aboriginal peoples. While they understand that because the overwhelming majority of residents of the North are Aboriginal, any Northern organization must and will reflect Aboriginal concerns and interests, they also acknowledge the existence of a distinct discourse that focuses on the interests shared by most Northerners, whether Aboriginal or not. Reviewing the KCDC's Headwaters application to Industry Canada's Smart Communities project and its submission to HRSDC in connection with its Workplace Skills Initiative, as well as business plans and other documents,[11] I was able to identify a discourse of "land, health, and jobs"—a phrase that key KCDC staff members agreed was an appropriate description of their priorities.

As the texts I examined reveal, the KCDC and its partner organizations feel that they are rooted in the land. Their values, interests, and activities are framed by the goal of enabling residents of northern Saskatchewan to engage in fulfilling lives despite living in geographically remote areas where they must cope with social isolation and relatively scant opportunities for employment. The documents also reveal a concern with physical and mental well-being, with health-related services delivered in the North through such means as Canada Health Infoway's Telehealth. Finally, the texts that focus on education and skills training aim at the creation of a skilled workforce whose members will be able to find jobs in northern Saskatchewan.

The KCDC telecommunications expert—himself a long-time resident of northern Saskatchewan who felt fortunate to have found a challenging job in his own community—very explicitly noted the linkage between telecommunications infrastructure, education, and good local jobs for Northerners:

> Math and science education, for example, in northern Saskatchewan is a real concern. The principal economic driver is mining. The skilled mining jobs—as opposed to equipment operators, which are semi-skilled—all require significant comfort levels with advanced science and math and post-secondary training that requires those as prerequisites. So you have both post-secondary school training needs and high school training needs in the maths and sciences which are difficult to fulfill [in northern Saskatchewan].

For the KCDC, then, the point is not to educate and train residents of the North only to have them move to larger, better developed urban centres in order to find work. Rather, the goal is to strengthen the social and economic fabric of the North by encouraging skilled individuals to remain in the area.

As the discussion of these three competing discourses demonstrates, none of the actors was fundamentally opposed to the dominant discourse of the KBES. Each, however, sought to modify that discourse to better suit their respective interests. In reaction to Industry Canada's preference for relying on market economies, minimal subsidies, and limited-term projects to expand broadband services throughout the country, the Province of Saskatchewan sought to ensure that room would be left for universal, sustained, and non-market-based programs that would support equitable service for all the province's residents. The Aboriginal discourse of ownership and control endeavoured to allow First Nations to engage actively with the KBES but in a manner consistent with their particular cultural and economic circumstances and objectives. The KCDC's discourse was concerned with bringing the full benefits of the KBES—social, educational, and cultural, as well as economic—to a specific rural and remote region via broadband telecommunications.

REVERSE ENGLISH

In billiards and pool, *reverse English* refers to the side spin that a player can put on the cue ball when striking it. The spin moves the ball into an advantageous position on the table in order to set up subsequent shots. By skillfully manoeuvring the cue ball in this manner, an expert player can sink every ball on the table.

The metaphor of reverse English offers a useful description of the strategies of resistance to the federal discourse of the KBES that the KCDC has employed, especially in connection with the BRAND program. Such a strategy is visible in the manner in which the KCDC tried to modify the rules governing the program and in the ways it built on earlier successes in an effort to win new grant competitions, as well as in the tactics it has used to draw jobs to northern Saskatchewan.

Community-based organizations such as the KCDC sometimes seek to modify the criteria according to which government policy and programs are designed and evaluated. This is one instance of the use of reverse English—attempting to alter the rules of the game so that future programs will be better suited to the CBO's objectives as well as to the constraints under which it operates. Commenting on the relationship that had evolved between the KCDC and the Saskatchewan-based staff of Industry Canada, the KCDC telecommunications expert noted that the arrangement allowed the KCDC some latitude. "Our entire Smart Communities program was based on bending the rules, not breaking [them]," he commented, "but where they didn't make sense, we bent them." He went on to say that Industry Canada staff members "were comfortable enough with us doing that, and we were comfortable enough that they were going to let us do it by the time we got to BRAND."

There is also an element of mutual dependence in the government's use of CBOs to deliver programs, which gives the CBOs a certain power. I asked the Saskatchewan-based Industry Canada policy analyst whom I interviewed what would happen if the requirements governing a particular program were so tightly designed and so stringent that no CBO was interested in becoming involved in program delivery. In response, she acknowledged that such a circumstance would create a severe problem for the government. She also noted that there has been increasing recognition that national programs must allow for tailor-made local solutions. "The Smart Communities project was a very innovative way of adapting one particular national project to a particular region," she commented. It "built on partnerships that identified various communities that are geographic communities of interest," while it also "set strategic outcomes and goals that would in fact address particular identified needs." In short, Industry Canada understood that, to achieve its own objectives, it needed to maintain some degree of flexibility.

The strategy of reverse English is also visible in the grant application that the KCDC prepared for submission to HRSDC's Workplace Skills Initiative program (Keewatin Career Development Corporation 2005). The KCDC proposed that it build on its existing expertise with video conferencing, acquired through its work as a First Nations SchoolNet RMO, to create a skills development and training organization. The organization would rely heavily on video conferencing and thus be available to any public or private sector group throughout northern Alberta and northern Saskatchewan, with a particular emphasis on small and medium-sized companies located in smaller communities. The application reviewed the KCDC's past accomplishments, presenting them as a logical sequence of development reaching back from the current BRAND, SuperNet, and CommunityNet broadband projects, to the teacher skills training and use of video conferencing it employed in its role as First Nations SchoolNet RMO, to the multi-level skills training that was part of the Headwaters Smart Communities project, and ultimately to the KCDC's very first project involving Internet-based skills training and support for employment counsellors in the North. Viewing its activities retrospectively, the KCDC was able to forge links between its earlier projects and the areas of expertise that would be required for participation in the Workplace Skills Initiative.

In so doing, the KCDC engaged in a certain sleight-of-hand. The WSI program had obviously not yet been developed when, for example, the Headwaters project was conceived. Although Headwaters did include a definite skills training and development component, the project was aimed primarily at novice ICT users, who were not the target audience of the Workplace Skills Initiative. The KCDC's strategy, however, was to position itself in the grant competition as an organization that could already claim considerable experience and success in the area of skills training and development. Even though its application for a Workplace Skills Initiative grant was ultimately unsuccessful, the KCDC's skill in presenting itself as an organization that could be entrusted with another large project was another instance of reverse English, one that allowed the KCDC to continue as a player in the game.

One factor in the KCDC's success in assuming a leadership role in the community was its experience with the Northern Labour Market Committee (NLMC). The NLMC, established in 1983, is made up of over eighty different government and private sector agencies in northern Saskatchewan, including Aboriginal organizations and industry-based groups, that are broadly involved with skills training, funding opportunities, and economic development. It meets quarterly and is a clearing house for anything of interest relating to employment and the economy. The KCDC was a member of the NLMC while the Headwaters project was underway and has maintained observer status since then. Through its participation in the NLMC, the KCDC was able to establish a reputation in the community as an organization noted for its technological expertise. As the senior KCDC staff member who was involved with the NBN application observed:

> Because of the Smart Communities program and the way we structured our matching funds, there was strong participation from both the school divisions and the municipalities for in-kind contributions. So they were very aware of what we had been doing already with Smart Communities at that point. We had been having some successes and making things happen, so we were definitely seen as the technological leadership group in northern Saskatchewan.

Finally, the KCDC's overarching policy objective has been to draw jobs to northern Saskatchewan, in particular, and, more generally, to keep people and jobs in the North. This goal is evident, for example, in the comment made by the KCDC telecommunications expert about the need for good mathematics and science training so that Northern residents will be qualified for skilled positions in the mining industry. The KCDC aimed to achieve this objective through its involvement with programs, such as BRAND, First Nations SchoolNet, and Breaking Barriers, that focused on connectivity. Participation in these programs was one way to keep the goals of employment and an improved quality of life in the North in play.

One continuing risk, however, is that by engaging in initiatives that emphasize broadband connections and video conferencing in support of job training, the KCDC is helping Northerners acquire skills that might ultimately encourage them to leave the region.

The NBN project actually did result in more jobs for residents of northern Saskatchewan, while simultaneously producing an increased revenue stream for the KCDC. SaskTel did not have much of a staff presence in northern Saskatchewan at the time, nor were there local companies who could do the required work of installation. The KCDC seized on the opportunity and was able to fill the gap with graduates of its youth IT trainee program, who carried out the final installation in local communities. As the KCDC telecommunications expert noted, during the implementation of the NBN project, the KCDC stood in a double relationship with SaskTel:

> So KCDC became in effect a SaskTel vendor, much the same as any big city [service retailer such as] Wireless Age. All of these different companies, if you go to them, they have "High Speed Dealer" in their window. Well, KCDC became a SaskTel High Speed Dealer for Northern communities. That put us in a business relationship with SaskTel, so we were in a slightly odd position, I suppose. On one hand we were the proponent, and on the other hand we were a subcontractor of the main vendor.

Although the KCDC was able to capitalize on this dual relationship, the NBN project was of limited duration, and a concern with the creation of skilled jobs remains one of the KCDC's priorities.

CONCLUSION

Three more observations can be made about the KCDC and its role in northern Saskatchewan. The first is that things change. The individuals associated with the NBN application and the subsequent installation of broadband services had a track record with each other that facilitated the project. But many of these people have now moved on, and new relationships have to be built. The funding environment has also changed. The KCDC senior manager noted that the organization now has "more of a straight business relationship" with one of the Saskatchewan tribal councils, "as opposed to a community development partnership." As he went on to explain:

> That's partly because that's the way that KCDC is evolving. Now our partners are business partners. . . . It's because the government programs have dried up, and we don't have any core funding at all. So we have to, in order to survive, go in the direction of providing commercial services in more of a business arrangement as opposed to program proposals. . . . It really changes the nature of your organization. It really takes you out of community development.

Second, in the environment of the development of broadband telecommunications in northern Saskatchewan and the BRAND program, there were, to paraphrase the Saskatchewan-based Industry Canada policy analyst, no secrets. With regard to SaskTel, he remarked: "You know, there are a lot of well-known secrets about SaskTel's infrastructure, what's already in the ground, and what was being put up . . . and [about] how aggressive they are in protecting their own territory, too." But the notion of "well-known secrets" applies more broadly. Whatever their formal organizational affiliation, the individuals involved in the BRAND proposals had worked with one another for many years. There was considerable back-and-forth as the proposals were being developed. Industry Canada provided feedback on the proposals as they evolved. SaskTel was actively involved not only as a respondent to the RFP but also in the ongoing development and evaluation of the two rounds of proposals. The KCDC talked with other applicants across Canada. The same is true of other government programs in which the KCDC has participated. Personal relationships had formed over time. There was confidence that the various parties could deliver on their commitments and obligations. In rural and remote areas, people often wear a lot of hats. Everyone knows what is going on. Although it is possible to distinguish specific discourses and analyze the relationships among the various actors, the fact remains that everyone knew everyone else's business and conducted themselves accordingly.

The third observation concerns the question of what affordable and equitable telecommunications might mean in rural and remote areas. In contrast to urban dwellers, residents of rural and remote areas typically do not have many choices when it comes to health services and education. They must rely on broadband connections for access to telehealth and on multicast video conferencing for advanced education and skills training. It is possible to argue that the goal of equity requires that rural and remote residents be provided with *better* telecommunications capacity and services than urban Canadians because they are so reliant on those services. Should this argument prevail, it makes the challenge of addressing market failure in these regions an even more pressing issue than it is currently assumed to be.

As a community-based organization located in a remote area of Canada, the KCDC has successfully faced numerous challenges, taken advantage of the opportunities available to it, and worked hard to create other opportunities. An initial examination of key texts has demonstrated that the KCDC was able to manoeuvre among competing discourses in order better to fulfill its mission of "bringing technology to the north." Closer examination of texts, as well as a dialogic analysis of the interaction of these texts with various social contexts, is necessary, however, to fully describe the KCDC's role in exploiting those discourses. It is my hope that the research described in this chapter will contribute to the skills that CBOs such as the KCDC routinely employ not only to ensure their continued survival but also to further their ability to serve their communities. I also hope that this research will contribute to the development of a knowledge-based public policy.

ACKNOWLEDGEMENTS
I wish to thank Michael Gurstein and Andrew Clement for their advice and suggestions.

NOTES
1. The NBTF report estimated the maximum cost of connecting all communities, homes, and businesses at $4.6 billion. In June 2001, David Johnston, the NBTF chair, clarified that the task force had proposed a two-phase process. The first phase, which would cost between $1.85 billion and $2.5 billion, would connect all communities by 2004. This cost would be shared by all levels of government and the private sector. The second phase, costing approximately $2 billion, would extend broadband connectivity to homes and businesses and would be funded primarily by the private sector (Johnston 2001). Minister of Industry Brian Tobin gained cabinet support for $1 billion in funding, but when the budget was presented in December 2001, the amount had been reduced to $35 million over a three-year period from 2004 to 2006 (Scofield 2001). This provoked a very public dispute between Tobin and Prime Minister Paul Martin that culminated in Tobin's high-profile resignation from the cabinet.

2   For more information, see "Broadband Canada: Connecting Rural Canadians," http://
    www.ic.gc.ca/eic/site/719.nsf/eng/home, and, in particular, the "Frequently Asked
    Questions" section (http://www.ic.gc.ca/eic/site/719.nsf/eng/h_00004.html#BPQ1).
3   *Community-based organization* is one of several terms used to describe organizations
    that are involved with the delivery of services and programs—typically, although
    not exclusively programs sponsored by governments—to individuals and groups in
    a community. Other terms include the *not-for-profit sector*, the *voluntary sector*, the
    third or *independent sector*, and the *non-government sector*.
4   This and additional information about the region is available at http://www.fnmr.gov.
    sk.ca/nad.
5   The KCDC's involvement with Alberta's SuperNet and Saskatchewan's CommunityNet,
    as the First Nations SchoolNet RMO responsible for both provinces, provided it with
    an insider's view of both initiatives at all stages, from public discussion, the formula-
    tion of program objectives, and systems design and delivery through to operational
    realities.
6   For a critical examination of this rather narrow interpretation, see Stevenson 2009.
7   Examining the impact of PowerPoint on organizational communication, Yates and Or-
    likowksi (2007) argue that PowerPoint presentations are coherent texts with specific
    characteristics that can be identified and tracked. The tendency for PowerPoint to
    encourage a somewhat simplistic and reductive form of thinking has also been noted
    (see, e.g., Parker 2001). In addition, everyday experience with presentations made by
    civil servants suggests that the "deck" is a carefully prepared script and that speakers
    rarely depart from or embellish the text accompanying the slides.
8   These statistics appeared in the December 2008 CommunityNet FAQ. CommunityNet
    remains a major priority of the provincial government, as was indicated by a grant to
    SaskTel in 2008 of $90 million (later quietly reduced to $45 million). This grant pro-
    vided partial funding for a $129 million SaskTel project to extend CommunityNet to
    even more communities, to upgrade existing facilities, and to add additional cellphone
    towers to support wireless broadband access. The next objective of the program is to
    bring high-speed broadband to farm gate and to communities that are exceedingly
    remote.
9   "This government" is that of Brad Wall and the Saskatchewan Party, which came to
    power in 2007. The previous government was that of the NDP, which governed Sas-
    katchewan from 1991 to 2007, with Roy Romanow and then Lorne Calvert as premier.
    Gary Lane was the minister responsible for telecommunications during the adminis-
    tration of Grant Devine and the Conservative Party (1982 to 1991).
10 Primary texts include, at the national level, Assembly of First Nations 2001b, 2004,
    and 2008, and, at the provincial, B.C. First Nations Technology Council 2005. I also
    examined documents from other Aboriginal organizations: Meadow Lake Tribal
    Council 2002; Northern Broadband Network 2003, 2007; K-Net 2004; Keewaytinook
    Okimakanak 2005. Also useful were consultation documents and reports of meet-
    ings that represent significant Aboriginal participation (Jock et al. 2004; Aboriginal
    Voice 2005; Nickerson and Kaufman 2005) and published academic research (Alex-
    ander 2001; Matiation 1999; Pannekoek 2001; J. Whiteduck 2010; T. Whiteduck 2010),
    as well as and briefs and submissions, such as a RICTA 2005.
11 Included among the numerous KCDC documents I examined were "Headwaters
    Project: Vision of the Future" (1999); "Headwaters Project Business Plan" (2000);
    "Headwaters Project 2004: Online Report" (2004); "Saskatchewan and Alberta

e-Communities: Rural, Remote and Aboriginal, Three-year Plan, 2006–2009" (2005); "Northern Innovation" (2005); "Workplace Skills Initiative: Submission to Human Resource and Skills Development Canada" (2005); and "Decreasing Rural Poverty Through Application of Information and Communication Technology (ICT): Presentation to the Senate Standing Committee on Agriculture and Forestry—Rural Poverty Hearing" (2007). In addition, between 2002 and 2005, I looked at various announcements in the News and Events section of the KCDC home page.

REFERENCES

Aboriginal Voice. 2005. *Aboriginal Voice national recommendations: From digital divide to digital opportunity*. Ottawa: Crossing Boundaries National Council. http://www.turtle island.org/resources/digiops.pdf.

Alexander, Cynthia J. 2001. Wiring the nation! Including First Nations? Aboriginal Canadians and federal e-government initiatives. *Journal of Canadian Studies* 35(4): 277–97.

Anderson, Robert B. 1999. *Economic development among the Aboriginal peoples of Canada: The hope for the future*. North York, ON: Captus Press.

Anderson, Robert B., Leo Paul Dana, and Teresa E. Dana. 2006. Indigenous land rights, entrepreneurship, and economic development in Canada: "Opting-in" to the global economy. *Journal of World Business* 41(1): 45–55.

Assembly of First Nations. 2001a. National chief endorses Broadband Task Force recommendations and initiatives. Press release, 18 June. Ottawa.

——. 2001b. Executive summary to the Government of Canada for the deployment of broadband services to First Nations communities. 29 October. Ottawa.

——. 2004. Resolution No. 65. Charlottetown: Annual General Assembly.

——. 2008. National Think Tank. First Nations ICT Mapping: Designing a National Strategic Framework. Ottawa. www.knet.ca/documents/AFN-MEETING-SUMMARY2-Connectivity-Think-Tank-March18-20.doc.

B.C. First Nations Technology Council. 2005. Submission to the Telecommunications Policy Review Panel. http://www.telecomreview.ca/epic/internet/ intprp-gecrt.nsf/vwapj/ BCFNTC_-_Submission.pdf/$FILE/BCFNTC_-_Submission.pdf. Accessed 26 January 2006. (The page has since been taken down.)

Binder, Michael. 2003. Innovation and inclusion in the network age. Paper presented at the Information Highway 2003 Conference, 24–26 March. Toronto.

——. 2005. Canada in the networked economy: Tomorrow's challenges, today. Paper presented at the Wireless Communications Association Global Harmonization and Regulatory Summit, 28 June–1 July. Washington DC.

Canada. Privy Council Office. 2001. Speech from the Throne to open the first session of the 37th Parliament of Canada. 30 January. http://www.pco-bcp.gc.ca/index.asp?lang= eng&page=information&sub=publications&doc=aarchives/sft-ddt/2001-eng.htm.

Canadian Radio-television and Telecommunications Commission. 2003. Status of competition in Canadian telecommunications markets: Deployment/accessibility of advanced telecommunications infrastructure and services. Ottawa. http://www.crtc.gc.ca/eng/ publications/reports/PolicyMonitoring/2005/gic2005.pdf.

Fairclough, Norman. 1995. *Critical discourse analysis: The critical study of language*. London: Longman.

Fiske, Gerald. 2010. Telecom Notice of Consultations CRTC 2010-43: Proceeding to review access to basic telecommunications services and other matters. Memo from Gerald

Fiske, Deputy Minister and Chief Information and Services Officer, Information Technology Office, Saskatchewan, to Robert Morin, Secretary General, CRTC. 26 April. http://www.crtc.gc.ca/public/partvii/2010/8663/c12_201000653/1386306.pdf.

Gibson, Kerri, Susan O'Donnell, and Vanda Rideout. 2007. The project-funding regime: Complications for community organizations and their staff. *Canadian Public Administration* 50(3): 411–35.

Hardy, Cynthia, and Nelson Phillips. 2004. Discourse and power. In *Sage handbook of organizational discourse*, ed. David Grant, Cynthia Hardy, Cliff Oswick, and Linda Putnam, 299–316. London: Sage Publications.

Hersche, Robert. 2005. Re: Telecommunications Policy Review: Response comments. Memo from Robert Hersche, Executive Director, Telecommunications, Information Technology Office, Saskatchewan, to Allan MacGillivray, Executive Director, Telecommunications Policy Review Panel Secretariat. 15 September. http://www.telecomreview.ca/eic/site/tprp-gecrt.nsf/vwapj/Government_of_Saskatchewan.pdf/$FILE/Government_of_Saskatchewan.pdf.

Himmelsbach, Vawn. 2000. Saskatchewan pools tech resources. *Technology in Government* 7(9) (September): 12.

Hull, Douglas. 2000. Building a global, knowledge-based society for the twenty-first century. Presentation delivered at the North American Day meeting on e-government, 12 October. Ottawa.

Ilcan, Suzan, and Tanya Basok. 2004. Community government: Voluntary agencies, social justice, and the responsibilities of citizens. *Citizenship Studies* 8(2): 129–44.

Indian and Northern Affairs Canada. 2009. Evaluation of the First Nations SchoolNet program: Final report, 16 February. Ottawa. http://www.ainc-inac.gc.ca/ai/arp/aev/pubs/ev/fns/fns-eng.pdf.

Jessop, Bob. 2005. Cultural political economy, the knowledge-based economy, and the state. In *The technological economy*, ed. Andrew Barry and Don Slater, 144–66. London: Routledge.

Jock, Richard, Mary Simon, Graham Fox, and Marcia Nickerson. 2004. Finding an Aboriginal digital voice. *Policy, Politics and Governance* 7 (July): 1–8. http://www.kta.on.ca/pdf/ppg7.pdf.

Johnston, David. 2001. Broadband critics are shortsighted. *Globe and Mail*, 27 June.

Keewatin Career Development Corporation. 2005. Workplace Skills Initiative: Submission to Human Resource and Skills Development Canada. La Ronge, SK. http://www.kcdc.ca/media/pdf/WSI-Proposalfinalxbud.pdf.

Keewaytinook Okimakanak. 2005. *Aboriginal e-community program concept: A national initiative partnering with regional Aboriginal organizations*. Fort Severn, ON. http://knet.ca/documents/EComm-concept-final.pdf.

K-Net. 2004. Re: Broadband connectivity in Aboriginal communities. Fort Severn, ON.

Lynch, Kevin. 1999. Building a global, knowledge-based economy/society for the twenty-first century. A presentation to the meeting of the SchoolNet National Advisory Board, 4–5 November. Ottawa.

Matiation, Nicole. 1999. A plea for time: Northern Aboriginal peoples advocate for the right to communicate on the Information Highway. MA thesis, Concordia University.

McBride, Stephen. 2000. Policy from what? Neoliberal and human-capital theoretical foundations of recent Canadian labour market policy. In *Restructuring and resistance: Canadian public policy in an age of global capitalism*, ed. Mike Burke, Colin Mooers, and John Shields, 159–77. Halifax: Fernwood Publishing.

Meadow Lake Tribal Council. 2002. Business plan submission for implementation funding. Meadow Lake, SK.

Moll, Marita. 1997. Canadian classrooms on the information highway: Making the connections. In *Tech high: Globalization and the future of education*, ed. Marita Moll, 33–64. Ottawa: Canadian Centre for Policy Alternatives.

Murray, Richard. 2002. CommunityNet: Connecting Saskatchewan. PowerPoint presentation. Information Technology Office, Government of Saskatchewan, Regina, SK. http://www.aboriginalcanada.gc.ca/abdt/lookups/cacwebsitegraphics.nsf/vDownload/richard_murray.ppt/$file/richard_murray.ppt. Accessed 30 April 2004. (The page has since been taken down.)

National Broadband Task Force. 2001. *The new national dream: Networking the nation for broadband access*. Ottawa: Industry Canada.

Nickerson, Marcia, and Jay Kaufman, 2005. Aboriginal culture in the digital age. *Policy, Politics and Governance* 10: 1–8.

Northern Broadband Network. 2003. Business plan submission for implementation funding. Meadow Lake, SK.

———. 2007. Final report for the Northern Broadband Network project. Prince Albert, SK.

Pannekoek, Frits. 2001. Cyber imperialism and the marginalization of Canada's Indigenous peoples. In *The handing down of culture, smaller societies and globalization*, ed. J-P. Baillargeon, 64–80. Toronto: Grubstreet Books. http://www.grubstreetbooks.ca/handingdownofculture/Resources/06_Pannekoek.pdf.

Parker, Ian. 2001. Absolute PowerPoint. *New Yorker* 77(13): 76. http://www.newyorker.com/archive/2001/05/28/010528fa_fact_parker.

Pike, Robert M. 1998. A chequered progress: Farmers and the telephone in Canada, 1905–1951. *Journal of Canadian Studies* 33(3): 5–30.

RICTA (Research on ICT with Aboriginal Communities). 2005. Submission to the Telecommunications Policy Review Panel. http://www.telecomreview.ca/epic/internet/intprp-gecrt.nsf/vwapj/RICTA.pdf/$FILE/RICTA.pdf. Accessed 23 January 2006. (The page has since been taken down.)

Rideout, Vanda N. 2007. No information age Utopia: Knowledge workers and clients in the social service sector. In *Knowledge workers in the information society*, ed. Catherine McKercher and Vincent Mosco, 133–46. New York: Lexington.

Rideout, Vanda N., and Andrew J. Reddick. 2005. Sustaining community access to technology: Who should pay and why. *Journal of Community Informatics* 2(1): 45–62. http://www.ci-journal.net/index.php/ciej/article/view/202/162/.

Rideout, Vanda N., Andrew J. Reddick, Susan O'Donnell, William McIver, Jr., Sandy Kitchen, and Mary Milliken. 2006. Community intermediaries in the knowledge society. Report of the Community Intermediaries Research Project. March. Fredericton: University of New Brunswick. http://www.unb.ca/cirp/En_CIRP.pdf.

Ritter, Teresa Leigh. 2006. Universal connectivity and market liberalization: Competing policy goals in government initiatives for broadband connectivity in rural and northern parts of Canada. MA thesis, York University.

Rooney, David J., Gregory N. Hearn, Thomas Mandeville, and Richard Joseph. 2003. *Public policy in knowledge-based economies: Foundations and frameworks*. Cheltenham, UK: Edward Elgar.

Russell, Bob. 2000. From the workhouse to workfare: The welfare state and shifting policy terrains. In *Restructuring and resistance: Canadian public policy in an age of global capitalism*, ed. Mike Burke, Colin Mooers, and John Shields, 26–49. Halifax: Fernwood Publishing.

Sanders, Larry. 2000. Widening the digital divide: The telecommunications policies of the Canadian Radio-television and Telecommunications Commission. Paper presented at the Ontario Library Association Superconference, 5 February. Toronto.

Saskatchewan. 2005. Telecommunications Policy Review Panel. Consultation paper response by the Government of Saskatchewan. 12 August. http://www.telecomreview.ca/eic/site/tprp-gecrt.nsf/vwapj/Govt_of_Saskatchewan_-_Submission.pdf/$FILE/Govt_of_Saskatchewan_-_Submission.pdf.

——. 2010. Changes to telecom foreign ownership rules must consider needs of rural residents. News release, 14 May. http://gov.sk.ca/news?newsId=aa14b020-972b-45a4-b4a1-0eb3172cefof.

Schnarch, Brian. 2004. Ownership, control, access, and possession (OCAP) or self-determination applied to research: A critical analysis of contemporary First Nations research and some options for First Nations communities. *Journal of Aboriginal Health* 1: 80–95. http://www.naho.ca/jah/english/jaho1_01/journal_p80–95.pdf.

Scoffield, Heather. 2001. Tobin pledges to keep up pressure for broadband network. *Globe and Mail*, 14 December.

Stevenson, Siobhan. 2009. Digital divide: A discursive move away from the real inequities. *The Information Society* 25(1): 1–22.

Taylor, Alison. 1997. Visioning education in the information economy. In *Tech high: Globalization and the future of education*, ed. Marita Moll, 15–31. Ottawa: Canadian Centre for Policy Alternatives.

Whiteduck, Judy. 2010. Building the First Nations e-community. In *Aboriginal policy research*, vol. 6, *Learning, technology and traditions*, ed. Jerry P. White, Julie Peters, Dan Beavon, and Peter Dinsdale, 95–103. Toronto: Thompson Educational Publishing.

Whiteduck, Tim. 2010. First Nations SchoolNet and the migration of broadband and community-based ICT applications. In *Aboriginal policy research*, vol. 6, *Learning, technology and traditions*, ed. Jerry P. White, Julie Peters, Dan Beavon, and Peter Dinsdale, 104–17. Toronto: Thompson Educational Publishing.

Wilson, Kevin G. 2000. *Deregulating telecommunications: U.S. and Canadian telecommunications, 1840–1997*. Lanhan, MD: Rowman and Littlefield.

Yates, JoAnne, and Wanda Orlikowksi. 2007. The PowerPoint presentation and its corollaries: How genres shape communicative action in organizations. In *Communicative practices in workplaces and the professions: Cultural perspectives on the regulation of discourse and organizations*, ed. Mark Zachry and Charlotte Thralls, 67–91. Amityville, NY: Baywood Publishing.

PART VI

Libraries and Community Networks

17 COMMUNITY NETWORKS AND LOCAL LIBRARIES Strengthening Ties with Communities

Nadia Caidi, Susan MacDonald, Elise Chien

Despite widely acknowledged similarities between community networks and public libraries, there are also challenges and constraints that hinder the potential for future synergies. Public libraries have a long-standing tradition of involvement with their communities, yet their circumstances and concerns differ from those of community networks (CNs). The mission of libraries is often rather narrowly focused and, when it comes to dealing with individuals and other organizations, their procedures can be somewhat rigid. In turn, CN practitioners, while institutionally more flexible, are sometimes too quick to dismiss the role of public libraries in the community, tending to view the library simply as a repository of books backed by public funding. Although both CNs and libraries are concerned with providing information services to the public, a dialogue seems to be lacking between the two communities.

In this chapter, we aim to contribute to an understanding of the areas of intersection between CNs and libraries, particularly in Canada, where specific public policies have contributed to shaping the playing field. With reference both to the existing literature and to the CRACIN case study sites, we examine the barriers to collaboration between CNs and libraries, and, in a few cases, the successes achieved by forging a relationship between the two. The main questions that drive our enquiry concern the ways in which public libraries and CNs compare in terms of their ideals and practices, whether there are identifiable dimensions along which to compare the synergies and tensions, and what the prospects are for new forms of partnering between libraries and CNs. The last requires an examination of the conditions under which such partnering is likely to occur, as well as a consideration of possible incompatibilities and, if such exist, how they might be mitigated.

As both information scholars and members of the CRACIN team, we were in a position to bring a distinctive perspective to bear on this research, and we aimed to do so with open minds in order to better understand the similarities and differences between libraries and CNs. However, the CNs that were the subject of CRACIN case studies were not chosen on the basis of any pre-existing connections with libraries, and in some cases the connections were very limited. All the same, over time, we were able to arrive at useful insights about the ways in which these two parties interacted (or not).

We set out to examine this relationship by reviewing the relevant literatures for evidence concerning the types and the scope of involvement between libraries and CNs. In her foundational work in this area, Stevenson (2008) describes two approaches to public access computing in Canada—that of community networking and community informatics (CN/CI), on the one hand, and of public librarianship and library and information science (PL / LIS), on the other—and compared the two in terms of their respective political engagement and scholarly research agendas. She calls attention, in particular, to their shared concern with "universal access to information and communication technologies," noting that "both communities recognize that, as a social problem, the digital divide extends beyond simple access" (Stevenson 2008, 19). In this chapter, we compare the two communities more broadly, in terms of their shared ideals and values, their financial resources and accountability models, and their approaches to outreach and the provision of services.

SHARED IDEALS AND VALUES

Despite differing developmental trajectories, CNs and public libraries have similarities that include their grassroots origins as well as their ideals and values when it comes to serving their constituencies. Among these values are an affirmation of the importance of public education, lifelong learning, affordable access to information and ICTs, and individual empowerment. In addition, both serve to provide social, public, and civic spaces (see table 17.1).

The library as a social, public, and civic space can be traced back to its early development in North America. Since their inception in the mid nineteenth century, public libraries have been thought of as "public goods," sharing with public schools the mission of supporting education (Valentine 2005). Principles of intellectual freedom formed part of the core values of libraries, which encouraged citizens to take an active role in democracy by providing access to public information resources and creating spaces that foster citizenship and community participation. These values translate into modern-day public library practices that support lifelong learning, including the public library's focus on community information services, Internet support, educational support, and literacy programs. Despite their popular branding as the "temple of the book," libraries are places of engagement, bringing people together (via reference desk encounters, book clubs, study circles, and so on), as well as sites of learning, where users have access to information, research, and knowledge (Fisher et al. 2007). In promoting values of access, equity, and diversity to all members of the community, the public library is a potentially vital contributor to the social economy, a sector that is primarily concerned with building community and with achieving overarching social goals (Canada 2004; Quarter 1992).

TABLE 17.1 Similarities between libraries and community networks

Environment	Social, public, and civic spaces
	Use of ICTs and provision of ICT resources and services
	Connection to geographic community
	Attention to community needs
	Skill in volunteer management
	Emphasis on outreach activities and partnership building
Ideals and values	Grassroots origins
	Support for public education, equity, diversity, and access to information
	Support for lifelong learning
	Support for affordable public access to the Internet
	Potentially vital contributors to the social economy
	Emphasis on fostering social capital and attention to issues of social inclusion
	Promotion of reading and literacy
Obstacles	Economic pressures
	Competition for consumers' attention
	Reduced and/or unreliable government funding

Typically, community networks are also rooted in a specific geographic location (Carroll and Rosson 2003), in some cases serving as a physical space that fosters social interaction and inclusion through face-to-face encounters with other CN users and volunteers. However, community networks offer more than low-cost public access to the Internet. In the United States, community networks grew out of the "community organizing" movement that developed into a particular strand of activism in the 1970s and drew its agenda from geographically based communities. The idea of "marrying geographic community-based activism with ICTs" was at the origin of the development of CNs (Kubicek and Wagner 2002).

Like CNs, public libraries also developed as part of a grassroots movement, but one that began nearly a century earlier.[1] In many cases, free public libraries started as rural township and women's social libraries. Valentine (2005) points to the central role that local women played in establishing hundreds of public libraries across the United States, in effect producing grassroots organizations that became part of and helped to produce local community narratives. In the 1970s, the growing need for community information resources and services led public libraries to find new ways to actively engage with their communities. They initially developed paper-based databases of community information, providing the public with referrals to social service agencies and other community resources (Durrance 1984). These community information services (CIS) later became networked and were eventually made publicly available online. Public libraries' grassroots connections to community seem to have shifted over the years, likely because of such factors as their formal institutional status and the evolving role of accredited library professionals.

Through the myriad of services offered, ranging from the provision of information to encouraging dialogue among community members and beyond, libraries and CNs have an important role to play in fostering social capital, promoting reading and literacy, and addressing issues of social inclusion. Given the clear parallels between public libraries and CNs in terms of responding to community needs for local information, resources and services, and despite calls for them to work more closely together (Bajjaly 1999; Cisler 1994; Das 1999; Durrance and Schneider 1996; Schuler n.d.), it is surprising to note that formal collaborations between public libraries and CNs are typically more the exception than the rule. For example, in 1999, a nationwide survey of American public library directors showed that only 14 percent of public libraries had relationships with CNs (Durrance and Pettigrew 2002). Despite this, many CNs owe their origins to some form of collaboration with public libraries (Mattison 1994).

As early as the 1970s, there were documented instances of public libraries collaborating with CNs, the best-known example being the Community Memory project in Berkeley, California, one of the earliest known community access networks (Cisler 1994). In 1973, the first community networking experiment in Canada involved the installation in the front lobby of the Vancouver Public Library of a terminal providing access to an online database of community and social service listings.

In Canada, the infusion of funding in the mid-1990s through the federal government's Community Access Program (CAP) aimed to create community-based Internet access points and marked the beginning of much library-CN collaboration. In 1997, a Canada-wide study of Internet connectivity in county and regional libraries found that 67 percent provided public Internet access, which was a dramatic increase from 3 percent in 1995 (Curry and Curtis 2000).

It is unclear how many of the libraries surveyed were involved in formal partnerships with CNs. Yet it may be telling that almost 50 percent of respondents reported that volunteers, such as community networkers, helped to train the public to use the Internet in public libraries. Former president of the Canadian Library Association Wendy Newman asserts that in the early to mid-1990s, libraries had technical expertise not found elsewhere in the community sector in Canada, especially in small towns and rural communities, because of their experience in developing electronic catalogues. However, libraries' participation in community networking was often quite invisible because of the informal nature of those partnerships and relationships (Wendy Newman, pers. comm., 26 April 2010). Consequently, it has been difficult to assess the extent to which public libraries, librarians, and CNs and community practitioners initiate, develop, and sustain collaboration and working relationships (Pettigrew, Durrance, and Vakkari 1999).

Despite their commonalities, there are various key elements that distinguish CNs from public libraries and that in some cases may act as deterrents to co-operation. Differences are visible in the areas of funding resources and accountability mechanisms, outreach and community development, and professional development and other staffing issues, as well as in differing orientations toward ICTs, all of which have influenced the developmental trajectories of CNs and public libraries (see table 17.2). We examine a few of these issues below.

Financial Resources and Accountability Models

Financial resources and accountability models are two elements that public libraries and CNs have to contend with on an ongoing basis. Libraries, while they may be chronically underfunded, tend to have more funding opportunities and more stability than CNs, thanks to their formal institutional structure. CNs are much more precarious, as their funding is dependent on such factors as shifting political agendas. (For further discussion, see chapter 19.) In some cases, the result can be collaboration between CNs and libraries; in other cases, it can lead to rivalry and competition for meagre funds. For example, in the United States, the funding structure for both public libraries and CNs in the 1990s incited "turf wars" about which group would best serve the public (Cisler 1994).

TABLE 17.2 Divergences between libraries and community networks

	Public libraries	CNs
Funding	"Public good" status and associated public funding	"Social utility and public good"
	Sustainability ensured but not always on par with needs (rising costs of serials, licensing fees, etc.)	Precarious funding structure largely dependent on political will
Institutional structure	Highly formalized bureaucratic structure (municipal institutions, enacted by bylaws, library boards, etc.)	Local systems, run by local people and organizations, utilizing local resources to meet local communications, educational, social, and economic needs (Shade 1999)
	Institutional status support mechanisms	Flexible, responsive, ad hoc
	Professional staff, unionized	Geographic community-based activism
	Membership required (through library card)	Civic spaces that lie somewhere between government and the private sector
	Need for staff to be proactive and reflective in their practice (Durrance, Fisher, and Hinton 2005)	Reliance on volunteer efforts
	Need for strategies to anticipate and respond to neighbourhood needs (Durrance, Fisher, and Hinton 2005)	
Practices	ICTs prevalent, but emphasis is on the role-based model of libraries and librarians	ICTs as key to the very existence of the CN
	Formal skill set: ability to organize and catalog information for more effective retrieval	Primary concern is with the community (e.g., shared problems, collective empowerment)
	Primary concern is with the individual ("ideologies of individualism," Stevenson 2008)	Lack of full-time skilled individuals, reliance on volunteers
	The book as a central "object" associated with the library and its practices	Can be technologically focused and thus exclusionary (Powell 2007)
	Tendency to make the marginalized more like the mainstream (generic user)	Traditional support of political and social reform not reflected in current user base
	Emphasis on in-person support	Informal, with opportunities for involvement
	Value of "neutrality" as a professional norm	
	Absence of a model for engagement with community and for providing civic information	
	Community comes to the library	

Ultimately, many public libraries were beneficiaries of funding initiatives to bridge the so-called digital divide, which led to increased collaborations between libraries, service providers, and other local groups including CNs. But, as Cisler (1994, 24) observes, public libraries were slow to realize that effective relationships in the community often meant "collaboration with groups and individuals who may know little about libraries and whose agenda may not fit .the style of some libraries."

The first CNs in Canada were established in 1992, in the form of the Victoria Free-Net and National Capital FreeNet, both modelled after the Cleveland Freenet. By 1998, there were sixty FreeNets across Canada (O'Brien 2001), many of which still rely on Industry Canada's Community Access Program (CAP) funding as their primary source of funding.[2] Public libraries also figured prominently in CAP as sites of public access and training for the public. In some cases, CAP funding allowed already existing CNs to expand (e.g., by increasing their number of computer terminals). It must be noted, however, that some public librarians felt that the government had simply "downloaded responsibility to libraries, without much planning or practical consultation of the actual delivery" (Anderson and Julien 2003, 13).

As for CNs, their paradox is that although they gained charitable status as a "social utility and public good" in 1996, this decision sharply contrasted with Canadian federal policy makers' vision of "national information infrastructures as existing in a privatized and deregulated environment" (Shade 1999). Shade notes that because CNs in Canada are civic spaces that lie somewhere between government and the private sector, one ongoing challenge for CNs is the risk of their place being eroded as a result of a lack of funding and the absence of a model that clearly distinguishes them from commercial competitors and securely roots them in the "local." Stevenson (2008, 12–13) observes:

> As a result of nationwide funding initiatives such as CAP, public libraries and community networks/centres have become discursively linked as public sites for access to and training on the new information and communication technologies. As well, both have been consistently constituted as important social safety nets for the "digitally divided" in Canada. . . . Given their differing genealogies, it is not surprising that these similarities have more to do with the discursive practices associated with public policy initiatives (applications for funding, site reports) than anything inherent to either community.

Other issues that contributed to an uneven playing field between public libraries and CNs include the fact that many funding initiatives did not recognize CNs as legitimate community organizations, targeting instead more formal institutions. Strover et al. (2004) and others have criticized the fact that, for example, in the United States the definition of public spaces is largely restricted to a focus on schools and libraries, which don't always meet community needs in the most effective manner, in terms of their hours of operation, the constituencies they reach, and so on. According to Strover et al. (2004, 483), "the very placement, staffing, and use of public access in [libraries and schools] largely replicated the power structure and access advantages that already were in place." Consequently, while the institutional status of public libraries identified them as worthy recipients of funds to support access to computers and the Internet, it was a mixed blessing with regard to engendering relationships with other community organizations, including CNs.

Libraries, like other institutions, encounter barriers in meeting the needs of their constituencies. The usual culprits include funding, staffing, sustainability, and the setting of priorities. For example, public libraries are viewed as vital contributors to the Canadian social economy, yet, because they have traditionally relied on public funding, they do not fit into this framework as businesses. In the past decades, libraries have increasingly faced pressures to respond to prevailing ideological shifts, most notably toward a "market-led" approach to the provision of services that calls for increasing efficiency (Buschman 2005; Durrance and Fisher 2003; Greenhalgh, Worpole, and Landry 1995), as well as related economic pressures from government. Service delivery and performance indicators were implemented, along with evaluation frameworks, in an effort to make the libraries more accountable and responsive to political requirements. The large bookstores also increased competition for consumers' attention, as did the advent of ICTs (digital content and services, social networking platforms, etc.), which have forced libraries to adapt themselves as organizations as well as to adapt their services in order to respond to these new challenges and opportunities. Like institutions in other sectors, to gain public and political support for increased funding, libraries have had to reexamine their role in the knowledge society, while also keeping up with the services that they have traditionally provided to their constituencies. The emphasis on managing their assets and identifying their competitive advantages in a knowledge economy—and the related business-like discourse—likely reflects the tensions that libraries face in pursuing their traditional mandates during a period of neoliberal ascendancy. Increasingly, libraries find themselves pulled between these measurements of productivity and performance and their involvement with grassroots community organizations and community networking. In that, they share similarities with CNs.

CNs have also been forced to deal with economic forces beyond their control. In the 1990s, the Web introduced competition in the form of commercial community information services. Carroll and Rosson (2003) observe that, during this period, CNs became less interactive and less community oriented. Where once the CN was locally hosted and managed with a focus on communication—through bulletin board systems and newsgroups, electronic discussion boards, and email—CNs increasingly became more like websites, thus competing with commercial providers. Further, the authors argue, the advent of social software and computer-supported co-operative work (the Web 2.0 environment) raised the bar for CNs since their users often expect to be able to interact online. According to Carroll and Rosson and others, what continues to distinguish CNs is their connection to geographic community. As such, CNs are often exhorted to incorporate models of place, to foster sociability, and to incorporate aspects of lifelong learning—all of which, in our minds, represents a clear connection with public libraries.

Outreach and Provision of Services

Libraries and CNs both perform a considerable amount of outreach activity and partnership building. Through their joined efforts, the external community is invigorated, and, as McCabe (2001, 116) writes, "Such a structure for collaboration will allow powerful new strategies for solving community problems to emerge." But there are limits to the nature and scope of involvement of both libraries and CNs in community initiatives.

Much has been written about the ability of libraries to foster social capital within the communities they serve, although few empirical studies have been produced to support this claim (Johnson 2009, 2010; McCook 2000). Established through relationships among and between individuals, groups, and organizations, social capital involves five key elements, as outlined in a report prepared by Middlesex University's Institute of Social Science Research: trust, reciprocity and mutuality, social networks, shared norms of behaviour, and a sense of commitment and belonging (European Commission 2003). In turn, these elements may foster a sense of community, establish identity, and encourage the practices of a civil society (Côté 2001; Farr 2004; Woolcock 2001). Beyond simply providing the community, including marginalized populations, with access to information, public libraries also strive to educate citizens in handling the information that they come across in an effective manner. As Kranich (2001, 41) observes, "It is from librarians that citizens learn how to find, evaluate, and use the information essential for making decisions that affect the way we live, learn, work, and govern ourselves." Educating library users to achieve the capacity to make effective use of the information and resources available is a central tenet of libraries. The measure of social inclusion, as outlined by Berman and Phillips (2001, 183), is to "tap into the skills and awareness of citizens," by asking "how aware are they of what is available?" As for CNs, they offer a gathering place, a more informal environment, and through their in-person support they enable the empowerment of users through active participation in the life of the CN.

Social capital, social inclusion, and solidarity are important issues around which libraries and CNs share some common ideals in a general sense, although the nature and scope of services of public libraries and CNs differ to some degree. As well, the ways in which they interpret these ideals often differ. For instance, it has been argued that libraries tend to treat social inclusion as a means of making the marginalized more like the mainstream (Caidi and Allard 2005). Furthermore, libraries "have at times only been seen as passive supporters of social change that only indirectly contribute towards changing the disempowered status, experiences, and realities of people on the margins" (Mehra and Srinivasan 2007, 125). In contrast, CNs, with their presumptions of technological prowess, may contribute to defining social inclusion in a rather narrow sense. For example, Powell (2007, 4), in a study of community wireless networking, concludes that "even though this civic participation contributes positively to local communities, Wi-Fi projects seem to contribute primarily to building communities—publics—of Wi-Fi geeks rather than emerging out of more widely constituted local communities." (See also chapter 11 in this volume.)

In the communications literature, there is a significant amount of interest in CNs as an alternative medium through which to promote active participation in democracy and movements for political reform, but there is little evidence that such an effect exists (Horning 2007; Kubicek and Wagner 2002; Longan 2005). Although Chewar, McCrickard, and Carroll (2005, 263) suggest that one of the primary goals of CNs is to foster the development of social capital, they conclude that "actual implementations of community networks do not yet seem to be effective in building social capital." Further, research has shown that the connection between CNs and their local community is in some cases being eroded. Kwon (2005), for instance, found that only 20 percent of CN members surveyed actually use CNs because of their community focus and ideals, while the majority were unaware of the differences between CNs and commercial ISPs, which suggested that CN administrators need to do a better job of clarifying and emphasizing their links to communities.

In contrast to CNs, the key tension for librarians seems to be over whether to maintain "the order of the book"[3] or to go to the places where people need information and figure out how best to address these needs. A steady stream of literature and research projects have examined this difficult tension, a discussion that Pateman (2005) termed the "reads" versus "needs" debate, referring to the question of the mission of the library. Is it to provide books and a space for users, or is it to focus instead on the needs of the users wherever they are, whether inside the library walls or out in the community? The exploration of this tension was at the centre of the project Working Together: Library-Community Connections (http://www.librariesincommunities.ca/). Funded by Human Resources and Social Development Canada, the project brought together the Vancouver Public Library, the Toronto Public Library, the Regina Public Library, and the Halifax Public Libraries in an effort to explore community development approaches to working with socially excluded individuals and communities. The objective was to work toward transforming the culture and attitudes of librarians toward socially excluded people and to remove systemic barriers that keep these individuals from using the public library. There are many valuable lessons that can be learned from the Working Together project, in terms of the effectiveness of community development techniques and the assumptions and prejudices inherent in traditional library service planning and delivery.

The Working Together project explored the idea of a community development librarian (CDL) who, by being positioned within the community, would bring the library to the user rather than the user to the library. An interesting distinction is made by the Working Together researchers between "outreach" and "community-based development," and they favour the latter. The project leader, Brian Campbell (pers. comm. 2006), stated that "'outreach' is about working in the community whereas community development is about working with the community." He went on to describe one of their key findings:

> Many librarians lack experience and awareness of the philosophies and techniques of working collaboratively with their communities. Many do not see collaborative community-library service development as different from traditional service planning. Traditionally, librarians assess various inputs and make decisions about what communities need—rather than asking people directly and involving them in the planning and delivering of library services and programs. Understanding this distinction and its philosophical foundation is essential if we are to create public libraries that accept and welcome socially excluded communities.

Summary

It is evident from the above review that libraries and CNs share many values and ideals. However, they also differ to some extent in their practices. As opposed to transforming themselves into telecomputing centres for local communities, libraries complement the technical infrastructure and associated content that CNs offer by providing human resources and a non-discriminating space. Libraries, however, are a different kind of space from CNs. Libraries are more durable, in that they have a longer history, a formal institutional structure (with related funding), and more public "branding" than CNs. Despite the relative invisibility of librarians' work, people usually know what to expect when they walk into a library: the acquisition of a library card for borrowing privileges, a cozy space for studying or leisure reading, learning opportunities, the use of computer terminals, in-person support, access to books and other materials, reference or readers' advisory services, and so on. The public library may also elicit childhood memories and is a place associated with both entertainment and learning—what Adria, in chapter 18 of this volume, refers to as the "library ideal." These elements contribute to making the public library a recognizable institution in society with well-understood practices and values.

However, the public library is confronted with many challenges in its attempts to serve its constituencies. Beyond issues of geographical location— physical access to library branches and associated resources and services—there may be additional barriers that limit the use of libraries by community members. These include a lack of knowledge of the services provided by libraries (pointing, for example, to a need for clearer signage, more effective outreach, better visual displays, pamphlets in various languages about services provided at the library) and a lack of services in minority languages, including multilingual search capabilities for the collections. (For example, only in 2006 did the Toronto Public Library expand the available translations of its "Guide to the Library" from four to ten languages.) These challenges exist at the logistical, financial, linguistic, and cultural levels, as well as in terms of human resources, empathy, training, and so on. This drives librarians to ask themselves a number of questions: whether they are assessing the needs and skills of their users accurately, and perhaps even enhancing them, whether the services provided by librarians necessarily need to be contained within the physical space of the library, and whether librarians view their role as extending to the facilitation of individual empowerment, civic engagement, and the development of social capital among community members.

The CN, in contrast, does not usually possess the same level of "branding" and public recognition. However, the characteristics that make the public library what it is also make it less flexible than its CN counterpart. As part of their mandate, libraries do not cater to particular groups of people the way that CNs do for specific geographic communities. Libraries also tend to take a systemic approach to service delivery. For instance, the Toronto Public Library is a large system, consisting of close to one hundred branches, and this broad reach requires a certain amount of standardization. As a result, libraries may appear to be much less welcoming than a community network that caters to the needs of the local community (Viseu et al. 2006). Enabling personal connections, face-to-face interaction, and the formation of social networks are major assets of CNs, which allow individuals to be involved and valued rather than simply informed or assisted (Chien 2005; see also chapter 9 in this volume).

CRACIN CASE STUDIES

Libraries' degree of involvement in the various CRACIN case study sites varied but in general was rather limited. As mentioned above, the sites were not selected on the basis of any prior connection to libraries. Rather, by examining cases in which connections developed between libraries and CNs, we sought to understand what came of the collaboration. Through conversations and interviews with people involved with the CNs, we also tried to grasp the prevailing attitudes toward and understanding of the library-CN connection.

Method

The method we employed was exploratory in nature. We conducted semi-structured interviews with key informants from each site and held informal discussions with other informants, including some at CNs that had no direct involvement with libraries. We shared our thoughts and preliminary findings at the CRACIN workshops held annually over the course of the four-year project. It was at these sessions in particular that we gained helpful insight from fellow collaborators.

For each of the sites examined—K-Net, St. Christopher House, VCN, the WVDA, Communautique, and the Alberta Library Project—we met with the CN's key coordinator, and, in some instances, with other individuals at the CN who worked closely with a local library. Even for case study sites that did not have a direct partnership with libraries, we were interested in the role of information professionals and what information practices were conducted at each site.

The questions we asked were intended to yield general information about the site's users, along with an indication of the most common uses of the site's services, as well as the users' most pressing needs. We also asked about the level and nature of the library's involvement at the site. We wanted to determine whether the public library was a formal partner in the community network (direct affiliation), whether it functioned more as a source of information and aid to which the site's users could be referred, or whether its involvement with the site was relatively limited. (For example, the only connection might be that the key coordinator or other staff members sometimes made use of library services in the course of their work.) Another set of questions pertained to who at the site was responsible for the organization, indexing, and/or evaluation of the information housed on the site, who made information available to staff and the public, and whether the site offered any training for users to create and evaluate the information provided to them.

It must be noted that all of our informants were CN practitioners. So, in effect, the data presented here is the picture of the relationship as perceived by CN participants rather than librarians. As researchers with a background in library and information science, we were the principal link to the library sector. We benefitted from the long-standing relationship developed through CRACIN to explore, and sometimes create, opportunities to talk about the role and potential value of libraries to community network practitioners. Although we were careful not to advocate for libraries, in at least one instance (K-Net), the CRACIN study provided the basis for further discussions about the relationship between libraries and CNs. A spin-off project evolved that aimed at examining the role of libraries in remote and isolated communities of Northern Ontario.

K-Net: Service Provision in Rural and Remote Communities

K-Net, whose primary constituents comprise people living and working in remote and rural First Nations across Northwestern Ontario, was one CRA-CIN site that had little to no affiliation with libraries. Yet the interest in, and need for, libraries is great in these geographical areas. With only 37 percent of First Nations communities having established libraries, and in view of diminishing operating grants to support the existing ones, First Nations libraries face a formidable challenge in serving the information and reading needs of their communities (Edmonton Public Library 2005; Lawlor 2003; Library and Archives Canada 2004). Not surprisingly, funding is among the major concerns. Public libraries in most Ontario First Nations are funded by the Ontario Ministry of Cultural Heritage and are typically governed by the councils or educational department of each community. Government funding for First Nations public libraries is allotted per capita, so if a First Nation community has a low population, there is relatively scant support for a community library. Since the late 2000s, funding programs and donations from organizations such as the Bill and Melinda Gates Foundation, Industry Canada (through the Community Access Program), the Southern Ontario Library Service, and the Ontario Library Association have enabled broader access to computers and connectivity to be established in libraries.

Another ongoing challenge is raising awareness among community members about the role and significance that a library might play within the community. Since many individuals in First Nation communities lack basic necessities such as proper shelter, clean water, and heating, it is quite understandable that a library would not be a top priority. Brick-and-mortar libraries, in particular, are difficult to establish because of the shortage of materials and space in Northern communities.

To investigate the options available to provide library services in connection with K-Net, Nadia Caidi worked with Brian Walmark, of the Keewaytinook Okimakanak Research Institute (KORI), to organize a workshop in November

2005, which brought together thirty-two researchers, librarians, band council members, academics, and government officials. (See http://research.ischool. utoronto.ca/dlac/DLAC-Summary.pdf.) The objectives of the workshop were to discuss best possible models for providing information resources and services to communities in remote areas of Northern Ontario and to devise a strategy for the creation of a digital library for elementary and secondary school students in Northern Ontario. Digital libraries offer users the opportunity to access materials that traditional brick-and-mortar libraries might not be able to provide. A large portion of the workshop was devoted to determining exactly what a digital library has to offer and how such a library might best operate in the context of a northern Aboriginal community. It was deemed essential that the digital library fit within the existing knowledge and learning environments of the Keewaytinook Okimakanak community, along the lines of the Internet High School or Telehealth services (Caidi and Walmark 2007).

In the workshop, a clear need was identified for a mixed approach to the provision of information services and resources through digital as well as physical libraries. Community partners and librarians at the workshop pointed out that children in First Nation communities often have limited access to print material and books and often resort to online resources to retrieve information. The need for "information literacy" skills—including the ability to assess the quality and authority of sources—was raised, as well as the challenges of relying solely on web content. In addition to a desire for books relating to curriculum content and development, community partners also expressed interest in creating a repository of culturally relevant works dealing with community knowledge and history, language scripts, and local artifacts. There was also an interest in other types of information, particularly health-related materials and resources, as well as children's literature and leisure reading materials such as fiction and cookbooks.

Discussions concerning the need for "help desk" services elicited strong interest from the workshop participants. Since many First Nations communities do not have a physical library, a virtual help desk was considered as a possible alternative. That is, by phone, email, instant messaging, or video conferencing, community members would be able to contact a trained librarian, who could provide assistance with reference questions, cataloguing, collection development, or other services related to the functioning of a library in the community. Many workshop attendees felt that such a service would be tremendously important and was even a necessity.

The workshop generated a lot of support and enthusiasm for developing a library project, with a mixture of digital and physical libraries, in Northern Ontario, and some concrete steps were suggested to explore the possibility of further collaboration between the community members at Keewaytinook

Okimakanak, the K-Net team, government representatives, library practitioners (such as Ontario Library Services North), and the information professionals at the University of Toronto's Faculty of Information. The workshop resulted in a follow-up project in the form of a feasibility study for the On-Demand Book Service (http://odbs.knet.ca).

The purpose of the On-Demand Book Service (ODBS) is to support the joy of reading in rural and isolated First Nations communities within the context of learning, knowledge sharing, and the recording of history. Modelled on the Internet Archive Bookmobile initiative, the ODBS seeks to bridge the gap between physical and digital libraries. The service builds on the power of ICTs to provide users with physical copies of public domain materials available on the Web, by enabling such works to be downloaded and printed using ODBS printing and bookbinding equipment (see Caidi and Walmark 2007; Caidi and Lam 2011). In addition, materials written by members of the community can be produced as printed books. Such an initiative points to the demand for library services that exists in these communities, as well as to the difficulties involved in procuring funding and establishing sustainable projects that address the particular needs of these communities.

Although the CRACIN project has come to an end, the development of the ODBS forged a relationship between K-Net and the University of Toronto's Faculty of Information that still continues. In March 2010, the university made funds available from the 2009–10 allocation to the Council on Aboriginal Initiatives for two initiatives related to the On-Demand Book Service: (1) the purchase and shipping of ODBS-related equipment to First Nations communities in remote areas of Northern Ontario, and (2) a public workshop on reading and literacy issues, which focused in particular on the provision of information resources and services and featured the ODBS and other related reading technologies and initiatives. By then, the ODBS had grown to become a web portal that allows students, community leaders, and members of the community to reflect together on issues of access to materials, reading, and library and information services in remote and isolated areas of Northern Ontario. While it remains a work in progress, it has also provided an experiential hands-on workshop that has allowed many students to engage in real-life projects and in community-based research.

With the funding received, three complete sets of ODBS equipment and related technologies were shipped to three Northern Ontario communities.[4] In addition, a selected list of possible titles for download was compiled by our students, in consultation with community partners, based on a survey of the reading preferences of community members that was likewise designed and administered by students. Finally, we were able to send students to the various sites—namely, Thunder Bay, Sioux Lookout, and Keewaywin—to meet with the community, assist in setting up the equipment, and generally serve as facilitators.

In addition to the shipping of the ODBS equipment, a public event was organized to raise awareness about reading in First Nations communities. The theme of the event, held on 29 March 2010, was "Reading in First Nations: Infrastructure, Access and Imagination." The goal was to explore the realities, barriers, and challenges to reading in First Nations communities, particularly in remote and isolated areas of Northern Ontario. The meeting was a hybrid of physical and virtual presence via tele- and video conferencing, with four nodes, one each in Toronto, Sioux Lookout, Thunder Bay, and Keewaywin, with bridges to Sandy Lake and other locations. The day included keynote speeches, roundtable discussions with members of various Northern Ontario communities who discussed the obstacles to reading in their communities, and general sharing of stories and experiences. In addition, there were demos of various initiatives aimed at enabling reading in First Nations communities, including the On-Demand Book Service and projects undertaken by individual libraries. The ODBS is a testament to the strong and meaningful relationships that have been built over the past few years as a result of the CRACIN study. The ODBS provides an alternative means to bring information resources and services to isolated communities. But many of these communities still long for traditional libraries, or at least for a combination of physical and virtual libraries, to fulfill the reading needs of local residents.

St. Christopher House

St. Christopher House, a well-established community and social service agency in Toronto, offers a sharp contrast to K-Net, notably in its relations to public libraries. St. Christopher House, or St. Chris, is a not-for-profit agency of the United Way that has served the southwest quadrant of downtown Toronto since 1912. St. Chris offers a range of services and resources to disadvantaged community members of all ages. These include computer and Internet access, employment services and skills training, information about nutrition, language and literacy courses, legal services, counselling, and recreational and housing support services, making St. Chris an essential resource for its community of users. St. Chris has seven locations that provide community access to training and over seventy computer terminals with high-speed Internet service. St. Chris has also developed a community learning network (CLN), a web-accessible content management system that uses a participatory approach to its design and development. By enabling users to create a shared physical and online space where individuals and groups can share ideas, network, and learn from one another, the CLN allows users to be both producers and consumers of content. (For more on the St. Chris CLN, see chapter 8.)

In its early days, St. Chris founded a children's library, which was taken over by the Toronto Public Library in 1921 and remained in operation for almost forty years. Today, however, St. Chris does not interact very much with the public library branches in its vicinity. From our discussions with St. Chris staff, it became clear that St. Chris views its mission as essentially different from that of a public library. Although staff members still refer users to the library whenever appropriate and collaborate with the library on occasion, St. Chris maintains its distinct presence and identity. There have been collaborations between the St. Chris team and information professionals and researchers on various aspects of the CLN and other endeavours, and those at St. Chris understand that librarians and information professionals can bring skills to the table that are a valuable addition to their own technical expertise. Over the years, a mutually beneficial and respectful relationship has thus been established, in the form of referrals and specific collaborations between St. Chris and the Toronto Public Library (as well as the University of Toronto's Faculty of Information). In the case of St. Chris, however, CN developers maintain a strong sense of what their identity and mission is and how it differs from that of the public library.

Vancouver Community Network (VCN)

The Vancouver Community Network (VCN) presents yet another scenario. A senior administrator at the Vancouver Public Library was a founding member of VCN. Over the years, the relationship between VPL and VCN has persisted, although it has assumed a different form. The Vancouver Public Library provides both space and bandwidth for VCN. In turn, VCN acts as a technical infrastructure, offering access to ICTs for thousands of individuals and groups who could not otherwise afford it. Funding is a mixture of donations to cover the telecommunications costs, special projects, and contracts, as well as public funds from the federal government and the city. In addition to user accounts, VCN provides content management services and meets the learning needs of its users, mainly in the form of IT skills. As a physical space, VCN plays an important social function by allowing individuals to gather and share information, broaden their social networks, and engage in various forms of civic participation. In chapter 9 of this volume, Diane Dechief characterizes VCN as a type of "third space" for new immigrants. She depicts the recent immigrants as a technically savvy "alternate civic core," made up of individuals who make a major contribution to VCN's volunteer program. In the process, they gain much needed Canadian work experience, as well as social networking opportunities, thereby improving their job prospects.

From our discussion with key respondents, the relationship between VCN and the Vancouver Public Library now seems to be limited largely to technical support. As has so often been the case, the relationship between the two depends heavily on existing contacts between particular individuals at the library, whose interests in VCN may be shifting. The philosophy of VCN revolves around providing access to information and ICTs to the economically disadvantaged. While the library community shares these ideals, the VCN respondents indicated that, as they see it, in practice librarians "do things differently." The prevailing sentiment was that libraries and librarians adhere to a more rigid, structured, and formal set of rules, preferring "to do things in particular ways" and otherwise "possessing a strong sense of ownership of the physical space of the library," and perhaps being constrained by it. There was no sense of competing interests between the two, but rather an acceptance that the two entities were different and were meant to achieve different purposes. An example was advanced regarding the provision of services to newcomers. Because of union rules, the library cannot provide such individuals with some of the same opportunities that VCN can offer them, such as the opportunity to volunteer. This local experience allows them to be involved in and contribute to the day-to-day activities of the CN, interact with a wide range of Canadian-born as well as immigrant individuals, hone their IT skills, and build their résumé, thus potentially enhancing their opportunities for paid employment.

In the case of VCN, we thus have a scenario in which a public library was, thanks to the commitment of a particular individual, a founding member of the CN. However, the relationship failed to develop beyond the sharing of technical support and IT equipment (e.g., server space). Ultimately, the two entities pursued different trajectories and came to be relatively estranged from one another.

Western Valley Development Agency (WVDA)

Despite having core funding, the Western Valley Development Agency (WVDA) closed down in 2005, when several of the constituent municipalities withdrew the funding needed to receive matching funds from provincial and federal agencies. (For details, see chapter 19.) In terms of the relationship between WVDA and the local library, two factors seem to have limited the interaction between the two: (1) the state of libraries in urban versus rural/remote areas, and (2) the reliance on one individual's time and commitment. The WVDA shared with K-Net the poor state of library services that so often prevails in rural or isolated geographical areas. This situation makes it hard for libraries, which are already underfunded, to find the resources they need to take on additional endeavours. At the same time, reaching out to other community organizations is critical to fulfilling the needs of the residents in such areas, and for making the best of what can be a challenging situation. In the case of the WVDA, once again a single individual acted as a bridge between the CN and the library. In this case, a librarian became involved in the CN efforts and was able to maintain a working connection between the two, until funding problems forced the WVDA to shut down. The benefits of this bridging were mutual. It conferred a deeper understanding of the commonalities between CNs and libraries, and it educated the users and staff of each about the resources and services available and delivered by the other. Such a rapprochement also demands, and thus encourages, a certain amount of creativity, in the use of space, for example, or in the delivery of services. However, on the down side, much rested upon the shoulders of one individual, which is inherently a precarious arrangement. If that individual were to leave, the relationship obviously would be jeopardized.

Communautique

Of all the CRACIN case study sites we examined, Communautique is the only one that was not involved with libraries. The Communautique team partnered with various other CNs and agencies, but this did not include the public library, despite the organization's strong emphasis on civic engagement (*l'Internet citoyen*) and a focus on using ICTs to empower citizens. As in the case of VCN and, to a certain degree, St. Chris, there was a sense that the mission of the CN and that of the library were complementary but essentially different, that their funding models differed, and that the institutional structure of the library system did not lend itself to the ways and practices of the CN. In our discussions with Communautique members, we noted a set of assumptions on the part of the Communautique team regarding what it is that libraries "do," with library practices viewed as distinct from the mode of operation of the CN. There was also a sense that libraries existed in a parallel but separate world from Communautique and other CNs. In this case, these perceptions may have hindered any potential for creative collaborations between the two entities. It is also possible that librarians harboured their own misconceptions about Communautique, although we did not speak to any librarians (as none were identified).

The Alberta Library Project

Perhaps the most concrete example of the potential of libraries to support community networking was found in the CRACIN case study titled "The Alberta Library and the Social and Organizational Implications of Broadband in Canadian Public Libraries." This research suggests that public libraries are moving beyond their roles as simple information providers to become places where communication, interaction, and social exchanges occur. The study, in which four rural public libraries took part, involved an innovative pilot project designed to demonstrate the possible uses of video conferencing technology in library settings. The project focused on the role of oral history in the preservation of community memory, in this case through intergenerational storytelling sessions aimed at Grade 3 children, some of whom participated in the sessions from remote locations, via video conference (Adria et al. 2007; Adria and Parrish 2005; University of Alberta 2004). In addition, through interviews with librarians and community members, the Alberta Library Project team was able to explore the perceptions of local community members regarding the place of new technologies in the delivery of library services. They discovered a mix of welcoming and unwelcoming attitudes, which suggests the areas in which barriers exist that will need to be overcome. (For analysis, see chapter 18.)

Although in this case local libraries collaborated with schools, rather than with existing CNs, the study has positive implications for the role of libraries in community networking initiatives. First, social capital might be generated through the development of new partnerships, formed through the use of broadband and other ICTs such as video conferencing. Second, a vast landscape such as Alberta's, which includes extensive rural areas, calls for enhanced cohesion and uniquely situates the public libraries, which are attempting to fulfill the needs of diverse users—often the most marginalized. Finally, engaging children in storytelling and allowing them to interact both with each other and with the storyteller by means of video conferencing promises to foster social inclusion. The case study richly illustrates how public libraries can harness the power of ICTs in novel ways both to provide traditional services, not only to disadvantaged users but to the entire community, and to build bridges among communities that are geographically distant from one another.

LESSONS LEARNED

The brief overview above of the literature on public libraries' involvement in community development and on community networks points to various issues that were subsequently examined in the context of the CRACIN case studies. As we have noted, because a relationship with a public library was not one of the criteria by which CRACIN case study sites were selected, there are limitations to these findings and how they may be generalized. Along the way, however, there were some lessons that could help funding agencies and policy makers alike to ensure that a community-based project will be carried out in a way that optimizes its chances of success. The overarching question concerns the prospects for future co-operative efforts between libraries and CNs.

Schuler and others have argued that CNs and libraries can work together to develop training programs, public access approaches, forums and roundtable discussions, advocacy positions, and policy recommendations. Schuler (n.d.) states that CNs and libraries should work together "to help do with electronic information and communication what the public library has done with print media," in order to safeguard public spaces and resources on the Internet. Citing Joan Durrance, Bajjaly (1999) suggests the following ways that libraries can share their expertise and skills with CNs:

- Librarians' ability to organize and catalog information for more effective retrieval
- Needs assessments of the community needs and experience in addressing the everyday life information needs, uses, and practices of various user groups (i.e., youth, seniors, immigrants, professionals, etc.)
- Skills in volunteer management
- Expertise in policy development
- Experience with collaboration (e.g., public library systems' rotating collections).

In addition, some lessons can be drawn from the CRACIN case studies. As the K-Net example illustrates, in remote and isolated communities, where no physical library exists, there may be opportunities for CNs to take on some of the traditional roles of libraries. As Shade (1999) reminds us, CNs are, by nature, sites for the exchange of information: they are "local systems, run by local people and organizations, utilizing local resources to meet local communications, educational, social, and economic needs." Funding programs could support such efforts by hiring librarians, archivists, or other information professionals to help CNs organize their databases, collections, classification schemes, and finding aids, so that these resources will be more easily accessible to users. Librarians could also work with CN practitioners to teach information literacy skills to community members to support their search for reliable online information. Furthermore, in many cases, CNs can contribute to keeping the collective community memory alive by archiving local materials and information pertaining to the history and fabric of the community. Librarians and CN staff could extend these opportunities in an urban setting through outreach to particular communities, especially vulnerable ones such as the urban poor, immigrants, seniors, youth, children, and small business entrepreneurs, who need access to a range of resources and services.

It seems likely that both libraries and CNs could benefit from each other's "branding." While some may perceive the dogged association of public libraries with print and books (Online Computer Library Center 2005), no one can argue with the "permanence" of their institutional status in society. It is possible that more formal associations between libraries and CNs could revive both. In the case of CNs, a home or at least some kind of physical presence in the library might provide the sort of public visibility that many have suggested is needed to set CNs apart from commercial service providers (Carroll and Rosson 2003; Shade 1999).[5] In turn, public libraries might benefit from the technology skills of community networkers, from more formalized ties with community organizations, and with access to digital information and services channels and distribution mechanisms. (Only slightly more than half of all respondents in a 2005 survey by the Online Computer Library Center were aware that public libraries provided remote access to electronic resources.)

As we have seen, co-operation between CNs and libraries has often been instigated by a committed individual—from the library, the CN, or both—who reaches out to the other side and acts as a bridge between the two worlds. More often than not, it is through these personal connections, rather than through more formal organizational design, that a relationship develops. However, these kinds of partnerships are inherently somewhat fragile, as they may be jeopardized by events in the personal life of the key individual(s)—loss of job, changing circumstances such as a move, death, or promotion, sacrifices in other aspects of one's life, burnout, and so on. In this regard, there is a need for longer-term planning to sustain these ties and types of collaborations.

In order to serve and meet the community needs, libraries and CNs need to recognize each other's potential as partners. One way for CNs to make their connections with local communities more explicit and to distinguish themselves from commercial providers is through stronger ties with libraries. To be more active in the community networking movement, libraries could broaden their scope and the nature of their involvement in community-based initiatives. They could rethink how they can best reach out to their constituency, even seeing themselves as engaging in "community-based development," and keep up to date with community members' needs, including directing them to other initiatives established by community networks. In addition, more awareness and renewed skills need to be taught to information professionals to enable them to work more closely with other community development professionals, practitioners, and members of the community.

NOTES

1 In the context of large urban centres, however, revisionist historians understand "the history of public library development within the history of the development of modern industrial capitalism" and the processes of institutionalization and professionalization that led to the formation of a middle class (Christine Pawley, "Foreword," in Garrison 2003, xxvii).

2 The 1990s in Canada also saw the injection of federal government funding to bridge the digital divide in the Connecting Canadians initiative. See chapter 1 for more details.

3　The reference, made by David Levy in "Cataloguing in the Digital Order" (http://www. csdl.tamu.edu/DL95/papers/levy/levy.html), is to Roger Chartier's *The Order of Books* (1994).

4　The full set of equipment included a computer station, an all-in-one colour laser printer and scanner, a thermo book binder, a do-it-yourself (DIY) book binder, a prototype of a DIY book scanner, portable e-tablets, and associated publishing and editing software.

5　As a possible model for CN presence in libraries, consider a recent initiative funded by Citizenship and Immigration Canada called the Library Settlement Partnerships (LSP), which places settlement workers in public libraries across the province of Ontario to provide services to new immigrants. See http://www.lsp-peb.ca/ for more information.

REFERENCES

Adria, Marco, with Lisa Grotkowski, Huijie Feng, Dan Brown, Cathryn Staring Parrish, and Lantry Vaughan. 2007. Talking about technology adoption in the public library: Final report. http://archive.iprp.ischool.utoronto.ca/publications/Adria_CRACIN-ASRA_ Report.pdf.

Adria, Marco, and Cathryn Staring Parrish. 2005. Community videoconferencing and Alberta public libraries. Presentation at CRACIN Workshop no. 3, 25–27 February.

Anderson, Sandra, and Heidi Julien. 2003. The public library in "Connecting Canadians." *Canadian Journal of Information and Library Science* 27(4): 5–29.

Bajjaly, Stephen T. 1999. *The community networking handbook.* Chicago: American Library Association.

Berman, Yitzhak, and David Phillips. 2001. Information and social quality. *Aslib Proceedings: New Information Perspectives* 53(5): 179–88.

Buschman, John. 2005. Libraries and the decline of public purposes. *Public Library Quarterly* 24(1): 1–12.

Caidi, Nadia, and Danielle Allard. 2005. Social inclusion of newcomers to Canada: An information problem? *Library and Information Science Research* 27(3): 302–24.

Caidi, Nadia, and Margaret Lam. 2011. Reading in First Nations and the On-Demand Book Service. In *iConference '11: Proceedings of the 2011 iConference* (8–11 February, Seattle, WA). New York: ACM, 2011.

Caidi, Nadia, and Brian Walmark. 2007. Developing an on-demand book service for First Nations communities in Northern Ontario. Background paper prepared for the CRACIN Final Workshop, 20–22 June, Montréal. http://meeting.knet.ca/mp19/file. php/20/Library/Caidi_Walmark_ODBS.pdf.

Canada. Privy Council Office. 2004. Speech from the Throne to open the first session of the 38th Parliament of Canada. 5 October. http://dsp-psd.pwgsc.gc.ca/Collection/ SO1-1-2004-1E.pdf.

Carroll, John M., and Mary Beth Rosson. 2003. A trajectory for community networks. *The Information Society* 19(5): 381–93.

Chewar, C. M., D. Scott McCrickard, and John M. Carroll. 2005. Analyzing the social capital value chain in community network interfaces. *Internet Research* 15(3): 262–80.

Chien, Elise. 2005. Involving and informing newcomers online: Users' perspectives of settlement.org. MA thesis, University of Toronto.

Cisler, Steve. 1994. Community networks on the Internet. *Library Journal* 119(11): 22–24.

Côté, Sylvain. 2001. The Contribution of human and social capital. *Isuma: Canadian Journal of Policy Research* 2(1): 29–36.

Curry, Ann, and Alison Curtis. 2000. Connecting to the Internet. *Library and Information Science Research* 22(1): 77–103.

Das, Malabika. 1999. Public libraries and community networks: Linking futures together? *Ariadne* 22. http://www.ariadne.ac.uk/issue22/das/.

Durrance, Joan C. 1984. Community information services: An innovation at the beginning of its second decade. *Advances in Librarianship* 13: 99–128.

Durrance, Joan C., and Karen E. Fisher. 2003. Determining how libraries and librarians help. *Library Trends* 51(4): 541–70.

Durrance, Joan C., Karen E. Fisher, and Marian Bouch Hinton. 2005. *How libraries and librarians help: A guide to identifying user-centered outcomes.* Chicago: American Library Association.

Durrance, Joan C., and Karen E. Pettigrew. 2002. *Online community information: Creating a nexus at your library.* Chicago: American Library Association.

Durrance, Joan C., and Karen G. Schneider. 1996. Public library community information activities: Precursors of community networking partnerships. http://www.laplaza.org/about_lap/archives/cn96/durrance.html.

Edmonton Public Library. 2005. *Library services to Aboriginal peoples: Task force report.* November. Edmonton: Edmonton Public Library.

European Commission. EU Research on Social Sciences and Humanities. 2003. *The contribution of social capital in the social economy to local economic development in Western Europe.* CONSCISE Project, final report. Luxembourg: Office for Official Publications of the European Communities. http://cordis.europa.eu/documents/documentlibrary/82608021EN6.pdf.

Farr, James. 2004. Social capital: A conceptual history. *Political Theory* 32(1): 6–33.

Fisher, Karen E., Matthew L. Saxton, Phillip M. Edwards, and Jens-Erik Mai. 2007. Seattle Public Library as place: Reconceptualizing space, community, and information at the central library. In *The library as place: History, community, and culture*, ed. John Buschman and Gloria Leckie, 135–62. Westport, CT: Libraries Unlimited.

Garrison, Lora Dee. 2003. *Apostles of culture: The public librarian and American society, 1876–1920.* Madison: University of Wisconsin Press.

Greenhalgh, Liz, Ken Worpole, and Charles Landry. 1995. *Libraries in a world of cultural change.* London: Routledge.

Horning, Michael A. 2007. Putting the community back into community networks: A content analysis. *Bulletin of Science, Technology and Society* 27(5): 417–26.

Johnson, Catherine A. 2009. A place where everybody knows your name? Investigating the relationship between public libraries and social capital. *Canadian Journal of Information and Library Science* 33(3–4): 159–91.

Kranich, Nancy. 2001. Libraries create social capital. *Library Journal* 126(19): 40–41.

Kubicek, Hubert, and Rose M. Wagner. 2002. Community networks in a generational perspective: The change of an electronic medium within three decades. *Information, Communication and Society* 5(3): 291–319.

Kwon, Nahyun. 2005. Community networks: Community capital or merely an affordable Internet access tool? *Journal of the American Society for Information Science and Technology* 56(8): 812–23.

Lawlor, Patty. 2003. Ontario's First Nations public libraries: An overview with observations. *Feliciter* 5: 240–44.

Library and Archives Canada. 2004. *Report and recommendations of the consultation on Aboriginal resources and services.* Prepared by Dale Blake, Libby Martin, and Deborah Pelletier. Ottawa: Ministry of Public Works and Government Services Canada.

Longan, Michael W. 2005. Visions of community and mobility: The community networking movement in the USA. *Social and Cultural Geography* 6(6): 849–64.

Mattison, David. 1994. Librarians and the free net movement. *Computers in Libraries* 14(5): 46–50.

McCabe, Ronald B. 2001. *Civic librarianship: Renewing the social mission of the public library.* Lanham, MD, and London: Scarecrow Press.

McCook, Katherine de la Peña. 2000. *A place at the table: Participating in community building.* Chicago: American Library Association.

Mehra, Bharat, and Ramesh Srinivasan. 2007. The library-community convergence framework for community action: Libraries as catalysts of social change. *Libri* 57: 123–39.

O'Brien, Rory. 2001. Research into the digital divide in Canada. http://www.web.net/~robrien/papers/digdivide.html.

Online Computer Library Center. 2005. *Perceptions of libraries and information resources: A report to the OCLC membership.* Dublin, OH: OCLC Online Computer Library Center. http://www.oclc.org/reports/pdfs/Percept_all.pdf.

Pateman, John. 2005. "Reads" or "needs"? The UK debate on the future of public libraries. *Feliciter* 6: 268–70.

Pettigrew, Karen E., Joan C. Durrance, and Pertti Vakkari. 1999. Approaches to studying public library networked community information initiatives: A review of the literature and overview of a current study. *Library and Information Science Research* 21(3): 327–60.

Powell, Alison. 2007. Wi-Fi publics: Community Wi-Fi and the production of community and technology. Paper presented at the Final Workshop of the Canadian Research Alliance for Community Innovation and Networking, Montréal, 20–22 June.

Quarter, Jack. 1992. *Canada's social economy: Co-operatives, non-profits, and other community enterprises.* Toronto: James Lorimer and Company.

Schuler, Doug. n.d. Public librarians and community networkers: A marriage made in cyberspace? http://www.tc.ca/libsnets.html.

Shade, Leslie Regan. 1999. Roughing it in the electronic bush: Community networking in Canada. *Canadian Journal of Communication* 24(2). http://www.cjc-online.ca/index.php/journal/article/viewArticle/1095/1001.

Stevenson, Siobhan. 2008. Public access computing in Canada: A comparative policy analysis of Canada's community informatics and public libraries communities. *Canadian Journal of Library and Information Science* 32(1–2): 1–33.

Strover, Sharon, Gary Chapman, and Jody Waters. 2004. Beyond community networking and CTCs: Access, development, and public policy. *Telecommunications Policy* 28(7–8): 465–85.

University of Alberta. Faculty of Extension. 2004. *Extension R&D report.*

Valentine, Jolie. 2005. Our community, our library: Women, schools, and popular culture in the public library movement. *Public Library Quarterly* 24(4): 45–79.

Viseu, Ana, Andrew Clement, Jane Aspinall, and Tracy L. M. Kennedy. 2006. The interplay of public and private spaces in Internet access. *Information, Communication and Society* 9(5): 633–56.

Woolcock, M. 2001. The place of social capital in understanding social and economic outcomes. *Isuma: Canadian Journal of Policy Research* 2(1): 11–17.

18 THE LIBRARY IDEAL AND THE COMMUNITY NETWORK
Prospects for New Technologies in the Public Library

Marco Adria

With its mandate to provide public, open space for the dissemination of information, through books as well as free access to the Internet, the public library
is well-positioned to support community networks. In very small and rural
communities, in fact, the public library already functions as the centre of the
community network, simply because the public library is *the* institution mandated to provide information to all citizens. Information and coordination of
issues of public interest are managed within the public library on behalf of the
community, through such facilities as bulletin boards that are used for posting meeting times and places, display areas for the distribution of pamphlets
and brochures, and access to public meeting rooms. As broadband arrives in
public libraries in small communities across Canada, the potential emerges
for a more widespread use of technology to expand the library's participation
in and support for the community network.

In this chapter I explore the meaning that community members associate
with new technology use in the public library. Using video conferencing as a
prototypical example of a technology to which people can respond in a concrete way, I seek to gauge the prospects for an expanded public library and an
enhanced community network, especially in rural communities. The case of
video conferencing and its possible introduction into the public library was

developed as a sensitizing concept, or guiding heuristic, for possible use in examining other technologies. Video conferencing is capable of presenting moving images, allows for two-way communication, and is "always on." Community video conferencing could be added to the standard menu of services available in the local public library, just as Internet access was added in the 1990s. Community video conferencing could support programming areas such as storytelling, local and regional history, public services, advocacy/interest groups, social services, and continuing education. Respondents saw potential uses of community video conferencing in the public library but identified social, organizational, and practical barriers to its possible implementation.

The research questions presented here were drawn from an analysis of the historical roots of the public library in North America and assessed in the light of a social constructivist approach to technology use, following the work of Gurstein and others, to develop the community informatics area (see chapter 2 in this volume). The public library is part of the social and cultural context of rural Canada. The interplay of politics, media, and public education in western Canada has been addressed in a number of historical and sociological studies (Faris 1975; Irving 1959; Laycock 1990; Schultz 1964). In an earlier publication (Adria 2010), I examined the roots of the use of ICTs for community development in the context of regional and national identity. Early radio broadcast experiments in western Canada, for example, were concerned with what the new technology of radio—and, by extension, the modern mediated social world—would introduce to the social and political culture of mid-century Canada. E. A. "Ned" Corbett, a University of Alberta educator, was involved in the establishment of the first educational broadcasting station in Canada, CKUA Radio, and, through his later work with the Canadian Association for Adult Education, the *National Farm Radio Forum* and *Citizens' Forum*. Both broadcasts were presented nationally on CBC radio, becoming a notable thread in the social, cultural, and political life of Alberta. Both broadcasts represented experiments in deliberative democracy for community development through what we would now call community informatics. They constituted early efforts to develop new media in ways that would draw on and expand local knowledge.

The public library was the hub of community learning in the early part of the twentieth century, and advocates of "extension" and "adult education" relied on the public library to support community learning (Corbett 1957; Faris 1975). Although highly popular, the model of media use represented by such programs was left aside for another model involving federal regulation of cultural content (Berland and Hornstein 2000). The research questions in this study are informed by the historical context of new media in the public library in Canada. They are concerned with the ways that local communities interpret and respond to new media, especially as those new media may contribute to the codification and expansion of local knowledge.

Respondents in the study were considered in their social context of technological development and use, forming a kind of community of practice. Their responses were interpreted within that framework. The research questions were as follows:

1. *How do library users and decision makers view the use of physical* space *in the public library?* This question was important for an understanding of how a new use of library space might displace an existing use.

2. *How do library users and decision makers view the use of new* technology, *understood as digital information and communication technology (ICT) in the public library?* This question was explored in the context of a broadband network, and specifically in relation to the potential development of community video conferencing.

3. *As technology adoption occurs, what changes in the relative importance of* information-seeking *activities, on the one hand, and* interaction *activities, on the other, are likely to take place in the public library?* This question addressed the primary advance that broadband offers over the dial-up Internet connection, which is the capacity to offer real-time interaction using moving images.

METHODS

Four rural communities in Canada were part of the study described in this chapter, involving about forty respondents representing a cross-section of local residents and officials associated with the public library. Qualitative analysis of interviews and focus groups revealed key ideas and themes expressed by respondents. The primary data collection methods were twenty-six semi-structured interviews and four focus groups (one in each community), which involved a total of forty participants, including librarians, trustees, citizens, and local politicians. The public libraries in four rural communities were selected as research sites. To provide interview and focus-group respondents with a reasonable assurance of anonymity, pseudonyms for these four Alberta communities are used here—Forestville, Prairietown, Collegetown, and Isletown. The four were chosen from the 429 communities to be connected by the Alberta SuperNet, a government-sponsored broadband network. The primary criterion for choosing these four communities was the potential for supporting an investigation into the potential adoption of new technologies in public libraries. In addition, the communities represent differing characteristics in terms of size, degree of technology adoption, and proximity to an urban centre. They range in population from 2,500 to 70,000. Prairietown, the community that has the largest population and is the most technologically advanced, has a branch library in addition to the main downtown library. The other three communities have one public library in the community. In the case of Collegetown, the closest city with a population of more than 100,000 is over 100 kilometres away. The Alberta Library, a network of almost all of Alberta's public and post-secondary libraries in the province, introduced the researchers to the libraries. All four libraries that were approached agreed to participate in the study. Respondents were generally well educated, working in professional occupations and earning moderate incomes. In that sense, they represented the broad middle class that constitutes the largest group of patrons and supporters of the public library (Berelson 1949). Table 18.1 shows respondents by professional or community role and by community.

TABLE 18.1 Respondents by professional/community role and community

Professional or community role	Community
Library staff and board members n = 17	Forestville n = 9
Municipal councillors and administrators n = 4	Prairietown n = 14
Economic development board n = 2	Collegetown n = 9
Social service agency staff n = 7	Isletown n = 4
Other citizens n = 10	Other communities n = 4
TOTAL: 40 respondents	

To provide respondents with a sense of what the abstract notion of "broadband networks" in the community could involve in practice, as well as to develop a level of engagement of both researchers and community members in the issues of interest, the researchers organized two events (one in each of two of the four communities) related to the use of video conferencing in the public library. Some of the interviews and all of the focus groups took place after these two events and therefore allowed respondents to make reference to the practical experience of the events.

First, two video conferenced intergenerational storytelling sessions in Forestville and Prairietown were organized in collaboration with the local public library and a local school in each community. Holding these sessions in only two of the four communities allowed for a reference point of technology use for all four communities: respondents in all four communities could discuss the video conferenced storytelling sessions, even though respondents in two communities would be commenting on events occurring in communities not their own. Each storytelling session was a technology-demonstration pilot project that linked Grade 3 students in Forestville and Prairietown and represented an instance of bringing oral history to life. Oral history resides in the memories of community members, rather than in printed accounts such as books and other records. The project provided an opportunity for community members to separate the opportunities for social interaction that a technology such as video conferencing provides from a concern with the hardware and complexities of the technology.

The relationship of storytelling to the technology of video conferencing is rooted in the continuous and synchronous characteristics of the technology (Bly, Harrison, and Irwin 1993). Video conferencing provides users the ability to present moving images. It allows for two-way communication and is "always on." In the technical sense, video conferencing provides opportunities for the immediate and continuous verbal, nonverbal, and visual cues that storytelling requires. As a consequence, community video conferencing could be added to the standard menu of services available in the local public library. The capacity of storytelling to bridge generations and allow for an exchange of expressed values and felt needs has been explored by sociologists who study aging (Meadows 2004), suggesting that video conferencing and intergenerational storytelling can be combined for community capacity building and for encouraging cultural cohesiveness.

The participative nature of the project ensured the involvement of many community members in meaningful ways. Participants included parents, children, museum staff, private information technology professionals, and local politicians, in addition, of course, to librarians, library staff, and library trustees. Local knowledge creation was at the heart of the project. A local storyteller in each community spoke to the local and remote students (linked by video conference) about their childhoods in Alberta. Children in each location also had the opportunity to greet one another using the video conferencing equipment and to ask questions of the storyteller. Videotaped recordings of the storytelling sessions were created and made available in each public library.

Second, a workshop on the use of video conferencing in the public library was held as part of a regional conference on library technology. Researchers made a presentation on the practical implications of establishing a community video conferencing program in their communities and discussed the potential use of video conferencing in their public libraries. This was attended by approximately thirty community representatives from across Alberta, including librarians, library staff, trustees, and other community representatives. The event widened the regional scope of the potential implementation of community video conferencing.

The next three sections of this chapter present the theoretical approach of the study. Community informatics as an area of study is rooted in an ethos of praxis, with practitioners and scholars concerned mainly with explaining the values by which a social movement may be sustained (Buré 2006; de Moor and Wiegand 2006; Schuler and Day 2004). Schuler (1996) has argued that the public library should continue to be in a complementary relationship to the community network. In chapter 17 of this volume, Caidi, MacDonald, and Chien suggest that the public library and the community network share some characteristics but differ significantly, arguing that the two should be regarded as complementary. In the absence of a particular theory of technology adoption in the public library for the purpose of community networking, three primary areas of related research are examined here: the history of the public library as an institution, the social construction of technology, and empirical studies of the uses of video conferencing.

HISTORY OF THE PUBLIC LIBRARY IN NORTH AMERICA

The contemporary public library's mandate, mission, and operations are rooted in the protocols of community governance established in Boston in the nineteenth century. The "Boston protocols," as they are referred to here, were based on a report by the library trustees in July 1852 (Pungitore 1995). The Boston protocols were adopted by other cities and towns in Massachusetts and then in the rest of the United States and Canada. They have remained relatively constant for 150 years and are often cited in the professional training provided for librarians (Raber 2007). Although they are not widely acknowledged or understood by the public, they provide a historically valid perspective on the evolution of the public library as a significant and politically vibrant organization that is part of the social life of even the smallest of communities in the United States and Canada. The protocols represent relatively simple principles that have had a remarkably potent and durable presence in the development of cultural life in the two countries. They constitute an institutional framework within which community members base their notions of organizational change in the public library. Notable in the protocols are the following components of the public library in modern history: space, technology, information seeking, and interaction. These are discussed in turn below.

Space

The Boston protocols for the public library were permissive rather than prescriptive. They allowed for or anticipated state legislation that would enable geographic districts or local government units to establish physical space in the community that would be devoted to offering the services of the public library. The legislation would not mandate the establishment or maintenance of libraries. However, if a public library were to be created in a particular locale, it was to be considered a "public good" and therefore supported on a continuous basis with local public funding. A public library became recognizable as such, and therefore deemed worthy of public support through tax allocations and other public grants, if it was dedicated to maintaining an information repository and if it was established as a public entity with a policy of universal access. The physical space opened by application of the Boston protocols continues to be modest in comparison to other civic institutions, but the open and free nature of the space, through offering universal access, remains a key characteristic of the public library.

Technology

The Boston protocols did not use the term *technology*, but in establishing a public library a community committed itself to the use of certain technologies—defined as basic tools, such as shelves for books, a cataloguing system, a record system for lending privileges, and the physical premises and systems by which the library's space and collection were secured for citizens' use. These technologies would change through adoption and innovation in subsequent decades. The public library's mandate and mission are broad, and there are many constituencies involved in shaping the organization's operations and its adoption of technology. The Boston protocols required that governance of the institution was to be carried out as a public trust, with a board of trustees mandated to set budget, maintain a staff, and set policy, including policy concerning technology for providing access to the public. A given technology may find wide application in the public library *only* if many individuals and groups arrive at a consensus about the meaning of the technology in relation to the library's mandate. As Servon notes in regard to the movement to establish public Internet workstations in North America, libraries have been early leaders in the "community technology movement" (Servon 2002, 231). However, if libraries have the mandate and the organizational capacity to adopt technology relatively quickly, there are limits to such actions. In part this is because a consensus must be reached among government, library staff, and the board of trustees before a new technology is introduced.

Information Seeking

The public library includes, as a core provision of its mandate, the policy of free access to residents of the jurisdiction that the library is chartered to serve. Access to the library is in significant part maintained for the purpose of finding information. Public libraries may provide the context for digital genres by the organization of materials (for example, displaying selections and bibliographies prepared by librarians) and by making available information and training materials related to digital literacy, that is, the skills needed to find and interpret digital information (Pawley 2003).

Interaction

The Boston protocols stated that the public library should have an educational purpose (Pungitore 1995, 17), and this implies something more than information seeking. Interaction has been part of the library's mandate from the beginning, and such a change would be a shift relative to other activities, rather than a new activity. The status of interaction has remained equivocal for a century and a half. Recently, Marcum (2002) called for a move from the concept of the library as a centre for information literacy, which he sees as overly broad and too firmly rooted in the information-system paradigm, to what he calls the library as a "discovery system," or the "learning library."

THE SOCIAL CONSTRUCTION OF TECHNOLOGY

Technology is adopted and used through a process that has come to be known as the social construction of technology (Bijker, Hughes, and Pinch 1987). In this view, the intrinsic properties of a technology are not the only means by which its adoption may be explained or predicted. Instead, relevant social groups contribute to the meaning that is eventually associated with a technology. These groups enjoy "interpretative flexibility" (Bijker 1995). They make judgments about how a technology is to be interpreted and what meanings should be ascribed to it. Interpretative flexibility decreases when the meanings ascribed to a technology become less ambiguous and more stable. Thereafter, the interpretation of a relevant social group finally becomes dominant, and closure occurs, thereby achieving a consensus about the meaning of the technology.

Professional norms and other cultural factors may influence the meaning that a technology assumes within a given organization. The purpose of a given technology can vary significantly, even within the same kind of organization. A Swedish study showed, for example, that, following from professional norms, social workers viewed information technologies as an "administrative evil." They therefore ignored the many functionalities of a new groupware system that had been promoted by the manufacturer and endorsed by management, preferring to use only the email function (Henfridsson 2000; see also Barley 1986).

VIDEO CONFERENCING

Video conferencing is a technology-mediated form of communication involving voice, video, text, and graphic data, which are exchanged electronically by participants at geographically dispersed locations. Many studies have demonstrated the uses, advantages, and disadvantages of video conferencing (Campbell 1997). Much of the literature on video conferencing is concerned with formal settings, such as business meetings. The informal settings represented by uses within the public library have not been examined in a systematic way. Tovey (2007) notes that the use of video conferencing in the library represents a competency that should be developed. However, the literature suggests that video conferencing should be viewed as a structuring technology, in that it will shape the uses and public image of the library. Through pilot programs and careful study, the potential use of video conferencing should be explored before full implementation is considered.

Uses

Video conferencing usage is continuing to grow in organizations because of the increasing globalization of commerce and the geographical dispersion of business units and customers, with the concomitant need for groups of people within these dispersed settings to work together in an effective and timely fashion. Svenning and Ruchinskas (1984) note that if video conferencing is to be adopted as a valid communication medium, there must be acceptance by both the organization and the individuals within the organization. Distance learning has been noted as an important use of video conferencing in the public library (Chandler 2001), which confirms the relevance of the concept of the "learning library."

Advantages and Disadvantages

A video conferencing system uses video images as well as sound to duplicate as closely as possible the experience of face-to-face meetings without imposing the burden of travel. In a video conferenced meeting, participants can see not only the reactions of their colleagues but also pictures, graphs, and three-dimensional objects, as they would in a traditional face-to-face meeting. Research suggests that as communication bandwidth narrows, as in video conferenced versus face-to-face meeting environments, a feeling of contact or social presence decreases and communication is likely to be best described as less friendly, impersonal, business-like, and depersonalized (Hiemstra 1982; Williams 1978). Within organizational and business contexts, there have been attempts to try to introduce or encourage the use of informal factors such as "small talk" and nonverbal language (Bly, Harrison, and Irwin 1993; Fish, Kraut, and Chalfonte 1990; Fish et al. 1992; Fish et al. 1993; Isaacs, Walendowski, and Ranganathan 2002; Landauer and Kraut 1990). The findings of research undertaken in organizational settings cannot be reliably generalized to other contexts such as public spaces. However, the benefits identified by research under favourable organizational conditions indicate that (1) meetings are shorter, as people tend to concentrate specifically on the task at hand, (2) meetings are more task-oriented, (3) meetings are better structured, (4) meetings are more orderly, even though less hierarchically organized and less status oriented, (5) there is generally more equality of participation, and (6) more opinion exchange occurs and persuasion is more successful.

In sum, concepts were drawn from the social and organizational structure of the public library and from a theory of human action involving the interpretative flexibility surrounding technology adoption. The Boston protocols constitute the public library's basic social dimensions of space, technology, information seeking, and interaction. The theory of the social construction of technology suggests that individuals and groups establish the meaning of a technology through discourse, and discourse provides the basis for the potential adoption of technology. Video conferencing offers a mode of interaction in which task completion may be enhanced, while certain communicational aspects of the context are reduced.

CODING AND ANALYSIS

The hermeneutic circle, which gives attention to the relationship of interdependent parts to the whole that they form, is a key principle in interpretive studies (Klein and Myers 1999). The hermeneutic process has been described in relation to Miles and Huberman's (1994) principle of alternating between cultivating theoretical concepts and returning repeatedly to what research subjects have said. In this way, the abstract concept of the adoption of technology in public libraries, which involves the social construction of technology as a fundamental theory of human action, is considered in a way that allows for potential generalization. In the study present here, the hermeneutic circle was developed through attention to the relationship of the theoretical perspectives of the transcripts through successive stages of analysis. Data analysis therefore proceeded in a tandem relationship with the activity of data collection, allowing each to inform the other. The analysis was carried out iteratively, tacking between examinations of data and development of a conceptual framework. In this hermeneutic process, analysis of respondents' statements corresponded to the *parts* of the emerging conceptual framework, while theoretical interpretations corresponded to the *whole*. The conceptual framework was structured according to the dimensions of the worldview associated with communities of practice: knowledge, values, meanings, assumptions, beliefs, and practices (Pawlowski and Robey 2004; Wenger 1998). Transcripts were coded according to rubrics corresponding to these dimensions, which are the *etic* level of the analytical coding system, corresponding to the "outsider's" point of view, which is that of the analyst.

The second level of analyses of respondents' statements is the *emic* level, or the "insider's" point of view. These indicate the division of the rubrics into subcategories representing the possible means by which a new technology might change the management, practices, and status of the public library in the community. The first three emic subcategories are space, technology, and information seeking. These subcategories correspond to the main elements of the public library as an organization and are abstract expressions of the Boston protocols. The remaining three subcategories related to *interaction* are based on the work of Lyytinen and Hirschheim (1988), who suggest that any information system provides three opportunities for accomplishing discursive action:

1. Establish *new channels* for communication (e.g., email made available using Internet stations in the library)
2. *Redistribute access* to existing information (e.g., allocating some portion of a video conference facility for the use of the disabled)
3. *Provide new information* that can act as "data" or "warrant" in a discourse (e.g., subscribing to an e-periodical on environmental issues that is used by community groups involved in advocacy).

Analysis of the data involved three steps. First, the audiotapes from the interviews were transcribed and notes made following an overall review of the transcripts. Second, transcript coding was carried out by the researcher and two research assistants. Third, a weekly discussion of the research team took place over a period of twelve weeks as coding proceeded, during which themes were identified and potential data representations considered. Data representation involved linking themes in a relationship of possible meanings and was accomplished through the use of graphical text boxes and arrows. The researcher had several opportunities to scrutinize the emerging themes and their relationships to one another (Miles and Huberman 1994).

The results of the study, which are presented in the next four sections, are organized according to the following themes, which were identified through transcript analysis: library space as an ideal, using technology to expand the library's space, and opportunities for information seeking and interaction in the library.

LIBRARY SPACE AS AN IDEAL

Ideal of the Public Library

In discussing the potential use of technologies such as video conferencing in the public library, respondents described the community use of library space as an ideal. The ideal of the public library was discussed in terms of three characteristics of the public library: Its capacity to address a wide range of public demands and needs, the perceived limitless range of activities that take place or could take place in the library, and the size, nature, and purpose of the library space.

Respondents described the library as a community-based organization that serves a diverse set of interests and a diverse range of people. A social service worker in Prairietown, for example, stated that every community needs a public library in order to serve the many needs and demands of the population. As a user of the public library in Collegetown put it, the public library "provides accessibility in many ways, shapes, and forms to people who don't have it." Respondents suggested that there were almost no limits to what the library did or could do. For example, the same individual stated that the library can provide information about leisure activities as a means of supporting and encouraging such activities: "If you don't have access to the Internet or your email . . . the library is a great place to do that. I've always wanted to know what to do with geraniums in the winter, so people can go to the library and do that. Maybe the gardening club could meet."

The diversity of interests and activities represented by the public library was based not only on what respondents observed actually taking place in the library but also on memories from childhood or youth. Respondents referred to an ideal of the public library, a view they had developed in some earlier stage of their lives (Altman and Low 1992). In their accounts, they compared this ideal to the changes in the library that might follow from the introduction and use of new technology. A manager of a community-based organization in Forestville mentioned the experience of her childhood and youth and that of her social contemporaries: "[For] the friends I know who are really into the library, it was something that they grew up with as being an important place in the community. They knew it was a source of information. If you didn't have it in your own library at home, then it would be a place where you could look for it."

The public library space was reported to be separate in some ways from other spaces, such as the university or school, but in other ways it was described as being related to these other spaces by its purpose of allowing for reflection. Reflection is possible in the public library not simply because of the relative quiet but because of the library's separateness from other spaces and its intimacy. Public libraries are smaller than other facilities, according to the ideal to which respondents referred. A trustee in Collegetown associated the size of the public library with the rural setting of the town, noting that "everyone knows the librarian."

In sum, respondents reported the public library to be a space in which exists an ideal of open and free access and a diverse range of many interests and demands, and in which activities take place involving interaction, as opposed to only information seeking.

A Place for "Other" People

As respondents discussed the potential use of technology in the public library, they created a consistently positive image of the library in the community. This consistency was maintained even in those instances in which the library was not seen as living up to the ideal role and operation of the public library. Respondents chose from among their knowledge stocks in order to select positive or sympathetic comments about the library. This was the case even if they stated, as the mayor of Isletown did, that they were not regular or even occasional users of the library: "[The library] doesn't appeal to me . . . but from the mayor's perspective . . . having a facility like that is incredible. And they continue to grow. We moved them about eight years ago from a space that was about half the size of now, to this space. They have had two expansions since and now are talking about another."

Respondents described the library as an ideal social space, but they often identified disadvantaged individuals and groups, not themselves, as the main beneficiaries of the public library's function. This identification established a limit on the ideal of the public library, since it specified a select group as enjoying the benefits of the public library. When they considered the adoption of new technologies in the public library, respondents stated some measure of approval for new technologies, as part of what may be called a "welcoming" approach, but this support was limited by references to the relatively limited group that would benefit by such technologies. Because the public library is managed, governed, and influenced in its policy by many individuals in the community, it is this wider context of technological development that is considered. Overall, there is a welcoming approach to technology that may be identified, which has contributed to the public library being an early adopter of technology (Servon 2002). However, the attitude to technology on the part of the community is also unwelcoming, and this is related to the community's adherence to a view of the public library as a kind of enchanted space—solitary yet communal (Morrill and Snow 2005), quiet but imbued with the autonomous agency of the patron (Suttles 1972) and with the symbolism of housing and protecting the venerable medium of the printed word, often in buildings of imposing civic architecture (Hummon 1990). As we saw, this view draws on quite durable and long-standing historical roots, as suggested by the enduring application of the Boston protocols.

The town manager in Forestville stated that although other members of his family used the public library, he didn't because he had a computer. It was therefore a place for "other" people. In this sense, the social function of the public library is complementary to the active membership of the community network, which, although in the abstract sense is open to all community members, in practical fact is given life by only a small portion of the population.

Learning and Literacy

In describing the primary role of the public library in the community, respondents referred to the educational function of the library as a broadly beneficial "public good." Indeed, the Boston protocols suggested that education is a key function of the public library. In the early stage of the development of the public library, education departments of government retained oversight of it. Though that structural aspect of library governance has changed, in that public libraries are not generally under the control of departments or boards of education, respondents stated that the main purpose of libraries is to encourage and facilitate learning. The kind of learning that goes on in the public library was diverse, according to the respondents, but the primary kind of learning, and the most appropriate in their estimation, was related to conventional literacy: reading and writing.

Social Levelling and "Filling the Gaps"

Although learning was properly a primary focus of the public library, according to respondents in the interviews and focus groups it has another major purpose. The library was also described as functioning as a kind of social services hub, a place in which "social levelling" may occur. Access to and use of technology in the library should support disadvantaged groups, such as the economically disadvantaged, for example, or those with reduced mobility or vision. One library staff member said: "One library I [visited] the other day is the only public facility in that community. They have a real need for a safe public place for kids to come to and kids who have maybe not the best home lives either. They first started off with just being a warm welcoming place."

In the same way that learning was to be limited by literacy, limits were established for the social-levelling activities in the library. Libraries were intended to "fill the gaps" in society, that is, to contribute to only selected social-levelling activities. In turn, the selection of these activities was to be accomplished by reference to literacy as the primary function of the library. The library in Prairietown, for instance, has its own family literacy department, which maintains relationships with social service agencies. Literacy was linked to wider social and economic needs that the library was reported to be in a good position to address. One social service worker said that the library is for kids who are learning about the written word and its relationship to the spoken word: "I encourage my clients to go and utilize [library] programs because they are really good. Children interact there in their age group and read the story or they hear the story to be read to them or do some other activities."

In summary, when respondents considered the space of the public library in relation to the adoption of new technologies, they reported on the ideal of a free and open space in which universal access to the citizenry is assured and a broad range of activities is to be encouraged. Learning and social levelling were two important means by which the public library accomplishes its socially progressive goals. Having described and endorsed a broadly inclusive space for the public library, respondents used literacy and the filling of gaps as a discursive means of limiting the purposes for which technology might be used in the public library. As a complement to the community network, the public library may therefore be in a good position, in terms of community views, to encourage and provide opportunities for interaction and learning through the use of video conferencing and other technologies and to contribute to social levelling.

USING TECHNOLOGY TO EXPAND SPACE IN THE PUBLIC LIBRARY

The welcoming approach expressed by respondents extended to the virtual spaces opened up by the Internet workstations and information databases available in the public library. However, concern was expressed that some activities involving interaction using technology (exchange of messages via email, for example) were not fulfilling the proper role of the public library, which was to provide information. A library employee in Isletown put it this way: "The teenagers are doing the informal chatting and the emailing and to me that's more recreational, which is a perfectly valid function in the library, but I guess I look forward to it being more truly informational."

However, this was not exclusively the view that respondents provided. In Centretown, which was the largest and most technologically advanced of the four research sites, the executive director of the local museum stated that libraries had an obligation to introduce and encourage technological literacies: "I think the public library here generally has a responsibility to bring a whole range of knowledge and information to make it acceptable to the community. . . . That's meant the traditional means of information, like books, but it also now means a variety of other ways of making information available to people."

Professional librarians, because of their training, education, and professional norms, may be expected to be supportive of unconventional access to knowledge and interaction in the public library. Other respondents consistently invoked conventional literacy as a means of limiting the adoption of technology in the library. To explain the resistance to developing technological literacies in the public library, the historical place of the library must be considered. For respondents, the "story" of the public library in their community and on a personal basis began in childhood and youth. At that time, books were the symbol of the enchanted space of the public library. Given the sometimes romantic tinge to respondents' narratives, it is perhaps not surprising that moving away from books and conventional literacy was seen as undesirable, or at least difficult to imagine or justify.

COMMUNITY OPPORTUNITIES FOR INFORMATION SEEKING IN THE PUBLIC LIBRARY

Social Context

Respondents stated that information seeking could be enhanced through the use of ICTs. A member of the public library board in Collegetown said that the library should adopt "technology to access information at the library or possibly from the library or maybe from their business. They would be able to connect to the library right from there and maybe they could even get some kind of help directly online or directly over voice, voice over IP, from the library staff."

As with the themes of learning and social levelling, respondents limited the use of information technology by referring to the social context of the public library. The economic development officer in Isletown, for example, linked the passage of time to the library's inability to provide the information people need: "I don't have kids at home anymore, but when they were at school, the library was one of the tools used, although as they got higher in their education, they turned more to the Internet for research. There just isn't the capacity in rural libraries to provide the resource material they need."

In other words, the public library was for certain kinds of information, but not for all kinds of information. The social context of the public library was limited, in that it shapes the kind of information that should be made available. Respondents identified information that would be of interest and use mainly to disadvantaged groups as particularly relevant to the public library's information resources.

Decommodification and Interlibrary Sharing

As respondents considered the potential adoption of technology in the public library, they referred to the library's traditional function in taking information, knowledge, and cultural products "out" of the economic market. The process of decommodification was linked to the character of the public library as a free and open space and not to the influence of new technology. In decommodifying information, knowledge, and cultural products, the public library was able in part to fulfill its mandate for social levelling. An additional aspect of decommodification that the library accomplishes is as part of a network of libraries in the region and beyond. Respondents noted that the broader access represented by interlibrary sharing was part of the appeal of the public library. The director of a social service agency in Forestville stated that sharing through libraries made information more accessible. When she was seeking a book, "[librarians] might not have it in the library but they can bring it in and that is really valuable."

COMMUNITY OPPORTUNITIES FOR INTERACTION IN THE PUBLIC LIBRARY

Interaction in the public library is facilitated and encouraged in part through the information technology of the public library. The three kinds of interaction opportunities that technology provides are new information channels (for example, video conferencing), redistribution of access among users (that is, the enfranchisement of groups that previously did not have access), and new information. In discussing the opportunities for interaction in the public library, respondents suggested that the first and third of these opportunities, *new information channels* and *new information*, would be desirable outcomes of the adoption of a new technology. These channels and information would be for everyone. The theme of the universality of the library's audience and group of users was given support in suggestions that the library should be "more proactive . . . so that [it is] available for everybody."

However, as they described the new information channels and information that the public library could make available, respondents emphasized the second of the opportunities for interaction, that of *redistribution of access*. Redistribution of access means a reconfiguration of an existing pool of resources, in this case the public library's space, technology, information seeking opportunities, and interaction channels. In adopting a technology, the public library would, in broad terms, move access from an existing group of users to a new group, primarily groups considered disadvantaged in some way. Respondents did not state directly and explicitly that redistribution was desirable. Instead, the analysis of the transcripts revealed two clear, separate, and related views. The first was that the scope and scale of the public library in the community should remain the same. In other words, its budget and resources should not significantly be increased. Second, any technology that would be adopted, such as video conferencing, should be provided primarily for the benefit of the disadvantaged, or groups that did not now have access to the technology. The list of the groups to which access could be redistributed was long, but included Brownies, families involved in home-schooling, literacy programs, and the schools. One library staff member said: "[Using technology,] there is potential for classes. . . . We have home-schoolers all throughout the province, so I could see that that would be something that they would really latch onto."

When they considered new opportunities for interaction in the public library that technology could make possible, respondents referred to reconfiguration—not expansion—of the existing opportunities for interaction. They stated that redistribution of access should be the primary means by which change should take place. In adopting a technology, the public library would shift access from one group of users to another, rather than enhancing or expanding access overall.

PROSPECTS FOR THE COMPLEMENTARY ROLES OF PUBLIC LIBRARIES AND COMMUNITY NETWORKS

As an ideal, the public library was regarded by respondents as a "solution" to a host of "problems" of disadvantaged groups. The problems included access to information and learning opportunities, income disparities, and illiteracy. Through a comparison of the library ideal with actual practices, limits were placed on the extent to which technology could appropriately be used to address these problems. The relationship of the various themes is represented in the conceptual framework provided in figure 18.1. The discursive contradiction represented by the figure reveals that a significant barrier to the wider use of technology in the public library is connected to a view of the public library as not fully a site for interaction and the exchange of ideas but rather primarily as a repository for the printed word and for information seeking. This is a barrier to immediate collaboration between the public library and the community network. The purpose of identifying discursive contradictions is in part to uncover them for actors within and outside the research site as a means of encouraging further dialogue and possible change.

FIGURE 18.1 Impact of technology adoption on library practices

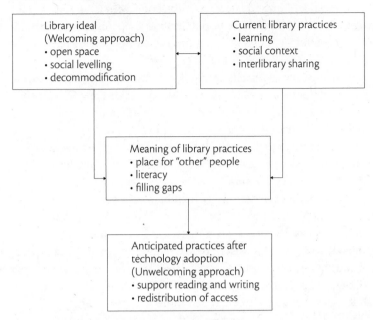

The *library ideal* is suggested by the themes of the free, open space of the library, along with its functions of social levelling and decommodification. The themes of the library ideal are shown in figure 18.1 to be in a state of constant comparison to *current library practices*. These practices involve the use of the library as a centre for learning, by the social context in which information is made available and by the sharing that libraries make possible through, for example, interlibrary loans and the common use of space and technology. It is noteworthy that the library ideal is complementary to and in harmony with the social ideals of the community network (Buré 2006). The conceptual framework presented in figure 18.1 could therefore be the starting point for considering a renewed collaboration between the public library and the community network. Such a collaboration could include the participation of disadvantaged groups as well as active and less active users of the public library, in addition to non-users, that is, those who were not part of the "community of practice" forming the sample for this study.

The comparison of the library ideal to current library practices contributes to the development of the themes identified under the category of the *meaning of library practices*. I have noted that respondents made a distinction when they referred to users of the public library, who were generally described as "other people." Prospective change in the public library's role or activities, including the potential adoption of new technology, would entrench this distinction by allowing the library to serve disadvantaged groups more exclusively. The functions of social levelling and decommodification, seen in another area of the discourse as part of the ideal of the public library, are limited by regarding literacy as the main form of social levelling and learning that takes place in the library and by the selective "filling of gaps."

In emphasizing conventional literacy and services to the disadvantaged, the public library may paradoxically reduce the likelihood that it will strengthen its role as a site within the community network. The community network as a movement affirms such goals as social levelling and decommodification through such initiatives as providing free or subsidized Internet access to community members and by exploring the use of open source software. However, in the public library the *anticipated practices after technology adoption* are limited or bounded by community members themselves. According to community members, technology may be properly used in the public library only when it supports the use of print materials (i.e., reading, writing, and conventional literacy) and to assist in redistributing access to interactive activities in the library, as opposed to expanding them. Respondents explored many existing and potential capacities of the public library in the context of new technologies, but they also identified limits on how technology should be used in the library. As a consequence, my second finding is that assessments of the value of technology adoption in the public library depend on a process by which individuals and groups alternate between what I've called in this chapter the welcoming and unwelcoming approaches to technology.

CONCLUSION

The question of how community video conferencing and other new technologies might find a home in the public library has been considered in this chapter to the extent that a discursive contradiction among the public library's stakeholders has been identified. Although community members expressed limits to the expansion of technology in the public library, two of the communities visited as part of this study subsequently considered expanding the public library space for the community, in part as a response to some of the issues raised in this study. In one instance, a new library building has been constructed. The design of the new space incorporates provision for flexible deployment of technologies in the future.

In order to create the conditions in which community networks may collaborate meaningfully with community networks, community views and opinions of the public library as a free and open space must deepen. They must take into account the practices, processes, and artifacts by which that ideal is maintained, including the ongoing adoption of ICTs for public use.

ACKNOWLEDGEMENTS

The author gratefully acknowledges the contributions of the research assistants who carried out interviews and helped with transcript analysis: Lisa Grotkowski, Huijie Feng, Dan Brown, Cathryn Staring Parrish, and Lantry Vaughan.

REFERENCES

Adria, Marco. 2010. *Technology and nationalism.* Montreal and Kingston: McGill-Queen's University Press.

Altman, Irwin, and Setha M. Low, eds. 1992. *Place attachment.* New York: Plenum Press.

Barley, Stephen. 1986. Technology as an occasion for structuring: Evidence from observations of CT scanners and the social order of radiology departments. *Administrative Science Quarterly* 31: 78–108.

Berelson, Bernard. 1949. *The library's public: A report of the public library inquiry.* New York: Columbia University Press.

Berland, Jody, and Shelley Hornstein, eds. 2000. *Cultural capital: A reader on modernist legacies, state institutions, and the value(s) of art.* Montreal and Kingston: McGill-Queen's University Press.

Bijker, Wiebe E. 1995. *Of bicycles, bakelites, and bulbs: Toward a theory of sociotechnical change.* Cambridge, MA: MIT Press.

Bijker, Wiebe E., Thomas P. Hughes, and Trevor Pinch. 1987. *The social construction of technological systems.* Cambridge, MA: MIT Press.

Bly, Sara A., Steve R. Harrison, and Susan Irwin. 1993. Media spaces: Bringing people together in a video, audio and computing environment. *Communications of the ACM* 36(1): 28–46.

Buré, Claire. 2006. Digital inclusion without social inclusion: The consumption of information and communication technologies (ICTs) within homeless subculture in Scotland. *Journal of Community Informatics* 21(2): 116–33.

Campbell, John. 1997. The impact of videoconferenced meetings on the pattern and structure of organisational communication. *Singapore Management Review* 19: 77–95.

Chandler, Yvonne J. 2001. Reference in library and information science education. *Library Trends* 50(2): 245–62.

Corbett, Edward Anand. 1957. *We have with us tonight.* Toronto: Ryerson.

de Moor, Aldo, and Hans Weigand. 2006. Effective communication in virtual adversarial collaborative communities. *Journal of Community Informatics* 2(2): 116–34. http://www.ci-journal.net/index.php/ciej/article/view/271/226.

Faris, Ron. 1975. *The passionate educators: Voluntary associations and the struggle for control of adult educational broadcasting in Canada, 1919–52.* Toronto: Peter Martin Associates.

Fish, Robert S., Robert E. Kraut, and Barbara L. Chalfonte. 1990. The VideoWindow system in informal communications. In *Proceedings of the 1990 ACM Conference on Computer-supported Cooperative Work* (7–10 October, Los Angeles, CA), ed. Frank Halasz, 1–11. New York: ACM Press.

Fish, Robert S., Robert E. Kraut, Robert W. Root, and Ronald E. Rice. 1992. Evaluating video as a technology for informal communication. In *Proceedings of the ACM CHI 92 Human Factors in Computing Systems Conference* (3–7 June, Monterey, CA), ed. Penny Bauersfeld, John Bennett, and Gene Lynch, 37–48. New York: ACM Press.

———. 1993. Video as a technology for informal communication. *Communications of the ACM* 36(1): 48–61.

Henfridsson, Ola. 2000. Ambiguity in IT-adaptation: Making sense of First Class in a social work setting. *Information Systems Journal* 10(2): 87–104.

Hiemstra, Glen. 1982. Teleconferencing, concern for face, and organizational culture. In *Communication yearbook 6*, ed. Michael Burgoon, 874–904. Beverly Hills, CA: Sage.

Hummon, David M. 1990. *Commonplaces: Community ideology and identity in American culture.* Albany: State University of New York Press.

Irving, John A. 1959. *The social credit movement in Alberta.* Toronto: University of Toronto Press.

Isaacs, Ellen, Alan Walendowski, and Dipti Ranganathan. 2002. Hubbub: A sound-enhanced mobile instant messenger that supports awareness and opportunistic interactions. In *Proceedings of the ACM CHI 2002 Human Factors in Computing Systems Conference* (20–25 April, Minneapolis, MN), ed. Loren Terveen, 179–86. New York: ACM Press.

Klein, Heinz K., and Michael D. Myers. 1999. A set of principles for conducting and evaluating interpretive field studies in information systems. *MIS Quarterly* 23(1): 67–93.

Landauer, Thomas K., and Robert E. Kraut. 1990. CHI in the applied research divisions at Bellcore. In *Proceedings of the SIGCHI Conference on Human Factors in Computing Systems: Empowering people*, ed. Jane Carrasco Chew and John Whiteside, 285–86. New York: ACM Press.

Laycock, David H. 1990. *Populism and democratic thought in the Canadian Prairies, 1910 to 1945.* Toronto: University of Toronto Press.

Lyytinen, Kalle, and Rudy Hirschheim. 1988. Information systems as rational discourse: An application of Habermas's theory of communicative action. *Scandinavian Journal of Management* 4(1–2): 19–30.

Marcum, James W. 2002 Rethinking information literacy. *Library Quarterly* 72(1): 1–26.

Meadows, Daniel. 2004. Digital storytelling: Research-based practice in new media. *Visual Communication* 2(2): 189–93.

Miles, Matthew B., and A. Michael Huberman. 1994. *Qualitative data analysis.* Thousand Oaks, CA: Sage.

Morrill, Calvin, and David A. Snow. 2005. Taking stock: Functions, places, and personal relationship. In *Together alone: Personal relationships in public places*, ed. Calvin Morrill, David A. Snow, and Cindy White, 225–46. Berkeley: University of California Press.

Pawley, Christine. 2003. Information literacy: A contradictory coupling. *Library Quarterly* 73(4): 422–52.

Pawlowski, Suzanne D., and Daniel Robey. 2004. Bridging user organizations: Knowledge brokering and the work of information professionals. *MIS Quarterly* 28(4): 645–72.

Pungitore, Verna L. 1995. *Innovation and the library: The adoption of new ideas in public libraries.* Westport, CT: Greenwood Press.

Raber, Douglas. 2007. ACONDA and ANACONDA: Social change, social responsibility, and librarianship. *Library Trends* 55(3): 675–97.

Schuler, Douglas. 1996. *New community networks: Wired for change.* New York: ACM/Addison-Wesley.

Schuler, Douglas, and Peter Day, eds. 2004. *Shaping the network society: The new role of civil society in cyberspace.* Cambridge, MA: MIT Press.

Schultz, Harold J. 1964. Portrait of a premier: William Aberhart. *Canadian Historical Review* 45(3): 185–211.

Servon, Lisa. 2002. *Bridging the digital divide: Technology, community, and public policy.* Oxford: Blackwell.

Suttles, Gerald D. 1972. *The social construction of communities.* Chicago: University of Chicago Press.

Svenning, Lynne, and John Ruchinskas, 1984. Organizational teleconferencing. In *The new media: Communication, research, and technology,* ed. Ronald Rice, 217–48. Beverly Hills, CA: Sage.

Tovey, Laura. 2007. Build a foundation for the list of competencies. *Library Technology Reports* 42(2): 18–26.

Wenger, Etienne. 1998. *Communities of practice: Learning, meaning and identity.* Cambridge: Cambridge University Press.

Williams, Ederyn. 1978. Teleconferencing: Social and psychological factors. *Journal of Communication* 28(3): 125–31.

PART VII

Public Policy

19 COMMUNITY NETWORKING EXPERIENCES WITH GOVERNMENT FUNDING PROGRAMS Service Delivery Model or Sustainable Social Innovation?

Susan MacDonald, Graham Longford, Andrew Clement

For more than a decade, community networks and the federal government in Canada have been entwined in a relationship of mutual but asymmetrical dependence. In spite of their grassroots origins and nature, as well as the critical stance they tend to adopt toward the federal government's vision for the information society, many community networks have over the last decade come to rely on the federal government for a majority of their funding. For its part, the federal government has offered varying degrees of support for community networking initiatives and, more recently, has relied heavily on community networking organizations to bridge the so-called digital divide by delivering ICT-related services on behalf of the federal government, allowing the latter to achieve its connectivity goals more generally. Since 1995, the federal government has invested roughly $900 million in its various connectivity programs, with community networks and other community-based organizations receiving substantial portions thereof (see table 19.1).

As grassroots, community-based organizations, community networks (CNS) have limited resources and are heavily dependent upon volunteers to carry out their activities. Partnerships with the federal government have injected substantial resources into the CN sector and broadened the size and scope of its activities, which benefits community networks and the communities they serve. Partnerships with community networks are also beneficial to government because they reduce overhead costs, while supporting connectivity initiatives in a climate of budgetary constraint, and represent alternative forms of service delivery for ICT access and training. But such partnerships have also had more ambivalent and unintended consequences, particularly for the community networks.

TABLE 19.1 Federal programs in support of community networking, 1995–2007

Program name	Department	Duration	Funding
Broadband for Rural and Northern Development (BRAND)	Industry Canada, Infrastructure Canada	2002–7	$90,000,000
Community Access Program (CAP)	Industry Canada	1995–2007	$337,000,000
CAP Youth Initiative (CAP YI)	Human Resources and Social Development Canada, Industry Canada	1996–2007	$41,000,000
Community Learning Networks (CLN) Initiative	Human Resources and Social Development Canada	1998–2005	$51,500,000 [a]
Francommunautés virtuelles		1998–2005	$9,000,000
National Satellite Initiative (NSI)	Industry Canada, Infrastructure Canada, Canadian Space Agency	2003	$155,000,000
SchoolNet	Industry Canada	1995–2007	$243,000,000
Smart Communities	Industry Canada	1999–2002	$60,000,000
VolNet	Industry Canada	1998–2002	$10,000,000 [b]
TOTAL			$996,500,000

a This figure represents the Office of Learning Technologies program contribution budgets from 2002 to 2005. From 2003 to 2004, the majority of this funding was directed to the CLN program. In 2006, OLT was integrated into the new Adult Learning, Literacy and Essential Skills Program (ALLESP). See Audit of the Office of Learning Technologies (OLT) Program, October 2006, http://www.hrsdc.gc.ca/eng/publications_resources/audit/2006/sp_664_10_06e/page03.shtml#_4.

b As reported in the Management and Financial Audit of Selected Programs in the IHAB Program (2000), contribution payments to VolNet were made in the amounts of $1.2 million and $4.9 million in 1998–99 and 1999–2000, respectively. The total figure reported here of $10 million for Volnet program spending is an estimate to the end of 2002.

SOURCE: Various Industry Canada, program websites, and news releases.

Like many other organizations in the non-profit and voluntary sector, community networks' dependency on federal government funding has imposed new pressures and obligations, such as performance targets, additional accountability and reporting requirements, and partnerships with the private sector or other community or government agencies. These new pressures put considerable strain on the organizational development, human resources, autonomy, and governance of community networks. In this respect, the experience of community networking organizations mirrors that of others in the non-profit sector (Scott 2003).

In this chapter we explore the nature and extent of federal government support for community networking initiatives in Canada over the decade of the 2000s and shed light on community networks' experiences with federal funding programs in terms of the latter's impact on their activities, accomplishments, and organizational development. Focusing on the experience of six of the CRACIN case study organizations, the findings presented here are largely based on a series of semi-structured interviews with key informants in senior administration positions in community networking organizations who have had significant experience with federal ICT funding programs as well as in partnering with the federal government to deliver ICT services in community settings.

UNDER STRESS: THE EMERGING IMPORTANCE AND INCREASING PRECARIOUSNESS OF THE VOLUNTARY AND NON-PROFIT SECTOR IN CANADA

Community networking organizations are part of Canada's broader voluntary and non-profit sector,[1] the growing economic and social importance of which has only recently been recognized. The sector comprises roughly 160,000 charitable and non-profit organizations that together employ over one million Canadians, mobilize hundreds of thousands of volunteers, and generate $77 billion in revenue (Goldenberg 2006). Until recently, however, little was known about the importance of the non-profit sector and its impact on communities. The sector creates employment and delivers programs and services that contribute to community economic and social development, encourage civic participation, and enhance local quality of life and well-being. Furthermore, in the context of the past decade of government program cuts and downloading of costs onto local governments, the non-profit sector plays an increasingly important role in the delivery of public services, providing innovative and locally sensitive solutions to problems faced by communities (Goldenberg 2006). Yet the sector's increasing role in delivering public services has been accompanied by increasing accountability and responsibilities that have taxed the resources and jeopardized the sustainability of community organizations.

The rising importance of the community non-profit and voluntary sector has been due in part to a significant restructuring of government programs and services along neoliberal lines. Under growing fiscal pressure in the early 1990s, the federal government began to look for ways to control costs and reduce its chronic deficit. As part of a major restructuring of public administration and the civil service in Canada, the federal government began to experiment with alternative models of service delivery, including contracting out to both the private and non-profit sectors (Tupper 2001). In the case of the latter, governments at both the federal and provincial levels sought to off-load the delivery of employment, social, and health care services (Evans and Shields 1998). Alternative service delivery was promoted by Treasury Board of Canada Secretariat (2002) as a means of controlling the costs of government, but it was also seen as a way to make service delivery more responsive to the needs of clients and communities, while also increasing Canadians' engagement with and involvement in addressing social problems (Ford and Zussman 1997).

For the non-profit sector, the attendant shift in the nature of government spending and the new roles and responsibilities attached to it have been a double-edged sword. While public sector restructuring has in some ways elevated the profile and importance of the sector as a partner in the delivery of services valued by communities, it has at the same time subjected the sector to new and growing pressures and strains. The sector's growing importance to and role within communities as an agent of government services is seldom matched by funding levels or administrative systems and rules that meet its need for long-term stability, cover the true costs of delivering the services they do, and match the organizational resources of typical community organizations (Gibson, O'Donnell, and Rideout 2007; Goldenberg 2006). The nature of funding itself has undergone a significant shift away from core funding and toward shorter-term and more narrowly focused contribution agreements, which involve conditional transfer payments subject to accountability and audit. Increasingly, project funding is in the form of competitive purchase of service agreements, a type of contribution allotted through competitive application processes and designed to fund specific services (Scott 2003).

The shift to short-term, project-based funding has placed significant pressure on the sector and its member organizations, who struggle with the strategic planning and human resources challenges of such an unstable funding and revenue environment (McMullen and Brisbois 2003; McMullen and Shellenberg 2002). Furthermore, organizations face a variety of funding gaps, such as the ineligibility of overhead, maintenance, or training expenses, which leave resource-poor organizations struggling to cover the true but unfunded costs of delivering services. Moreover, at the same time that funding has been reduced or made more tenuous, pressure to meet government-mandated performance targets and accountability requirements have placed additional administrative demands on community organizations. A seminal study of the non-profit sector found that "at a time when it faces increased insecurity about its own funding, the non-profit sector is facing pressures to meet an expanding range of needs and to generally contribute to the strengthening of civic values. The sector is being called on to undertake these tasks in a way that will satisfy public expectations for high standards of accountability" (Canadian Policy Research Networks 1998, 25).

In recognition of the difficulties that the non-profit and voluntary sector faces in responding to the expectations of government and the public, *An Accord Between the Government of Canada and the Voluntary Sector* was signed in 2001. The principles underlying the accord (Canada 2001) acknowledge the value of the voluntary sector to the economy and society by recognizing the importance of building sustainable capacity in these organizations; facilitating close co-operation and collaboration with government; fostering innovation in government and the voluntary sector; providing diverse and equitable access to funding; and promoting accountability, transparency, consistency, efficiency, and effectiveness. Two codes of good practice followed in 2002 as part of the Voluntary Sector Initiative under Chrétien's Liberal government (Canada 2002). Despite such initiatives, however, the non-profit sector continues to be plagued with many of the same difficulties.

Two recent studies in particular confirm the ongoing plight of the non-profit sector in Canada. In the 2003 report *Funding Matters: The Impact of Canada's New Funding Regime on Nonprofit and Voluntary Organizations*, Katherine Scott documents and analyzes the impact of government funding trends over the past decade on the non-profit sector, particularly with regard to the "capacity of organizations to pursue their missions and achieve their sustainability" (Scott 2003, 3). Paradigmatic changes on the funding side include the replacement of core funding for organizations by project-based funding with shorter time horizons, increased reporting requirements, interorganizational competition for service contracts, and the increasing requirement that funding recipients seek out partnerships or submit joint applications. Scott's study (2003, xiv–xv) identified seven major impacts or implications for the health, success, and long-term sustainability of the community-based, non-profit, and voluntary sector as a result of these trends:

Volatility—a situation in which need to diversify funding sources as a result of the withdrawal or absence of core funding produces swings in revenue that affect organizational stability, including the ability to plan and retain experienced staff

Mission drift—a tendency on the part of organizations to adapt organizational missions and goals to conform to narrowly defined funding parameters and government policy objectives, which can lead to loss of credibility in the community

Loss of infrastructure—the frequent result of non-program based, overhead, or administrative costs being insufficiently covered by project-based funding

Reporting overload—the situation in which organizations do not have the administrative infrastructure they need to handle different funder or multiple reporting requirements, which vary in terms of frequency and format

House of cards—the situation in which required partnerships produce interdependencies that are susceptible to collapse if one partner withdraws

Advocacy chill—the situation in which organizations avoid being outspoken so as not to risk negative media attention that could influence funder decisions

Human resource fatigue—a common situation in the non-profit sector in which employees are typically underpaid (in relation to both government and private sector employees), overworked, and stressed because of the precariousness of employment that results from project-based funding with short time horizons.

Scott's findings illustrate the disturbing implications of the neoliberal funding regime for community organizations, in which government funding requirements have increased their burdens of accountability and the challenges of sustainability. The specific implications of and experiences with the new funding regime for community networking organizations in Canada are discussed at length below, in the section "The Funding Experiences of Community Networks."

The second study of relevance is the 2006 report of the federally appointed Independent Blue Ribbon Panel on Grants and Contributions Programs titled *From Red Tape to Clear Results*, written by Frances Lankin and Ian Clark. This study, commissioned by the Treasury Board Secretariat of Canada, made thirty-two recommendations about the federal government's grants and contributions budget, calling broadly for fundamental change in the way government funding programs are designed, managed, and held to account. The report asserts that administration can be simplified *and* accountability can be increased and that sustained leadership is needed at the political and public service levels. However, Lankin and Clark (2006, 6) observe that despite commitments by government for "sustainable multi-year funding, streamlined application processes, and improved consultation," little action to date has taken place.

COMMUNITY NETWORKS AND GOVERNMENT FUNDING IN CANADA: AN OVERVIEW

In Canada, community networking initiatives date back to the early 1970s. By the mid-1990s, thirty-five community networks provided Internet access, ICT training, email hosting, and other services to as many as 600,000 members across Canada (Shade 2002). Community networks take a variety of organizational forms, but typically comprise a few paid staff members, a voluntary board of directors, and a larger group of volunteers who contribute to activities such as training, technical support, fundraising, and content development. Early on, funding and other forms of material support were typically provided through a pastiche of membership fees, cash and in-kind donations, volunteer labour, and equipment donations from corporate benefactors. Early community networks often maintained close ties with public institutions, such as universities and libraries, that shared the former's commitment to universal access to knowledge. (On the relationship between public libraries and CNs, see chapter 17.) Community network ties to the public sector were strengthened and deepened significantly by major government investments in connectivity programs, beginning in the mid-1990s, with dramatic impacts on the nature, budgets, activities, and fortunes of community networking organizations.

For its part, the federal government first demonstrated interest in community networking initiatives in the 1970s, beginning with the Department of Communication's support for the Telidon pilot project, which involved using Videotex technology to create a television-based community information system for home use (Clement 1981; Shade 2002). Federal involvement in community networking increased dramatically in the 1990s with the growing importance of computer and Internet use, culminating in the announcement of the Connecting Canadians initiative in the mid-1990s, including a suite of programs designed to promote public access to the Internet and close the so-called digital divide. Led by Industry Canada, the agenda included initiatives such as SchoolNet, the Community Access Program (CAP), and the Smart Communities program, which aimed primarily at providing technical connectedness to the Internet for underserved areas and populations. Other federal programs have pursued related goals, such as rural broadband connectivity, online training and education, and the development of Canadian content online. Altogether, over $900 million has been invested in these programs since the mid-1990s, providing funding assistance to nearly 10,000 community-based initiatives. (Table 19.1 provides a snapshot of federal programs and funding for connectivity and community informatics initiatives in Canada over the past decade or so. For a complete description of the various Connecting Canadians programs, see Appendix C.)

Community networking organizations were major recipients of federal funding under the Connecting Canadians initiative and became lynchpins in the development and delivery of government-funded connectivity services, including the provision of public Internet access, computer training and technical support, and community-based online content development. The majority of CRACIN case study sites were the recipients of funding through one or more of these federal funding programs (see table 19.2). While the involvement of community networks in the Connecting Canadians initiative has not been without its tensions, particularly around issues of access philosophy, funding, and sustainability, community networks have played a pivotal role in ensuring its success (Moll and Shade 2001). Declining federal government commitment to universal access, and to CAP in particular, has severely affected community networking organizations, in which dwindling and unreliable funds had as of 2002 caused more than 50 percent of the approximately 8,800 CAP sites to close (Moll 2007). In 2010, the future sustainability of the fewer than 4,000 remaining CAP sites was unclear.

TABLE 19.2 CRACIN case study sites and federal funding received

	BRAND	CAP	CAP YI	CLN	FC	NSI	SchoolNet	Smart Communities	VolNet
Vancouver Community Network		X	X	X					
K-Net		X	X	X		X	X	X	
St. Christopher House		X		X					
Communautique		X	X		X				X
Western Valley Development Agency		X	X					X	
SmartLabrador	X	X						X	

METHODS

Our study of government funding of community networking relies mainly on in-depth interviews with key informants and documentation from six CRACIN community partner organizations: St. Christopher House, K-Net, Vancouver Community Network (VCN), the Western Valley Development Agency, Smart-Labrador, and Communautique. The informants were chosen on the basis of their experience as senior managers of non-profit organizations and, in particular, their experience in dealing with a range of government funding bodies and programs. All our informants are well known as strong advocates of the non-profit sector. Janet Larkman was the executive director of the WVDA. At the time of the interview, Maureen Fair was the acting executive director but is now the executive director of St. Christopher House. Sheila Downer is currently the executive director of SmartLabrador, and Brian Beaton is K-Net services coordinator. The interviews are supplemented with findings from CRACIN's national survey of administrators of community technology centres, which included several questions about program funding (see chapter 3 in this volume). We asked interviewees about

- their sources of funding and how well these sources matched the organization's needs
- how well the various funding sources worked together
- the affect of losing core funding on their organization
- their strategies for sustainability
- their experiences with partnerships
- how the Connecting Canadians programs compare to other funding programs.

Transcripts of the interviews were produced from audio recordings and analyzed for common patterns and themes.

In addition, we situate our findings in relation to Scott's (2003) framework for understanding funding experiences and challenges in the non-profit and voluntary sector more generally. While we frame our findings in terms of the seven major impacts of the current funding paradigm identified by Scott (see above), in some cases we expand these themes in order to capture the particular experience of community networks. The CRACIN research builds on Scott's findings by exploring the distinctive organizational impacts on recipients of funds under the federal Connecting Canadians suite of programs. Furthermore, Lankin and Clark (2006) provide guidance in offering promising ways to improve the design, management, and administration of government funding programs in all government sectors. With the Lankin and Clark report in mind, we conclude this chapter with a series of recommendations for the improvement of funding programs aimed at community networking organizations, drawing recommendations from our CRACIN key informants and the results of the CRACIN survey of community network administrators. The following CRACIN community partners participated in this study:

- St. Christopher House, a social services organization serving downtown Toronto
- K-Net, an Aboriginal-owned and -controlled community network that serves sixty remote First Nations communities in Northern Ontario and Québec
- Vancouver Community Network (VCN), the owner, operator, and promoter of a free, publicly accessible, non-commercial community computer utility in the Lower Mainland of British Columbia
- Western Valley Development Agency (WVDA), based in Nova Scotia, which worked on community economic development and local ICT infrastructure projects until its demise in 2005
- SmartLabrador, a regional community-based ICT organization that represents thirty-two communities in rural and remote Labrador
- Communautique, a community-based organization in Montréal that supports community informatics initiatives across the province of Québec.

(For more detailed profiles, see chapter 1 and Appendix A.)

As can be seen in table 19.2, each of the CRACIN community partners received funding from a variety of the Connecting Canadians programs. The single common denominator was that all received CAP funding, which in many cases represented an organization's initial foray into ICTs and/or into the world of government funding. Other factors such as location (rural versus urban), access to resources, organization size, and scope of mission make the experiences of each organization unique. But, in conducting this research, we found that common themes arose, similar to those identified by Scott (2003) to describe the experience of organizations in the non-profit sector more broadly. In the following section we provide illustrations of the particular ways these themes resonate with community networks. Furthermore, we build and expand upon them to inform future public policy as it relates to community-based ICT initiatives.

THE FUNDING EXPERIENCES OF COMMUNITY NETWORKS

Community networks, like most other non-profit organizations, rely on government funding, the goodwill of volunteers, and various partnerships to sustain their activities. Although community networks share many of the challenges identified by Scott (2006), there are some distinctive aspects, such as the scale and focus of funding programs and the nature of ICTs in general, that introduce new levels of complexity for this part of the non-profit sector.

Volatility

Scott (2003) found that non-profit and voluntary sector organizations experience volatility when they are dependent on diverse, and sometimes unreliable, sources of funding. Fluctuations in revenue affect an organization's ability to "provide consistent, quality programs or services, to plan ahead, and to retain experienced staff" (Scott 2003, 4). Community networking organizations dependent on Connecting Canadians programs often fall victim to the kind of volatility in the funding environment that Scott describes. In fact, the very nature of CAP's implementation and administration contributed to such volatility to a considerable degree. One interviewee from an organization with a wealth of federal funding experience stated that the CAP program in particular was "one of the worst examples of federal funding ever." Many of our community partners talked about the stress they experienced when funding did not come exactly when it was needed and expected, with employees often suddenly finding themselves "hanging in limbo." In recent years, CAP funding recipients have been subject to extreme uncertainty in the face of the program's repeatedly rumoured closures and last-minute reprieves, which has become an annual ritual. When new funding is announced, moreover, potential recipients are expected to submit competitive bids for funding that are subject to tight deadlines (Moll 2007).

In the CRACIN national survey of community network administrators, 79 percent (n = 11) reported that their funding was unstable (that is, it was not certain it would be renewed), and 92 percent (n = 12) did not have core funding. Maureen Fair, executive director of St. Christopher House, suggested that cash flow problems are especially difficult for smaller agencies that simply do not have the resources to sustain "activity with months and months [of expenses] uncovered." One survey respondent recounted that "staff at [a] partner organization took out personal loans for their cash-flow projects," echoing a report from the coordinator of the Vancouver Community Network. With more than half of the original 8,800 CAP sites closing because of inadequate funding, these hardships were widespread.

Many community networks expected that the various Connecting Canadians funding programs were designed to work together. For example, the Community Learning Network (CLN) initiative was perceived by many in the non-profit sector as a logical means by which to build upon and help sustain the ICT infrastructure established through CAP funding. However, anticipated synergies between CAP and the CLN programs were largely unrealized because the two programs did not work together. The organizational cultures of the two federal departments that housed the respective programs did not mesh, and neither did their reporting timelines or reporting requirements.

This was the experience at St. Chris, where, Fair commented, despite a good potential fit, "CAP and CLN have been administered by separate federal government departments. While each funding program has its own merits, we could have a more streamlined and efficient way to close the digital divide if funders coordinated amongst themselves more."

CRACIN findings emphasize that a volatile funding environment produces organizations that, while priding themselves on their ability to be flexible, ultimately risk becoming quite fragile. Even K-Net, one of CRACIN's most financially successful community partners, sees itself as vulnerable to the volatility inherent in project-based government funding and what Brian Beaton, K-Net services coordinator, called "the directions" of government, referring, of course, to the government's tendency to change course.

Community networks have developed a number of coping strategies to offset some of the swings in revenue experienced under the existing funding regime. Staff at the Vancouver Community Network and Communautique have deliberately sought to diversify their funding sources across programs and levels of government in order to prevent overdependence on any single funding source (Bodnar 2005; Proulx, Lecomte, and Rueff 2006). K-Net's model for sustainability, meanwhile, involves reliance on the human and financial resources of the communities it serves. In the face of unstable government funding, Beaton said, "[we] can still always go back to our base, which is the communities—the communities are carrying this network."

Mission Drift

One-third of the organizations that Scott studied experienced mission drift, in which governments' targeted approach to funding leads organizations to redefine their organizational goals in order to qualify for grants. CRACIN community partners also experienced this, though "drift" may be too mild a metaphor—in one instance it could even be described as "mission explosion." Two organizations, both with broad regional development mandates, talked about the process of qualifying for large ICT infrastructure grants in the Smart Communities program and the often unanticipated consequences that can result. In one case, the competition for a Smart Communities grant was so fierce that the applicants made what seemed in retrospect to be an unrealistic proposal. Sheila Downer, the executive director of SmartLabrador, the winning proposal in Newfoundland and Labrador, warned: "Be careful what you wish for. We so wanted to be selected as a Smart Community because we saw it as the answer to meet the IT needs of Labrador. . . . But then [when] we got awarded it, we said, 'Oh God, now we have to do what we said we would do.' We had a huge infrastructure component in this program, a huge skills and training component, plus we had an enormous suite of services we had to build."

Similarly, the Smart Communities grant awarded in Nova Scotia to the Western Valley Development Agency (WVDA) had both positive and negative consequences. In the opinion of Janet Larkman, the former executive director of the now defunct organization, winning the highly political Smart Communities program competition contributed to the demise of the organization:

I have no doubts whatsoever that the Smart Community Project was in part instrumental in the ultimate fate of the organization. Probably if that huge wonderful thing hadn't happened, [the WVDA] would probably be plugging along like every other RDA (regional development agency) but, the fact was that the organization did carry on with all of those core mandate activities. ... But it didn't necessarily appear that way because there was this very large, very glittery component related to ICTs that got a lot of media attention, had a lot of money ... [and] staffing.

Larkman describes the process of making applications for government funding programs as "reinvention" and attributes the ability of an organization to secure funding to the maintenance of an intentionally broad mandate. However, given the way the funding programs are designed, achieving a good fit between the parties is an elusive goal. She stated:

Reinvention was something we essentially did every time we put in a proposal. Our mandate was broad enough that we could cover a lot of ground but the reinvention process usually means that it's not 100 percent perfect for either the funder or the fundee in that a lot of times the funding programs that are put out there don't have a perfect match, so an organization comes forward that sort of looks like a match and so well, off it goes—but there's a lot of contortions that have to be gone through in order to get funding, period. It's not easy.

As the WVDA experience illustrates, the challenge of adapting to ever-changing government policy trends and funding priorities can place considerable strain on community organizations as they reinvent themselves to fit within them. One risk of this continuous process of organizational reinvention and repositioning is that community organizations can lose credibility with key stakeholders and clients. This was clearly the case with WVDA. As Peddle also demonstrates in chapter 15 in this volume, the large injection of funding received through the Smart Communities project meant that the organization devoted greater than normal amounts of staff and energy to ICT-related development projects. The organization's municipal partners negatively perceived the focus on ICT projects to be a distraction from their core economic development activities, such as business recruitment and retention. Unfortunately,

WVDA was unable to alter the perception that its core activities had been compromised or to convince their constituents that these activities were, in fact, compatible with ICT projects.

Not all community networks have suffered the same fate as a result of funder-induced pressure to adjust their organizational mission. Northern Ontario's Aboriginal-owned K-Net has managed to skillfully adapt to evolving government funding and policy priorities while maintaining both funder and community support. K-Net administrators attribute the growth and development of the network to a certain "constellation of good fortune," under which the network was able to align its activities with a succession of federal government policy priorities—connectivity, e-government, learning, and health—in order to secure a steady stream of funding and support (Fiser, Clement, and Walmark 2006; see also chapter 14 in this volume).

Loss of Infrastructure

From the standpoint of community organizations, government-funded projects can be both a blessing and a curse, in that the funding frequently does not cover the cost of overhead. As Scott (2003, 14) observes: "With the move to project funding and the tightening of restrictions on administrative costs that are covered by funders, some organizations are losing their infrastructure. They are becoming a series of projects connected by a hollow foundation."

Owing to the nature of the Connecting Canadians agenda, the primary focus of most of the programs, especially those emanating from Industry Canada, is capital investment in ICT infrastructure. Consequently, CRACIN community partners typically had limited access to resources for administrative and human resource costs related to these initiatives. With regard to CAP, for example, little consideration was given to additional expenses related to troubleshooting, maintaining and repairing hardware, Internet service charges, and salaries for staff. The executive director of St. Chris stated: "We were subsidizing CAP with our fundraising dollars." She went on to explain that even when the program was fully funded by Industry Canada, "it would just barely cover staff salaries. . . . The ongoing replacement of computers was hit and miss, so some years we got it, some years we didn't." In the experience of some CRACIN partners that received large grants, the problem of infrastructure is compounded. Receiving in excess of $5 million from Industry Canada programs such as Smart Communities and BRAND requires a comparable administrative infrastructure, large enough to handle the sizable funds received. Larkman, the former executive director of the WVDA and recipient of Smart Communities funds, observed that the money they received was very paperwork heavy, so that means resource and expertise heavy, but [it] also assumed that there would be a huge infrastructure to support it. Like, for example, most programs that we tapped into had no money for the purchase of computers or desks or phones, and most didn't even have money to support phone lines and Internet access and a lot of the overhead things, never mind an office and administration infrastructure and all of that. But because we had core funds, core staff, and we had a big building that we were renting, we had a much bigger capacity to access programs than any organization that didn't have all that infrastructure.

The experience of SmartLabrador, which received both BRAND and Smart Communities funding, was that not enough time was factored into the timeline of the project to permit the commensurate administrative processes to be put into place. This point is linked to Scott's next theme, regarding an overall increase in reporting requirements, which is also the experience of CRACIN's community partners.

Reporting Overload

Scott (2003) notes that the non-profit and voluntary sector is increasingly forced to deal with the inconsistent and competing reporting and accountability requirements of multiple funding bodies, each with its own administrative rules and forms and its own performance measurements, evaluation processes, and reporting requirements and timelines. On the one hand, as noted above, this affects community networks and other small community-based organizations that do not have access to the requisite resources and administrative infrastructures. One CRACIN interviewee echoed Lankin and Clark's 2006 Blue Ribbon report when she observed that "every one of [the funder requirements] was different; there was so much paperwork and there was absolutely no consistency, not within departments, not within programs" and called for "one set of criteria for all programs in terms of reporting." On the other hand, it is the common experience of CRACIN's community partners that large ICT-related grants shifted attention away from managing relationships with their other partners. For example, in dealing with the administration of a $5-million Smart Communities grant, the WVDA's former executive director stated: "For our municipal partners, it was probably extremely difficult for them to understand what was going on because we were answerable to so many different groups who had so many different criteria. So while we were trying to keep our core local funders happy, we were also probably spending more time answering to all of these larger funders." It was, she said, "a paperwork nightmare!"

Again, however, the experience of CRACIN's community partners was not always uniform in this regard. In order to simplify application and reporting processes for funding recipients, for example, the Federal Economic Development Initiative for Northern Ontario (FedNor) provides financial administration support and capacity building to community organizations such as K-Net. Brian Beaton, K-Net services manager, stated: "FedNor paid for an auditor to come in on a quarterly basis to take a look at our program report, our financial reports for five Smart Communities. It reassured the federal government, but what it did was for us as an organization [was that] it allowed us to learn from these accountants, it allowed us to be able to develop the financial systems that could manage these programs on an ongoing basis."

Furthermore, Beaton notes, as a result of this experience, K-Net was able not only to produce its own reports but also to develop a new financial system that was later shared with other First Nations and Tribal Councils as a model. Beaton argued that "if it's kept local, we benefit, everyone benefits [and] then it's accountable." Indeed, the practices of FedNor and other federal regional development organizations were singled out in the Lankin report as examples of "best practices" in the delivery of federal funding programs that should be generalized across government. Such practices, including tailoring reporting requirements to the size and purpose of the contribution and the capacities of the recipient, and the avoidance of excessive or duplicative audits, would provide significant relief to overstretched community networking organizations.

House of Cards

Scott describes the phenomenon of a "house of cards," in which the loss of one contract or partnership can lead to the loss of others, since they are often interdependent. Under such funding obligations, worthwhile community initiatives and organizations can be threatened by the loss of a key partner. Federal funding of community organizations in general, and community networking initiatives in particular, have increasingly mandated the pursuit of partnerships and joint funding submissions, including with the private sector. Both the Smart Communities and BRAND programs, for example, made the development of partnerships with the private sector an explicit criterion for successful applications. While such partnerships can prove fruitful and mutually beneficial, this is not uniformly the case, especially for partnerships in which organizational priorities clash—universal access versus profit making, for example. Partnerships with other levels of government or other community organizations are not immune from such clashes either.

The experience of the Western Valley Development Agency (WVDA) offers a poignant lesson on the perils of partnership. From the time it was created in 1994, the WVDA successfully contributed to the sustainability of its local rural economy by fostering community-based innovation in the face of high unemployment (Peddle 2007). Janet Larkman attributes much of the WVDA's success to its ability to establish and maintain partnerships within the local community as well as with various levels of government. Despite having core funding, however, the WVDA closed in 2005 when several municipalities withdrew the funding the organization needed to receive matching funds from provincial and federal funders. Over the history of the organization, the WVDA had been very successful in attracting ICT-related funds, participating in nearly all the Connecting Canadians programs, including CAP, the Smart Communities Program, and BRAND. Reflecting on these successes with funding and on their results in the community and local economy, Larkman recalled: "We never saw ourselves as being fragile. We had this illusion that the organization was really going to be around for a very long time and was very stable in terms of long-term funding commitments, and all of the ingredients were there to view it as a really stable institution if you will, and it turns out that it wasn't." In hindsight, despite being a core-funded organization, it is clear that WVDA's existence was inherently precarious because it depended for its existence on a system of matching government grants, where the loss of support from one level of government entailed the withdrawal of support by all.

Many of the Connecting Canadians programs required private sector partnerships with telecommunications companies. Some recipients of both Smart Communities and BRAND program funding reported their experiences with private sector partners to be problematic. Private sector and community networks have fundamentally different agendas, which played out in varied ways. In one instance, the recipient of a Smart Communities grant notes that these partnerships were ultimately unsuccessful "in part because their agenda was profit and our agenda was community development, and ultimately they weren't entirely compatible agendas." The profit-driven agenda is illustrated in the experience of SmartLabrador, an organization that desperately wanted to bring connectivity to the rural and remote regions of Labrador. The director of SmartLabrador was told in 1995 by the local telecommunications company, and in no uncertain terms, that "local dial-up access and cellphone services are never going to come to Labrador communities . . . because the business case is simply not there to sustain it." WVDA also experienced difficulty in negotiating and concluding successful partnerships with the private sector. The WVDA eventually withdrew from the BRAND competition, for example, over divergent values and priorities between it and the local private sector telecommunications carrier with whom it would be required to work. The WVDA went on to build and operate a community-owned fibre ring through partnerships with local public-sector organizations, including a local community college.

Advocacy Chill

Scott describes advocacy chill in the new funding paradigm as a tendency for organizations to become afraid to take risks (speaking against government, for example) for fear they will not be awarded funding in the future. Several of the CRACIN community partners are active advocates on behalf of their clients, such as St. Christopher House, which provides opportunities for community members to engage with social policy experts on such issues as income security. However, organizations that depend for their survival on government contracts may understandably be reluctant to "bite the hand that feeds them." Some of our interviewees indicated discomfort with being critical "on the record" about anything related to their funders and the various funding programs. Evidence of this sentiment among community networkers is felt in more formal settings as well. The 2005 Telecommunications Policy Review Panel was the first comprehensive review of Canadian telecommunications policy in fifteen years and provided an opportunity for public input on the future of federal connectivity policy and funding. As Longford, Moll, and Shade demonstrate in chapter 21, there was minimal direct community network involvement in this process. While it is likely that reticence to speak out in such a forum contributed to low participation, it is also clear that government did not encourage communities to participate. Most of the consultation proceedings took place over the summer of 2005, when many people have other commitments, and no funding was made available for citizens or community groups to participate in face-to-face public fora held in Whitehorse, Yukon, and in Ottawa.

Human Resource Fatigue

Project-based funding often barely covers staff salaries, putting pressure on both organizations and staff. Scott (2003, 106) reports that over 90 percent of surveyed non-profit sector organizations were "experiencing greater demands on staff and volunteers related to changes in the funding environment (n = 49)." Both employees and volunteers experience increased levels of stress, a high burnout rate, low wages, and a lack of benefits, all of which affect their quality of life. Human resource fatigue also makes it difficult for organizations to recruit and retain talented staff and ultimately undermines an organization's ability to realize its mission. Organizations are forced to invest scarce resources (human and otherwise) into a time-consuming process of hiring (and in some cases, rehiring) staff on short-term contracts. It is increasingly difficult for non-profit sector organizations to retain skilled staff, such as managers and financial personnel, who may be attracted elsewhere by a more secure and stable work environment. The result is that core or permanent employees often end up "wearing a number of hats" to bridge gaps across the organization.

CRACIN community partners reported similar experiences. Larkman observes that the project-based funding environment can produce competition within an organization such that some staff are left "hanging in limbo" while others have more secure positions. "It was very difficult in that there was definitely sort of a hierarchy," she said. "We didn't want there to be one, but inevitably there were people that realized that their position was very much less stable than [those of] their colleagues." Even in "permanent" positions, stability and adequate financial compensation are hard to find. The CRACIN administrator survey revealed the prevalence of volunteerism, especially at the level of senior management, with 50 percent (n = 7) of all respondents indicating that their positions were either volunteer, part time, or some combination of paid and volunteer. As is frequently the case in the non-profit sector, the core staff often bridge gaps when funding shortfalls arise. One survey respondent stated: "We are the volunteers—we don't have any volunteers outside of staff, spouses. When we are short of funds, we volunteer our time until new funding is found."

There were also some notable differences from other non-profit sector organizations with regards to human resources. For example, 86 percent (n = 12) of CRACIN administrator survey respondents indicated that staff turnover rates were typically quite low, which is the opposite of what Scott found. Low turnover rates can be explained in the three cases where public libraries house community networks, since employees are full- or part-time librarians with relatively secure jobs. But in the majority of cases, CN administrators attributed the low turnover rate of staff, despite low wages and little job security, to the commitment of individuals to the goals of these organizations.[2] Respondents provided explanations that included: "Staff feel a strong connection with the programs and participants," and "Staff strongly endorse the objectives of the network and find the work very rewarding. There is a spirit of striving for continuous improvement."

DISCUSSION

As we have noted throughout this chapter, community networks face many challenges similar to other organizations in the non-profit sector. But there are also some distinct differences, which we summarize below.

First, in many cases, community networks have had better, relatively more generous funding opportunities than other non-profit sector organizations. Except in the case of the notoriously underfunded CAP, most of the Connecting Canadians programs offered substantial sums of money for large infrastructure-focused initiatives. In particular, BRAND and the Smart Communities programs offered millions of dollars in funding with which to build large technical infrastructures in what were often small, rural communities. The experiences of CRACIN community partners WVDA and SmartLabrador speak to the mixed blessings that can result from winning these highly competitive awards. In some cases, organizations made ambitious proposals that ultimately were difficult to realize. In other cases, these technology-focused initiatives appeared to distract organizations from their core goals, causing tensions within organizations and communities. The WVDA's former executive director, Janet Larkman, remarked that in this regard that a lot of energy was spent "managing expectations" of community members, many of whom were disappointed when benefits did not flow directly to them.

Another factor that was characteristic of the Connecting Canadians programs was the expectation by many funding recipients that the various programs were designed to work together by building on one another. This was particularly the case with CAP and the Community Learning Network initiative, in which the former was seen as providing the basic technical infrastructure upon which the latter would build by developing applications to facilitate community learning. While synergies do arise between funding programs, these are often hard won. Considerable effort and skill on the part of community organization are required to knit together the disparate funding regimes into coherent and viable programs on the ground. This also calls for the organization to be locally embedded, especially in terms of partnering connections; Brian Beaton, manager of K-Net, suggested that viability often depends on finding local solutions:

> In my experience, successful community networks tend to require a local champion who has the vision and willingness to include others in the development and ongoing operation of both the infrastructure and applications that address local needs and priorities. With the proper vision and support, the community network usually is able to sustain itself based on the partnerships, resources and opportunities that are shared among the local membership.

Second, community networking and ICT-related initiatives introduce new and unfamiliar levels of complexity to organizations, which can significantly affect outcomes. As we've noted, these funding programs typically offer substantial funds to cover capital expenses. However, with computers and other new forms of technology, rapid obsolescence is a common and ongoing problem, and this fact is not accounted for in the design of ICT-based funding programs. CNs must use their own fundraising dollars to replace outdated computers or rely on donations of used equipment from other organizations.

Furthermore, there are rarely any funds available for maintenance of technical equipment or training of staff.

Finally, in many respects these government-funded ICT initiatives differ from other funding programs because there is a strong experimental element to them, most obviously in terms of the new technologies but in connection with new service delivery models as well. Funding recipients as well as government recognize this to some extent, but there are recurring and so far unresolved tensions over the dual character of federally funded ICT projects, which are at once experiments in socio-technical innovation and a means to provide ongoing services. Fixed-term project funding is appropriate for supporting experiments, but, as noted earlier, it is problematic for dealing with continuing service needs. One CRACIN community partner stated: "There's room for project funding and experimenting, but it's really not fair to turn all funding into special project funding [because] some . . . communities really need . . . some programs just . . . to exist on an ongoing basis and the federal government needs to shoulder that responsibility."

While the experimental nature of funding models for social innovation in the community networking sector is commonly understood, there are crucial aspects of an experimental approach that are missing. One is how "unsuccessful" outcomes are dealt with. The government's emphasis on quantitative methods to measure outcomes in relation to expected performance (e.g., the number of users or uses of a community network) might be counterproductive in this context. Within a service model, failure to meet targets is typically viewed as a problem, a potentially embarrassing sign of incompetence, and it risks undermining an organization's ability to win the next funding award. However, when viewed from an experimental perspective, falling short of targets is an opportunity for investigation of causal factors and a refinement of method for the next time. An experiment is only a "failure" when nothing of value is learned. However, it requires a willingness to openly discuss actual performance when it isn't as expected. The reluctance of many of our community partners to air their views about possible shortcomings offered a clear sign that they regarded this as too risky. This has the unfortunate effect of sabotaging the potential to learn, which is vital to achieving sustainable innovation. Where a community organization had good relations with their federal program officer, who understood the local situation, the risk of reporting lower-than-expected results was mitigated somewhat, but it didn't address the more fundamental questions: What can we learn from "failure"? How can this information be used to improve future CN practices and funding programs?

This brings us to another key aspect of the experimental approach that was largely missing from many of the Connecting Canadians funding programs:

the lack of systematic attention to learning from experience. For example, the funding criteria for CAP emphasized the prospect of self-sustainability at the end of the funding period but gave much less attention to how the experience of the project could be shared with others and used to improve either the future community networking initiatives or the funding programs themselves. As a result, there was an enormous amount of "reinventing the wheel," which seriously undermined the long-term prospects for sustainability. In the later stages of the CAP program, attention was paid to linking CAP sites in regional networks, which helped with spreading the expertise developed through experience, but this appeared to be aimed more at cost saving and rationalization, rather than as way to help diffuse innovation. Another sign of the failure to treat community ICT initiatives as potentially valuable experiments was the complete absence of a research component. There was no systematic study of the CN initiatives in their early days, and it was mainly external research projects coming late in the funding programs' history that enabled in-depth studies to be conducted. This CRACIN project, for instance, was funded in 2003 via the Social Sciences and Humanities Research Council.

CONCLUSION

As noted earlier in this chapter, Lankin and Clark (2006) made a series of broad recommendations intended to improve how federal government funding programs are designed, managed, and held to account. The essence of these recommendations is summarized as follows: funding recipients should be accorded respect as partners in a shared public purpose supported by programs that are accessible, understandable, and useful; reporting requirements should be simplified; and, finally, innovation should be encouraged by embracing a sensible, in some instances case-by-case, regime of risk management. In this light, we offer CRACIN community partner recommendations as they relate to the funding of ICT initiatives in community networks and more broadly in the non-profit sector.

While CRACIN community partners have praised the success of federal government programs in achieving their objective of improving and increasing high-speed connectivity across Canada, there are several messages that clearly resonate about the practical realities of implementing and sustaining community-based ICT initiatives. First, with ICTs it is important to avoid "reinventing the wheel" through careful study of both the successes and the failures to see what worked and what did not. As Brian Beaton put it: "I think what you have to do is build on the examples . . . of what has worked . . . instead of focusing on what's not working or where the problems are. There are some good concrete examples . . . and that I think needs to be celebrated."

Second is the need to consider local solutions and, in some instances, to consider individual organizations on a case-by-case basis. This is an issue for rural and remote communities in particular where, as Sheila Downer suggested, a cookie-cutter approach is not going to be as suitable as it is "in an urban area that has [a large] population and much broader volunteer and organization base. That's not the same in a rural community because you've got a much smaller user base to work with and often much smaller leadership to draw from in terms of planning and implementation. [So] there needs to be some awareness and input from the rural perspective." Janet Larkman concurred when she stated that "the most successful funding programs are those that have flexibility to receive innovative ideas from communities."

Finally, in the spirit of the Lankin and Clark report and its call for horizontal integration of policies and practices across federal government departments, Maureen Fair appeals for the integration and promotion of ICT initiatives across the entire non-profit sector. Fair notes in particular that "ICTs change so rapidly that many disadvantaged communities and their community social services agencies are lagging behind. There are relatively few community networks still surviving and complementary direct service community agencies are not usually equipped to adopt and adapt new ICT for community use." Fair further notes that it is time for governments to help other organizations in the voluntary sector to find ways to use ICTs to enhance social services delivery and to send the message that "community development work . . . could be strengthened by use of ICT."

We conclude by reflecting on the question we posed in the title of this chapter: Were the Connecting Canadians funding programs simply alternative forms of service delivery, or did they in fact produce exemplary forms of sustainable social innovation in ICT use in the non-profit sector? Drawing from the lessons learned as outlined by our key informants above, we concur that CNs have successfully furthered the Connecting Canadians goals of providing services to the public by offering ICT training and providing support to citizens learning to navigate online government programs and services. However, as our key informants have also illustrated, the successes have been hard won and required a great deal of experimentation (and in some cases, failure) to achieve rewarding outcomes. We have seen that in many cases CNs were pioneers in both innovating and contributing to early digital infrastructures in Canada, but they did so with few resources. As the Connecting Canadians programs wind down and the federal government gears up for another major impetus under the "digital economy" banner, we ask: How will the efforts of such vibrant non-profit organizations be sustained and built upon? Will the presumably forthcoming funding regimes that support community-based ICT initiatives learn from a decade of experience through the

2000s and be able to craft programs that do a better job of combining social-technical innovation with sustainable service offerings in ways that reflect the complex realities of contemporary community life?

NOTES

1   A variety of terms are often used interchangeably to refer to organizations in this sector, such as the *voluntary, non-profit, third, non-governmental, community-based,* or *charitable* sector (Canada 2001). In this chapter we predominantly use *non-profit* to refer to the sector designated by this cluster of terms.

2   Both survey respondents who reported high rates of staff turnover reside in remote and northern locations (Nunavut and Northern Ontario), where, as one administrator observed, "once a technician receives training and is able to demonstrate sufficient skills, they are able to obtain better paying positions either in the community in a different capacity or in another community (usually an urban environment—i.e., brain drain)."

REFERENCES

Bodnar, Christopher. 2005. The Vancouver Community Network, social investing and public good models of ICT development. CRACIN Working Paper no. 9. November. Toronto: Canadian Research Alliance for Community Innovation and Networking. http://archive.iprp.ischool.utoronto.ca/cracin/publications/pdfs/WorkingPapers/CRACIN%20Working%20Paper%20No%209.pdf.

Canada. Voluntary Sector Initiative. 2001. *An accord between the Government of Canada and the voluntary sector.* December. http://dsp-psd.pwgsc.gc.ca/Collection/CP32-75-2001E.pdf (accessed 7 June 2010).

——. Voluntary Sector Initiative. 2002. *A code of good practice on funding: Building on an accord between the Government of Canada and the voluntary sector.* October. http://www.vsi-isbc.org/eng/funding/pdf/codes_funding.pdf.

Canadian Policy Research Networks (CPRN). 1998. *The voluntary sector in Canada: Literature review and strategic considerations for a human resources sector study.* Report submitted to Patricia Mosher, Human Resources Partnership Directorate, Human Resources Development Canada, 27 April. http://cprn.ca/documents/24997_en.pdf.

Clement, Andrew. 1981. Community computing. *Journal of Community Communications* 4(1): 10–15.

Evans, B. Mitchell, and John Shields. 1998. "Reinventing" the third sector: Alternative service delivery, partnerships and the new public administration of the Canadian post-welfare state. Centre for Voluntary Sector Studies, Faculty of Business, Ryerson University. Working Paper Series no. 9. May. http://www.ryerson.ca/~cvss/WP09.pdf.

Fiser, Adam, Andrew Clement, and Brian Walmark. 2006. The K-Net development process: A model for First Nations broadband community networks. CRACIN Working Paper no. 12. February. Toronto: Canadian Research Alliance for Community Innovation and Networking. http://archive.iprp.ischool.utoronto.ca/cracin/publications/pdfs/WorkingPapers/CRACIN%20Working%20Paper%20No%2012.pdf.

Ford, Robin, and David Zussman. 1997. *Alternative service delivery: Sharing governance in Canada.* Toronto: Public Administration of Canada and KPMG Centre for Government Foundation.

Gibson, Kerri, Susan O'Donnell, and Vanda Rideout. 2007. The project-funding regime: Complications for community organizations and their staff. *Canadian Public Administration* 50(3): 441–35.

Goldenberg, Mark. 2006. *Building blocks for strong communities: A profile of small- and medium-sized enterprises in Canada.* A research report prepared for Human Resources and Social Development Canada. March. http://library.imaginecanada.ca/files/nonprofitscan/en/misc/building_blocks_for_strong_communities_small_and_medium_sized_enterprises.pdf.

Lankin, Frances, and Ian Clark. 2006. *From red tape to clear results: The report of the Independent Blue Ribbon Panel on grant and contributions programs.* December. http://dsp-psd.pwgsc.gc.ca/Collection/BT22-109-2007E.pdf.

McMullen, Kathryn, and Richard Brisbois. 2003. Coping with change: Human resource management in Canada's non-profit sector. CPRN Research Series on Human Resources in the Non-profit Sector no. 4. December. http://www.cprn.org/documents/25445_en.pdf.

McMullen, Kathryn, and Grant Schellenberg. 2002. Mapping the non-profit sector. CPRN Research Series on Human Resources in the Non-profit Sector no. 1. December. http://www.cprn.org/documents/16373_en.pdf.

Moll, Marita. 2007. CAP in crisis: From high priority to policy limbo. *The Straight Goods,* 12 April. http://archive.iprp.ischool.utoronto.ca/cracin/alttelecomcontent/Moll%20Straight%20Goods%20April%2007.pdf.

Moll, Marita, and Leslie Regan Shade. 2001. Community networking in Canada: Do you believe in magic? In *E-commerce vs. e-commons,* vol. 1 of *Communications in the public interest,* ed. Marita Moll and Leslie Regan Shade, 165–81. Ottawa: Canadian Centre for Policy Alternatives.

Peddle, Katrina. 2007. Smart Community, community informatics, ideology, and governance: The experience of the Western Valley Development Agency. CRACIN Working Paper no. 20. February. Toronto: Canadian Research Alliance for Community Innovation and Networking. http://archive.iprp.ischool.utoronto.ca/cracin/publications/pdfs/WorkingPapers/CRACIN%20Working%20Paper%20No.%2020.pdf.

Proulx, Serge, Nicolas Lecomte, and Julien Rueff. 2006. A study of Communautique: Portrait of a Québec organization's focus on the social appropriation of information and communication technologies in the community sector. CRACIN Working Paper no. 10. February. Toronto: Canadian Research Alliance for Community Innovation and Networking. http://archive.iprp.ischool.utoronto.ca/cracin/publications/pdfs/WorkingPapers/CRACIN%20Working%20Paper%20No%2010.pdf.

Scott, Katherine. 2003. *Funding matters: The impact of Canada's new funding regime on nonprofit and voluntary organizations.* Canadian Council on Social Development. http://www.ccsd.ca/pubs/2003/fm/index.htm.

Shade, Leslie Regan. 2002. Community networking in Canada: A status report. *Canadian Issues/Thèmes Canadiens* (June): 42–47.

Statistics Canada. 2006. *National survey of community sector organizations.* http://www23.statcan.gc.ca:81/imdb/p2SV.pl?Function=getSurvey&SDDS=5023&lang=en&db=imdb&adm=8&dis=2.

Tupper, Allan. 2001. The contested terrain of Canadian public administration in Canada's third century. *Journal of Canadian Studies* 35 (Winter): 142–60.

Treasury Board of Canada Secretariat. 2002. Policy on alternative service delivery. http://www.tbs-sct.gc.ca/pubs_pol/opepubs/TB_B4/asd-dmps1-eng.asp.

20 COMMUNAUTIQUE Action and Advocacy for Universal Digital Access

Nicolas Lecomte, Serge Proulx

In his work in the history of science and technology, Andrew Feenberg offers a critique of essentialist views of technology, which tend to present technology as an independent force over which human beings ultimately have little control. As Feenberg (2004) demonstrates, social relations are in fact central to the creation of technological goods and processes. The innovation process can be influenced by various human dynamics, such as workers' grievances (for example, over accidents with steam engines) or user-driven adaptations (such as the two-wheeled bicycle). In other cases, presiding institutional interests can lead to questionable organizational choices, as was the case in some US academic institutions where various "grassroots" distance learning initiatives that originated with the faculty were smothered by the administration (Feenberg 1999).

In the 1990s, information technologies (ITs) were presented as the cornerstone of the "new economy," the engine of the "knowledge-based," "information," or "learning" society. Presented by experts and political and private actors as a necessary technological shift, the diffusion of ITs was "the way to go" for all industrialized countries participating in the global economy, and various projects relating to technologically driven social institutions were proposed (see Lemire 1998). But who should be responsible for these projects? Should they be considered to be strictly technical and therefore something to be managed only by administrators and technical experts?

In Québec, after several years of deliberation, the first formal government initiatives that focused specifically on information and communication technologies (ICTS) and on the development of the information society (see Québec 1995) clearly targeted infrastructural issues and the creation of public access points to the Internet (described in several examples below). Surprisingly, seldom did any public debate emerge regarding which social categories and communities should be targeted and thus included in the soon-to-become information society, who should be in charge of the information network (should it be public or private?), or, more generally, what the information society should be like. In fact, as we have mentioned, infrastructural development was the main issue, and discourse on the information society was tainted by an underlying assumption that ICTS would naturally have a positive economic, social, and cultural impact (Lemire 1998).

If popular awareness of the economic and social implications of ICTS seemed to be absent, a handful of public interest advocacy groups quickly formed and mobilized around social issues such as communication rights, universal access, ownership, and skills development. When, in the mid-1990s, the Government of Canada declared that all Canadians should have the means to access the "information highway," thus granting universal access the status of a key public policy goal, several not-for-profit organizations pointed out that certain groups, such as lower-income Canadians and rural and remote communities, had not been adequately taken into account, or even consulted, in policy-making circles, including the influential Information Highway Advisory Council (IHAC) appointed by Industry Canada. More ambitious proposals for ensuring universal access went beyond the federal government's narrowly technological focus on access to hardware and bandwidth and were articulated by groups such as the Coalition for Public Information and Telecommunities Canada (Clement, Moll, and Shade 2000). While such public interest proposals fell on deaf ears in Canada, they were taken up in other forums, including the 2003 World Summit on the Information Society in Geneva (Moll and Shade 2004). In Québec, Communautique has been one of the few groups to work explicitly on the social, cultural, and political issues that are raised by the development of an information society.

As Aldo de Moor (2009) puts it, community informatics research places great emphasis on contextual issues, and "much attention is paid to assessing the community values driving the development and uptake of these technologies. Such values include soft but key notions such as passions, energy, empowerment, legitimacy, and social inclusion." Our case study is mostly concerned with understanding the values and interests that are particular to the context of Québec's community organizations, whose concrete actions are embedded in a tradition of social activism and conflicting relations with the government (White 2001). Our research shows that Communautique carries this tradition into the domain of community informatics, making information technologies a social and political issue.

As we will argue, Communautique demonstrates a rare ability to lead concrete projects while engaging in political advocacy on behalf of universal access and digital inclusion. In fact, this organization could be considered one of the most active and successful grassroots organizations involved in the ICT sector in Canada. In this chapter we focus on the relationship between Communautique and the formulation and implementation of ICT policy and programs in Québec and Canada. Through a description of the group's activities as they relate to provincial and federal public policies, we intend to establish the mutual influences between Communautique and this policy domain.

A FEW WORDS ON COMMUNAUTIQUE

Communautique was originally a joint project created and managed in its early years by La Puce communautaire (http://www.puce.qc.ca/) and the Institut Canadien d'Éducation des Adultes (ICÉA) (http://www.icea.qc.ca/). In 1995, Communautique was launched to facilitate the integration of ITs into community groups' daily activities and, more generally, to democratize access. Back then, very few groups in Québec were using ITs, and many of them had no idea of what was at stake. Communautique rapidly evolved from a project in 1995, to an association in 1997, to a non-profit corporation endowed with independent legal personhood in 1999. It goes without saying that this last step increased the group's autonomy and fundraising ability.

Communautique's activities build on a double concern. First, the ICÉA brought to the table experience and analysis of the media's educational role, advocating for the adoption of an information highway policy that takes technological exclusion into account (Institut Canadien d'Éducation des Adultes 1995). In this regard, Communautique has fostered policy-related debates around the information society, creating public spaces (whether face-to-face meetings or virtual forums) in which community groups and citizens can express their views. Second, starting in the 1980s, La Puce communautaire developed a great deal of technical and educational expertise, notably by offering computer training activities in Montréal's Hochelaga-Maisonneuve area, which is characterized by lower-income, underprivileged households. Communautique's pilot projects involving public access points built upon the technical expertise of La Puce. Since its creation, Communautique has also undertaken numerous knowledge transfer activities, from sensitization to professional training, and has built various types of support mechanisms for citizens and community organizations willing to embrace technological change.

Communautique's general objective of digital inclusion is pursued through a community-oriented strategy, where the transfer of skills and knowledge is realized through already existing groups. Such a strategy requires a strong partner base, political recognition, and government support. From a modest experiment, Communautique would eventually spearhead a movement for IT appropriation in the Québec community sector at large.

UNDERSTANDING PUBLIC POLICIES AS PROCESSES

Vincent Lemieux provides a range of concepts that can help shed light on Communautique's activities as they relate to public policies. According to Lemieux (2002, 19), the development of public policies can be analyzed as a set of decisions in which actors try to use their resources to influence a variety of issues, as the real power of actors consists in controlling the decision-making process according to their preferences."[1] Four successive steps characterize the process of policy making:

1. *Emergence:* Public policies generally emerge after a series of issues and problems are identified, be it by policy makers, administrators, or interest groups. This phase is typically characterized by the creation of pilot projects and funding programs and consultation with experts and the public at large, with the objective of raising the government's and the public's awareness of the issue at stake.

2. *Formulation:* This second step refers to decisions that concern policy objectives, funding initiatives, and eligibility. Usually the process of formulation is conducted inside the government's administration, and policy-interested actors play a limited role compared to government agents and officials. Status, norms, information, and relations are among the most crucial assets actors bring to bear at this stage of the policy-making process.

3. *Implementation:* Implementation refers to how the policy is organized and put into action through the funding of programs and projects. Various groups of policy-interested actors seek to be taken into consideration and try to negotiate with government agents and officials.

4. *Evaluation:* This last step examines the efficiency of governmental programs in addressing the problems that initially led to the formulation of the policy.

Lemieux considers that, within the domain of public policy, an actor's legitimacy and influence in the decision-making process largely depend on the personal or informational resources that he or she possesses. The way that those engaged in policy making use their resources contributes to the definition of problems. We cannot consider policies solely as processes, however, because they translate into concrete programs that sustain (or lack) a vision. Lemieux's perspective is helpful in describing the evolution of ICT policies in Québec and Canada. It is also helpful in understanding the status of a group such as Communautique and its potential influence during the different phases of public policy making.

The following pages provide a description of Communautique's projects in the context of provincial and federal public policies. A substantial document review of the organization's activities between 1995 and 2005, along with a series of interviews conducted with key actors, has shown that these larger projects are highly representative of the group's activities, even though smaller projects were also crucial for the organization's development.

COMMUNAUTIQUE'S PROJECTS IN THE REALM OF PUBLIC POLICY

Space does not allow us to describe the full range of Communautique's activities, which include various local projects as well as policy *mémoires*, or position papers. Below, we describe only some of Communautique's more significant activities, those related to Québec's Information Highway Policy and Ottawa's Connecting Canadians initiative. (For more information on Communautique's activities, see Proulx, Lecomte, and Rueff 2006.)

Québec: Information Highway Policy

Québec's provincial Information Highway Policy was officially launched in 1998, although the formulation process began in 1992, with the subsequent creation of an Information Highway Secretary and an Information Highway Fund in 1994. In 1995, an action plan—*Inforoute Québec: Plan d'action pour la mise en oeuvre de l'autoroute de l'information,* commonly called the Rapport Berlinguet (Québec 1995)—was published by an advisory committee, followed by additional works by the secretary for the Information Highway, which finalized the general objectives and strategies of the policy. Essentially, Québec's Information Highway Policy and its related funds stand on five pillars (see Québec 1998):

Access: ITs should be available to all citizens living anywhere in Québec, even in remote areas, and regardless of their social and economic status.

Education: Access to training opportunities can be improved through the use of ITs, and pedagogical strategies and methods can be modernized.

Culture: The rise of communication technologies is an opportunity to further promote Québec-based cultural content and, more generally, to expand the use of the French language on the English-dominated Internet.

Economy and employment: ITs should lead to the transformation of the business world, work, workers' skills, and employment opportunities. Technologies could also be used to enhance Québec's regional development.

The state and public services: The government will use new technologies to ensure the provision of quality and timely services to its citizens.

Several ministries and public institutions are engaged in managing the province's technological development. These include the Ministère de la culture et des communications, which deals with online cultural content and copyright issues, the Ministère de la santé et des services sociaux and the Ministère des relations avec le citoyen et de l'immigration, which are concerned, respectively, with the online provision of health and social services and of information regarding citizenship and immigration, and the Office québécois de la langue française, which oversees French language on the Internet.

Between 1994 and 2004, $98 million was spent by the Information Highway Fund, with $48 million in the 1994–95 period alone, for development of telecommunications infrastructure. In general, a large majority of non-profit organizations received support in comparison to private companies. Nevertheless, between 1994 and 2003, the average amount of money allocated to a non-profit organization was half of what a private company received (Québec 2005).

Emergence and formulation phases. During its first years, which coincided with the period when the Information Highway Policy was in its early phases, Communautique was active primarily in Montréal, receiving funding from local sources. The organization played a central role in creating the first public Internet access points in the city, an undertaking that dovetailed well with the government's emerging goal of improving public access to ICTs. Located in community group facilities, schools, and libraries, these access points offered free Internet access and training sessions to citizens and community activists interested in learning how to use computers and the Internet. These were pilot ICT experiments, which helped to bring the population into direct contact with technologies new to them. Creating these access points also provided Communautique with a good opportunity to analyze barriers to appropriation as they arise in practice.

Communautique's programs and services were soon in high demand from community groups who wanted to integrate ICTs into their operations, as the organization rapidly accumulated expertise in domains such as website creation, professional training, and technical support. Thanks to these achievements, the organization quickly came to the attention of the Québec government.

Policy implementation. Starting in 1999, several important programs were launched, marking the implementation of the Information Highway Policy. While lobbying for more community-based projects and a more inclusive political vision, Communautique was able to develop its expertise in technology-based service provision on a much larger scale, through its participation in a number of major projects mounted by the provincial government, such as Courrier.qc.ca and Inforoutes–Points d'accès.

Courrier.qc.ca. In October 1998, the Québec government launched a pilot project called Courrier.qc.ca, designed to offer an email address to all Québecers. Communautique was invited by the Québec minister of Culture and Communications to take part in the "user training," "technical," and "director" committees of a planned pilot project that would distribute email addresses to the citizens of Montréal's Ste-Marie–St-Jacques, Hochelaga-Maisonneuve, and Baie-Comeau neighbourhoods. Beyond the training itself, Communautique coordinated the project's activities in two Québec ridings. Although the project was only partially successful, the fact that Communautique was given such responsibilities certainly contributed to the organization's growth and visibility.

Inforoutes–Points d'accès. The Inforoutes–Points d'accès project was launched at the beginning of 2000, supported by the Anti-Poverty Work Reinsertion Programme and the Québec Youth Fund. The project was designed to create public access points in every region of Québec, diversify the range of locations from which the information highway could be accessed, ensure the transfer of expertise in leadership training, and produce training material. The project adopted an innovative strategy, whereby technologies would be distributed gradually to the population through community groups that partnered with the project.

Communautique again played a major role, taking on the coordination of all the groups involved, the provision of ongoing support to these groups in administrative matters, and the creation of a reference library related to the use of certain software, as well as offering technical support itself, jointly with La Puce. In addition, Communautique was responsible for training operations. Its training program was composed of five modules running over four weeks. It was pitched to activity leaders who were asked to work at various access points, helping them round out their ICT knowledge and equipping them with oversight strategies. Those leaders, who could be considered multiplier agents, were part of Communautique's goal to develop training expertise that is affordable and readily available to serve community groups' daily needs. Inforoutes–Points d'accès also provided the organization with an opportunity to develop partnerships throughout Québec. In the course of the project, Communautique established twelve regional partnerships in nine Québec regions, for a total of ninety-eight access points. According to data compiled by the organization, more than 50,000 people across Québec were introduced to ICTs.[2] In 2002, Communautique was recognized for its role in the community and its expertise as a trainer when the group received core funding from the Ministère de l'éducation. This funding enabled Communautique to offer regular training sessions in its own facilities.

Québec's Information Highway Policy funded some of Communautique's projects, but the group also benefitted from funding from local or federal sources. Communautique was eligible for a variety of funding programs because its activities were varied: training, website development, research and analysis, equipment provision, networking, technical support, partnership, dialogue with community groups, and so on. This variety prevented Communautique from becoming dependent on a single ministry or funding source, reducing the group's vulnerability to the kind of fluctuations in funding and revenue that have plagued other community networks (see chapter 19 in this volume).

Connecting Canadians Projects

The Connecting Canadians initiative was launched in September 1997 by Industry Canada with the objective of making Canada "the most connected country in the world." This program started off with large amounts of money devoted to building infrastructure, including the establishment of public Internet access points. Public interest organizations closely followed the emergence and formulation phases of the new agenda (Clement, Moll, and Shade 2000). Communautique did not initially participate in these debates, but it eventually led (and still leads) several projects linked to the Connecting Canadians policy.

On the national scene, Communautique did not play an active role during the emergence and formulation phases of Ottawa's new initiative. But the fact that the group received funding from several key federal programs shows that, through its activities in Québec, it achieved national recognition.

VolNet. The goal of Industry Canada's VolNet program, which formed part of the broader Connecting Canadians initiative, was to offer connection services, computing equipment, and Internet training to thousands of volunteer and community organizations. Communautique was involved in the project between 1999 and 2002, as part of a consortium bringing together Économie communautaire de Francheville (ÉCOF) and Atena, and later known as Communautés branchées (Wired Communities). The VolNet program facilitated Internet access and ICT training for more than 11,000 non-profit groups across Canada. In Québec, Communautique and its multiple partners equipped, connected, and trained almost six hundred groups from various regions over a period of three years. It was the first time that a project led by Communautique had specifically targeted the need of community organizations for computing equipment.

CAP. The Community Access Program (CAP) was launched by Industry Canada as another component of the Connecting Canadians initiative, with the objective of connecting groups and citizens and, ultimately, to promote strategic uses of new technologies. Central to the CAP program was the creation of community access centres to the Internet (CACI), which are basically community sites equipped with computers and an Internet connection, the specific function of which is to offer training. Communautique provided training for staff and volunteers from several CACIs. An eighteen-hour training course was designed for activity leaders who would work in existing community access points and at newly created CACIs. As in the Inforoute project, Communautique offered basic Internet training and also identified pedagogical strategies that would allow activity leaders to address the diversity of the population they would train. In 1999 and 2000, Communautique established sixteen CACIs in Québec. By 2004, this number had grown to seventy-four. A group of trainers was organized to support these community access centres.

Since 2003, Communautique has also been active within the CAP Youth Initiative (CAP YI) in the Montréal region, providing youths with work experience while allowing them to develop their skills in IT training throughout the CACI network. The skills they learn are diverse and include technical maintenance and support, computer and Internet training, and website management. Hundreds of youths have been trained in community access settings since 2003.

CACI networks gave birth to new practices among community groups, as each CACI could provide citizens with a place to access the Internet and use office applications, which required new training and supervision skills on the part of host groups. The CAP initiative also stimulated partnerships among community groups, schools, libraries, local businesses, foundations, government agencies, and others. These successful partnerships have yet to translate into long-term funding for the CAP program, however, as the government has progressively decreased its budgetary envelope for this program since 2004 (see chapter 21).

GI-TI. Communautique has been involved with the GI-TI project, an offshoot of the federal Voluntary Sector Initiative, since 2004. The project originally promoted the diffusion and efficient use of technological innovation in community groups. One of the main short-term objectives was to promote affordable technical support resources and make them easily available to community groups. The project gave birth to a free phone line, as well as a website (http://giti.ca) that lists companies and community groups that offer free or inexpensive technical support services.

Summary

As this survey of projects indicates, Communautique has been efficient and successful in delivering key government-sponsored projects—projects that were also congruent with the group's mission and objectives. During the emergence and formulation phases of Québec's Information Highway Policy, Communautique's activities improved the group's visibility and political legitimacy. This had a snowball effect in terms of funding secured for the first programs that accompanied the policy's implementation phase, such as Courrier.qc.ca and Inforoutes–Points d'accès. Communautique's early access point initiatives also increased its chances of garnering federal support.

RESEARCH: INFORMING THE ACCESS DEBATE THROUGH NEEDS ASSESSMENT

Throughout the years, Communautique has conducted three large studies among Québec's community groups and citizens (Communautique 1997, 2001, 2004), assessing digital divide issues such as equipment, training, and technical support. These studies provide an understanding of how social and community ICT needs evolved over time and how efficiently policies responded to them. Ultimately, in the realm of public policy, these studies would be used by Communautique as expert resources to inform the debate on two of the government's five objectives regarding the information highway: access and education.

The Impact of the Digital Divide on Community Groups (1996–97)

In 1996, when Communautique initiated its first research among Québec's community groups, its main goal was to evaluate to what extent networking tools, such as computers and fax machines, were available and actually used (Communautique 1997). Among other issues, Communautique investigated Québec community groups' degree of interest in devoting resources to ICT acquisition and training and whether they had considered the potential for ICTs to facilitate the accomplishment of their goals. Communautique sent surveys to approximately six hundred community groups but collected only eighty responses. For further exploratory discussion, three public events were organized, which served as a public space in which to share ideas around the theme of the emerging information society. A total of thirty-two groups participated in these events.

Several conclusions followed from this research. First, many community groups wanted to be equipped with computers and new communication tools, and some of them already owned devices that they wanted to upgrade, but the majority lacked the financial resources to do either. Second, most of these groups were eager for more training, especially because, in most cases, no staff member had the ICT skills or competence needed to integrate new technologies into the group's daily activities. This research also revealed that, while a majority of community groups was willing to use computers and networking, a significant portion expressed concerns about issues such as privacy, security, and political control. In short, community groups agreed that they needed to "go with the flow," but not at all costs: they would remain careful, if not wary, with regards to the implementation process. In addition, it was clear that substantial financial support would be necessary to answer even basic equipment and training needs.

Several disparities surrounding the question of access to ICTs were also revealed. Those who were using ICTs typically lived in urban settings (Montréal or Québec City), were well educated, and were generally well off. In rural areas and among lower-income populations, however, such technologies were clearly used to a lesser extent. To address this divide, community organizations were identified as potential hubs for democratizing digital access, which led Communautique to advocate for improving the availability of affordable equipment and training to these organizations.

This research, the first of its kind to be conducted in Québec, demonstrated that the issue of access was not limited to a lack of equipment and that community groups were greatly affected by the digital divide. This research was also instrumental for the group itself, as it provided a strong foundation on which Communautique could shape its own mission and objectives, at a time when the group was still on the early stages of its development. Last but not least, this study constituted a body of facts that would be helpful in informing Communautique's lobbying efforts.

Progress Made (1999–2001)

In 1999, Communautique evaluated how the use of ICTs had evolved since 1996 among community groups (Communautique 2001). This time approximately three thousand surveys were sent out across Québec, generating 450 responses. Public workshops were again organized, encouraging groups to share their experiences with technologies. The research objectives were to assess the diffusion of ICTs and their concrete impact on activities and organizations.

This study showed that the level of informatization of community groups varied considerably, although the vast majority of the responding groups considered the integration of ICTs into their activities to be strategically important for their development. Many groups reported difficulties managing the introduction of ICTs into their daily activities and in coping with the rapid obsolescence of equipment. The study also demonstrated the persistence of basic training needs (although these had diminished since 1996), as well as the emergence of new needs. For the most part, staff members had received basic training, but additional expert support was necessary in order to allow them to keep up with the rapid evolution of devices and software. One of the study's recommendations was that a means be found to provide community groups with better access to computer experts.

In 2001, results of the study were publicized and discussed with several community groups during a set of meetings called Forum rencontres, which eventually led to a public conference called "Où mènent les TIC: Rêve ou réalité?" ("Where do ICTs lead: Dreams or reality?") (Institut Canadien d'Éducation des Adultes 2000). A public-oriented vision of digital access gradually developed, culminating eventually in Communautique's *Plateforme de l'Internet citoyen*, to be discussed below.

Advanced Training and Technical Support Resources (2004)

In order to start the GI-TI project, Communautique produced another needs assessment study (Communautique 2004). This study had the same objectives as the one conducted in 1999, but a focus on technical support was added: What are community organizations' needs? What solutions could be developed in order to answer these needs? Approximately five hundred groups were contacted by phone, and 415 agreed to participate in the research and were sent a survey. An impressive total of 194 surveys were sent back, for a 47 percent response rate.

Most if not all of the organizations that participated in the study owned at least one computer, while 75 percent of them had an intranet. It appeared that the staff of most organizations had acquired basic computer and networking competencies, with many employees now looking for more targeted, objective-driven training. Indeed, respondents often identified training needs, such as the advanced use of office automation tools, text editors, and database or spreadsheet programs. Numerous groups indicated that they were ready to take the next step and use the Internet to its fullest potential, as they wanted strategic training such as website creation, communication tools, specialized search engines, and so on.

Concerning technical support, community organizations' recurring problem was the day-to-day functioning of equipment. Especially in the case of geographically isolated groups, equipment failures sometimes took long periods of time to resolve. The study also looked into the groups' satisfaction levels with the technical support services they had already received. Even though most respondents professed satisfaction with the efficiency of support services in resolving their problems, the cost of these services was identified as a major problem.

As we have seen, the GI-TI project would give birth to a phone line and an electronic database listing free or affordable technical support services. Communautique considers technical support to be one of the main factors in the sustainable development and empowerment of community groups within the information society.[3]

Persisting Needs: A Call for Long-Term Funding

With reference to Lemieux's analysis of how various actors influence the development of public policy, we can see that Communautique's needs assessment studies constituted important "informational resources" for the organization. They contributed to its acquisition of knowledge, information, and expertise, thereby building its political legitimacy.

Communautique's studies demonstrate the persistence of certain needs among citizens and community groups, in particular, for training and technical support. Equipment has to be regularly renewed, given the constant innovations that characterize digital devices and software. The question then is, can equipment, training, and technical support be considered systemic issues in the context of the information society? If access is to be universal, such a question is appropriate, as social inequalities will not disappear in the near future. That is why Communautique calls upon the government for long-term funding, or core funding, which would help community groups keep pace with rapid technological change and make up-to-date technology available to everyone.

The research described above proved useful to Communautique for at least three reasons. First, it provided a general overview of the evolution of ICT diffusion and use in Québec, particularly in the community sector. Second, it played a strategic role in Communautique's own development as an organization, helping the organization to define its mission and goals (1997), evaluate the impact of its activities (2001), and investigate specific issues (2004). Third, it raised social issues rather than technical ones, which contributed to a better way of addressing the issue of the digital divide and to conceptualizing access in terms of the public interest. It illustrates the fact that community groups' needs have shifted from basic training to more precise and strategic uses of ICTs, from getting equipped to the effective use of digital technology, defined by Gurstein (2004, 229) as "the capacity and opportunity to successfully integrate ICTs into the accomplishment of self or collaboratively identified goals."

COMMUNAUTIQUE, A POLITICALLY ENGAGED ACTOR

Leading projects and conducting research are not Communautique's only areas of expertise. The organization is also very active in the political arena, advocating for an inclusive and democratic information society in which community organizations and citizens would be actively involved. As Lemire argues, the public claims made by politicians, experts of one sort or another, and journalists regarding the information society are far from being apolitical. Based on broad ideals of technical, political, economic, social, and cultural progress, these claims spread the illusion that the information society is an imperative and that the government has this process of technological change well under control. In addition, any form of debate that questions the official implementation of the information society is deemed at best irrelevant, and even illegitimate (Lemire 1998). In this context, Communautique's contribution is all the more interesting because it brings social problems such as economic inequalities back into the debate.

La politique québécoise de l'autoroute de l'information

In 1998, Communautique created a coalition that advocated for greater participation of community organizations and the public at large in the development of policy and for equal and universal access to the information society. The coalition produced a critical analysis of Québec's Information Highway Policy (Pelletier and Tousignant 1998), which the province had most recently laid out in a document titled *La politique québécoise de l'autoroute de l'information* (Québec 1998). It solicited input from various community groups, social economy organizations, workers' unions, student federations, and even consumers' rights associations, whose members identified specific issues and possible consequences of the information society that Québec's policy did not address. For example, fears were expressed regarding the possible widening of social disparities because of unequal access to technologies. Some community partners were concerned with the effects of technologies on the organization of work. The expected impact of technologies in the education sector could be problematic, and the status of scientific knowledge needed to be further discussed among all interested stakeholders. Finally, there was no concrete strategy concerning the security of personal data during online transactions with public or private organizations. The coalition subsequently called for a more inclusive information highway policy, in which community groups would receive government funds to participate in democratizing digital access and citizens from all social backgrounds would be recognized. Communautique's coalition appeared on several occasions in the media, serving as one of the few voices from the civil society sector that expressed interest in ICT-related social issues and stressing the urgent need for critical discussion of the Québec government's vision of the information highway.

Plateforme de l'Internet citoyen

Drawing on several of its position papers pleading for the recognition of the digital divide in various areas of public life, Communautique refined its community-driven vision of the information society in a document titled *Plateforme de l'Internet citoyen* (Platform for a citizen-based Internet) (Communautique 2002). This document synthesized Communautique's values and beliefs regarding the promised information society and the way in which the government was handling its implementation.

According to Communautique, "the digital divide should be considered in its broadest sense, in terms of the ability not merely to access the Internet but to contribute to knowledge disseminated by the Internet." [4] The main theme developed in the *Plateforme* concerns access rights (*droits à l'accès*), which stand as a response to the digital divide. To put it briefly, Communautique argues that if technologies are to play a central role in core social institutions such as culture, education, health care, the government, and the economy, access rights need to be instituted as basic rights granted to every citizen.

The ability to participate in the information society depends on more than just infrastructure (such as equipment and carriage). Other factors—social and economic inequities, level of education, geography, age, gender, physical handicaps, and so on—can impede access. Communautique's arguments embrace all the dimensions of Clement and Shade's (2000) "access rainbow" model, in which access is presented as "a multi-faceted social-technical phenomenon." The *Plateforme* reminds us of the social and political issues implicit in the development of the information society, and it strongly criticizes the government's response to the problem of the digital divide, in which the notion of access tended to be reduced to a matter of hardware and connectivity. The document calls for a collective debate around the place of ICTs within society and makes concrete political demands, which include calling on the government to provide long-term funding programs related to access and training, to promote accessibility norms for building websites, and to address the ethical and political aspects of connectivity, such as the protection of privacy.

The *Plateforme de l'Internet citoyen* is an inclusive vision of the information society in which grassroots initiatives play a central role, the infrastructure is designed and driven by citizens, and the content and services available are not simply a function of consumerism but also contribute to the effective social and political representation of people, communities, and cultures.

Communautique and e-Government

Following Minister Henri-François Gautrin's June 2004 recommendations, Québec's government announced the implementation of a major e-government initiative, the aims of which included a fundamental transformation in the relationship between citizens and the state (see http://hfgautrin.com). The initiative was intended to contribute to the modernization and increased transparency of the state. Minister Gautrin's task force was asked to investigate and advise the government about the following objectives:

- Allow citizens access to the information that the state holds on them through a so-called "citizen page"
- Develop an ICT-enabled state administration and bureaucracy
- Develop processes for e-democracy (online voting)
- Enable Internet-based public services.

Communautique did not wait long to initiate public discussions. For an entire month, public conferences and workshops were held in eight regions of Québec, open to community groups and citizens willing to learn and to express their views. Communautique also developed a website (http://consultations. communautique.qc.ca/consultations/) in order to collect opinions on the government's project. Five themes were discussed during the regional and online consultations: public services online, the creation of a "citizen page," electronic voting, the use of the Internet as a public forum, and the role of the community movement in the context of e-government.

The public's overall participation in this discussion process was rather small, especially in the case of its online component. Nonetheless, highlights from these conferences (Communautique 2007) reveal that the public's primary concern was the issue of personal data security during their transactions with the government. Consequently, Communautique called for rigorous legislation guaranteeing the security and confidentiality of personal data in the context of online government services. The problem of protecting citizens' anonymity was also pointed out as one of the main shortcomings related to e-democracy. At the time the conferences took place, problems had arisen with the use of voting machines in both the United States and

Québec (see Feldman, Halderman, and Felten 2006), undermining citizens' trust in the process.[5]

Communautique is still leading several projects linked to e-government and e-democracy. Most notable are the Formation à l'inforoute citoyenne project, the Communautaire en ligne (an association of community groups), and the Comité d'étude sur la démocratie en ligne.[6] These programs are meant to keep citizens and community groups informed about developments surrounding the government's IT policies and regulations and to provide otherwise rare opportunities for the emergence of public discussion and action.

CONCLUSION

Through its various projects and its contribution to public debates during the emergence, formulation, and implementation phases of public policies, Communautique has been critical toward the provincial government's view of the information society.[7] At the same time, the group had to align with and adapt to government policy goals in order to receive funding. Communautique straddles a position between the government's objectives and the social needs of local communities, which may turn out to be an uncomfortable position. Communautique considers the recognition of community needs to be the basic condition for a democratic information society, and its actions have helped the community sector to cross the digital divide and make effective use of new technologies, while its research and reflections have preserved a much-needed critical stance regarding the policy that numerous citizens and civil society representatives have progressively endorsed. Communautique well illustrates the fine line that exists between the role of community organizations as service providers for the government, on the one hand, and, on the other, their role as social activists who promote public discussion and engage in political advocacy.

The case of Communautique and its interactions with information society policies also showcases the problems surrounding the recognition that community groups and civil society initiatives have a legitimate part to play in the development of public policy. Particularly in Québec, the community movement's history and identity can be understood by considering the evolution of its relationship with the state, as it is characterized by what sociologist Deena White calls "conflicting co-operation." For example, the very notion of a community "sector" (*secteur communautaire*) shows how this relationship has gradually been rationalized and bureaucratized (White 2001). As is true for CRACIN case study sites, as well as for many other community organizations, government funding can be a "double-edged sword" (see chapter 8). Nevertheless, the increased administrative burden that accompanies such funding has not kept Communautique out of public debates—far from it. By diversifying its funding sources, Communautique has been able to adopt and maintain its critical but constructive stance in relation to provincial government policy, insulating itself from the dangers of advocacy chill, which has tended to silence other community networks (see chapter 19). In contrast, the group has continued to champion the values of social justice that are inherent in the community movement in Québec. These values have coloured the organization's public positions, whether they concerned the Information Highway Policy in the second half of the 1990s, the policy on workforce training in 2003, or the e-government initiative in 2005, or, more recently, its lobbying on behalf of the *Plan numérique,* which calls for Québec to adopt a broadly inclusive strategy regarding ICTs. This commitment to social justice is one of the distinctions that can be drawn between two types of activists in the domain of information technologists: techno-activists, who are interested in shaping information systems by means of technical mastery, and social activists, whose interest lies with civic participation and political recognition of excluded social categories (Proulx, Rueff, and Lacomte 2007).

Communautique's actions and analyses are based on community needs and public debates, which may also be valuable to the field of community informatics (Gurstein 2006). Communautique directly calls for "effective use" and "effective access," as its actions within communities take into account "the fact that access is a socially situated behaviour and phenomenon" (Gurstein 2004). Quantitative studies, coupled with the collection of various experiences of technological appropriation (see chapter 5), contribute to mapping effective use. In this sense, Communautique's actions and critiques have contributed to our understanding of the digital divide and to developing the concept of universal access. One could wonder about the lack of participation and media interest during Communautique's 2005 public workshops on e-government, however. One possibility could be that the ideal of universal access is still in its embryonic phase: "Analogous to the state of ecological awareness 40 years ago, there are the first warnings of systemic malfunctioning, but little general concern or mobilization" (Clement, Moll, and Shade 2001). Communautique may have been successful in terms of both demand and supply of community participation, but, as noted by Thakur (2009), "perhaps the greatest challenge . . . is to integrate, feasibly and legitimately, [ICT] projects into local political structures while still creating enough space for genuine participation." Then again, perhaps the fact that the government's agenda regarding e-government was already set discouraged community participation in the discussion process. In this regard, empowering community members through direct involvement in gathering and shaping information appears to be a promising avenue.

To conclude, what can we say about Communautique's influence on policy making? Did the group induce a noticeable shift in IT policy? At the very least, as regards the emergence and formulation phases of the policy making process, Communautique's critical analysis of the Information Highway Policy prevented the information society from being planned without any form of democratic debate, by urging other civil society groups to engage in the process of building this "new" society. To its credit, the provincial government's *La politique de l'autoroute de l'information* (Québec 1998) acknowledges the importance of providing universal and affordable access to all residents of the province. Communautique's advocacy work, along with that of its partners, is likely to have played a role in flagging the digital divide as a legitimate social issue worthy of government attention. As we have shown, a community-oriented vision of access was concretely tested in the field through government-funded projects that characterized the implementation phase of both federal and provincial IT policy.

In Louis Maheu's (1983) view, one of the roles of Québec's *groupes de base* (which include community organizations) has been to protest against the political appropriation of social experiences and practices. The case of public policies in the domain of information technologies is no exception, because groups such as Communautique have questioned the state's technocratic vision—now reduced to the management of public goods—to promote a citizen-led information highway. As such, the case of Communautique is an example of how social innovation is vital to the process of technological development.

NOTES

1 All translations from the French are our own.
2 From an internally circulated Communautique document, "Projet de formation à l'inforoute citoyenne" (23 September 2003), Appendix A.
3 From an internally circulated Communautique document, "Projet CITES—Document de réflexion à l'attention des partenaires du projet" (2005).
4 « La fracture numérique doit être considérée dans son sens le plus large comme la différence qui existe tant dans la capacité d'accéder que dans celle de contribuer à la production de connaissances véhiculées sur Internet. »
5 In Québec, the Directeur général des élections, Marcel Blanchet, criticized the way electronic voting was carried out during the 2005 municipal elections and imposed stricter rules for future elections. See http://www.electionsquebec.qc.ca/francais /actualite-detail.php?id=2015 and http://www.electionsquebec.qc.ca/francais/ actualite-detail.php?id=2145.
6 For a description of the Formation à l'inforoute citoyenne project, see http://www. communautique.qc.ca/projets/projets-actifs/inforoute-citoyenne.html; for Communautaire en ligne, see http://www.communautique.qc.ca/projets/projets-actifs/ communautaire-en-ligne.html.

7   Some of the projects mentioned in this chapter are still active, such as CAP Youth Initiative, Formation à l'inforoute citoyenne, and Communautaire en ligne. A list of *Communautique*'s current projects is available at http://www.communautique.qc.ca/ projets.html.

REFERENCES

Clement, Andrew, Marita Moll, and Leslie Shade. 2001. Debating universal access in the Canadian context: The role of public interest organizations. In *E-commerce vs. e-commons: Communications in the public interest*, ed. Marita Moll and Leslie Regan Shade, 23–48. Ottawa: Canadian Centre for Policy Alternatives.

Clement, Andrew, and Leslie Regan Shade. 2000. The access rainbow: Conceptualizing universal access to the information/communication infrastructure. In *Community informatics: Enabling communities with information and communication technologies*, ed. Michael Gurstein, 32–51. Hershey, PA: Idea Group Publishing.

Communautique. 1997. Rapport de l'étude de besoins. http://www.communautique.qc.ca/ reflexion-et-enjeux/appropriation/etude-besoins.html.

——. 2001. Le monde communautaire et Internet: défis, obstacles et espoirs. Résultats de l'enquête auprès des groupes communautaires. http://www.communautique.qc.ca/ reflexion-et-enjeux/appropriation/monde-communautaire.html.

——. 2002. Plateforme québécoise de l'Internet citoyen. http://www.communautique. qc.ca/reflexion-et-enjeux/internet-citoyen/plateforme.html.

——. 2004. Enquête sur les besoins en GI-TI. http://www.communautique.ca/reflexion-et-enjeux/appropriation/enquete-giti2.html.

——. 2007. Rapport synthèse sur les consultations de Communautique sur le projet gouvernemental de gouvernement et de démocratie en ligne. http://www.communautique. qc.ca/reflexion-et-enjeux/internet-citoyen/rapport-synthese-consultations.html.

de Moor, Aldo. 2009. Moving community informatics research forward. *Journal of Community Informatics* 5(1). http://www.ci-journal.net/index.php/ciej/article/view/ 546/434.

Feenberg, Andrew. 1999. Distance learning: Promise or threat? *Crosstalk* (Winter). http:// www.sfu.ca/~andrewf/TELE3.htm.

——. 2004. *(Re)penser la technique: Vers une technologie démocratique*. Trans. Anne-Marie Dibon. Paris: La Découverte. Originally published as *Questioning technology* (London and New York: Routledge, 1999).

Feldman, Ariel J., J. Alex Halderman, and Edward W. Felten. 2006. *Security analysis of the Diebold AccuVote-TS Voting Machine*. Princeton University, Center for Information Technology Policy. http://citp.princeton.edu/pub/ts06full.pdf.

Gurstein, Michael. 2004. Effective use and the community informatics sector: Some thoughts on Canada's approach to community technology / community access. In *Seeking convergence in policy and practice*, vol. 2 of *Communications in the public interest*, ed. Marita Moll and Leslie Regan Shade, 223–43. Ottawa: Canadian Centre for Policy Alternatives.

——. 2006. Notes Towards an Integrative Agenda and Community Informatics Theory. CRACIN Working Paper no. 14. February. Toronto: Canadian Research Alliance for Community Innovation and Networking. http://archive.iprp.ischool.utoronto.ca/ cracin/publications/pdfs/WorkingPapers/CRACIN%20Working%20Paper%20No% 2014.pdf.

Institut Canadien d'Éducation des Adultes. 1995. *Une nouvelle voie d'expression, de communication et d'apprentissage.* Submission to the Canadian Radio-television and Telecommunications Commission's first-stage consultation on the information highway, prepared by Francine Pelletier and Lina Trudel. January.

———. 2000. Où mènent les TIC: rêves ou réalités? Conference proceedings, Montréal, 30 November–1 December. http://bv.cdeacf.ca/bvdoc.php?no=2004_12_0579&col=EA& format=htm&ver=old.

Lemieux, Vincent. 2002. *L'étude des politiques publiques: Les acteurs et leur pouvoir*, 2nd ed. Québec: Presses de l'Université Laval.

Lemire, Marc. 1998. Les représentations sociales dans le discours public sur les autoroutes de l'information. *Politique et sociétés* 18(2): 83–100. http://id.erudit.org/iderudit/040174ar.

Maheu, Louis. 1983. Les mouvements de base et la lutte contre l'appropriation étatique du tissu social. *Sociologie et sociétés* 15: 77–92.

Moll, Marita, and Leslie Regan Shade. 2004. Vision impossible? The World Summit on the Information Society. In *Seeking convergence in policy and practice*, vol. 2 of *Communications in the public interest*, ed. Marita Moll and Leslie Regan Shade, 45–80. Ottawa: Canadian Centre for Policy Alternatives.

Pelletier, Francine, and Philippe Tousignant. 1998. Spécial: Politique québécoise de l'autoroute de l'information. *CommInfo* 1(8). http://www.communautique.qc.ca/reflexion-et-enjeux/comminfo/volume1no8.html.

Proulx, Serge, Nicolas Lecomte, and Julien Rueff. 2006. Note de recherche: Portrait d'une organisation québécoise orientée vers l'appropriation sociale des technologies de l'information et de la communication en milieu communautaire. Centre interuniversitaire de recherche sur la science et la technologie (CIRST). http://www.cirst.uqam.ca/Portals/0/docs/note_rech/2006_01.pdf.

Proulx, Serge, Julien Rueff, and Nicolas Lecomte. 2007. La redéfinition du tiers secteur québécois à l'aune du militantisme technique. *Hermès* 47: 107–14.

Québec. 1995. *Inforoute Québec: Plan d'action pour la mise en ouvre de l'autoroute de l'information.* Comité consultatif sur l'autoroute de l'information, Conseil de la science et de la technologie.

———. 1998. *La politique québécoise de l'autoroute de l'information: Agir autrement.* http://www.msg.gouv.qc.ca/documents/gel/politique_autoroute.pdf.

———. Ministère des services gouvernementaux. 2005. "Subvention moyenne accordée selon le type d'organisme pour les phases I, II et III." http://web.archive.org/web/20051218192915/http://services.gouv.qc.ca/fr/enligne/societe/tableau/tab5.asp. Accessed 18 June 2010 (but no longer available).

Thakur, Dhanaraj. 2009. ICTs and community participation: An indicative framework. *Journal of Community Informatics* 5(1). http://www.ci-journal.net/index.php/ciej/article/view/473/437.

White, Deena. 2001. Maîtriser un mouvement, dompter une idéologie: L'État et le secteur communautaire au Québec. *Isuma: Canadian Journal of Policy Research* 2(2): 34–46.

21 THERE AND BACK TO THE FUTURE AGAIN Community Networks and Telecom Policy Reform in Canada, 1995–2010

Graham Longford, Marita Moll, Leslie Regan Shade

Community informatics initiatives take place within wider political, economic, and societal contexts that can generate atmospheric conditions, ranging from the supportive to the outright hostile, which affect the former's growth and development. Among the more important of these wider contexts are the ideological, political, and policy-making currents and processes that together shape how societies integrate new technologies into collective life and who benefits from them. This is particularly the case in countries such as Canada and the United States, where community networks have historically been nourished by "public interest" traditions in telecommunications regulation and by large-scale public funding for universal access initiatives, while simultaneously being buffeted by the winds of ideological change and neoliberal trends in public policy making toward more market-oriented approaches, which threaten the very existence of such networks (see chapter 4 in this volume). Indeed, the more that community networks come to rely on government funding and programs to grow and sustain themselves, the more vitally important it becomes for them to pay attention to and seek to influence developments within the wider context of the governance and regulation of ICTs, lest the existence and value of CNs be called into question. In this, as we shall see, community networks are not now and have seldom ever been passive spectators but rather very active (if not always successful) participants in ideological and public policy debates concerning the societal adoption and integration of new ICTs.

In this chapter, we focus on what is at stake for Canada's community informatics sector in light of recent trends in telecommunications policy making favouring more market-oriented approaches to telecommunications regulation, drawing on the experiences and activities of community networks in Canada from roughly 1995 to 2010. This period encompasses a time in which the telecommunications regulatory regime in Canada underwent significant change while the community networking movement enjoyed rapid growth and transformation, followed by a sharp contraction. To its credit, and despite a definitive regulatory shift toward telecommunications deregulation in the 1990s, the federal government of Canada made a significant commitment to supporting community-based ICT initiatives, allocating close to $1 billion in spending on universal access programs between 1995 and 2005 (see chapter 19). Community networking organizations flourished as a result but were at the same time transformed from grassroots volunteer organizations into increasingly institutionalized and professionalized organizations dependent on government funding programs and responsible for delivering government services and programs in the field of ICT access, training, and applications development (for example, e-health). As MacDonald, Longford, and Clement make clear in chapter 19, the community informatics sector's growing involvement in delivering the federal government's connectivity programs and services during the 2000s was a double-edged sword, until recently increasing the sector's access to funding while burdening it with increasingly onerous paperwork and threatening to impose the government's agenda on the sector's work within communities. Meanwhile, beginning in 2004, the federal government's commitment to universal access began to wane, and major funding cuts to universal access programs were implemented, as the federal government increasingly looked to market forces to solve the problem. Since that time, the community informatics sector in Canada has been in a state of crisis, and hundreds of organizations and initiatives have since disappeared. The lessons of the Canadian experience for community informatics research and practice are difficult to overlook. The future of community informatics is inevitably entangled with the evolution of telecommunications policy and regulatory frameworks and the extent to which the ideas of community and the public interest are championed within them.

After an initial overview of telecommunications policy reform in Canada since the mid-1990s and the role played by community networks in seeking to influence those reforms, in this chapter we focus on the federal Telecommunications Policy Review Panel (TPRP) and its 2006 final report, which has cast a shadow over telecommunications policy and regulation in Canada ever since,

with ambiguous implications for the status and future of community informatics initiatives across the country. We conclude with an examination of the
responses to the TPRP report by community networks and other public interest organizations in Canada and articulate an alternative public policy agenda
that protects the public interest in telecommunications regulation and carves
out a space for community-based, government-supported initiatives to ensure
both access to and effective use of new ICTs in communities across Canada.

TELECOMMUNICATIONS POLICY IN CANADA

Canada has a long history as a world leader in the development of advanced
telecommunications networks. In recognition of their importance to economic
development, cultural identity, national sovereignty, and communication
rights, these networks have been subject to a legislative and regulatory framework that safeguards the interests of all Canadians. Indeed, section 7 of the
Telecommunications Act (1993) affirms that "telecommunications performs
an essential role in the maintenance of Canada's identity and sovereignty" and
that "the Canadian telecommunications policy has as its objectives," among
other things, "to facilitate the orderly development throughout Canada of a
telecommunications system that serves to safeguard, enrich and strengthen
the social and economic fabric of Canada and its regions." Such legislative and
regulatory recognition of the public interest in telecommunications has helped
protect the interests of users and consumers of telecommunications services,
including those in under-served communities, through recognition of common carriage provisions, the importance of Canadian ownership, consumer
protection, and the adoption of cross-subsidization to finance hard-to-serve
areas. While such protection has been far from absolute, it has provided a foundation for public interest policy and regulatory provisions and a framework
for claims making on behalf of the public interest (Babe 1990). Coupled with
this have been legislative and regulatory institutions, such as the Canadian
Radio-television and Telecommunications Commission (CRTC), and reform
processes marked by relative democratic openness and responsiveness to the
claims of Canadian citizens and communities (Barney 2004).

During the 1990s and 2000s, however, telecommunications policy in
Canada has been driven by a neoliberal agenda focusing on deregulation
and economic competitiveness, at the expense of the public interest, cultural
sovereignty, and social well-being of Canadians (Rideout 2004). Beginning in
the 1980s, calls were made for the deregulation of the telecommunications system. In 1992, the long-distance telephone industry was deregulated. Canada's
Telecommunications Act was amended in 1993 to encourage increased reliance on market forces. This was followed by the deregulation of long-distance

services in 1997 and the CRTC's stunning 1998 decision on new media to forego regulation of the Internet altogether.

While deregulation was designed ostensibly to increase competition and unleash market forces in order to increase consumer choice and lower prices, Canadians continue to face a market oligopoly comprising a very limited number of powerful incumbents (White 2008). As a result, Canadians live in the worst of both worlds, enjoying neither the benefits of real competition nor the benefits of an industry regulated to serve the public interest. The Canadian telecommunications market lacks competitive vitality and has fallen behind other markets in terms of price, consumer choice, and penetration rates for services like cellular telephony and broadband. "In Canada, telecom history shows that we don't go from monopoly to competition—it's always the other way around. We had five wireless providers a few years ago and now we have three. The market has already spoken on this topic," said Lawrence Surtees, telecom consultant and author of a history of Bell Canada (McMurdy 2007). The Organisation for Economic Cooperation and Development report *Communications Outlook 2007* supports this assertion (OECD 2007). Summarizing the report, Geist notes that "Canada ranked second [to] last in the OECD for the total number of mobile subscribers," that "Canada placed far behind other countries for innovation," that "Canadian investment in telecommunications was average, trailing countries such as the US, Australia, Japan, and the UK," and that "the report reconfirms Canada's sinking ranking in broadband subscribers along with its relatively high prices for broadband" (Geist 2007). Little progress has been made in the late 2000s. As of 2009, Canadian wireless consumers paid the third highest rates among developed countries, while high-speed broadband consumers paid the second highest rates, according to the OECD (Nowak 2009). While deregulation may well have been good for corporate bottom lines at incumbent telecommunications giants such as Bell and Telus, it is difficult to discern how the public interest has been served. In spite of this, the mantra of deregulation continues to prevail.

CONNECTING CANADIANS

If there has been a bright spot in the recent history of telecommunications policy and the public interest in Canada, it would be the federal government's response to the challenges posed by new ICTs. Concerned about the challenges Canadians would face in a new digital economy, the federal government established the Information Highway Advisory Council (IHAC) in 1994, under the auspices of Industry Canada, to formulate a broad-based strategy for adapting Canada's economy and society to the new realities of the digital age. After a series of closed consultations dominated by industry groups, and with only token representation from civil society groups and communities with a stake in the issues, IHAC (Industry Canada 1995) recommended, among other things, that the development of Canada's digital infrastructure—including the Internet—be left to market forces and without government interference or regulation. While in its composition, proceedings, and final recommendations IHAC was an industry-dominated affair concerned primarily with the competitiveness of Canada's ICT industries (Barney 2004), its work nonetheless had the effect of galvanizing and uniting a broad and diverse constituency of civil society organizations, including community networks, around a common agenda of universal access and effective use (Clement, Moll, and Shade 2001). While the concerns of these groups fell on IHAC's deaf ears, they continued to organize and to lobby officials within Industry Canada, arguing that a strictly market-oriented approach to the development of Canada's digital infrastructure would leave millions of low-income Canadians as well as residents of rural and remote communities out in the cold, because there would be little market incentive for telecommunications companies to provide service to them. Some form of government intervention would be necessary to bridge the digital divide, they argued, and would be consistent with decades of telecommunications policy and regulation designed to meet the needs of all Canadians, including low-income groups and residents of high-cost service areas.

While the federal government adopted a great many of IHAC's recommendations, including an overall commitment to allowing the private sector to lead the development of Canada's digital infrastructure, it also recognized the need for government to play a role in ensuring universal access to computers and the Internet, as well as supporting programs enabling Canadians to acquire the necessary skills to use them, especially in rural and remote regions of the country. In September 1997, the federal government announced its Connecting Canadians agenda, a suite of programs the objective of which was "to make Canada the most connected nation in the world—to make Canada a world leader in developing and using an advanced information infrastructure to achieve our social and economic goals in the knowledge economy" (Manley 1999). It was a wide-ranging initiative that included made-in-Canada, online access programs such as SchoolNet, the Community Access Program (CAP), VolNet, and Smart Communities, as well as support for e-commerce, web-based Canadian content, and government online projects (see Appendix C).

The CAP program was one of the cornerstones of the Connecting Canadians initiative, and it became central to the development of community networks and community informatics projects across the country over the next decade. When first introduced, CAP was described as a program to "help provide Canadians with affordable access to the Internet and the services and tools it provides" (Industry Canada 2005a). The program's goal was to have all

Canadians and communities participate fully in the knowledge-based economy. While initially targeted at rural and remote communities, CAP funding was eventually extended to include organizations serving the needs of low-income Canadians in urban areas as well. CAP sites were most commonly located in schools, libraries, community centres, and friendship centres and operated through partnerships with provincial and territorial governments and non-profit organizations. Community networks were logical CAP partners of both the federal government and a diversity of community organizations hosting CAP sites, providing space, training, and technical as well as administrative support to site administrators, volunteers, and users. Industry Canada (2005a) documents peg the cost of the CAP program between 1995 and 2006 at $337.2 million—a relatively modest sum of money dedicated to some very lofty goals. A companion program, the CAP Youth Initiative (CAP YI), funded through Human Resources and Social Development Canada, was launched to provide paid work experience to youth at CAP sites, where they provided training and technical support to users. Together with the assistance of thousands of volunteers, CAP YI workers helped support the CAP sites so that communities could bring all members—including immigrants, seniors, youth, First Nations individuals, and the socially and economically challenged—up to date with new communications tools (see Appendix B).

Within two years of its inception, the goals associated with Connecting Canadians and CAP had moved well beyond the idea of connectivity as access and infrastructure for economic development, to the idea of connectivity as a vehicle for social cohesion. According to then Minister of Industry John Manley, "Connectedness is about our vision of the Canadian society we want in the 21st century—one with a strong, dynamic, competitive economy, and a strong lifelong-learning culture, but also one that uses connectedness to promote social cohesion, cultural expression and to build new linkages between citizens and government" (Manley 1999). Whatever the rationale presented, CAP was clearly set up as a community capacity building project—a multifaceted, grassroots-driven, nation-building project. At its apex, CAP funding helped to sustain 8,800 sites across Canada and maintained a footprint in communities across the country that was greater than all the Tim Hortons and Starbucks coffee shop chains combined (Industry Canada 2005a; Moll 2007). While, as MacDonald, Longford, and Clement discuss in chapter 19, the nature and administration of government programs such as CAP posed significant challenges for the community networks that benefitted from them, the period from 1997 to 2004 constituted something of a golden age in the history of community networking in Canada in terms of its access to resources and the number of projects launched.

By 2004, however, federal interest in universal access had begun to wane.

With household Internet access rates at 65 to 70 percent, the continuing relevance and necessity of public Internet access services were called into question. Federal and provincial governments began to withdraw significantly from supporting community networking and public Internet access. The major Connecting Canadians programs, such as CAP, SchoolNet, the Broadband for Rural and Northern Development (BRAND), and the National Satellite Initiative (NSI) were wound down or closed. The 2004 federal budget announced a two-year extension on CAP and SchoolNet, but with greatly reduced funding and a new strategic direction away from general public access and toward a more narrow focus on "digital divide" communities. The BRAND program allocated all available funds without any plans for new spending, despite the fact that thousands of rural and remote communities remained unconnected. With the imminent withdrawal of the federal government from community networking and public Internet access promotion, thousands of community-based ICT initiatives across Canada were plunged into crisis, since most of them relied on the CAP funding to support the cost of computers and Internet access, which underpinned the other services and programs they offered. By 2007, the Connecting Canadians initiative was a shadow of its former self. The CAP program was put on life-support, existing on drastically reduced funding from $25 million in 2004–5 to approximately $9 million in 2007. Once encompassing 8,800 sites across Canada, the number of active sites declined precipitously to fewer than 4,000 by 2005 (Industry Canada 2005b).

BACK TO THE FUTURE: THE TELECOMMUNICATIONS POLICY REVIEW PANEL

In this rather bleak climate of funding cuts and insecurity surrounding the hundreds of community informatics projects across the country, community networking advocates and practitioners greeted the federal government's announcement of a major review of telecommunications policy and regulation in 2005 with a mix of hope and trepidation. In April 2005, Minister of Industry David Emerson, a Liberal, appointed a three-member panel to conduct the first major public review of Canada's telecommunications policy framework since 1993.[1] The task of the Telecommunications Policy Review Panel (TPRP) was to consult with relevant stakeholders and then recommend policy changes that would "ensure that Canada has a strong, internationally competitive telecommunications industry that delivers world-class services and products for the economic and social benefit of all Canadians" (Telecommunications Policy Review Panel 2006, iii). Still smarting from the IHAC experience, community networking advocates nonetheless seized on the TPRP process as an opportunity to once again advance a broader community informatics agenda and resuscitate the many initiatives that had fallen victim to funding cuts to CAP and other programs. Alas, from both a substantive and a procedural point of view, as we shall see, the community networking sector's engagement with the TPRP was very much a "back to the future" scenario, replicating the experience of its attempts to engage with the IHAC process in the mid-1990s.

The TPRP was asked to consider three specific areas within the context of recent changes in technology, consumer demand, and market structure: regulation, access, and information and communications technologies (ICT) adoption.

Regulation. Given a rapidly changing telecom environment (Wi-Fi, Internet protocol-based services, mobile technologies, and broadband) coupled with increasing consumer demand, the panel was asked to make recommendations on the implementation of an "efficient, fair, functional and forward-looking regulatory framework that serves Canadian consumers and businesses, and that can adapt to a changing technological landscape" (Canada 2005).

Access. Canada's 1993 Telecommunications Act mandates the provision of reliable and affordable telecommunications for Canadians across the country and various sectors of the economy. The panel was asked to make recommendations on "mechanisms that will ensure that all Canadians continue to have an appropriate level of access to modern telecommunications services" (Canada 2005).

ICT Adoption. The 1993 Telecommunications Act includes provisions to safeguard, enrich, and strengthen the social and economic fabric of Canada. Given the reliance of the Canadian economy on ICT service provision, the panel was asked to make recommendations on "measures to promote the development, adoption and expanded use of advanced telecommunications services across the economy," along with recommendations on the current appropriateness of Canada's ICT investments (Canada 2005). The importance of this area of the panel's inquiry was not lost on the community networking sector. Clearly at stake, and explicitly in question, was whether and to what extent a continued role for the federal government in connectivity investments and initiatives such as CAP was still warranted.

Included in the TPRP's activities was a series of consultations designed to solicit input from stakeholders as well as the public at large. A consultation paper was issued in early June 2005, with interested parties invited to make submissions on the paper by 15 August 2005 (called Round One). A second round of submissions commenting on the first round of submissions was invited for 15 September 2005. The panel received a total of 198 submissions.

The consultation paper itself ran sixty pages in length and included over a hundred questions for consideration (Telecommunications Policy Review Panel 2005a). The paper was divided into a number of key sections. The first part offered a brief description of the current state of telecommunications technologies and markets and discussed current trends and future developments. The second part explored the basic questions of why governments intervene to regulate telecommunications markets, what the policy objectives of such government intervention should be, and the types of economic, technical, and social regulation required to meet them. A third section discussed government institutions best equipped to achieve the intended objectives, as well as various regulatory tasks such as policy development, rule making, authorization, dispute resolution, enforcement, and appeals. The fourth section dealt with Canadians' access to broadband services and advanced ICTs, reviewing recent initiatives to expand broadband access (e.g., BRAND and NSI) and posed the question of when and how the government should proceed to ensure that more Canadians have access to broadband and other advanced telecommunications services. The panel invited stakeholders to consider the desirability of increased reliance on market forces in the telecommunications sector to complete the job of ensuring universal access to advanced telecommunications services, including broadband. The Telecommunications Policy Review Panel asked:

> Is government or regulatory intervention required to expand Canada's telecommunications network connectivity—or should this be left to the market? Given the level of competition in the broadband access market, as well as the fact that new access and IP technologies are reducing costs for consumers and improving the business case for service providers, is government or regulatory intervention still required? (Telecommunications Policy Review Panel 2005a, 51)

While framed as a question, the intent lying behind the query was transparent: the TPRP was calling on the federal government to reconsider its connectivity programs while reviving IHAC's suggestion that unencumbered market forces would solve the problem of the digital divide.

Other sections of the consultation paper dealt with ICT adoption across a variety of sectors within Canadian society, including business, government, and the home. A final section of the consultation paper examined questions of implementation of the policy and regulatory changes considered by the panel. Overall, the panel's consultation paper reflected the regulatory concerns of key industry stakeholders as opposed to those of public interest and other community organizations and was informed by an unmistakably neoliberal worldview professing faith in market forces and disavowing the role of government and regulation.

Following the release of its consultation paper, the public consultation and discussion phase of the TPRP was skewed, both substantively and procedurally, in favour of business and industry participants. Submissions to the panel's consultation paper came overwhelmingly from business and industry stakeholders. The short timelines that stakeholders were given in which to respond favoured business and industry participants with the paid staff and the resources needed to produce well-researched and professionally written submissions in a short period. A survey of TPRP submissions for Round One (15 August 2005) and Round Two (15 September 2005) revealed that Aboriginal, consumer, women's, and community groups represented only 15.5 percent of the total submissions, versus 60.1 percent for industry groups (see table 21.1).

TABLE 21.1 TPRP submissions Round One (15 August 2005) and Round Two (15 September 2005)

Source of submission	Round One submissions (n = 109)	Round Two submissions (n = 89)	Total submissions (n = 198)
Industry	29 (26.6%)	28 (31.4%)	57 (28.7%)
Industry-related associations	16 (14.6%)	11 (12.3%)	27 (13.6%)
Industry-related consultancy firms	1 (0.9%)	1 (1.1%)	2 (1.0%)
Employee associations/unions	2 (1.8%)	3 (3.3%)	5 (2.5%)
Governmental bodies (federal or provincial)	14 (12.8%)	8 (8.9%)	22 (11.1%)
Consumer groups (including one consortium of groups)	2 (1.8%)	2 (2.2%)	4 (2.0%)
Community groups	9 (8.2%)	8 (8.9%)	17 (8.5%)
Aboriginal groups	3 (2.7%)	5 (5.6%)	8 (4.0%)
Women's groups		2 (2.2%)	2 (1.0%)
Business-related associations or councils	11 (10%)	3 (3.3%)	14 (7.0%)
Educational institutions	2 (1.8%)	1 (1.1%)	3 (1.5%)
Individuals (includes academics, high-tech entrepreneurs, and small business owners)	14 (12.8%)	13 (14.6%)	27 (13.6%)
Miscellaneous (includes associations, institutes, cultural or professional organizations)	6 (5.5%)	4 (4.4%)	10 (5.0%)

SOURCE: Telecommunications Policy Review Panel submissions archive. Statistics compiled by Rachel Miles, Concordia University.

The TPRP also held two in-person public forums featuring invited guest speakers, expert panel discussion, and limited opportunities for stakeholder groups to attend and participate. A public forum on rural and remote broadband was also held in Whitehorse, Yukon, in September 2005, but public attendance was limited and subject to the discretion of the panel's executive director. In addition, the prohibitive costs of travelling to and within Canada's North discouraged many interested stakeholders from attending. No travel subsidies were offered to community groups wishing to attend (Telecommunications Policy Review Panel 2005b). The panel's other public forum was held in Gatineau, Québec, in the fall of 2005. The meeting agenda was dominated by industry and government concerns, such as competitiveness, productivity, and deregulation (Telecommunications Policy Review Panel 2005c). Industry giants Telus, Bell Canada, and Nortel issued urgent appeals for the government not to regulate, to let market forces reign, and to promote telecommunications for economic efficiency—all tenets of the neoliberal agenda—but not for social and cultural betterment (Telecommunications Policy Review Panel 2005d). Faced with an unexpected group of tenacious researchers and community networking advocates, forum organizers scheduled a hastily organized civil society panel at the end of the final day's session, which was conducted while the majority of forum participants filed out of the conference room and the proceedings of which were not reflected in the summary report on the forum proceedings produced by TPRP staff. The marginalization of community and public interest advocates in the proceedings of the October policy forum served to underscore the extent to which their concerns were an afterthought to the whole process.

COMMUNITY NETWORK RESPONSES TO THE TPRP

Submissions to the TPRP from community networks and public interest groups insisted that government had a continuing role in ensuring equitable access to network infrastructure and technologies and in ensuring that all Canadians have the necessary skills, resources, and confidence to take advantage of the potential benefits afforded by them. Community and public interest organizations, including CRACIN, participated in the review process by making written submissions and presenting and participating in the two policy forums in Whitehorse and Gatineau (Clement et al. 2005a, 2005b). On the whole, community submissions stressed the following:

- The important role played by the community networking sector in supporting access to and effective use of ICTs in Canada's telecommunications infrastructure as a whole

- The persistence of a multi-faceted "digital divide" within Canadian society afflicting various regions and populations
- The ongoing need for government intervention to regulate market actors and to support local, community-based telecommunications solutions.

Responding to the panel's provocatively worded question about the continuing need for government investment in connectivity infrastructure and supporting programs, CRACIN researchers made several recommendations in two separate submissions. In the current climate of decreased government funding for ICT programs, CRACIN recommended the following:

- The imminent cuts to and/or closure of connectivity programs such as CAP and BRAND should be reconsidered. New resources and, if need be, new programs should be dedicated to connecting Canadians and to strengthening community-based ICT organizations and the programs they offer.
- Connectivity policies and programs should be designed and implemented to support the necessary social structure of universal access and to encourage effective use of ICTs by individuals and communities.
- Connectivity policy and programs should be designed and implemented with a strong community-based component in mind. This means not only better funding for community-based ICT initiatives but also involving communities and community organizations in connectivity policy making, in defining access needs, in designing programs, and so on.

In a second submission to the panel, commenting on the first round of submissions, CRACIN acknowledged the significant role played by private industry and market forces in the build-out of Canada's advanced ICT infrastructure but cautioned that "reliance upon an unregulated market to ensure equitable and effective access to increasingly essential telecommunications infrastructure and services by all Canadians would be irresponsible and potentially damaging to Canadian society" (Clement et al. 2005b, 4). In CRACIN's opinion, experience and research demonstrate that "when left to free market imperatives, the evolution of Canada's telecommunications infrastructure fails to meet the needs of many Canadians, including the disabled, rural communities, Aboriginals, and the urban poor" (Clement et al. 2005b, 4). Because private sector investment in providing products and services to such groups and communities is deemed uneconomic, the latter have often been faced with poor service, high costs, or exclusion from service altogether. CRACIN reiterated that "in an increasingly networked economy and society, in which being connected is a necessary condition of economic, social and political participation, such market-based forms of discrimination and exclusion are unacceptable" (Clement et al. 2005b, 4). Beyond a need to address these various market failures,

CRACIN endorsed as a *communication right* that all Canadians have access to and benefit from advanced telecommunications infrastructures that increasingly serve as the gateway to economic, social, and political participation in the information society.

In a follow-up letter to the TPRP, CRACIN reiterated the importance of community networks in fostering citizen-centric ICT initiatives. Community networking solutions offer distinctive models and advantages to communities and users that the private sector does not afford and that warrant being supported and promoted by governments, including:

- Local control of network development and management
- Content and applications development based on locally determined social needs and active community participation
- Development of local skills and capacity for innovation based on local resources and local opportunities
- A commitment to equitable access for all community members.

CRACIN then reiterated to the panel the following recommendations:

- Affirm, preserve and improve existing policies and programs to support and promote community-based networking solutions as consistent with the objectives of the Telecommunications Act as specified in section 7.
- Support communities, municipalities, and local organizations that wish to develop and maintain their own community-based networking infrastructure, services, and applications.
- Resist the use of regulation and legislation to suppress community and/ or municipal networking solutions, as had recently been witnessed in the United States (e.g., community/municipal Wi-Fi).

CRACIN's submissions and presentations also pointed to the persistence of ICT access gaps afflicting various populations in Canada, including low-income families, rural residents, Aboriginals, and the disabled. As they further reiterated to the panel:

The minister of Industry has a statutory responsibility under section 7 of the 1993 Telecommunications Act to implement policies and programs that ensure affordable access to high-quality telecommunications networks for all Canadians and that safeguard, enrich, and strengthen the social and economic fabric of Canada and its regions.

Policies and programs that support ICT network access, adoption and effective use by Canadians need to be maintained and strengthened, and these should be backed by adequate and stable long-term funding to meet the present and future access needs of Canadians as new technologies arise.

DÉJÀ VU ALL OVER AGAIN: THE TPRP FINAL REPORT

The final report of the TPRP was released in March 2006. By then, the government had changed hands as a result of the 2006 federal election, changing to a Conservative minority government led by Stephen Harper. Not surprisingly, the report called for bold steps to deregulate telecommunications industries and to maximize reliance on market forces in order to promote growth and competitiveness. Industry groups were pleased with the report. Said Bell Canada executive Lawson Hunter: "This is a landmark report that will ignite a key driver of Canada's economy. . . . Important is their recognition of the urgent need to allow market forces to prevail in order to ensure Canadian consumers and businesses receive the full benefits of competition and innovation" (Bell Canada 2006). Perrin Beatty, then president and CEO of Canadian Manufacturers and Exporters, called it "one of the most comprehensive and authoritative reviews of telecommunications policy ever conducted anywhere" (Beatty 2006). That said, the panel's recommendations also included an acknowledgement that market forces alone would not ensure timely access to broadband infrastructure for many of Canada's more remote communities, and it endorsed the creation of a new program to ensure broadband connectivity for such communities. The following is a brief summary of the major recommendations made in the TPRP final report, with a focus on those with the greatest potential to impact the community informatics sector, for better or worse.

Deregulation of Canadian Telecommunications

The panel contended that market competition has served telecommunications consumers well and that further economic deregulation was warranted. The panel specifically recommended eliminating from the Telecommunications Act any requirements that telecommunications services be regulated unless the CRTC rules otherwise and imposing a heavy burden of proof on the commission to justify regulation. The panel also recommended limiting economic regulation to geographic areas where it is demonstrably required to protect consumer interests and/or the maintenance of competitive markets. The position endorsed by the panel is that the whole Canadian regulatory framework should move from what it called a "presumption of regulation" to a "presumption of deregulation" (see Telecommunications Policy Review Panel 2006, 4 and 3-12).

Consumer Protection

The panel recommended that the Telecommunications Act be amended to explicitly obligate telephone companies to continue to provide basic telephone service to their customers, that a Telecommunications Consumer Agency be established to deal with various consumer complaints, and that violations of network neutrality for anti-competitive purposes be prohibited. This would involve an amendment to the Telecommunications Act so that Canadian consumers would continue to have the right to access publicly available Internet applications and content, with the CRTC able to respond to any infractions by telecommunications companies.

Ubiquitous Broadband and the U-CAN Program

While the panel believed that competition and market forces had served Canadians well, in areas where it is too expensive to justify a market-led plan, such as rural and remote regions, the panel recommended a narrowly targeted subsidy program managed by the federal government and dispersed by way of "least-cost subsidy" auctions, awarded to bidders that are financially and technically sound but that need the least subsidy. The panel also recommended the creation of a specific targeted program, the Ubiquitous Canadian Access Network/Ubiquité Canada (U-CAN). Its role would be to provide broadband access to geographic areas in Canada that are not well served by commercial providers, who are unlikely to offer service for economic reasons. U-CAN would replace the BRAND program, providing ubiquitous broadband across Canada by 2010. While the U-CAN program recommendations signalled an important concession to the role of government on the panel's part, the narrowly geographic way in which the panel conceived of the digital divide failed to address the ongoing connectivity needs of other groups, including low-income and new Canadians. Furthermore, the fine print made it quite clear that the U-CAN program, if implemented, would bare scant resemblance to the CAP program in terms of the role to be played by community organizations in providing and managing connectivity infrastructure and services. The terms and implementation of the proposed program, including the financial and other obligations imposed on subsidy recipients, guaranteed that applicants would have to come primarily from the private sector and that few, if any, non-profit community organizations would be able to participate.

National ICT Adoption Strategy

To its credit, the TPRP also recommended the development of a joint federal-provincial-territorial-municipal National ICT Adoption Strategy, in collaboration with the private, public, and not-for-profit sectors, to strengthen ICT adoption by small and medium-sized enterprises (SMEs), enhance ICT uses by governments, promote ICT research and development and adoption, improve consumer confidence and trust, and achieve ubiquitous access to broadband networks and services. In the section of the TPRP report on ICT adoption, the panel remarked:

Physical access to ICTs at the community level, together with improved broadband network connectivity, is a prime means for spreading the social and economic benefits of information technology. A new generation of ICT applications allows communities to adapt ICTs to their own situations, develop local content, and access and use content created by others. However, none of this will happen in the absence of e-literacy and technology skills at the community level.

The Panel believes a vibrant ICT private sector not only is important for creating opportunities throughout the economy, but also is an engine for building e-literacy and ICT technology skills at the community level. (Telecommunications Policy Review Panel 2006, 7-43).

The TPRP also acknowledged CRACIN's submission:

The Canadian Research Alliance for Community Innovation and Networking noted in its submission to the Panel that community networks and other community-based organizations provide both technological and social infrastructures for ICT access, adoption and use. Community networks also act as important sources of local economic development and innovation. Through training programs, for example, they help ensure that all Canadians, particularly those most at risk of being left behind, have the necessary skills to participate in the networked economy. (Telecommunications Policy Review Panel 2006, 7-43)

The panel thus recognized that universal access and effective use are needed alongside the physical infrastructure associated with ICTs. It takes the social infrastructure—the training, support, relevant applications, and human beings on the ground—to make effective use a reality.

Telecommunications Policy Objectives: Amendments to Section 7 of the Telecommunications Act

One of the most controversial and, from a community informatics and public interest perspective, most alarming recommendations was the panel's suggestion for amending section 7 of the 1993 Telecommunications Act, which lays out the fundamental policy objectives of the act. In general, the panel recommended reducing and narrowing the meaning of the social and cultural concerns addressed in the policy objectives of the existing act, effectively truncating them. Section 7 of the existing act reads as follows:

It is hereby affirmed that telecommunications performs an essential role in the maintenance of Canada's identity and sovereignty and that the Canadian telecommunications policy has as its objectives:

(a) to facilitate the orderly development throughout Canada of a telecommunications system that serves to safeguard, enrich and strengthen the social and economic fabric of Canada and its regions;

(b) to render reliable and affordable telecommunications services of high quality accessible to Canadians in both urban and rural areas in all regions of Canada;

(c) to enhance the efficiency and competitiveness, at the national and international levels, of Canadian telecommunications;

(d) to promote the ownership and control of Canadian carriers by Canadians;

(e) to promote the use of Canadian transmission facilities for telecommunications within Canada and between Canada and points outside Canada;

(f) to foster increased reliance on market forces for the provision of telecommunications services and to ensure that regulation, where required, is efficient and effective;

(g) to stimulate research and development in Canada in the field of telecommunications and to encourage innovation in the provision of telecommunications services;

(h) to respond to the economic and social requirements of users of telecommunications services; and,

(i) to contribute to the protection of the privacy of persons.

In its Recommendation 2-2, the panel suggested amending section 7 to read as follows:

It is hereby affirmed that telecommunications performs an essential role in enabling the economic and social welfare of Canada and that Canadian telecommunications policy is based on the following objectives:

(a) to promote affordable access to advanced telecommunications services in all regions of Canada, including urban, rural and remote areas;

(b) to enhance the efficiency of Canadian telecommunications markets and the productivity of the Canadian economy; and

(c) to enhance the social well-being of Canadians and the inclusiveness of Canadian society by:

(i) facilitating access to telecommunications by persons with disabilities;

(ii) maintaining public safety and security;

(iii) contributing to the protection of personal privacy; and

(iv) limiting public nuisance through telecommunications.

(Telecommunications Policy Review Panel 2006, 2-9)

In other words, the panel recommended gutting most of the broader social objectives of the previous act, such as cultural sovereignty and social cohesion, in favour of a much more limited and circumscribed list of social concerns, including access for persons with disabilities, privacy, and the protection of users from cybercrime and spam. What was immediately recognized by community informatics and public interest groups was the threat posed by the panel's section 7 amendments to the very grounds upon which citizens and public interest groups made claims upon the government to regulate the telecommunications sector in the first place. Amending the section 7 provisions in the ways suggested by the panel would have the effect of eliminating much of the purchase that such groups enjoyed on the system of telecommunications regulation in Canada and their ability to have a voice within it (Lawson 2008).

CRTC Policy Directive

The panel's report also contained a series of practical suggestions for implementing the recommendations contained in it. Recognizing that an overhaul of the Telecommunications Act of 1993 was a relatively distant possibility under the minority parliament of the time, the panel recommended that the federal cabinet issue a policy directive to the CRTC in order to expedite the process of deregulation by performing an end run around legislative hurdles. "In addition to clarifying the policy objectives," the panel wrote, "the *Telecommunications Act* should establish the following new guidelines for government and regulatory action," which should be made binding on the CRTC immediately:

- Market forces should be relied upon to the maximum extent feasible as the means of achieving Canada's telecommunications policy objectives.
- Regulatory and other government measures should be adopted only where market forces are unlikely to achieve a telecommunications policy objective within a reasonable time frame; and only where the costs of regulation do not outweigh the benefits.
- Regulatory and other government measures should be efficient and proportionate to their purpose and should only minimally interfere with the operation of market forces to meet the objectives. (Telecommunications Policy Review Panel 2006, 4)

THE ALTERNATIVE TELECOMMUNICATIONS POLICY FORUM: CITIZENS AND COMMUNITIES RESPOND TO THE TPRP

Public interest advocates and community networks were alarmed by many of the TPRP's recommendations, arguing that they threatened the Canadian public's right to an affordable, universally accessible, and democratically accountable telecommunications system. In order to provide a forum in which to articulate and discuss these concerns, the CRACIN research group convened the Alternative Telecommunications Policy Forum, which was held in Ottawa in October 2006. The forum was born from a recognition of the fragmented nature of the telecommunications "counter-publics" attentive to the issues at stake, of the need for a more citizen-centric and community-oriented forum for the discussion of telecommunications policy and regulation in Canada, and of the need for a more coordinated and collective response to the TPRP report on the part of citizens and communities.

The forum attracted sixty participants representing community and public interest groups, academic researchers, cultural organizations, and practitioners from community networks and CAP sites from across Canada. Participants met for two days to hear and discuss expert presentations on various aspects of the Telecommunications Policy Review Panel (TPRP) final report, issued the previous spring. The forum panels and discussions focused on the following key themes and topics:

- Regulation versus market forces in ensuring the public good in telecommunications
- Rethinking institutions of telecommunications governance
- Sustaining community ICT programs
- Network neutrality.

As participants grasped the implications of the TPRP's recommendations for amending the policy objectives of the Telecommunications Act, section 7, these became a central preoccupation as well. What follows is a brief summary of the recommendations that came out the forum discussions, with an emphasis on those most pertinent to the sustainability of community informatics initiatives and guarding the public interest in telecommunications.

The convenors of the Alternative Telecommunications Policy Forum summarized the substance and recommendations of the forum proceedings in a press release and follow-up letter to then Minister of Industry Maxime Bernier. On the subject of deregulation to enhance the role of market forces in the development of Canada's telecommunications system, forum participants expressed skepticism and concern. The letter reiterated the point that greater reliance on market forces to ensure universal access to telecommunications infrastructure and services "would be irresponsible and potentially damaging to Canadian society" (CRACIN 2007). As community and public interest group submissions to the TPRP made abundantly clear, the convenors pointed out, Canadian consumers have not always been well served by market forces in telecommunications services, especially in areas such as price, consumer protection, and the rollout of broadband infrastructure. "The United States," they argued, "which has pursued telecom deregulation more vigorously, should also serve as a cautionary example—American broadband consumers face some of the highest prices and poorest service in the OECD" (CRACIN

2007). "Canada would do well to learn from the mistakes already made south of the border in the United States, where we embraced aggressive deregulation sooner," suggested forum guest speaker Ben Scott, policy director for Free Press, a media policy think tank based in Washington DC (quoted in CRACIN 2006). Scott went on to point out that, since 2001, the United States had fallen from fourth to twelfth in OECD rankings for broadband penetration. The convenors noted:

> There was concern about the tenor of the proposed policy directive to the Canadian Radio-television and Telecommunications Commission (CRTC). . . . Shifting too sharply towards a market-based approach to implementing the Telecommunications Act has the potential to sideline many Canadian citizens without affordable and effective telecommunication services. Participants felt that the CRTC played an important role in the implementation of Canadian telecom policy and that its role should not be arbitrarily diminished. (CRACIN 2007)

On the subject of ICT access, adoption, and use, and the related question of whether or not there was an ongoing role for government in supporting them, forum participants

> acknowledged a number of positive findings and recommendations from the TPRP report, including the latter's recognition that community-based organizations provide important technological and social infrastructure for access to and the adoption and use of information and communications technologies (ICTs) at the community level. . . . The need to further promote and support this valuable community-based infrastructure, much of which originated with the "Connecting Canadians" agenda, was emphasized. To lose it now would be to destroy an asset that the rest of the world would like to emulate (CRACIN 2007).

The convenors went on to note the forum participants' enthusiasm for the TPRP's proposed National ICT Adoption Strategy (Recommendations 7-2 to 7-4), integrating research, a coordinated skills adoption plan, and a connectivity agenda, which they argued "could go a long way towards supporting these essential services and is a step in the right direction for community groups whose important work is being complicated by short-term funding decisions by government" (CRACIN 2007).

Forum participants also expressed tentative support for the TPRP's recommendations for the U-CAN targeted subsidy plan to connect all communities to broadband by 2010 (Recommendations 8-1 to 8-20). The implementation of such a plan, they noted, including multi-stakeholder consultations, could propel Canada to the forefront of broadband penetration among developed countries. Concerns were expressed, however, about the geographic bias implicit in the TPRP's understanding of the digital divide, which recognizes only distance, low population density, and remoteness as the primary barriers affecting Canadians' access to broadband. The TPRP's fixation with geography threatens to obscure the role of other barriers that also call for intervention, including poverty. In addition, participants worried that the eligibility criteria and administrative burdens associated with the TPRP's implementation plan for U-CAN (Recommendations 8-13 to 8-19) would disqualify many community networks and not-for-profit organizations from eligibility for funding (CRACIN 2007). Participants argued that the major benefactors of the U-CAN subsidy would in all likelihood be the large telephone companies rather than communities. "The outlined financial obligations are simply too onerous for any other group to play," said Garth Graham of Telecommunities Canada, a group that supports Canadian community networks. "That leaves communities unable to pursue their own ideas and choices about connection and development" (Telecommunities Canada 2006). Overall, there was a strong consensus among forum participants that policies and programs that support ICT network access, adoption, and effective use by individuals and communities in Canada need to be maintained and strengthened, and these need to be backed by adequate and stable long-term funding in order to meet the present and future access needs of Canadians as new technologies arise.

Proposed changes to the policy objectives of the Telecommunications Act as laid out in section 7 were discussed and debated at length during the forum. There was considerable unease among participants about the TPRP's proposed revision to the section (Recommendation 2-2). Participants felt that the proposed amendments would truncate the act's concern with the social implications of telecommunications in Canada by focusing more narrowly on (albeit significant) matters such as access for the disabled, public safety, and spam. Philippa Lawson, then executive director of the Canadian Internet Policy and Public Interest Clinic, noted:

> The proposed rewrite of section 7 of the *Telecommunications Act* would eliminate important policy goals such as reliable, high quality service and the protection of consumers from telecom-specific marketplace abuses. It would also remove key provisions including the requirement for just and reasonable rates and the rule against unjust discrimination. Without these goals and basic ground rules, we can expect lowest common denominator approaches to telecommunications service in Canada and widespread marketplace abuses. (Quoted in CRACIN 2006)

In their follow-up letter to the minister of Industry, the forum convenors urged the minister to "retain the statutory responsibility under section 7 of the Telecommunications Act to implement policies and programs that ensure affordable access to high quality telecommunications networks for all Canadians and that safeguard, enrich and strengthen the social and economic fabric of Canada and its regions" (CRACIN 2007). The forum also expressed concern that the TPRP's section 7 recommendations would dilute the federal government's responsibility for preserving Canadian cultural and economic sovereignty in telecommunications.

Finally, network neutrality was an important topic of discussion at the Alternative Telecommunications Policy Forum, as many participants were increasingly aware of the public debate and legislative activity on this issue in the United States at the time. The TPRP addressed the issue of network neutrality as well. In its report, the TPRP (2006, 6-16) wrote that Canadian telecom policy and regulation "should include provisions that confirm and protect the right of Canadian consumers to access publicly available Internet applications and content of their choice by means of public telecommunications networks that provide access to the Internet." The panel made a number of recommendations, including a strong regulatory mandate for the CRTC to review complaints and establish rules with respect to content blocking and service degradation (Recommendation 6-5). The forum participants recommended that Recommendation 6-5 of the TPRP report include a statement that would strengthen network neutrality protection in Canada: "Notwithstanding any other provision in this paragraph, network operators shall not discriminate against content, applications, or services on broadband Internet services based on their source, ownership or destination." In addition, forum participants disagreed with the TPRP's recommendation (Recommendation 3-13) to strike section 27 of the Telecommunications Act, which protects network users and consumers from discrimination and unfair pricing. On the contrary, legislation prohibiting unjust discrimination must be maintained and even strengthened in order to provide consumer protection and to control anti-competitive behaviour on the part of network owners and operators.

Upon forwarding a summary of the forum proceedings to the minister of Industry, the convenors received a prompt, if somewhat vague, response from the minister. On the subject of policies and programs to encourage ICT access, adoption, and use, Minister Bernier professed to share the forum's view that "ICTs and other advanced technologies are important to Canada's long-term prosperity and well-being" (Minister of Industry 2007). At the time of writing, however, the minister informed the convenors that "no decision has yet been reached on how to proceed" with programs to address this issue (Minister of Industry 2007). Despite the apparent urgency of the subject, it would take two more years for the government to finally come to a decision, with the announcement of the Broadband Canada program in 2009. On the question of amendments to section 7 of the Telecommunications Act, again, the minister declined to reveal the government's hand, stating that "no decision has been taken on the timing or substance of any possible amendments" (Minister of Industry 2007). Given the sensitivities that such amendments might arouse among cultural nationalists, and the government party's own minority status in Parliament at the time, it is no surprise that it did not immediately pursue the panel's legislative recommendations. In any case, aggressive implementation of the policy directive to the CRTC and the cabinet's own power to overrule CRTC decisions on regulatory matters (e.g., VOIP and Globalive decisions) meant that the government did not need to go the legislative route in pursuing its agenda of further deregulation. In his letter to the forum convenors the minister insisted that "the purpose of the Policy Direction is not to reduce the role of the CRTC" (Minister of Industry 2007), a claim that seemed belied by the policy directive's rejection of the "presumption of regulation" in favour of deregulation and the cabinet's subsequent attempts, as we shall see, to prevent the commission from regulating in key areas such as discriminatory practices and foreign ownership. Finally, on the subject of enhancing the role of market forces in the telecom sector, the minister agreed that this "should not come at the expense of key social considerations," which he defined narrowly as "public safety issues and the needs of disabled Canadians" (Minister of Industry 2007). On the subject of the many other social objectives that the forum participants put forward—such as universal access, effective use, cultural sovereignty, and Canadian identity—the minister was silent.

While grateful for the acknowledgement that their input and work on these issues received from both the TPRP and the minister of Industry, the convenors and participants in the Alternative Telecommunications Policy Forum felt a distinct sense of déjà vu. Many forum participants were veterans of the proceedings of IHAC in the mid-1990s, during which a coalition of community networks, arts and culture groups, trade unionists, library professionals, and public interest and privacy organizations attempted to carve out a space for greater public participation and input into the IHAC consultations. More than a decade later, the sense that their concerns were being marginalized in the process, that their voices were not being heard, and that government was not really interested in a serious engagement with them was as strong as ever. At the same time, the forum did have the intended effect of reestablishing and strengthening connections amongst the various groups that make up Canada's telecommunications "counter-public"—groups who, together, have remained in contact and have since actively lobbied government and the CRTC on a variety of other issues, including the future of the CAP program, copyright, network neutrality, and foreign ownership.

DEREGULATION IN THE WAKE OF THE TPRP

Although, at the time this chapter was written, many of the TPRP's recommendations were still under review by the Conservative government, a number had been adopted and implemented rapidly through cabinet orders. In June 2006, the federal minister of Industry at the time, Maxime Bernier, tabled a policy directive to the CRTC, ordering the commission to rely on market forces to the "maximum extent feasible" in its rulings. "Tabling this document," the minister declared, "signals the government's intention to direct the CRTC to rely on market forces to the maximum extent feasible under the *Telecommunications Act* and regulate—where there is still a need to do so—in a manner that interferes with market forces to the minimum extent necessary" (CBC News 2006b).

In addition, where, in the view of the federal cabinet, the CRTC fails to adhere to the directive, the cabinet has not hesitated to invoke its power to overrule the commission's decisions. The cabinet has already rewritten the terms of a number of CRTC regulatory decisions in the name of market forces, one on Internet telephony and another on foreign ownership. In 2006, for example, the federal cabinet set aside a CRTC decision on the regulation of discriminatory practices in the provision of Internet telephone services (VOIP) in favour of less regulation (Canadian Radio-television and Telecommunications Commission 2005; CBC News 2006a). In January 2007, the cabinet appointed federal court Justice Konrad von Finckenstein, former head of the Competition Bureau, to chair the CRTC. Finckenstein was a staunch opponent of corporate concentration during his tenure at the Competition Bureau, and his appointment to the CRTC chair's position was seen as a precursor to the federal government's efforts to open the telecom sector to increased competition. In 2008, meanwhile, Industry Canada presided over a key wireless spectrum auction in which spectrum licenses were auctioned off in the hopes that a new player would emerge in the Canadian market for advanced wireless services (Longford 2008). One of the successful bidders was Globalive Inc., an Egyptian-owned firm. When the CRTC rejected Globalive's bid to operate its new wireless network on the basis that the company did not satisfy legislative requirements on domestic ownership and control, the cabinet intervened in 2009 and overruled the CRTC's decision (Industry Canada 2009b). In overruling the CRTC, the federal cabinet effectively lowered the bar for foreign-controlled companies to qualify as domestic participants in Canada's telecommunications services market, opening the Canadian market to increased foreign competition and control. Indeed, in the March 2010 Speech from the Throne, the federal government made an explicit commitment to lowering existing legislative barriers to foreign ownership (Curry and Marlow 2010).

The federal government's agenda has received plenty of push from the private sector as well. In an extraordinary move, Bell Canada and Telus funded TPRP member Hank Intven and former deputy minister Mary Dawson to draft a "model telecommunications act" based on the recommendations of the TPRP. Published by the law firm McCarthy Tétrault, which currently includes Intven among its legal experts, the "model act" was unveiled at the 2007 Canadian Telecom Summit, an annual meeting of the powerhouses of the Canadian telecommunications industry (Intven and Dawson 2007). This is a disturbing precedent that passed largely unnoticed by the media or public interest advocates. While rather moot at the time, given what was then a minority parliament, the Intven-Dawson "model act" provides the Tories, who now hold a majority, with a template for legislative reform. How tempting will it be for those who are truly tasked with bringing forward legislation on these issues to start with a neatly prepared industry-friendly document rather than starting from scratch to address the needs of Canadians as a whole? How can communities match the resources and expertise of the private sector and friends in government in order to put forward credible alternatives? Together with other TPRP recommendations still under consideration by the government, these moves represent an unprecedented attempt to diminish the ability of Canadian citizens, through their democratically accountable legislative and regulatory bodies, to ensure that Canada's telecommunications system meets the needs of all Canadians.

The federal government's September 2009 launch of a long-awaited program to extend broadband service in rural and remote areas was perhaps the lone bright spot in what had been, for community networks and public interest advocates, a discouraging few years. Called Broadband Canada: Connecting Rural Canadians, the $225-million program was announced as part of the government's stimulus package in response to the severe economic downturn that began in 2008 (Industry Canada 2009a). It was, perhaps, also a response to the TPRP's call for the U-CAN program to replace the lapsed BRAND program. However, once the terms and conditions of the new program were understood, it became clear that it falls far short of addressing Canadians' access needs or the needs of the community organizations that can effectively address them. As part of an economic stimulus plan, first of all, Broadband Canada will most likely be a short-lived affair, with funds drying up at the first hint of economic recovery. Second, with its exclusive emphasis on connecting rural and remote communities, the program is targeted exclusively at overcoming geographic barriers to access, rather than recognizing and addressing other barriers identified in community submissions to the TPRP, including poverty, low educational attainment, and immigration status. Finally, many of the administrative details of the program discourage community organizations from applying for funding, including a requirement that 50 percent of the value of subsidies be matched by other sources of funds and that applicants submit a five-year sustainability plan (see chapter 4 in this volume). Indeed, few of the successful applicants announced in the spring of 2010 were not-for-profit community organizations. Instead, the vast majority of Broadband Canada funding recipients turned out to be for-profit private sector companies, including Vidéotron Ltée and Barrett Xplore Inc. (Industry Canada 2010). While the funding for Broadband Canada will offer technical access to thousands of additional households in rural and remote communities, the new program lacks any support for the social infrastructure of access and effective use that was central to the success associated with CAP's community-based initiatives.

Meanwhile, in the March 2010 federal budget funding for the CAP program was cut from $15 million to a mere $2 million, igniting a wave of protest across rural Canada. At the time, CAP administrators received a letter from Industry Canada informing them that only CAP sites more than 25 km from a public library would be eligible for funding as of 1 April 2010. This would have effectively wiped out a majority of CAP sites in Canada. An administrator (pers. comm.) in the province of Prince Edward Island noted that under such conditions there would not be a single site left in the province. Although the program, by now, had suffered many near-death experiences, this was very close to the real thing. In an intense three days, CAP administrators, users, and supporters contacted MPs and the press, seeking support for the program. The issue hit the floor of the House of Commons, and various media began reporting on the work done at CAP sites across the country (e.g., Marlow 2010). Stung by criticism from rural communities and MPs, the federal Tories scrambled to reassure rural Canadians that the funding cut to CAP would be offset by funds from the newly announced Broadband Canada plan (CBC News 2010). While community networking advocates and CAP site administrators were relieved by this short-term resolution of the crisis, they continued to worry that the funding for access and other community informatics initiatives had become more unstable than ever. Under the current scenario (as of late 2010), once the Broadband Canada fund is depleted, the CAP program will no longer have a base in government policy or in practice. In government, it is much more difficult to start up programs than to continue them.

Reviewing developments in Canadian telecommunications policy and regulation in the wake of the TPRP, then, the trend toward deregulation is obvious. At the same time, notwithstanding the TPRP's nod to community informatics and the launch of the Broadband Canada program, the status of community informatics and public interest perspectives within Canada's telecommunications system has been dealt a series of setbacks that jeopardize thousands of worthwhile initiatives and organizations and diminish democratic governance and accountability within Canada's telecommunications system.

CONCLUSION: THROWING COMMUNITY OUT WITH THE BATH WATER?

In this chapter we set out to consider the role that public policy can and has played in both nurturing as well as undermining community informatics initiatives within the Canadian context. As we have seen, when visionary governments commit resources and energy to achieving goals such as universal access, community informatics initiatives and organizations can flourish. On the other hand, when they adopt policies and regulatory decisions that privilege the interests of incumbent telcos, such as bans on community or municipal wireless projects, community informatics initiatives and the collective aspirations they embody can be thwarted.

The period from roughly 1995 to 2004 represented something of a golden age for community networks and other community informatics initiatives in Canada, one in which supportive public policies and programs designed to promote connectivity brought government and the community informatics sector into a mutually beneficial partnership to promote universal access and effective use in thousands of communities. This is not to say that community informatics initiatives cannot flourish and succeed without government funding and support, as the case of Montréal's community wireless collective, Île Sans Fil, has demonstrated (see chapter 10). Neither, as MacDonald, Longford, and Clement demonstrate in chapter 19, is government funding in and of itself a panacea. The legacy of the Connecting Canadians initiative has been somewhat mixed, with thousands of community organizations receiving financial support while being strained and transformed (not always for the best) under the weight of additional administrative burdens and the expectations of communities and funding partners. Nonetheless, with a tradition of greater government intervention for social development, at least compared to the United States, and with a comparatively small philanthropic sector to provide an alternate source of funding (Moreno and Plewes 2007), community informatics initiatives and organizations in Canada have become increasingly dependent on government largesse and therefore increasingly vulnerable to significant ebbs in its flow.

The dire financial predicament of community networks and other community informatics initiatives in Canada can be traced to a number of developments in telecommunications policy and government programs over the course of the late 2000s, which we have discussed in detail. The first signs of waning government interest in funding connectivity initiatives appeared in 2004, with cuts to programs such as CAP and SchoolNet under the previous Liberal government. The TPRP, however, with its enthusiasm for allowing market forces to determine the further development of the telecommunications system and its explicit questioning of the need for government intervention to ensure universal access, cemented the grip of neoliberalism within telecommunications policy-making circles in Canada.

While the TPRP laid the groundwork for questioning the need for government intervention to achieve universal access, it took the decidedly ideological Conservative government to implement its recommendations and drain the lifeblood from the community networking sector. Granted, the legislative review conducted by the TPRP was overdue in light of the fact that the Telecommunications Act had not been updated since the inception of new technologies such as the Internet and wireless broadband. However, even the TPRP recognized the need to maintain at least a limited role for government in order to ensure access for communities on the margins of Canadian society, suggesting that the message from community informatics and public interest groups had been heard to some extent. Thus, to a modest degree, the TPRP refused to throw community out with the "bathwater" of outdated telecommunications policy and regulation.

The same could not be said for the federal government elected in 2008, which delayed introducing any significant connectivity initiatives until three years into its mandate, and then only grudgingly, as part of a short-term stimulus package that ran against the grain of its neoliberal commitments. Absent the recent financial crisis, in all likelihood the community informatics sector would still be waiting for a decision on access programs from the Conservative government, and gradually withering in the process.

NOTE

1   The three panel members were Dr. Gerri Sinclair, former academic and now Internet technology consultant to industry and government; Hank Intven, partner in the Toronto office of McCarthy Tétrault LLP, a Canadian law firm and former CRTC commissioner; and André Tremblay, president and CEO of Microcell Telecommunications Inc.

REFERENCES

Babe, Robert E. 1990. *Telecommunications in Canada.* Toronto: University of Toronto Press.
Barney, Darin. 2004. The democratic deficit in Canadian ICT policy and regulation. In *Seeking convergence in policy and practice*, vol. 2 of *Communication in the public interest*, ed. Marita Moll and Leslie Regan Shade, 91–108. Ottawa: Canadian Centre for Policy Alternatives.
Beatty, Perrin. 2006. Choose not to regulate. *Ottawa Citizen*, 19 April, A19.
Bell Canada. 2006. Statement re: telecom policy report. Press release, 22 March. http://bce.ca/news-and-media/releases/show/bell-canada-statement-re-telecom-policy-report.

Canada. 2005. Appointment of members to the Telecommunications Policy Review Panel. Press release. http://telecomreview.ca/eic/site/tprp-gecrt.nsf/eng/h_rx00096.html. Accessed 6 July 2010 (but no longer available).

——. 2006. Order issuing a direction to the CRTC on implementing the Canadian telecommunications policy objectives. P.C. 2006-1534, 14 December. *Canada Gazette* 140, no. 26. http://www.gazette.gc.ca/archives/p2/2006/2006-12-27/html/sor-dors355-eng.html.

Canadian Radio-television and Telecommunications Commission. 2005. CRTC decides on limited regulation for VoIP telephone services to foster competition. Press release, 12 May. http://www.crtc.gc.ca/eng/com100/2005/r050512.htm.

CBC News. 2006a. CRTC reaffirms VoIP decision, will review regulations. 1 September. http://www.cbc.ca/news/technology/story/2006/09/01/crtc-voip.html.

——. 2006b. Ottawa directs CRTC to rely on market forces. 13 June. http://www.cbc.ca/news/business/story/2006/06/13/crtc.html.

——. 2010. Internet access funds not cut: Clement. 16 March. http://www.cbc.ca/news/canada/story/2010/03/16/cap-internet-funding.html.

Clement, Andrew, Michael Gurstein, Christie Hurrell, Graham Longford, Marita Moll, and Leslie Regan Shade. 2005a. Canadian Research Alliance for Community Innovation and Networking (CRACIN): Written Submission to the Telecommunications Policy Review Panel, 15 August. http://archive.iprp.ischool.utoronto.ca/cracin/CRACIN_TPRC_Submission.pdf.

——. 2005b. Canadian Research Alliance for Community Innovation and Networking (CRACIN): 2nd Round Submission to the Telecommunications Policy Review Panel, 15 September. http://archive.iprp.ischool.utoronto.ca/cracin/TPRP_Sept15_%20submission_v2.pdf.

Clement, Andrew, Marita Moll, and Leslie Regan Shade. 2001. Debating universal access in the Canadian context: The role of public interest organizations. In *E-commons vs. e-commerce: Communications in the public interest*, ed. Marita Moll and Leslie Reagan Shade, 23–48. Ottawa: Canadian Centre for Policy Alternatives.

CRACIN. 2006. Proposed telecom policy places too much faith in market forces, Citizens' Forum warns. Press release. Alternative Telecommunications Policy Forum, 26 October. http://media.mcgill.ca/en/alternative_telecommunications_policy_forum_press_release.

——. 2007. Letter to the Honourable Maxime Bernier, Minister of Industry. 6 February. http://archive.iprp.ischool.utoronto.ca/publications/publications/Alt_Forum_to_Bernier.pdf.

Curry, Bill, and Iain Marlow. 2010. Ottawa to open telecom sector to greater foreign ownership. *The Globe and Mail*, 3 March. http://www.theglobeandmail.com/report-on-business/ottawa-to-open-telecom-sector-to-greater-foreign-ownership/article1488414/.

Geist, Michael. 2007. Canada's communication outlook: Average at best. 17 July. http://www.michaelgeist.ca/content/view/2104/125/.

Industry Canada. 1995. *Connection, community, content: The challenge of the information highway. Final report of the Information Highway Advisory Council*. Ottawa: Minister of Supply and Services.

——. 2005a. Departmental Performance Report, 2004–2005. http://www.tbs-sct.gc.ca/rma/dpr1/04-05/IC-IC/IC-ICd4506_e.asp. Accessed 25 September 2009. (The report is no longer available at this URL but can be accessed through http://www.collectionscanada.gc.ca/webarchives/20060116230539/www.tbs-sct.gc.ca/rma/dpr1/04-05/0405dpr-rmr_e.asp.)

——. 2005b. Strategic outcome: Competitive industry and sustainable communities. Departmental program review, 2004–2005. http://www.tbs-sct.gc.ca/rma/dpr1/04-05/IC-IC/IC-ICd4503_e.asp#pri17. Accessed 25 September 2009 (but no longer available).

——. 2009a. Broadband Canada: Connecting Rural Canadians. Updated 6 November 2010. http://www.ic.gc.ca/eic/site/719.nsf/eng/home.

——. 2009b. Government of Canada varies CRTC decision on Globalive. Press release, 11 December. http://www.ic.gc.ca/eic/site/ic1.nsf/eng/05211.html.

——. 2010. Broadband Canada: Connecting Rural Canadians. List of Projects. http://www.ic.gc.ca/eic/site/719.nsf/eng/00066.html.

Intven, Hank, and Mary Dawson. 2007. *A model act to implement the regulatory recommendations of the Telecommunications Policy Review Report*. Montreal: McCarthy Tétrault.

Lawson, Philippa. 2008. Gutting the Telecom Act. In *For sale to the highest bidder: Telecom policy in Canada*, ed. Marita Moll and Leslie Regan Shade, 17–26. Ottawa: Canadian Centre for Policy Alternatives.

Longford, Graham. 2008. Spectrum matters: Clearing and reclaiming the spectrum commons. In *For sale to the highest bidder: Telecom policy in Canada*, ed. Marita Moll and Leslie Regan Shade, 95–107. Ottawa: Canadian Centre for Policy Alternatives.

Manley, John. 1999. Canada and the Internet revolution: Connecting Canadians. Speech to the annual meeting of the Trilateral Commission, Washington DC. http://www.wisetel.com.br/biblioteca/doc_de_referencia/trilateral/john_manley.htm.

Marlow, Iain. 2010. Ottawa ends computer funding for Community Access Program. *The Globe and Mail*, 16 March. http://www.theglobeandmail.com/report-on-business/ottawa-ends-computer-funding-for-community-access-program/article1501674/.

McMurdy, Deirdre. 2007. Less regulation helps competition—unless it doesn't. *Ottawa Citizen*, 27 June. http://www.canada.com/ottawacitizen/news/story.html?id=b4c74ef9-603a-4167-b414-f983ff40dbab.

Minister of Industry. 2007. Letter from the Honourable Minister of Industry, Maxime Bernier, to Ms. Leslie Regan Shade, Co-Investigator, CRACIN. Received 14 March 2007. http://www3.fis.utoronto.ca/iprp/cracin/alttelecomcontent/Bernier%20Letter%20p.%201.pdf. Accessed 9 July 2010 (but no longer available).

Moll, Marita. 2007. The good news about CAP. *Making Waves* 18(2): 10–13. http://www.tc.ca/GoodNewsaboutCAP.pdf.

Moreno, Esperanzo, and Betty Plewes. 2007. *Thinking globally: Canadian foundations and trends in international philanthropy*. Montreal: Philanthropic Foundations Canada. http://pfc.ca/en/wp-content/uploads/files/resources/grantmaking/Thinking_globally_plewes_sept07.pdf.

Nowak, Peter. 2009. Canadian cellphone rates among world's worst. CBC News, 9 August. http://www.cbc.ca/technology/story/2009/08/11/canada-cellphone-rates-expensive-oecd.html.

Organisation for Economic Cooperation and Development. 2007. *OECD Communications outlook 2007*. July. http://www.oecd.org/document/17/0,3343,en_2649_34225_38876369_1_1_1_1,00.htm.

Rideout, Vanda. 2004. *Continentalizing Canadian telecommunications: The politics of regulatory reform*. Montreal and Kingston: McGill-Queen's University Press.

Telecommunications Act. 1993. *Statutes of Canada*, 1993, c. 38.

Telecommunications Policy Review Panel. 2005a. Consultation paper. 6 June. http://www.telecomreview.ca/epic/site/tprp-gecrt.nsf/en/h_rx00015e.html. Accessed 11 July 2010 (but no longer available).

——. 2005b. Broadband Access Policy Forum. 9 September. http://telecomreview.ca/eic/ site/tprp-gecrt.nsf/eng/rx00040.html. Accessed 12 July 2010 (but no longer available).

——. 2005c. October Policy Forum: Reviewing the Telecommunications Policy Framework. 24–26 October. Gatineau, Québec. http://www.localret.cat/revistesinews/broadband/ num11/docs/3num11cat.pdf.

——. 2005d. *October Policy Forum: Summary Report.* http://telecomreview.ca/eic/site/ tprp-gecrt.nsf/vwapj/Summary_Document_e.pdf/$FILE/Summary_Document_e.pdf. Accessed 12 July 2010 (but no longer available).

——. 2006. *Telecommunications Policy Review Panel: Final Report 2006.* http://www.ic.gc.ca/ eic/site/smt-gst.nsf/vwapj/tprp-final-report-2006.pdf/$FILE/tprp-final-report-2006.pdf.

Telecommunities Canada. 2006. Letter to Leonard St. Aubin re: Order under Section 8 of the Telecommunications Act. August. http://www.tc.ca/TC-TPRPrecs34.pdf.

White, Julie. 2008. Keeping Canadian culture: Why Canadians need self-determination of our telecom industry. In *For sale to the highest bidder: Telecom policy in Canada*, ed. Moll, Marita and Leslie Regan Shade, 37–54. Ottawa: Canadian Centre for Policy Alternatives.

APPENDIXES

A COMMUNITY PARTNERS PROFILE

Graham Longford

THE ALBERTA LIBRARY
(HTTP://WWW.THEALBERTALIBRARY.AB.CA/)

The Alberta Library is a province-wide library consortium that works with its members to promote universal, barrier-free access to the materials and resources in Alberta's libraries. Between 2004 and 2007, researchers from the University of Alberta's Faculty of Extension partnered with the Alberta Library and a number of libraries from communities across the province in order to explore the potential uses of new technologies, such as broadband and video conferencing, to increase social interaction and participation among users and to assist governments and libraries in the development of appropriate policies for the adoption of new technologies in public libraries (Adria 2007). The research project is of particular importance to libraries in rural communities, which are expected to become important hubs for broadband connectivity and services in such communities. Research was conducted at public libraries in four rural Alberta communities slated for connection to the province-wide Alberta SuperNet broadband network.

The Alberta Library–University of Alberta project explored a number of questions related to broadband networks and public libraries, including how library users and decision makers view the use of physical space and broadband technology in the public library and what changes are anticipated in the relative importance of *information-seeking* versus *social interaction* activities (e.g., video conferencing, civic engagement) as a result of the adoption of broadband technology in the public library. The research project was specifically designed to pilot the development and evaluation of socially interactive activities such as intergenerational storytelling via video conference links.

Key research activities included an intergenerational storytelling demonstration pilot project conducted between two communities, a regional workshop on technology in the public library, and a series of semi-structured interviews and focus groups involving some forty participants, including librarians, trustees, citizens, and local politicians (Adria 2007). In the storytelling project, elementary school students in two communities were linked via video conference to each other as well as to elderly participants in the project who recounted stories of their childhood to the students.

COMMUNAUTIQUE
(HTTP://WWW.COMMUNAUTIQUE.QC.CA/)

Communautique is a Montréal-based non-profit urban community network founded in 1995 to assist low-income individuals and families and other groups potentially excluded from participating in the information society. It provides Internet access and other ICT services and training throughout the province and has assisted with the installation of more than eighty Internet access points in communities across Québec. Until recently, Communautique also managed a CAP Youth Initiative program that allowed youth facilitators to be hired in various communities to provide information and training sessions on the use of ICTs to socially marginalized populations, including low-income, new immigrant, and elderly individuals. Overall, Communautique's Internet initiation and new technologies workshops have been attended by over a hundred thousand people and have played an important role in combatting the digital divide in Québec society.

Communautique also plays an active and visible role advocating on behalf of universal access and community networking. In 2002, for example, it issued its *Plateforme québécoise de l'Internet citoyen*, which articulated the basic principles of community networking—emphasizing the importance of overcoming the digital divide and enabling full participation in the information society—and called upon government to develop and implement policies and programs that recognize universal access as a basic right of citizenship and that support the role played by community networks in democratizing the information society. The *Plateforme* is supported by more than 350 community groups and individuals. In addition, Communautique has raised public awareness of the potential impact of the provincial government's online initiatives on the voluntary sector and the populations it serves.

Communautique is also active in building ICT capacity within the voluntary sector itself in order to enable community groups to work more effectively to accomplish their goals. Communautique is a founding member of Réseau Maillons, a network that brings together actors in the non-profit sector interested in the development of the Internet in Québec. Since 2006, Communautique has led a research program on digital inclusion, intended primarily to establish a qualitative portrait of the inclusion/exclusion experience of Québec citizens who are handicapped or who have a limited degree of familiarity with the use of Internet for information and communication purposes, as well as to establish priorities that will encourage their inclusion.

ÎLE SANS FIL MONTRÉAL (HTTP://WWW.ILESANSFIL.ORG/)

Île Sans Fil (ISF), also based in Montréal, is one of Canada's most successful and innovative community wireless networks. Founded in 2001 by two university students and now comprising an administrative board of ten members and a core membership of some forty to fifty people, ISF is a completely volunteer-run initiative. A bilingual organization, Île Sans Fil has both francophone and anglophone volunteers and works with both French and English organizations. With over 150 hotspots and 60,000 registered users in downtown Montréal, ISF has become the dominant provider of public wireless access points in the city, while it has also emerged as a key player in the city's open source software and community media landscapes.

Île Sans Fil describes itself as a non-profit organization dedicated to "the development of a free communication infrastructure to strengthen local communities in the greater Montréal region" and to the use of wireless technology "to empower individuals and to foster a sense of community." To achieve these goals, ISF members focus on a number of key activities. The first is the deployment and maintenance of free Internet-access hotspots in public spaces (cafés, parks, etc.) throughout downtown Montréal. ISF has adopted a "venue-sponsored" model in which local businesses, public institutions, and community organizations agree to share their existing broadband connection with their customers, clients, and neighbours for free via wireless hotspot technology that ISF volunteers install and administer at no charge. ISF was operating 155 hotspots as of 2008, making it one of the largest community wireless networks in North America.

ISF is also actively engaged in developing locally relevant content for delivery via unique captive portal pages at each of its hotspot locations. When users connect to the ISF network, they see an initial portal page unique to the location, which is used to disseminate local content and to encourage interaction among hotspot users. In collaboration with local artists, community groups, and volunteer programmers and developers, for example, ISF has participated in a number of projects featuring local content on its portal pages. Additional functionality, such as the delivery of local services, is currently under development.

The dissemination of local content via ISF's hotspot network was facilitated by its WiFiDog authentication server software, developed by ISF technical volunteers. The WifiDog software initiative has been a highly successful open source software development project in its own right, with WifiDog software having been adopted by more than fifty community wireless networks and other organizations spanning four continents (http://dev.wifidog.org/). In October 2010, WifiDog migrated to a new technology, AuthPuppy, a new open source platform for authentication.

KEEWATIN CAREER DEVELOPMENT CORPORATION (HTTP://WWW.KCDC.CA/)

The Keewatin Career Development Corporation (KCDC) is a non-profit organization formed in 1996 by a group of fourteen career and educational service-providing agencies in northern Saskatchewan. The partners are a mixture of K–12, post-secondary, Métis, First Nations, and provincial government agencies. The KCDC's broad mission is to use information and communication technologies (ICTs) for the social and economic benefit of the residents of northern Saskatchewan. Operations are overseen by the general manager and carried out by paid staff.

Northern Saskatchewan includes roughly 37,000 people inhabiting forty First Nations, Métis, rural, and remote communities scattered across a heavily forested region interspersed by thousands of lakes, rivers, and streams. Approximately 85 percent of its residents are of Cree, Dene, or Métis descent. The regional economy depends primarily on mining, logging, and forest products, on tourism, and on government administration sectors, with the potential for tar sands development in the northwest. The economy is underdeveloped, and socio-economic conditions are challenging. Both household income and educational attainment are much lower than the national average, and unemployment rates are high. Access to health, educational, and employment services is limited by the remoteness and small size of the region's communities.

Since its founding in 1996, the KCDC has engaged in several different but complementary initiatives. These include successfully applying to be the

Saskatchewan demonstration site for Industry Canada's Smart Communities project. The KCDC's Smart Communities project, Headwaters, ran from 2000 through 2004 and supported initiatives in distance education, community Internet access, e-commerce, telemedicine, e-government, video conferencing, and heritage preservation. In 2002, the KCDC became the regional management organization (RMO) responsible for administering Industry Canada's First Nations SchoolNet programs in Saskatchewan and, until 2009, in Alberta. In this capacity, the KCDC assisted First Nations schools in managing their connections to CommunityNet and SuperNet, the provincial government broadband connectivity programs in Saskatchewan and Alberta, respectively. From 2003 to 2005, the KCDC worked with the Saskatchewan Association of Northern Communities (New North), the Prince Albert Grand Council, and Meadow Lake Tribal Council to implement the Northern Broadband Network, a $9-million initiative, carried out as part of Industry Canada's Broadband for Rural and Northern Development (BRAND) pilot program, that brought broadband Internet services to northern Saskatchewan.

The KCDC operates in several distinct areas, with an overarching focus on the networked delivery of career services, with particular expertise in multicast video conferencing. The KCDC also continues as the First Nations SchoolNet RMO for Saskatchewan. It operates the CanSask Career and Employment Services site for northern Saskatchewan and, in connection with its Breaking Barriers series, has produced numerous videos on various occupations in the North. The Keewatin Academy of Information Technology (KAIT) offers several Cisco Networking Academy technical certifications that are delivered through video conferencing. Largely as a result of the decline in public funding, there is greater emphasis today on commercial pursuits, such as KCDC Media Services, which offers a wide variety of video, website, web streaming, video conferencing, and video capture services. Through its Headwaterstech division, the KCDC is also a successful SaskTel mobility and Internet services dealer.

KUH-KE-NAH NETWORK (HTTP://KNET.CA/)

The Kuh-ke-nah Network (K-Net) is an Aboriginal-owned and -controlled community network that currently serves sixty First Nations communities across Ontario and Québec. K-Net Services is the telecom and ICT arm of the Keewaytinook Okimakanak Tribal Council (the Northern Chiefs), an Aboriginal organization representing six First Nations communities located in northwestern Ontario. K-Net primarily serves remote and sparsely populated First Nations communities that inhabit the Sioux Lookout district in northwestern Ontario. The Sioux Lookout district is part of the Nishnawbe Aski Nation (NAN), a political territory that includes fifty-three First Nations across northern Ontario. NAN communities vary between 100 and 2,000 people and are extremely remote. Many are only accessible by air, while others are accessible via temporary winter roads. As a result, community members are compelled to travel great distances in order to receive advanced medical and educational services, at a considerable financial and social cost. Indubitably, distance and isolation shape the social fabric of NAN communities.

K-Net's telecom infrastructure consists of a C-Band Public Benefit transponder, IP video conferencing and telephony, web and email server space, and a variety of terrestrial wireline and fixed wireless links that effectively connect small, scattered First Nations communities with each other as well as with the wider world. In the space of less than a decade, these K-Net communities have gone from a situation in which it was common for there to be but a single public payphone in a settlement to the point where forty of these communities have high-speed Internet service available to private households.

But K-Net is far more than a provider of basic carriage services. Rather than be a seller of products, it is a facilitator for First Nations organizations and communities. In this capacity, it brokers relationships among various agencies to provide a wide range of public and civic services to remote communities, including access to Telehealth, Indian and Northern Affairs Canada's First Nations SchoolNet, the Keewaytinook Internet High School, personal homepages and email addresses, Keewaytinook Mobility, video conferencing and webcasting and archiving of public events. K-Net's myknet.org free website hosting service, for example, allows community members to create personal and community websites. MyKnet has been enthusiastically embraced by First Nations communities and beyond, with currently over 30,000 sites created. A more recent initiative is the On-Demand Book Service (ODBS), designed to support the joy of reading in rural and isolated First Nations communities within the context of learning, knowledge sharing, and the recording of history. In late 2010, radical capacity changes appear to be in store for twenty-six K-Net-affiliated communities. An $81-million agreement between the Nishnawbe Aski Nation, the Province of Ontario, Industry Canada, and Bell Aliant is scheduled to build a network that will enable speeds up to fifty times faster than Bell Aliant's and K-Net's current systems.

First Nations community ownership and control over local loops means that each community can adapt broadband services to address local challenges and priorities. The aggregation of demand from disparate users creates economies of scale and allows the dynamic reallocation of bandwidth to meet social priorities (Internet high school classes, remote eye examinations, residential connectivity). While K-Net's achievements reflect the technical savvy and political acumen of the network's creators, they also derive from its First Nations roots. This influence is seen in its decentralized structure, which encourages resource pooling, knowledge sharing, and respect for local autonomy.

K-Net thus constitutes a (nearly) full-spectrum, community-driven, vertically integrated service provider oriented toward meeting the social and economic development needs of its primary constituents.

SMARTLABRADOR
(HTTP://WWW.SMARTLABRADOR.CA/HOME/)

SmartLabrador was Newfoundland and Labrador's demonstration project under Industry Canada's Smart Communities Program. It was an extension of the Labrador Information Technology Initiative (LITI), a grassroots community technology project created in 1997 as a joint partnership in local development (Peddle 2007). SmartLabrador was designed to pilot the use of new ICTs in this remote part of Canada, an area inhabited by roughly 30,000 Inuit, Innu, Métis, and settler peoples living in thirty-two isolated settlements, many of which face economic and social challenges that include high unemployment, low educational attainment, and high rates of violence and substance abuse. Initiated in the fall of 2001, the SmartLabrador network combined satellite, terrestrial, and wireless technologies to connect forty-one sites in twenty-five communities spanning an area of 300,000 square kilometres, an area roughly the size of Sweden, making it one of the largest broadband networks in Canada.

The SmartLabrador network provided the technical platform for a variety of services and applications, including video conferencing, distance education, telemedicine, e-government, and e-commerce. The SmartLabrador project piloted video conferencing applications in areas such as training, health care, and justice in order to explore the potential cost-savings of new technologies in a region where long-distance travel by any means is expensive and at times hazardous. SmartLabrador also developed an e-commerce site called the Heritage Mall, which enabled Labrador businesses to market their products and services to the outside world. One key priority was to ensure equal access to services in all communities connected by the network. To accomplish this, SmartLabrador installed regional staff to provide technical and IT development support and training at the community level. Although Industry Canada funding for SmartLabrador came to an end in December 2007, the project continues under the auspices of LITI, which seeks additional funding and new partnerships to sustain the project and its related services.

ST. CHRISTOPHER HOUSE
(HTTP://WWW.STCHRISHOUSE.ORG)

For nearly a century, St. Christopher House (St. Chris), a non-sectarian social services agency in west-central Toronto, has provided a range of services and support with the goal of "enabling less advantaged individuals, families and groups in the community to gain greater control over their lives and within their community," according to their mission statement. To this end, St. Chris delivers a broad range of community-based social services to over 15,000 clients a year, of all ages, through drop-in centres, employment and skills training (including computer and Internet training), language and literacy courses, and legal, recreation, and supportive housing services. St. Chris's holistic approach focuses on individual and community development and also advocates for the rights of the less advantaged through the development of social policy.

The St. Chris catchment area is one of Toronto's most diverse and changing neighbourhoods, characterized by a range of income levels and residents who represent over sixty ethno-cultural backgrounds and speak some forty different languages. St. Chris has responded to the changing needs of the community with a variety of innovative programs. For example, the Employment Preparation Program (EPP) supports the unemployed with individualized Return-to-Work Action Plans that take into account language and literacy skills and that identify other barriers (housing, daycare, transportation, and so on) to finding good, long-term jobs. EPP is among the many programs at St. Chris that take advantage of free access to computers and the Internet.

In 1999, St. Chris launched its Bang the Drum program, with financial assistance from the federal Community Access Program. Bang the Drum provides access to more than seventy computer terminals with high-speed Internet service across St. Chris's seven locations. St. Chris later envisioned an online community portal that would complement the organization's programs and activities and would be based on content provided by staff, volunteers, program participants, and the wider community. Launched in 2005, the federally funded Community Learning Network (CLN) initiative resulted in an organization-wide, open source content management system, designed using a participatory approach, to support user-generated content, information sharing, online communication, and self-directed learning.

VANCOUVER COMMUNITY NETWORK
(HTTP://VCN.BC.CA/)

Founded in 1993, Vancouver Community Network (VCN) offers a variety of free networking services to individuals and non-profit groups in Vancouver and elsewhere in British Columbia, including dial-up Internet access, computer training, email accounts, listservs, and website hosting. As many as 11,000 individual users and more than 1,200 non-profit groups have made use of its services. vcn hosts over a hundred listservs on its Sympa system, enabling individuals and groups to set up electronic mailing lists in order to share information and discuss issues of mutual interest and concern, ranging from the arts and culture to politics, health, and sports. The organization has a volunteer board of nine members, over fifty active volunteers, and a thousand donors. Encouraging broad civic participation in the use of electronic public space is one of vcn's primary missions. vcn provides network access, training, and technical support to community-based non-profit groups with a view to enabling them to more effectively accomplish their goals in the areas of community development and civic participation. In partnership with the federal government, among others, vcn launched the 604 Connect! program, through which over four hundred non-profit groups in the area acquired Internet access, along with training and support.

In 2001, vcn launched its Community Learning Network pilot program, which was designed to explore the effectiveness of community networking in support of community development and local civic participation. It worked closely with numerous community groups and community centres to develop interactive websites that would allow their programs to become better known and more accessible to the local community.

Many of vcn's public computing initiatives focus on using new icts to organize and empower marginalized individuals and groups. As part of the federal cap program, vcn has coordinated as many as 250 public Internet access sites throughout the region. Many of these sites are situated and designed to serve the poor, new immigrants, youth, and the homeless, including the residents of Vancouver's Eastside neighbourhood, one of the country's poorest urban areas.

In 2003–4, in conjunction with the West Coast Democratic Workers' Association, vcn helped to develop and run the Computer Literacy Project computer training program, which is specifically designed to meet the needs of domestic workers. Other vcn projects have included the development of a Spanish-language portal containing community, health, and legal information and resources, and, in partnership with the 411 Seniors Centre, the Seniors Gateway to Legal Information and Resources, which seeks to empower seniors and their advocates by providing them with better access to benefits, services, and programs.

In 2010, vcn was able to move its six-workstation Special Projects office to the restored Woodwards Building on West Hastings Street, after the Vancouver City Council approved the organization's application to use a portion of the building. This move to a more central location helped to extend the VCN's outreach to a broader community.

Operating CAP and the CAP Youth Initiative is an ongoing and rewarding focus of the staff at VCN. Recent concerns that federal funding to CAP may come to an end has the staff and the board of directors searching for means to continue the significant positive outcomes of the program should funding be discontinued. Another ongoing concern lies with the availability of faster Internet services to VCN members. While in many cases dial-up service is adequate, the staff and board members are aware of its limitations and stay abreast of potential alternatives, which have thus far proved prohibitively expensive.

WESTERN VALLEY DEVELOPMENT AGENCY

The Western Valley Development Agency (WVDA) was a non-profit organization based in Cornwallis, Nova Scotia. As one of thirteen Regional Development Authorities in the province, the WVDA was supported by federal, provincial, and municipal funding. Organizationally, the WVDA was made up of a volunteer board of directors, six core staff, and a variety of project staff whose numbers fluctuated depending on the programs that were being run through the WVDA at any given time. The WVDA was created in 1994, at a time of intense economic crisis for the rural Western Valley region and its roughly 45,000 inhabitants. The groundfishery, which had been an important source of employment throughout the history of the Western Valley, had suffered collapse in 1992. Additionally, the federal government had announced the closure of CFB (Canadian Forces Base) Cornwallis, which, at the time the WVDA was founded, employed more than seven hundred people. Clearly, given the high levels of unemployment, the WVDA was facing an uphill battle (Peddle 2005).

The WVDA focused on community economic development across all areas of the local economy. Much of the organization's activity focused on information and communication technology development. The organization was involved in supporting thirty-five Community Access Program sites, as well as in the creation of three digital collections websites, the delivery of the federal VolNet program (which supports technology adoption in voluntary organizations), the creation of a virtual community resource centre, and an e-business support program. By far the largest and most ambitious community informatics project that the organization undertook was its Smart Communities demonstration project, FUNDYweb, supported by a $5-million grant from Industry Canada's Smart Communities program. The centrepiece of FUNDYweb project was the deployment of a community-owned broadband network, jointly owned by the seven Digby and Annapolis municipalities and the Nova Scotia Community College, consisting of 144 kilometres of dark fibre that completes the area's broadband loop from Halifax to Yarmouth and back along the South Shore. On the strength of these and other initiatives, the WVDA received numerous awards from a range of organizations, including UNESCO, the Province of Nova Scotia, and the Intelligent Communities Forum (MacNeil 2004).

Meanwhile, the activities and growth of the WVDA coincided with the economic resurgence of the region. Ten years after the formation of the WVDA, the economy of the Western Valley had diversified, and the former CFB Cornwallis had become a business park employing over nine hundred people. Unemployment in the region had declined significantly as well, from 16.3 percent in 1996 to 12.2 percent by 2001. While the organization did not claim exclusive credit for this dramatic shift toward a rejuvenated, sustainable rural economy, it prided itself on stimulating community-based innovation (MacNeil 2004).

Owing to a confluence of factors, including governance struggles and ideological conflict, the WVDA closed permanently at the end of August 2005. Currently there is no comparable community economic development association serving the Western Valley from Middleton to Digby Neck. The FUNDYweb broadband network remains in operation, despite the absence of its former host organization. Responsibility for the network has been assumed by the municipalities, as have the other former functions of the WVDA.

WIRELESS NOMAD CO-OPERATIVE INC.

Founded in 2005, Wireless Nomad Co-operative Inc. was a small co-op Internet service provider (ISP) that primarily served residents and small businesses in the greater Toronto area. Wireless Nomad was incorporated February 2005 and began operating its network soon after that. It resold Digital Subscriber Line (DSL) Internet service from Bell Canada, initially providing subscribers with a DSL modem and a wireless router. The wireless router was a modified commercial unit (802.11g standard) that allowed for signal sharing among other Wireless Nomad account holders, both those who paid for their subscriptions and those who held free accounts. Paid account members became part of the Wireless Nomad co-operative, which convened meetings of its members every few months to discuss the status and direction of the ISP, as well as wireless access issues more broadly. The Wireless Nomad sharing system worked on a priority access model. The "owner" of the wireless router (a node) received full bandwidth access to their Internet connection via wired or wireless use. Other Wireless Nomad co-operative members could connect to the wireless signal broadcast via the router and thus access the Internet. Anyone who could detect the Wireless Nomad signal could also connect to the Internet for free, albeit at a reduced bandwidth rate. Ideally, this would have created a self-expanding network of wireless access for Wireless Nomad users. Increasing numbers of nodes would mean that more people would become aware of the benefits and, by becoming subscribers, would increase the value of membership, and so on through a network effect.

At its peak, in early 2007, Wireless Nomad had grown to include 126 physical wireless nodes, with a total of over 3,500 users (both paid and free accounts). However, a series of technical setbacks, including server failures and connectivity issues, led to a gradual decline in paying users. Wireless Nomad ceased operations in March 2009, after transferring all remaining members to Teksavvy Solutions Inc., a private independent ISP.

REFERENCES

Adria, Marco, with Lisa Grotkowski, Huijie Feng, Dan Brown, Cathryn Staring Parrish, and Lantry Vaughan. 2007. Talking about technology adoption in the public library: Final report. http://archive.iprp.ischool.utoronto.ca/publications/Adria_CRACIN-ASRA_Report.pdf.

MacNeil, Ryan. 2004. *Information and communication technologies and community economic development: Lessons for governance at the Western Valley Development Agency.* Cornwallis Park, NS: Canadian Research Alliance for Community Innovation and Networking.

Peddle, Katrina. 2005. Updated case study history: Western Valley Development Agency. Presentation at CRACIN Montréal Workshop, 8–9 December. http://archive.iprp.ischool.utoronto.ca/cracin/research/WVDA%20Case%20Study%20Profile_2005.pdf.

———. 2007. Smart community, community informatics, ideology, and governance: The experience of the Western Valley Development Agency. CRACIN Working Paper no. 20. February. Toronto: Canadian Research Alliance for Community Innovation and Networking. http://archive.iprp.ischool.utoronto.ca/cracin/publications/pdfs/WorkingPapers/CRACIN%20Working%20Paper%20No.%2020.pdf.

B A BRIEF HISTORY OF THE COMMUNITY ACCESS PROGRAM
From Community Economic Development to Social Cohesion to Digital Divide

Marita Moll

First introduced in 1995, the Community Access Program (CAP) was one of the cornerstones of the federal government's Connecting Canadians agenda. Industry Canada (2010) described CAP as a program that "aims to provide Canadians with affordable access to the Internet and the skills they need to use it effectively." The program's initial goal was to establish 10,000 community access sites by 2001 so that all Canadians, in communities everywhere, could participate fully in the knowledge-based economy. CAP sites are most commonly located in schools, libraries, community centres, social service centres, and friendship centres and operate through partnerships with provincial or territorial governments and non-profit organizations.

Industry Canada's Departmental Performance Report for 2005–6 (the last year in which cost breakdowns were reported) showed that the CAP program had cost $337.2 million between 1995–96 and 2005–6 (Treasury Board 2007). A companion program, the CAP Youth Initiative (CAP YI), now funded through Human Resources and Skills Development Canada, provides employment opportunities to Canadians between the ages of 15 and 30 at CAP sites across the country. Assisted by thousands of volunteers, the CAP YI workers are the backbone of the CAP sites, working with immigrants, seniors, youth, First

Nations, the socially and economically disadvantaged—in fact, with anyone needing assistance in negotiating the new communications landscape.

In the 1997 Liberal Party policy platform, CAP was presented as a community economic development (CED) initiative: "The rapid changes taking place in information technologies present new opportunities to individuals and communities for learning, interaction, and economic development. Business and local development possibilities are becoming less dependent on location and more reliant on access to information technologies" (Liberal Party 1997, 41). The platform promised that, by the year 2000, all rural communities with a population of 400 to 50,000 would be connected to the Internet.

Within two years, the goals associated with Connecting Canadians and CAP had expanded well beyond the idea of connectivity as access and the creation of an infrastructure to support economic development to include the goal of connectivity as a vehicle for social cohesion. According to then Minister of Industry John Manley: "Connectedness is about our vision of the Canadian society we want in the 21st century—one with a strong, dynamic, competitive economy, and a strong lifelong-learning culture, but also one that uses connectedness to promote social cohesion, cultural expression and to build new linkages between citizens and government" (Manley 1999). This might be described as the "golden age" of connectivity policy in Canada, when the vision, policy, and financial support mechanisms aligned to bring about a program that was highly successful and served as a model for similar programs around the world.[1] Unfortunately, the golden age was short lived.

In 2004, the goals of the CAP program were substantially narrowed from the vision Manley described in 1999. The target audience was refocused "to channel limited resources into the communities that have the most pressing needs" (Treasury Board 2007). Internal Industry Canada reports showed that, during the 2005–6 fiscal year, CAP site services were focused on digital divide groups as follows: low income (69%), rural (68%), seniors (59%), francophones (39%), limited education clientele (65%), recent immigrants (37%), Aboriginal Canadians (26%), and persons with disabilities (49%) (Treasury Board 2007).

Despite the differing policy objectives articulated over the years, various evaluations of the CAP program indicated that it regularly exceeded expectations. An extensive 2004 evaluation commissioned by Industry Canada concluded that "CAP has been having success at bridging the gap in public Internet access and capability. There is a consensus that the formal program objectives continue to be relevant" (Ekos 2004, 41). All the same, the CAP program was scheduled to sunset on 31 March 2004. Since then, it has been kept alive on annual renewals, largely in response to intensive grassroots campaigns in affected communities. These efforts have been accompanied by a great deal of uncertainty, however, with program renewal hanging upon a slender thread each year. In 2007, for example, the funding that ended on 31 March was not formally renewed until 6 June, leaving CAP site administrators, volunteers, and users across the country in limbo for nine weeks.

In March 2008, the program was shuffled from the Spectrum, Information Technologies and Telecommunications (SITT) branch to the Regional Operations branch of Industry Canada. Supporters hoped that CAP had finally found a good home, now that the program was located within a department tasked with encouraging community economic development, supporting the social economy, and promoting participation in the digital economy. But as Garth Graham, one of the directors of Telecommunities Canada, a national alliance of community networks, cautioned in an email to the group mailing list: "We'll have to wait to see whether the orphan CAP has now been adopted by loving parents or merely warehoused in foster care."

Foster care appears to be the case. After 2007–8, CAP no longer appeared in the annual departmental performance reports filed by Industry Canada with the Treasury Board (Treasury Board 2009, 2010). For fiscal year 2009–10, the funds allocated to CAP came not from the Regional Operations branch budget but from a $225-million infrastructure fund, Connecting Rural Canadians, designed specifically to extend broadband coverage to rural and remote areas. This funding was part of a $62-billion Economic Action Plan—the federal government's response to the 2008 economic crisis. It was a financial "shot in the arm" for an ailing economy, not a fund to support ongoing programs. It was a subtle move that caught little attention until the next shoe dropped.

In the second week of March 2010, CAP administrators across the country began receiving letters advising them that their funding would end on 31 March 2010 unless their sites were more than 25 kilometres from the nearest public library. From a focus on community economic development and social cohesion to the provision of Internet services chiefly for "at-risk" populations, the scope of CAP had now been narrowed further, to a matter of finding short-term solutions to the problem of rural and remote access. The new 25-kilometre requirement would have wiped out a majority of the remaining CAP sites in Canada. Once again, the CAP community marshalled its resources and contacted members of Parliament and the press seeking support. Over an intense three days, the issue was raised during Question Period by members of all three opposition parties in the House of Commons. On 16 March, Iain Marlow, of the *Globe and Mail*, visited the CAP site at St. Christopher House, a social service agency in downtown Toronto and a CRACIN community partner. In a resulting story, a 38-year-old woman explained how the site was helping her complete high school. "It would be difficult to do any of the programs without computers," she said. "It ties it all together. You can't really make a résumé unless you know how to use the Word program" (quoted in Marlow

2010). In a quick turnabout, Minister of Industry Tony Clement announced that there had been a bureaucratic misunderstanding and that the funding had never really been withdrawn. The program was good for another year, but it was again funded through the temporary Connecting Rural Canadians infrastructure program.

Once encompassing 8,800 sites across Canada (Treasury Board 2003), the number of active CAP sites in 2004–5 was 3,786 (Treasury Board 2006) and was probably hovering around 3,000 by 2009. From $30 million per year in its early days, the CAP budget has stood at $14 million since 2004 (Marlow 2010). These funds can be accessed only by established CAP sites; there is no provision for establishing new sites. Without a powerful champion in a governing party, this program "may have used up its nine lives by now," said Peter Frampton, a member of the Telecommunities Canada board, in an email message to the author. Its long-term status is more uncertain than ever.

John Manley's 1999 vision of the CAP program as supporter of "social cohesion" and "cultural expression" reflected the policy environment of the time. According to Canadian policy analyst Jane Jenson, definitions of social cohesion include the concept of a process, or set of processes, leading to the development of a community based on shared values, mutual recognition, and a sense of belonging. Of particular interest to the Canadian policy research environment, she suggests, is the definition offered by the federal government's Policy Research Subcommittee on Social Cohesion: "The ongoing process of developing a community of shared values, shared challenges and equal opportunity within Canada, based on a sense of trust, hope and reciprocity among all Canadians" (Jenson 1998, 29).

Placing the interest in social cohesion in a political context, Jenson argues that the policy focus on social cohesion in the late 1990s stemmed from the government's recognition that the neoliberal economic policies of the 1980s and 1990s were damaging to communities and societies. As she points out (1998, 7), "Neoliberalism privileges the market for distributing resources and power, seeks to limit the role of the state, and emphasizes individual (and family) freedom as the core value." Rejecting state action to address social problems, the voluntary sector became, under neoliberalism, "the only legitimate locale for realising collective goals" (1998, 7, emphasis in original). Jenson quotes an observation made by Ronald Hirshhorn (1997) regarding the non-profit sector: "The sector is being compelled to transform itself, frequently along the lines of market principles of the 'new managerialism'; nonprofits have to become more like any ordinary firm, focussed on the bottom line rather than social projects of other parts of their mission" (1998, 7). No doubt many community networking practitioners would immediately agree.

As already noted, a shift of focus from social issues to business operations has been the trajectory of community-based networks funded through Industry Canada's CAP program. In a study based on CRACIN research, Chris Bodnar investigates the status of community networks in the context of an increasingly prevalent social entrepreneurial model that calls for market integration of the non-profit sector:

> As the remaining Community Networks explore new funding avenues, some groups are investigating the relationship between fee-for-service options and the financial viability of the organizations. Whether fee-for-service models compromise the nature of Community Networks may require a rethinking of the public good understanding of Community Networks as non-profit organizations. (Bodnar 2007)

For the time being at least, the Canadian policy pendulum has swung back to the neoliberal context described by Jenson. Remaining community networks may be increasingly pushed to seek different partners, or pushed toward the fee-for-service model that Bodnar mentions, or pushed out altogether. The battle for survival is clearly far from won.

NOTE

1   In its heyday, the Connecting Canadians suite of programs was routinely showcased at international gatherings of government officials. The telecentre movement, which was modelled on the CAP experience, is still supported in some countries by Canadian development funds through the International Development Research Centre.

REFERENCES

Bodnar, Chris. 2007. The Vancouver Community Network, social investing and public good models of ICT development. *Journal of Community Informatics* 3(4). http://ci-journal. net/index.php/ciej/article/view/307/378.

Ekos Research Associates. 2004. *Evaluation study of the Community Access Program (CAP): Final report.* Prepared for Industry Canada, Audit and Evaluation Branch. 16 January. http://archive.iprp.ischool.utoronto.ca/cracin/policy/policy/polmap-ic1.pdf.

Hirshhorn, Ronald, ed. 1997. *The emerging sector: In search of a framework.* CPRN Study No. CPRN/01. Ottawa: Canadian Policy Research Networks.

Industry Canada. 2010. What is CAP? Formerly available at http://www.ic.gc.ca/eic/site/ cap-pac.nsf/eng/00006.html.

Jenson, Jane. 1998. *Mapping social cohesion: The state of Canadian research.* CPRN Study No. F/03. Ottawa: Canadian Policy Research Networks. http://cprn.org/documents/15723_en.pdf.

Liberal Party of Canada. 1997. *Securing our future together: Preparing Canada for the 21st century.* Ottawa: Liberal Party of Canada.

Manley, John. 1999. Canada and the Internet revolution: Connecting Canadians. Speech to the annual meeting of the Trilateral Commission, Washington DC. http://www.wisetel. com.br/biblioteca/doc_de_referencia/trilateral/john_manley.htm.

Marlow, Iain. 2010. Ottawa ends computer funding for Community Access Program. *Globe and Mail,* 16 March.

Treasury Board of Canada Secretariat. 2003. Departmental performance report, 2001–2002, Industry Canada. Appendix A: Detailed activity information. http://www.collections canada.gc.ca/webarchives/20060122022035/http://www.tbs-sct.gc.ca/rma/dpr/01-02/ ic/ico102dpr10_e.asp#appendix_connectedness (but no longer available).

———. 2006. Departmental performance report, 2004–2005, Industry Canada. Section 2: Analysis of performance accomplishments by strategic outcome. http://www. collectionscanada.gc.ca/webarchives/20060120070822/http://www.tbs-sct.gc.ca/rma /dpr1/04-05/ic-ic/ic-icd4503_e.asp (but no longer available).

———. 2007. Departmental performance report, 2005–2006, Industry Canada. Section 2: Analysis of performance accomplishments by strategic outcome. http://www. collectionscanada.gc.ca/webarchives/20071222154140/http://www.tbs-sct.gc.ca/ dpr-rmr/0506/ic-ic/ic-ico2_e.asp (but no longer available).

———. 2008. Departmental performance report, 2006–2007, Industry Canada. Section 2: Analysis of program activities by strategic outcome. http://www.tbs-sct.gc.ca/ dpr-rmr/2006-2007/inst/dus/dus09-eng.asp.

———. 2009. Departmental performance report, 2007–2008, Industry Canada. Section 2: Analysis of program activities by strategic outcome. http://www.tbs-sct.gc.ca/ dpr-rmr/2007-2008/inst/dus/dus02-eng.asp#sec2.3.

———. 2010. Departmental performance report, 2008–2009, Industry Canada. Section 2: Analysis of program activities by strategic outcome. http://www.tbs-sct.gc.ca/ dpr-rmr/2008-2009/inst/dus/dus02-eng.asp#sec2.1.

C THE FEDERAL CONNECTING CANADIANS INITIATIVE, 1995–2007
A Brief Overview

Graham Longford, Marita Moll

> Connecting Canadians means making sure Canadians have access to the Internet, through SchoolNet and the Community Access Program; it means creating Smart Communities where all economic and social organizations are linked together to stimulate growth and create jobs; it means increasing Canadian content online, including tele-health and tele-education; it means Canadian governments providing citizens with 24-hour-a-day access to integrated services online; it means promoting investment in a connected Canada; and it means building an environment where electronic commerce can flourish. (Manley 1998)

Connecting Canadians was a multi-pronged national strategy intended to make the government of Canada "a model user of information technology and the Internet" (Canada 1999). According to a government report delivered in October 2000 to an international audience in the Netherlands, the Connecting Canadians vision included the following:

• The Government On-Line (GOL) Initiative, the government's plan to deliver electronic access to government information and services by December 31, 2004;

- Strategic Directions for Information Management and Information Technology: Enabling 21st Century Service to Canadians, a strategy outlining broad-based visions and plans for a more citizen-centred government. It outlines a series of priorities to lever the government's significant investments in Information Management and Technology and move towards a more integrated, collaborative model of government;
- Electronic Commerce Strategy, the policy framework to engender trust in electronic transactions. This includes legislation to protect personal information in private sector transactions, and to provide legal certainty for the use of electronic signatures and records, as well as a policy encouraging the use of cryptography for electronic commerce;
- Canada On-line, a variety of programs to increase public access to the Internet. Canada was the first country in the world to connect all its schools and libraries, and is now in the final stages of setting up 10,000 access points in communities across Canada through the Community Access Program, 5,000 [in] rural and remote communities and 5,000 in urban neighbourhoods. The next step is to connect as all classrooms;
- Cultural Content On-line, a plan to bring Canadian culture into the digital age. Through consultations three areas were identified as key:
  - digitizing significant collections and setting up the virtual museum of Canada;
  - assisting new media producers to create innovative cultural content; and
  - improving access to Canadian cultural content through better visibility, branding and distribution.

(Government of Canada 2000, 2–3)

The programs gathered under "Canada On-line," which originally comprised CAP, SchoolNet, LibraryNet, and VolNet but later expanded to include programs such as Smart Communities and BRAND, were major recipients of federal funding under the Connecting Canadians initiative. These programs have become lynchpins in the development and delivery of government-funded connectivity services, including public Internet access, computer training and technical support, and community-based online content development. The majority of CRACIN case study sites received funding through one or more of these federal programs (see table 19.2 in this volume). While the involvement of community networks in the Connecting Canadians initiative has not been without its tensions, particularly around issues of access philosophy, funding, and sustainability, community networks have played a pivotal role in ensuring its success (Moll and Shade 2001). A brief overview of Canada On-line and related programs follows.

BROADBAND FOR RURAL AND NORTHERN DEVELOPMENT (BRAND) PILOT PROGRAM

Between 2002 and 2007, a total of roughly $90 million was allocated under the BRAND Pilot Program, which was designed to promote the extension of broadband Internet access to unserved rural, remote, and Aboriginal communities. Under the BRAND program, unserved communities were encouraged to develop business plans for the deployment of broadband access in partnership with the private sector. Successful proposals were selected on a competitive basis. As of March 2005, fifty-eight projects representing 884 communities had been selected for funding. BRAND was launched and administered jointly by Industry Canada and Infrastructure Canada.

COMMUNITY ACCESS PROGRAM (CAP)

The Community Access Program (CAP) was launched by Industry Canada in 1994. In 1995, it became a cornerstone of the Canada On-line portion of the Connecting Canadians initiative and still constitutes the federal government's principal "digital divide" program. As of 2006, CAP had dispersed almost $340 million. Since 2004, however, the program has been constantly threatened by budget cuts and rumours of impending closure (see Appendix B). Originally intended to provide affordable Internet access to rural communities so that they could participate in the knowledge-based economy, CAP was expanded in 1999 to include sites in low-income urban communities. CAP operates on the basis of partnership agreements between provincial or territorial governments and the voluntary sector. (For further information, see chapter 19.) CAP supports the maintenance of public computing and Internet access sites located in schools, libraries, and community centres across the country. At its peak, in 2003, CAP supported 8,800 sites, although, owing to funding cuts, this number has dwindled in recent years to under 3,000. Community networking organizations such as the Vancouver Community Network, Communautique, K-Net, and the Western Valley Development Agency are or have been important voluntary-sector participants in CAP, receiving significant funding in exchange for managing extensive networks of CAP sites, staff, and volunteers.

CAP YOUTH INITIATIVE (CAP YI)

An important supplement to the original program, the Youth Initiative has become a key component of CAP by providing sites with the staffing needed to continue operations. Now funded by Human Resources and Skills

Development Canada (formerly Human Resources and Social Development Canada) and administered by Industry Canada as part of the federal Youth Employment Strategy, CAP YI provides work internships for young Canadians who have ICT skills and is designed to give them career-related work experience that will help them to succeed in the rapidly changing knowledge-based economy. Program participants receive short-term placements with schools, NGOs, CAP sites, small businesses, and employment agencies, where they engage in a variety of activities including the delivery of ICT training, tech support, and website development. Community networking organizations played an important role in the placement, training, and supervision of CAP YI interns. Roughly $41 million was allocated to CAP YI between 1996 and 2006. CRACIN case study sites that participated in CAP YI include VCN, K-Net, and Communautique.

COMMUNITY LEARNING NETWORKS (CLN) INITIATIVE

The Community Learning Networks Initiative was launched in 1998 by the Office of Learning Technologies, a branch of what was then Human Resources Development Canada. The CLN Initiative, which was allocated $29.7 million over its first three years, was designed to "help targeted groups of adult learners benefit from skills development and lifelong learning opportunities. It supports community-based projects that use network technologies in innovative ways to allow individuals to participate fully in the labour market and in their communities" (Human Resources and Social Development Canada 2007). The CLN Initiative supported the development of more than 135 community learning networks (Human Resources and Social Development Canada 2005). CLN projects sought to develop physical, social, and electronic public spaces that would foster community values and technological literacy while offering a supportive learning environment, especially for those without computer access at home. The projects also helped community members to develop new skills that would enable them to participate actively in a knowledge-based economy and society. The CLN Initiative, which came to an end in 2006, aimed beyond the relatively simple Internet connectivity provided by the CAP program to promote effective uses of ICTs by and within communities. CRACIN case study sites that were recipients of CLN funding include VCN, K-Net, and St. Christopher House.

FRANCOMMUNAUTÉS VIRTUELLES

Launched by Industry Canada in 1998, Francommunautés virtuelles was designed to support the development of French-language applications and content services, to promote networking among francophone and Acadian communities, to stimulate the development of a French-Canadian multimedia industry, and to support and develop the use of information technologies in francophone and Acadian communities in Canada. Roughly $9 million had been allocated to the program by 2005, which ended on 31 March 2008. Communautique received funding from this program.

NATIONAL SATELLITE INITIATIVE (NSI)

Introduced jointly by Industry Canada, Infrastructure Canada, and the Canadian Space Agency in 2003, the $155-million National Satellite Initiative supports the development of satellite broadband infrastructure in communities in the far to mid-North and in other isolated and remote areas where satellite is the only option for broadband connectivity.

SCHOOLNET

In partnership with other governments, schools, NGOs, and the private sector, Industry Canada launched SchoolNet in 1995 "to position Canada at the global forefront of e-learning readiness, to support the innovative use of ICTs for lifelong learning, and to promote the competitiveness of the e-learning industry." In conjunction with the Computers for Schools program, School-Net was intended to ensure affordable access to computers and the Internet in all schools across Canada. Although the Computers for Schools program—which provides refurbished computers for schools, libraries, and non-profit organizations—is still operating, SchoolNet ended in 2006. Over its ten-year lifespan, the program received $243 million in funding. Of the CRACIN case studies, K-Net was a participant in SchoolNet through the companion First Nations SchoolNet program.

SMART COMMUNITIES

Announced in 1999 by Industry Canada, the $60-million Smart Communities program funded the development of twelve Smart Communities demonstration projects over a three-year period, one in each province, one in the North, and one in an Aboriginal community. The purpose of the program was to encourage the development of innovative uses of information technology in order to promote community development. Three CRACIN case study sites were selected as Smart Communities demonstration projects—K-Net, the WVDA, and SmartLabrador—each of which received $5 million from the program.

Governments at the provincial and municipal levels have also played an important role in supporting various connectivity initiatives, including community informatics projects. The Alberta SuperNet, a partnership involving the government of Alberta, Bell Canada, and Axia SuperNet Ltd., connects 420 Alberta communities to the Internet. A joint project of the New Brunswick provincial government and the federal government, in partnership with Aliant Telecom Inc., extended broadband coverage to 327 communities throughout rural New Brunswick. Saskatchewan's CommunityNet I and II and Northern Broadband Network initiatives provide broadband services to over 450 communities in that province. Municipalities have also invested in community wireless and broadband networks, adopting a variety of funding and deployment models ranging from free, city-owned wireless hotspots in Fredericton to Toronto Hydro Telecom's for-profit subscription wireless broadband service in downtown Toronto. Together these investments and initiatives total at least $600 million.

REFERENCES

Canada. Privy Council Office. 1999. Speech from the Throne to open the second session of the 36th Parliament of Canada. 12 October. http://www.pco-bcp.gc.ca/index.asp?lang =eng&page=information&sub=publications&doc=aarchives/sft-ddt/1999-eng.htm.
Canada. 2000. Report on Canadian government on-line activities. Leiden, Netherlands. October. http://www.governments-online.org/documents/Canada_Leiden.pdf.
Human Resources and Social Development Canada 2005.
——. 2007.
Manley, John. 1998. Presentation to the Industry Committee on Bill C-54, *The Protection of Personal Information and Electronic Signatures Act*. http://www.ic.gc.ca/eic/site/ ecic-ceac.nsf/eng/gv00218.html.
Moll, Marita, and Leslie Regan Shade. 2001. Community networking in Canada: Do you believe in magic? In *E-commerce vs. e-commons: Communications in the public interest*, ed. Marita Moll and Leslie Regan Shade, 165–81. Ottawa: Canadian Centre for Policy Alternatives.

GLOSSARY

Aboriginal Peoples Television Network (APTN) Launched in 1999 and headquartered in Winnipeg, APTN blends news and public affairs with multilingual programming devoted to the history and culture of Canada's First Peoples. A vital resource for Northern communities, APTN is available on cable and satellite. See http://www.aptn.ca.

Access rainbow A socio-technological model that describes the multiple dimensions of access to the Internet, taking into account both the technical infrastructure (e.g. hardware, software) and the social infrastructure (e.g. literacy, governance).

Actor-network theory An approach to social theory that developed out of science and technology studies (STS), which grants agency to non-human factors as well as to human beings and attempts to map relationships between the material and the semiotic.

Afya A participatory action health informatics project developed for African American women in partnership with the graduate program in Library and Information Science at the University of Illinois at Urbana-Champaign.

Backbone The Internet backbone refers to the principal data routes between large, strategically interconnected networks and core routers in the Internet.

Backhaul The backhaul portion of the Internet comprises the intermediate links between the core network, or backbone, and the small subnetworks at the "edge" of the Internet.

Berkeley Community Memory Project One of the first public access bulletin board systems, the Berkeley Community Memory Project was founded by Lee Felsenstein, Efrem Lipkin, and Ken Colstad in the 1970s to "harness the power of the computer in the service of the community."

Broadband for Rural and Northern Development (BRAND) An Industry Canada program, BRAND was piloted in September 2002 to deploy broadband to unserved rural and remote Aboriginal communities and to isolated areas in Canada's far and mid-North. A $105-million pilot project, it lasted until 2007.

Bulletin board system (BBS) An early computer system that allows users to connect via a modem and terminal program to a system for uploading and downloading files, exchanging information, and reading news and information posted by users.

Canadian Heritage A department of the Government of Canada, Canadian Heritage has responsibility for policies and programs pertaining to the arts and culture, media and communications networks, official languages, the status of women, sports, and multiculturalism. One of the CRACIN government partners.

Canadian Radio-television and Telecommunications Commission (CRTC) A federal regulatory agency created by the Broadcasting Act of 1968 as the Canadian Radio-television Commission. Its name was changed in 1975 when its mandate was expanded to include telecommunications. The CRTC grants and may revoke licenses for radio and television stations, television networks, cable companies, specialty and pay channels, satellite distribution systems, and multi-point microwave distribution systems. Since 1975, it has also overseen the telephone and telecommunications industries. The CRTC has established

Canadian-content rules for both radio and television and has set forth numerous regulations on such issues as sex-role stereotyping, television violence, and editorial independence. The CRTC consists of up to thirteen full-time and six part-time commissioners appointed by order in council. The federal cabinet maintains the right to give directions to the CRTC, to set aside its decisions, and to refer decisions back to it.

Capacity building The ability of community groups to define, delineate, and deploy actions that address community concerns in a positive and empowering fashion.

Captive portal software An authentication system that obliges an HTTP client on a Wi-Fi network to log in before accessing the Internet.

Community informatics The use of information and communication technologies (ICTs) to enable communities to reach their social, economic, cultural, and political goals. The term refers to both a body of practice and a research area.

Community Learning Networks (CLN) Initiative Launched in 1998 by Human Resources Development Canada, through its Office of Learning Technologies, the CLN Initiative aimed to encourage adult learners to acquire new skills and engage in lifelong learning. It offered support to projects that made use of community learning networks—shared access, web-based, content management systems that are locally controlled and are designed to serve the learning needs of a community. St. Christopher House received funding from the CLN Initiative.

Community network A means of providing public and low-cost or free access to the Internet, often oriented to serving the information and communication needs of a geographically based community.

Community technology movement Organizations and individuals involved in creating community networks and organizational infrastructure to support community networks.

Connecting Canadians initiative A suite of programs initiated by Industry Canada in the mid 1990s to bring Internet access to Canada. These included the Community Access Program (CAP), SchoolNet, First Nations SchoolNet, VolNet, and Smart Communities.

Counter publics Networks of individuals and groups excluded from the dominant regimes of power and policymaking.

Digital divide A term popularized in the mid-1990s to refer to the fact that socioeconomic factors, including income and educational levels, geographical location, gender, ethnicity, and age, influence participation to the Internet. Implied in the term is the recognition that digital technologies not only confer benefits but also contribute to social inequalities. Not everyone has equal access to digital technology and, even among those who do, not everyone is equally competent in its use.

Digital economy A term popularized by the Canadian federal government to refer to the use of ICTs (information communication technologies) for economic development.

Digital Ontario A program of the Ontario Ministry of Government Services aimed at investigating the use of broadband in Ontario for social and economic development.

802.11 standards A set of standards developed by the Institute of Electrical and Electronics Engineers (IEEE) for the implementation of wireless local access network (WLAN) communication. Available at http://standards.ieee.org/getieee802/download/802.11-2007.pdf.

E-Rate The subsidy program in the United States that provides federal funds for Internet access to libraries and schools under the 1996 Telecommunications Act.

FLOSS (or FOSS) movement An acronymn for Free/Libre and Open Source Software, referring to a group of designers and users who create, modify, and promote the use of open source software.

FON / Fonero FON is a crowd-sourced global Wi-Fi community that operates using the Fonera wireless router. A "Fonero" is a member of the FON community. There are three kinds of Foneros. An "Alien" does not have a Fonera router to share but must pay for access on a per-use basis. A Bill (named after Bill Gates) shares his or her router but charges others for its use, whereas a Linus (named after Linus Torvalds) shares his or her router freely and gets free roaming at any FON spot. See http://corp.fon.com/en.

Freenet movement An activist movement, which reached a peak in the 1990s, that advocates for free and public community networking.

Global information society A vision of human society based on the global use and coordination of ICTs (information and communication technologies), including the programs and policies that support such a vision.

Hotspot A physical space where Wi-Fi access is available.

Hub-and-spoke system A Wi-Fi configuration, in which one radio signal (the hub) sends and receives data for several users (the spokes).

Human Resources and Skills Development Canada (HRSDC) A department of the Government of Canada that is responsible for developing, managing and delivering a variety of social programs and services, including those related to skills and development, information technology, and education. HRSDC originated in 1993 as Human Resources Development Canada (HRDC), which in 2003 was split into the Department of Human Resources and Skills Development and the Department of Social Development. The two departments were recombined in 2006 under the name Human Resources and Social Development Canada. Toward the end of 2008, the name was changed to Human Resources and Skills Development Canada. HRSDC was one of the CRACIN government partners.

Industry Canada Industry Canada is the department of the Government of Canada that has responsibility for regional economic development, including tourism, trade, and investment in small businesses, and for scientific and technological innovation, research, and development. Its stated mission is to "foster a growing, competitive, knowledge-based Canadian economy," which includes responsibilities for telecommunications policy. One of the CRACIN government partners.

Information highway A term popularly deployed in North America by the media and government during the 1990s to refer to the Internet.

Information Highway Advisory Council (IHAC) A federal research body established in 1994, under the auspices of Industry Canada, to investigate the economic, social, and cultural dimensions of the 'information highway" and to formulate a strategy for adapting Canada's economy and society to the digital age. Among other things, IHAC recommended that market forces be allowed a free hand in the development of Canada's digital infrastructure, with minimal government interference.

Information Highway Applications Branch (IHAB) An arm of Industry Canada that operated programs at the local, regional and national levels to assist Canadians in accessing the Internet. Notable programs included the Community Access Program (CAP).

Information society A term that originated in the 1960s and that refers to the widespread use of information and communication technologies for economic, cultural, political, and social activities.

Keewaytinook Okimakanak Tribal Council A tribal council that represents six First Nations in Northern Ontario. The Keewaytinook Okimakanak Tribal Council was instrumental in the creation of the Kuh-ke-nah Network (K-Net) and has been a strong advocate of the use of ICTs to promote education and social cohesion among isolated Aboriginal communities.

Local area network (LAN) A network that connects computers located in a fairly circumscribed space, typically within the walls of a single building (an office or a school, for example). Various technologies can be used to build LANs, but Wi-Fi and Ethernet are the two most common.

Mobile Digital Commons Network (MDCN) A joint research project launched by Concordia University and the Banff New Media Institute, with support from Canadian Heritage, to investigate the use of mobile media for culture and arts. Île Sans Fil received funding from MDCN for some of its projects. See http://mobilelab.ca/mdcn/.

MSAT Developed by the National Research Council of Canada, MSAT (for "Mobile Satellite") is a mobile telephony satellite service supported by companies in the US as well as Canada.

National Broadband Task Force (NBTF) Established by the Canadian federal government in 2001 to develop a strategy for the deployment of broadband in Canada, with the goal of making broadband available in every Canadian community by 2004. The task force explicitly recommended that priority be given to rural and remote regions, as well as to Aboriginal communities.

Participatory action research (PAR) A scholar-community research methodology in which research questions, studies, and evaluation frameworks are developed in partnership with the group or organization under study.

Participatory design A design methodology based on the principle that those who will be using a given technology should be involved in its initial design, development, and diffusion.

Point of presence (POP) A point of presence is a location from which the entire Internet can be accessed. It consists of servers, routers, call aggregators, ATM (asynchronous transfer mode) switches, and other such equipment and necessarily has a unique IP (Internet protocol) address. Large Internet service providers (ISPs) typically have many POPs, and the number of POPs an ISP operates is one measure of its size.

Social capital A sociological concept that refers to the collective social and economic value generated by social networks, that is, by the connections among individuals and groups. A related concept, human capital, refers to the knowledge, skills, and experience held by specific individuals.

Spectrum policy Policies governing the allocation, use, and management of spectrum, that is, bandwidths of a particular length.

Telecommunications Policy Review Panel (TPRP) A federal initiative to review the status of telecommunications in Canada and make policy recommendations regarding its "modernization."

Wide area network (WAN) In contrast to a LAN, a WAN links computers that are geographically remote—in another city or province or country. They enable businesses and governments to transmit information instantaneously across long distances and can also be used to connect geographically distant LANs.

WiFiDog WiFiDog is an open source embeddable captive portal solution used to build wireless hotspots, developed by Île Sans Fil.

ZAP Zone d'Accès Public, an organization that supports a series of public access Wi-Fi hotspots in Québec. See http://www.zapquebec.org/category/zones-dacces-public/ and http://www.zaplanaudiere.org/anglais/index.html.

PUBLICATION CREDITS

Chapter 2 Michael Gurstein, "Toward a Conceptual Framework for a Community Informatics" Portions of this chapter appeared in Michael Gurstein, "Towards a Critical Theory of Telecentres: In the Context of Community Informatics," in *The Political Economy of the Information Society*, edited by Parminder Jeet Singh, Anita Gurumurthy, and Mridula Swamy, Information Society for the South Series, vol. 1 (Bangalore: IT for Change, 2010), 9–24.

Chapter 5 Serge Proulx, "Information Technology as Political Catalyst: From Technological Innovation to the Promotion of Social Change" Earlier versions of this essay appeared in *Innovating for and by Users*, edited by Jo Pierson, Enid Mante-Meijer, Eugène Loos, and Bartolomeo Sapio (Brussels: COST [European Cooperation in Science and Technology] Office, 2008), 121–31, under the title "Social Innovation Among ICT Users: Technology as Catalyst in Promoting Social Change"; and in *Global Media and Communication* 5(3) (December 2009): 293–307, as "Can the Use of Digital Media Favour Citizen Involvement?"

Chapter 6 Katrina Peddle, Alison Powell, and Leslie Regan Shade. "'The Researcher Is A Girl': Tales of Bringing Feminist Labour Perspectives into Community Informatics Practice and Evaluation" An earlier version of this chapter appeared in 2008 as "Bringing Feminist Perspectives into Community Informatics," *Atlantis: A Women's Studies Journal* 32(2): 33–44.

Chapter 8 Susan MacDonald and Andrew Clement, "Systems Development in a Community-Based Organization: Lessons from the St. Christopher House Community Learning Network" This chapter is a much expanded version of "Participatory Tensions in Developing a Community Learning Network," a brief paper presented at the Participatory Design Conference 2008, Bloomington, Indiana, 30 September–4 October, and available in *Proceedings of the Tenth Anniversary Conference on Participatory Design*, edited by David Hakken, Jesper Simonsen, and Toni Robertson (New York: ACM, 2008), 234–37.

Chapter 10 Alison Powell and Leslie Regan Shade "Community and Municipal Wi-Fi Initiatives in Canada: Evolutions in Community Participation" An earlier version of this chapter was published in 2006 as "Going Wi-Fi in Canada: Municipal and Community Initiatives," *Government Information Quarterly* 23(3–4) (2006): 381–403.

Chapter 11 Alison Powell, "Wi-Fi Publics: Defining Community and Technology at Montréal's Île Sans Fil" An earlier version of this chapter was published in 2008 as "Wi-Fi Publics: Producing Community and Technology," *Information, Communication and Society* 11(8): 1068–88.

Chapter 13 Brandi L. Bell, Philipp Budka, and Adam Fiser, "'We Were on the Outside Looking In': MyKnet.org—A First Nations Online Social Environment in Northern Ontario" This chapter is a revised version of Philipp Budka, Brandi L. Bell, and Adam Fiser, "MyKnet.org: How Northern Ontario's First Nation Communities Made Themselves at Home on the World Wide Web," *Journal of Community Informatics* 5(2) (December 2009), http://ci-journal.net/index.php/ciej/article/view/568/450.

Chapter 21 Graham Longford, Marita Moll, and Leslie Regan Shade, "There and Back to the Future Again: Community Networks and Telecom Policy Reform in Canada, 1995–2010" This chapter is an expanded version of "From the 'Right to Communicate' to 'Consumer Right of Access': Telecom Policy Visions from 1970–2007," in *For Sale to the Highest Bidder: Telecom Policy in Canada*, edited by Marita Moll and Leslie Regan Shade (Ottawa: Canadian Centre for Policy Alternatives, 2008), 3–16.

CONTRIBUTORS

Marco Adria is a professor at the University of Alberta, where he directs the graduate program in Communications and Technology. He has served as president of the Canadian Association of Library Trustees and as chair of the Edmonton Public Library Board and is the author of *Technology and Nationalism*.

Brandi L. Bell is a graduate of the joint PhD program in Communication at Concordia University. Her doctoral research examined the changing perspectives on Canadian youth as participatory citizens between the late 1960s and the present. Her work is inherently interdisciplinary, building upon a background in critical new media and mass media studies but also encompassing sociology, education, and health. She continues to focus on investigating the intersections of youth, socio-political participation, health, and technology and the media in her current role as research coordinator in the Comprehensive School Health Research Group at the University of Prince Edward Island.

Philipp Budka is a social and cultural anthropologist interested in media and communication technologies, indigenous media, transnationalism, social and cultural theory, ethnicity, the production and transfer of knowledge, and ethnographic methods. He is PhD candidate and part-time lecturer with the Department of Social and Cultural Anthropology of the University of Vienna. His dissertation investigates indigenous media technology practices in Northwestern Ontario from a sociocultural anthropology perspective.

Nadia Caidi is an associate professor in the Faculty of Information at the University of Toronto. Her primary research interests are information policy and the influence of culture on the production, distribution, and use of information and on its institutions and technologies. Caidi has been exploring the information practices of vulnerable communities and marginalized populations, including newcomers and immigrant groups and Aboriginal communities in Northern Ontario. In addition to her CRACIN research, which focused on the relationships between community networks and public libraries, she has also been involved with other initiatives such as RICTA (Research on ICTs with Aboriginals). Her numerous articles have appeared in venues such as *The Information Society*, *Library and Information Science Research*, the *Journal of Information Science*, *The Library Quarterly*, and the *Government Information Quarterly*.

Elise Chien graduated from the University of Toronto's Master of Information Studies program in 2005 and also holds a graduate certificate from the collaborative program in Knowledge Media Design. Her MA thesis, "Involving and Informing Newcomers Online: Users' Perspectives of Settlement.Org," examined the ways in which newcomers to Canada make use of new media technologies in the process of becoming settled. She is currently a consultant with a firm that specializes in health information management, benchmarking, and evaluation and continues to pursue interests in the areas of community networking, library studies, health care, and immigration.

Andrew Clement is a professor in the Faculty of Information at the University of Toronto, where he coordinates the Information Policy Research Program. With a PhD in computer science, he has had long-standing research and teaching interests in the social implications of information and communication technologies and human-centred systems development. In the early 1970s he was the programmer and project leader of the first online public access community networking service in Canada, based on the model of the Berkeley Community Memory Project. His recent research has focused on public information policy, the role of the Internet in everyday life, privacy, surveillance, digital identity constructions, public participation in the development of the information and communication infrastructure, and community networking. Clement was the principal investigator of the Canadian Research Alliance for Community Innovation and Networking and a co-investigator in the Community Wireless Infrastructure Research Project. Clement is currently a co-investigator in a major research collaboration, The New Transparency: Surveillance and Social Sorting.

Diane Dechief earned her MA at Concordia University and is currently a doctoral candidate in the University of Toronto's Faculty of Information. Her interests lie with the experiences of immigration and settlement for people who migrate to Canada, particularly their interactions with state-led programs and institutions and use of state-supported information infrastructures. Her current research focuses on the motivations underlying personal name changes among immigrants to Canada. Her MA thesis, "Recent Immigrants as an 'Alternate Civic Core': Providing Internet Services, Gaining Canadian Experiences," examined volunteerism amongst recent immigrants as a means of integration.

Adam Fiser earned his PhD in the Faculty of Information at the University of Toronto and is currently a Social Sciences and Humanities Research Council postdoctoral fellow at the Ted Rogers School of Information Technology Management at Ryerson University. His research examines how next generation networks develop in rural, remote, and Aboriginal communities.

Melissa Fritz received her MA from the School of Journalism and Communication at Carleton University and is a doctoral candidate at the University of Toronto's Faculty of Information. Her interests lie in the area of policy analysis and, in particular, with the politicization and determination of needs in policy discourse. Her research has focused on issues of digital divide, telecommunications policy, gender and technology adoption, and motherhood and child care in Canada.

Michael Gurstein is currently executive director of the Centre for Community Informatics Research, Development and Training in Vancouver, Canada. He is the editor-in-chief of the *Journal of Community Informatics* and foundation chair of the Community Informatics Research Network. He is an advisor to the EU-funded N4C project, which looks at telecommunications services for underserved and indigenous peoples in Northern and Central Europe. He has served as a consultant to the governments of Canada, Australia, New Zealand, Malaysia, Nepal, and Jordan, to the Ford Foundation, the Hewlett Foundation, the UN Development Program, and the European Union, and to Nortel, Mitel, Bell Canada, and Intel, among others. He has been a member of the board of the Global Telecentre Alliance, Telecommunities Canada, the Pacific Community Networking Association, and the Vancouver Community Network and is a member of the High Level Panel of Advisors of the (UN) Global Alliance for ICT for Development. His blog, "Gurstein's Community Informatics," can be found at http://gurstein.wordpress.com.

Heather E. Hudson is director of the Institute of Social and Economic Research and professor of public policy at the University of Alaska Anchorage and was founding director of the Telecommunications Management and Policy program at the University of San Francisco. She has planned and evaluated communication projects in northern Canada, Alaska, and more than fifty developing countries. Her work focuses on applications of ICTs for socio-economic development, on regulation and policy issues, including universal access, and on policies and strategies designed to extend affordable access to new technologies and services, particularly to rural and remote areas.

Nicolas Lecomte currently teaches in the sociology program at Champlain Regional College–Lennoxville, in Sherbrooke, Québec. At the time the CRACIN research was conducted, he was a graduate student at the Université du Québec à Montréal. Since 2005, he has been part of Serge Proulx's LabCMO research group, working on the Communautique case study and participating in related research activities, and is the co-author of several academic papers that focus on Québec's community organizations in the context of the "information society." He has also been involved in projects related to the use of distance learning, particularly e-learning, in post-secondary institutional settings.

Graham Longford was the CRACIN postdoctoral research fellow in community informatics in the Faculty of Information Studies at the University of Toronto from 2004 to 2007. His research and published work have focused on the social and political implications of new ICTs, e-governance, and telecommunications policy in Canada. In addition to his postdoctoral work with CRACIN, Longford was a co-investigator with the Community Wireless Infrastructure Research Project and held a Canada Research Chair Postdoctoral Research Fellowship in citizenship studies at York University. He holds a PhD in political science from York University and has taught at Trent University, York University, and Wilfred Laurier University.

Susan MacDonald was trained as a librarian and is currently a doctoral candidate in the University of Toronto's Faculty of Information. Her dissertation research involves a case study of the Library Settlement Partnerships (LSP), through which she explores partnerships with public libraries and community-based organizations in immigrant settlement service provision in Ontario and examines government interest in partnerships designed to accelerate immigrant settlement and integration processes.

Marita Moll is a freelance writer and public policy researcher in the field of telecommunications policy. She is a research associate with the Canadian Centre for Policy Alternatives (CCPA), a non-partisan research institute concerned with issues of social and economic justice, as well as a board member of Telecommunities Canada, a Canadian alliance of community networking practitioners. She lectures at Carleton University in the Department of Technology, Society and Environment Studies and was a co-investigator in the CRACIN project. Together with Leslie Regan Shade, she has edited a number of collections on telecom policy published by the CCPA.

Katrina Peddle holds a PhD in communication from Concordia University. Her research interests include rural youth cultures and sexualities, Métis identities and ICTs, and the rights of prisoners in Canada. She has worked extensively in community-based research in rural areas throughout eastern Canada and as a researcher in Cree territory for the James Bay Cree Public Health Department. Currently studying law at McGill University, Peddle has interned at the Canadian HIV/AIDS Legal Network and has worked as a legal information coordinator at the Centre for Community Organizations in Montréal.

Alison Powell is LSE Fellow in Media and Communications at the London School of Economics and Political Science and a research associate at the Oxford Internet Institute, where she held a Social Sciences and Humanities Research Council postdoctoral fellowship. Her research explores digital media policy "from the bottom up," examining how technical activism and digital advocacy influence the structure, function, and policy environment of the Internet. She also studies open source production cultures, teaches communication and social theory, and writes at http://www.alisonpowell.ca.

Serge Proulx is a professor at the École des médias of the Université du Québec à Montréal and research associate at the Department of Economics and Social Sciences at Telecom ParisTech, in Paris. A sociologist by training, he has authored more than a hundred articles on the uses of media, technologies, and communication. He is co-director of the Laboratoire de communication médiatisée par ordinateur (LabCMO). His recent publications include *Web social: Mutation de la communication* (co-edited with Florence Millerand and Julien Rueff) and *L'action communautaire québécoise à l'ère numérique* (co-edited with Stéphane Couture and Julien Rueff).

Christian Sandvig is an associate professor in communication and media at the University of Illinois at Urbana-Champaign, as well as a faculty associate at the Berkman Center for Internet and Society at Harvard University. His research investigates the development of new communication technology infrastructures, particularly the role of public policy in that process. Sandvig was previously named a "next-generation leader in science and technology policy" in a junior faculty competition organized by the American Association for the Advancement of Science and has received a Faculty Early Career Development Award from the US National Science Foundation in the area of human-centered computing.

Leslie Regan Shade is an associate professor in the Department of Communication Studies at Concordia University. Her research focuses on the social and policy aspects of ICTs, with particular emphasis on issues of gender, youth, and political economy. She is the co-editor (with Katharine Sarikakis) of *Feminist Interventions in International Communication*, the two volumes of *Communications in the Public Interest* (with Marita Moll), and *For Sale to the Highest Bidder: Telecom Policy in Canada* (also with Moll), as well as the editor of *Mediascapes: New Patterns in Canadian Communication*.

Frank Winter is a PhD candidate in the Faculty of Information at the University of Toronto. His dissertation research focuses on discourses surrounding the deployment of ICTs in the service of the knowledge-based economy and society, with particular reference to the goal of universal broadband access in northern Saskatchewan. He has held a number of positions at the University of Windsor Library and the University of Saskatchewan Library, including two terms as director of the latter, where he is currently employed. Winter was also a member of the Health Canada Advisory Council on Health InfoStructure and was involved in the development of information policy for the Canadian Association of Research Libraries and the Association of Research Libraries.

Matthew Wong was a research associate with CRACIN while working on his MA thesis in the Faculty of Information at the University of Toronto. He is currently working toward his PhD in business administration at the Richard Ivey School of Business at the University of Western Ontario. His research focuses on issues related to organizational culture and the role of the founder in small businesses and entrepreneurship.